1903

W. E. B. Du Bois article "The Talented Tenth" published.

1906

Alpha Phi Alpha founded at Cornell.

1908

NAACP founded.

1929

JANUARY 15 Martin Luther King, Jr., born in Atlanta, Georgia.

1932

MARCH 12 Andrew Jackson Young, Jr., born in New Orleans.

NOVEMBER 8 Franklin Roosevelt elected to first term as president of the United States.

1936

AUGUST 9 Jesse Owens wins four gold medals at Berlin Olympics.

1938

JUNE Joe Louis defeats Max Schmeling.

1941

DECEMBER 7 Bombing of Pearl Harbor brings United States into World War II.

1943

MAY Andrew Young graduates from Valena C. Jones Elementary School.

1947

APRIL 10 Jackie Robinson joins Brooklyn Dodgers.

MAY Andrew Young graduates from Gilbert Academy.

1948

Completes freshman year at Dillard University in New Orleans, enrolls at Howard University in Washington, D.C., as a sophomore.

1950

Pledges Alpha Phi Alpha fraternity.

1951

MAY Graduates Howard University with B.S. in Biology.

SEPTEMBER Begins taking classes at Hartford Theological Seminary while working as a youth organizer with the Connecticut Council of Churches.

1954

MAY 17 *Brown v. Board of Education of Topeka* desegregation case decided by U.S. Supreme Court overturning "separate but equal" doctrine.

JUNE 7 Andrew Young marries Jean Childs at First Congregational Church in Marion, Alabama.

1955

JANUARY Graduation from Hartford Theological Seminary with B.Div. degree.

Begins pastorate at Bethany Congregational Church in Thomasville, Georgia.

AUGUST 3 Daughter Andrea Young born in Thomasville.

DECEMBER 1 Montgomery bus boycott begins.

POCKET NEXT PAGE

1956

Andrew Young spearheads voter registration drive in Thomasville.

An Easy Burden

Also by Andrew Young

A Way Out of No Way

Andrew Young

An Easy Burden

The Civil Rights Movement and the Transformation of America

HarperCollins*Publishers*

HarperCollins books may be purchased for educational, business, or sales promotional use. For information please write: Special Markets Department, HarperCollins Publishers, Inc., 10 East 53rd Street, New York, NY 10022.

FIRST EDITION

Designed by Alma Hochhauser Orenstein

Library of Congress Cataloging-in-Publication Data

Young, Andrew, 1932–
    An easy burden : the civil rights movement and the transformation of America / Andrew Young. — 1st ed.
       p.   cm.
    Includes index.
    ISBN 0–06–017362–9
    1. Young, Andrew, 1932–   . 2. Civil rights worker—United States—Biography. 3. Afro-Americans—Civil rights. 4. Civil rights movements—United States—History—20th century. I. Title.
E840.8.Y64A3   1996
323'.092—dc20   96-22928

96 97 98 99 00 ❖/RRD 10 9 8 7 6 5 4 3 2 1

To the ground crew
who gave flight to the movement
and
To the wives and mothers
without whose faith, prayers, and willingness to sacrifice
we never would have had the courage to try

Come unto me, all ye that labor and are heavy laden, and I will give you rest. Take my yoke upon you, and learn of me; for I am meek and lowly in heart: and ye shall find rest unto your souls. For my yoke is easy, and my burden is light.

—MATTHEW 11:28–30

I want young men and young women who are not alive today but who will come into this world, with new privileges and new opportunities, I want them to know and see that these new privileges and opportunities did not come without somebody suffering and sacrificing for them.

—MARTIN LUTHER KING, JR.

Contents

PART III   1968–1972

Photo sections follow pages 182 and 374.

PROLOGUE

We Have Come So Far

We have come so far, yet we still have a long, long way to go. "Freedom is a constant struggle," says the Negro spiritual. "We've struggled so long, that we must be free." And we are free. That is the lesson of the American civil rights movement. We are as free as we dare to be.

There were many who made the American civil rights movement possible: men and women, preachers and laypeople, students and workers, young and old. But in the 1960s, the Southern Christian Leadership Conference (SCLC), the organization I was involved with during the civil rights movement, was largely made up of thirtyish, Southern-born, Negro preachers. We were children of the New Deal of Franklin Delano Roosevelt. We spent our adolescence enjoying the rise of the United States as a defender of liberty and democracy in World War II. Our high school and university life was defined and colored by the social responsibility of the Marshall Plan, a sense of world community signaled by the founding of the United Nations and, yes, the successful liberation of India from British colonialism—without violence.

Even with the nuclear clouds above us, racial segregation surrounding us, and crippling seeds of inferiority sown within us by a thoroughly racist society, we were able to lay claim to a heritage of faith in God, confidence in the undiminished potential of our country, and hope for better tomorrows for ourselves and our children. We believed because we sensed the power and grandeur of the ideals of this nation. We lived in the South, in the midst of its horror and shame, but our eyes were on the prize of freedom; we were willing to pay the price for freedom, we were willing to die for freedom, but we knew that the freedom to which we aspired could never be achieved by killing.

We began our struggle as a means of survival against the oppressive racism of our time. We were all confronted daily with disadvantages imposed on us simply by the color of our skin and the texture of our hair. Our religion taught us that we too were created in the image of God. Our schoolbooks taught us that we were "endowed by [our] Creator with certain unalienable rights." Yet our society determined to legally deprive us of self-respect, educational opportunity, political power, and economic access. Because we believed in this nation, we sought to remove the barriers that separated us from white society—not out of a need to be close to white people, but to gain the same access to society's benefits that they enjoyed. Whites and some blacks assumed this would mean the assimilation of traditional white values and culture. But we knew there were no intrinsically "white values" and that in an open relationship the power and meaning of our black experience would stand on its own merit and enrich the larger society.

We believed in spite of it all, that as children of God and agents of history we could redeem the soul of America. In the Old Testament, the redeemer was a kinsman who bought back land that one had lost. In the New Testament, the Redeemer is Jesus Christ, who paid for the sins of all believers with his life. The former slave and abolitionist Frederick Douglass described the effort to end slavery as a struggle to save "black men's bodies and white men's souls." It was in this tradition that the preachers who founded the Southern Christian Leadership Conference decided its mission was "to redeem the soul of America." It was an ambitious mission for a small band of Negro preachers, a mission that could only be conceived in faith. That soul we saw less in America's actions than in its ideals: freedom, equality, justice. While we endured segregation, we knew that America had shed the blood of hundreds of thousands of its sons and daughters in a war that ended slavery. We knew that America had risen up out of the depths of a Great Depression to defeat fascism. We had cheered the exploits of Dorie Miller and the Tuskegee Airmen and other colored soldiers who refused to let racial segregation prevent them from offering their lives for freedom and for America, and we were inspired by their example. Dorie Miller was told he could only be a cook's helper, but he dared to believe he could shoot down enemy aircraft. The Tuskegee Airmen dared to believe black men could fly.

We were thought to be naive, but in truth we were visionary. We dared to believe that America could be healed of the gangrene of racism. We saw America as we could become, not just as we were. We believed that people could change, because we were constantly aware of how far we had come, personally. But most of all, we believed that a free society was constantly changing and that we could influence those changes to accommodate the needs and aspirations of all of our citizens, and that race, creed, gender, and national origin could be strengths rather than problems.

We began with the limited goal of ending racial segregation. But we came to understand segregation as just one aspect of the barrier confronting black Americans in American society. The March on Washington became a march for jobs and freedom, because in a nation based on free enterprise, access to jobs and money are an essential component of freedom. We came to see the war in Vietnam as a symbol of the destructive role America was playing in suppressing the cause of freedom for people of color not just at home, but around the world. As America made the world safe for democracy, we had to make America's democracy safe for the world.

Racism, war, and poverty were anchors dragging on our society, preventing us from reaching our full potential, as if anchors from a nineteenth-century sailing ship had been attached to the space shuttle. We accepted the challenges of detaching those anchors. We knew it was a burden, but we believed it was an easy burden in a country as great as ours. We believed that God didn't give anyone more burden than he or she had the strength to bear. Our faith made our burdens light, because we never carried them alone. Our understanding and clarity of vision was a blessing, and I was taught that God requires us to use the gifts that we have been given. Racism, war, and poverty were heavy burdens, to challenge injustice was an easy burden.

We possessed a fundamental faith in democracy and free enterprise. We learned to address the nation through a free press; we made our claims on the economy by word and deed. We believed in our American heritage—a great people in a great nation that was ready to lead humankind in a new way of thinking and working. We believed in a future that we would help to create from our faith in spite of very real fears. Martin expressed it for all of us when he constantly reminded us that "the moral arc of the universe is long, but it bends toward justice."

Each of us came to the civil rights movement by a different path and our backgrounds influenced our styles of leadership and approaches to the challenges we faced. I begin by sharing my personal history, because of its impact on the role I chose to play in SCLC, to give some sense of life for American Negroes before the civil rights movement, and to share the spiritual and cultural values of the black community that were the foundation for our efforts.

I hope this book will foster a better understanding of our intentions and our tactics, our struggles and weaknesses, and in so doing will help all of us recognize that our struggle continues, that the rise and fall of enthusiasms is a necessary rhythm of social change. Energy and vitality come with vision, and at this moment we do not see clearly.

But perhaps a brighter vision of our future can be inspired by a better understanding of our recent past.

PART I

1932–1961

1

===

Don't Get Mad,
Get Smart

We are climbing Jacob's ladder, soldiers of the Cross.
—AFRICAN-AMERICAN SPIRITUAL

I was born at the beginning of an era of enormous change, change
so great it would be called the second American Revolution. Of
course, America has always been a changeable nation, with a constant flow of new people, all pushing toward new frontiers. But the
conquering of these frontiers was seldom good news for all concerned—the Native Americans who lost their land, culture, and lives;
the Africans stripped of all contact with their homeland and all rights
as human beings; the women who had no right to their own property
or children; the poor whites who were on the vanguard when these
perilous frontiers were penetrated and pushed aside when it was time
to distribute the wealth.

The year was 1932. In that year Franklin Roosevelt was elected
president, the Bonus Marchers—veterans who found themselves victims of a depression they had no hand in creating—came to Washington, Hitler was the leader of the largest political party in Germany,
Prohibition was coming to an end, and the Great Depression was in
full force. The modern world was in crisis and with that crisis would

come an opportunity for my generation to change America in a way that was good news for all Americans. We would try to change America, morally: we would redeem the soul of America.

I was born in a New Orleans shotgun-style house to Andrew Young, a dentist, and Daisy Fuller Young, a former schoolteacher. We were middle class, which in 1932 meant my parents owned our home and had food enough to share with those in need. In those days of the Great Depression, Jim Crow was the law of the South and in polite society we were known as "colored people." My parents believed in three things: God, hard work, and education. Their faith in a righteous and loving God sustained their unwavering belief that they and their sons would prevail over the harsh restrictions of segregation.

It was the desire for education that brought my father to New Orleans from Franklin, Louisiana, a small town one hundred miles west of New Orleans. My grandfather, Frank Smith Young, owned a popular café and other small businesses in Franklin, and he served as a state officer of several influential black organizations, including the Knights of Pythias and Prince Hall Masons. He was an educated man who started out teaching at a mission school for blacks near Franklin, lived near the rail line, and saved the money he earned on the side picking up the U.S. Mail from the train to go into business.

Frank Young wanted his son to continue his education beyond the eighth-grade level, all that was possible at the local mission school, and sent him to New Orleans to attend normal school at first Southern University and then Straight College. Straight had its origin in Reconstruction with the assistance of the American Missionary Association, an antislavery society founded by Congregational ministers and laypersons in 1846. The AMA promoted opposition to slavery and assisted freedmen and fugitives in the Northern and border states. With the Civil War, AMA missionaries, mostly teachers, established schools for freedmen as the Union soldiers liberated the South and restored the Union. Where there were Union garrisons and Freedmen's Bureau agents during Reconstruction, there were generally AMA schools and churches. Two generations after the Civil War, the best education for blacks in the South was still to be had from schools founded by the AMA or other Northern church missions.

From Straight College, my father went to dental school at Howard University in Washington, another school founded by Congregational abolitionists after the Civil War. At Howard, my father was one of a group of talented young men from Louisiana, who partially financed their education by working in resorts in the Catskills during the summer. They provided entertainment by playing baseball and worked as waiters and dishwashers, as well. The best players were assigned tables where the better-tipping guests were seated. If a player was in a hitting slump, he would find himself relegated to the kitchen washing dishes. Two members of the Louisiana gang married my father's sisters: Laddie Melton married Bessie Young and opened a dental practice in Beaumont, Texas; and Ulric Price married Lola Young and opened a pharmacy in Lake Charles. Daddy graduated from dental school in 1921 and returned to New Orleans to begin his own practice.

In those days my father was a handsome toffee-colored man, a dapper dresser with a university education and the trim body of an athlete. One of his first acts upon returning to New Orleans was to visit the campus of Straight College to see "what caliber of young ladies they had now," as my mother put it. Mother was working on her two-year teaching certificate at Straight. Daddy saw a young woman who was vivacious, olive-skinned, and shapely. He moved fast, and within a short time after meeting they were engaged. Mother was self-possessed, strong-willed, and determined even as a young woman, and although they could not afford to marry for many years, she was always proud that she was a virgin on her wedding night. I believe my father was proud, too.

My parents had absorbed the conservative New England culture of the Congregational schools in which they were educated, and in turn my values were tremendously influenced by my parents' Puritan ethic; my life as a middle-class African-American was the direct result of my parents' hard work and frugality. But to truly understand my parents, it must be said that they recognized that their ability to reap the just rewards of their hard work was due in large part to the sacrifices and commitment of the Northern white missionaries who founded Straight College. Like a lever, education lifted the value of their labors. And my parents' commitment to Straight and to the Congregational church never faltered. In my family, faith and a good education were intertwined with the commission to serve others. To that end I was raised on Luke 12:48: "From everyone to whom much has been given, much will be required." A burden of responsibility, but an easy burden.

Mother was the product of a New Orleans family of classic Creole complexity. The youngest of eight children, she hardly knew her father, who died when she was still very young. Mother can trace the family back to the 1840s or so when a ship captain by the name of Brown bought and freed her great-grandmother in order to enter into

a "placage" relationship (an interracial union unsanctioned by matri-
mony) with her. Interracial marriages were, of course, illegal, but
they lived together for all intents and purposes as husband and wife
and produced several children, an arrangement quite common in
antebellum New Orleans. When Captain Brown lost his life in an
accident at sea, great-grandmother Brown and her children were left
with nothing, although the captain died a wealthy man. For a time
Brown's attorney who controlled the estate made small payments to
the Brown children, but soon even that meager support faded.

Now, according to my mother, all the children from this union
except one went "passe-blanc"—they passed for white. The one who
retained a "colored" identity was my mother's grandmother, who
formed a union with a Polish Jew named Czarnowski. One of their
children was my grandmother, Louisa, who married Joe Fuller, a
black man who worked as a distributor for a cigar company.

My grandmother raised eight of her own children and informally
adopted others as well. All of her children were fair-skinned, and
knowing there were tremendous economic disadvantages to being
black, several of my mother's siblings avoided declaring themselves
"colored" in order to receive better jobs. Once that happened, they
began to move away from the family. One of my grandmother's children was the manager of Rubenstein's Men's Shop, a carriage trade
store on Canal Street, where black customers were not encouraged
and under no circumstances were they permitted to try on or return
the clothes. This job was only available to him because he went
"passe-blanc." I remember my grandmother telling me, "You don't
need to go in there." She was not bitter about his choices, but knew
that he could no longer acknowledge us without causing harm to
himself.

Joe Fuller died before the older children were able to complete
secondary school, and my uncle Walt left school and began working
to help support the family. Other siblings joined him in the work-
force, while "cousins" and siblings who passed into the white world
left the Fuller family to fend for themselves. Education became a luxury my mother's siblings could not afford, but as the youngest child
who showed real academic promise thanks to their sacrifices, my
mother became the only one of the children to receive a high school
diploma. With their moral and financial support, she also attended
college and obtained a certificate to teach.

Mother says her sisters advised her not to marry Andrew Young
because, according to them, a dentist couldn't possibly support her.
Color was also a factor. As light-skinned, mixed-race Creoles, my

mother's family had more options than darker-skinned people. Her sisters may have looked at their fair-skinned mother's marriage to a black man whose death had left them in poverty. Had my father been rich, color would have mattered less, but his future prosperity was doubtful, in their minds. Caste and color were intertwined in an unmistakable preference for lighter skin. They wanted their well-educated, good-looking sister to make a good match and had their doubts that my father was the best she could do. But she was determined, and in 1931 they married, using her savings (she was always a scrupulous saver) to make a down payment on the "shotgun" frame house on Cleveland Avenue where they could begin a family and Daddy could establish his practice. Each room followed the other in railroad car–style, hence the designation "shotgun" (I suppose because if you shot through the front door the pellets would go through every room of the house). Daddy's office was a small addition adjoining the second room, just big enough to house his dental chair and equipment. The living room and dining room of the house became the waiting room for the dental office. It was only natural that they would settle there, for it was the neighborhood in which my mother had grown up as well as the historic neighborhood of Straight College and the community of blacks who settled around it.

I was born in March 1932. Within two years, my brother, Walter, was born, so we were raised virtually together and were treated as a pair by relatives: "Andrew 'n Walter." During my parents' long courtship, Mother's sisters had learned to appreciate Daddy and accept Mother's decision to marry him. Since Mother's sisters and brother were all childless, they adopted us as theirs, and my earliest memories are of my mother's relatives, who rallied around my parents, visited often, and gave us the feeling we were part of an extended family. Mother's mother, Louisa Czarnowski Fuller, came to live with us in our small six-room house very soon after I was born.

My parents were sociable, and there were always people around the house. Of Mother's brother and sisters our favorite was Walter, for whom my brother was named. When my mother's sisters had advised her against the wisdom of marrying Andrew Young, it was Uncle Walt who encouraged her to go ahead and said he would help her with wages from his job as a waiter at the Roosevelt Hotel. He and his wife, Phena, had no children. Uncle Walt, especially, treated Walter and me like his own children, buying us everything he could afford, and spending time with us when our parents were busy.

*　　　*　　　*

Daddy's practice grew at a snail's pace; needless to say, building a dental practice in the early 1930s was very difficult for a black man. Ironically, some blacks felt a black dentist or physician could not be as competent as his white counterpart. This form of racial self-denigration had firm roots in the historic perversity of slavery. The assumption was that if black professionals had been taught by other black professionals, their training couldn't be very good. It took my father years to overcome these innuendos and assumptions of inferiority. Moreover, the kind of cosmetic dentistry that is quite common now was unknown at that time, and few people had the money to pay for a dentist, so if a tooth hurt, you simply got someone, rarely a professional, to pull it.

To supplement his practice, Daddy worked in an innovative program developed during the administration of Governor Huey P. Long to offer free dental treatment to indigent patients in rural areas of Louisiana. Taking the position meant that he was away from home for long periods during the two or three years he worked in the program, but it was the only way he could support his family. The state of Louisiana purchased several house trailers and fitted them as dental clinics. They were hitched behind an automobile and towed from parish to parish. The state also employed public health nurses who visited homes throughout the rural areas and arranged for patients to come to the courthouse for free dental checkups, fillings, and prophylaxis. It was quite a visionary project. Huey Long showed great concern for the poor, and his programs helped black citizens as well as white.

Sometimes in the summer we would join my father as he traveled around in his dental trailer, setting up shop from town to town with his assistant. We would visit our grandfather in Franklin and his second wife, Ma Mae. Daddy's mother died while he was at Straight College and her sister came to Franklin to help take care of Frank and the girls. She was an educated woman and I remember her as tall and handsome. It wasn't long before they were married. The house in Franklin had a big front porch with a swing shaded by oak trees trimmed in Spanish moss and a grove of pecan trees. I was also impressed with his immaculate, big green Buick. It seemed to me that it must be the largest car in town, but I never saw him actually drive it. My grandfather was proud and independent in a way that only an entrepreneur can be. He had made a living for his family, sent his children to school, and provided employment for others at a time when jobs were scarce.

These trips around Louisiana were my first exposure to the rural

South. Outside of New Orleans, Louisiana was scarcely different from Mississippi or Alabama. But my father traveled from parish to parish, an itinerant black dentist, without fear. Through his example of quiet courage, my father taught me I need not fear rural Southern whites. Self-control, unflagging courtesy, and compassion toward those who were rude were his guides for navigating those small towns. Later, in my civil rights career, when I began to enter new and hostile towns in the South, I would remember my father's example and feel confident that I could handle any situation.

The state dental work made it possible for my father to slowly build a professional reputation. There was some prestige in doing "state" work, and when he returned to his New Orleans practice full time, he had enough patients to squeeze out a marginal living. Mother worked as his secretary and receptionist, and with her unflagging efforts at economizing, and her sense of discipline and organization, my father's fortunes rose. Despite all the doubts among blacks about the abilities of a black professional, Daddy's reputation as a dentist took giant steps forward when a white neighbor rang the bell one night with a horrible toothache. Daddy woke up, took him into his office, pulled the tooth, and somehow relieved the pain. Word of this "miracle" spread like wildfire throughout the neighborhood, and a few more whites began to trickle in, always in emergency situations, and usually by cover of night. But more blacks began to come too, blacks other than their Straight College friends, on the assumption, I suppose, that if Daddy could treat whites he was good enough to treat them.

Strangers in the house were a reality I was always prepared for. I don't ever remember our front door being locked until it was time to go to bed. The thought that someone might enter the house to harm us was, in those days, beyond comprehension. My father's business depended on the goodwill of the public and his personal reputation, and I had to do my part from the time I was a child.

Because I was the oldest son, my father gave considerable attention to teaching me how I should behave, although he was never overbearing. When I entered the front door of our house, if there were patients waiting in the front room, I had to stop and greet each of them. If I thought he wasn't noticing my entrance and I ran straight through to the rear of the house, he would stop drilling or whatever he was doing, come to the rear, and make me return and do the greeting, introducing myself to each person as "Andrew Young, Junior." At first this was annoying and seemed like a heavy obligation to put upon me—after all, they were his patients, and had nothing to do with me—but in time, I came to accept this ritual as a matter of course. It was probably my first introduction to the art of politics.

This attitude of welcome in our home was not only that of my father but also that of my grandmother. After informally adopting several children whom she raised along with her own, she was always taking people in throughout her life. Mother inherited that trait from her; I suppose I inherited it from all three of them.

Gran had a reputation in the neighborhood for feeding people who came to our door hungry. She would feed anybody. Beggars and hoboes, many of whom had just arrived in the city on the railroads that ran only a few blocks from Cleveland Avenue, apparently passed the word among themselves that if you were really desperate, you could go to 2224 Cleveland Avenue, where some friendly colored people lived, ask for an old light-skinned woman named Mrs. Fuller, and most likely get something to eat, even if it was only a slice of French bread and butter. Feeding the needy seemed to be my grandmother's self-appointed task, and she was never happier than when acting as great-mother-of-the-lost. There were a number of people like that in New Orleans when I was a child—helping the needy had not yet become completely institutionalized—and those who volunteered themselves did so with no fear they would be victimized or taken advantage of.

The food my grandmother made and offered was old-style New Orleans, with plenty of French bread, and a lot of red beans and rice, fried fish, shrimp, and oysters. Seafood was extremely plentiful and inexpensive in New Orleans in those days. Shrimp were only fifteen cents a pound and crabs were purchased by the bushel. The very idea of buying seafood in a market was considered unnecessary and extravagant; most people caught their own and gave the excess to friends. This vast variety of excess seafood was the origin of seafood gumbo, today an expensive New Orleans delicacy. *Gumbo* is a West African word for okra, which often formed the base for the thick broth. Before the advent of freezers, you couldn't keep seafood on ice for more than a few days, so at the end of the week you had to cook all the leftovers, preferably in one pot. My favorite food was red beans and rice—the New Orleans red beans. Gran used to make red bean sandwiches—red beans heavy with juice, highly seasoned, poured between the shells of bakery fresh French bread with the inside pulp removed—a delicious, gooey mess! And it filled you up: one of those sandwiches would satisfy us for the whole day no matter how much running and playing we did.

I remember an elderly white man who came to our door for a free meal one day. He was obviously not from New Orleans, and my grandmother fixed him a red bean sandwich. He sort of looked at it quizzically, and finally said, "I don't eat that. Do you have something else?" Gran stiffened with indignation, then shot back, staring straight out the window: "Humph! That's what we eat. We eat it all the time. If it's good enough for us, it's good enough for you."

I always associated my family's openness, their willingness to help others in need, with Gran's and my parents' strong religious faith. It was a living faith that guided every aspect of their lives. They were conscientious Christians and sought to live in service to God and their community. My parents were active members of Central Congregational Church, the "home" church of Straight College, which met in Straight College's auditorium when I first attended as a child. Every week we went to Sunday school; Mother taught our class. Daddy held court out in front of the church every morning, greeting members and visitors as they came in the door. He sang tenor in the choir and almost never, if ever, missed a Sunday until the last year of his life, when he became too physically incapacitated to attend. Even then, he left his sickbed and struggled out in a wheelchair to attend what would be his last Easter service.

Mother chaired the diaconate at Central at a time when it was unusual for women to be on a board of deacons. She visited sick and shut-in members, always taking along some Coca-Cola and a casserole for the family. Communion was good for the spirit, but the body needed real food. Mother believed that food would cure any ailment. If you weren't feeling well she asked two questions: Have you eaten? Have you made a BM? She was a faithful Christian in the Martha mold, always tending to the practical, physical needs of any of God's children.

When Walter and I were old enough, we went through confirmation, and had to sit through church, or a good part of it, following Sunday school. The Central services, however, under the leadership of Rev. Dr. Norman Holmes, a professor of philosophy and religion at Straight College, later Dillard University, were not nearly as lengthy as the day-long services common in Baptist churches. Our services were modeled on the New England Congregational order of worship. We used the Pilgrim Hymnal with its English and German hymns. The congregation intensely disapproved of black praise songs and emotional outbreaks. The only element of the service that reflected the particular culture of the congregation was the inclusion of Negro spirituals. The choir sang "We Are Climbing Jacob's Ladder," "Steal Away," "Lord, I Want to Be a Christian," and other songs from the African-American tradition. These songs had helped our ancestors endure and triumph over the adversities of slavery. Arranged for classical choral presentation, they were another legacy of the American Missionary Association.

At home, I was taught to get down on my knees and pray every night. There was no other posture for nightly prayer. Ironically, it was a habit I abandoned only after I entered Hartford Seminary. My grandmother required that I read her Bible to her every day, and we gave thanks for every meal after being asked to recite a Bible verse. No alcohol was served in our house, but dancing and cards were permitted. My mother was the founder of a bridge club that included many of her college girlfriends—that club stayed together as long as there were enough members to sit a full table, more than fifty years.

My parents' relationship recalls an old Moms Mabley joke in which she affirms that her husband is the head of the household and makes all the big decisions, like who'll be president, while she makes all the small decisions, like where they live and what they eat. My father was the head of our household, and my mother ran his life. Daddy was gregarious and sociable and had exposure to the world beyond the confines of New Orleans, but it was my mother's management of the dental office that made it successful as a means of supporting the family. She kept the business accounts and made sure that patients' bills were paid in a timely manner. Since my parents were both busy with the dental office, it was my responsibility after school to start preparing dinner. Mother was the chef and I was her kitchen aide—peeling potatoes, fetching a quart of oysters, boiling the rice, chopping onions and celery. I also ran errands downtown to the dental supply shop. Mother insisted that I wear a shirt and tie for these errands—without those symbols of middle-class status, she feared I would be accused of stealing. I often helped Daddy in other ways, preparing his instruments, laying out charts, and mixing the compounds for fillings. My parents believed that idle hands were the Devil's workshop. They were constantly in motion—working, caring for us, volunteering in church and community efforts—and they expected us to stay busy as well.

I learned to enjoy reading, a pursuit that was encouraged by my parents, but I didn't like it structured for me and did not take well to textbooks. I most looked forward to reading the newspapers, particularly the black weeklies that Dad subscribed to, which carried news of the black community from all over the country: the *Louisiana Weekly*, which was published in New Orleans, and the *Pittsburgh*

Courier, printed on brown paper and probably *the* most popular national black weekly. Through them we learned about the way the black community was relating to World War II, which began about the time I began reading seriously, and how black troops were being treated, the effort to protect the rights of blacks in the extremely lucrative war industries, and the progress of blacks in the armed services, as well as outrages committed against them in the South, where the treatment of black soldiers could be brutal. We could also read about the tremendous contributions that black soldiers were making in the war effort: the Tuskegee Airmen, the valor of Dorie Miller at Pearl Harbor, and the bravery of a black platoon at the Battle of the Bulge. And we pored over stories about Dr. Charles Drew and his blood plasma, which saved the lives of countless Allied soldiers.

Of course I read the funnies first, and then the sports. The *Courier* had a cartoon called "Bootsie" and a wonderful columnist, Evelyn Cunningham, who wrote "For Cullud People Only." On the sports page I learned about great black baseball players of the Negro leagues, like Satchel Paige and Josh Gibson, and news of Joe Louis, Jesse Owens, and Ralph Metcalf. Joe Louis and Jessie Owens were special heroes. They represented the power and potential of black men and refuted the notion of black inferiority. At a time when Hitler was talking about the Aryan master race, blacks across America cheered as Jesse Owens went to the Olympics in Berlin and won four gold medals. I was thrilled when Joe Louis, the Brown Bomber, defended his title as Heavyweight Champion of the World, defeating Max Schmeling in 1938. We stopped everything to listen to his fights on the radio. It was only in the black newspapers that I could read accounts that did justice to the accomplishments of my African-American heroes.

Daddy read the columnists faithfully, and he taught me to read editorials. When my parents finally had a private living room, he would sit in an armchair before dinner, carefully reading the news of the day. He appreciated Drew Pearson's and Wendell Wilkie's columns. In fact, the first adult book I read was Wendell Wilkie's *One World*.

My friends and I also read boys' books. The boys in the books were all white, but we enjoyed their adventures and imagined ourselves in similar escapades. I also read *Black Boy*, Richard Wright's powerful autobiography. Daddy subscribed to *Life* magazine, and I remember they ran a section on *Black Boy*, with photographs of Wright. The book left me with mixed feelings, and I couldn't finish it. The violence and suffering he described were just too much for me.

When I'd begin to feel anger and bitterness boiling up within me, I'd just quit reading and turn to something else.

The reality Wright was describing was very different from what I had known or was experiencing—almost as if we were in different countries. On the other hand, we were from the same country, the same South, and Wright's beginnings were just a few miles from my own. But my parents and their friends didn't talk about Richard Wright. It was almost as if the reality he had laid bare was an embarrassment. By depicting the world of his upbringing in Mississippi so starkly, and by honestly portraying the frustrations of the race, Richard Wright was bringing into consciousness uncomfortable realities—realities about which many blacks possessed dangerous feelings that had to remain submerged.

The attitude of my parents' generation, of our teachers, seemed to be that we should not waste our time complaining about the way blacks were treated—that wouldn't achieve very much. Instead, we should concentrate our efforts on "improving the race," not only improving the level of education but also improving moral behavior. They felt we had to disprove the oft-heard accusations, repeated endlessly by blacks themselves, that as a race we were uneducated, shiftless, lazy, overly emotional, given to hopelessly stretching the truth, talented only at singing and dancing, and sexually undisciplined and immoral. "Niggers is hopeless," is what it seemed to mean. We were bombarded with this denigration, condemnations heard in one form or another every day in school, in church, and on the streets among blacks themselves. The message was that we had best address ourselves to uplifting ourselves before we leveled criticisms against the powers that be for our second-class status.

The idea that blacks alone are responsible for their impoverished condition has resurfaced in the voices of the new black conservatives. But, the notion that blacks must prove themselves worthy of social, political, and economic equality with whites is nothing new. My parents and grandparents adopted that strategy. Their lives were exemplary in every respect. They were educated, responsible, hardworking, taxpaying, church-going Americans. But no matter how hard they worked, or how much they achieved, segregation made no exception for them.

My formal schooling began at the age of six at Valena C. Jones Elementary on Galvez and Annette Streets in the Seventh Ward, a public school for blacks under the old racially segregated school system. Despite being a segregated school, Jones (named for the late wife of

Methodist Bishop Robert E. Jones) was considered top rate. The principal, Miss Fannie C. Williams, was an early careerist in black education. A handsome, dark-skinned woman with pressed, white hair, she believed in strict discipline and patrolled the halls of the three-story brick structure observing classes and seeing for herself that everything was in order. Miss Williams went about her task of uplifting the race and bringing unruly boys and girls under control with great gusto and an almost legendary determination, pacing the halls with her thick ruler ever at the ready. But the obstacles were formidable. New Orleans was still in the midst of the Great Depression and the social and economic pressures on blacks from segregation were unrelenting. One application of Miss Williams's philosophy of uplift was her constant presentation of positive racial "role models" before the student body; she invited every black celebrity who visited New Orleans to come over to Jones School, and most came, from Joe Louis to Marian Anderson. Miss Williams would halt classes and march the entire student body in class formation down to the basement assembly room, where we would stare at the "role model" and listen to him or her say a few words of inspiration while Miss Williams beamed. Then we would be marched back up to the familiar routine of classes once again. To the students at Valena C. Jones, Miss Williams had the bearing and charisma of Mary McLeod Bethune. I remember that Miss Williams had purchased one of the last Oldsmobile sedans assembled before war production began. Such was her Puritan thrift that she was driving that same car to church in her nineties.

Though I was exceptionally small for my age, Miss Williams started me in the third grade instead of the first (under the assumption I was too "advanced" for first grade, having experienced some preschooling at Central's nursery school), so by the time I graduated from Jones, having finished the seventh grade, I was only eleven years old.

It was at Jones School that I became an ambassador. The neighborhood around the school was rough and fights were so frequent the school's nickname was "bucket of blood." Of course, our fights were fistfights and the blood came mostly from noses rather than bullet holes. I wasn't at Jones School very long before I realized I could survive among larger children if I made friends with a few other boys. Since there were no students there who I might have known from the Cleveland Avenue area, which was a good twenty blocks away, I couldn't depend on familiarity, my father's notoriety as a dentist, or any previously formed alliance. But thanks to my father's coaching I liked people and knew how to introduce myself to strangers. And in this case the practical advantages of having my own group of friends were obvious: if someone jumped *me* to try and take my lunch money, they had to fight *us*.

It didn't take me long to make friends with some other boys who, like myself, hated eating in the school cafeteria, even though Jones provided free lunches. I couldn't stand the daily menu of lima beans and Spam or jelly sandwiches. So I suggested to my new friends that if we pooled our change and slipped across the street to the grocery, we could do a lot better. A half-loaf of raisin bread, a few slices of bologna, one of those huge Mr. Big Colas, which we all drank from, did the trick—we ate like little princes for about twenty cents. At least half the money was mine. The other boys contributed a few pennies or we scrounged up bottles to return for deposit.

World War II started while I was attending Jones School. I remember the worry and apprehension of my parents as we sat around the radio in their bedroom listening to news reports and the soothing speeches of President Franklin D. Roosevelt. But I was really too young to know what war meant; I read war stories in the newspapers and heard them on the radio, but it didn't touch my world in any perceptible way. For all I knew, "war" was merely an excuse for new and exciting games for my friends and me. The war was thrilling, for it carried with it an air of foreboding and unpredictability, particularly among the adults. As children, we had no way of knowing what war meant: we saw no one killed, no bombs exploded in our neighborhood; there were hardships like rationing of food supplies and gasoline, but to us that wasn't so difficult to adjust to since only adults could stand in the long ration lines.

At school Miss Williams insisted that the entire student body, in a great rush of excitement and alarm, play a new game called *air raid*. We would all scramble into the basement: nothing happened once we got there, which was something of a disappointment, but it did break the boredom of the nine-to-three day. *Air raid* was almost as exciting as *fire drill*, where the fire bell rang and everyone virtually knocked one another over spilling out of the building, class by class, with Miss Williams shouting orders like a grand drill sergeant.

Cleveland Avenue was about twenty city blocks from Jones School, and I often walked home from school, though I sometimes took the bus. Walking through a neighborhood where you were not known was fraught with danger during those days in New Orleans. Adults did not prey on children, but children preyed on other children who were strangers. There was a kind of fierce neighborhood territoriality. Neighborhoods had developed like separate towns that were divided by canals and railroad tracks, so there was limited interneighborhood experience before automobile traffic became universal. The Cleveland Avenue neighborhood, for instance, was only about six square blocks, but there was hardly ever any need to leave except to go to school or downtown to Canal Street. There was a bakery, a butcher, a well-stocked small grocery, a cleaner's, a bar, a playground (the neutral ground, green space with palm trees separating north and south traffic lanes on Galvez), and a typical New Orleans seafood house that sold fresh shucked oysters for fifteen to twenty cents a pint, all within those six square blocks. However, the public schools brought us into contact with kids from different neighborhoods, since there were never enough schools, particularly for blacks, to serve each distinct neighborhood. When I walked home and boys I didn't know caught sight of me, they would give chase, threatening to beat me up and take my money. I learned to talk tough, which was mostly a bluff, but I really tiptoed around where I wasn't known, and my ability to run came in handy.

When I had to venture "back of town," which was only a few blocks from Cleveland Avenue but between Tulane Avenue and the railroad tracks in the tough "tenderloin" district where Louis Armstrong grew up, I was always afraid, even when I was on my bike. The key to safe passage in any hostile neighborhood was the existence of a blood relative who lived there and the quick presentation of his or her name and address. Even a distant blood relative, like a second cousin, would do the trick. If the person who was checking you out actually *knew* your relative, his attitude might abruptly change to one of warm friendship, as if both of you were blood relatives. But, unfortunately, I didn't have relatives who lived "back of town" or in the area between Jones School and Cleveland Avenue. So I learned to stay alert and try to see any challenge before it saw me. Negotiating city streets has always been like survival in a jungle. Then, as now, if it wasn't other kids, it could be hostile police.

Cleveland was called an avenue, but it was really a very narrow street. To us, however, it was more than that, it was our playground. We played touch football, baseball, and hockey on roller skates with tin cans and the branches of palm trees: the street was a marvelous skating rink. If we wanted to risk tackle football, we walked half a block to Galvez Avenue where the neutral ground became a small grass playing field. Later, with some of my friends, we dug a hole and raised a basketball goal, so we could convert our yard into a short basketball court. It was quite an achievement, going to the lumber yard and hauling wood back on bicycles and wagons. We built it ourselves with skills learned in shop classes in school.

Despite the rigid segregation in New Orleans, our neighborhood was a real jambalaya. It was there I learned to appreciate diversity. Delahay Dunn and Harry Hannan were Irish, Eddie Pontiff was Italian, Ralph Guelfo was German, Jimmy Ray was Cajun, and Israel Kitt was black. On the corner of my house was the Deutsches house, a German cultural center. We would sneak around the back and look through the windows. They had a flag with a swastika, and we would watch as they sang Hitler's anthem "Deutschland über Alles" and heiled Hitler. Sophie and Ginger Watts were Creoles who lived around the corner. They were Catholics and, of course, we were Protestants. I can remember having arguments with the Watts girls over the correct way to say the Lord's Prayer.

There was an Irish grocery and an Italian bar, Penninos. Miss Lottie Eel ran the Irish grocery and she gave credit. She kept all the accounts in a book behind the counter. My uncle Johnny would send me over to Penninos to get him a bottle of beer. Johnny was the family ne'er-do-well—it was whispered that he had been a bootlegger during Prohibition. He was a grasshopper, a happy-go-lucky type that everybody helped. He was lovable and nice, but completely irresponsible, and he mostly lived from the resources of his siblings, all hardworking people. To me he was wonderful—fun and exciting. He told me things about the world that my parents considered improper and impolite. Uncle Johnny was a good man, but some would say he was good for nothing.

Everything I needed to know I learned on that block. We had Protestants and Catholics, blacks, whites, and Creoles, Nazis and American patriots—it was a microcosm of so many of the world's differences and conflicts. When you grow up with the world in your community you are prepared to deal with difference, diversity, and conflict. Walter and I played with all the boys on our block; their parents may not have liked it, but we had very few problems with families in our immediate neighborhood. The white girls never played with us, however. They didn't speak to Walter or me, nor did we speak to them. That was taboo, even for children. And our neighbors' relatives were not so comfortable with the racial interaction that took place on Cleveland Avenue either. I had a regular playmate who lived above the store at the corner of Galvez and Cleveland. We were playing basketball in my yard one day when he said, nonchalantly, "Would you believe what my uncle said to me?" His uncle didn't live in our neighborhood. "He said, 'I'll give you a quarter if you stop playing with those little colored boys, and for Christ's sake, stop going over to their house.' I took his quarter," he added, "that's why you didn't see me yesterday." We laughed together about it. That boy later became a priest. I told Daddy what my friend said; he only shook his head and muttered, "I feel sorry for those folks."

Daddy taught me that racism was a sickness and to have compassion for racist whites as I would have compassion for a polio victim. Racism wasn't a problem with me, he told me, it was a problem they had. Daddy had a genuine turn-the-other-cheek attitude, although he didn't believe in becoming a victim. My mother and Gran were not quite so gentle.

Sometimes white kids would walk through our block who were not from our immediate neighborhood, who didn't really know us. Two brothers, about the ages of Walter and me, could not walk past our house without yelling "Niggers!" or "Alligator bait!" Sometimes they would see us playing, yell "Nigger," and run away. None of the white kids we knew called us names; they would just ignore these kids and act like they didn't hear them.

I frequently read the Bible to my Gran in the evening, as she was very religious and her eyesight was failing. I was just learning to read myself, so I practiced by reciting the Bible. I read our family standard, "From those to whom much has been given will much be required," as well as "I was young, and now I'm old but I've never seen the righteous forsaken or his seed begging bread" and "Be not deceived, God is not mocked, whatever a man soweth, so shall he reap." I also read the Daily Devotion to her, and "Lil' Orphan Annie," which I didn't understand at all.

"Gran," I said one night while reading the Old Testament to her, "there's these boys that come by calling us 'Niggers.'"

Gran sat up straight in the bed. "If they call you 'Nigger,'" she said sternly, "you got to fight 'em. If you don't fight 'em when they call you 'Nigger,' I'm gonna whip you myself if I find out about it."

So the next time those brothers came on Cleveland Avenue yelling, "Look at those niggers," Walter and I lit out after them, and, surprise of surprises, the boys ran. They were prepared to call us names, but they weren't prepared to fight. One day soon after we started chasing them, the father of the boys came to our house looking for my father. Dad wasn't home, so he complained to Mother.

"Every time my sons walk past this house your sons try to beat them up," he said. "Yes, and they're gonna continue to chase them," my mother snapped, "because your boys call my boys names, and they are not going to take that. Nobody else around here acts like that."

The man just left. After that, the name-calling stopped, probably to Walter's regret, because he loved to run after them, stalking them, yelling, "I dare you to say that word. Now go ahead and say it." Walter was small and always getting picked on. He enjoyed turning the tables for a change.

"You have to fight," Gran had said, and Mother and even my gentle father supported her. They didn't want us to become targets for every bully in the area. Daddy began play-boxing with me while I was still very young, trying to teach me the principles of manly self-defense. He'd slap-jab me in the face lightly while we were sparring and I'd get so confused, so frustrated and mad, that I'd flail away with my small arms, totally without purpose.

"Stop," Daddy would yell. "Don't get mad, get smart. Learn to move in circles away from my left so I can't hit you."

Then he would show me how to do it. "Never lose your head when you get hit," he said. If there was anything he hated it was to see someone carried away with anger, and he didn't want to see that in us, even though we were only children. A man didn't lose his temper, for then he was out of control. He taught me that the most powerful weapon you have is your mind. Your emotions tend to turn off your thought processes. In very practical terms, he literally slapped those lessons into me. "In a fight," he said, "if you get wild or lose your cool you lose the fight." "Use your head, think" was an early IBM slogan that he gave me to put up in my room. I didn't realize it until much later, but Daddy had given me my first lessons in nonviolence. Later, I had a seminary professor who was a pacifist and also allowed his son to learn to box. His belief was that pacifism was a philosophy for the brave, not the fearful. Only when fighting is a genuine alternative does the decision not to fight represent a higher ethic.

One of the first patients to see my father regularly was Eddie "Kid" Brown, a well-known local boxer who lived near our neighborhood. Eddie Brown, understandably, had plenty of problems with his teeth, and not much money, so my father proposed that he pay for his dental work by giving Walter and me boxing lessons. Eddie jumped at this opportunity with enthusiasm. Every Saturday we met him at the old Coliseum gym, where he put us through a serious training regimen, including jabbing the punching bag and jumping rope. I loved the conditioning, and the boxing lessons, but I never entertained the thought of becoming a professional boxer, not after seeing the condition of Eddie's teeth.

Another of Dad's patients was Ralph Metcalf, the Olympic track star who was then coaching at Xavier University, an outstanding black Catholic college that was founded in New Orleans in 1915. Daddy asked Metcalf to train us in track, so Walter and I also had lessons on the technique of running dashes. I suppose Daddy figured if we didn't take to boxing, we'd better learn how to run.

Outside my parents' sober and disciplined world of home, school, and church and the confines of our little block was the exotic and pulsating city of New Orleans with its riverfront worldliness, French, Spanish, and African heritage.

The Mississippi River became the main transportation route for trade for the American heartland that grew in the basin of the great river. New Orleans was the gateway to the rest of the world. Sugar and cotton plantations demanded the import of slaves, primarily from West Africa and Santo Domingo. By 1800, New Orleans was the major slave market for the Mississippi Valley; by 1830, the city had as many as two hundred slave auction houses.

The heavy influx of slaves into Louisiana and New Orleans left it with a strong African presence: in 1800, according to census reports, the black population, slave and free, actually outnumbered the white population. This African influence has left an indelible imprint on the black culture of New Orleans, particularly in its music, dress, speech, the abundance of social and fraternal organizations, and foods like gumbo.

But black New Orleans was also notable for the phenomenon of its large Creole population, which was produced by liaisons between white men, usually French or Spanish, and slave women, who they usually manumitted, and whose children were therefore born free, though not with the same rights as white citizens. By 1850, Louisiana and New Orleans had the largest number of free blacks of any slave state or slave city—almost all of them light-skinned people who were called Creoles. These people, many of whom inherited property and assets from their white relations, sought to set themselves apart from the slave community as a distinct French-speaking, Catholic community, even when they had blood relatives who were still slaves. After emancipation and the imposition of segregation laws, when all persons with more than one thirty-second of African blood were declared legally black, the Creoles remained generally aloof from social intercourse with the freedmen and continued to speak French for the remainder of the nineteenth century and well into the twentieth. Many eventually went "passe-blanc," and some even emigrated to France to escape the harsh post-Reconstruction segregation laws.

The heavy presence of the Creoles at one extreme, and blacks who could probably trace their ancestry directly back to West Africa at the other, has made New Orleans black culture and history interesting and diverse. Nevertheless, conditions for blacks in New Orleans after emancipation were harsh, in part as a backlash against the remarkable achievement of black and Creole political power during Reconstruction: a black-dominated legislature and more key black state officials than any Southern state except South Carolina. Three blacks, P. C. Antoine, Oscar J. Dunn, and P. B. S. Pinchback, were elected lieutenant governor during Reconstruction. Pinchback served as acting governor for about forty days. This exercise of newfound power and influence was so great that the ruling white oligarchy of Louisiana went out of its way to enforce disenfranchisement and segregation so that those of African descent would never so strongly assert themselves again.

The vital African, Indian, and European heritage of New Orleans is symbolized by its famous Mardi Gras celebration. When I was growing up, the Mardi Gras parades were an invitation to all people to celebrate their ancestry. Each crew had an ethnic link: some chose to connect with their Indian ancestry, ordinary blacks reveled in their African past with the Zulu crew, the Italians put on Roman togas. My parents took us to the parades, but Mardi Gras was part of a Catholic tradition and we were Protestants. They didn't drink and Mardi Gras was a time of pervasive public drunkenness. In truth, my parents believed themselves above the emotional outburst that was Mardi Gras. They looked down on jazz and the blues and only barely tolerated other people's dancing. My mother's primary expression of her Creole heritage was in her cooking.

In many respects, my parents remade themselves in the image of the Congregational teachers of the American Missionary Association. They were New England Puritans, who cultivated an emotional reserve, a strong work ethic, and high moral standards for behavior. Education was their armor and shield against the degradations of segregation, enabling them to rise above the economic limitations segregation placed on most blacks. Just as important, education helped them feel superior to whites who treated them in an offensive or discourteous manner, shielding them from much of the psychological harm that came from segregation.

My parents were proof that success was possible for a black boy, but education was the key. My mind was my best defense and my best vehicle to overcome segregation. Self-control, thinking rather than reacting, would help me to avoid the pitfalls, toils, and snares that awaited young blacks in the larger world. Most important, I was taught that once I was properly trained and prepared I would have the power to determine my own fate.

2

Among the Talented Tenth

The Negro race, like all races, is going to be saved by its
exceptional men.

—W. E. B. Du Bois

In 1943, at the age of eleven, I graduated from Valena C. Jones
Elementary School, having completed the course of study offered
there. Due to the vagaries of New Orleans's segregated educational system, Jones had no eighth grade and I went directly to the
freshman class at Gilbert Academy. I had heard wonderful things
about the school, which was located near the elegant and prestigious
Garden District on oak-lined St. Charles Avenue, from the children of
my parents' friends and I was excited about entering.

Founded in the Reconstruction era, Gilbert evolved from a rural
mission school to an urban preparatory school for New Orleans's
Dillard University. The Gilbert campus, which the school once shared
with Dillard, then occupied an entire city block. The main building
was an old four-story brick structure facing St. Charles Avenue, used
for classrooms, the administrative offices, the library, and the auditorium. Behind the main building was a deep, open field, big enough
for a football field, basketball court, and small tennis court. Flanking

the side streets were several modest faculty houses. The block behind the campus housed Peck Hall, the former New Orleans University women's dormitory, which served as a dormitory for out-of-town Gilbert girls and unmarried women teachers.

The campus was quite beautiful, with ample, though never luxurious, facilities and plenty of space behind the main building for outdoor activities. St. Charles is still one of New Orleans's most beautiful avenues and Gilbert's location there lent it an enhanced sense of spaciousness and a peaceful atmosphere in an environment that was uncrowded and unhurried.

The principal of Gilbert Academy was Mrs. Margaret Davis Bowen, whose husband, John Wesley Edward Bowen, was a prominent Methodist bishop. A combative woman with a sharp tongue, Mrs. Bowen was tireless in raising money from Methodist churches and other philanthropic sources in New Orleans to keep the school open, enabling students to pay a small tuition of only $3.50 per month. Mrs. Bowen was strict about payment, otherwise you were "delinquent," a word she had the ability to make reverberate with unimaginable horrors. Every student who attended Gilbert remembers long, tortuous, sweating lines of students in the hallway, waiting to pay tuition at the business office and finally receive the prized signed receipt to take home to parents. The receipt seemed more valuable than money, and it felt good in our pockets.

Three dollars and fifty cents per month was no hardship for my father, but for the parents of many of my classmates $3.50 represented wages from several hours or even days of labor cleaning, ironing, scrubbing, working in private homes or commercial kitchens. There was a fierce pride behind the act of sending their children to school, which I am convinced was not misunderstood by their children. This pride was strong and permanent enough to sustain many of those students through the ambiguities, troubles, and tribulations of their teen years.

Though Mrs. Bowen could be frightening to us, our parents saw through her stern exterior and loved her. She found many creative ways to help families whose fees were delinquent. Several parents traded services to the school in lieu of tuition, cooking lunches, helping with chores, assisting with the almost endless Gilbert extracurricular affairs and fund-raisers. At the time, I could not appreciate her achievement of keeping a private school operating and making it available to scores of children who could barely even afford tuition of $3.50 a month. If "work is love made visible" then Mrs. Bowen loved us more than we ever knew.

Mrs. Bowen was committed to the improvement of each student. Her educational philosophy stressed excellence and achievement along with preparation for adjusting to living and surviving in the segregated South. She and Miss Williams at Jones School were of like mind. These were black finishing-school women, and they walked with their backs ramrod straight. They seemed to believe the path to freedom was found in manners and diction as much as intelligence and morality. It was an illusion, that somehow if you really got yourself together nobody could enslave you. One of my colleagues in the civil rights movement, Randolph Blackwell, prided himself in being able to recognize any important classical music composition. He believed that when he knew European culture backward and forward white people would accept him. He became disillusioned when, despite all his efforts, he was denied the right to vote. The reality was that Mrs. Bowen could help us rise to the top of separate but equal, so long as we didn't try to mix socially. And, even when one had risen that far, there were no guarantees that you would be safe.

Mrs. Bowen was more aggressive than Miss Williams and a little more imaginative, perhaps because she could do more with her older students. Her philosophy was drawn from both W. E. B. Du Bois and Booker T. Washington, but not necessarily the best from each. Gilbert was the epitome of the Du Bois talented tenth, in the sense that we were an elite group among blacks. Du Bois's theory was that through the education of a talented ten percent, these leaders could in turn bring about the uplift of the entire Negro race. He said that by developing our abilities we not only helped ourselves but were prepared to lead our people to a new day and a better way of life. Mrs. Bowen aimed to do just that, but I did not understand her objectives. When oversimplified, Du Bois's elitism can easily drift into a destructive class consciousness, and I reacted strongly to this kind of elitism as I saw it in Mrs. Bowen and my parents.

Once I entered high school, my parents became concerned that I associate with young people of their social class and position. I saw less of my neighborhood friends, because of our racial differences and because my parents wanted me to socialize with the children of their friends from Straight College. They organized a club for us, like Jack and Jill, and the children of black professionals gathered at one another's homes or took outings to Portia's, a black-owned soda shop in an old mansion. At Portia's we could sit at tables, eat ice cream sundaes, and hang out like other American teenagers. Dolly Deselle Adams, who became the national president of The Links, Inc., a black women's Junior League, and Sybil Haydel Morial, whose husband was the first black mayor of New Orleans, were part of that group. I enjoyed my bourgeois friends and the girls were as beautiful as they were smart, but I also felt an inner conflict over the way we were being set apart from other black kids. We were so comfortable, while so many other blacks were so poor.

Looking back, I realize that it was a complex task preparing children for leadership, giving them a sense of being special, and also inculcating in them a sense of social responsibility. My parents were diligent in their service to others, through their church and work in civic organizations, but they did not invite my participation in their service work. We were being sheltered and nurtured, but it often felt like being smothered.

In her desire to protect us, Mrs. Bowen adopted the most tragic element of Booker T. Washington's approach to racial progress: accommodation with the racial policies of the time. In a famous speech intended to ease the fears of whites Washington was interested in befriending, he scolded those who would claim social equality and asserted, "In all things that are purely social we can be as separate as the fingers, yet one as the hand in all things essential for mutual progress." From Mrs. Bowen I sensed no expectation that we would challenge or resist segregation; rather, there was a naive hope that by proving ourselves as good as whites, we would somehow demonstrate that segregation was unnecessary.

At the same time, my education neglected the positive entrepreneurial message of Washington and the early American Missionary Association. The emphasis in our education focused on preparing us for professional occupations rather than developing independent businesses as my grandfather had done. The early mission schools taught self-reliance and industry—they saw no contradiction in teaching bricklaying and Shakespeare to the same students. The early AMA teachers were pragmatists and promoted a balanced model of what we would today call "community development." However, in the debate over the best path to black advancement, that balance was lost. While Du Bois was correct that blacks should not accept anything less than full social and political equality, Washington was correct in asserting a need to develop the skills that were the bedrock of the American economy such as agriculture, skilled crafts and mechanical skills and developing black institutions—schools, farms, and businesses.

As part of the talented tenth, we were encouraged to develop self-respect and prepare for a life of leadership and dedicated community service through the school's extensive and varied extracurricular activities. The school square hummed all day long with athletic practices, choir and band rehearsals, student government meetings, special assemblies to hear guest speakers, and rehearsals for the annual performance of *Kermis*, Gilbert's own operetta, written and produced by Mrs. Bowen, with a cast of the entire student body, the faculty, and the principal herself. Rehearsals began in September and lasted throughout the school year until the spring gala performance. Three o'clock hardly meant the end of the school day; practices and rehearsals continued until nightfall. As if that wasn't sufficient, we had to return on Saturdays.

In Mrs. Bowen's push for excellence, she gave the more creative teachers free rein to be as innovative as they wished. Two or three teachers in particular left indelible impressions on me. They taught us in a way that would be impossible today under a more structured academic system. Miss Marie Blakely, our English teacher, was a thin, dark-skinned, earnest, and serious lady who began teaching us Shakespeare during our second year. I was twelve when I struggled through *Julius Caesar*, *Hamlet*, and *Macbeth*, and though there was no way we could fully understand Shakespeare's plays at that age, we were able to figure out what the stories were about and to capture some sense of his magnificent and poetic language.

Mrs. Rudolph Moses, who was still in her twenties and on her first job, was our other English teacher. She introduced us to African-American literature. Innovative teachers had to reach out on their own to find black literary material to weave into their classes in the same way black choral directors wove spirituals into their repertoires. Through Margaret Walker's epic racial poem "For My People," which chronicles the history, variety, and struggle of African-Americans to achieve strength and stability, we gained a sense of the literary excellence of our people. And in keeping with the preoccupation with extracurricular activities, Mrs. Moses decided to create a voice choir. "For My People" was one of the first poems she used.

In the textbooks available to us, African-American history was hardly touched upon; when it was, we read in a few sentences of the long painful past that was slavery. The sustained, varied and heroic battles against slavery by black and white abolitionists and those of our ancestors who had escaped to freedom were absent. The story of the South included in our textbooks was more a collection of myths and legends than actual history. It was closer to *Gone With the Wind*: the South from the perspective of a few privileged white families, not the full story of stolen slaves, relocated Acadians, and displaced Indians that was New Orleans. The books described the War Between the States as a defeat rather than the victory that it was for my people. The achievements of blacks during Reconstruction, which were spectacular in Louisiana, were completely ignored in any book or class, and were, I believe, sadly, generally unknown even among our teachers.

Within the confines of his poorly equipped physics lab, the dour and brilliant Aaron C. Dutton taught everything from math to philosophy, and alternately lectured and lashed us with his sharp wit. Dutton's classes never started on time, nor did they end precisely at three o'clock. He and Mrs. Dutton lived in one of the small faculty houses on the campus, so he was always available, either in class or in his darkroom, where he moonlighted as a photographer. He taught us the magic of radio by having the entire class make crystal sets; we learned photography from his darkroom; he arranged theatrical demonstrations to illustrate chemical principles. Dutton's genius was his ability to make us question and wonder.

"What created the universe, Mr. Dutton?" someone asked one day. We all watched intently as Dutton drew dots in a design on the blackboard. Then he stepped back, satisfied.

"Now, if you went to the beach, those of you who've ever seen a beach, and you saw pebbles arranged like that, what would you think about how they got that way?"

One of the girls in the class hesitantly raised her hand. "If they were like that, just like you put those dots up, I would say someone arranged the pebbles on the beach."

"Good," answered Dutton. Then he pulled down his chart of the solar system. The arrangement of planets was roughly similar to the design Dutton had drawn on the blackboard. "Then what do you say about how the solar system got the way it is?"

We could only conclude someone had arranged the planets that way.

"Then I agree." Dutton smiled. "And if everything in the universe is moving, including the Earth, in certain patterns, the someone who did that might have been God, if there's a God. Or some supreme being, because there's a sense of order and purpose to everything in the universe, though man doesn't always understand it."

Dutton talked openly about the racial limitations on our futures. He seemed to have a sense of racial history and possibly a suppressed bitterness. Despite his natural skepticism, he urged us on, but never like a cheerleader. He was not simplistic and he did not expect miracles. Once as we sat silently (it was Dutton's intellect, not his insistence on class decorum that commanded silence), I remember him saying, in an extremely reflective mood, almost to himself, "Despite everything, I wouldn't want to be white. Too pale."

Though I had a passion for sports and was a natural athlete I was too small and too young to play on Gilbert's teams, which dominated every sport among the black high schools in the entire state of Louisiana while I was there. My exclusion from high school sports was due to the superiority of the black high school teams. I remember reading in the newspaper the times for fifteen-year-olds in the 100-yard dash and the 220-yard dash in a whites-only track meet in City Park. While I wasn't good enough to run for Gilbert, I could have beaten any white fifteen-year-old boy at that meet. My body simply hadn't developed enough. Coaches Joel Blakely, the brother of Miss Marie Blakely, and Leonidias Epps knew I had ability—they saw me running and playing basketball on the school athletic fields—and every summer Coach Blakely paid a visit to our home to see if I had "grown any" so I could play for him. But when I was at Gilbert I never grew; I reached my present height of 5'8" only when I was in college.

If segregation hurt me in track, it indirectly contributed to the strong teaching staff that we had at Gilbert. Scholars like Dutton, Miss Blakely, and Mrs. Moses, and coaches like Blakely and Epps would probably not have been working at Gilbert in an open society with equal opportunity. Teachers of their talents seldom work in high schools today. Prior to desegregation they were forced to work at places like Gilbert because most positions were closed to them simply because of race. Ironically, in this case, we students benefited from the unfairness of the system.

We were neither trained nor expected to protest against racial injustice, for that was not considered possible, or even desirable. It was generally assumed nothing could be done to change the situation, so any attempt to do so was "unwise"—and wisdom was one of Mrs. Bowen's eternal goals. It was wisdom that would enable us to survive, not courage or the unpleasant and uncomfortable emotions evoked by honesty.

Along with academic achievement, appropriate behavior was key to Mrs. Bowen's educational philosophy. She emphasized first and foremost to students and parents that we must come to school properly dressed and well groomed. That meant clean and pressed clothes, worn the way she thought decency and modesty required. The girls' skirts could not be too short, not above the knee, or they couldn't come in the school door. Mrs. Bowen actually stood in the door in the mornings carefully appraising her students' appearance. Knees must not be ashy; if they were too ashy you had to Vaseline them down, though I never understood the reason for that. Blouses must be modest; the newly blooming bosoms of young womanhood must be concealed.

As for the boys, we had to wear clean shirts and pressed trousers. T-shirts were not permissible, except on the athletic field. When zoot suits and draped trousers came into brief but raging fashion around 1945, the boys in New Orleans wanted to rush to South Rampart Street to buy drapes. Zoot suit jackets were made with extremely wide, padded shoulders, in flaming colors. Drapes had wide knees and ankles cut so tight you could hardly slip your feet through the legs. The tighter the ankles and the wider the knees the more "hip" you were. Mrs. Bowen was not amused. High in her pantheon of evils to be avoided at all costs was South Rampart Street and everything it stood for. It was not long before she was standing in the front entrance of the school with a tape measure comparing the width of ankles and knees, and sending boys back home with a stern "Tell your Mama to take those knees in and let those ankles out or you can't come in this door." I never knew what her dimensions of decency were, but she had them.

Personal deportment and behavior were an important part of Mrs. Bowen's curriculum and she would use corporal punishment to enforce it. She never whipped me, but she made an example of her son, whipping him before the entire school. Coach Epps delivered my only whipping at Gilbert Academy. There was a group of boys shooting dice in the bathroom and I stayed to watch. Coach Epps walked in and said, "You want to roll dice, I'll show you how to roll dice." He made each boy roll the dice and whatever number came up, that's how many licks they got. When it was time for me to roll, I said, "No Coach, I was just watching, I went in to use the bathroom." He said, "But you stayed here to watch." I said, "Yes, I watched, but I did not roll any dice." He said, " Well, you get one lick for watching." I was so ashamed, I still get a twinge of guilt when I roll dice to play Monopoly.

Mrs. Bowen called frequent assemblies of the entire student body, which she invariably concluded by conjuring the most horrible image of the New Orleans she wanted us to avoid: the pimps and prostitutes on South Rampart Street. Many of the negative images of blacks had to do with sexuality, and it was an unshakable tenet of Mrs. Bowen's philosophy that we must disprove the common myths and allegations of sexual licentiousness. Sensuality in dress, speech, and dance was strictly forbidden. Fancy dress by the boys indicated tendencies toward pimpdom. (This no doubt explained her horror of the drape pants.) Loose dress and behavior by the girls would lead to a life of strolling South Rampart in search of customers, she assured us, and warned, "Many a good girl has fallen." We were constantly admonished with her favorite foreboding aphorism: "A hint to the wise is sufficient." She ran the words together as if they were one: "Ahinttothewiseissufficient" . . . building the phrase to a crescendo, as if she were swinging a mighty sword with the word, reaching the climax of its arc at the "FISH" in sufficient.

Gilbert gave us an education in proper behavior. All the little things—dress, speech, the way we conducted ourselves in public—received as much emphasis as academics. Academics were important, but the value of an education could always be undermined by rude and improper deportment. It was important to go along with the etiquette required by segregation, we were told. Arrogant, insolent Negroes would not be tolerated, no matter how brilliant they might be. The thrust of Mrs. Bowen's message was: "If you expect to survive in the South, if you expect to avoid the fate of the great mass of blacks, you must learn to accept the realities of a racist society, and it's better that you learn this now when you're young than later, when it might be too late."

Now, years later, I realize that one of the reasons behind the protective education of Gilbert Academy was to help us avoid the notice of the police. Blacks were particularly subject to the scrutiny of the omnipotent police, who enforced segregation laws and responded to violations of racial protocol. In New Orleans, as in many other Southern cities, the police were notoriously corrupt and racist, so the fear the black masses felt for the police and their traditional role of "keeping blacks in line" was real. Though lynching of blacks was less common as I was coming of age, hangings, shootings, and burnings of blacks still occurred—we read about them frequently in the pages of the national black weeklies.

Very early I learned to handle police with caution and self-control. I remember the police cruising through Cleveland Avenue one night, stopping when they noticed me hanging out with the white kids from the neighborhood. We weren't doing anything, just talking. The policeman got out of his car, came over, looked at us, looked at me, then looked at us again. He asked what we were doing. "Nothing, just talking," we said and explained that we lived in the neighborhood. I pointed and said calmly and politely, "That's my house right over there, Officer." He looked at me hard, and said, finally:

"You, go home. The rest of you all, be careful." I went home without any more discussion. It was not fair, but I didn't expect the police to be fair.

Once, during my early childhood, our family was riding in Dad's car in New Orleans. Dad ran a stop sign within view of a motorcycle cop, who quickly signaled for him to pull over. We were all nervous because even a simple traffic violation could explode into a major encounter, depending on the mood and personality of the policeman. The policeman came to the window of the car and asked Daddy for his license. Daddy gave him the license, adding that he was sorry, he simply missed seeing the stop sign. The policeman looked at the license, looked at Daddy, then began to ask questions designed to find out who he was. Dad explained that he was "Dr. Andrew Young," a dentist on Cleveland Avenue. The policeman seemed very satisfied, then apparently decided maybe it wasn't necessary to give Daddy a ticket after all, but he wanted Daddy to say he didn't run the stop sign, which of course wasn't true. To the policeman I sup-pose it was his way of being nice, but Daddy kept insisting he had run the stop sign, though he hadn't meant to. Finally the policeman tired of playing the game and wrote a ticket. It took me a little while to grasp why Daddy didn't accept the offer of a little white lie, but I came to understand that his self-respect and his respect for honesty were more valuable to him than the cost of the traffic ticket. My father's stand was particularly significant to him and to us since so much of the application of law to blacks by the police was arbitrary, and he didn't want to benefit from the same system that victimized so many of us.

At the time of this incident, civil rights organizations such as the National Association for the Advancement of Colored People were simply asking the courts and the Congress that blacks be treated fairly and equally under the law. "Equal protection under the law" was guaranteed under the Fourteenth Amendment to the Constitu-tion, but the withdrawal of federal troops from the South after Reconstruction marked the end of any pretense of equal protection for blacks, and the beginning of Jim Crow, separate and unequal. By refusing to lie to the police officer, my father was insisting that the law be applied as written; he had broken the law and he would accept the consequences as a matter of principle. Like the black sol-diers in World War II, he would shoulder the full responsibilities of citizenship despite being denied the full benefits of that citizenship. He wanted his sons to understand that segregation did not lessen our duty to be good citizens.

Even powerful and upstanding Mrs. Bowen was vulnerable to the arbitrariness of the police. One day, after one of New Orleans's minor hurricanes, a group of students decided to sneak away from school in the confusing aftermath of trees blown down and lights short-circuited, and headed downtown to the movies at the Orpheum Theater. Students were not allowed to leave school before three o'clock, and even that was too early for Mrs. Bowen. Somehow, through her vast grapevine, the principal got wind of what was going on. She enlisted our huge basketball coach, Leonidias Epps, who had recently been discharged from the military, and together they went down to the Orpheum, demanded entrance, and climbed the long steps up to the top balcony. There, Coach Epps and Mrs. Bowen searched every row of the colored balcony with flashlights, ferreting out the Gilbert students, who were trying to recede into the shadows, and demanded that they get up and come back to school immediately on threat of expulsion. Fortunately for me I had remained in school, but the "Orpheum capture" was the talk of Gilbert for a long time and we all heard the many versions of the tale. Some of the boys ran into the men's room to hide, but Epps followed them in and grabbed them anyway.

When the manager of the Orpheum heard what had happened, he was not enthused about such harassment of his paying customers. A few months later, when Mrs. Bowen went back to the Orpheum during the school day to look for students, the manager refused to cooperate with her effort to keep her students in school and would not let her in. This dignified, middle-aged school principal, impeccably groomed and well spoken, insisted that her students attend school rather than his matinee; the manager's response was to call the police. She was arrested.

The entire incident was an example of how the least little dispute could instantly explode into a police matter if a black person was assertive. Such explosions very often ended in tragedy, for blacks were completely helpless before the whims and unlimited authority of the police. Despite the unspoken promises of Mrs. Bowen's and Gilbert's approach to education, the truth was that all our efforts to make ourselves acceptable Negroes could not keep us safe. In a confrontation with white authority, the odds were clearly against us.

At the end of every school day, we boarded the St. Charles streetcar to return to our homes. The hour spent at the streetcar interchange on Canal Street was one of the most satisfying times of the day. We met classmates, watched the girls, and drank in the excitement of the hustle and bustle of cars, people, and shops. Canal Street was the central shopping area for New Orleans—our family purchased practically everything we owned there, although no blacks whatsoever worked as store clerks.

Canal Street was where I received one of my first lessons in economic exploitation. It was during the summer that I worked for my aunt Florestine Collins in her photography studio. I started work on a Monday, cleaning the shop, setting up trays of chemicals, greeting customers. On Wednesday, Aunt Florestine hired a young woman about twenty years old and asked me to show her the ropes. At the end of the week, she was paid fourteen dollars and I was paid five dollars. I was so offended by that injustice that I quit. But quitting was not an option for the black adults who regularly endured that kind of injustice on their jobs.

The street that catered to black customers was the legendary South Rampart strip, despised by Mrs. Bowen, but fascinating nevertheless. On South Rampart there were cafés where blacks could eat, along with bars, large and small hotels, barbershops, juke joints, black fraternal offices and small businesses, a plethora of tailors (South Rampart Street was the trendsetter in black street fashion), shoeshine stands, the sound of Louie Jordan records—"Saturday Night Fish Fry," "Caldonia," and "Run Joe"—prostitutes and pimps, and nightclubs, particularly in the vicinity of Perdido Street, where the greatest New Orleans musicians, from Buddy Bolden to Louis Armstrong and their descendants, performed. I was too young to enter the clubs, but the spirit of the music echoed all through the street.

Rampart Street was a sensual parade: the dress, the women, the music blowing from jukeboxes, the smell of fish frying and red beans cooking heavy with cayenne pepper. Rampart Street might have been "sinful," as Mrs. Bowen exclaimed, but it was exciting. It was the center of economy for people who were living on the edge; despite their flashy dress—zoot suits, blazing colors, fancy shoes, flamboyant hats—the people inside the clothing were mostly poor.

I got my hair cut at Levi Hartman's barbershop on Rampart Street, and listening to the stories and jokes and observations in the barbershop provided an education as fundamental as the one I was getting at Gilbert. Listening to the men and women in the barbershop, I realized that they recognized every level of injustice they were subjected to as blacks. Some were veterans of World War II and had been away from New Orleans and the South. They knew from experience that racial attitudes were different elsewhere—that segregation as it existed in New Orleans and the South was considered unfathomable in most Western European nations. Yet, there was no organized way in which the average black person could express his or her discontent. For much of its existence, the NAACP was devoted to the modest goal of stopping lynching. NAACP Executive Secretary Walter White began his career with the organization documenting the scourge of lynching and issuing yearly tallies. Publisher and journalist Ida Wells-Barnett reported on the economic basis of lynching and mob violence against blacks. In the forties, the NAACP shifted its focus to Charles Houston's and Thurgood Marshall's brilliant legal strategy to erode the separate-but-equal doctrine by which the Supreme Court ignored the Fourteenth Amendment and permitted segregation. But the fruits of that strategy were still to come.

During those years, the Dryades Street Young Men's Christian Association, the black community YMCA, played a crucial role in my development. My parents were strong supporters of the YMCA, and friends of its innovative entrepreneurial director, William H. Mitchell. Mr. Mitchell made the YMCA building available for city-wide meetings, organized an active youth program and summer camp, and, in his later years, began a business school, giving training otherwise unavailable to black youth. Mr. Mitchell insisted that we have classes to learn about some of the great African-American leaders of the past. He had an early interest in Africa, and was the first black American I knew to travel to Africa regularly, often bringing back African students whom he helped enroll in American schools. I think of him now as a man far ahead of his time, and it was a great misfortune for the New Orleans community that he died in the 1950s while still in the prime of his life.

Such experiences and involvements, all by the time I was fifteen years old, gave me a rich and varied cultural foundation despite the subjugation and discomforts of the legally segregated South. I grew up with a sense of a strong, intact community that provided me with enough psychological support to not simply survive, but to dream of the promise of a better future.

Before I was really ready, graduation from Gilbert was upon me. I was fifteen years and two months old, and I was just beginning to enjoy high school; now it was time to move on. It had become a ritual among the friends in my class to walk from the campus over to the Mississippi River on the last day of school each year. When we reached the river, we walked on top of the levee toward uptown for about two miles until we reached spacious Audubon Park. This was always a nostalgic hike because we knew we wouldn't see one another until the beginning of school next year. Now we were graduating and we knew we might not see one another ever again, for we were headed in different directions. Some of us would enter college, some of us would take jobs, some of us would volunteer for the military, some of us would be leaving New Orleans. Graduating from high school was an important crossroad in our young lives.

As we walked, chatting excitedly about our hopes and dreams, we looked over at the massive Mississippi, while the big ships plowed upriver and downriver, destined for worlds that still remained a part of our imaginations. The docks along the levee buzzed with activity; they were the source of New Orleans's riches, but we knew they would not make us rich.

"I know you're going to college, Andrew," one of my friends said. "You'll probably be a dentist like your father." Yes, I would attend college, that was a parental expectation I did not question. Besides, by the time we had gone through four years of Gilbert, most of us knew our future was limited in the society we lived in if we did not have a college education. That idea had been drummed into us steadily by Mrs. Bowen and our teachers. Our parents lived in a circumscribed world, a world from which we and they dreamed we might free ourselves. But the question that haunted me haunted all of us: if our parents sacrificed to send us to school so that we might achieve what they were not allowed to achieve, how could we still relate to the world of our parents and be happy? And what of my friends who would not be going to college because their families could not afford to send them? Most of them would have to find jobs now or join the army to relieve the family financial burden.

So there was a certain pain that accompanied the pleasures of graduation. Our paths were diverging: I felt not guilt, but a heavy responsibility, because of the opportunity provided for me by my parents' means, to make whatever I might achieve through education meaningful not just for me, but for all of us who rode the St. Charles streetcar to and from Gilbert Academy. I wanted to go to college and looked forward to new experiences and new challenges eagerly, but my passage was fraught with many questions, and a pain of parting it was difficult if not impossible to talk about.

My parents were not anxious for me to leave home at such a young age, so I began my college career at their alma mater, Dillard University. By this time, we had moved out of the rooms behind the dental office to a two-story brick house just two blocks from Dillard's green and white campus. It was very much like going to Gilbert, except that I missed the trolley rides every afternoon. The sense of decorum was even more strict than at Gilbert. The campus, with its spotless white brick buildings nestled in a broad swath of bright green grass, stretched along Gentilly Boulevard.

I could see clearly that New Orleans thrived on laws and practices that were unfair to me and unfair to my friends. Part of my estrangement from education was that so much of Miss Williams's and Mrs. Bowen's philosophy had to do with accommodating myself to the injustices I saw all around me. I could not square that philosophy with what I read to Gran from her Bible. It was one thing to be trained as one of the talented tenth, but how did that translate into uplift for my classmates and the folks on Rampart Street?

In my sophomore year I transferred to Howard University. I was still younger than most of my classmates, and there were a lot of older students at Howard, veterans who were taking advantage of the GI Bill to get an education. I liked them because they were more sociable and down-to-earth than the bourgeois class of student I was used to associating with. They were quite content to wear army fatigues and blue jeans to class, which was fine with me. I made friends with some of these older guys, perhaps knowing that I could use a couple of big brothers.

I joined the track team at Howard, and my love of the sport inspired me to finally commit myself to achieving excellence in an endeavor. Because of my youth, I had little confidence in myself around the sophisticated young women at Howard, and my academic performance fluctuated up and down—I did well with subjects and professors I found engaging and poorly with others. I felt anonymous in the large classes of one hundred students that were common in many courses. I remember it was my brother, Walter, who helped me gain confidence in my ability to run. He was attending Princeton High School in New Jersey and came down to visit me during the spring of my first year at Howard. Gilbert Academy had closed and my parents sent Walter to live with their dear friends in Princeton, the Waxwoods, to attend the integrated school near them. Walter was running track for his high school, and tagged along with me and the rest of the Howard team for a meet with the marines at Quantico Marine Corps Base.

For some reason, the track coach at Howard, Tom Hart, did not take me seriously. There were no scholarships; the school just gave athletes equipment, which in track meant shoes. But Coach Hart would not give me shoes, so I was using borrowed track shoes. As I watched Walter warming up with the Howard team and doing very well, I realized he was my little brother and I could always beat him. I was not scheduled for any events, so I asked permission to join in some of the early time trials. Running on a cinder track in borrowed shoes my time was 21.4 seconds, beating the Marine Corps record in the 220-yard dash.

Track was a wonderful discipline for me. I did the 440-yard run as well. To win the 440 one has to run all out, but it is too long a distance, and the runner invariably runs out of air before the finish line. You have to be able to dig deep and find a second wind to get you to the finish line. It's confidence as much as air that takes you through.

I made the Howard track and swimming teams, becoming in my senior year the number-one dash man on the track team, and winning my events in several meets. My body finally matured at nineteen years, and all the potential I knew I had at Gilbert and during my earlier years at Howard finally came to fruition, though, for some unknown reason, I was never really accepted by the track coach. Coach Hart had his favorites, and it amuses me even today that he seemed so outdone that I outran his chosen few that he never did give me a pair of shoes.

Despite my love of sports and other aspects of my time at Howard, the atmosphere on campus was imbued with a haughtiness and pretense that I found unappealing. This was the first place I had been where people didn't speak when they passed one another on campus. The girls were society-conscious to an extreme—some even wore high heels, cocktail dresses, and fur coats to class, as if their sole purpose was to snare a future physician or attorney. Boys wore suits and ties, not just on special occasions, but often to class. Mrs. Bowen would have loved it.

As at Gilbert, I was sporadic and undisciplined in my attention to academics at Howard, finishing with something like a C+ cumulative average, though I continued my high school practice of doing quite a bit of reading on my own. The only course I made an A in was speech. I have never been afraid to talk or state my opinions. I could also organize my thoughts rather quickly and express them with some coherence. I still get butterflies when I have to make a speech, but even in college I had confidence in my ability to communicate.

I found myself seeking out students who had the sense of purpose that I lacked. One I admired greatly was Emmanuel Latunde Odeku, from Nigeria. Odeku was brilliant and possessed a certain arrogance toward American blacks typical of some Nigerians. In his case, though, he really *was* superior, and did the work to make himself so. He would sleep for two hours after dinner, arise and study until three or four in the morning, then sleep two hours in the morning and take a nap for an hour after lunch. He was incredibly disciplined and organized. He did not have very much money, so he had to make every semester count. Odeku was a scholar, an athlete, and a true gentleman. He completed his studies at Howard in two and a half years, finishing *summa cum laude* in chemistry and physics; then he went to medical school at McGill University in Montreal and also finished at the top of his class. He went home to Nigeria and was the only neurosurgeon in West Africa. After independence was attained in 1960 he became the dean of Nigeria's medical school, ran the public health service, and still performed operations in the morning before he went to one of his offices. Tragically, he died prematurely at age fifty-five. He just worked himself to death. Odeku impressed me because he knew precisely what he wanted to achieve and why. His courage and commitment are one reason I continue to have hope that Nigeria, despite its tumultuous history, will fulfill its destiny as one of the world's most prosperous and influential nations.

As I proved my abilities to myself, grew in confidence, and gained friends, I learned to appreciate Howard. I developed my black bourgeois credentials and learned the rules and regulations and amenities that go along with being part of the black middle class. Eventually I discovered the joys of college social life. The girls at Howard may have been pretentious husband-hunters, but they were quite alluring. Many girls had a string of guys following them around, pursuing an almost universal extracurricular activity. These were the days before sexual liberation and there was not much sexual activity. My romances consisted mostly of talking and flirting, and when they went beyond that you could still get no further than the panty girdle. It was the era of the panty raid; we would serenade the girls and they would throw their panties out of the window. The trick was to remember to take the name tag out first. I think we got a much bigger thrill from seeing panties fly from the dorm windows while the girls' laughter floated down with them than today's young guys do from seeing girls wear their underwear on public streets.

By senior year I had a steady girl. Sylvia was an only child of a local physician, and she was beautiful and stylish but emotionally very demanding. I was a biology major and everyone expected that I would go to dental school and go back to New Orleans to work with my daddy, and that scenario fit perfectly with Sylvia's personal ambitions. With graduation approaching, our relationship became a source of worry; she was imagining our wedding and I knew I wasn't ready.

I graduated from Howard not *magna cum laude* but "Oh, thank you Lordy." Howard had a rule that if you had forty-five hours of D's you were automatically expelled. If I had made even one D my last semester, I would have experienced that fate. I was nervous about my parents coming to graduation, and my parents didn't understand why I didn't want them to come or why I seemed embarrassed about graduating. The truth was I believed I didn't deserve my degree and felt tremendous guilt for having wasted so much time as well as their hard-earned money.

In retrospect I realize my years at Howard were important to my personal development. I was mature enough upon graduation to regret the lackadaisical attitude I had toward my studies when I started college, but it was college that helped me mature. By the time I graduated from Howard, I had learned to embrace the strengths of the black middle class. I learned to interact in formal social settings, refined my manners and conversation skills, and began to carry myself with self-assurance. Howard picked up where Mrs. Bowen and Gilbert Academy left off. It was the same philosophy—academic achievement and exemplary behavior. I had not fully mastered either concept, but I had grown to appreciate the wisdom of having those abilities in one's repertoire.

Had I failed to come to terms with my identity as a middle-class black person, I would never have accomplished very much in the civil rights movement or won elective office. We could not have persuaded the white establishment to accept social change if we hadn't first worked on persuading the black establishment. Middle-class blacks achieved within the system of segregation and were legitimately concerned about any changes that integration could bring. But they were also in a position to reap the most benefits from any improvements in the status of blacks. I understood the anxieties of the black middle class, but I also knew their most treasured hopes. I spoke the language of middle-class aspirations: it was my parents' language and it had become mine, as well.

For the integration of my own personality, Howard helped me to understand there was a social and cultural reality that was both black and middle class, a tradition that went beyond my parents and Gilbert Academy. I learned it was possible, even desirable, to have a black identity without being poor. My parents and their friends had shown me this, but only at Howard did I accept that part of myself.

The summer before my senior year, back home from college, I

had an encounter with a childhood friend that reminded me how fortunate I was. When the first swimming pool for blacks opened around 1950 at Hardin Playground, I worked there as a lifeguard. One day when I was on duty, a young man came to the pool, put on his swimsuit, and then, as I watched, he staggered rather than dove in and went straight to the bottom as if he didn't know how to swim at all. I dove in and pulled him from the pool and laid him on his stomach to recover. He hadn't been down long, so he coughed up a little water. As he began to get his wits about him I realized that his face was familiar. It was Lincoln.

At Jones School, Lincoln had been one of my best friends, one of my lunch-period buddies. He lived only a few blocks from Jones School. I remembered that one day at Jones School Lincoln and I were playing in the back of a classroom—I think we were in the third grade—sticking an ice pick into the floor in a game of mumblety-peg, and the teacher got upset and sent us to Miss Williams's office. The punishment was most severe: either we brought our parents to Miss Williams's office or we were expelled. We were sent home immediately. "Bring your mother back to talk to me," Miss Williams said sternly, "or you can't remain at Jones School." Miss Williams was a faithful and respected member of Central Congregational Church, so she knew my parents very well. The entire situation was extremely embarrassing for me.

I walked home, the longest way possible, and finally told Mother what had happened. That same afternoon, she brought me back to school, spoke to Miss Williams in her office, and I was readmitted after a strong lecture. But I never saw my friend Lincoln again, and I had never been able to find out what had happened to him.

As soon as Lincoln got the water out of his system and rested for a while, I said to him, "I believe I know you from somewhere. I think we were in school together at Jones School."

He said he had gone to Jones School, but he didn't remember me.

"Yes, you know me," I repeated. I asked him his name. He said his name was Lincoln. I told him that we were put out of school together.

"Yeah," he said, after looking at me for a long time. "You must be Lil' Andrew! Whatever happened to you?" We both cracked up.

Lincoln said that when he went home that day, he never returned because he couldn't get his mother to come back to school with him. "She just never had the time on school days. She had to work. She

worked uptown for white folks and she only made a dollar a day
with nine children, and she couldn't afford to miss work to see about
me messin' up in school."

When I asked him about his father, Lincoln looked at me as if I
was a fool. "I didn't have no father. I'm still tryin' to find his ass. It
was just my Moms, that's all."

Then Lincoln told me the sad story of his young life. He was
older; I was eighteen, he was twenty-two. When we were expelled, he
was ten. After he left Jones School he began stealing and was caught,
committed and interned at one of the boys' homes for juvenile delin-
quents. He virtually grew up in these homes, which hardly corrected
his problems; when he came out he went back to stealing and was
soon caught and committed again. Finally, after exhausting the limits
of the juvenile court system, and being considered incorrigible, he
was sentenced to the state prison at Angola while still a juvenile.

As I listened, I knew that "there, but for the grace of God, go I."
I didn't realize it when I was a child, of course, but the reason I
stayed in school and was now in college was because my mother was
able to come to see Miss Williams, and, in a deeper sense, because my
parents knew Miss Williams. It wasn't really because they cared more
about me than Lincoln's mother cared about him, but because my
parents' circumstances allowed them to do something about their
caring. I realized all the more there was something wrong with a society and an educational system that cared more about the Andrews
than the Lincolns. "There are plenty out there like me," Lincoln said.
"You have to tell my story, because I don't know how to tell it."

The memory of Lincoln remained with me. My parents had
given me more opportunities than any of my poor black friends, or
even white friends, had. Along with the privilege came responsibility.
"From everyone to whom much has been given, from them will much
be required." And as I left Howard, there was a restless place in my
soul asking, "What will be required?"

3

Somebody's Calling My Name

I will lift up my eyes to the hills, from whence will my help come? My help cometh from the Lord who made heaven and earth.

—PSALM 121:1–2

My parents drove up to Howard for graduation, and after the ceremony was over Daddy, Mother, Walter, and I began the long trip southward to New Orleans. It was a journey I had made many times during the last few years. Driving along the rolling Southern hillside always provided me with an occasion for reflection, for contemplation. I thought of it as a trip between worlds, from the Upper South to the Deepest South, from the "world out there" to home, New Orleans.

I was not ready to move on. Once again, I was graduating too young, and leaving just at the time I was beginning to enjoy myself. Daddy and Mother expected me to pursue dentistry eventually, following in Daddy's footsteps, but I had not applied to dental school. Discussion of my future had been carefully avoided, but I feared that on this long, close-quarters trip the subject would somehow surely come up. I knew I was not interested in dentistry, but I simply didn't have the heart to tell that to my father. I felt like I was playing a part. Just a few weeks before, at the Alpha Phi Alpha fraternity dance, I had given my fraternity pin to my girlfriend, which was traditional, but also an indication that we were serious. I liked her very much, of course, but I was not committed—that is, I knew I was not ready to be contemplating marriage. The cornerstone of my self-confidence, my accomplishments in track, had suffered already from trying to fulfill the roles I believed others had assumed for me. I had gone to the Alpha dance because I felt I had to for my girlfriend and my friends, even though I had a major track meet—the Central Intercollegiate Athletic Association relays—the following afternoon. Tired and sluggish, I had cinders kicked in my face by George Rhoden, the great Jamaican runner who held the world's record in the 400-meter run. So, my sensational season at Howard ended with a humiliating defeat.

As we worked our way southward in Dad's Oldsmobile, I felt overwhelmed with other people's expectations and the sense that they differed so dramatically from what I passionately wanted. Daddy wanted me to be a dentist. My girlfriend wanted to get married. I wanted to run and spend the summer training, in the hope I could qualify for the 1952 American Olympic team in track.

Our plan for the drive home was to stop en route at Kings Mountain, North Carolina, where the Convention of the South of the Congregational Church was holding its annual summer conference at Lincoln Academy. The Convention of the South was comprised of all the Southern black churches founded as a result of the Congregational Church's mission effort during the Reconstruction era. Lincoln Academy began as a school but its use by the 1950s was limited to special meetings. Rev. J. Taylor Stanley, the superintendent of the convention, planned and organized the conference in the old Christian camp meeting style. Each year my family attended the conference at Kings Mountain or a summer conference at Camp Knighton at Morbihan, Louisiana, near my father's hometown. Through these annual gatherings, black Congregationalists from Virginia to Texas renewed friendships formed at the American Missionary Association colleges and academies. For most of the pastors and lay participants, this was summer vacation. For their children it was camp.

When we arrived at Lincoln there was a private room set aside for my parents, and Walter was placed in a dorm room with other teenaged boys. I was assigned a room with a young white minister, John Heinrich, who had been a classmate at Yale Divinity School of Rev. Nicholas Hood, our new pastor at Central Church in New Orleans. John was on his way to a Congregational mission in Rhodesia, and he was taking his wife and a newborn baby with him. His sense of purpose struck a powerful chord with me and seemed a sharp contrast to my confusion. His commitment rekindled all the questions that were festering in the back of my mind since the swimming pool encounter with my old friend Lincoln, and his mere presence as an example caused me to intensify that questioning. We never discussed what I, or he, should do with our lives. Nor did we have a conversation about God or Jesus—in fact, he didn't seem the least bit religious to me. What I remember is that he was a good softball player. That impressed me. "The Lord works in mysterious ways, his wonders to perform," as my grandmother used to say.

I found similarly unexpected inspiration in Nick Hood, who was also attending the Kings Mountain conference. He too was very young, only in his twenties, and full of enthusiasm. I had liked Nick since he first came to Central. Nick broke the mold of the traditional black preacher simply by his youth and made an instant impression on me and other young folk in Central, though he may have been disconcerting to some of the older members. His discipline and dedication particularly impressed me; he arose at five every morning to read and study. His sermons, which were down-to-earth, straightforward, soft-spoken in a tenor voice, and sincere, dealt with the application of theology to the concerns of our everyday lives. He was not otherworldly, yet he possessed a depth of spirit that could move the congregation, and under his youthful tutorship Central was full on Sunday mornings. But while I admired Nick, a personal relationship between us did not develop easily. I studiously avoided extended conversations with him—which I felt were sure to include unanswerable questions about my future—and he did not press me.

While we were at Kings Mountain, a group of us decided to skip Bible study and climb to the top of the mountain. The school sat just at the sloping base, and it was maybe a half-mile walk to the peak. When we reached the winding path to the peak, someone suggested we race to the top. Well, I was in top physical condition, and though it was a hot summer day, I just started running down the road. Not jogging, but running. There's no more exhilarating feeling than running when your body is conditioned for it.

I reached the top of the mountain exhausted and looked out at the valley. I was simply stunned by the beauty of everything around me. It seemed as if questions about my direction, what would happen to me, raced through my head in no conscious, organized way as I stared in wonderment at the vista below me; I felt at one with the earth and the heavens.

Mr. Dutton's pattern lay before me. There is such a splendid order to the universe, there is such awesome beauty, I thought, surely there is a God, the creator of heaven and earth. Suddenly, from the top of Kings Mountain my whole life began anew. An awakening occurred. "The earth was the Lord's, and I was God's child." If everything else in the world was a part of God's order, then so must I be a part of some plan of the Creator. The valley was in full bloom. It was the clearest of June days. The greens and yellows of cultivated fields blended with the uncultivated landscape, in harmony. The harmony out there in the valley was what I sought for my own inner being. From the moment of that transcendent experience I thought about a religious purpose for my life that was in tune with my nature, a personal religious purpose that would be at the center of my life.

Later, I didn't say anything to anyone, but in that moment I had begun to think of myself in a new way. Until that point I had lived my life simply as the child of my parents. Now I realized that I didn't *belong* to my parents, but neither did I belong to me. I belonged to something or someone beyond me—the Creator of this universe was also my Creator.

The next day the conference ended and we were back on the road to New Orleans. For the first time I noticed the beauty and peacefulness of the rural South: the rich green expanse growing out of the red clay of Alabama, the Alabama of Tuskegee Institute and Booker T. Washington and the struggle to make Tuskegee a great school, struggles I had read about, heard my parents talk about. We stopped to visit Tuskegee, with its ancient buildings, the old brick baked, and structures built by the earliest students. All that seemed a different time, a different age. Then down through the hills from Montgomery to Mobile, a town set on bays and canals, we descended from the hills like we were gliding to earth in an airplane to the flat basin of the Gulf Coast.

From Mobile, driving westward, there were no elevations as we rode along the Mississippi Gulf Coast, a Mississippi of white beaches and brilliant sunshine, not the mythical Mississippi of frightening swamps and tortuous cotton fields. But we couldn't use those beautiful beaches along Highway 90. I remembered that when we attended the Dryades Street YMCA camp in Waveland, Mississippi, as children, we were warned to maintain a low profile for fear of racial incidents: "Behave, you're in Mississippi now." We drove through Biloxi, Long Beach, and by the entrance to Waveland without stopping; soon we were crossing the Pearl River at its isthmus with its many branches into Louisiana.

I felt joyous and sad at the same time as we crossed the familiar Rigolets bridges, then on to New Orleans. Soon we approached our new brick home on Annette Street near Gentilly Boulevard. We had completed the trip, but the subject of my future had still not been discussed.

Once back in New Orleans, I sensed that whatever my life's work would be, I would never accomplish it at home. As my own father had grown beyond Franklin, I felt my destiny lay outside of New Orleans. My parents had created a wonderful, nurturing society for themselves, with their Straight College friends, Central Church, the YMCA, Mother's bridge club, and Daddy's club, the Boulé. They had carved out a pleasant niche in segregated New Orleans. I was proud of what they had achieved, but I could not live my father's life anymore than he could live his father's.

One of the most difficult decisions for any young person is to determine that Father and Mother may not know best. For several years I had been reading "On Children" from Kahlil Gibran's *The Prophet* and quoting it in letters to my mother, as if to signal my independence of thought and purpose: I may have been unsure about my direction, but I knew I did not want my parents to decide it for me. It said what I needed to say to my parents about what I felt were their heavy-handed attempts to direct my life:

> *Your children are not your children.*
> *They are the sons and daughters of Life's longing for itself.*
> *They come through you but not from you,*
> *And though they are with you yet they belong not to you.*
> *You may give them your love but not your thoughts,*
> *For they have their own thoughts.*
> *You may house their bodies but not their souls,*
> *For their souls dwell in the house of tomorrow, which you cannot*
> *visit, not even in your dreams.*
> *You may strive to be like them, but seek not to make them like*
> *you.*
> *For life goes not backward nor tarries with yesterday.*
> *You are the bows from which your children as living arrows are*
> *sent forth.*

I didn't know what I wanted for my life, but I knew that somewhere God had a plan for me, if only I could find it. Daddy seemed oblivious to my inner struggle. Mother was supportive and sensitive to my searching for God's purpose in my life, but she saw no conflict between serving God and going to dental school to join my father's practice.

My father's single-mindedness about my future as a dentist was related to his abiding fear that he would not live long. He had no illusions about the financial position of his family if something were to happen to him. For that reason, he pushed me through Gilbert and on to Howard, although I was young and immature. I envied Walter's less pressured path, his freedom to attend high school in Princeton. I had asked to do the same when I finished Gilbert Academy, to give myself a year to grow up before starting college, but my father had refused. He was determined that I would finish dental school in the shortest possible time, join his practice, and provide an added layer of economic security for my mother and brother.

I felt that I was unworthy of the high expectations my parents had of me. The vision that I had on Kings Mountain was a direct line into my feelings of confusion and inadequacy. Somehow I had to find the courage to respond to the call of that vision.

For the first few weeks after our return to New Orleans, I did little or nothing. The long-anticipated and feared family discussion about my future had not taken place. I had made no application to graduate school, nor was I looking for a job. With nothing else to occupy me, Nick Hood asked me if I would be interested in helping him drive to Texas, where he planned to attend a weeklong church retreat at a camp near Lake Brownwood. I was in the mood for a journey, but I asked Nick, "Where in the world is Lake Brownwood, Texas?" He said it wasn't far from San Antonio. I decided to drive Nick to the conference and then go down to San Antonio and spend the week visiting my roommate at Howard, Bob Hilliard.

Lake Brownwood turned out to be a very long drive from New Orleans, six or seven hundred miles. It was also a lonely drive, for once we passed Houston, we were seeing fewer and fewer people, and, incidentally, hardly any black faces. As we approached the conference on wooded back roads, night had already fallen and I was feeling as if I was entering a strange and forbidden place. Nick and I began joking about this being our *last* ride. We weren't actually lost, but it felt as if we were.

The conference was an interdenominational retreat sponsored by the United Christian Youth Movement, which included teenagers from some twenty-five Protestant denominations. The organizers had intended it to be an interracial experience, but Nick was the only black pastor to accept their invitation. Later in the week, several black students came from Abilene Christian College, a Disciples of

Christ school. But when we arrived that night, I was the only black young person on the premises, so Jane Alexander, the conference director, and Bob Fudge, a seminary student, begged me to stay on. They had fifty or sixty white students and only Nick to make the conference "interracial." "Nick is great as a minister, but we need you desperately as a participant," they pleaded.

Well, I thought about it. By then it was virtually midnight and I would have to make the long drive to San Antonio alone. As I walked around the site, I became intrigued. There were young whites attending who seemed to be eager to relate to me on a level that I hadn't experienced before with whites. And the place was beautiful and restful. I decided I would stay for a day or so, and see how I felt about remaining.

I look back now on what became a full week at Lake Brownwood as one of the pivotal experiences of my life. It was there for the first time that I read the Bible seriously. I believe that Nick developed his Bible study series for the conferences with me in mind, hoping I would be talked into remaining. In fact, the entire trip might have been a plot on his part. The biblical passages he emphasized in his daily sessions are some of the most intimate passages of New Testament theology, and are still some of my favorites:

> Do not be concerned about your life. Consider the lilies of the field, how they grow; they toil not, neither do they spin. And yet I say unto you, that even Solomon in all his glory is not arrayed like one of these. Wherefore, If God so clothe the grass of the field, which today is, and tomorrow is cast into the oven, shall he not much more clothe you, O ye of little faith?

And:

> For whosoever will save his life shall lose it; but whosoever shall lose his life for my sake and the gospel's, the same shall save it. For what shall it profit a man, if he shall gain the whole world, and lose his own soul?

And an old favorite of Gran's, which I recall when problems mount:

> Be not anxious for your life, let the day's own trouble be sufficient unto the day thereof.

It was Nick's practice to begin each day with a hymn, read a carefully selected Scripture, then make commentary on his selection. Those of us in his class then took an hour to ourselves to meditate on the deeper meaning of his reading. The camp area was undeveloped, with natural rustic beauty, so I always chose to sit alone on a rock overlooking Lake Brownwood during the hour of meditation. I was nineteen, and I don't believe I had ever sat quietly for an hour—or even fifteen minutes. My life, like the lives of most young people, had been a constant beehive of activity. It was all related to growth, learning new skills and strength, but never had I focused on inner strength and development in any concentrated way.

The quiet time at Lake Brownwood opened the door of my inner life, the life of the soul. I was amazed at the way I could sense new things and answers to questions. A quiet confidence and peace about life began to replace the doubt and confusion that had been with me for the past few years. I did not know the answers to my future, but I knew that it would be all right. I still couldn't understand or explain what was happening within me. I knew, however, that there was a spiritual dimension to my life that was gradually awakening.

In retrospect, I can see that I was not only straining to discover a role for myself in life, but trying to acquire the psychological strength to break from the career expectations of Daddy and Mother. My newfound religious purpose provided me with an Authority to support my break. Moreover, that Authority was in keeping with everything my parents had always said they believed, so I knew it would be difficult for them to reject my commitment to work in an area of religious service. I was now prepared to confront Daddy and tell him I was not interested in becoming a dentist. Armed with these strong convictions and a deeper self-knowledge, I began to be open to unexpected and unanticipated possibilities.

Later that summer, I discovered through reading that many creative people did not find their life's work, or receive societal recognition, until they were well along in age. Albert Einstein and Albert Schweitzer were both over forty when they made their mark, so I decided that fifty-five was my target. I could work slowly but steadily until I was fifty-five, and by then I should know what my contribution to life must be. While it may sound amusing to imagine a nineteen-year-old planning his major contribution thirty years down the road, the realization came as a tremendous relief; I no longer had to be the child prodigy.

It also meant I was no longer a burden to myself: this was the heaviest load to be lifted from me. While I had been a model child and went through all the motions of religion—praying, abstaining from alcohol and promiscuity—it was piety without purpose. I no longer felt the burden of weighing my wants versus my parents' designs for my life; I needed only open myself to God's purpose. I ceased to feel so *anxious* about myself, whether I would be rich or successful or important; I didn't care about that. Now I felt I belonged to another set of values. "From them to whom much is given much will be required" began to acquire a real meaning for me beyond what I had been taught as a child.

At Lake Brownwood there were six bunk beds in each cabin, and quite often at night we would lie awake and talk. The whites were mostly from Texas and Oklahoma; a few were from Louisiana. They all spoke with strong Southern accents, the very kind of people I had supposed would be the most prejudiced. But at night, during our talks, we searched for ways to understand one another, to transcend racial and cultural differences. This was the first time I had had such intimate contact with white youth outside of those from my Cleveland Avenue neighborhood, certainly the first time I had met whites who were trying to deal with the reality of racism, who were questioning what they had been "taught" to believe. The amazing thing to me was that it was their religion that was challenging them to question and change. Religion really made a difference in their lives.

One of the people I met that summer, Jim Waite, later became dean of Candler School of Theology at Emory University in Atlanta. Another, Don Shriver, recently retired as president of Union Theological Seminary in New York. They were the future leaders of the new South. As a young Methodist minister, Jim signed an ad, along with eighteen others, calling for adherence to the Supreme Court's school desegregation decision in *Brown v. Board of Education of Topeka* as the law of the land. All the signers of the ad were run out of Mississippi. But it worked out well for Jim—he got his Ph.D. and later returned to the South to teach at Candler.

I came away from Lake Brownwood thinking seriously that I might want to attend seminary and become a minister. When I shared my thoughts with Nick, he seemed a little surprised, despite the fact he had been influencing me in that direction by his own example. "Don't rush," he said. "If you make such a decision, be sure to do so at your own pace." Nick always denied that he was trying to recruit me into the ministry, but I have never believed him.

In early July, very soon after returning home, I received a call from the National Council of Churches' Youth Department. They were recruiting thirty young people to work as volunteers for six months to help organize and empower youth through the United Christian Youth Action. The National Council had sponsored the Lake Brownwood conference, and the Brownwood organizers recommended me. I jumped at this opportunity. They mailed an airplane ticket with instructions to report to Camp Mack, in Indiana, where I was to receive training as a field-worker. Our mandate was to unite one million young people of all denominations to commit themselves to Christ and to become active in their own local churches. There was a national conference going on concurrently; altogether I was to be in Indiana for two weeks.

Camp Mack was sponsored by the Church of the Brethren, one of the historic Peace churches. I was the only African-American attending. There was an African student from Mozambique, Eduardo Mondlane, who later became famous as the founder of Frelimo, the Front for the Liberation of Mozambique. Tragically, Mondlane was assassinated by letter bomb in Dar es Salaam during the 1970s, just before Mozambique became independent. At Camp Mack, Mondlane and I struck up an instant friendship, and we spent a lot of time talking, exchanging ideas and discussing the future.

At Camp Mack I was also exposed, for the first time, to nonviolent theory. Don Bowman, a graduate of Manchester College and a Church of the Brethren layman, gave me a copy of a little book by Jawaharlal Nehru on Gandhi; after I finished that he passed along a collection of Gandhi's articles called *Nonviolent Resistance,* which was published by the Quakers. These books shed new light on coping with the segregated South in which I grew up. While I had been taught that education was an effective way to adjust, Gandhi was pointing a way to change an oppressive system without violating deeply held religious convictions about the use of aggressive violence. Reading these books raised my consciousness; I recognized many of the issues Gandhi had confronted in faraway India and I found myself thinking, "This can work here."

Reading Gandhi, I understood that the Gospel could be applied to a political situation. My parents' faith inspired them to social responsibility, but theirs was an individual effort, helping one person at a time. Good works and personal salvation impacted the social order only indirectly. I realized that it was going to take more than good works to change segregation: it would require a change in the social order. Gandhi described a way for a spiritually based movement to effect such change. I began reading with more and more excitement, continuing with Gandhi's *Autobiography* and any book on or by Gandhi that I could lay my hands on.

It was almost as if my experiences at Kings Mountain, Lake Brownwood, and Camp Mack were a predestined series of related events. I knew I was headed in a meaningful direction; all I really had to do was follow my instincts where they led me. My guilt and anxiety were supplanted by a sense of peace that came from giving my life over to God. I looked forward to the days ahead, not with dread, but excited anticipation and a wondering sense of exploring a new world—my own life. I was excited by what was happening to my life.

After my internship at Camp Mack, Don Newby, an executive with the Division of South Ministry, assigned me to Hartford, Connecticut, where I would work as an organizer in Connecticut and Rhode Island for United Christian Youth Action. When I arrived in Hartford and reported to the Connecticut Council of Churches office, I was sent to live in one of the dormitories of the Hartford Seminary.

There were many World War II veterans registered in the school who, as I had experienced at Howard, in no way acted like my stereotype of a seminary student. I was immediately attracted to their lifestyle, and to the school itself. These were New England Congregationalists who went out drinking on weekends and knew how to have a good time. This was quite a revelation for me. I was going through a period, right after Lake Brownwood, when I was refraining from any sort of mood-altering beverages as part of my new religious self-discovery. I have never smoked, but I wasn't even drinking coffee, tea, or soft drinks. I believed that "the body is the temple of the Holy Spirit," and that I shouldn't partake of any substance that would defile my body. I didn't date or even go to the movies. I took seriously Gandhi's notion of self-denial as a way of controlling one's passions. I decided to live a life of celibacy, listening to the call of the Holy Spirit. That period lasted an entire year, and when I look back on it now I laugh at myself, but I appreciate the discipline and dedication as something I needed very much.

I had been carried on a wave of events from the time I reached Kings Mountain at the beginning of the summer to my assignment at Hartford in the fall. My parents did not interfere, although I was under no illusions that they had accepted that I was unlikely to go to dental school. The three of us maintained a conspiracy of silence regarding my future. I was still nineteen, and they were indulging me, giving me what would later be described as time to "find myself." In their minds, my fate was already decided.

I liked the atmosphere at Hartford and I was intrigued by the students. I decided to enroll in two courses for the fall semester: Philosophy of Religion and New Testament. The classes at Hartford were small and intimate, and professors led discussions instead of lecturing from a distant podium. It was intellectually electrifying. Although I was working as a youth organizer, I woke early to study and came to every class prepared. I read the assigned materials and asked for more reading. I sat in the dining hall with other students and argued over the religious concepts: grace, salvation, social gospel. It was as exhilarating to my mind as track was for my body.

Late in the semester, I approached Dean Tertius Van Dyke about enrolling as a full-time student. My professor had recommended me and apparently had high regard for me and the quality of scholarship I had demonstrated. The dean gave me an application packet that included a release form to obtain my transcripts from Howard and assured me that I would be a welcome addition to the student body at Hartford.

Just before the Christmas break, I received an urgent summons to the dean's office. When I arrived, Dean Van Dyke was frowning at a piece of paper—my Howard transcript had arrived. He cleared his throat. "Mr. Young, this is highly irregular. Normally, an undergraduate record of this kind would not meet our standards for admission." I started to speak in my own defense, but he continued. "However, your record at this institution contradicts these marks and you will be admitted to our Bachelor of Divinity program. Don't give me reason to regret this decision."

I wanted to run around the campus and hug all the trees, but it was time to prepare for my trip home. Admission to Hartford had been the easy part, the culmination of the journey that began at the top of Kings Mountain. Now I had to explain it all to my parents.

4

Jean

And the oak tree and the cypress grow not in each other's shadow.

—KAHLIL GIBRAN, *THE PROPHET*

When I returned home from Hartford for Christmas in 1951, I knew I could avoid a confrontation with my parents no longer. They had been slightly put off by my decision to go to Camp Mack, then on to Hartford, but when I talked with them by telephone they seemed to feel I was merely going through a "phase" and were hoping I would soon come to my senses. After all, there was still "plenty of time" for me to right myself around and apply to dental school; I wouldn't be twenty until March, and they may have thought a year of searching and experimentation was not such a bad idea.

When I confronted Daddy with my decision, he was enormously hurt, and so was Mother. Mother minced no words—she was always emotional and assertive in her opinions. Nonetheless, I knew it was time to break away from her control and take charge of my own life.

When Mother became protective, there was no limit to what she might do. When Walter and I had first left home to go to elementary school, she began going to a Catholic church every day to say novenas for our welfare, despite the fact she was a staunch Congregationalist. And while I was at Howard she concocted a way to continue doing my laundry—in New Orleans. A neighbor on Cleveland Avenue worked on the Southern Railroad, and every week I went to the train station in Washington and presented this man with a bag of my dirty clothes. He took them all the way to New Orleans, a journey of more than a thousand miles. He would deliver them to Mother, then pick up my clean clothes to carry back to Washington when he was ready for his return trip. I thought this was going a little far in motherly protection and dutifulness, but I didn't have the nerve to stop her. Besides, it was better than doing the laundry myself. Fortunately, few of my classmates knew about this arrangement, or I would have been the laughingstock of the dormitory. Those who did know about it were bribed with the occasional piece of homemade angel food cake or oatmeal cookies that were often stashed away with my laundry.

While I was prepared for my mother's emotional responses, I had always been able to reason with my father. Mother *told* you what to do, Daddy made suggestions. But this time was different. One night during the Christmas holidays the three of us got into a terrible argument that ended with my normally soft-spoken father actually shouting at me. "It seems as if I've just wasted all this money sending you to Howard, expecting you to be a dentist. Now you're telling me you want to be a preacher." His words cut like blades. I started crying and Mother burst into tears. I felt as if I had let him down in some terrible way, for I knew how much emotional energy Daddy had invested in what he hoped I would be. My parents had lived, scraped, and saved for Walter and me. But hurt as I was, painful as the confrontation was, I knew I had made up my mind and I just wasn't going to change it. Daddy finally threw up his hands and said if I wanted to enter Hartford then to go ahead, but he wasn't going to pay one penny toward my tuition.

Walter treated me like I was losing my mind, which was funny to me, even at the time, because Walter, who was attending Baldwin-Wallace College in Cleveland, had been much more active in the church, both in Cleveland and in New Orleans, than I had ever been. He was even minoring in religion at Baldwin-Wallace. We had always had a sort of natural sibling rivalry, but in this matter I had hoped for his support. Instead, he taunted me: "Andrew, if you're gonna be a preacher, I'm gonna open up a pool hall saloon across from your church and I guarantee you I'll outdraw you, even on Sundays."

From that point on, Walter and I seemed to switch careers. Walter decided he would be the one to follow Daddy into dentistry, and I defected into ministry. Like my father, Walter was strongly influenced by his faith throughout his life. When he became a dentist, he donated dental treatment to civil rights activists, and today he is a deacon in the church we attend. And eventually both my parents came to accept that I would not become a dentist, marry a nice Creole girl, and settle in New Orleans to relive my father's life. Although they hadn't envisioned me, their eldest son, as a minister, they were devout church people and they couldn't very well reject me for taking seriously the values they taught in their home. In my parents' middle-class New Orleans social set, the ministry didn't carry the social status and esteem they wished for their children, and certainly didn't promise the economic security they valued, but I wasn't worried about that. Now I was freed from the responsibility of fulfilling their expectations.

Despite all the trauma at home surrounding my decision, I was eager to return to Hartford to formally begin school and be on my own for the first time in my life. Mother made sure I returned to Hartford with clean clothes, some transitional money, and a parcel of food. Since Daddy had said he would not pay my tuition, I requested and received a partial scholarship from Hartford. I also took on three part-time jobs: washing dishes in the school cafeteria, working in the library, and cleaning and tending the furnace of an apartment building with my roommate, Hardy Carroll. To my utter surprise, I ended up with more spending money than I ever had in my days at Howard.

The Hartford campus, with its traditional New England architecture—stone and brick—exuded age, crustiness, and inflexibility. But this impression contrasted sharply with the vibrant and innovative spirit of the place: Hartford was brimming with new ideas and was a center of ecumenical and humanistic theology. I liked the interracial, multiethnic atmosphere of the campus. The school was famous for its expertise in non-Western cultures and attracted many students from Africa, the Far East, and the Mideast. My first real interest in world affairs began in the multinational atmosphere at Hartford Seminary. I was also comforted by the closeness and companionship of the African-American students on campus. With them I could feel the pressures of interracial expectations and anxieties fall away—with them I wasn't on trial, nor did I feel I had to "prove" myself.

At Hartford, it seemed, being "different" was the rule rather than the exception. Even the white students differed from the white American norm in their beliefs about race, nonviolence, and service. There were Americans who planned to become missionaries and students from Africa, Asia, and Europe who planned to return home to become religious leaders. We were alike in that we were Christian nonconformists.

I had always thought becoming a minister would mean I would have to be a different person—aloof, otherworldly, and dignified. Now I was reconceiving a life role for myself within the church in which it would be possible for me to retain all the elements of my personality. I could be gregarious and down-to-earth and maintain all my interests, even those not strictly theological, like my athletics. I joined the seminary basketball team while continuing with my running almost as seriously as I had been when I was on the track team at Howard. I realized I could weave things I knew and believed into a new me. I could use all of my talents and abilities toward my new sense of mission, my calling to do God's work in the world.

The public speaking style I adopted for my sermons was just as individual. When I first came to Hartford, while still with the United Christian Youth Action, I had addressed the Connecticut State Conference of Pilgrim Fellowship of the Congregational Christian Church in Bushnell Auditorium, the city auditorium in Hartford. I had a slide presentation with carefully prepared notes on index cards to explain the goals of Christian Youth Action to the more than three thousand young people assembled there. But when I began, to my dismay, the slide projector did not work, and the audiovisual person was operating out of a booth too far away for me to be able make eye contact with him. I was afraid my entire presentation would collapse right in the middle, and I would just be stuck up there, speechless. So with only ten minutes to do something, I dispensed with the index cards and began to describe the call to Christian Youth Action, as the slides were meant to do. I had a thorough knowledge of the subject and had been conducting workshops all around the state of Connecticut with Methodist, Presbyterian, and other youth groups from denominations that were members of the Connecticut Council of Churches. It went over so well that no one would have known there was supposed to be a slide presentation if the slides hadn't come on near the end of my talk. I began to believe the words of Jeremiah, "Now, I have put my words in your mouth" (Jer. 1:9). What I learned then is that material truly well planned in your head and believed in your heart always works better before an audience than reading from a text, even if one reads from a text extremely well. I've heard too many written speeches that went unlistened to because there was no attempt by the speaker to communicate personally with the audience and because the words lacked emotion.

During my first spring at Hartford I continued to train seriously in the hope I could join up with the Pioneer Track Club in New York and prepare for the 1952 Summer Olympic trials in the 200- and 400-meter dashes. I was delighted with the way the semester had progressed and whether I made the Olympic team or not, I was set to reenter Hartford in the fall. However, Mother, who was trying to heal the wounds opened up in our family over my decision to enter the seminary, had, on her own, concocted a plot to lure me back to the South for the summer. When she realized I would not be deterred from my decision to enter the ministry, she contacted Rev. J. Taylor Stanley, the superintendent for the Convention of the South of the Congregational Church, to ask him to obtain a summer job for me, preferably as close to New Orleans as possible.

Thus in May 1952, before I could work out plans to go to New York, I received a call from Reverend Stanley telling me of a small country church in Marion, Alabama, that needed a summer assistant. He asked me if I would be willing to set up a Bible school and recreation program. Occasionally I would also be asked to conduct vespers services. My salary would be five dollars a month. Well, spending the summer in rural Alabama was not at all what I had in mind. Furthermore, I felt Mother's meddling was largely responsible for the proposal. I wasn't that excited about running a Bible school, but I did perk up at the words "recreation program." In fact, that's all I heard. Ultimately I decided I might as well go—they obviously did need someone, Mother's machinations aside. It would not reflect well on my commitment to the ministry if I refused the first assignment offered by Reverend Stanley, who was essentially my bishop. Unfortunately, I would simply have to give up my dream of running in Helsinki.

As I drove home to New Orleans to prepare for my summer in Marion, I took the opportunity to stop in Washington to see my college sweetheart, Sylvia. I had not seen her very often since graduation, but I had kept up a regular correspondence with her, sharing all my dreams for my future as a minister, missionary, and social reformer. This had not been part of Sylvia's plan. Rather than sharing a joyful reunion, Sylvia returned my fraternity pin and broke off our relationship. In many ways, I was relieved. I knew that she was the perfect wife for a socially prominent dentist, but the wrong mate for a Christian missionary. Nevertheless, I was a long way down U.S. 29, the road that led south from Washington, before I stopped crying.

Nothing that had happened to me in the last year—Lake Brownwood, Camp Mack, Hartford, Marion—had been planned. I didn't really want to go to Marion. I did it because I thought I ought to, they needed a minister. I was developing a notion that if you do what you *ought* to do, you'll find that maybe it's better for you than what you wanted to do. That is, assuming you have a clear sense of what you ought to do. Theologically, the question of what one "ought" to do is called "discernment," or trying, in the most profound sense, to discern God's will for your life, but it was only later that I began to discover the theological language and principles behind my own personal beliefs.

Marion, Alabama, is a small town in the middle of the state's black belt a few miles north of Selma, in Perry County. Although not far from a major highway, Marion felt remote and out of the way. Nevertheless, it was and is an interesting and unusual town. It had been the home of Lincoln Normal School, one of the strongest of the early American Missionary Association Reconstruction schools. Lincoln was no longer functioning as a private church-run school, but its presence was still evident in the high educational level of Perry County's black citizens dating back to the postemancipation period. By the 1950s, more black Ph.D.'s had come from Perry County than from many Southern states.I was amazed to discover this rich intellectual tradition in such a rural area.

When I arrived that summer in Marion, I discovered that the church was being repaired and the congregation was temporarily meeting at Phillips Memorial Chapel on the Lincoln Normal grounds, just as Central Church had held services in the Straight College Chapel before the new church was built on Bienville Street. I also discovered, to my dismay, that since the church had no minister they were expecting me to conduct regular Sunday services, even though I was just beginning my seminary training.

I was to live with families in the community who had agreed to lodge and feed me for one week each. After a few weeks of that I set up housekeeping on my own in the old, unused dormitory of Lincoln School.

The first family I was assigned to share meals and lodging with were Mr. and Mrs. Norman Childs, one of the oldest black families in the county. The Childses were immediately warm and generous, and I became more impressed by them as I learned to know them. Mrs. Idella Jones Childs had been a teacher in a one-room school back in the days when she had to fight with the plantation owners to allow kids out of the cotton fields so they could go to school. Her husband, Norman Lorenzo Childs, came from a family that had a long and interesting history. Mr. Childs's great-grandfather, Stephen

Childs, was one of the founders of the Congregational Church and Lincoln Normal School. Stephen's father, James, was a shoemaker who had purchased his own and his wife's freedom before the war, but Stephen went to the Civil War as his owner's body servant. After the Civil War, he sold cotton as far as Mobile, traded cotton futures on the New York Stock Exchange, and opened a grocery store and bakery on Main Street across from the Perry County Courthouse. Stephen encouraged other families of freedmen and freedwomen to purchase land for a school. After one school was burned down by angry whites, Stephen and other leaders, with the assistance of the American Missionary Association, succeeded in establishing Lincoln Normal School.

Norman, the only child to remain in Marion, graduated from Lincoln Normal and continued in the family business. He married Idella Jones, a young widow he'd known all of his life. A certificate from Lincoln Normal permitted Idella to teach school in Perry County, but she never gave up her dream of earning a college degree. By attending school in Selma and Montgomery in the summer, Idella earned that degree the same year her youngest daughter graduated from high school.

The Childses talked to me about their five children, who were on their own or away at college. One afternoon, I began to wander around their house, since they had told me to make myself at home. While looking through one of the children's bedrooms, my attention was drawn to a senior lifesaving certificate on the wall, made out to a Jean Childs. This interested me because I didn't know many black women who could swim at all, and you had to be a very strong swimmer to qualify for a lifesaving badge. Due to segregation, there were very few pools or beaches open to blacks. The girls I knew who might have had the opportunity were usually too concerned about their hair to spend that much time in the water. I began to look at the books that were in the bookcase by the bed. Among her books there was a Revised Standard Version of the Bible, which had been published just a few years earlier by the National Council of Churches. Passages in her Bible were actually underlined, with handwritten notes in the margins.

At that very moment I figured that the Lord intended that I be in Marion, Alabama, to marry this girl whom I had never met, whose belongings I found so intriguing. It didn't hurt that her mother was a striking woman and her father resembled Clark Gable. Even her grandmother had lovely legs, which she proudly displayed by wearing high heels with her elegant Sunday dresses.

Our first meeting took place on the first day of summer, Jean's mother's birthday. I drove with Mr. and Mrs. Childs in their Chevrolet to Tuskegee to pick up Jean, who was helping her brother, Bill, and his expectant wife, Barbara, with their two active children. When we pulled up to the new, brick ranch-style house, Jean came through the kitchen door and walked across the thick, green lawn to meet us. She was wearing a plain cotton dress, with her hair pulled back from a face that looked as if no makeup had ever dared mar its freshness. She possessed such a pure and simple beauty, it was as if she stepped out of my dreams into reality. I wanted to rush out and throw my arms around her. When we were properly introduced, I shook her hand and didn't let go. She had to tug her hand out of my grasp. When she drew away, I realized that my enthusiasm was making her uncomfortable. Although I had been dreaming about her, asking her parents every detail about her childhood, I was a stranger to her. I had to give her time to get to know me, but as I followed her into the house for cake and ice cream, I was even more convinced that she was going to be my wife.

A few days later, arriving at her house, I was startled to find Jean out in the fields milking a cow. She was barefoot, wearing cutoff blue jeans and a raggedy-looking pullover. I didn't mean to offend her, but when I saw her, my first thought was to run back to my car, grab my camera, and ask her if I could take her picture. She *really* got mad! She told me I was treating her like "a little country hick," and that I was the city slicker who was going to take pictures of this country girl and then show them to my friends. Sometime later Jean told me her first impression of me had been that I was too collegiate, too clean-cut, for her. It was only after decades of marriage that she revealed that she had been attracted to me from the beginning, but she didn't want to be the city boy's summer romance. So we got off to a rough start. But at least I had overcome the dreaded preacher image.

Somehow we got past the picture-taking incident and kept talking. Jean had promised her mother that she would help me with the Bible school, so maybe I was getting some inside assistance. Jean was a wholesome country girl, fresh, energetic, and unpretentious. She looked like Hollywood's version of a farmer's daughter in a checked shirt and cutoffs. She was captivating, but she mocked me relentlessly. One day I was helping her carry water in the fields to the cow trough, when she impulsively stopped to pick and eat some pears from a pear tree. She would throw the pear core at me, then grab another one, take a bite, and throw the next and the next at me. So I reached for the bucket of water and told her, "If you throw another pear at me, I'll dump this water on you." Of course, she didn't believe me. I ducked when she pitched the next pear and doused her with the bucket of water, just as I had promised. Jean ran into the house and told her parents I had thrown water on her. She wouldn't even change into dry clothes. She walked around all afternoon wringing wet, telling everyone who saw her, "You see what Reverend Young did to me; he drenched me with a bucket of water."

Our relationship developed over the summer as we spent a great deal of time walking, talking, sharing our hopes and dreams. I told her the story of my life and shared with her my conviction that she would be important to my future. I would pour out my heart and she would just shrug and say she didn't know about the future. That made her even more attractive to me. Jean told me of her problems at Manchester College in Indiana (a Church of the Brethren college), where she felt lonely and isolated as the only black student. She wanted to transfer to Fisk, but her two older sisters, Cora and Norma, had graduated from Manchester, so she was following in their footsteps. I encouraged her to stay at Manchester, mainly, I suppose, because I knew I would have a lot of competition from all the young medical students if she transferred to Fisk. Meharry Medical College in Nashville was noted for training black doctors, and Fisk, on an adjacent campus, for providing the doctors with wives. I figured she'd be kept pretty safe for me out there with the Hoosiers.

Jean surpassed my expectations when it came to athleticism. At Bible school, when recreation period came, she always wanted to play basketball with the boys, and play opposite me. She was a good basketball player, and had been a member of her high school team. Once we were in a place where there was a Ping-Pong table and I said, "Come on. I'll beat you a game of Ping-Pong." She shot back, "No mere man beats me doing anything." She was competitive and she was good. If we decided to walk down the road and jog back, the jogging always ended up in a little race.

Our courting took on an interesting ritual. Jean had a pet cow called Queen, which she had raised from a calf. It had won fourth prize in a contest. Almost every evening when I came to visit her she would be looking for Queen, who had wandered out of the pasture. So I would help her look and we'd end up walking through the woods. The Childses lived on the outskirts of town, on about ten or twelve acres of land, and there were plenty of woods nearby. We spent a lot of time walking through the woods, talking, supposedly looking for the cow. We never found Queen. We'd always come back about dark, and the cow would be in the pasture, without any help from us.

I may have been getting along well with Jean, but I had problems being accepted in Marion as a minister. I was only twenty years old and I looked even younger. The members of the congregation, particularly the elders, were very aware of my youth, and though generally supportive they immediately adopted a paternalistic attitude toward me. I wore tennis shoes and everyday clothes except when conducting services, and even then I shied away from black suits. Such a nonconformist image and my youthfulness were the occasion, I suppose, for a wealth of comments in the town, and some challenges too. I'm sure they were a little put off by my tendency to want to get things done right away without going through the protocol of consulting the deacons.

Some of the challenges had a humorous side. In many ways Marion was like the Cleveland Avenue of my childhood. In my old neighborhood everyone knew me and there was no privacy or anonymity, and Marion was very much like that. When I first moved into the Lincoln Academy dormitory, I wrote to Mother and asked her to send some sheets and pillow cases, as there were none there. The next day everyone in Marion was bringing me sheets and saying, "Why didn't you tell us you needed sheets and pillow cases. We would have given you some." For the life of me, I couldn't figure out how they suddenly knew I needed sheets. Then I remembered I had written Mother a postcard! Apparently, someone in the post office had read the card, told someone else who told someone else, and the next thing I knew my business was all over town.

Once I was waiting to get a haircut in the downtown black community barbershop when a fellow came in drunk and cussing. Someone pointed at me and said, "Don't be cussing in front of him. Don't you know he's the new preacher in town?" The drunk staggered over to me and said, "You a preacher, boy?" I said, "Yes." Then he began quoting the Bible. He said, "And Jesus said come unto Me all ye that labor and are heavy laden, and—" then he pointed to me to finish it. So I replied, "I will give you rest." Then he said, "Blessed are the pure in heart—" and pointed to me to complete the verse. So I said, "For they shall see God." He stood there for what seemed like an hour, though it was only three or four minutes, starting every Bible verse he knew, then pointing to me to finish it. I knew I was being tested; if I couldn't quote Scripture with the town drunk I was in real trouble! It turned out that this man was a veteran and had a master's degree, but had never found employment that permitted him to use his intellect. He had turned to drink in despair.

This was perhaps one of the most striking lessons of that summer. The oppression of segregation was felt not just by those at the bottom at the economic and educational ladder. Even a relatively successful and well-respected family like the Childses suffered from the pressures of segregation. Since the turn of the century, the family had owned a bakery and grocery on the main square in Marion, a legacy of the opportunity that existed during the brief period of Reconstruction. When Jean was in high school, her uncle Amzie sold the family business and Jean always blamed him for the pain it caused her family. But I suspected that Amzie was under a great deal of pressure to sell that property. Whites in Marion had always been uneasy with the presence of prosperous, educated blacks in their midst. A local white banker now lived in the classic Southern house built by her grandfather Stephen, and the Perry County school board had destroyed the most historic buildings at Lincoln Normal when the mission gave the property to them. No level of education or accomplishment would induce whites in Marion to accept the Childses as equals. Rather, their success was an affront to the ideology of segregation.

Amzie's divestment had a terrible effect on Jean's father. Her father had worked all his life in the family bakery and confectionery, even traveling around Alabama during the depression to sell the special peanut brittle they made. Suddenly, that business was gone. Norman Childs began to drink heavily as he floundered in his search for a new career. Finally, he learned a new trade and purchased a shoe repair business. Once he settled on a new path, the drinking stopped. Jean adored her father and was deeply pained by his drinking. When we met, Mr. Childs had regained his full dignity as a breadwinner and business owner. But it was always a reminder to me that no one, no matter how proud the family, was immune to the pressures and injustices of segregation.

As the end of the summer approached, I was even more certain that Jean was the reason the Lord sent me to Marion. We promised to stay in close touch with each other throughout the following school year. Jean understood my desire through religious commitment to dedicate my life to service; I understood and appreciated her intent to serve in the same manner through teaching, and we shared a wish to live and work in the South. We were also sharing a similar educational experience. I was in seminary, and the rules at Manchester were even stricter—students were not allowed to smoke, drink liquor, or dance on campus. Underlying such proscriptions was a religious philosophy that extolled the virtues of a simple, unornamented life, and a rejection of materialism and ostentatiousness that fit hand in glove with the discipline I was imposing upon myself during that period.

Jean and I were both from middle-class black families who had persevered over generations to make a comfortable life in the South, despite the racial restrictions. Both of our families were well rooted in the Congregational Church, and both believed in the value of education as the key to the improvement of conditions for the next generation. Jean and I wanted to use our advantages for the betterment of not just our family but the entire black community. This was the bond that really brought us together and which kept us together, despite our personality differences.

In Marion I had my first on-the-job test of the life role I had chosen for myself, and it was my first experience working in the rural South. When I arrived in Marion at the beginning of the summer, I had no idea what to expect, other than that I would carry out the wishes of the church by setting up small summer programs. When I left at the end of the summer, I felt reassured in the "correctness" of my personal direction. I even began to enjoy preaching. Living in Marion sparked a desire in me to return to the South to live and work, not only because the South was my home, but also because I was convinced that the South, particularly its rural, hardworking blacks, represented a more pure, unpretentious, solid folk force I could learn from and work with than the urban South in which I had grown up.

When it was time for us to return to school, Jean accepted my offer to drive her back to Manchester College in Indiana. We drove first to Chicago to meet Bob Polk, my close friend and classmate from Hartford, and then the three of us went on to Manchester. Bob and I then drove hurriedly back to Hartford to resume our studies.

Jean and I wrote regularly; I sent about three letters a week her way, spilling out my ideas, dreams, and anxieties. When spring came, Jean was elected May Queen of Manchester College, and I drove over to Indiana to be her escort for the occasion. It was an honor for Jean and reflected well on her classmates' commitment to overcome racial prejudice. It probably didn't hurt that the Childs girls had been the loveliest on campus since her sister Norma had entered Manchester seven years before—the Childs women were beautiful in their appearance and Christian spirit. Forty years later, it is still part of the school's lore that Jean was May Queen. Whenever I meet a Manchester graduate, he or she is proud to remind me of it.

Since dancing was forbidden at Manchester, the official occasion was a banquet in honor of the Queen and her court, attended by almost the entire student body. Everyone was friendly and unpretentious, and the hall was transformed with festive decorations. Jean's mother made a beautiful dress for her. After this very formal banquet, Jean and I went back to her dormitory, and with a devilish twinkle in her eye she said to me, "Come on, let's go to the college woods!" She quickly changed into jeans and came downstairs carrying rolled-up blankets and signed out in the housemother's office. "Now, wait a minute," I said, "you all don't drink, don't smoke, don't even dance, but after events everyone heads for the woods?" Well, the "college woods" turned out to be an all-too-wholesome bonfire down by the river, where the students sang lively songs, toasted marshmallows, and cuddled up for a little necking. In New Orleans, the "college woods" would have suggested something a lot more provocative.

That summer Jean was awarded a six-week fellowship from the Church of the Brethren to go to Europe to work in an Austrian refugee camp sponsored jointly by the Brethren and the Society of Friends. The rebuilding of Europe after the devastation of World War II was still in progress. I had hoped to see Jean during the summer, so I borrowed money from my parents to make the trip too. We went by boat, the *Arosa Kulm,* with four hundred other students on a ten-day trip across the Atlantic to Le Havre-de-Grâce, France. It was a rough trip, and Jean was seasick for several days. There was no recreation on board, as this was not a pleasure ship—we were unpaid volunteers going to rebuild Europe by way of the cheapest transportation available.

We traveled around Europe by bus and to Austria through East Germany via military train. The windows of the train were covered with sheet metal that appeared to have been nailed down, and they reminded me of Winston Churchill's use of the phrase "iron curtain" in his famous address at Westminster College in Fulton, Missouri. We were told that the East Germans had not done as good a job in repairing the damage of the war as had been done in West Germany, so they didn't want the area to be seen or photographed.

After a short train ride we hitchhiked in groups through Austria to our separate destinations. Jean was assigned to Linz, and I to Ried, in the Austrian Alps. These were camps for the refugees streaming into the West from points in Eastern Europe, mainly Romania and Yugoslavia. Jean worked with children in her camp. I helped build a community center in Ried. The two camps were thirty miles apart.

We really wanted to be together, but we were the only African-Americans in the entire group, and the leaders wanted us to split up so there would be two camps with interracial teams. We decided to accept the "burden of the race" and go to different camps.

In Ried I was an instant celebrity and curiosity, and I'm sure Jean was in Linz, for in this area of Austria the people seldom saw blacks. It was a more open, honest curiosity and wonder than either of us had ever experienced with white Americans, who were much more repressed and covert about their racial curiosity. For instance, when my hair became so long and unruly I could no longer comb it, I decided to try to get a haircut in Ried, which caused an unbelievable commotion. There I was, in a barbershop for both men and women, trying to explain to the barber in my broken German how to cut my hair. All the women simply stopped what they were doing and came over to watch. Whenever the barber shaved off a little hair with his clippers the shoeshine boy picked it off the floor and gave away pieces of my locks to the spectators. People even came in off the street to watch!

The European summer created interesting dynamics in our personal relationship. We both established close friendships with others under much freer and less inhibited circumstances than had existed when we had met in Jean's community of Marion the previous summer. I was a little taken aback when Jean reported her innocent but admiring friendship with a Croatian exile who had sailed dramatically across the Adriatic Sea to freedom. I suppose my ego was slightly bruised. Jean pointed out that I had formed close friendships with other women, and if she needed to accept my friends, I would have to accept hers. We were forced, in effect, to recognize that our being in love did not change the fact that we were two separate individuals. All our interests or inclinations would not and could not coincide. It was time to read Kahlil Gibran to myself, "For the pillars of the temple stand apart/And the oak tree and the cypress grow not in each other's shadow."

We grew, both individually and as a couple, that summer. In our heated discussions as we traveled through Europe, we were forced to adjust our romantic notions of each other to a more realistic appraisal. I vividly remember one particularly telling event. After our arrival in Europe, the men and women checked into different hostels and met for an evening exploring Munich. Jean and I split off from the larger group to enjoy private time that would be all too rare that summer. When the time came to take her home, I discovered Jean didn't know where she was staying, not the name of the hostel, not the address. I was exasperated beyond belief! This was Jean's first time being on her own in a new place without someone else to take care of her. Even her first year at college, her older sister Cora was with her.

Toward the end of the summer we returned to Berlin to join Jean's oldest sister, Norma, who had received her master's degree in social work and was living in Berlin working with YMCAs and USOs. Norma was the most adventurous of the Childs girls. Nearly six feet tall and strikingly beautiful, she had the confidence of a smart woman with a memorable appearance. She had friends everywhere. With Norma as our guide, despite our meager funds, we took off on a wonderful tour through Germany and Italy before returning home.

In Europe, we were permitted to eat in restaurants, stay in hotels and youth hostels, freely explore museums, and purchase tickets to concerts without reference to a "colored" section. We were subject to a lot of curiosity, but none of it was hostile. It was an enlightening experience, helping me realize how much I had always carried my own sense of freedom within myself. My parents had taught me never to internalize other people's prejudice. So while I enjoyed Europe, there was no sense of euphoria from being away from Jim Crow. I had always felt free.

Once we returned to school Jean and I continued to write to each other. Now our letters said "when we get married," not "if we get married." In my letters I wrote of my hope to avoid the pitfalls of marriage. I knew there would be marital problems but felt we should try to anticipate them. In my earnestness I even decided to write my senior thesis on the Christian view of marriage. I was reading all the different theologians and I had books stacked three feet high around my desk. I wrote Jean, partly as a way of discussing issues with her, and partly to work through my own beliefs. Emil Brunner argued that love was too fickle and transient a notion to serve as a basis for Christian marriage. In marriage, one had to remain true and loyal even when a spouse was not lovable. Marriage had to be a commitment based on rational process. Jean was very strong-willed and possessed an unwavering conviction that she would preserve her own identity and separate personality. It was the fifties and the pressures for women to find fulfillment solely through marriage were enormous, so I felt at the time that she went overboard to protect herself. She had to have a different opinion on any subject, no matter how minor. If I said the sun was bright, she would point out that it was covered in a haze. She was also very competitive, and I knew that I would have to have a strong ego if our marriage was to succeed. In our favor, we had complementary callings. At the time I wanted to serve in Africa, and her goal was still to serve in the South, but we were both committed to serving black people. I wanted to engage in a Gandhian program for social change, and she wanted to end oppression through education. Our challenge was to reconcile our goals without sacrificing our basic integrity, and I felt we could do that.

I was also a little apprehensive about the physical side of marriage, and I sent her a couple of manuals on lovemaking in marriage. When she sent them back, there were fingerprints and smudge marks on what I felt were the important pages, so I figured we would be all right.

We had planned to see each other over the Christmas holidays. First, I went home to New Orleans and told my parents what they already suspected, that I planned to propose to Jean and hoped the wedding could be in the early summer. I think Mother still had hopes I would marry a New Orleans girl and come back there to live. But, true to form, Mother's feelings were expressed in her actions rather than her words. She gave me a beautiful small diamond that had belonged to Grandmother Fuller, my beloved Gran. From this diamond I had an engagement ring set in white gold. Then I drove over to Marion to join Jean and her family. Soon after I arrived at the Childses' home I said matter-of-factly to Jean, "Your Christmas present is in my duffel bag, why don't you go search for it." She found the package, unwrapped it, ran back into the living room, and punched me playfully on the shoulder. "What a strange way to propose to somebody!" she said. "Anyway, you have to ask my father for my hand." And so I did, though there was no surprise—I believe everyone in the house knew exactly why I was there.

We immediately set a date of June 7, 1954, for the wedding, in Marion, after Jean's graduation from Manchester College. Then we spent the next few days eagerly discussing the details. We wanted to do something a little different: instead of having a traditional wedding, we wanted to be married by Nick Hood, as part of the regular Sunday morning church service. At the point where the minister asks, "If there is anyone who wishes to make an announcement or join the church, they should now come forward," we would both come forward and say, "Yes, as a matter of fact, we would like to get married now."

This scenario did not sit well with either of our mothers, however. Jean's mother sang a sad song: "Oh, Cora eloped, and Norma isn't married and this is going to be the only wedding I'll have for one

of my daughters and now you all are going to deprive me." My
mother complained too: "All these people we've been giving wedding
presents to all these years are going to want an opportunity to give
you all presents. And you're going to need some, as poor as you're
going to be. You all have to have a real wedding." Mother also said
she wanted to have a reception for us in New Orleans, though Jean
wanted the wedding to be in Marion. So we decided to compromise:
scrap our novel low-key wedding, have an early-morning ceremony
at the church in Marion, and then, with the contingent of out-of-
town guests, drive to New Orleans for a reception at my parents'
home. It was a six-hour drive, across narrow rural roads, and
although it could be done, it would be an arduous day for all concerned. But at least both families would be satisfied.

That's exactly what we did. Nick performed the morning ceremony. Many of my friends and relatives drove over from New
Orleans. Hardy Carroll, my roommate from Hartford, came down
for the occasion, and four of Jean's classmates drove down from
Manchester College. Mrs. Childs had a fine brunch after the wedding
for all the guests. Then we all climbed into about twenty-five cars to
make the long drive southwestward to New Orleans.

Everything went fine until we reached Purvis, Mississippi, which
is near Laurel. Somehow our wedding caravan got ahead of a driver
from Chicago who decided he wanted to pass all the cars in our
party. In doing so he ended up going about ninety and was pulled
over by the police at Purvis. But the policeman decided to stop not
only him but *all* of the cars in our party. We all received speeding
tickets, though we were not speeding, and we had to go to the courthouse to pay the fines.

Actually, it was kind of funny to us; we were in such an ecstatic
mood that something like this, which happened all the time in Mississippi, was not about to ruin our day. The only potentially serious
problem was with Jean's friends from Manchester, who were traveling together and were flagged down along with the rest of our caravan. When the ticketing policemen reached their car, they were so
certain these white girls were not with us they waved them on. The
girls didn't know what to do, so they pulled over to the side of the
road and idled, waiting to follow us wherever we were taken. Thankfully, quick-thinking Uncle Walt, without the policemen observing
him, told them, "You all go on down the road a few miles and wait
until you see us pass to rejoin us. Don't follow us into Purvis!" Uncle
Walt knew that this not-too-bothersome rip-off to fatten the town
coffers could turn nasty if the officers discovered they had flagged

down an interracial wedding party. We might never get out of jail, and there was no telling what might happen to the girls.

When we drove into Purvis, the justice of the peace was sitting on a barrel outside this rural town's country store wearing bib front overalls and a wool cap with a farm product logo on it. As the sheriff passed by he gave a two-fingered whistle and the justice of the peace stood up and ambled over to the courthouse.

Since I had only thirty-five dollars to my name, Uncle Walt volunteered to pay the $17.25 fine. When we arrived at the courthouse and they realized we were a wedding party, the justice of the peace got playful and began to tease us about making us spend our wedding night in separate cells. Then he gave me too much change from the twenty-dollar bill I gave him for the ticket and I very proudly pointed out his mistake and gave him back the extra change. Everyone remained calm and eventually they sent us on our way. Once again I had reason to thank my father for teaching me to stay in control. One cross word said in frustration, and we might well have spent our honeymoon in a Mississippi jail. More important than our anger was our desire that this incident not ruin our wedding day.

Fortunately, Mother and Daddy had left Marion a little ahead of us, since she needed time to prepare for the guests. That night Mother had her reception in grand style, as if nothing whatsoever had happened. She invited all of her friends from Central Church, her bridge club, The Links, the Carousels, and Straight College alumni to fill the house. Mother stacked the many presents in their silver and white wrapping paper on the pool table, because every table surface on the first floor was covered with bowls and platters of Creole delicacies. Jean and I cut the traditional three-tiered cake with white frosting and fed each other pieces as a symbol of the life we would share.

When we were thoroughly feted, toasted, and teased, Jean and I left the reception to go to Uncle Walt's log cabin in Slidell for a brief honeymoon hideout. My bride was too embarrassed to wear the frilly nightgown she had been given for that night. She wore pajamas that her mother made from the cloth of Purina chicken-feed sacks. So it was, we began our forty years of life together. Every day a challenge. Every day a blessing.

5

Serving Bethany

Jesus on the main line, tell Him what you want.
—AFRICAN-AMERICAN PRAISE SONG

After our honeymoon in Slidell, I returned with Jean to the place where I had begun the path that led me to her: Kings Mountain. It had been only three years since I had arrived at Kings Mountain a confused teenager, tied to my mother's apron strings, facing an uncertain future. In those three years, I had learned to listen for the still small voice of God and to put my life in God's hands. I returned to Kings Mountain married to the woman I believed God had chosen for me, seeking guidance for the next destination on my journey of faith.

Jean and I caused quite a stir at the summer gathering at Kings Mountain. Our status as newlyweds seemed to thrill the teenagers, but also we were a young couple committed to ministry in the South, something that was in short supply. Founded to prepare teachers, pastors, and leaders to serve the communities of newly freed slaves, American Missionary Association schools like Fisk and Howard were now capable of offering an expanding array of professional programs. The older graduates of AMA schools, who themselves didn't have such opportunities, began to encourage their children to enter professions more lucrative than the ministry or teaching. The excellent education offered in the AMA's primary and secondary schools made it possible for their high school graduates to leave the South and to prosper in the Northern industrial cities. As a result of these migrations, small Congregational churches were losing members and finding it difficult to recruit leadership. To the shrinking pool of black Congregational ministers, the growing, affluent congregations in cities like Atlanta or Chicago were more attractive than the small mission churches of the South.

Leadership development for the churches in the Convention of the South was one of Rev. J. Taylor Stanley's biggest concerns, and he took great care in his recruitment and placement of new ministers. As the superintendent of the Convention of the South, he functioned as our "bishop." In the polity of the United Church of Christ, each congregation retained the authority to call its own pastor, but few churches questioned Reverend Stanley's wisdom in his selection of recommended candidates. Matching clergy and congregations was one of his many gifts. I went to Kings Mountain to receive my summer assignment from Reverend Stanley, without any idea what it might be. When Jean and I found out we were assigned to Bethany Congregational Church in Thomasville, Georgia, we got in our car, already packed with everything we would need for the summer, and drove directly from North Carolina to southwest Georgia.

We arrived in Thomasville to discover that the parsonage was in significant disrepair. On the small stipend we received from the church and the Convention, renting a house was impossible, even if one had been available, so the church leaders arranged for us to live in the home of a member, Mrs. Mosey Flipper. Jean and I continued our still new married life in the back room of Mrs. Flipper's small frame house. We worked together much as we had that summer in Marion, organizing a vacation Bible school for the children and youth in the community that included sports as well as Bible study. I think it was the first time the pastor's wife had ever been seen on the basketball court. I preached at Sunday services; we got to know the members and they got to know us.

Jean and I knew we wanted to serve a church in the South and Thomasville seemed a likely place. It had a sizable black community, including an educated group of teachers and businesspeople, and we found the parishioners warm and loving.

When the summer came to an end, we had to return to Hartford so that I could complete my seminary education and earn the Bachelor of Divinity degree that would qualify me for ordination in the United Church of Christ. Jean was able to secure a teaching position at Arsenal School, an inner-city primary school with mandatory showers three times a week. The administrators were trying to ensure good hygiene with the shower policy, but it was a real hardship for one little girl in Jean's class who came to school neat as a pin, her hair painstakingly pressed. The showers ruined the child's hot-combed hair and Jean, a new teacher and still very timid, tried to intercede on her behalf, but to no avail. Jean had been supportive of my attempts to work with the parishioners in Thomasville, and this was my opportunity to support her work in the harsher environment of the Hartford public schools.

My tiny student apartment seemed luxurious after our summer in one small room, but we soon discovered it lacked one amenity: Mrs. Flipper's cooking. So it was that I discovered that my new wife was entirely sincere in explaining that she did not know how to cook. The first time Jean cooked breakfast, she actually burned the toast. It was such an absurdly classic newlywed experience that I couldn't stop laughing. In disgust, she threw half a glass of milk in my face, which only made the situation more hilarious to me. When we both calmed down, I persuaded her that it was only fair that I do the cooking, first, because I knew how, and second, because I was a student and even with my part-time jobs I had more flexibility than she did working at the school all day.

Jean adjusted without complaint to my bachelor friends from Hartford Seminary, who had the habit of dropping by at all hours. While we had always visited back and forth, a couple of my buddies seemed to be hanging around more than they had in the past. One, Bob Polk, had known Jean's sister Cora in Chicago. I think Jean was a reminder that he had let a good woman go when he couldn't work up the courage to ask Cora to marry him.

As I was finishing seminary I learned that the Congregational Church in Birmingham needed a minister, but Reverend Stanley did not suggest I apply there. I was hurt at the time, but Reverend Stanley was very deliberate when it came to the development of clergy in his domain. He steered me toward rural churches to broaden my experiences and deepen my understanding of Christian spirituality. By this time Nick Hood had moved to Detroit and he urged me to go to a Congregational Church in Gary, Indiana, that was looking for a minister. But Jean was eager to return South and I respected Reverend Stanley's advice.

With my degree from Hartford and a "call" from Bethany Congregational Church, I was entitled to seek ordination. My mother, who had lost the battle to have my wedding at Central Church in New Orleans, would not consider that I could be ordained anywhere else. Mother organized my ordination ceremony and virtually every prominent black Congregational clergyman in the South participated in my consecration to ministry: Reverend Stanley, Nick Hood, Homer McEwen from First Congregational Church in Atlanta, and Harold Long of First Congregational Church in Birmingham. As I knelt before the altar, heard the charge, and felt the hands pressing on my head, I truly felt the energy of the Holy Spirit and an affirmation that I was treading the path God had chosen for me.

So it was that we went back to Thomasville from Hartford in January 1955, ready to settle down. I was nearly twenty-three years old, and this was my first full-time job. My pastorate now included Bethany Congregational Church in town and Evergreen Congregational in the hamlet of Beachton, a few miles outside of town.

Thomasville was located in the black belt of southwestern Georgia, which W. E. B. Du Bois described in detail in *The Souls of Black Folk*. It is an area where for generations blacks made their livelihood working massive plantations owned primarily by wealthy Northern absentee landlords. George Humphrey, secretary of the treasury in the Eisenhower administration, owned one of the plantations, as did John Hay Whitney, a chairman of the board of Yale University, and other prominent Northern whites. The crops were basically okra, peanuts, and cotton; corn was planted for animal feed.

Our first project when we returned to Thomasville was to rehabilitate the parsonage, which was on the second floor of a two-story building on Fletcher Street, across from the church. We were grateful for Mrs. Flipper's hospitality, but we needed our own home. We spent the next month putting up Sheetrock, laying tile, and renovating a dump into a livable dwelling. We planted azaleas and camellias in the yard and laid a lush lawn of St. Augustine grass.

Once Jean and I had settled into the old parsonage, I plunged into learning as much as I could about the area, my new churches, and the people in the congregations. It did not take me very long to discover that the two churches, though both Congregational in name, were distinctly dissimilar in style. Bethany was much like the Congregational churches I grew up with. Evergreen, in Beachton, was Congregational in name, but black Baptist in style. Traditionally, the Congregational Church service is extremely restrained, befitting its New England Puritan origins. The tone of the service is one of rationality and intellectual appreciation of the Lord and His works. There is rarely, if ever, a passionate expression by the minister, and seldom any outbursts from members overcome with the spirit. The Congregational services are usually short, to the point, with a spare liturgy and ritual, and follow a planned order of service.

Raised a Congregationalist of the staid variety, I often reflected on how the presence of Congregational churches in the black South, though related to our educational history, was nevertheless a cultural anomaly: the northeastern, rational Puritan style is at an opposite pole of cultural expression from the emotional, dramatic African-American style. However, the Congregational churches were introduced to black Southern communities on the wings of the missionary school for the freedmen movement after the Civil War. Wherever there were historic AMA schools like those in New Orleans, Kings Mountain, Marion, Thomasville, and Beachton, there was community pride associated with the educational legacy of these schools. Congregational churches were founded to serve as the home church for these schools. By the mid-1950s, many of these schools had become precious memories, but the churches often survived. This was true in Thomasville and Beachton, as well as New Orleans, Kings Mountain, and Marion.

The history of Evergreen Church fascinated me. The Evergreen congregation had moved to south Georgia en masse from Alabama. They were forced to flee in 1911 when their minister, who was trained in an AMA school, was discovered teaching his members to read, write, and count. The local whites terrorized the minister and gave him twenty-four hours to leave the county. He left, but only to find a new home for the entire congregation. He came back, and one amazing night the entire congregation packed their belongings and left Alabama forever, settling in Beachton, Georgia, not far from the Florida state line. I learned from Mrs. Flipper that they chose Beachton because the Allen Normal School was there. They wanted their children to be educated even though then, as now, the only employment in the Thomasville area was work on plantations.

Evergreen Church forced me right away to modify the laid-back style of service I had so carefully groomed at Hartford Seminary. I was soon caught up in the warmth and emotion of my congregation. Their spontaneous songs and fervent amens were a real confidence builder. My training at Hartford Seminary taught me to develop a simple, direct message and a tightly organized order of worship. This approach never worked at Evergreen. Any time there was a brief lull in the service, the congregation automatically slipped into one of those old-time gospel hymns. Pretty soon they had worked up a steady rhythm, clapping and tapping their feet, which left me trying to figure out how to regain control of the service without asking the congregation to be quiet.

After a few tries at delivering a sermon that would have been acceptable to my seminary professors, I was given this advice by the deacon of the congregation: "Some of our folks don't trust a preacher with a whole lot of paper. The Lord doesn't need that paper to make Himself heard. They see paper and they think the devil has gotten up in your preaching." That deacon's insistence that I preach from the heart and not the paper turned out to be a real blessing. I had studied the "three point" sermon style in seminary, but it was not an authentic approach for me. Evergreen gave me license to experiment and develop my own true style, which I modeled on jazz improvisation. Rather than preach three points on a text, I chose one, then developed three variations on the theme. In many ways, it required more preparation, because I had to memorize my key themes rather than jot them on note cards. But the Evergreen congregation was so loving and accepting that I quickly became comfortable with this new style. No matter what I said, Deacon Spearman hummed "True," or "Well, *praise* the Lord!" They got their rhythm going, pulled me into their rhythm, and before long I found my own rhythm. And gradually, I learned the very old hymns and ancient spirituals that are not written down, like "Jesus on the Main Line, tell Him what you want." I grew to be more at ease with them and to love the church's softly hummed communal chants. I even learned how to adjust the Order of Worship so that it could be integrated into the traditional folk structure the Evergreen congregation already knew.

Once again, my youth drew a lot of attention. The nontraditional clerical lifestyle Jean and I followed was startling to some people in the Thomasville area. I thought I should be measured by my works, though, and was determined to remain the person I had always been. I also knew that my concept of a nontraditional ministerial role helped make my marriage work, for Jean had always made it clear she was not going to be a typical "minister's wife." As Jean told our friends in Thomasville, "I don't sing, I can't direct the choir, I don't play the piano, and I'm not interested in being a social butterfly." Jean taught Sunday school because she liked teaching, but she felt no obligation to conform in other ways. On Sunday afternoons after church, Jean and I played ball with the kids, we attended dances given by friends, and Jean wore shorts in our yard. Not surprisingly we were criticized for it.

I remember in particular that some of the older, more traditional ministers didn't take kindly to the fact that I played guard on the YMCA basketball team. After we played a game one Friday night, one of the ministers denounced me from the pulpit the following Sunday in another church, proclaiming that a "true preacher" had no business "running up and down some floor half naked." But, while I would alter the style of the church service to make it more comfortable for the congregation, I was determined not to be a slave to what I felt was simply mindless and petty tradition. If I was forced to conform in that way, I was prepared to leave. The words spoken by Rev. Homer McEwen of Atlanta in my Ordination Charge seemed quite real to me now: "Preach with your bags packed because if you *really* tell the truth, people will be offended and you'll have to move on to the next town." Well, I learned then to keep my bags packed and tell the truth, and that has remained a constant in my character in the decades since.

I did finally come to accept the fact that folk in the rural black South were quite formal. In Thomasville I was called "Reb" or "Rev" or "Rev. Young." No one called me "Andrew," which would have been fine, or "son," which I would have hated. I made it a practice to address adults as Mr. or Mrs. because local whites called them by their first names, which they deeply resented. I only called people by their first names if I was on very intimate terms with them; and if they were my elders, never. It was insulting to hear whites calling an elderly black woman "Betty" or "Daisy" or "Rometta" when they were hardly acquaintances, much less friends. Jean was called by her first name fairly often, but mostly she was "Mrs. Young," even though she was considerably younger than most of the women in our churches.

My salary was $40 a month from Bethany in Thomasville and $50 a month from Evergreen in Beachton. The AMA office subsidized us with an additional $100 per month. As in Hartford, Jean was able to obtain work teaching at the segregated Thomasville elementary school, earning about $250 a month; so, once again, she earned most of the money.

Our oldest daughter, Andrea, was born our first year in Thomasville. While Jean was at school, Mrs. Laura Hayes, a wonderful friend, helped baby-sit. During services, Jean scarcely had a chance to hold the baby because the women passed her around the congregation. People in Thomasville had that small-town openness and friendliness; because so many friends helped take care of Andrea she was raised as the "community baby."

The pace in Thomasville was relaxed, and though I had my hands full with church activities—conducting Sunday services, visiting and getting to know each family in both congregations, initiating recreation programs, and carrying forth with other traditional church activities, conducting weddings and funerals—there was still ample time to expand my reading. I remember I got so wound up in Dostoyevsky's *Brothers Karamazov* I hardly left the house until I finished it, and it's a long book. I was also becoming interested in the theology of Paul Tillich, and read as much of his works as I could, while continuing my reading of and about Mohandas Gandhi. I think I read more during those years in Thomasville than at any other time. And it was only then that I really began to understand the books that I had merely read for credit while in school.

Throughout the Bible there are periods of testing and wandering: forty days in the Ark for Noah; forty years in the wilderness for the Israelites leaving Egypt; forty days in the wilderness for Jesus. My Thomasville pastorates provided an opportunity for me to test and prove to myself that I could achieve without my parents' reputation to back me up. I did not know where it was leading, but trusting in the Lord had provided a wife and a profession. I continued to trust, and remain open to God's plans for my life. Remaining open to God, I learned a great deal from my parishioners.

Many of our church members lived on farms and it helped my relationship with them to show an interest in farm life. If I went to visit a family and they were in the field, I would go out to the field too. Sometimes I spent half the day working in the field with a family. Often we cut okra—a plant that is extremely irritating to the skin, so gloves are necessary for protection. In ninety-degree heat sweat drips down into your gloves, so at the end of each row I'd have to pour out the liquid collected in my gloves. Peanuts are harvested by shaking the root of the plant, and they're a dirty mess. That's why in West Africa they're called "groundnuts." I also picked a little cotton and a few peas. Sometimes on a visit the family would take me out to their fields and let me pick watermelons or pull up some sweet potatoes to take home. If they had slaughtered a hog, they'd give me some of that, and if someone had shot a deer, we'd get a piece of venison. Poor as the people were, they knew how to live well off the land, how to treasure it and cultivate it. And they were always generous.

Working in the fields was new to me, and I loved it. Having been born and raised in the city, I had never done this kind of work and of course I knew nothing about it. So this was a chance to share with my parishioners work they had been doing all their lives, to become one with them in this way, and to learn from them. It made me feel good to imagine the twinkle in an elder's eye when one of his friends came by while I was out in the fields and he would say: "That's our young preacher out there, cutting some okra."

I learned a lot from an old blind man, Uncle Joe Metcalf, who was legendary in those parts. Uncle Joe was a farmer. Until he was nearly seventy-five he could still load a log into a truck, Uncle Joe grabbing one end and his son the other. He had huge hands, strong and weather-beaten from decades of tilling the soil. Once when I went to visit Uncle Joe, I had with me a copy of *Christ and Time* by Oscar Cullmann. It was a study of concepts of time, the various terms for time in the Bible, and the Greek terms, *Kairos* and *Khronos*. Uncle Joe was sitting on his front porch swing, surrounded by corn fields, a watermelon patch, and collard greens. I placed the book on the swing between us and he felt for it and picked it up.

"What's this, Preacher?" he asked.

"It's a book," I said.

"What's the name of it?"

"*Christ and Time.*"

"Oh, yeah," he said, "there's God's time and when God gets ready, you got to move. You can do anything you want to in those fields, Preacher, but it's not until God's time that the flowers bloom and the trees bear fruit." And he sat there talking, in his black folk idiom, about essentially what Oscar Cullmann, the German theologian, had attempted to document through biblical scholarship. It was amazing to me to listen to him give a lecture on time, and on the life cycles of nature, based on his experience as a farmer and his faithful reading of the Bible.

Uncle Joe had cancer and yet he would sit there on the porch, never taking any medicine for pain. Sometimes he would be talking and he'd reach down and grab his chair or the chair next to him which someone was sitting in. Even though he was almost ninety, he was still so strong that when he squeezed he would move that chair. You could tell he was in pain, but when you'd ask him, "How you feeling, Uncle Joe?" he'd answer, "Oh, pretty fair." I could feel, through him, the power of ordinary people to survive and endure hardship.

The trustees of the Evergreen Church also furthered my "education," but in a different way. When I began pastoring the church in Beachton, it had an outdoor toilet. A year or so later, the toilet caved in. So I had to build another one, which was something of a problem because the state had recently passed a law raising the minimum quality standard for outdoor toilets; concrete linings were now required. You couldn't just dig a hole anymore and throw a shack over it.

When I looked into the expense of building the new outdoor toilet it dawned on me that it was about the same as building an indoor toilet. We already had a well and a pump that wasn't working, so I figured out how much it would cost to get the pump fixed, then went to the hardware stores and in great detail priced secondhand plumbing fixtures. Finally, I worked the cost of building an indoor toilet down to less than the cost of a new outdoor toilet.

So into the next trustee meeting I strode with my plan to build an indoor toilet, my figures researched to the last penny. However, after I proudly presented my proposal everyone sat there and no one said a solitary word. When it came time to vote, the trustees voted against an indoor toilet. Unanimously. I just couldn't understand it.

Finally it occurred to me that indoor toilets were considered quite a luxury and there were a number of church trustees who themselves did not have indoor toilets. They were not exactly thrilled with the idea of the church having one when most of the people in the church still had outdoor toilets. But no one told me that. I also realized my mistake in bringing in the plan as my idea; possibly if I had just suggested it to a trustee before the meeting, and that trustee had picked it up as *his* idea, it would have been different. From then on, when I had an idea I wasn't sure would fly I discussed it with a selected few trustees as a possibility, only a possibility, but never proposed it myself in the larger meeting. Sometimes, to my surprise, and when I least expected it, the idea would surface as the proposal of this or that trustee and it would soar like a bird. That strategy served me well years later during the hectic infighting at the Southern Christian Leadership Conference.

In this way, I learned about the realities of my parishioners' lives and something, as well, about the larger economic structure that undergirded their livelihood. One of the many unnecessary tragedies of the South was created by the structure of the farm subsidy programs. Essentially, these programs paid farm owners not to use the land; the result was that folks like my parishioners lost their jobs and their homes. The tenant farmers and sharecroppers never earned enough cash money from their hours at work picking, but the plots of land they had access to on a plantation allowed them at least to provide sufficient, even plentiful food for their families. The federal programs required all that land to lie fallow. When the big farmers went on "welfare," eventually their former workers were driven to welfare too. The only difference was that there was no shame in the former. In the late 1950s, when I was in Thomasville, the full impact of these programs was just beginning to be felt, and a black farmer working a small piece of land could still make an adequate living, but it was a dying way of life. Those who prospered from their labor on the land earned invaluable wisdom.

It depressed me to see the frustrations of the talented and brilliant black men who remained in small Southern towns, particularly those who had no opportunity to find work commensurate with their abilities, who were forced to work menial jobs all their lives even though they might have graduated as valedictorians of their high school classes. These men often turned to drink, drowning their frustrations in alcohol. This was brought home to us vividly by the case of one man in Thomasville who was an alcoholic, a failure by every standard with which we measure success. Townspeople pointed to him behind his back, whispering, "He was a brilliant man." So much of the promise of the black community had been invested in this man in his youth, but somewhere along the way he seemed to have simply self-destructed. And no one quite understood why.

At first I thought this man's problems could be addressed through counseling, one of the traditional roles of the minister, but I soon came to realize no amount of counseling could solve his problem, for it was rooted in the inequities of the society—being treated as a "boy" all his life, being forced to do menial work when he might have been an outstanding scientist, mathematician, researcher, or poet. Some men could take it, adjust to it, laugh it off as "white folks' hell," or absorb it while secretly living for the day when their children could escape the ravages of racial oppression—but not everyone. It was as if the most gifted young blacks were the ones who suffered the most. They were the ones who felt most keenly the denials of equal opportunity. The valedictorians who could not escape northward were the ones who committed suicide, either in one tragic moment, or slowly throughout their despairing years.

For my first Mother's Day sermon I had planned to preach on the Christian family. Coincidentally, that Saturday night Deacon Ervin Hadley came home drunk. His wife, Leola, was furious, but when she fussed at him he slapped her and went to bed. Leola waited until he'd gotten in bed under the covers, got an ax handle, and started beating him. Ervin got up to take the ax handle away, and in the struggle gave Leola a black eye.

When I got to Sunday school the next morning, everyone was buzzing about the big fight the Hadleys had had the night before. They both showed up for church the next morning, still visibly bruised from the fight. I wondered how I was going to preach on the Christian family with the Hadleys sitting in the front. But I decided it wouldn't be right to change my sermon.

Later I talked with some of the other men, trying to find out what happened to Ervin Hadley; he didn't have a reputation for abusing alcohol or violence. I was told that Hadley was the foreman on a nearby plantation; he was over forty years old and they were paying him $45 a week. Recently he had been training a nineteen-year-old white boy who had been working there for a few weeks. When the paychecks were passed out, Hadley saw that the white boy was paid $125 a week. He couldn't afford to get angry and perhaps lose his job altogether, but he couldn't ignore the the insult either, so he just got drunk. When he came home, his wife had no idea what had happened.

So much of the dysfunction and self-destructive behavior that I saw was caused by despair. It was not a crisis of faith that caused them sometimes to lose the ability to cope. Faith isn't meant to accommodate people to injustice, but rather to give them the means to challenge it. Individual protest was unwise, Mrs. Bowen had reminded us constantly at Gilbert Academy. But, increasingly, I began to see and believe how concerted action in the black community had produced results: a bus boycott in Baton Rouge and direct action by the Congress of Racial Equality in Northern cities. Perhaps the brightest ray of hope shining through the pine trees around Thomasville was that the Supreme Court had begun to rule against segregation. The NAACP, under the leadership of Thurgood Marshall, had developed a legal strategy to lay the groundwork for the elimination of the doctrine of "separate but equal," which in the South was considered carte blanche for the oppression of people like my parishioners.

In *Sipuel v. Oklahoma* in 1948 and *Sweatt v. Painter* in 1950, the NAACP persuaded the court to require the admission of black students to graduate schools that were part of the state university system, in the former case because there was no state graduate school for blacks, and in the latter case because the segregated law school hastily established for blacks to comply with *Sipuel* was found unequal to that of the University of Texas. The NAACP won its most profound victory with the momentous May 17, 1954, Supreme Court decision in *Brown v. Board of Education of Topeka* that overruled *Plessy v. Ferguson* and the doctrine of "separate but equal." But there was no dramatic change in the South immediately in the wake of the Supreme Court decisions. In Thomasville in 1955, the tremors of *Brown* had yet to be felt in the town's segregated schools. Southern political leaders were shouting—in editorials, speeches, proclamations, and by their actions—that they would defy the Supreme Court and never desegregate. Yet, with the *Brown* decision, there was a change in our belief in what was possible.

On the heels of the inspiring decision in *Brown*, came the resolute men and women of the Montgomery bus boycott. We had been in Thomasville nearly a year when the boycott began in December 1955 and we followed its progress with avid interest. The boycott was sparked by the arrest of Rosa Parks, an NAACP activist who refused to give her seat to a white man. Well respected in Montgomery's black community, the lovely and dignified Mrs. Parks was a worthy symbol of the hardships caused by segregated buses. Martin Luther King, Jr., the young minister who emerged as the spokesperson for the Montgomery Improvement Association, was married to Coretta Scott of Heiberger, Alabama, a village just north of Marion, whom Jean had known as a student at Lincoln School, although Coretta was older and several classes ahead of Jean. We had no direct contact with the boycott activities. However, like every thinking black person who knew the South, we understood the issues and identified with the struggle there. We relied on black publications like *Jet* and national broadcasts and periodicals for information on the Montgomery boycott and Supreme Court decisions. Our local newspaper was unreliable as a source of information on matters of particular concern to black citizens.

Thomasville engaged in a gentler form of segregation than the surrounding counties in southwest Georgia, but it was no less real. One incident in particular occurred around the time I was coordinating the annual March of Dimes drive for the black community. Jean and I had gone up to see President Franklin Delano Roosevelt's Little White House in Warm Springs and I was deeply distressed by the rows of iron lungs—huge cylinders that encased an entire body so that the person inside could breathe. I was eager to do something about polio when the March of Dimes project presented itself. When I was ready to give my final report to the chairperson for the drive, who was white, I went to the front door of his house and knocked. I turned in my materials and went home. I soon heard from my deacons that they were upset that I had violated racial protocol in Thomasville. They said I should have gone around back, or if I knocked on the front door, I should have stepped back down off the porch and waited to be invited onto the porch. I can only assume that the chairman of the local March of Dimes suggested to my deacons that I needed to be briefed on appropriate behavior.

At Thomasville's annual Festival of Roses parade, the town's approach to race relations was clearly illustrated in a parade float by one of the county's largest employers. The Sunnyland Packing Company float featured two huge egg cartons. One carton had twelve white children and a sign that said GRADE A WHITE. The other carton had twelve black children and a sign that said GRADE A BROWN. That was Sunnyland's version of separate but equal. The sad thing was, we thought it was good.

My parishioners had such small dreams and goals for improving their lives, most would have been more than satisfied if separate were genuinely equal. I was becoming a little discouraged because I had arrived in Thomasville believing strongly, and perhaps naively, in the inherent virtue of the rural black masses: it was my intention to devote my ministry to working to improve their conditions, and to build a strong ministry around them. True freedom, I hoped, would emanate first from the struggle of the masses, from the folk of the South, not from the black middle class of which I was a product. The black middle class, I felt, was too involved in their own materialism, and hardly ready to risk the little they had achieved by engaging in broad social demands for further change.

But my experiences in Thomasville altered this view, and left me somewhat frustrated. I became increasingly aware that the dream of people on the lowest economic levels was to become the middle class, and, if they could, to possess all the things they thought economic success would bring. My parishioners aspired to the very materialism I had the luxury to reject. The parents of the most talented kids in Thomasville urged their children to go away to college so as to obtain better jobs and become professionals—and probably never return—in the same manner that so many of my generation had departed New Orleans, never to return. It was as if they had to go through a full cycle of material acquisition before they could evaluate what they had been through and where they were going.

Ironically, my own efforts supported that system. I remained active in Christian Youth Action (CYA), and when I led sessions at their conferences and camps I would bring along some of my more interested youth group members. The CYA gatherings were always integrated, and it was the first interracial experience for our Thomasville kids. I also took them with me when I was invited to speak at colleges like Talladega and Tuskegee. This exposure made our youth all the more eager to leave Thomasville, as I knew it would. One of the kids in my youth group was the son of Norvella and Doc Hadley. Robert and his parents were determined to see him escape his father's fate. Robert went to Talladega College, an AMA school, in 1958, and after he graduated, he joined the Peace Corps as one of its first volunteers. I was very proud of Robert, but at the same time the constant migration of the best and the brightest made it difficult to strengthen organizations that had the potential to press for social change. We were losing the fresh blood.

I soon realized that nothing would stop the train carrying young people away from towns like Thomasville until something strong enough, or important enough, happened in rural towns to attract the youth. Whether it was Rampart Street in New Orleans, or Marion, Alabama, or southwest Georgia, broader solutions were required if there was to be any substantive change. Thus while still in Thomasville I leaped eagerly into my first attempt to organize a voter registration drive.

Our drive was organized around the presidential campaign of 1956, in which Adlai Stevenson was running against President Dwight Eisenhower. A few blacks in Thomasville had always voted— it was not nearly as repressive an area as the hotbed of Klan activity just north of us, Terrell County, which would be known as "Terrible Terrell" during the civil rights movement. The heavily Northern absentee land ownership created a somewhat more tolerant attitude toward blacks than was common in most of the rural South, though, of course, blacks had no input into the political control of the town or county.

In preparation for our Thomasville campaign, I was invited to come to Macon, Georgia, for a meeting at the Prince Hall Lodge, where the Masons were training and recruiting organizers for a statewide voter registration drive. At this meeting I agreed to cochair the Thomasville voter registration drive along with the Thomas County Business and Civic League. The Business and Civic League had taken over civil rights functions in the county because the NAACP was such a red herring to the white power structure that anyone who admitted membership in the NAACP was sure to get fired if not run out of the county. We had a spirited meeting, and John Wesley Dobbs, who was a legendary orator, agreed to come down and speak to kick off our drive.

For Jean and me, being active in this voter registration drive seemed perfectly natural, as it was not only consistent with every-thing we believed in and an integral part of my concept of an activist ministry, but also the type of thing we thought we should be doing as young black people with the advantages of an education. This was the first presidential election since we had turned twenty-one, and we were determined that we would register and vote, now that we were old enough. Jean's father was one of six black men who had paid the poll tax to vote in Perry County, Alabama, and my parents had voted as far back as the 1930s, though they didn't belong to any political organization. The Supreme Court decision in *Brown* and the Montgomery bus boycott encouraged us to believe our registration efforts would make a difference. We didn't even take into consideration possible repercussions, and we didn't quite realize what we were getting into.

The Saturday before John Wesley Dobbs was to speak at our rally, Jean and I drove to Albany, which was very near, to do some shopping. On our return trip in our little Nash Rambler, we came around a curve at Doe Run, Georgia, and passed what we realized, to our shock, was a small army of Ku Klux Klansmen convening on the highway. I had always heard of the Klan and seen pictures of them in their white robes, but this was the first time I had actually encountered them in person. We passed them without incident, and by the time we arrived back in Thomasville we learned that the Klan had been gathering from all over southwest Georgia, and their destination was Thomasville, where they were going to try to intimidate us. We had publicized our planned registration rally quite openly and expected a large attendance, so it was no surprise that the Klan knew about us. Klan activity was nonexistent in Thomasville, but it had also been a long time since blacks had held a rally there to register voters.

That night I went through a sort of psychological trial by fire. I had now become a believer in nonviolence from my study of Gandhi and other nonviolent teachings at Hartford, but I was also just then reading Reinhold Niebuhr, particularly *Christian Realism and Power Politics*. Niebuhr advocates negotiating from a position of strength, which struck a chord with me; that's what I had learned to do back at Jones School in New Orleans. So by the time Jean and I arrived at the parsonage I had worked out a little scenario to deal with the likely possibility we would be paid an unfriendly visit by the Klan.

We had fixed up the old church parsonage with Sheetrock, bathroom facilities, and asphalt floor tile. Jean and I had done this pretty much by ourselves with the help of some church members and Uncle Walt, who, in his tireless spirit of giving, had driven all the way from New Orleans with his car loaded down with tile. But despite our improvements, it was still an old frame house that, if a match was struck to it, would go up in flames instantly. We certainly had reason to feel vulnerable should the Klan come looking for us.

Part of my plan involved Jean. On the way down to Thomasville from Hartford after graduation, Jean and I had stopped off for a few hours at Coney Island Amusement Park in New York. We were both attracted to the shooting gallery. Jean, being a country girl, was experienced with rifles, and she liked to shoot. We took turns at the target and Jean shot sixteen out of twenty at a moving target and I shot eighteen out of twenty. So I knew we both could shoot, and we had rifles and shotguns at the parsonage.

As soon as we arrived home I told Jean, "Look, if the Klan comes here, they're coming to intimidate us. And we're not safe in this house. So if they come I'm going downstairs and confront them outside in our front yard. Now, I want you to sit in the upstairs window with the rifle and when I identify who the leader is, I'm going to point to him and say, 'Let's talk this over.' I'm going to tell him, 'Now it's obvious you're the leader and I want you to know my wife is sitting in the window back there, and she's got a rifle trained between your eyes. So if you mess with me, then you're going too.'" I concluded, "If we do this we can deal with them from a position of strength as equals."

Jean looked at me hard, as if she were looking *through* me. "No, Andrew, I'm not going to touch that gun."

"Wait a minute," I yelled. "What's the matter? You can shoot. I saw you hit sixteen out of twenty at Coney Island."

"I'm not going to point a gun at another human being."

I pleaded with her as hard as I could. "Listen, Jean, you have a three-month old baby here in the house and the child is helpless. If they do something to us I don't mind dying, but Andrea needs a chance."

"Well, you preach all this resurrection business," she said, "you preach life after death. Don't you believe God is able?"

I really became furious. "Damn woman, what the hell you talking about?" I shouted.

"If you're going to preach it," she answered calmly, "you ought to live it."

And that stunned me, stopped me right in my tracks. I had been so proud of living my faith, but now I was hysterical and Jean was calm enough to see it clearly, and demand that we live our faith, otherwise there was no purpose in having it. We finally agreed that because it wasn't safe in the parsonage, we would go over to the home of our close friends, Bill and Lucille Morris. They were the only black folk in town who had a television set, and we hoped to get some news about what the Klan actually planned to do. As we were driving through town en route to the Morrises', we could see the Klan gathering in the Thomasville courthouse square. I was stunned to see black folk hanging around also, watching the Klan to see just what they planned to do.

Nothing happened that evening and we went forward with our voter registration rally at the local high school. John Wesley Dobbs came as planned and gave a masterful speech, in the tradition of powerful black oration and leadership. I discovered later, however, that an elaborate negotiation had taken place without my knowing it. When it was discovered there might be violence or threats by the Klan, the black elders of Thomasville went to the white business community leaders and, in effect, told them, "If you let these Klansmen come into our community and harass us you can forget about us shopping at your businesses from now on. So you all stop them before they get started." Blacks were poor, but the margin of profit for most of those businessmen was their heavy black clientele. The white business leaders demanded that the sheriff rein in the Klan, and he did. There were no more public Klan gatherings in Thomasville. Hubert Thomas, the president of the Civic League, Elijah Hill, who ran a service station, and our close friend Bill Morris, an insurance executive, were the black leaders who took the message to the white businessmen. Though I was probably considered too young and too new to the community to be asked to join them, I did not forget how quickly their economic message got through to those businessmen.

I have also never forgotten Mr. Dobbs's speech. Taking note of the advent of integration, he said sagely, "Stick with this 'Blue-eyed Boy,' but watch him." He went on to make the observation that there were things in white America that black America needed, and said we therefore should maintain a close relationship with white America, but we couldn't put all our trust in them. "You can't trust white folks with your life, 'cause you can't trust him with his own," he said, with heavy innuendo. The implication was that prejudice and fear prompted white Southerners to act counter to their own interest to maintain the subjugation of blacks. The Civil War was a case in point: poor white Southerners gave their lives defending a system of slavery from which they received no economic benefit. The people in the audience knew what he meant, and years later, through so many trials and tribulations with Martin, I came to understand his meaning even more profoundly. Segregation was choking off the economic lifeblood of the South, yet it took lawsuits, demonstrations, arrests, beatings, and killings to persuade white Southerners to do what was really in their own interest.

Our voter registration drive was not as successful as we had hoped—we were able to register only a handful of people. But our efforts helped Eisenhower carry Georgia by increasing the rolls even a little and encouraging those who were registered that it was an important election. Black voters in the South were still voting Republican, although most made an exception for Franklin Roosevelt. I voted for Eisenhower too. The Southern segregationists were all Democrats, and it was the black Republicans like John Wesley Dobbs, John Calhoun, and Q. V. Williamson who could effectively influence the appointment of federal judges in the South. The best civil rights judges in the South were the Eisenhower appointees: Frank Johnson in Alabama; Elbert Tuttle on the U. S. Court of Appeals; Brian Simpson, who would save my life in Florida; Minor Wisdom; and Skelly Wright on the D.C. Court of Appeals were all Republicans. These judges are among the many unsung heroes of the civil rights movement.

Bethany was a small rural church, but in the Convention of the South it had a proud history. One of its pastors, Henry S. Barnwell, went on to become the superintendent of black Congregational churches in the South under the auspices of the American Missionary Association. I came to understand that in sending me to Bethany, Reverend Stanley was signaling to leaders of AMA institutions and my clergy colleagues that he considered me a person of great promise. As a result, and because of my background in youth work, I was often invited to preach for the traditional chapel services that were a feature of AMA colleges.

The Alpha Phi Alpha fraternity chapter at Talladega College in Alabama provided my first opportunity to meet Martin Luther King. Alpha Phi Alpha was my fraternity at Howard University, and the president of Talladega, Arthur Gray, was an Alpha and a Congregational minister. I accepted President Gray's invitation in the spring of 1957 to speak for the Alpha Phi Alpha's annual program at Talladega College in northern Alabama. When I arrived I discovered I was one of two speakers. Martin King was the other. I looked forward to hearing him speak and to meeting him with great anticipation.

Martin was the morning chapel speaker, I was the evening speaker; that afternoon we participated in a panel discussion together. After the event, Martin invited me to visit him in Montgomery before I returned to Thomasville, and I accepted his invitation with pleasure. I had read in his interviews and public statements that his ideas of nonviolent social protest originated from Gandhi and the pacifist movement in India, which had helped bring the downfall of British colonialism. In fact, Martin later spent time in India pursuing his Gandhian studies. His ability in sermons and writings to place the Montgomery protest within the context of theological social action elevated that struggle to a level that won worldwide respect, and he made many allies among those who were not on first-hand terms with the racial unrest in the South. I, too, was inspired by Gandhi's story, and there were many similarities between Martin's and my theological training. I was eager to have a chance to talk with him about how he had applied his academic training to the practical situation in the South. I was also interested in discussing the work of the theologian Paul Tillich; I had read somewhere that Tillich was the subject of Martin's doctoral dissertation.

After so much buildup in my mind, and such great expectations as to the in-depth discussions we would have, our actual visit was nice enough, but an extreme disappointment to me. Martin was not inclined to discuss anything philosophical. He was mostly interested in talking about Yoki, his and Coretta's new baby. His only comment on Tillich was, "All that's behind me now," or something to that effect. I learned later that was not quite what he thought, but he was moody and into his more private self, and he didn't feel like acting out the role of the Reverend Dr. Martin Luther King, Jr.

I realized later I had expected too much from such a casual meeting. Martin was exhausted, and he wanted to be just plain Martin, a side of him I would learn to know and love. Since then I too have come to know very well the same exhaustion, the disinclination to "live up to the image" in relaxed meetings with new acquaintances. I also came to know the necessity of muting academic theories under the pressure of dizzying, daily traumas; Martin's sighed "All that's behind me now" came to have a far more profound meaning for me later than I could have possibly imagined that fine spring day nearly forty years ago.

Shortly after the meeting with Martin in May 1957, the national civil rights leadership held a Prayer Pilgrimage in Washington on behalf of the civil rights bill being debated in Congress. I was excited about the prospect of participating and encouraged other ministers as well as laypeople who had worked on the voter registration drive in Thomasville to drive to Washington with me. I was very disappointed when only one of the ministers felt the Prayer Pilgrimage was important enough to attend. But once there, we were part of the then-largest civil rights demonstration in American history. I was so tired from the long drive from south Georgia to Washington, which took place before Eisenhower initiated the interstate highway system, that I scarcely remember the pilgrimage. I was proud to be there, though, to stand up for civil rights. The bill we supported was modest, but it

established an independent civil rights commission and civil rights
division in the Justice Department to enforce the bill's voting rights
provisions. As it turned out, the Civil Rights Division at the Justice
Department would be an invaluable liaison between the civil rights
movement and first the Kennedy and then the Johnson administration. I had to preach that Sunday, so after the march we got back in
the car and, once again, drove all night to Thomasville.

During June 1957, while I was in Lakeland, Florida, leading Bible
study at a conference sponsored by United Christian Youth Action,
an offer came from Don Newby at the National Council of Churches
to move to New York to work as an NCC associate director in their
Youth Department. United Christian Youth Action was affiliated
with the National Council and was centralized in the Council of
Churches offices in New York. Don Newby, who was the director of
youth, proposed that I become one of his three associates, and a
national representative of the United Christian Youth Movement.

     Don was very persuasive. He had watched my development from
a nineteen-year-old with no sense of purpose into an accomplished
pastor. He reminded me that I had come to ministry through youth
work and I had a real gift for working with young people. Through
the NCC, I could help more young people find God's purpose for
their lives. He confided to me that there were almost six hundred
executives in the National Council office, only one of whom was
black, and he was assigned to the Department of Race Relations. He
very much wanted me in his office.

     I was appreciative of the invitation, but not all that eager to
leave Thomasville. After two and a half years we were comfortably
settled, had made many friends, and were satisfied to be in the rural
South working with black people. I felt keenly my commitment to
those two churches, however unimportant they might have seemed to
someone else. Jean was at home in rural Georgia; it wasn't that different from the Alabama she had grown up in. There was a sense of
community and warmth there that she liked very much. We were
raising Andrea in Thomasville under wholesome circumstances, and
though there was barely enough money, we had just about everything
we needed to live comfortably. Jean was also pregnant with our second daughter, Lisa. "Despite all that," Jean added, "if you decide you
want to take the job in New York I'll support you. It's your decision."

     In Thomasville I was working in a local situation satisfying the
needs of a small ministry; with the National Council my work could

have potentially national impact. I agonized trying to make a decision, putting it off as long as I could. Never have I struggled over anything like I did over whether I should leave Thomasville.

For a period of several weeks in July, trying to make a decision occupied my every thought. I was virtually unable to do anything other than think about what I should do. I finally decided to attempt to re-create the climate of inner peace I loved so much at Lake Brownwood and withdraw into seclusion until I could come to a decision. I was afraid Jean would think I was being ridiculous, but thankfully she understood. In fact, she even encouraged me to withdraw. "You're not much good around here until you figure out what you want to do," she said. It happened that the parents of one of our friends in Evergreen Church owned a small cabin out in the woods near Beachton, and they generously allowed me to camp out there for a period of three days.

I devoted those three days entirely to reading, walking, running, and assessing. I was so consumed with questioning that the idea of food did not cross my mind, even though my friends had stocked the cabin with provisions. I walked for hours and hours. Sometimes I ran, running for miles at a time, even at night. Running through the woods seemed to help me penetrate to the depth of my psyche. I could hear my father's voice imploring me to think my way through life and give it purpose. It seemed as if the sweat rolling off my body was a purifying of both the physical and spiritual—freeing me to deal only with the essentials of my life's promise and to see the problems clearly, shedding the unnecessary and the self-destructive. I ran as if I were chasing my own true course in life, trying to run down an indication of the route life held in store for me, for I somehow knew that whichever path I chose, from this crossroad my choice would be irreversible.

Did the National Council want me as a "token" black, visible but voiceless and powerless? I wasn't interested in doing that, but such racial "tokens" were very much in vogue. I had felt like a "first" with the United Christian Youth Movement, but it had in turn offered me an avenue through which to develop my own sense of religious purpose. I was the only black American youth at Camp Mack, one of only a handful at Hartford Seminary, and as a young minister in Thomasville, I had interacted with whites on equal terms whenever I came into interracial situations. Maybe, if I went to the National Council, I would become a "token" if I had no active role, but what Don Newby seemed to be offering was an opportunity to interact meaningfully with youth and church officials throughout the nation in meetings and ecumenical retreats, in the hope that we could foster an interracial and multiethnic experience. I believed that was worth being a part of. White Americans, particularly white American youth, desperately needed to be confronted with new ideas that challenged a narrow WASP concept of reality, and they needed to hear blacks speaking freely, and on equal terms. The historical roots of American racism are conscious and deliberate, but sheer ignorance perpetuates it without any extra effort; most white Americans don't even know the history of slavery and the long continuing struggle of blacks to overcome it. Middle-class white youth knew nothing of the harsh conditions suffered by the underprivileged. It seemed to me, the more I thought about it, that it was well worth attempting to make an impact on a new generation of white youth with a more balanced, realistic, and democratic sense of America, for many of them would become the next generation's leaders of their religious, business, and political communities.

If their racial attitudes began to change just a little, if they began to question some of the assumptions held by their parents, if they became concerned about the conditions of the less fortunate among them, some positive change might filter down even to the Thomasvilles of America. To follow this route would be a long, slow journey, revealing only small changes. It promised no revolution in attitudes or conditions, no immediate, quickly discernible change— but real change can occur only through education, and is always slow. I felt a strange calm imagining myself in such a role. Working for the National Council would be akin to the trips I had taken to downtown New Orleans to purchase dental supplies for my father— trips across the racial line, with me as his emissary—doing business where blacks were usually prohibited from treading. In those days my parents had demanded that I present an image consistent with their values. Now, as an adult, if I performed a similar role I must design my own image, sacrificing none of my awareness, questions, experience, or humor in the process. If I took this streetcar ride, I wanted to have considerably more control over how I rode, what I said, how I presented myself, and what I hoped to accomplish.

But what about Thomasville? Wouldn't I be abandoning my mission there? In a sense I knew that I would be, but I wondered if I hadn't done all I could in Thomasville, even if I remained another decade. Fundamental problems there were inextricably entwined with broader social problems that I could not myself solve. I considered the men who became alcoholics out of their frustration over not becoming what they were capable of: attacking the alcoholism would be helpful, but it would not address the root of the problem. What was gnawing at their innards were social and psychological conditions of which alcoholism was only the symptom. The same held true for the men who beat their wives every day, and the women who abused their children. These were individual problems that had larger social dimensions. And I was realizing that I was more attracted to broader social action work than to personal "soul-saving" or parish ministering. The direction I liked was one in which I felt myself moving ever outward, creating a new consciousness, developing new relationships to address individual and specific problems.

When I finally returned home I had decided to take the job with the National Council in New York. After considerable thought Jean said, "Andrew, I'll accept your decision. But you have to realize for me the South is home and I feel very apprehensive about moving to New York. If you take this job, I want you to promise we'll return South in four or five years." I agreed—and it was on that basis that I began my work for the National Council of Churches.

6

The Establishment
at Prayer

Living just enough for the city . . .

—STEVIE WONDER

In the late 1950s New York was still the glamorous town of the pearly luminescence of black-and-white movies. Washington may have been the political capital of the free world, but New York was the cultural and business capital of the West. Hartford was a short train ride from New York City, so I was familiar with Manhattan, Harlem, and the cultural riches the city had to offer. If Thomasville was off the back roads of America, New York was the crossroads for the whole world and it was thrilling to ride the subway to the National Council of Churches office in midtown, near the new United Nations Headquarters, and enter a building so tall it required an elevator. No one here thought indoor toilets were an unseemly luxury. New York was as exhilarating as a long run, and as my heart beat faster to the city's rhythm, I realized I was a city boy.

But Jean was a country girl, and moving to New York was an enormous change for her. Getting settled in New York proved to be fraught with problems. Lisa was born on July 19, 1957, in the middle of our preparations to depart. So there we were, with a two-year-old and a newborn, but no new home; in fact, we didn't have a home at all. Bethany had had no problem securing a replacement for me. So while we were inclined to postpone our departure until Lisa was several weeks old, my successor, Rev. James Crutcher, was ready to move into the parsonage with his family and it was absolutely imperative that we move immediately. Jean and I therefore decided that I should go on to New York by myself to begin work at the National Council. Jean would take Andrea and baby Lisa to New Orleans to live with my parents until I could secure housing in New York for all of us.

Shortly after I arrived in New York and began working, Wilson Cheek, who was my new boss and director of Adult Ministries, graciously helped me find a house in Jamaica, Queens. The price was sixteen thousand dollars; a very small down payment of, I believe, two thousand dollars was required, which my parents gave us.

Jean and the children left New Orleans and came on to New York. I had taken a small two-room apartment in the Cornish Arms Hotel on Eighth Avenue and 23rd Street near the National Council offices. But as soon as Jean arrived and we attempted to finalize the sale on the house, all kinds of problems came out of the woodwork. The savings and loan company wouldn't approve our mortgage. For three months we waited for their approval. Jean was miserable with two babies in the tiny, shabby hotel apartment. The place was really a dump. I came home one day and Andrea proudly showed me fifty cents. She said a sailor gave it to her.

For Jean, the one saving grace of New York was that her sister Norma also lived there. Norma had married the conductor, Leonard dePaur, and settled in Manhattan. She had a toddler and was expecting another baby, so she and Jean enjoyed spending afternoons together in the park. Jean would take the subway to Norma's apartment on 87th Street just off Central Park West. With an energetic toddler on a leash and a baby in a heavy, cumbersome stroller, Jean would struggle down the subway stairs and wait on the platform for the train to Norma's. When the next train came, she got on. Later, when we moved to Queens, she discovered that two trains ran on that platform and that the A train went uptown, but the E train would have taken her out to Queens. I got some idea of how stressful that period had been for Jean, when she told me, "If I had ever gotten on the wrong train, I might have kept going all the way back to Marion!" She was only half-joking. Thankfully, although she always caught the first train that arrived on the platform, through some luck it was always the train to Norma's.

Finally, as we were becoming truly desperate, my boss, Wilson Cheek, who had himself just purchased a house only three blocks from the one he helped me find, decided he would go to the mortgage company officials and confront them. It had only taken a few days for him to have his mortgage approved. "This is just racism, straight out," Wilson said angrily. "There aren't any blacks living on 200th Street in Queens and they don't want an integrated neighborhood."

When we went in to see the loan officer, there was no sign of anger. I was about to see a master negotiator at work. In a very calm voice, Wilson patiently explained that he and I worked for the same church organization and my job was guaranteed. Then he leaned forward, looked the loan officer in the eye, and said quietly, "Now, if this was my home, North Carolina, I would understand what was going on here, but this is New York." The loan officer began to squirm and stammer and offer reassurances that the loan would be approved.

It was a classic example of how, through subtle, complicated obstacles, blacks are discouraged from purchasing homes in neighborhoods where the neighbors don't want them. The obstacles are always thinly disguised as additional "requirements that must be met." Race was never mentioned. So much for one of my first experiences as a black church "executive" in New York. It reminded me of a truism about the difference between racism in the North and racism in the South: In the North they don't care how big you get, but they do care how close you get; in the South they don't care how close you get, but they do care how big you get.

Just shopping was a trial. In Thomasville, when we made our first major purchase, a convertible sofa, the white shop owner was very solicitous, gave us throw pillows at no extra charge, and wished us a long and prosperous married life. When we purchased a refrigerator in New York, the white salesperson all but sneered as he begrudgingly answered our questions about the different models. Jean was becoming increasingly upset, but we had to have a refrigerator. When we finally returned home, she burst into tears. "What a horrible man. If this is the liberal North, I'd rather be back in Georgia with the racists!" It took us a while to adjust to the cold aggressive manner of New York and to realize that it was not racial. They treated everybody cold.

New York was a big change in our lifestyle and the practical aspects of our day-to-day relationship. In Thomasville I was the one who was usually home during the day, who did the shopping, worked around the house, and picked up Andrea while Jean was at school. Now that situation was reversed. I left every morning for Manhattan on the subway and didn't return home until nightfall. To make matters worse, I developed a habit of hanging around the National Council offices with coworkers or friends after work, which meant sometimes I got home very late. At the end of the working day, colleagues would go out to a nearby bar for a drink, and in that way we were typical young executives. That was where fresh ideas were exchanged; it was the kind of intellectual banter that I had missed in Thomasville. The long subway ride from our office on 23rd Street to 200th Street in Jamaica, Queens, provided time to read, and I would arrive home satisfied with a long day's work and ready to relax. I suppose Jean sometimes felt I had brought her all the way to cold, indifferent New York City only to abandon her, and throw upon her all the responsibilities of the house and two small children. She would prepare dinner, but much too often I wouldn't be there when she expected me. When I arrived home, she was ready for stimulating conversation and I had had my fill of it. I just wanted to bounce and tickle the girls and go to sleep.

To make our adjustment even more difficult, my job required that I begin traveling almost immediately. "These days, whenever I need you, you're never available," Jean complained. She felt a discomfort in New York in those first weeks that was impossible to relieve. I was traveling so much that Lisa, the baby, didn't seem to remember me when I came home. That first year, when I returned from a trip and tried to hug her, she would scream for her Mama until she was red-faced and Jean begged me to put her down. It hurt to realize I was such a stranger to my small daughter.

Meanwhile, I had looked forward to my new job at the National Council eagerly and was glad to discover that my working conditions and the office staff were quite congenial. Wilson Cheek helped smooth my way in the office, as did my coworkers in the Department of Youth, Don Newby, John Wood, and Al Cox. My closest colleagues made me feel as if my being there was the most natural thing in the world, though I was one of only two blacks. Even so, I felt everyone's eyes followed me wherever I went. The challenge was to know this and not let it worry you: being sensitive but not self-conscious. Later, Wilson Cheek would tell me that my appointment had been somewhat controversial. The board ratification of executive selection was typically fairly routine, but my appointment had been carefully examined. "Are you sure you aren't just hiring him because he's black?" Wilson was asked. Even before "affirmative action" policies were a reality, the merits of my selection were questioned solely because of my race.

The National Council of Churches was at the center of American religious life at a time when the mainline Protestant churches were bursting with the families of the postwar baby boom. A new Interchurch Center was being built on the Upper West Side with funds from John D. Rockefeller that would place the offices of the National Council of Churches and several denominations under one roof. The vision of ecumenism was a companion to the hopes for the new United Nations—that having experienced terrible world war, people would strive to be united around our common beliefs rather than divided by our differences.

Much of what we take for granted in the structure of the postwar world was possible because of the active support of the National Council of Churches. We often joked that the NCC was the "establishment at prayer," because so many of the lay leaders of the member denominations were corporate and government leaders. The chairman of the Council was J. Irwin Miller, the president of Cummins Engine Corporation, Secretary of State John Foster Dulles was a Presbyterian elder and, of course, John D. Rockefeller, an American Baptist, was a major patron of the NCC in the 1950s. Many of the denominations had sister churches in Europe: the Lutherans in Germany, Presbyterians and Congregationalists in Britain and the Netherlands, and the Church of the Brethren in Germany and Czechoslovakia. Those connections led the NCC and its humanitarian arm, Church World Service, to become involved in the rebuilding of Europe and to encourage U.S. government support for that cause. The belief was strong in our churches that America, by virtue of its mainline religious values, was the leader of the free world and that peace and prosperity were possible for the people of the world. In the wake of the victory in World War II there was a pervasive idealism that America could and should lead the world into a future that was free of war and want. This was my introduction to foreign policy.

In the Youth Division of Christian Education our mission was to develop a ministry relevant to the concerns of American youth, and to the rapid social and political changes taking place in the world in the mid- and late-twentieth century. My special role, as I had expected, was to create an interracial awareness at church youth conferences, not so much by continually bringing up the issue of race, but just by being there, and often by acting as group leader: white youth would have to relate to me without the subject of race even coming up.

The church's coming to terms with the issue of racism, even in limited ways, along with a concomitant positive reevaluation of the meaning of the black American experience, was part of a growing sensibility in white liberal circles during the late 1950s. Most of the mainline Protestant churches had their own separate and unequal Negro divisions, largely the result of mission work after the Civil War. These Negro divisions were now self-supporting, and their leaders well educated, yet the attitude toward them was often patronizing. By their very presence and dignity, Rev. J. Taylor Stanley and Bishop John Bowen and others like them exposed the limits of the liberal church's acceptance of their African-American members. The most gifted of the Negro clergy would be unwelcome in most of the white churches, except as exhibits of the congregation's mission largess. Reverend Stanley would not attend denominational meetings at Elon College, an institution closely related to the United Church of Christ, because he was permitted to enter the president's home only through the back door. Several denominations had split along the Mason-Dixon Line over the issue of slavery in the nineteenth century, and there was a creeping awareness in the formerly abolitionist denominations of their hypocrisy on contemporary racial issues.

Many of our regional conferences were held in the South, and we worked hard to insist that they be interracial. In such situations I dealt with the subject of race indirectly, focusing discussion around questions of the meaning of Christian maturity in contemporary America, which we felt must include an attempt to challenge and confront racial prejudice—both in ourselves, and in the society at large. Everyone knew racism and segregation were the critical problems in the South, but at such interracial meetings it was amazing how skillfully the issue was skirted. Only in private conversations, usually at night in camp settings, would participants let comments slip such as "If my parents knew I was sharing a cabin with a Negro, they probably wouldn't let me back in the house" or "If my parents had known I was coming to a meeting where there would be Negroes they would have never let me come in the first place." Nervous laughter would follow. But these confessions let me know they were, deep down, attempting to deal with these new experiences, no matter how trivial they may seem today.

After all, blacks and whites were accustomed to interacting in the South—far more than in the North—but the terms of social contact had been clearly spelled out by Southern society since slavery. Whites always occupied a superior position by virtue of race alone and this was backed up by Southern state law. Now we were attacking that presumption in our meetings, and equality was assumed. These were "breaking the ice" sessions, and they proceeded with great sensitivity. We did not, and I did not, try to force new ideas down the throats of white youth. That wouldn't have worked. Instead, we hoped that given exposure to blacks each person would grow naturally to challenge the myths and prejudices of prior generations and mature at his or her own pace. We felt this approach would better prepare white youth for the confrontation over segregation that was sure to come, and for the more racially equitable and just society toward which the South must inevitably move as blacks became more politically and economically assertive.

Ironically, it was during the heyday of the NCC that we began losing contact with our young people. One book that was influential in the Youth Division was *Middletown, USA*, a study of a small town in Ohio. It reported that virtually all the youth activities in the small-town church—Y programs, Scouts, and extracurricular school activities—touched the same thirty percent of the youth population, while a full seventy percent of the young people were unserved. In large cities, there were even more young people adrift, lacking the active intervention of adults in their lives. The purpose of Christian Youth Action was to reach out to young people, to remind them of the importance of faith to their process of growing into adulthood. We tried to engage them in a dialogue around traditional values without condemning everything in the emerging youth culture. I worked with state and local councils to help them develop approaches to the young people in their own communities.

One of my most challenging assignments was in Little Rock, Arkansas. In 1957, I went there to meet with the Little Rock Council of Churches soon after President Eisenhower had to send in troops to enforce the Supreme Court's school desegregation decree. The local Council, the Friends Service Committee, and Little Rock pastors were looking for a way to calm the situation at Central High School. In our analysis of the problem, we discovered that the kids involved in the violent incidents at the school were by and large those with a history of causing other kinds of trouble. And none of the mainline churches had any contact with these unruly teens through any of their youth programs.

We began to meet with school officials to persuade them that they didn't have an integration problem, they had a discipline problem. The usual troublemakers were getting support from adults who opposed integration, but basically they were the same kids who disrupted classrooms and broke rules before integration began. With the real issues properly identified, the local churches looked for ways to build bridges and help the kids in Little Rock understand the reasons for desegregation. I was finding that my work with the NCC placed me at the center of the emerging social order in race relations, able to influence events that I had only read about in Thomasville.

Having said all this, I must quickly add: no matter how much we may think we have overcome our own prejudices, there's always room to learn. After we had been in New York a few years and had made several friends among our neighbors along 200th Street, a Puerto Rican family purchased the house next door to us and moved in. I never got to meet them because at the time they moved in I was constantly on the road. I learned about them when I returned from out of town late one night to discover that Lisa wasn't home. When I asked Jean where Lisa was Jean said, "Oh, she's spending the night with our next-door neighbors. I've gotten to know them and we've become friends. Their daughter has been baby-sitting for me."

Well, I became very upset because Jean had let Lisa stay with a family I didn't know. "Why didn't you invite them over here so I could meet them before you let her spend the night," I complained. I just went on and on about it, despite Jean's assurances that Lisa was fine. After a long argument, finally Jean shot back at me, "Andrew, you know, your problem is you're prejudiced. Are you afraid your daughter's gonna marry one of 'em?" This stopped me short. Here I was flying around the country preaching brotherhood and cultural interchange on the grand scale, but worried about my own young daughter naturally experiencing the same kind of cultural interchange and enrichment I was working so hard to foster through the church. Living by our principles means being honest with ourselves, and holding ourselves to a standard that is harder to do than it is to say.

Jean and I had an understanding that she would continue her career as a teacher even after we started our family. Both of our mothers had worked while their children were growing up, which was very common among black middle-class families. When Andrea started kindergarten, it seemed like a good time for Jean to enter Queens College to obtain her master's degree in education so that she might resume her teaching career in New York. Within a year she had earned her degree, but by that time we were expecting our third child. Paula was born on June 6, 1961, just one week after Jean completed her master's thesis. She never was able to resume teaching in New York.

In time, as we made friends and got to know New York a little

better, we came to understand it not so much as one huge monolith
of a city, but as a conglomeration of thousands of small towns organized according to interests or neighborhoods—each one not that different from Thomasville or Cleveland Avenue, though in New York it
was possible to remain anonymous if one chose to.

I found much that was fascinating about New York as a microcosm of the world, and all the world's cultures, crammed into much
too small a space. Because of its diversity and its status as the economic and entertainment capital of America, we became involved in
an exciting new world of literature, theater, music, and education
available in no other city. In the National Council office everyone
seemed to have cultural interests, everyone seemed to be reading
something. Even on long subway trips in New York it was quite common to see people reading serious books, as well as newspapers,
something you rarely see in any other city in the world. Some of our
secretaries were aspiring actors and actresses, or attended night
school or pursued some interest besides merely holding a job. People
on our staff went to the theater as a matter of course, so we began to
go also. This was all new for us; there simply was no live theater for
blacks to attend in the South other than black college productions in
towns where colleges existed.

One of the young women on our staff was in the cast of the first
production of Langston Hughes's play *Simply Heavenly*. We made a
point of going to Harlem to see it, and this experience sparked my
interest in the great writer's other work, of which I had seen only bits
and pieces. I came to love his poetry and his "own home" Jesse B
Simple stories. On Broadway we saw Lorraine Hansberry's play,
Raisin in the Sun, starring a young Sidney Poitier. I remember reading
with avid interest James Baldwin's *Giovanni's Room*, a sensitive
novel about sexual insecurity and homosexuality, without realizing
until later that Baldwin was black. *Giovanni's Room* helped me to
understand young men I was coming into contact with in New York
who were struggling with issues of their own sexuality. I knew how
to joke about sex, but nothing had prepared me to consider sexuality
as a serious issue in people's lives. Later I read almost all of James
Baldwin's works, and came to know him well during the movement,
for he became a strong and faithful supporter of our cause.

I began to reread Sartre for the first time since Hartford, particularly *No Exit*, to try to understand his philosophy of existentialism.
Continuing my reading was important to me, and I felt a wide range
of reading was necessary for making our work at the Youth Department meaningful, although religious conservatives might consider

such secular intellectual interests antireligious and ungodly. I had learned about the limits of personal piety in Thomasville when trying to preach salvation to parishioners who experienced insults to their humanity every day of their lives. Personal piety was only part of a mature faith, and mature faith had to engage the secular world, its pressures and its ideas. If we were serious about trying to reach disaffected and alienated young people, particularly young whites, we had to understand the pressures in their world, which were as real for them as segregation was to Ervin Hadley, my parishioner in Thomasville. We believed that part of what the most serious of them were going through, or struggling toward, was a firmer sense of reality about themselves and the nation itself, demonstrated by their anxiety and by the kind of questions they asked. We sought to encourage an atmosphere of questioning, so that resolution would bring more meaningful answers. Sometimes we used short plays or skits to help us confront the questions and contradictions that lay at the root of modern American life, and I wrote some short scripts myself. This was all in tune with the world of New York City at that time, in the late fifties, when it seemed to be bursting with creativity and tradition-shattering artistic activity.

Jean and I were captivated by the world of movies. We saw first-run movies and the new wave of European films that were just then hitting New York. The availability of a variety of serious and impassioned newspaper and journal articles on serious cinema was altogether new for us; at the National Council and at home we discussed and argued about the movies we had seen. We were beginning to sense the emerging power of the media. Television was a qualitatively different medium from the radio of our childhood. Radio's ability to convey images was limited by the imagination of the listener, but television controlled the image that appeared in the viewer's mind. Jean and I really agonized over the purchase of our first television. We wanted our children to love books, not television. Even years later, we were the last people we knew to get a color television, and for a long time after that we had only one. I still think it's better for a family to argue over what to watch than for everyone to retreat to their own separate rooms and televisions.

As we grew to understand the ability of both cinema and television to shape images and ideas, I became very interested in helping with the development of *Look Up and Live,* the Youth Department's new Sunday morning television series, sponsored jointly by the Columbia Broadcasting System and the National Council of Churches. Al Cox, the program director, used me frequently as narrator for our dramatic skits, which provided me with an excellent introduction to television both behind and in front of the camera. Television was demanding and unforgiving. We had sixty seconds to open and close the program. In that time, we had to get across the main point we wanted to impress upon the audience, what we wanted them to take away from the program. It couldn't be sixty-two seconds and it shouldn't be fifty-eight seconds, it had to be exactly sixty seconds. This was excellent practice for me. Later, in the civil rights movement, the discipline and experience of *Look Up and Live* gave me the skills to help Martin King to communicate effectively through the media.

During this period of reading and intellectual excitement, I tried my hand at some creative writing, particularly poetry. My poems were not intended for publication, but they provided me with a form of personal catharsis. I believe they helped me develop a sense of myself in the world, to sharpen my sense of identity in the midst of all the new experiences to which I was trying to adjust. Working for the National Council of Churches was as fine a job as I guess I might have had at the time, and I was working with whites who were unusually sensitive to me as a young black, but it was still quite an adjustment. I was accustomed to being in charge of my days, my own time. In Thomasville, I was the congregation's pastor and a prominent member of a small community. At the NCC I found myself a junior member of an extensive bureaucracy. Everything was decided by committee after seemingly exhaustive discussions of the most minute details. It gave me a new appreciation of the efficiency of the trustees at Bethany and Evergreen. I often endured these long, boring meetings by playing with the lines of poems. When I felt frustrated by organizational politics I wanted to run, my old stabilizer, but that was not as easy to do in New York as in Thomasville. Jogging had not yet become a popular pastime and there were no long country roads to run down. I just couldn't see running on New York streets, stopping at the end of every block. So I wrote poems instead.

Ironically, working in a nonblack atmosphere intensified my appreciation of African-American music and culture. In New York I really discovered the blues of the rural South I had just left: Muddy Waters, Sonny Boy Williamson, Little Walter, John Lee Hooker, and finally, Ray Charles, who is a native of Southwest Georgia. Of course, I had grown up listening to rhythm and blues in New Orleans—it was impossible to have the radio on and not hear Paul Gayten, Johnny Moore and the Three Blazers, Roy Brown, and especially Louis Jordan and the Tympany Five. (Fats Domino did not become popular until the fifties, after I had left New Orleans.) However, in New York I was really *listening* to the blues for the first time. It seemed to me that the blues performed by masters like Hooker, Lightning Hopkins, and Muddy Waters was more poetic than rhythm and blues; the themes of blues lyrics are adult in a way R&B is not always. I also began listening to the new contemporary jazz: Miles Davis, Cannonball Adderly, Nina Simone, Thelonious Monk, John Coltrane, and Oscar Brown, Jr. We bought all their records and carried them with us each time we moved.

Simultaneous with our growing cultural consciousness, Jean and I were excitedly aware that there was truly a new day dawning for people of African descent around the world. We observed new African nations come into being and their leaders shed the yoke of European colonialism; Azikiwe in Nigeria, Nkrumah in Ghana, Kenyatta and Tom Mboya in Kenya. Africa's emergence from centuries of colonialism made us as African-Americans feel part of a world movement for the liberation and self-determination of subjugated peoples.

All these things were elements for us, and for many other blacks like us, of a new positive image of what it meant to be black. This image stood in sharp contrast to the messages subtle and otherwise we and our children received on a daily basis from white society. When little Andrea ran home one day, and cried out to Jean, "Mama, is it true I'm black and nasty?" we realized some playmate had called Andrea a name. We were caught a little off guard. Jean was in graduate school and had access to the test that black sociologist Kenneth Clark had used to reveal the impact of segregation on black children that formed part of the basis for the Supreme Court's decision in the *Brown* school desegregation case. She administered the test to Andrea. The test asked the child to color two pictures, one of a white child and one of a black child. Andrea used her crayons and colored the white child very carefully. When it was time to color the black child, she took a purple crayon and ripped up the paper. Even at the age of four, she had absorbed negative messages about her skin color. Segregation and racial prejudice did tremendous damage to our children, even when we thought they were rarely exposed to it. Luckily, we had more ammunition to combat the impact of prejudice and negative images than our parents had had, and we decided to begin then to instill in Andrea and Lisa as much as we could what was positive about being an African-American.

Years later, when I was at the United Nations, I made a remark about the existence of racism in the United States, mentioning

Queens, New York, specifically, which offended several people. My remarks reflected the reality of my experience when I lived there. The overall impact of our experiences in Queens, despite the friends we eventually made, conveyed to us the message, in countless ways, that we were not supposed to be living there. It wasn't the clear-cut, explicit "blacks not allowed" racism we had encountered in the South. In the South the reality was one of legal segregation, which individuals of both races occasionally ignored or deliberately violated, often softening and humanizing its impact. In Queens, nothing was ever explicitly stated, but a series of small encumbrances, sudden obstacles, hard stares, or refusals to notice or acknowledge your presence added up to the message: "blacks not welcome."

Two particular incidents stand out in my mind. Soon after my neighbor Charles Smith moved into his house on 200th Street, we became close friends and developed a habit of going to a nearby playground in the afternoons after work to play basketball. One afternoon, after I got home from the playground, Jean said, "You know, they're registering voters at the public schoolhouse down the street at P.S. 134. I already registered this afternoon, and if you hurry over there before they close you can register too. After today you'll have to go all the way into Manhattan to register." I still had on my sweatshirt and a pair of jeans and my basketball shoes, and without bothering to change I drove over to the school, went in and tried to register. I assumed there would be no problem whatsoever, since Jean had registered earlier by merely providing her name and address. But they gave me a hard time. They looked me up and down with an air of distaste, then they asked me to produce my high school diploma. I said, "Well, I don't have a high school diploma with me; I went to high school in Louisiana. My college diploma is probably in Louisiana, also." I added, "I'm a resident and a homeowner in this community." That didn't do a bit of good. The woman in charge told me never mind all that, I'd have to go into Manhattan to take a *literacy* test. If I had gone in wearing a shirt and tie, and announcing I was a minister, they might have registered me with no trouble. But I looked like someone off the street—someone not deserving of a vote.

I went home and told Jean what had happened. She said, "Your seminary diploma is around here somewhere, why don't you take it over there and show it to them. If you show them you finished Hartford Seminary maybe they'll realize you graduated from high school." We were very matter-of-fact about these requirements. I didn't get angry; that would have wasted time and not accomplished my objective, which was to register. Compared to the Klan rally we had experienced in Thomasville, digging out my Divinity degree was a minor inconvenience. So I returned to the registration office with my Divinity school diploma, and they finally let me register. But they were in no way apologetic about causing me so much trouble. I got the distinct impression they registered me only because I was persistent, and they felt they had to.

The other incident I recall vividly also indirectly involved basketball. Once again I was playing with Charles Smith in our neighborhood court. Usually it was open until ten at night, as it was lighted. But one Friday the fellow who managed the playground said he had to leave early, so he wasn't going to turn on the lights. It was a summer evening and still bright enough to play, however. So he said, "Listen, I'm going home. If you guys want to stay it's okay with me, but you'll have to jump the fence when you leave because I have to lock the gate."

We played basketball until it was almost dark, then we sat on the court and talked for a while. It was almost completely dark when we began climbing the fence to go home. At the very moment we reached the peak of the fence a police car screeched around the corner; the officers spotted us and threw their spotlight on us. There we were, frozen at the top of the fence looking absurd, not quite knowing what to do. Charles whispered, "Lord, Andy, I can see it on the front page of the *Daily News* now: Young Executives from NBC and National Council of Churches Arrested for Breaking In and Out of Queens Playground." His remark cracked me up and we both started laughing and couldn't stop, while still perched on top of the fence. The policemen, who had been just watching us, burst out of their car when they saw us laughing and ran over toward us, looking furious. Charles and I decided it was better to come down off the fence and try to talk to them than perch there like sitting ducks, especially now that they were mad because we were laughing. It was a tense situation that made me feel like I was back in the South again. They finally understood the situation, and there was no trouble. They said they had made a "mistake." Only a small thing. But that kind of encounter was and continues to be all too common; it is very easy to end up in jail or even dead because of a police "mistake" when you're black in a large American city.

There was no way to escape race consciousness; it was an ever-present part of our lives. From the vantage point of New York, Jean and I watched the growing conflict in the South over desegregation. Attempts to enter previously all-white schools were the first stage of implementation of desegregation across the board, but such efforts usually brought strong repercussions, and sometimes violence. Black parents and their children were forced to bear the burden of initiating desegregation in Southern schools, despite the Supreme Court ruling, and then had to defy threats, intimidation, and the concerted power of local school boards and governments, who did everything they could to subvert and frustrate federal court desegregation orders.

In 1960, violence erupted over public school desegregation at the Frantz Public School in my hometown of New Orleans. Once again the level of hatred was clear for all to see, as federal marshals had to be called in to protect four little girls. These scenes are unpleasant to recall and difficult to believe today, when public school desegregation in the South transpires without fanfare. But then they were like fear-laden steps down a long treacherous road that we knew must be traveled at that time.

The new assertiveness of black Americans was part of a growing global trend of people of color rising up against oppressive structures. I eagerly followed events in Africa because of my African friends at Howard and the strong presence of global ministries in the National Council of Churches. The newly built Interchurch Center on Riverside Drive housed the NCC as well as the overseas mission boards for the United Methodists, American Baptists, Presbyterians, and my own United Church of Christ. At the time, these denominations supported hundreds of missionaries and sustained extensive mission complexes abroad: schools, churches, hospitals, publishing houses, agricultural and feeding projects. The humanitarian arm of the NCC, Church World Service, had grown tremendously in response to the need for direct assistance to Europe after the war. The wood-paneled common executive dining room in what was irreverently referred to as the "God Box" was always populated with visitors from mission churches in Africa, recently returned missionaries, as well as visitors from European and Asian churches. Luncheons and chapel services featuring speakers from mission churches were a daily feature of the vibrant intellectual and spiritual exchange in the Interchurch Center. Council staff and board meetings always involved decisions relating to international issues and events.

John Foster Dulles, secretary of state under President Eisenhower, was a Presbyterian elder who had participated in the predecessor to the NCC, the Federal Council of Churches. In naming him Man of the Year in 1954, *Time* magazine referred to Dulles as a "practical missionary of Christian politics." As a staff member of the NCC, I attended meetings at which Dulles explained the Marshall

Plan and outlined the rationale for U.S. foreign assistance to block the expansion of communism. He recruited the support of the mainline denominations for foreign aid, which persuaded Eisenhower to propose foreign aid legislation. Dulles has his detractors, but in a time when there was no clear consensus on any direction for U.S. foreign policy, he crafted one. His was the operative policy until the fall of the Berlin Wall, with some modifications on human rights during President Jimmy Carter's administration. From the Marshall Plan to the Anti-Apartheid Act, when the United States has proved itself capable of an enlightened international policy it has been largely due to the influence of the mainline Protestant denominations.

President Carter's human rights policy originated from his own understanding of his faith and statements and policy positions of the National Council of Churches and its member denominations. When Carter first ran for president, I had not intended to support him, although he was a former governor of Georgia. But on a campaign trip to California a black student asked him a question about his policy toward Zimbabwe. Carter was embarrassed that he did not even know what Zimbabwe (the black nationalists' name for white-ruled Rhodesia) was, much less have a policy on it. I was a member of Congress from Georgia, Carter and I had worked together on local issues, and he needed guidance from someone sensitive to the perception of Africa policy among black voters. He asked me to give him some policy guidance and I didn't have time to write anything. So I pulled together various policy papers on foreign assistance and human rights in southern Africa that I received from the NCC and the United Church of Christ. Candidate Carter read these papers and they formed the basis of his thinking on southern Africa and the importance of human rights in American foreign policy.

When I became President Carter's U.S. Ambassador to the United Nations, many of the young leaders I had met during my tenure at the National Council of Churches were then engaged in the final phases of struggle for the liberation of their people. For example, the leaders of the liberation movements in Rhodesia (Zimbabwe) were Joshua Nkomo, who was a Presbyterian elder, Robert Mugabe, a devout Roman Catholic, and N'dabinge Sithole, a United Church of Christ minister. All were educated at mission schools, as was true of most of the movement leaders. I represented the Youth Department of the National Council of Churches for several World Council of Churches meetings in Geneva, and through the Programme to Combat Racism (PCR) of the World Council of Churches I got to know many of these men personally.

I was very impressed by the work of the Programme to Combat Racism—the churches were responding to the needs of Christians in Africa that they had educated and converted to Christianity. The church recognized that when you teach someone they are a child of God, they want to be free. The Programme to Combat Racism was the Western churches' acknowledgment of the justness of the cry for freedom.

Many years later, Mike Wallace badly distorted the mission of the Programme to Combat Racism in a piece for the television program *60 Minutes*. The PCR assisted the humanitarian efforts of many of the liberation movements in southern Africa, such as Robert Mugabe's Patriotic Front and Nelson Mandela's African National Congress, organizations that were illegal inside Rhodesia (Zimbabwe) and South Africa. These organizations took responsibility for thousands of refugees and exiles fleeing racist governments determined to imprison or assassinate even nonviolent opponents of white minority rule. They were also focused on developing their own leadership capability for the time when they would rise to govern the countries of their birth. PCR assisted in these efforts, enabling farms, schools, and health care for exiled communities. This was an extension of the Christian commitment begun in the missionary era. Yet Wallace juxtaposed black South West African People's Organization guerrillas in full combat gear with a white, U.S. congregation passing the collection plate, as if PCR was funding combatants rather than schoolteachers. There was nothing sensational about the truth that church funds were supplying liberation movements with schools and clinics for needy exiles, so it didn't get covered. In treating an establishment church organization as if it were a fly-by-night mail-order house, Mike Wallace did irreparable damage to the PCR and the National Council of Churches.

When I worked at the NCC, Mike Wallace did what I felt was an equally irresponsible hatchet job on the African-American freedom fighter Malcolm X. I met Malcolm X in the home of friends Louis Lomax and Bea Spencer. Bea worked at the National Council and her husband Louis was a prominent scholar of American folk culture. Malcolm was just then becoming known for his ministry in Harlem. I was impressed with Malcolm's intelligence and also his gentleness. When I saw the provocative Mike Wallace interview, I couldn't believe this was the same person I had met in the Lomax home. Even today, this misleading interview is one of the most widely used. Yet, it is a terrible distortion of the character of Malcolm X, who I believe was a good and just man attempting to address the legitimate grievances of African-American people. Television can be a powerful tool for promoting understanding, but it is a polarizing force when complex ideas are oversimplified for the purposes of sensational entertainment. Advocates of new and threatening ideas have to possess sophisticated media skills to convey their message accurately.

World Council meetings were an ideal way to find out what was really going on in the world. As it turned out, the new leaders of African liberation movements were probably the most important people I met. Many of the liberation movements sent delegates to World Council meetings to inform us of conditions in their countries and to seek aid. I met representatives from the African National Congress and the Pan-African Congress of South Africa. These latter representatives impressed me as quiet, studious, thoughtful; they were never the wild revolutionaries portrayed by the American press.

Over the course of several meetings I could see the African representatives growing increasingly impatient with the meager results won from colonial regimes through their nonviolent protests and negotiations; nor were they all that thrilled with the restriction of World Council assistance to only food and medicine. I remember almost to the word the wry comment on this policy made by one of the representatives from Mozambique. "Yes," he said, "we get the food and the clothing and the bandages from the Christians of the West. But the Portuguese get the guns, and the napalm. Not long ago," he added, "we were thrilled that we received a shipload of medicine from Canada. But then our men shot down an airplane that was strafing us, and when we went to the wreckage we discovered that the airplane was *made* in Canada. That's the way you Christians are. You're good people in the midst of a sick society. But it's dangerous to deal with the Christians because we begin to believe that everyone in the West is like the World Council of Churches. Then we discover that America and the West is arming our enemies. So we've learned what to expect along with the food and clothing and bandages. If you didn't give our colonizers weapons, we wouldn't need your bandages." This was said without hostility, but its matter-of-fact tone made the message all the more powerful.

Ironically, the American Missionary Association in the 1870s was a bit more pragmatic than the World Council of Churches in the 1960s and 1970s. The original Lincoln School in Marion, Alabama, was burned down by local whites hostile to a school to educate freedmen and freedwomen. When the school was rebuilt, Northern supporters sent a large box conspicuously marked "Bibles." When opened, the box did indeed contain Bibles, but beneath the Bibles were rifles and ammunition. The enclosed letter stated the hopes of the contributors that the mission would only have use for the Bibles.

As the African liberation movements became more and more committed to armed rebellion and guerrilla tactics in the sixties, and as I became more and more identified with Martin Luther King in America, the pressure was heavy on me in World Council meetings to denounce violence as a means of liberation from the old European colonial regimes. In many cases, I did speak about the inherent advantages of nonviolent societal change, but I refused to condemn those leaders who felt they had run out of nonviolent options. I pointed out that even Martin Luther King, in his interpretation of Gandhian philosophy, drew distinctions between "aggressive violence" and "defensive violence." Martin argued that when needed for defending one's home it is "defensive violence." He often cited the case of a black woman in rural Georgia who fired on KKK members who, in attacking her home, were about to break down her front door. Even the local courts admitted she was in the right in this case, despite the prevailing local prejudices. On the other hand, Martin never supported aggressive violence, and he believed that violence on the part of the protester was not acceptable in a demonstration against societal and moral evil. In addition, any retaliatory violence was vigorously condemned.

Most of the African leaders I met felt they had been forced into a position of armed resistance because more peaceful protests were not, for them, bringing substantive results. They had all been jailed for their work in passive movements and for things like advocating strikes for improved pay and better working conditions. In one of our meetings I remarked: "If I were in a similar situation, I would want to look for a nonviolent way to come into full citizenship without going to war, but I don't live in Mozambique or Angola or South Africa. How they liberate themselves is a decision which must be made by the people who bear the brunt of the suffering."

My opinion now—many years and many battles later—is that ultimately one cannot organize a purely military rebellion that successfully engages the masses. Most people simply aren't interested in, nor are they capable of, armed resistance. For a social revolution to truly succeed there must first be an awareness of the ideas and issues most crucial in the lives of the people, and an effort must be made to educate the people in effective methods of resistance. Unless the ideological mandate for change is clear and compelling even a successful armed rebellion will not, in the long run, sustain real change. There must be a strong vision of a better life to come, not just the wreaking of vengeance or a mere trading of one form of exploitation for another, or one oppressor for another.

By the late seventies, many of the delegates I met at World Council of Churches meetings had become national leaders, especially in Third World countries. My journeys to interdenominational ecumenical conferences in Europe and Latin America had helped widen my social and political perspectives, and gave me a much better sense of what was going on in the world than I might have obtained from the news media and other purely American sources. My realization grew that as long as there is sickness, poverty, ill health, or political and economic injustice in the world community, Americans are affected, however much we may want to hide from those realities.

In the summer of 1958, I attended the meeting of International Youth in Lausanne, Switzerland. There I met Philip Potter, Albert Vander Heuvel, Jacques Beaumont, and Ernest Lange, all influential theologians with a strong interest in an activist church working for social change. Ernest Lange made a particularly strong impact on me. A young theologian from Berlin, he was my gracious host on several occasions when I traveled to Germany for World Council conferences. I always tried to go a little early so that I could spend time with him and his family prior to our meetings. Lange was one of the few West Berliners who had permission to move back and forth between East and West Berlin in the late fifties and early sixties due to his church responsibilities in East Berlin, and he had been instrumental in helping Christian churches to define their role in the new East European postwar communist societies.

On a later visit, during the sixties, Lange took me with him to East Berlin Technical University, where I was asked by the students to say a few words. Christian students were under pressure to exclude anything that might be construed as political from their meetings, as any comment critical of the government could be used to rescind their scholarships. I therefore attempted to lead a thoroughly sanitized Bible study, reading Scriptures that I felt were relevant to the black struggle for freedom in America. But this seemed only to present more difficulties; for instance, the Scripture dealing with Moses leading the children of Israel out of bondage in Egypt, which has strong overtones of racial freedom for African-Americans, might also be interpreted as antigovernment there. So I found myself stopping midstream. I then decided to try to teach the students some Negro spirituals. But our spirituals also have strong freedom movement connotations—most of them are rich with travel images—traveling to another, better land, or traveling from the slave South to the slaveless North. The more I talked, and the more I searched for an innocuous approach to this Bible study, the more I realized how well the Bible speaks to the needs of oppressed people everywhere and in all times. I think I finally just gave up and took questions from the students.

The East German students possessed some knowledge of the condition of American blacks. They knew about Paul Robeson, who was the most well-known African-American in all of Eastern Europe and Russia, not only because of his difficulties with the American government, but for his great artistry on the concert stage and in theater. It seems as if Robeson had done *Othello* all over Eastern Europe before World War II. Most of their information about black Americans, however, was limited to stories of atrocities and lynchings. They knew, for example, about the recent Emmett Till and Mack Parker lynchings in Mississippi. They were also under the mistaken assumption that conditions for blacks in the South had not changed since slavery, and they were anxious to hear about the growing activism to combat segregation and injustice in the South.

I remembered those meetings decades later when I was thrilled by the news that when the Berlin Wall came down, a group of East Germans sang "We Shall Overcome." Many leaders of the democracy movement in East Germany were Christians and pastors. The determination of the U.S. Protestant churches to nurture relationships and understanding with East German Christians surely helped to bring down that wall.

Along with international affairs and the emerging youth culture, National Council of Churches staff were conscious of the growing crisis in America's cities. We look back at the early sixties as a time of urban prosperity, low crime, and strong neighborhoods, but already the signs of decay were present as federal government policies began to use the wealth created by the cities to subsidize the growth of the suburbs. The NCC funded the East Harlem Protestant Parish, which became a model for urban ministry. Archie Hargraves and Don Benedict took that model to Chicago and founded the City Mission Society, now the Community Renewal Society. The concept of urban development pioneered by the East Harlem Protestant Parish and the overall organization became the basis for Martin Luther King's movement in Chicago in the mid-sixties.

One of the founders of the East Harlem Protestant Parish, Dr. Bill Weber, later started a prison ministry as president of New York Theological Seminary. Prisons are masquerading as policy for urban and rural development: take urban kids and lock them up in a rural prison for a few decades with guards who hate the city and fear the inmates from the city; after a few decades of brutal treatment, release the prisoners back into their urban communities. Bill Weber succeeded in providing theological training for inmates at New York prisons, and turning their lives around. The trend toward keeping human beings in small cells for years on end, only to release them into the community without training or education decades later, is a prescription for social chaos. Meanwhile, these men, and increasingly women, have families that they have left behind—another generation growing up without hope. I began to understand the challenge of urban poverty and decay during my years in New York, but I could not have predicted that after tremendous achievements in civil rights, the problem of urban poverty would only loom larger.

A modern, Christian view of urban policy emerged at the NCC. Throughout the Bible are images of the city of God, a shining city on a hill. While the popular media in the late twentieth century evoke the model of the biblical Sodom in their portrayal of cities, there stands in contrast the city of Jerusalem, the holy city. For generations of African-Americans from the rural South, the cities of the North were the "promised land." I had watched the most gifted and energetic young people in Thomasville leave for the North as soon as they could. For them, the rural South was a land of oppression. The sharecropping system was a direct descendant of slavery and Jim Crow was slavery's first cousin. For those who found factory jobs or were well educated enough to work in the post office, the North was a land of opportunity. But many found themselves trapped in subsistence jobs, strangely reminiscent of sharecropping—the more you worked, the more you fell behind. The problems of the South, especially the rural South, contributed to problems in the cities.

In Thomasville I observed the challenges facing America in microcosm, from the level of the family, church, and household. As an executive with the NCC I was able to gain a global and national perspective on these same challenges. I traveled across the United States and met business leaders and young people who would become influential religious leaders in their communities. I traveled to Europe and met with religious leaders from Eastern Europe, Latin America, and Africa. I met leaders of African liberation movements in the early days of the evolution of the African continent from a series of colonial enclaves to independent nations. I learned about the emerging force in communications known as television, and how to shape information to meet its demands. This was all preparation for what was to come.

7

Look Away Dixie

Hear that freedom train a-coming, coming, coming . . .
—AFRICAN-AMERICAN SPIRITUAL

Early in 1961 Jean and I were in our Queens home enjoying after-dinner conversation with our semipermanent houseguests Tom Dent and Carmel Collins. Jean had served her famous lasagne. Our two daughters were tucked in bed upstairs.

The two-story house in Queens was the first home that Jean and I owned, and it was our pride and joy. There was a fire in the fireplace; the flames cast shadows on the forest green walls of the living room. I sat on the floor, as usual, enjoying the feel of the plush green wall-to-wall carpet. I leaned against the Castro convertible sofa that was the first piece of new furniture Jean and I purchased together with her first paycheck from the Thomasville school board. The room was furnished with more artwork and books than furniture. There was a bookcase that I made myself when I was in Thomasville, Georgia. The windows across the front of the house made the room seem bright, despite the dark walls and carpeting. Even the walls in the adjacent dining room were green with red Chinese figurines that were in awful taste. But we weren't in a position to spend money on anything as frivolous as new wallpaper. It was a comfortable room, great for reading by the fire with one of the girls in my lap or sitting quietly with Jean after one of my frequent trips away from home.

We were sharing a bottle of wine. Tom was a writer and Carmel an artist and they fancied themselves sophisticated intellectuals. In fact, most of the art on our living room walls was by Carmel or Jean. I particularly liked Jean's painting of Cinque, the leader of the Amistad rebellion that helped to motivate New England Congregationalists to oppose slavery. The church's abolitionists formed the American Missionary Association, which played a big role in my life and Jean's.

Tom liked to drink expensive wine, although for a long time he couldn't seem to afford his own apartment. I used to like to pour jug wine into one of Tom's fancy wine bottles and laugh while he enjoyed his "fine wine." At the time I saw nothing unusual in Tom and Carmel living with us for nearly a year. Tom was my childhood friend from New Orleans and Carmel Collins was the nephew of a Howard Dental School classmate of my father's. I was raised in an open household. Fortunately, Jean and I had resolved any tension over an open-house policy during our months in Hartford and long-term houseguests continued throughout our marriage.

That night, NBC aired an hourlong program called "The Nashville Sit-in Story." We were very excited about watching the program. It was rare enough that black people were featured on television, but the story of the Nashville student action against segregation was extraordinary.

The student sit-in movement began on February 1, 1960, when four students from North Carolina A&T College in Greensboro decided to make a witness against segregation. These four freshman students—Joseph McNeil, David Richmond, Franklin McCain, and Ezell Blair—decided simply to sit at a Woolworth's lunch counter. The store's employees were completely unprepared for this peaceful, dignified act of defiance. The waitresses refused to serve the young men, and the black cook was recruited to shame them into leaving. The four sat politely until the store closed. The next day twenty-five more students went to sit at the lunch counter; the third day, more than eighty students went. The sit-in movement spread like wildfire and by the end of February sit-ins had been initiated by black college students across the South.

The most successful and well-organized student sit-in effort took place in Nashville, Tennessee. Nashville was the home of Fisk University, one of the great schools established after the Civil War to educate newly freed blacks. Founded in 1866 by the American Missionary Association with assistance from the Tennessee department of the Freedmen's Bureau, Fisk had a long tradition of excellence, persistence in the face of adversity, and a deep religious tradition. The famous Fisk Jubilee Singers were formed in 1871 when the school was in dire financial straits. This small, eleven-member chorus had its debut in Rev. Henry Ward Beecher's Plymouth Congregational Church in Brooklyn. Singing songs that told of freedom and good news during slavery, the Jubilee Singers raised money to keep the school open and in the process established the "Negro spiritual" as a treasured American art form. Later, the slave songs preserved by the Jubilee Singers were transformed into the freedom songs of the civil rights movement.

With Fisk, Tennessee State, Meharry Medical School, and the National Baptist Seminary, Nashville was, in retrospect, a logical site for a student movement. It had long been a center of black achievement and excellence. The students there were so disciplined that they regularly engaged in serious Bible study and discussed theories of social transformation before breakfast and the school day began. Already familiar with Gandhi and the principles of nonviolent resistance, young ministers and students in Nashville realized it was time to act when the Greensboro sit-in began.

The NBC white paper "The Nashville Sit-in Story" profiled the leaders of the student movement. Jim Lawson and C. T. Vivian were men I knew from my youth work with the National Council of Churches. Jim was a Methodist minister, and C. T. was a professor at the Baptist Seminary in Nashville. For some time before the Greensboro sit-in, Jim had been holding morning discussions on nonviolence and social change at his church near the Fisk campus. Students from Fisk, the Baptist Seminary, and Tennessee State came to his morning discussions. The NBC profile featured several students who would continue in the civil rights movement: John Lewis, Bernard Lafayette, Jim Bevel, Diane Nash, Angela Butler, and Marion Barry. I cannot overstate how impressive and inspiring these young men and women were to us. Their actions were rooted in deep personal faith and conviction. While the Montgomery bus boycott was a noncooperation with segregation, and in a sense consisted of passive nonviolence, the sit-ins were direct, nonviolent confrontation with segregation.

There is a passage in the fourth chapter of the Book of Esther— "And who knows whether you have not come to the kingdom for such a time as this?"—that certainly seemed to apply to Jim Lawson. Jim had been a conscientious objector during the Korean War. He was a strong athlete and all-around American boy from Massillon, Ohio. He refused to register for the draft and went to jail as a result of his convictions. After spending considerable time in jail, he went to India to a Methodist mission as alternative service. That put him in India in the wake of Gandhi's successful nonviolent freedom movement and India's independence. Jim was active in the National Conference of Methodist Youth and well known in national church circles. His stand on the Korean War was courageous and unusual in the African-American community. He was one of the first African-Americans that I knew about who was committed to nonviolence.

Jim went on to attend Oberlin, which had a long history of liberalism—it was the first coeducational college and had been a stop on the Underground Railroad. While there, Jim met Martin Luther King, and in Nashville, he organized the Nashville Christian Leadership Conference, an affiliate of King's Southern Christian Leadership Conference.

James Bevel was another of the students profiled. Bevel had been in the navy and had returned to study ministry at the Baptist Seminary. When he heard Jim Lawson speak about Gandhi, Bevel went to the library and found all the books it had on Gandhi. The books were all dusty and hadn't been used. He walked out of the library with every single one of them. He said that he was going to put them to good use. In Bevel's way of thinking, "Gandhi was about changing the world, books on the shelf ain't never changed nothing." So he read them and started passing the books around to other students.

Diane Nash was from Chicago. She looked like the kind of young woman who would be a cheerleader or homecoming queen—popular on campus, pretty, light-skinned, and from a middle-class family. She rebelled against the sorority activities that her parents probably expected and took up with these preachers instead. She spoke with great clarity in the television piece, and that clarity of purpose would remain a trademark of her leadership.

Kelly Miller Smith was pastor of the First Baptist church where the students held their first mass meeting. Strikingly handsome and dark-skinned, he had the rich, deep bass voice associated with Old Testament prophets. Smith opened the television program and set the moral context. He said that Nashville was called the Athens of the South. Like Athens, Nashville was a place of great glory and tragedy: glory was its university—Vanderbilt—and its "tragedy was its race relations." It was powerful, but not threatening; rather, he spoke with tremendous compassion, even sadness and regret.

The students in Nashville nearly perfected the sit-ins. It was a well-balanced movement that included demonstrations, boycotts, voter registration, mass marches, and negotiations with the white business community all working in concert. In the use of various strategies, it was also the most comprehensive of the sit-ins. Moreover, the sit-ins were interracial, with a few students from Peabody and Vanderbilt involved, as well as exchange students from Northern schools who were attending Fisk and Tennessee State. The elements that came together in Nashville would have a long-term impact on the course of the civil rights movement. I didn't realize that at the time. But it was clear that through the student sit-ins, a powerful force for change had been unleashed.

As I watched the program, other images ran through my mind, images of young Tom Mboya; the students I met in World Council of Churches meetings; Albert Luthuli's Nobel Prize. These men, many of them no older than I, were risking their lives for the freedom of their people. A new wind of freedom for people of color seemed to be sweeping the world. Gandhi's monsoon, the independence of India, was stirring up tornadoes in America.

The sit-in movement caught on like wildfire with blacks as well as with many supportive white young people all across the South. These youth accepted the principles of nonviolent protest, following the example of the Montgomery bus boycott. They submitted to arrest peacefully, even though violence was often committed upon them while they demonstrated. This was the beginning of the direct-action movement for civil rights, and all across the nation those of us who knew the South and were eager to see it change to a more equitable society realized that the sit-ins marked an important crossroads in the struggle. We were seeing the beginning of a movement that transcended the decades-old legal strategies of the NAACP, which in itself had been effective, but which had achieved all it could without additional help. Few of the new student demonstrators were members of the NAACP, so the student activism represented the introduction of a totally new and energetic force into the civil rights movement.

Such initiative coming from young people was thrilling; I knew from our experiences in Thomasville that there would be no real change until young people became involved, motivated by a more promising future *in* the South, not outside of it. Now this was finally happening. The youth seemed to sense that they could do more at that moment through massive demonstrations than the elders could by themselves through traditional piecemeal efforts like lawsuits, "human relations" negotiating committees, or the use of political pressure, given the low black voting percentages in the South in 1960.

When the television program ended, Jean and I knew that it was time to return home, to the South. It really didn't require any discussion. We had vowed when we left the little church in Thomasville, Georgia, that we would be in New York for only a few years. We were committed to living and working in the South, and we realized that the moment had come.

It was not that I was dissatisfied with my job at the National Council. In my three years there I had, as expected, made friends and had the opportunity to meet many theologians who were prominent behind-the-scenes supporters of the civil rights movement. I had seen our Youth Department program expand and achieve a high level of effectiveness through our almost perpetual conferences (in three years I had visited virtually every state in the union) and through our *Look Up and Live* television series, with which I had become increasingly involved.

But now, with the new and exciting developments in the area of civil rights, the broad focus of the Youth Department was no longer most important for me. As I wrote my close friend Rev. Bob Spike, when informing him of my decision to redirect my energies to the Southern movement, "I've had about enough of 'church work' and am anxious to do the work of the church. In our present situation you must be a little outside the structure of the church to do the church's work, otherwise you get caught up in the grinding wheels."

Shortly after the television special on the Nashville movement, Chuck Boyles, a former national president of the United Christian Youth Movement and then editor of *Motive*, a progressive church journal, and *Power*, a daily devotional journal, wrote to me at the Council to ask for our support for the Highlander Folk School in Tennessee. I was a regular contributor to *Motive* and *Power*—I enjoyed writing for a progressive church audience and the twenty-five-dollar honorarium allowed me to take my wife out to dinner. I considered Chuck a great friend who had not only fostered my professional career, but, more important, helped me stay in good graces with my wife. So I was predisposed to look favorably on any request from Chuck.

Highlander was founded at New Market, Tennessee, in the 1930s by Myles Horton, a liberal white Southerner who was attempting to work with the fledgling CIO unions. In the forties and fifties Highlander was one of the few places where concerned whites and blacks could discuss movements for equal justice in the South in an interracial setting. I was very receptive to the Highlander program, and within a few weeks I was invited there to participate in a student civil rights conference. The conference in February was titled "New Alliances in the South." The meeting brought together thirty-one representatives of organizations founded in the student sit-ins of 1960 who would then study the lessons of the Nashville and Atlanta sit-in movements. I was asked to conduct Bible study.

Highlander was like a twentieth-century oasis in the Tennessee Mountains. It reminded me of Lincoln Academy, the school for freed slaves founded in my wife's hometown with the help of the American Missionary Association. In one little block there were white frame buildings and well-groomed lawns. It looked like a small college campus. The few resident staff had homes in the woods, away from the main buildings. While there I recall visiting the home of Myles Horton's secretary, a college graduate who had married a young man from the mountains. Their house was deep in the woods and could not be seen from the main campus. It had a large, shady front porch, and we sat out on the porch at sunset having Highlander's version of the cocktail hour—drinking a martini out of a Vienna sausage can, complete with an olive.

Many of the Nashville sit-in leaders I had seen on television were present at the Highlander meeting. I was even more impressed with them in person. They had all read Gandhi (Jim Lawson was an expert on Gandhian philosophy), and their lives were constantly being risked in support of their beliefs, given the ever-present dangers of challenging the Southern segregation system. I felt more sure than ever that they were making history, that they were the vanguard of a movement that would only grow and gather strength. I wanted to join them, but I did not yet know what role I could play in what they were doing. I was an adult, not a student. I had children to support, so joining the movement was not as simple as dropping everything and rushing South.

Shortly after my visit to Highlander I decided I would write to Martin Luther King in Atlanta to tell him I wished to work in the South with the movement, and ask his advice as to where I might best fit in. At the same time, Myles Horton of Highlander was considering asking me to join his staff. In pursuance of that idea Myles wrote to Martin in Atlanta to ask him if he knew me. Martin's reply, recently given to me by Myles, I later had framed and placed on my living room wall:

April 25, 1961
Dear Myles,
    Please accept my apologies for being so tardy in my reply to your letter of March 24th. Absence from the city and an accumula-

tion of a great deal of mail accounts for the delay. I cannot for the world of me place Andrew Young! I am sure that I know him, but the name slips my memory. Please let me do some thinking back to see if I can recollect at any point my relationship with him. As soon as this is done I will be writing you concerning my impression of him as a full-time staff member at Highlander. I am sure that he must have a great deal of confidence since he is serving as Associate Director of the Department of Youth Work of the National Council of Churches of Christ.

Sincerely yours,
Martin

Someone on Martin's fledgling Southern Christian Leadership Council staff must have taken it upon himself to write this response to Horton's letter because by the time I received the letter, I already had a phone call from Stanley Levison. Levison was Martin's close friend and adviser who ran SCLC's fund-raising operation in New York. He did this out of his commitment to social justice and never received any material compensation. Stan called me in New York during the spring of 1961 and asked Jean and me to come over to his house to meet informally with him. This meeting seemed to go very well, and a letter from Martin soon followed asking me to come to Atlanta and work for his newly created Southern Christian Leadership Conference.

However, at that time I did not feel ready to join SCLC. I preferred to continue working with young people, but perhaps more important to me at the time, I hoped to be the first participant at a revolution to have the opportunity to record it as it was unfolding. I knew that working directly with SCLC would demand all of my time and energy, leaving none left for writing. Moreover, Martin King had already been on the cover of *Time* magazine. He was a national leader, while I was working behind the scenes at the National Council of Churches. I didn't feel that I had the kind of experience needed for such a high-profile operation. In addition, his organization was dominated by emotional Baptist preachers and I was a self-contained Congregationalist.

So I declined the offer. Very shortly after my communications with Martin, a letter came from Myles Horton and Chuck Boyles asking me to join the Highlander staff full-time to run their leadership training program, which was funded by a grant from the Field Foundation. This program trained adults to read and write as preparation for widespread Southern voter registration drives. This sounded like just the thing. Anyone who knew the South knew there could be startling changes if large numbers of blacks were able to register and use the ballot well.

In the spring of 1961 Jean and I discussed the idea of moving to Tennessee. She visited Highlander with me and agreed that it would be ideal. To this day I do not know how we intended to educate our three daughters in the backwoods of Tennessee. There were no other black families at Highlander and the local elementary school was certainly segregated. I accepted Horton's offer and I informed Wilson Cheek and my coworkers at the National Council that I regretted leaving, but was determined to move back South. We put our house up for sale, and began packing.

Meanwhile, back in New Orleans, my parents were very upset with my decision. They were proud of me as a young executive at the National Council of Churches, a very visible kind of black success in the white world, but they didn't know a thing about Highlander Folk School and not much more about what was now being called the Southern civil rights movement. They were not the least bit thrilled about my leaving job security for the dangerous unknown, particularly the dangerous unknown of civil rights activism. It only made matters worse when my parents heard that Highlander was controversial, slandered as a place of communist influence, and was under escalating attack from segregationists all over the South. The fact that Eleanor Roosevelt had been associated with Highlander made it somewhat more acceptable to my folks, however.

I was a little concerned myself about the allegations of "communist" activities at Highlander, even though I knew very well that "communism" was a worn-out epithet used by racists and segregationists in the South to try to destroy any black or white movement for social justice. But to assess the situation better, I asked Bill Stringfellow, an attorney and close friend who had been involved with the East Harlem Protestant Parish, to undertake on my behalf inquiries about Highlander. "I don't want to give in to this McCarthy-type of red-baiting," I told him, "but neither do I want to have people hounding me about Highlander Folk School for the next fifty years." Bill Stringfellow wrote to the FBI, the Internal Security Committee of the House of Representatives, and the Senate Un-American Activities Committee to inquire if they had evidence Highlander was a communist institution, or if there was any reason why I should not be associated with it. It was interesting that each of these government agencies, all known for their tendency to provide a cover of "respectability" to spurious allegations of communism, replied they had no evidence of communist influence or affiliation at Highlander Folk School. The real motive behind the charges of "communism," which were emanating solely from segregationists and right-wingers, was to hinder Highlander's role as host for progressive, interracial meetings.

Just after the sale of our house in Queens went through, the state of Tennessee moved, through the courts, to close Highlander and confiscate their property. The indictment the state brought would have been at home in the world of grand opera: the charge was that Highlander was a front for a bootlegging operation. In the surreal "trial" that followed it was charged that the legendary Septima Clark of Charleston, South Carolina, a member of Highlander's staff, was serving drinks to guests in violation of the Tennessee dry law. The liquor, according to the state's allegations, was brewed at Highlander. Mrs. Clark, a no-nonsense black schoolteacher in her sixties, and hardly a bootlegger, had previously been fired from her job in the Charleston public schools for her refusal to state whether she was a member of the NAACP. Highlander lost in the state courts, and the school was temporarily closed.

Jean and I were all packed and ready to go, but now there was no school to go to, and it looked like it would be a long time before Highlander could secure a reversal in the federal courts. So the idea of joining a program there was out. I was desperate. Once again, we had a new baby and I had neither home nor job.

Despite this new roadblock, I was determined that the citizenship programs continue in some manner, somewhere. The work was important and I needed a job. The Field Foundation grant could not go directly to SCLC because it was not classified as a tax-exempt organization. With Rev. Bob Spike of the National Council, I went to Dr. Wesley Hotchkiss of the American Missionary Association Division of the United Church Board for Homeland Ministries to ask if the United Church would be willing to take over as sponsor of the Leadership Training Program at an alternate site, with me as coordinator, as had been suggested by Myles Horton. Instead of the Field Foundation grant going to Highlander, it would go to the United Church. Wesley Hotchkiss was extremely receptive to my proposal. He and Bob Spike seemed to jump at the chance to give some support to the emerging struggle for civil rights. It was as if they had just been waiting for the right opportunity. Hotchkiss agreed to administer the Field Foundation grant and placed me on the staff of the Board for Homeland Ministries. My salary would be paid by the United

Church of Christ and all the Field money would go to the citizenship program.

I went looking for an alternate site for the citizenship schools and recommended that we choose either Penn Community Center on St. Helena Island, South Carolina, or the Dorchester Center in Dorchester, Georgia, near Savannah. Both were the sites of black Reconstruction church-related schools, retained usable old structures, and were the repository of memories of the kind of hopes and aspirations we planned to revive through the citizenship schools. The deciding factor was that the United Church Board for Homeland Ministries held title to the Dorchester school, which was occasionally used for summer camps and gatherings of the Convention of the South. So, in addition to my salary, the Board for Homeland Ministries would make improvements at Dorchester to facilitate its use for the citizenship schools.

My proposal that the UCC board sponsor the citizenship programs was approved: the Field Foundation agreed to the new arrangement, and it was also decided that the program would relocate itself administratively to the offices of Martin King's SCLC in Atlanta. So, despite my best efforts to avoid it, I found myself led by the Spirit to Atlanta to work with the famous civil rights leader. We would live in Atlanta and I would commute the three hundred miles to Dorchester each month for our one-week sessions.

The citizenship schools were a natural extension of the historic role played by the American Missionary Association. The seeds of the AMA were planted in 1839 when the slave ship *Amistad* entered the waters of Long Island Sound following a mutiny by the captives. Antislavery church leaders argued that the captive slaves, under the leadership of Cinque, should be allowed to return to Africa. Cinque had led a rebellion on board the slave ship and was endeavoring to return to Africa when the ship entered American waters. The Amistad Committee was formed to assist in the defense of the captives. Eventually, the captives were tried and the case appealed all the way to the U.S. Supreme Court where former President John Quincy Adams argued the case for Cinque and his followers. The captives were set free and the Amistad Committee raised funds to settle Cinque and his followers in Sierra Leone.

Lewis Tappan, an original member of the Amistad Committee, became a founding member in 1846 of the American Missionary Association, an antislavery mission society dedicated to carrying "Christian enlightenment to the oppressed and the disadvantaged of all races." The AMA opposed the fugitive slave laws and pressed for the abolition of slavery, but its mission activity was unable to reach captives in the South until the beginning of the Civil War. As the war began, AMA missionaries followed the Union Army to liberated territory. The first AMA school in the former Confederacy was founded by Mary Peake, an African-American woman educated in Washington, D.C. The second school was opened at Hilton Head, South Carolina. Within five years of the end of the Civil War there were three hundred mission schools for blacks. These schools influenced my life time and time again: Straight College, where my parents were educated; Lincoln Academy, where my wife and her forebears, as well as Coretta Scott King, were educated; Howard University; Fisk University; Lincoln at Kings Mountain; and, now, Dorchester.

I was very satisfied with this arrangement, which was finally worked out in August 1961. During June and July I had been almost constantly on the road back and forth between New York and Atlanta, and between Atlanta and prospective sites. I was most pleased by the commitment of the United Church to the program. I planned to maintain my old contacts in my new work, acting as a conduit for those in the movement who needed help from national church officials, and for those in the National Council who wished to interact with and support the Southern movement.

My parents were even more alarmed over my association with Martin King than they were over my decision to go to Highlander. One of my mother's good friends, Euretta Adair, was living in Montgomery at the time of the bus boycott. Married to one of the richest black doctors in Montgomery, she had a doctorate from Howard, so she viewed Martin and the Montgomery Improvement Association through the eyes of the city's black bourgeoisie. When Euretta heard that I was going to work with SCLC, she called my mother and pleaded with her not to let me get involved with that bunch because "they were going nowhere." It was a great reassurance to Mother and Daddy when I told them that I was still on the staff of the church, this time the United Church of Christ. The way they saw it, that offered more security.

In Atlanta I stayed at the Butler Street YMCA (hotels were not desegregated in 1961) until I could find a house for us. The red brick Butler Street Y was and remains an Atlanta institution. I didn't have much money to spend on housing, as I was paying for a house in New York. The Y provided a clean and reputable rooming house for men who were in Atlanta on business or to look for work. Jean's cousin, Arthur Childs, lived at the Y for decades while he worked in an insurance company and took the Greyhound bus home to Marion every weekend. In those conservative times, the YMCA's reputation for high moral standards was as important as its reputation for clean showers and towels.

The dangers associated with moving South for civil rights work had finally begun to assert themselves in my consciousness. As I looked for a home for my family, I realized I wanted them to be safe while I was on the road. There were large, affordable homes on the outskirts of Atlanta, and I saw one on Fairburn Road on three or four acres of land. I remember the owners were asking twenty-three thousand dollars, but I was not comfortable leaving Jean and the girls out there. The house I found was near the Atlanta University Center in an established neighborhood of middle- and working-class black families. The homes were brick ranch-style houses with Atlanta's trademark generous lots. Our house had three bedrooms, one bath, an eat-in kitchen, garage, and unfinished basement. The backyard was enclosed, with a stone barbecue pit, and a peach tree that actually bore small, sour peaches. The living room had a picture window where we would place our Christmas tree, and the dining room was large enough for the heavy mahogany table given to us by Wilson Cheek. I felt confident this was a secure and close-knit neighborhood whose members looked out for one another. The address was 177 Chicamauga Place—the street was named for one of the battles to take Atlanta during the Civil War. The modest but comfortable lifestyles of the street's black residents were clear proof that the Confederacy lost the battle and the war.

Once I identified a house, I discovered the advantages of using a black-owned bank for my mortgage. Citizens Trust Bank processed my loan application quickly and without a lot of red tape. I sold my house in New York for eighteen thousand dollars, purchased my Atlanta home for sixteen thousand dollars, and had money left over to pay for the actual moving expenses. Andrea had started first grade in New York, so rather than interrupt the school year we would move near the end of the fall semester.

The Butler Street YMCA where I stayed was in the heart of the black business district around Auburn Avenue. In New York I was accustomed to walking, so Ebenezer Baptist Church, the Citizens Trust Bank, the old Carnegie Library, and the SCLC offices were an easy stroll. Sweet Auburn was like Rampart Street, full of vitality, but here many more of the businesses were black-owned. Beyond the usual black-owned funeral homes and beauty parlors were insurance companies, pharmacies, restaurants, and nightclubs, like B.B. Beamons and the Royal Peacock, even a radio station. Along with the

Jewish professionals in the office buildings were the black graduates of Meharry and Howard Medical Schools.

The Southern Christian Leadership Conference was founded in 1957 after Martin's tremendous success in the Montgomery bus boycott. A group of mostly Baptist ministers came together to form SCLC as an organization comprised of local affiliates committed to "redeem the soul of America" from the sins of injustice. With Martin the obvious choice for president, his partner in the Montgomery boycott, Ralph Abernathy, was selected as vice president and treasurer. Joseph Lowery, a Methodist from Birmingham, was named chairman of the board of directors. Martin proposed Atlanta as the headquarters for the new organization, where he could join his father at Ebenezer and be relieved of the full responsibility of pastoring a church, thus devoting more time to SCLC.

The first SCLC office was in a small building overlooking the Royal Peacock Lounge. The office was quiet and professional. Wyatt T. Walker was executive director then, and he ran a very tight ship. Wyatt had come to SCLC from a disciplined and successful movement that he'd led in Petersburg, Virginia, the home of Virginia State University. A brilliant young Baptist minister, his efforts led to the creation of the Petersburg Improvement Association, modeled after Martin Luther King's Montgomery Improvement Association. Wyatt was tall, tan, good-looking, and sharp-featured, and, like a hawk, he had the instincts of a well-trained hunting bird. Once, in Petersburg, Wyatt led a demonstration to desegregate the public library. Wearing his clerical collar, Wyatt approached the main counter of the library and asked the librarian for a copy of the biography of Robert E. Lee.

This was Martin King's second attempt at building an administrative staff for SCLC. Initially, he had asked Ella Baker, an NAACP organizer in Georgia, to administer the office, but that had not worked out. These were young Baptist preachers in their late twenties and early thirties. Ella Baker was a determined woman and she reminded them of the strong Mommas they were all trying to break free of. The Baptist Church had no tradition of women in independent leadership roles, and the result was dissatisfaction all around. Ella Baker was being asked to perform miracles with no staff, no money, and less authority. A woman of tremendous ability, she left SCLC and began to work with the students from the sit-in movement who had come together at Shaw University in April 1960 to found the Student Nonviolent Coordinating Committee (SNCC).

Wyatt brought his own staff from the Petersburg movement: Dorothy Cotton, director of education, and Jim Wood, the press secretary. When I arrived, everyone was still finding their places. Wyatt and his secretary Edwina Smith (now Moss) were in one corner; Dorothy Cotton, Septima Clark, Bernice Robinson, and I shared an office with our secretary, Bernite Packer; Martin and his secretary, Dora McDonald, were across from us, and Ralph was in another corner with Lily Hunter, his secretary as well as SCLC's bookkeeper.

Martin's secretary, Dora McDonald, was a jewel of a woman, with dark mahogany skin, a dazzling smile, and a bosom as generous as her spirit. She was also a miracle of efficiency and well connected to Atlanta's black establishment. She had worked with J. J. Blayton, a CPA who had the first black-owned radio station in the South. She had also been secretary to Benjamin Mays while he was president of Morehouse. It was Mays who asked her to leave Morehouse to work with Martin Luther King. He knew that Martin needed a person like Dora McDonald, a polished professional who was well versed in the nuances of Atlanta's social, academic, and business circles.

Internal politics were difficult at SCLC almost before there was an organization. I figured that as a Congregationalist among Baptist preachers with large egos, the best approach for me was to take low and avoid ego battles. One day I had some good news about the repairs to Dorchester and Martin was standing in the doorway to his office talking with Dora. I was excited about our progress and I went over to tell him about it. Later, Wyatt said to Dora—he didn't say it to me—that I was not to talk to Dr. King unless it came through Wyatt. That kind of jockeying for position was all too common, so I tried to cooperate with the lines of accountability Wyatt was attempting to establish. That was his concept of the organization, although no one else shared it—everyone there saw themselves working directly for Martin Luther King. Wyatt also insisted that we all call Martin "Dr. King." This was important because he was so young— and looked younger. If we didn't show him an exaggerated respect, the concern was that others would not show it to him either. In the South in those days, formality was the rule and we made every effort to demonstrate our respect for "Dr. King." The rest of us were on a first-name basis with one another.

The staff of the Citizenship School Program consisted of Septima Clark, Dorothy Cotton, Bernice Robinson, and myself. Septima was much older than I and had developed the citizenship school model. Dorothy was about my age, but had had direct movement experience in Petersburg, which I lacked. Mrs. Clark was the one who initially acquired the commitment from the Field Foundation, but I had found a way to save it. I was deeply aware that I could easily spend months in a power struggle, and I worked very hard at setting up a nonhierarchical staff structure. I controlled the budget, but I endeavored not to use that fact as leverage to control the program. I knew that I could learn a lot from Septima and Dorothy.

The training I had received from the National Council of Churches in human dynamics and the status of women within the Congregational Church helped as well. My seminary classes included women, who were candidates for ordination, and the area of the NCC in which I worked also included women in professional positions. In the Congregational tradition, women were ordained, served on diaconates, and were active in every area of church life. That set me apart from the more authoritarian Baptist-style of most of SCLC's senior staff. In an SCLC staff meeting, Dorothy would be expected to get coffee, but in a Citizenship School staff meeting, I was as likely to get the coffee as any of the women.

It must be admitted that Martin was oblivious to the existence of any issues on his staff regarding gender equity. He would flatter and charm Septima for her work, in the same manner he charmed members of Ebenezer's Altar Guild. He was not aware of his tendency to ignore her substantive comments or undervalue her work. And for the most part, while Septima knew she deserved more recognition than she received, she still beamed at his kind words. However, Septima and Dorothy would grumble privately about how women were treated in SCLC. There were certainly stirrings of the coming feminist revival in the early days of the civil rights movement, but mostly the women talked among themselves and didn't confront even the most paternalistic among us.

I wanted Mrs. Clark to work with us, even though at sixty-five she might have retired, because she had set up, along with Esau Jenkins, the prototype for the Citizenship Education Program on Johns Island, South Carolina, in the late fifties, and had further developed the program at Highlander. The Johns Island program was a classic example of what can be accomplished with both community and individual initiative. A barrier island across the bay from Charleston, Johns and adjacent James Island had huge black populations, a legacy of antebellum rice and sugar plantations. The islands were famous for the strong African cultural traits of the black population, who spoke Gullah, a West African–English dialect. But the isolation that preserved their unique culture also deprived the residents of improvements in education and their livelihood.

Esau Jenkins, a native of Johns Island, founded a bus service that for years served as the only means of travel between the island and jobs in Charleston. Mr. Jenkins, while driving the workers back and forth, began to talk to them about the necessity of their registering to vote if they really hoped to see betterment of conditions on Johns Island. Mr. Jenkins himself was about the only black on Johns Island who had registered, which had to be done in Charleston. He began coaching workers, while on the ferry from the island to the mainland, to help them pass the county registrar's special test, which required applicants, or at least black applicants, to read aloud from the text a certain section of the South Carolina state constitution. Most of the workers could not read, so Mr. Jenkins hit on the idea of having the men memorize that section of the constitution so they could pass the test successfully, disguising the fact they could not read or write. Since the ferry ride was an hour long, Jenkins had ample time to teach the daily lesson.

Over in Charleston, Septima Clark heard about Esau Jenkins's imaginative efforts with the Johns Island workers, and offered to help set up a school to teach the workers how to actually read. She also asked Myles Horton at Highlander if there was anything Highlander could do to help set up an adult education program on Johns Island. She wanted the school to be nontraditional, interesting, and aimed specifically toward voter education and the most immediate needs of the people. They wished to stay away from the public night-school type of adult education programs, which had proved to be extremely ineffective.

The first citizenship school was founded in 1956, meeting during only three months of the year—December, January, and February— when islanders did not have to work in the fields (the "laying by" season). Bernice Robinson, Septima's younger cousin, became the first regular teacher, inventing and discovering new ways to effectively impart knowledge as she went along. She based her lessons on questions from the students, assuming correctly that they would learn most quickly what they most wanted to know, whether it had to do with language or counting.

Dorothy Cotton had come to SCLC from Petersburg, Virginia, where she had been a protégée of Wyatt Walker. A graduate of Virginia State, Dorothy received a master's degree from Boston University and was working at Virginia State University when the Petersburg movement began. When Wyatt moved to Atlanta in 1960 to become executive secretary of SCLC, Dorothy followed soon after to join the new staff, expecting to stay only a few months. She remained for more than ten years, serving as a key leader on the SCLC executive staff during the great days of the movement. Pecan-brown with dancing eyes, she was full of energy, devotion, and talent as both a speaker and singer, and her laughter was a musical trill that could be heard across the Dorchester campus.

There was an SCLC convention in August and we wanted to be able to make an exciting report on the citizenship schools by then. Two weeks before the convention, we set off on a road tour of the South, scheduled to end in Chattanooga, Tennessee, for the start of the SCLC convention. Septima, Dorothy, and I set out in Dorothy's green two-toned Buick to discover, as we called it, "the natural black leaders of the South" and to bring them to Dorchester Center for training. We were looking for "those with Ph.D. minds, but third-grade educations." To find these "natural leaders" we decided to make a Southwide scouting and recruiting tour by automobile to meet people, inform them about our program, and work on the logistics of bringing those who were interested to Dorchester. I imagine we looked, to those who didn't know us, like a mother and her two children. We departed from Dorchester, drove over to Macon in central Georgia, down to Thomasville, to renew my friendships there and to recruit, then across to New Orleans to the home of my parents, where we rested and met with Rev. A. L. Davis and other ministers who were prominent in the New Orleans movement. But while A. L. Davis was a key figure in New Orleans, and SCLC had been organized in 1957 in his church, we had little success recruiting in my hometown.

From New Orleans we journeyed up the fabled Highway 61, paralleling the Mississippi River to Natchez, and then over to Canton, which two years later would become the site of one of the South's most violent and bitterly fought voter registration campaigns of the Mississippi movement. At Canton we met Mrs. Annie Devine, a courageous former schoolteacher who was just becoming active in the movement. Later Mrs. Devine, along with Victoria Gray of Hattiesburg, and Fannie Lou Hamer of Ruleville, became great women of the Mississippi movement and the Freedom Democratic Party. From Canton we went down to Jackson, where we met Medgar Evers, the aggressive and fearless Mississippi field secretary of the NAACP, who two years later was brutally murdered for his efforts on behalf of the cause of full equality. From Jackson we went up to Mound Bayou, the historic all-black town in the Delta, then a few miles further up Highway 49 to Cleveland, where we met Amzie Moore, a longtime NAACP stalwart. We then traveled across the cotton-rich, flat, sparsely populated Delta to Greenwood, which would become the central focus of the Mississippi movement within the next year. From Greenwood we went down to Meridian, then eastward to Tuscaloosa, Alabama, and finally down to Marion to rest and visit Jean's parents. A day later we were in Birmingham to meet members of the Alabama Christian Movement led by Fred Shuttlesworth, then on to Chattanooga, Tennessee, for the 1961 SCLC board meeting.

In talking about the citizenship program and trying to interest people in coming, we learned it was crucial to tell people right away we would pay their expenses, for cost was the determining factor for most people who were interested. Most of the people we spoke to had never left their home states before to go anywhere. Now we were asking them to travel all the way to the Georgia Atlantic coast—it must have sounded to them like we were asking them to come to the moon—for citizenship training.

We had a good meeting with longtime Mississippi activist Aaron Henry of Clarksdale. State president of the Mississippi NAACP, Henry was determined to remain in Mississippi despite persistent persecution. From the beginning he believed that black folk and white folk ought to be able to get along, even in Mississippi. He never became a black separatist when the Mississippi movement went into that phase. His drugstore in Clarksdale was and still is his headquarters. In the sixties it was an unpainted store with a simple soda fountain and a few plain display cases holding notions for sale. During the more than three decades since I first met him, Mr. Henry has become, step by step, one of the most important black political figures in Mississippi, and one of the most respected. He has provided intelligent and strong leadership in a state where, in the early sixties, he was jailed for leading a boycott of segregated stores, and where, four decades ago, any black who even thought about voting or using the vote to better the conditions of the people was lynched or run out of town. Aaron Henry was eventually elected to the Mississippi legislature, but that official position never reflected the extent of his political influence. Vera Pigee, a beautician who worked with Henry in the State NAACP, really ran the operations. She became one of our first citizenship school recruits.

Amzie Moore, until his untimely death a few years ago, survived in the Delta as a well-known NAACP representative from the time of the Emmett Till case in the 1950s. I remember especially a story told about his bravery in the fifties. Amzie was a postal worker in Cleveland, Mississippi. This was a federal job with strong job-security provisions; otherwise, he surely would have been fired for his civil rights activities. It is said that one day a group of whites converged on the post office armed with shotguns, determined to "get" Amzie because of something he had said. His superior came up to him and whispered, "There's a bunch of men coming up the steps with shotguns, they're looking for you. Why don't you slip out the back and get out of town soon as you can." But that wasn't Amzie. He went right out to the front steps of the post office, saw the men, and shouted loudly, "Somebody out here looking for Amzie Moore?" They yelled back, "Yeah, where is the nigger?" Amzie answered, "I'm Amzie Moore, can I help you?" and just stared them down. The men didn't even touch him. They grumbled about how he'd "better not interfere in white folks' business" or something, but they were afraid to make a move to harm him. Finally, they turned around and walked away. I liked that story.

It was the Amzie Moores, the Fannie Lou Hamers, the Vera Pigees, the Septima Clarks, and the uncommon common black people of the South who, year after year, through their dedication and sacrifices made the Southern civil rights movement possible. They were not the publicized leaders of the media, spokesmen like Martin King, but they were the core of the movement.

As we traveled across the South, one problem we faced was that we were relatively unknown to those we were attempting to recruit; trust could only be built over a period of time, a period of testing. So although at first the response to our program was quite enthusiastic, we realized it would take time to really build the program to the level we desired. We arranged to rent a Greyhound bus, which originated in New Orleans, and traversed the black belt, picking up participants in Mississippi, Alabama, and Georgia, finally arriving at Dorchester. We didn't have to worry about recruiting in South Carolina because Septima Clark and Bernice Robinson were so well known there all they had to do was send out the word about Dorchester Center, and we would receive enthusiastic participation.

The basic idea at Dorchester was to establish voter registration using a few key people in 188 crucial counties that had black majorities across the Deep South but almost no black registered voters. Our hope was that the first people registered would in turn begin registration campaigns in their own counties. Our Southwide focus was on the Mississippi Delta, the black belt of Alabama, scattered areas of Georgia and Florida, the eastern shores of North Carolina and South Carolina, and the Tidewater area of Virginia.

Following our tour of the South, we made our report to the

SCLC convention in Chattanooga. In the beginning, it must be said that our project was not taken very seriously by the SCLC board and many of SCLC's most prominent preachers. Septima was often frustrated that she was not invited to sit in on high-level strategy sessions. I was not in those meetings either, initially, but I had resolved to focus on the Citizenship School Program and steer clear of internal SCLC politics. I knew that the citizenship schools were laying the foundation for a Southwide movement and I was content to spend my energy on training rather than engage in struggles for recognition within the organization. I never thought that board meetings and conventions were the real work of the movement anyway. So, having made our report, we finalized details and launched the first citizenship school at Dorchester Center.

The site of an American Missionary Association school, Dorchester Center was located about thirty miles south of Savannah, very near the Atlantic coast. It was quite an historic area of Georgia—Dorchester had been the southernmost outpost of the Puritan settlements that migrated from New England. Established in 1754 with 280 whites and 536 blacks held in slavery, the Midway Congregational Church at Dorchester included two signers of the Declaration of Independence: Button Gwinnett and Lyman Hall. Midway's early pastors included the fathers of Samuel Morse and Oliver Wendell Holmes. Over time, the connection with New England Congregationalism loosened; the Congregationalists at Midway continued to hold slaves as abolitionist sentiment grew among their Northern kin. Midway opposed secession from the Union, although its members eventually fought with the Confederates, and blacks were required to worship in the balcony of the white frame Puritan church. When General William T. Sherman cut his path from Atlanta to the Atlantic, he stopped at Midway, and the missionaries following in his wake started a school adjacent to the grounds of the old colonial church. The freedmen and freedwomen built their own church amidst the moss-covered oaks and continued many of the Congregational traditions.

By the end of the summer, with help from people living in nearby towns and funds from the United Church of Christ, we had been able to fix up the dormitory so it could satisfactorily house sixty people. The building's high ceilings and tall windows created an airy feel. The UCC purchased a new stove for the kitchen and we hired cooks from the neighboring black community to prepare familiar Southern meals. The community was very supportive and proud that the campus that had been used to educate many of their forebears was again being used to advance the cause of freedom. We never had any problem finding help. The auditorium, our meeting rooms, and the bedrooms were clean and fresh. When the preparations were completed, we arranged a charter bus to pick up students throughout the black belt of Alabama and Mississippi and bring them to Dorchester.

From the beginning we established a pattern of having each group arrive by bus on a Sunday night, so that we could begin early Monday morning. We had one building that enclosed the kitchen and an auditorium that doubled as a dining hall: on the first floor there were classrooms, an office, and women's bedrooms, and on the second floor were the men's rooms. The rooms were fitted like a barracks with several rows of bunk beds. There were communal showers and toilets, no air-conditioning, and precious few fans. The grounds were beautiful, with Spanish moss–covered live oak trees that kept the direct sunlight off the building. Nevertheless, we made available handheld church fans—large cardboard fans with pictures of praying hands or biblical scenes stapled onto an oversized Popsicle stick—and there were plenty of opportunities to use them.

We began Monday morning with a real Southern breakfast and lots of grits. First on the schedule was a plenary session in the auditorium where Dorothy, Septima, and I shared the story of Montgomery to put our efforts in context. Then later in the week we broke into smaller groups, one in the auditorium and two in the classrooms, to work on civics, education, and organizing techniques. Jean developed a phonics curriculum for us.

We didn't hold formal classes on the first afternoon since people had just come off a long bus ride and were tired. We would take people over to see the old Midway Church and drive over to the Civil War fort in Savannah, and the trainyard where more history was made—it was the site of a Revolutionary War battle in which the largest-ever contingent of black soldiers fought.

Our evening presentation was a filmstrip of "The Nashville Sit-in Story." The NBC program that drew me back to the South also inspired countless others. The genius of that program was that it let the students tell their own story, and that story was a powerful inspiration to the participants in our citizenship schools. We wanted to give our students a sense that people had power and could change things without guns and without money, drawing only on the power in their own souls. Throughout the week we followed the pattern of organizing techniques, education, and politics in the morning, relaxing in the afternoon, and filmstrips or discussion in the evening. We didn't push people too hard, because they worked so hard in their everyday lives. Our schedule gave them space to absorb new information and new understanding. On Saturday nights, the last day of each weeklong workshop, we held a banquet, which later Martin often attended as our featured speaker. The bus left after the banquet so that people could be in their own churches Sunday morning to share the good news they had heard at Dorchester and begin recruiting for their own classes.

Our Dorchester sessions brought together different people from all over the South and we never knew what kind of situations might present themselves when a new group of students came in. Once, there was a white college girl with SNCC at Dorchester who had come South to work in Mississippi. She was under the misguided impression that she was going to identify with the poor by being dirty. Now, the poor rural black people I knew made a fetish of cleanliness. They didn't stay dirty and sweaty one moment longer than they had to. Some of the women sharing her room came to me complaining, but I told them I couldn't touch it. So they went to Septima. Septima made a big show of placing her hand on the young woman's forehead, telling her she had a fever and needed a nice warm bath to make her well. Septima went through this elaborate charade to get the young woman in the bathtub. Septima thought she had solved the problem, but later, one of the girl's roommates came back, whining to Septima, "Mrs. Clark, that girl got out the tub and put those same blue underpants back on."

Once we had a veteran from Arkansas, a pulp mill worker, attend one of our sessions. He was a great big man with a bodybuilder's physique. In one of Bernice Robinson's classes, he started getting agitated and told Bernice, "Sit down, I'm taking over this class." He started asking people questions, mimicking our teaching style, but when folks gave an answer, he would point his meaty forefinger at them and ask in a challenging tone, "Would you stake your life on that?" Now, this scared folks to death and someone came to get me. One of the SNCC kids was very high-strung and had some prescription tranquilizers. I told him to make some tea and bring it to everyone in the class, but make sure he put tranquilizers and lots of sugar in the tea he handed to this brother. I think he put six tranquilizers in the tea. I went into the classroom and talked with the brother calmly, humoring him. I knew he was crazy and I knew he could kill if provoked. We all drank our tea and it knocked him out. While he was asleep, the guys who brought him loaded him in their car and started driving back home to Arkansas to check him into the veteran's hospital there. Truly, very few of the students we saw were as challenging as those two in their own special ways.

The first rule of Septima's adult education technique was to treat our students as adults, experienced in the practical skills of life. We taught by asking questions: "What do you think is the purpose of the Constitution of the United States?" "What does it mean to be a citizen of the United States?" These were adults who knew a lot about life; it was merely certain knowledge about citizenship they needed, basically because such knowledge had been denied them. Each person had a chance to say what he or she thought the Constitution was ("a set of rules," "what was set down in the beginning," etc.) or what the rights of citizenship were ("to be a part of the state") and from the discussions that followed we tried, slowly, to arrive at fundamental but practical definitions we could understand and accept. If we had asked the question "What does it mean to be a citizen?" we would then steer our discussions toward what it meant to be a black Southern citizen. The process of learning involved group sharing, group catharsis. By comparing similar experiences (the Mississippi sheriff versus the Alabama sheriff) we attempted to introduce pertinent new facts: the role of the courts in the American system of government, the hierarchy of the courts, the differences between federal and state law, and finally, what it means to be a citizen, and the basic rights guaranteed by the federal Constitution to each American citizen. "Practical civics" is what we called what we were teaching, and we ourselves learned as we taught.

We tried to improve literacy skills by using the daily newspapers, common signs, and labels as our textbook. The adults from farm communities were mostly functionally illiterate, since they were only allowed to attend school when it didn't interfere with farmwork. They could read, write, and figure just enough to get by, but they had no confidence in their abilities and didn't practice the skills they had acquired through intermittent schooling. We encouraged people to trust their abilities and showed them that they already possessed the ability to sight read many complicated words. We used the actual common forms that they needed to use in their everyday lives, such as IRS forms, Social Security forms, job or driver's license application forms. To familiarize participants with basic principles of banking and handling of money we asked a banker from the nearby town of Hindsville to do a session for us, and he came faithfully to each new session.

To augment our "practical civics" we added short courses in black American history, particularly political history, and an intro-

duction to nonviolent protest philosophy, including an exposure to
the ideas of Gandhi. To provide background understanding of Southern segregation laws, we employed a brief overview of the black
American experience, beginning with the slave ships, the long dark
period of slavery, the abolitionist movement, the opposition to slavery culminating with the Civil War, the Emancipation Proclamation
of 1863, and the special meaning of the Thirteenth, Fourteenth, and
Fifteenth Amendments, which abolished slavery, made us citizens,
and empowered us with the right to vote.

Then we zeroed in on some of the facts about Reconstruction in
a lecture and discussion on black history brilliantly conducted by
Jack O'Dell, a former labor organizer and SCLC fund-raiser who
commuted down from Atlanta for his sessions. Reconstruction had
been ignored in the public schools of the South, probably out of a
desire by Southern whites to erase it from memory. It shocked our
people to learn that blacks, from Emancipation until 1876, had voted
quite extensively in the South, had been elected to state and congressional offices, had enjoyed a degree of civil and political rights, and
had spoken out and fully participated in furthering their political and
civic interests. All of this was hard for us to believe in 1961 in south
Georgia, so far backward had things gone. It was important that our
people know that the civil and political rights exercised during
Reconstruction had been taken away by the activities of violent white
supremacist organizations like the Ku Klux Klan and the Knights of
Camelia, ancestors of the Citizens Councils and the Klan of the
1960s.

It was also important that we learn about the abandonment of
the national commitment to the protection of the rights of black citizens in 1876 and thereafter. The Hayes-Tilden Compromise paved
the way for the election of Rutherford B. Hayes to the presidency in
exchange for a withdrawal of federal troops from the South. Blacks
in the South discovered they had rights on paper, but no way to effectively enforce those rights. By 1883, the Supreme Court found the
Civil Rights Act of 1875 to be unconstitutional, and in 1896 the
Supreme Court decided the infamous case *Plessy v. Ferguson*, giving a
green light to Jim Crow and segregation under the doctrine of "separate but equal." The segregation laws we were combating in 1960
were a product of that success in destroying the progress won by
blacks in the period after Emancipation, and to keep blacks in a state
of perpetual subjugation. To make our "practical civics" real, it was
necessary for us to know that history.

But it was not all serious work. At least once during our sessions we chartered a bus and everyone went to the beach, usually over at Hilton Head Island in South Carolina, about an hour's drive away. Hilton Head is full of expensive resorts now, but then it was largely black-owned and undeveloped, perfect for the kind of outing we desired. And it was important to do this: most of our participants had never seen the ocean in their lives, and never thought they would.

Each night, we gathered for evening vespers in the auditorium. After prayers, Dorothy lifted her lovely soprano voice and led us in group singing. These were wonderful sessions that took the form of praying, singing, and testifying like the old deacons at Evergreen Church in Beachton. The music was a way of freeing individuals to tell their own stories. We sang and we sang: sorrowful songs, happy songs, freedom songs, made-up songs, like

If you miss me from the cotton patch
If you can't find me no where,
Come on down to City Hall
I'll be working over there

which was greeted with bursts of laughter and delight—for in the small, isolated black belt towns of the South, no blacks worked in city hall for any reason other than to sweep and mop. The music prevented us from becoming depressed about our individual situations. Coming together we could learn about and share one another's griefs, frustrations, dreams, and hopes for a better time.

People would testify about their attempts to register to vote, the first awakenings that had led to their activism. Dorothy Cotton told the story of the woman who had opposed her son's participation in the sit-in movement, but then she too slowly found herself becoming involved. This was often the case—parents who became activists in support of their children after warning them to "stay out of that mess in the streets." June Johnson of Greenwood, Mississippi, a fifteen-year-old student when she first came to Dorchester, testified that her mother had forbidden her to visit the SNCC project office in Greenwood established by Willie Peacock and Sam Block in 1961–62. When her mother found she could not stop her daughter she began attending meetings herself to "see what they were." She liked what she heard and started cooking for the SNCC volunteers. After a while she opened her home to them; her house became a noted "freedom house" in Greenwood. Eventually Mrs. Johnson was jailed in a demonstration, along with her daughter. Another woman who had at first opposed her son's participation in the movement testified one night that her son had questioned her closely about whether she felt it was right to be considered a second-class citizen in America and "just accept it" as a matter of course. "Finally, the cobwebs commenced a-movin' from my brain," she testified. Everyone in the hall knew what she meant.

James Bevel often spoke of this newfound consciousness as consisting of two phases: "picking up one's soul, and walking with one's soul." It was "picking up" and "walking" toward a new personal commitment to make our society just and equitable that we were working to enhance at Dorchester, by expanding knowledge of the historical and philosophical dimensions of the growing civil rights movement. During these nights of "testimony," of expressions of humble, heartfelt commitment, I realized that all the winding roads I had thus far traversed in my life, sometimes not knowing where they would lead, had led me to the right place at the right time. I was grateful to be part of this historical, spiritual transformation of the South, for we were certain that was what we were experiencing.

Once they returned home and continued or increased their movement activities, many of those who had come to our Dorchester sessions were marked by the controlling white community: often they faced threats to their lives and property, and the loss of their jobs. The movement career of the remarkable Fannie Lou Hamer, for example, was distinguished by her determination not to bow to pressures to keep her from speaking out for civil rights.

Mrs. Hamer had visited our first Dorchester sessions and become our most effective recruiter of Mississippi participants. We knew immediately there was something special about her: the sharpness of her mind, the force of her spirit, her special blend of black folk speech, a unique poetry of oral expression, the amazing strength of her gift for song. She spoke with the power of experience and vision. And she could really sing—she knew all the old church songs of the Mississippi Delta; music was really her entree into the movement.

When James Bevel, Sam Block, and Willie Peacock began to organize in the Mississippi Delta in 1960 and 1961, they often brought in singing groups to movement-friendly churches as a first step in their efforts. They were natives of the Delta and they knew how little chance they stood of gaining the people's trust if they presented themselves straight-out as organizers; people were too afraid to respond to that approach. So they organized gospel groups and hit the road. Both Peacock and Block were fine lead singers; under the cover of a musical group they sang and spoke their way through the black communities of the Delta, from Greenville to Greenwood.

Mrs. Hamer, who lived near Ruleville in Sunflower County, was recruited at one of their musicals, and in a very short time she was singing with them and speaking out too. At Dorchester she told us how they would begin with gospel songs, and then move on to the new freedom songs, which sounded like gospel songs with a slight twist of language, then they would ask the congregation to join in. Finally, they would speak about voting and ask for volunteers to meet at a certain time for the attempt to register.

When Mrs. Hamer returned to Mississippi after her first trip to Dorchester, she immersed herself in the movement, especially voter education and registration. She led a group of black Sunflower County residents to the central courthouse and asked to register. When she returned home, her employer gave her an ultimatum—either withdraw from the voter rolls or be fired. When she refused to be intimidated she was summarily dismissed from her job as a plantation timekeeper, a job she had held for fifteen years. She and her family were immediately evicted from their extremely modest plantation shack, and her furniture was put out on the highway. She took refuge with a family in Ruleville and the house was shot into. Bevel called me in desperation from Mississippi to ask if there was some way we could help Mrs. Hamer. We wired a hundred dollars—Bevel rented a truck for twenty dollars to move the Hamer family's possessions, paid two months rent on a house in Ruleville at thirty dollars a month, and gave Mrs. Hamer the remaining money for expenses.

The night we heard what had happened to the Hamers, sleep was impossible. I got up, dressed, and found myself wandering listlessly down the dark road leading from the school. Remembering how the bus carrying Mrs. Hamer had departed as we softly sang the old spiritual "This May Be the Last Time," I just collapsed into tears. This was perhaps the first time I felt deeply and personally how serious the business we were embarking upon would become. This was no play school, no play citizenship, no play freedom we were working for: people would pay with blood, with their lives, for doing what we maybe too comfortably were urging them to do. I had wanted to be part of this, and now I was, but the responsibility was heavier than I by myself could handle. Never had I needed my faith more; for we knew, prophetically, that the sacrifices necessary to make change possible would be more than some could bear. As surely as the next few years portended accomplishments and a taste of victory, they also held promises of tragedy.

Mrs. Hamer went on to become one of the most forceful leaders of the Southern movement, her unique eloquence providing unforgettable testimony of the suffering of black people in the South and the meaning of the struggle to alleviate that suffering. When she succumbed after a long illness in 1977, I returned once more to the small Delta hamlet of Ruleville to eulogize her life and spirit.

As I saw the incredible gathering of friends and movement veterans that came to Ruleville for Mrs. Hamer's funeral (held in two churches simultaneously to hold the masses who attended), I could not but reflect on the irony that this black woman, despised by the rulers of the Delta for her efforts in the service of human dignity, this woman who lacked wealth, education, and social status, had brought an importance to this spot on the planet never before even imagined. From near and far, by every means of transportation available, young militants and veteran warhorses, common folk of the land, the committed from around the nation, from every divergent wing and ideology of the movement came that day to pay their respects. Her life was eternal proof that the hands that had once picked cotton, given a fair chance, had the power to choose the future course of the South, and the progressive future of this nation.

There were very few models for what we were doing, so we tried to improve the Citizenship Program as we went along. Our community leaders were supposed to recruit their own students, hold classes, send new students to Dorchester, and send us information on their progress. Even without the added risks, we had very high expectations of these people. After Mrs. Hamer's experience, we began to give our community trainers and organizers a small stipend of thirty dollars a month. When the program began, we weren't giving them anything, but when people started suffering, we had to at least try to cover their expenses. Eventually the Field Foundation would give us an extra fifteen thousand dollars to pay teacher expenses. In the meantime, thirty dollars was a piddling amount of money, but it could make all the difference. Technically, we were in violation of the grant by even sending Mrs. Hamer that emergency assistance. But when you are surrounded by so many people in need, the terms of a grant seem far less important than the moral obligation to help people who are under tremendous pressure.

I was always grateful that I came to SCLC with a separate budget that I basically controlled. I knew Baptist preachers had a strong authoritarian streak. Ralph Abernathy was Martin King's close associate since the Montgomery bus boycott and served as the treasurer of SCLC. I did not want to have to justify myself to Wyatt or Ralph Abernathy every time I made a decision. It frustrated Ralph and Wyatt that they couldn't control me and there were always rumors about what I was doing and how I was handling the money, but fortunately it was under my authority from the United Church of Christ. The Field Foundation had provided thirty-five thousand dollars for us to train two hundred people, but before the grant cycle was over we had spent all the money and trained four hundred people. I called Wes Hotchkiss at the United Church and he advanced fifteen thousand dollars more. Field approved and eventually reimbursed the United Church of Christ, but Ralph and Wyatt were upset that I had money again, when they thought we had run out.

There was a great push to encourage voter registration across the South at this time, and our policy was to train everybody who came, regardless of whether they were affiliated with SCLC, SNCC, NAACP, or any other civil rights effort. We encouraged the community leaders we trained to get involved with local voter registration and education drives, and most of the voter registration drives were run by volunteers with no money, just as my voter registration drive in Thomasville had been run with a local preacher and a few volunteers. So even the small amount of money that our folk could contribute for gas or flyers could make a big difference. Often, these individual volunteers who became the leaders of the voter registration effort gained new status and respect in their communities. We did not preserve records of the students who came to Dorchester, but I have met many in subsequent years who became elected officials or helped a child or relative achieve elective office.

We always deliberately sought out the natural leaders who had not had the opportunity to attain much formal schooling. Mr. Steptoe, a fiftyish, rural farmer from Amite County, Mississippi, came to our program, and really absorbed it like a dry sponge. He went back and began organizing classes at his church. The Mississippi literacy test used all sorts of irrelevant big words, so he had his students practice words such as *miscegenation, fornication,* and *prevarication.* When he thought his class was ready—they were prepared to write and spell and answer questions that would be put to them by the Amite County registrar—he loaded the class in a horse-drawn wagon and drove into town. When he got to town and got out of his wagon in front of the courthouse, the sheriff stopped him and said, "What do you want, boy?"

Mr. Steptoe said, "I came to redish."

The sheriff pulled his gun and asked again, "What did you say?"
Mr. Steptoe said, "I aim to redish."
The sheriff cocked his gun and asked, "What did you say, boy?"
Mr. Steptoe said, "If I lives, I aims to redish."

You don't have to be able to read to know that if you vote your streets get paved and if you don't vote you drive through mud when it rains. You don't have to be literate to know that police respect you a little more when you vote. When the farm programs were enacted, paying big farmers not to plant food and fiber, no one thought of the farmworkers, because they didn't vote. Governments collect taxes without regard to literacy and education, and voting is the only way ordinary people have to determine how their resources are spent. The restrictions this nation still places on voting are a disgrace to democracy—residency and registration requirements discourage young, poor, and working-class citizens from voting. Elections should take place on weekends, when fewer citizens would have to take time from work to vote. Given the low voter turnout we consistently experience, no recent president has had the genuine consent of the governed.

At Dorchester our concern was not with ideology, but with cutting across ideologies to enhance people's sense of self-worth, to instill in them a belief that they had a right, despite historical hardships and oppression, to participate in their government and to exercise control over their own lives. My work in the Citizenship Program helped prepare me for a deeper involvement in the civil rights movement in ways I could not possibly have anticipated when I returned South. It left me with a sense of who the people were who would be in the movement, an appreciation for their dedication and intelligence, and a widespread network of warm contacts and friendships that lasted throughout the movement, and even until today.

Dorothy Cotton took over the Citizenship Program after I became executive director of SCLC in 1964. From 1961 to 1966 we trained more than six thousand people at the citizenship schools. When the movement underwent its "black power" phase, several of the Dorchester participants were young militants. One day, Dorothy said, one of the young people remarked that we needed to "burn down the system," then rebuild it. She told the young man, "Before you decide on that, why don't you take a walk with Miss Lucy over there." Miss Lucy was in her seventies, from rural Alabama, and had sacrificed everything she had to participate in the movement. "You take a walk through the grounds out there with Miss Lucy," Dorothy insisted. "Tell her what you think, and when you come back tell us what she said." Dorothy liked to call this the "trust walk." The young man returned reporting not what Miss Lucy said, but what *he* had said to Miss Lucy. "Did you listen to what *she* said?" Dorothy asked. "If you want change, if change is to mean anything, the people whom the change is intended for have to want it, and have to be part of the decision. Now, go with Miss Lucy again, and find out what *she* wants."

The movement that began in the South like a series of brushfires was the culmination of several new factors that had converged to ignite a dramatic escalation in the drive for racial justice. I had seen the first sparks of this change in Thomasville; as young people became aware that a better life was possible, their discontent increased and with it the pressure for change. At Dorchester we could sense a new attitude, a new determination in the air, in the voices of the people, in the music, a new spring in the steps of old and young, who had heretofore been downtrodden, depressed, devoid of hope.

There were several reasons for this optimism. First, there was the tremendously increased involvement of youth. For the first time in the twentieth century, black Southern youth were determined to stay in the South and sacrifice their lives, if necessary, to work for real change. This new generation, many of them college students with the advantages of education, were no longer willing to suffer the indignities and limited economic opportunities of their parents' and grandparents' generations. They were not willing to return to the plantations and follow in their fathers' footsteps in the fields, or work in towns as janitors and handymen. Their teachers may not have taught them this new defiance, but defiance against the status quo was the natural reaction, once the young people were exposed to the lifted horizons and greater aspirations made possible by education.

Second, there was a new attitude among those in the above-thirty age group, who were gradually straying away from the plantation system. They were streaming into the towns from the countryside, as the country offered them less and less opportunity to make even subsistence-level livelihoods. Blacks who could no longer "just make it" in the area around Thomasville were now moving to towns like Albany, and those in the Mississippi Delta were streaming into towns like Greenwood and Greenville. These migrants became desperate and restless because there were no jobs for them in the towns either. If they could not enjoy even a modicum of economic opportunity, they were now ready to go to jail as part of mass demonstrations in the hope that such drastic action would force change.

There was also by now a small but dedicated group of middle-class black professionals who had achieved independent economic means. Though subject to reprisals, intimidation, and sometimes outright violence, this small group was becoming much more defiant and determined to push for change, particularly those individuals who were not dependent on the white power structure for their economic livelihood.

At the same time, an entirely new factor was introduced in the wake of Supreme Court and subsequent federal court decisions that dismantled the constitutional underpinnings of the segregation system. For example, in Montgomery, it was the federal district court that first ruled that segregation in the Montgomery bus system violated the U.S. Constitution, a decision that was later upheld by the U.S. Supreme Court. The Court's decision in *Brown* set off a series of related lower-court decisions as activists attempted to implement these new rights in their own communities. These court decisions provided the protesters against de facto local segregation with more than just moral support: they also gave demonstrators a powerful claim to being within the law, while placing local and state officials on the moral and legal defensive.

Finally, there was now, with the emergence of Martin Luther King and other nonviolent protest theorists, a new philosophical and tactical basis for demonstrations—one that blacks could rally around with discipline and a sense of moral imperative that had not existed since the moral onslaught against slavery. Nonviolent civil disobedience in the service of a greater societal good carried with it, in 1961, a certain excitement and novelty, as well as a sense of history-in-the-making that had the potential to attract supporters who were not Southerners and who were not black. This philosophical basis gave us the feeling we were not alone. The clear and shining example of Gandhi's campaign in India against colonialism also aided tremendously in fostering a new togetherness, a new communion among those who were willing to accept the burdens of protest. No more was there the feeling that lonely, individual, uncoordinated, modest protest actions or voter registration drives in out-of-the-way towns would only bring about reprisals or violence to no greater end. Now even when such protests were carried out by individuals, those individuals felt part of a larger whole that was moving—thus the deeper connotation of the term "movement."

There was also a new binding—and we could feel it from the vantage point of our Citizenship Program—across class and educational lines, across generations, across localities and dialects and family backgrounds. We could hear this unity in the singing voices and speaking voices of the people; it seemed we could even hear it in the earth itself, like a soft rumbling, a rhythmic beating of drums from all over the South. It was a knowing, with undeniable and unshakable conviction, that our time had come. The South would never be the same again.

Part II

1961–1968

8

The Singing Movement

Woke up this morning with my mind, stayed on
freedom. . .

—AFRICAN-AMERICAN SPIRITUAL

By Thanksgiving 1961, I was finally able to move Jean and our
three girls into the brick house with green trim at 177 Chicamauga Place. I had been in perpetual motion going from
Atlanta, to rural Mississippi and Alabama, down to Dorchester, back
to Atlanta, up to New York to see Jean and to report to the Field
Foundation and Wes Hotchkiss. Mother was so grateful that we were
back in the South that she took the train over from New Orleans to
help Jean get unpacked. She was not pleased to see the bare wood
floors in our new house, however. It was nearly winter and I imagine
she had nightmarish visions of her grandchildren coming down with
pneumonia. So, her housewarming gift to us was a blue carpet for the
living room.

It was a tremendous relief to have the family all together again.
We enrolled Andrea in first grade at Frank L. Stanton Elementary
School and Lisa attended preschool on the Spelman College campus.
It was more than a little ironic that in leaving New York to fight segregation, I took my own children from integrated schools in Queens
to segregated schools in Atlanta. Despite our efforts to end segregation, we could not protect our families from its continued existence.

The Atlanta school board was being sued by the NAACP for its resistance to desegregation, so, initially, all of our children attended segregated schools. Of course, had any of us put the short-term welfare of our families first, we would not have been in SCLC and probably not in the South at all.

We joined the First Congregational Church, where Jean soon became active as a Sunday school teacher. The pastor, Dr. Homer C. McEwen, had preached the sermon at my ordination and many of the members were people we had known for years from Congregational church gatherings. The members of First Church were college professors, educators, business owners, doctors, and other well-educated professionals, members of Atlanta's black elite. Jean was neither impressed by nor disdainful of one's status, but was always drawn to the person beneath the social trappings. She became very popular, due in large part to her lack of pretension. In those days she was still fairly timid and shy, so petite and sweet-faced she looked more like a teenager than a mother of three. It was as if the matrons of First Congregational decided that Jean needed their guardianship, especially since her husband was working with that controversial King fellow.

First Congregational was at the center of a wide network and Jean and the girls soon had their own active social lives. At a Christmas party Jean met Daisy Harris, a teacher who became a dear, lifelong friend. When Daisy discovered Jean had a master's degree in education, she urged Jean to teach in the Atlanta public schools and walked her through the application process. When the next school year began, Jean had a position teaching at Whiteford Elementary School.

I made every effort to be home on weekends, but that was not possible when we had classes at Dorchester. When I wasn't working, Atlanta became a sanctuary, a place to relax and enjoy small pleasures like attending First Congregational Church and then driving down Hunter Street to Paschal's Restaurant for a Sunday dinner of fried chicken or crispy fried shrimp. I was proud to be seen with my wife, who looked beautiful even in the most inexpensive outfit, and our three daughters, hair combed smoothly into buns and wearing the matching dresses my mother liked to send them. Paschal's was one of several black-owned restaurants that thrived in segregated Atlanta and it was famous in the black community throughout the South as a gathering place for politicians, professors from Atlanta University, and other members of Atlanta's large black middle class.

In Atlanta, I was nurtured by my family and drew strength and comfort from being an attentive daddy to my little girls, tending to chores around the house, courting my wife. I liked being able to take a break from the intensity of the citizenship schools and SCLC and I had little interest in the desegregation battles taking place in Atlanta. Home was my sanctuary and I didn't want to become a controversial person in Atlanta by joining picket lines or attending strategy meetings of local civil rights groups. Whenever I went outside of Atlanta, I had to be constantly on guard for hostile law enforcement officers or ordinary whites who opposed civil rights. I needed to be able to let down my guard at home, and if I became involved in local civil rights actions, my home would cease to be a place of rest and relaxation. It was often frustrating for Jean that I did not want to talk about work when I was home. She wanted to know more about the citizenship schools and how the classes were going, but I just wanted to leave all that outside our front door when I was home. But Jean was ever strong and silent and didn't complain much.

When Ralph Abernathy moved from Montgomery to Atlanta he and his wife, Juanita, purchased a home near ours on the west side of Atlanta. Juanita was a vivacious and attractive woman with glowing, coffee-colored skin and a figure that belied the fact that she had borne three children. She made a real contrast with Ralph, who was tall and jowly with a generous waistline and an expansive personality to match. Where Juanita was quick and sharp, Ralph was plodding and easygoing. Their two daughters were the same age as my two oldest girls and the four became good friends. Martin and Coretta King lived in an old wooden frame house near Ebenezer Baptist Church and the home where he grew up, in what was known as the old Fourth Ward. There was nothing fashionable about his neighborhood, it was all but a slum. But Martin viewed living modestly as part of his commitment to social justice. He never accepted a salary from SCLC, and most of his speaking honoraria went to support the movement, so the small salary from Ebenezer was about all he and his family lived on. It was not easy for Coretta to keep shoes and clothing on their three rapidly growing children. She also worried about the neighborhood, since she and the children were alone there most of the time, and unlike Martin she had not grown up there. In Heiberger, a tiny community near Marion, Alabama, her parents still left their doors unlocked and even left the car keys in the ignition as searching for keys was more troublesome than the risk of theft. Adding to her concern were her memories of the bombing of their home in Montgomery.

During the fall of 1961, Martin's second attempt at forming a staff at SCLC was beginning to come together. He was traveling constantly, making speeches, holding fund-raisers, and organizing SCLC affiliate chapters. But SCLC, in the four years since its founding, had yet to develop a clear direction or any major initiatives. The staff was still being consolidated in Atlanta and, given the renown of Martin King, it had very few paid employees. It was an open question whether Martin King would be able to duplicate Montgomery successes in any other venue. In the meantime, the momentum of direct action in the movement had shifted to the students.

The daring student sit-ins had not originated with SCLC, although the students called on Martin to give support to their desegregation initiatives and the sit-ins were clearly inspired by the effectiveness of direct action in the Montgomery bus boycott. Martin had hoped that the students would form a youth arm of SCLC, but gave his blessing when it was clear that the students wanted their own organization. In a meeting at Shaw University in North Carolina in April 1960, the Student Nonviolent Coordinating Committee (SNCC) was born. As a student organization, SNCC had even less infrastructure than SCLC and came to depend on SCLC for support of its programs.

This set the stage for a virtually inevitable conflict. SNCC endeavored to be totally independent of SCLC, yet, as a matter of practice, SNCC came to SCLC for money. When they came to SCLC, they came to Wyatt Walker, an authoritarian Baptist preacher whose insistence on accountability was an affront to SNCC's more laid-back style of administration.

Wyatt was rightly concerned that SCLC be able to account for the funds that it spent. SCLC had given five thousand dollars to SNCC for one of their projects and had never received any itemization or reporting of how the funds were spent. He refused to give SNCC any more money until they fully accounted for those funds. Wyatt had also heard that a SNCC organizer had taken a trip to Mexico, and Wyatt was concerned that he might have used SCLC money to finance his vacation. Wyatt was right to be concerned, but it antagonized the students and they accused SCLC of trying to control SNCC. It was in the midst of this controversy that a group of SNCC students, Charley Jones, Charles Sherrod, Cordell Reagon, and Bernard Lee took a bus from Atlanta to Albany to test segregation in Albany's bus station.

What became known as the "Albany movement" began as a spin-off from the Freedom Rides of the winter of 1961, an effort by small interracial groups led by the Congress of Racial Equality

(CORE). CORE was founded by James Farmer as a nonviolent organization in Chicago in 1942. Farmer, a graduate of Howard School of Divinity and race relations secretary for the pacifist Fellowship of Reconciliation, knew that many tactics necessary to fight the de facto segregation in the North were unacceptable to genuine pacifists. While pacifists approved of nonviolent passive resistance, many considered demonstrations aggressively provocative and, therefore, unacceptable. CORE planned to test implementation of the December 1960 Supreme Court decision in *Boynton v. Virginia*, which extended the prohibition of segregation in interstate travel to train and bus terminals. This meant there should be no more COLORED and FOR WHITES ONLY waiting rooms, no more separate rest rooms, water fountains, lunch counters, and so forth, with the facilities for COLORED always inferior. It also meant that no more would blacks be confined to the front car of the trains, or seated at separate tables hidden behind a curtain in train dining cars, all common elements of the world I had grown up in, and a staple feature of Southern culture since the turn of the century. No form of segregation was more visible or more keenly felt than that in the world of public transportation.

But all over the South, particularly in the smaller cities and towns, the FOR WHITES ONLY signs were not coming down—local governments were simply refusing to abide by the Supreme Court decision. Blacks were continuing to use the COLORED facilities, fearful of what would happen if they defied local segregation laws and customs. Blacks who defied these customs and survived the brutality of the police (who were enraged at the very prospect that black citizens, once docile and controllable, were becoming "uppity") had little chance for redress in the local courts.

It was into this charged atmosphere that the courageous Freedom Riders rode during the spring of 1961, determined to deliberately challenge segregation on the buses and in terminals. They hoped that a planned defiance of the unconstitutional practice of segregated persons in interstate commerce action would force the executive branch to shore up the *Boynton* decision.

And indeed the beatings and arrests suffered by the Freedom Riders in the spring and summer of 1961 focused national and world attention on the South in a way not seen since the Montgomery bus boycott of 1955. This spotlight forced the new John F. Kennedy administration to at least attempt to protect the constitutional rights of the riders, and to implement *Boynton* administratively with an Interstate Commerce Commission (ICC) order of September 22 expressly prohibiting segregated facilities in interstate travel, effective November 1. This seminal ICC ruling precipitated the demonstrations in Albany, a small, previously docile southwestern Georgia town.

My interest was instantly attracted because I knew Albany fairly well; it was only sixty miles north of Thomasville and we had frequently gone there to shop. Albany was one of the reasons black folk in Thomasville hadn't complained too much—they had only to look to Albany to consider their own status tolerable. A small, isolated town of fifty-six thousand, Albany was ruled firmly by a long-established white oligarchy that was determined to vehemently resist any threat to the status quo; it had undergone none of the even slightly progressive social and economic changes experienced by a few other Southern cities.

Albany's economy was built around agriculture: peanuts and corn—it was the merchandising center for these crops farmed in neighboring counties. The population was about forty percent black. Most of them were dirt-poor, but there was a small professional class that had become relatively well-to-do. The pattern of black poverty was also broken by the presence of Albany State College, a state land-grant institution maintained for black students in the segregated Georgia state university system. The administrators of Albany State were overseen by the state Board of Regents and as a result divorced themselves from the realities of day-to-day racial conditions in the city. Like many of my old instructors, they urged the students to uplift the race by improving themselves. But there was a growing awareness among many black college students there and elsewhere who were tuned in to the new mood for racial justice.

After the ICC order was issued in September 1961, a group of Albany's black ministers sent a very deferential letter to the city government requesting that biracial meetings be created to discuss desegregation in Albany and asking that there be movement toward compliance with the ICC's order. In reply, the Albany *Herald*, James Gray's extremely conservative paper, published an indignant editorial condemning the ministers for writing such a letter. Not long afterward, the home of one of the ministers was bombed.

The hateful and violent responses to the simple request that the city obey federal laws served as a catalyst to the loose group of black community leaders. Dr. William Anderson, a local osteopath, became the president of the Albany movement, a coalition of community associations, ministers, NAACP members, and other individuals and organizations. A determined activist, Dr. Anderson contacted SNCC workers in Atlanta who had been involved in a boycott of downtown Atlanta businesses that had refused to hire black clerks the previous year, and asked SNCC to travel to Albany to challenge the still-segregated bus station there. Although CORE initiated the Freedom Rides, it did not have chapters in Georgia and the SNCC boycott was news across the state.

Early in November, just after the ICC decree took effect, in response to Anderson's request six SNCC students boarded buses in Atlanta bound for Albany. When they arrived they attempted to use the whites-only waiting room facilities and were instantly arrested. A few sympathetic students from Albany State had been made aware of the demonstration, and they quickly took the place of the initial group, and were also arrested. Each wave of arrests resulted in another wave of students sitting in at the bus station in the main waiting area reserved for whites and being arrested as well. Dr. Anderson then organized a committee to publicize the demonstrations and secure support for the arrested students.

Soon there were hundreds of students in jail and tension was running high. As part of a citywide support effort that continued to build throughout November, Anderson decided to invite Martin Luther King to speak at Shiloh Baptist Church on the night of December 15, to further dramatize the effort. Anderson and Martin had been friends since they were classmates at Morehouse. Martin was unable to refuse, although we were basically unfamiliar with the organizational structure of their movement. Martin planned to go to Albany, make a quick speech for his friend, and return to Atlanta. Up until that time, the events in Albany were primarily a local matter, and had not come to the attention of the national media as a major story. In inviting Martin, with his great prestige and charisma, Anderson hoped to focus national and international attention on conditions in Albany, thus forcing the hand of the city administration and creating some forward movement.

By this time the situation in Albany was building toward a crisis; the initial arrests had engendered an unprecedented mobilization of the entire black community—six weeks into the demonstrations, some two thousand students were now in jail. The Albany jails were absolutely jammed with student demonstrators. Although the demonstrations had been sparked by a single issue, by December the demands had broadened to include many more. But the city administration was absolutely impervious: they refused to even talk with representatives from the Albany movement.

The night Martin and Ralph arrived, there was a huge crowd at two churches, Reverend Grant's Shiloh Baptist Church and Reverend Gay's AME Church, with the crowds overflowing into the street in between. Those attending included NAACP activists, SNCC activists, students, and others not affiliated with any national organization. Martin spoke forcefully and eloquently to them, and the audience responded enthusiastically. Then, at the conclusion of the meeting, without first asking Martin's permission, Anderson announced that everyone should return to the church the next morning (a Saturday), and that Dr. King, Ralph Abernathy, and Ruby Hurley, the NAACP field director, would lead them in a march to city hall. Martin and Ralph were in effect trapped—after building everyone up to such an enthusiastic pitch there was no way they could now bow out of leading a march. Ruby Hurley said she hadn't come to march and she headed out of town. Martin felt like he'd been put in a trick. He had not come to lead a movement, but only out of friendship for Dr. Anderson.

The next morning, Martin and Ralph fulfilled their obligation, and with Anderson they led a crowd of two hundred to the Albany City Hall to pray. The entire group was promptly arrested for trespassing and taken to several jails. The arrests of Martin, Ralph Abernathy, and Dr. Anderson brought, as expected, tremendous attention to Albany from the national press.

The jails in Albany were already packed to the rafters, but Police Chief Laurie Pritchard was determined to break Martin Luther King on his turf. To that end he recruited the support of sheriffs in the surrounding counties, divided the protesters into groups, and bused them to jails in Sumter, Terrell, and Baker Counties. Conditions in these prisons were harrowing. The sheriffs who supervised the prisons were brutal, and in their minds, blacks had few, if any, rights. Martin, Ralph, and Anderson were taken to Americus, in Sumter County, thirty-six miles north of Albany. Sumter County, like neighboring Terrell County (dubbed "Terrible Terrell"), was infamous as a hellhole for blacks. Conditions in the Americus jail were so bad several demonstrators had to be bailed out because they simply could not withstand the discomfort and constant abuse. The marchers had not been prepared to go to jail and the morning of the march it had been fairly warm, so many of them had been arrested in light jackets, even shirtsleeves. Then a cold wave hit. When Martin asked Sheriff Chappell for blankets for the marchers, the heat was turned off, the few available blankets were removed, the windows were opened, and even the fans were turned on. Martin once said that Sheriff Chappell was "the meanest man in the world."

Years later, when I first met Jimmy Carter, whose hometown of Plains was in Sumter County, I told him, "The only person I know in Sumter County is Sheriff Chappell." Carter said innocently, "He's a good friend of mine." It took a long time for me to change my opinion of Jimmy Carter after that. But that was one of the many tragedies of segregation, that many otherwise decent people could behave with such inhumanity to persons of another color. Jimmy Carter never saw the side of Sheriff Chappell that I experienced.

Martin and Ralph, who were initially reluctant to march, now had their reputations on the line and became determined to remain in jail, possibly through Christmas, unless the city at least promised to meet with negotiators from the black community. However, within a day or two after the arrests, Dr. Anderson became physically ill in his icy cell, and his condition steadily worsened. Martin became extremely concerned and urged Anderson to accept bail and return home to receive treatment. In addition to his deteriorating physical condition, Anderson's nerves were shot. He had been under extreme pressure for a month, trying to hold together a movement that was showing signs of splintering and confronting a city administration that was not yielding. Such stress would have been enough to drive even the most experienced leader to the brink, but Anderson was a volunteer leader serving at great personal sacrifice to himself and his family. Nevertheless, he steadfastly declared he wasn't bailing out of jail until Martin decided to accept bail—even if they remained there a year. The more strenuously Martin insisted that he should bail himself out for much-needed treatment and rest, the more strongly Anderson insisted that he must remain, lest he betray the movement and the worthiness of the cause.

Meanwhile, without consulting Anderson, Martin, or any of those in jail, a more conservative faction of the Albany movement local leadership began negotiating with the city administration immediately after the arrests on December 16. They arrived at a shaky agreement with the city on December 18, which called only for desegregation of the bus terminal and for discussion of the desegregation of other public facilities after January 23, 1962. Nothing was said in the agreement about the status of the two thousand people then in jail.

When Martin, over in Americus and cut off from communication with events in Albany, heard an agreement had been reached, he decided to accept bail, his prime motive being to get Anderson out, though he did not announce that to the press once he was released. But when he read the terms of the agreement his extreme disappointment conveyed a sense of having been betrayed. He decided then and there that it would be necessary to return to Albany to wage a hard fight for real progress toward desegregation, fully utilizing the resources of SCLC and inviting other civil rights organizations and concerned ministers from around the nation to participate. Not having come into Albany prepared for a long campaign, however, Martin felt that he and SCLC should withdraw until they could fully assess the situation and build up national support.

The lack of real organizational structure in Albany had become apparent with the independent negotiations. Events had impelled a movement, but it was little more than a mass of loosely cooperating organizations held together by the strength of Anderson's will. There was no long-range plan, no generally agreed-upon goal. The effort began with desegregating the bus station, but as the community response mushroomed the standard for success grew beyond the initial target. This time around it would have to be different.

After the initial crisis was over, I decided to go to Albany myself to do what I could toward the long-term effectiveness of that movement. During the previous six months of sharing the same office as SCLC, increasingly I felt a part of the organization, identifying with their aspirations, problems, and tension. Although I had been busy with the Citizenship School Program, I knew that it had never been Martin's intention to become so involved in Albany. But now that Martin had become entangled there, I saw that I could be of service by identifying some of the student activists and local leaders and bringing them to train at Dorchester.

In the fall of 1961 SCLC had a very small staff but, far out of proportion to its size and support, the public interest in Martin was enormous. Though he was only in his early thirties, he was already a legend. I only rarely had the opportunity to talk with Martin in the offices, as he was almost constantly on the road speech making and fund-raising for SCLC. Even under normal circumstances he wasn't the easiest person to get to know intimately, despite his outward friendliness. I was not primarily interested in becoming an intimate of Martin's, however. There was already too much competition among those who wanted to be Martin's special confidant. Ralph Abernathy in particular saw himself and Martin rather like civil rights twins, brothers of the spirit, a replay of the biblical David and Jonathan. My interest was to contribute to the work of the movement and stay out of internal intrigue. This was one of the reasons I was always grateful that I had an independent budget, which permitted me to avoid petty struggles with SCLC staff. But I was always looking for ways to help, for ways that the Citizenship School Program could complement SCLC's work. One way I made myself useful was in offering to answer some of King's mail. SCLC was well connected through the black Baptist preachers, especially in the South, but my strength was that I knew the white liberal church community in the South and across the country and how best to explain our work to them. As a national movement, we needed to be able to communicate effectively with liberal churchmen who were inclined to be sympathetic.

Throughout the early months of 1962, the students and young people in Albany, supported by concerned adults, continued their marches and demonstrations. I realized that with its wide-scale demonstrations, Albany was an excellent place to make the citizenship training we were providing in Dorchester practical and meaningful through immediate "on-the-job training." So Dorothy Cotton and I went to Albany and set about reestablishing relationships with families we knew there, recruiting, and setting up citizenship training workshops and a temporary headquarters in Shiloh Baptist Church, where nightly meetings and rallies were held.

The training session at Dorchester for the Albany students was the liveliest week we ever had. Albany was an SNCC project, so we had Charles Sherrod and Charley Jones and the young people they had organized in Albany. We discovered an uncut diamond among the Albany students in sixteen-year-old Bernice Johnson. During our first evening session, she and Rutha Harris and some of the other students started to sing. It seemed as if all the kids could sing, but Bernice's voice was as rich as the soil around Albany, with the texture of all the suffering of black folk that made the crops grow. Their singing brought a special spirit to the movement. More than anyone, to this day Bernice Johnson Reagon has preserved the freedom songs and the spirit of the movement with her group, Sweet Honey in the Rock.

That first evening just set the tone for the whole week. The previous workshops at Dorchester had brought older people, mostly from Mississippi. These young people were so spirited, we sang, and after the singing, we danced. I like to dance and I encouraged them to teach me the latest dance steps and they loved it. We brought out the limbo pole, which Harry Belafonte had helped make hip at that time, and we did the limbo, "how low can you go." They thought of me as old at twenty-nine, but I was in good shape and I could go as low as any of the college guys.

Jack O'Dell came down from Atlanta and gave his lectures on African-American history using W. E. B. Du Bois's *The Souls of Black*

Folk. Du Bois invited the reader to accompany him on a tour of the "Black Belt." "How curious a land is this, how full of untold story, of tragedy and laughter, and the rich legacy of human life; shadowed with a tragic past, and big with future promise." *The Souls of Black Folk*, published in 1903, still provided the most accurate analysis available of the sociology and political economy of the black belt in the rural South in the early 1960s. In fact, even today, as we approach the twenty-first century, Du Bois's analysis is stunningly and tragically relevant. Reading Du Bois was tremendously affirming for the students, for all of us. The civil rights movement would later trigger an interest in African-American history in the nation's great universities, but at that time such scholarship was rare. Du Bois's assessment of Reconstruction ran directly counter to the version taught in Southern schoolrooms: Du Bois saw Reconstruction as a time of remarkable progress, while mainstream historians dismissed Reconstruction as a corrupt failure.

As we explored Du Bois's material with the students, the movement began to fall into historical and political perspective. The notion that we were in a period that had the potential to be a Second Reconstruction emerged in this workshop. We still had not made up the ground lost when Reconstruction ended, but we were beginning to see the outlines of a genuine change in the legal status of African-Americans. It must be remembered that in 1962 integration was a fairly radical concept, even in the African-American community. Until the Supreme Court decision in the *Brown* school desegregation case, only the most forward-thinking blacks considered integration even plausible. Virtually everything in their social environment told Southern black kids that they were inherently inferior to whites. It required a tremendous leap in consciousness, an ability to disregard the show of contempt experienced in any encounter with white institutions for these young people to demand real equality in American society. Du Bois's writings affirmed the rightness of their new consciousness and reassured the students that not only were they on the right track, but their efforts were long overdue.

We didn't talk organizational politics in Dorchester, we talked about the movement and the contribution the students could make and had made to it. For me the session with the Albany students was especially rewarding, because I had spent years working with mostly white youth groups. This was a chance to use that experience with courageous young black people who were committed to social change and social justice. I felt tremendous admiration for the students, for they had a sense of purpose and direction that I had not felt or experienced when I was their age. I admired their achievement. No matter what the press said about Albany, I knew how difficult and dangerous it was to be organizing for civil rights in southwest Georgia. By mobilizing black people in Albany to express their discontent, the students had accomplished a great deal.

I enjoyed the students—I respected their intelligence and their energy, and as a result I got along well with them. I also had many more social dealings with the SNCC kids than did most of the SCLC staff members. When I went to Albany, I stayed with Bo and Goldie Jackson, old friends from my days in Thomasville, who also put up many of the SNCC folks. Goldie was a professor at Albany State and Bo was a naturally bright and good-hearted brother without much formal education. One night I remember I shared their couch with Cordell Reagon and Charles Sherrod, the back of which folded down to make a double bed. I was asleep in the middle when the couch pulled apart and I found myself cradled in a kind of sling in the middle. It struck me then and now as an apt metaphor for the way I acted as a link between SNCC and SCLC. Unlike some of the more authoritarian SCLC staff, I had specialized in youth ministry and had a lot of experience dealing with prickly young adult males who were still trying to assert their own manhood. I had money that I could give them for specific things, and because they knew I respected them and didn't question their abilities, I had no problem getting them to account for it.

The situation in Albany was so polarized that the white leadership of the city would not even talk with the movement leaders. Eliza Paschal and Frances Pauley, middle-aged white women who had been asked to speak on behalf of the Georgia Human Relations Council, attempted meetings with the white leadership, and even their overtures were rebuffed. No matter the color of their skin, they were perceived as proponents of a change in race relations, and this was unacceptable to the Albany establishment.

Since they wouldn't talk to us face-to-face, we needed to find some other way of discerning what the white establishment thought of our efforts, and what chance there was of them bending to our pressure. I had an idea of someone who could help us. A Harvard Ph.D. candidate, Jim Laue, had been to Atlanta to interview us for his dissertation on the sit-in movement and his theories about conflict resolution. I asked Jim if for the price of a plane ticket and somewhere to stay, he would come to Albany and just try to interview some of the businesspeople, not as an advocate, but as a scholar. He too met a brick wall of resistance. They would not share their thoughts, but they anxiously picked his brain and he readily explained how the movement in Nashville and Atlanta had led to a new level of progress and prosperity. They were curious but not interested.

For months Albany had been a major focus of SNCC, whose volunteers had initiated the demonstrations with the first sit-ins at the bus station, but they were simply unable to make headway in forcing the city to negotiate. The fact that SNCC workers felt they had started the Albany movement and were the cadre that kept it going created quite a bit of resentment among them toward Martin and SCLC, particularly concerning the media attention given Martin when he was arrested. As a result, there were mixed feelings among those working in Albany when Martin and Ralph prepared to return during the spring of 1962 for their trial on the December arrests, and the interest of the news media predictably peaked once again.

Ralph Abernathy had been Martin's partner since the Montgomery bus boycott. It was not apparent to the casual observer why a Boston-educated sophisticate like Martin King was so close to a common preacher like Ralph. They had a bond that transcended those superficial differences, though, and in the planning for the next phase of Albany, I began to understand the importance of that relationship to Martin's ability to lead.

The decision to return to Albany was Ralph's finest hour. Martin and Ralph's trial had been deliberately scheduled around Easter; the powers-that-be in Albany knew that ministers would naturally feel an obligation to be in their pulpits. To debate the pros and cons of what to do, a meeting was held in the SCLC offices and there were all kinds of theoretical, tactical arguments flying about; everyone was intellectualizing various scenarios, offering conflicting viewpoints on whether to go back to Albany. Different responses were proposed: Martin could request to postpone the trial, but that would seem like cowardice to the activists in Albany; Martin could ignore the trial date and forfeit bail; or there might be some avenue to get the case to federal court. Ralph just got up in the midst of all these arguments. Martin looked at him in surprise and said, "Where are you going, we haven't decided yet." Ralph said, "You decide, I'm going to tell the deacons at West Hunter Church I may not be with 'em for this Easter Sunday, and I need to start explaining to them why." That pretty much settled it. Martin King was going back to Albany.

Ralph's constancy in that moment of confusion reflected the very important role he filled for Martin Luther King. Many know of Martin's legendary willingness to be imprisoned for as long as it took to win freedom for his people, but few realize that to do so he had to overcome an almost paralyzing fear of being alone in jail. Soon after Martin moved to Atlanta in 1960, sheriffs took him to jail in De Kalb County on the absurd charge of violating probation on a previous sentence for driving without a Georgia driver's license, with the clear intention of harassing him into leaving the state. He was in the De Kalb County jail alone, when in the middle of the night he was taken out of his cell, placed in a straitjacket, thrown in the back of a paddy wagon, and driven across the state to the Georgia prison at Reidsville. All this was done without any explanation. Though it was not something he talked about very often, Martin told me late one night that when being driven across those rural Georgia roads in the middle of the night, "I knew I'd never see anybody again. That kind of mental anguish is worse than dying, riding for mile after mile, hungry and thirsty, bound and helpless, waiting and not knowing what you're waiting for, and all over a traffic violation." Martin never quite got over that experience. He always knew that in jail alone, he was extremely vulnerable, and he was more afraid of that kind of prolonged mental anguish than he was of dying.

It was a phone call to Coretta from then presidential candidate John F. Kennedy during Martin's pointless imprisonment in De Kalb County prison that swung the traditionally Republican black vote to Kennedy in his race against Richard Nixon. Perhaps it's difficult to understand in the present day what a courageous thing it was for a white presidential candidate to do. King was as controversial to Southerners then as Louis Farrakhan is in all of America today. Harris Wofford, a campaign aide, gave Kennedy Coretta's phone number and told him, "You just do what your heart tells you to do." After speaking with Coretta, Kennedy asked Morris Abrams to intervene. Working with Griffin Bell, who was running Kennedy's campaign in Georgia, Abrams located Martin at Reidsville and persuaded the appropriate authorities that imprisoning a well-known civil rights leader for driving with an expired license was imprudent. Martin was released. The word that Kennedy had called Coretta spread through the black community like wildfire. Daddy King publicly announced, "I've got friends who keep the votes in a suitcase and I'm going to tell them we gon' vote for this Kennedy boy, now. Of course I was worried about him being a Catholic." I was still in New York during the Kennedy-Nixon election and met John Kennedy one afternoon when he was campaigning in the parking lot of a middle-class black apartment building in Chicago. I was impressed with Kennedy then, and had already committed to him, so I wasn't surprised that he possessed that kind of courage and decency.

Martin's sojourn at the Reidsville prison brought out the best in John Kennedy, but it left scars on Martin that never healed. Martin came to rely upon Ralph for a feeling of security in jail, and an unspoken reassurance that he wasn't alone. Ralph was Martin's companion and confidant in strange hotels in unfamiliar cities far from home. Ralph would joke, "Martin has a war on sleep." He would go to bed late at night, one or two o'clock in the morning, and rise at four or five A.M. to read for his next sermon or worry about the next step in a movement. When the burdens of his leadership role kept him unsettled and awake with worry, Martin needed people close to him. More often than not, that person was Ralph Abernathy. When Martin moved SCLC to Atlanta, he basically insisted that Ralph move to Atlanta from Montgomery, and to Ralph's credit he went. To do so he gave up a bigger, more prosperous church than West Hunter, the pastorate he took in Atlanta. And while it might seem today that it was a small sacrifice to be a confidant to Martin Luther King, Jr., in 1961 the civil rights movement was no one's idea of a path to prosperity. Ralph was far more than a companion. Martin's ascension during the Montgomery bus boycott was largely due to Ralph's support. Ralph had had the larger church and had been in Montgomery longer. Adept at the internal politics among black Baptist preachers, Ralph was able to protect and promote Martin among the other preachers, freeing Martin to lead. A mass movement begins with two or more people willing to make the commitment and sacrifices necessary to create change. Without Ralph, or someone to fill that role, the Montgomery movement would have disintegrated into bickering among the preachers about who should lead, and the moment for change would have been lost. Ralph's solid support of Martin was one of the critical ingredients that made Montgomery a success.

Now Martin was faced with trying to grasp the reins of a movement that had been put together by others in a fairly haphazard manner. Ralph's support was crucial to Martin's sense that going back to Albany was the right thing to do. Martin and Wyatt Walker viewed their participation in Albany as somewhat of an accident, but they also knew that multifaceted oppression was glaringly evident, and Albany was as good a place to begin waging a battle for across-the-board desegregation as they might find. They also recognized that strategies could be developed, even articulated, but this was not SCLC's movement and no amount of effort on our part could make it so. This was a movement staged by a committee of committees, a tricky, tenuous, contentious coalition of several local groups, crossing age, class, economic, and ideological lines: the Criterion Club (an elite black group, headed by Dr. Anderson), the Ministerial Alliance, the Baptist Ministers' Alliance, the Federation of Women's Clubs, the Negro Voters League, the NAACP, the NAACP Youth Council, SNCC, and SCLC. Rev. Samuel Wells was a movement preacher who served as a link between SNCC and the big preachers, but his was a small rural church and his influence with the big preachers in Albany was limited. Some of these groups wanted Martin in Albany because they hoped his presence and national prestige would benefit their cause; others, particularly some of the younger folk, thought Martin's presence was a detriment—cameras would roll while he was there, but after he was gone everything would return to the way it had always been and Albany would not be changed.

Because I had become well acquainted with many of the young people in the Albany movement, I attempted to bridge some of these gaps. I didn't try to tell them what to do, nor did I believe I had a right to, which helped to build positive relationships. However, the students lacked a long-range strategy and sufficient preparation for their demonstrations. Their idea seemed to be that stirring up conflict alone would produce change. That may have worked in some cases, but Martin and Wyatt were convinced that when the movement created conflict, there should be a clear idea of what was to emerge in a resolution of the conflict.

I listened to bitter personal complaints, both then and later, from SNCC members about Wyatt, and the way he ran things when he was in town. Wyatt tended to operate like a military commander in the field—issuing directions and orders to young people who had just a few short years previously freed themselves from being ordered around by their parents, and, not surprisingly, they didn't like it.

But Wyatt and SCLC had the budget, so despite the fact that the SNCC volunteers resented elders like Wyatt, Martin, and Ralph, they were dependent upon SCLC to help them out. There was always unpleasantness when Wyatt insisted on following formal financial procedures like collecting vouchers and receipts. Wyatt knew that what SCLC spent would be closely scrutinized, and he took very seriously his responsibility to ensure propriety in the handling of monies. A major, bothersome legal case against Martin and the officers of the Montgomery Improvement Association had just concluded with an acquittal on allegations that funds were mishandled during the bus boycott, a case brought by the state of Alabama. Although it was not in his nature to be overly concerned with financial and budgetary matters, Martin was thereafter extremely conscious of the need to handle funds raised almost exclusively from contributions with impeccable accountability. Wyatt was trying his best to protect Martin's and SCLC's interests, but his style in doing so had a way of leaving negative impressions on certain people.

Despite the multitude of conflicts of interests and approaches, Martin and Ralph decided that if convicted on the charges they would remain in jail as long as it took to force the Albany conflict toward a more productive conclusion. And as expected, after a trial replete with long delays, Martin, Ralph, and Dr. Anderson were found guilty on July 10 and sentenced to forty-five days in jail and fines of $178 each.

It fell to me to visit Martin and Ralph in the Albany jail. On my first visit, dressed in suit and tie, I asked politely to see Dr. King. The deputy looked at me disdainfully and yelled back toward the cells, "There's a little nigger out here, wants to see that big nigger back there." I was stunned, but I made a point to look at his name tag, and the next time I came to the jail I addressed the deputy by his name, Sergeant Hamilton. "How are you this afternoon, Sergeant Hamilton," I said, using a little of my Thomasville drawl. He looked startled as he answered, "I'm just fine." I said, "You just can't predict this weather, can you? Hot in the morning, cold before evening. They tell me this is good hunting weather." Before long he was telling me about his wife and kids. After that, I had no more trouble. It was my father's teaching coming through—show compassion to those who have no idea how to behave properly.

I went in and out of the jail several times a day over the next few days, and Chief Laurie Pritchard began to call me into his office to talk. He had recently converted to Catholicism and apparently knew that what he was doing was wrong in the eyes of God. He tried to explain himself and justify his actions as following local laws, and he even confided that he was trying to get a position as a federal marshal so he could get out of Albany. It got to the point where I had to run a gauntlet of confessions to get to see Martin. Several years later I got a call from black leaders in High Point, North Carolina, where Pritchard was seeking the chief-of-police job. I took the leap and gave him a good recommendation on race matters. He was hired and did a good job of integrating the police force in High Point.

Martin's intentions notwithstanding, Ralph, Anderson, and he were in jail only three days before they were bonded out by parties unknown. We suspected it was someone acting on behalf of the city of Albany itself, wishing to avoid the attention and sympathy Martin would surely attract while in prison. Once they were out of jail, we began to organize with renewed vigor and drummed up support for more continued demonstrations.

In response to the threat of new demonstrations, in what was becoming a sort of backwoods Georgia chess game, the city went to the federal district court to get an injunction against further marches. Around that time, when no SCLC staff members were in Albany, a demonstration got out of hand and people started throwing rocks at the police. That was all the excuse that was needed to shut us down, and an injunction was granted on July 20 by District Court Judge J. Robert Elliot, a recent Kennedy administration appointee.

Martin was at the Andersons when he heard about the injunction, but he didn't want to be served until he had decided what to do about it. Constance Motley from the NAACP Legal Defense Fund was representing Martin in Albany and he wanted to speak with her and Jack Greenberg about the consequences of different options. So, to avoid making a premature decision, when word came that Judge Elliot had ruled, Martin and Ralph jumped over the Andersons' back fence. Now, Martin was in pretty good shape, but Ralph was over two hundred pounds, and the fence was four feet high, so it was quite a sight seeing them jump that fence. For a few hours, there was a little mystery about the whereabouts of Dr. King.

The extremely broad injunction, which specifically banned Martin, Ralph, and Anderson from demonstrating or marching, created a serious problem. There was no question that Martin felt he was within his constitutional rights to continue demonstrating against segregation, already clearly declared unconstitutional by the Supreme Court, but he had vowed he would never violate a federal court injunction. His reasoning was that federal courts had led the way in breaking down racial segregation, in stark contrast to state and municipal courts in the South, which were upholding segregation statutes. While Martin believed that the federal courts were being misused by Judge Elliot in this case, he was forced to weigh the negative consequences in the press, and among his supporters, if he violated the injunction.

How to resolve this dilemma was one of the most difficult problems Martin had ever faced. This was the first time I had ever seen up close the way he worked, and I was a little taken aback at how loose his style was. He approached decisions in an extremely circuitous way. For instance, a staff meeting was called to consider what to do about the injunction, whether to follow it or ignore it. Martin didn't show up for the meeting. We didn't know where he was and we couldn't find him. I learned later he had gone to a fish fry or something, as if there were no crisis at all. Years later, after observing him repeat this pattern many times, I came to accept that this sort of escape was his method of working through problems, in the same way running or isolated contemplation was for me. Martin plunged into social activities that seemed, on the surface, to have nothing to do with the immediate crisis he was facing. To whomever he was with, the occasion was probably considered purely social. But whenever Martin returned from these escapes, he had made his decision about whatever was bothering him. The fact is, Martin loved people. He could relax in the comfortable repartee of black folk, and often over a pot of greens or a pan of neck bones or ribs he would seem to recharge himself, as if drawing spiritual, emotional, and intellectual sustenance from the food and culture of his childhood. Psychologists today would call it comfort food.

In the end, Martin decided he must abide by the injunction. But he was deeply upset. I remember him on the telephone arguing bitterly about the injunction with Burke Marshall, head of the Civil Rights Division at the Kennedy Justice Department, who we believed spoke for Kennedy personally. Martin listened courteously for a long time while Marshall was asking him to stop the demonstrations. It was one of the few times I saw Martin really upset and agitated. He told Marshall, "The time is always ripe to do right." One of the reasons Martin was so disturbed was that he was convinced that even if Kennedy had not actually ordered Judge Elliot to issue the injunction, he had at least given his tacit approval. Martin's belief was that Elliot, a very recent appointee, would never have violated the wishes of the president and the attorney general, and had probably, directly or indirectly, checked with them about what they wanted him to do. The Kennedys were concerned about the upcoming Georgia gubernatorial election, which they wanted Carl Sanders to win. Sanders's opponent in the primaries was Marvin Griffin, a Dixiecrat who was considered a potential opponent of the national Democratic administration. Sanders, on the other hand, was a Kennedy man. Martin believed that the Kennedys were so eager to bring demonstrations to a halt because they were frightened of a huge segregationist backlash vote for Griffin.

We believed Sanders's election was important too, and were busy helping to register black voters, always a by-product of any of our campaigns, but we didn't feel it was necessary to accept continued injustices in the hope conditions would suddenly improve if Carl Sanders became governor of Georgia. It was the black vote the Kennedys should have been after, we felt, rather than attempting to appease the whites who opposed civil rights. Sanders did ultimately win, by about the same number of votes as the number of blacks we registered, but not surprisingly his victory didn't improve conditions much for the black people of Albany.

In the end, the Albany movement wound down inconclusively, without us winning any substantial or noteworthy achievements. The district court injunction was eventually overturned by the federal court of appeals with lawyers from the NAACP Legal Defense Fund arguing on our behalf, but after so many starts and stops and aborted beginnings it was impossible to really get the movement going again.

While not a great success when compared to our later efforts, Albany's importance, it turned out, was as a test run for the direct-action phase of the movement, which was about to begin in earnest. The campaign there possessed characteristics that were present in all of the later campaigns: efforts to bring disparate elements of the black community together; the legal roadblocks that would recur time and time again, such as court orders designed to stop demonstrations; conflicts over tactical decisions between the youth and the older leaders; and the crucial support of friendly churches, with nightly meetings to encourage and inspire participation.

In terms of Martin's own career, Albany represented a period when almost everything he attempted to do was thwarted. This forced him to seriously reconsider how he would approach future campaigns, and indeed even *if* there would be any future campaigns. I believe he left Albany so depressed he went through an agonizing reappraisal in the months that followed of just how aggressive a role he should assume in the civil rights movement. Claude Sitton of the *New York Times,* writing in the *Times*'s magazine, seemed to delight in writing the obituary of nonviolence and Martin's leadership. It was as though this was too noble an ideal to succeed in America, particularly among blacks in the South. We were supposed to be angry, bitter, and violent; that would be understandable. This restrained, reasonable spirituality was just too naive to succeed in the violent twentieth century. Sitton's analysis was logical, but it did not count on the deep and abiding religious commitment of blacks and whites in the American South, or Martin's inner strength.

One thing Martin was very concerned about was his relationship with youth volunteers and the leaders of SNCC. They began derisively referring to Martin as "de Lawd" after a character in "Green Pastures," a Hallmark Hall of Fame television program. I remember a long discussion he held one night with SNCC leaders Charles Sherrod, Chuck Jones, Cordell Reagon, John Lewis, and Diane and Jim Bevel at Dr. Anderson's home, where Martin and Ralph were staying. The meeting took place, as did many of our meetings, on the patio in Anderson's backyard. Martin said, "Listen, I understand where you're coming from, and I'm not trying to take over your movement, but no matter what I do there'll be a certain amount of press coverage. So we may as well find ways to use that constructively." But despite this and other meetings and the real affection Martin had for the student leaders, there was never a completely satisfactory resolution to this problem. The real problem was not between him and the students—though there were surely differences of generational perspective—but was the tendency of the press to concentrate almost solely on Martin, a factor that Martin himself could not control unless he chose to completely bow out of an active role in the movement. In Albany, Martin made a great effort to fit in by participating in community affairs and talking with anyone who wanted to meet him, but despite all his efforts to downplay his celebrity, everyone still saw him as Martin Luther King, Jr., "Movement Savior," and there was nothing he could do to escape the glare of the public eye.

My fondest memories of Albany are the freedom songs we sang. Whenever someone mentions Albany I can hear again the hauntingly beautiful strains of "We'll Never Turn Back":

> We've been 'buked and we've been scorned
> We've been troubled sure as you're born
> But we'll never
> Turn back.
> No we'll never
> turn back
> Until we walk in peace.

"We'll Never Turn Back" was written by Bertha Gober in memory of Rev. George Lee, an NAACP leader who was murdered in Mississippi along with Lamar Smith in 1955 because they refused to take their names off voter registration lists. It became a theme song of the movement in Albany. Songs like "This Little Light of Mine," "Woke Up This Morning with My Mind on Freedom," "We Shall Not Be Moved," "Oh Pritchett, Oh Kelly" (sung to the tune of "Oh Mary, Oh Martha"), and "We Shall Overcome" also became movement anthems in Albany. These new freedom songs were adaptations of our original freedom songs, the spirituals, old hymns, and labor

Andrew Young, Jr., ten-months-old,
photographed in January 1933.

Andrew Young, Jr.,
Daisy Fuller Young, and
Walter Young, 1938.

Andrew 'n' Walter, 1940.

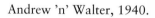

*(Unless otherwise noted, all photographs
are from a private collection.)*

Visiting Grandfather Frank Young (*rear center*) in Franklin, Louisiana. At the right is Andrew and second from right is Walter.

Andrew stands in the center with hands folded for a group picture at the Congregational Church Conference at Camp Knighton in New Iberia, Louisiana, 1942. Andrew Young, Sr., is sixth from the right, and between the two seated adults, fifth from the left, is Walter.

Family portrait, 1944.

Andrew, Sr., and Daisy, circa 1944, dressed for a club dinner.

The pledge line at Howard's Alpha Phi Alpha fraternity, 1949. Andrew is seventh from far right; pledge master David Dinkins is at the far left.

Pictured for the Howard University track team, 1951.

At the Manchester College (Indiana) crowning of May Queen Jean Childs, 1954.

The wedding in Marion, Alabama, June 7, 1954. The maid of honor, Jean's sister Cora Childs Moore, is third from left. Nick Hood is in the rear center, the best man Tom Dent is third from right, and Walter Young is second from right.

Ordained in
New Orleans, 1955.
Facing Andrew
(*left to right*) are:
Rev. Harold Long,
Rev. Homer C. McEwen,
and Rev. Nick Hood.

Dinner in Queens, New York, 1959. Norma Childs de Paur, Jean's oldest sister, is seated to the left of Andrew. Second from left at the table is Andrea, to the right of Andrew is Norma's daughter Lynn de Paur, and just behind her is Lisa.

In Savannah in
1961, recruiting
"natural leaders"
for the Dorchester
Citizenship School.

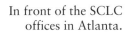

Dorothy Cotton,
when she was director
of education for SCLC.

In front of the SCLC
offices in Atlanta.

In Albany, Georgia, 1962, Andrew at left with James Forman of SNCC (*second from left*) and Wyatt T. Walker (*second from right*). *(photo courtesy of St. Louis Post Dispatch/Black Star)*

SNCC member Eddie Brown being arrested by Albany police during an Albany sit-in. *(photo courtesy of Danny Lyon/Magnum Photos)*

Investigating the bombing of a church outside Albany with (*from left*): Bernard Lee, Martin King, the church's pastor, Wyatt Walker, Ralph Abernathy, and James Bevel.

Dr. William Anderson, holding hands with Martin and Coretta King, and Ralph Abernathy during an Albany church gathering of demonstrators.

Jean with Andrea (age seven), Lisa (age five), and Paula (age one) in front of the house on Chicamauga Place in Atlanta, spring of 1962.

Hosea Williams in Savannah, 1962.
(photo courtesy of Danny Lyon/Magnum Photos)

Demonstrators kneel in prayer during a sit-in in Birmingham, Alabama, in 1963. *(photo courtesy of Bruce Davidson/Magnum Photos)*

Police arrest a demonstrator in Birmingham. *(photo courtesy of Charles Moore/Black Star)*

Opening the fire hoses on demonstrators in Kelly Ingram Park, March 1963.

Woman knocked down by fire hoses.

(photos courtesy of Charles Moore/Black Star)

ABOVE: Fire hoses used on unresisting demonstrators in the central business district of Birmingham. BELOW: Dog attacking a marcher in Kelly Ingram Park.
(photos courtesy of Charles Moore/Black Star)

Jim Bevel at a citizenship school workshop in Birmingham. *(photo courtesy of Vernon Merritt III/Black Star)*

Fannie Lou Hamer at the SNCC office in Greenwood, Mississippi, in 1963, not long before she was arrested and beaten in Winona, Mississippi. *(photo courtesy of Danny Lyon/Magnum Photos)*

A meeting of civil rights leaders in the Oval Office the morning of the March on Washington. Present are Floyd McKissick of CORE (*second from left*), Whitney Young of the National Urban League (*fourth from left*), Dr. Martin Luther King, Jr., of SCLC, John Lewis of SNCC (*in the shadow*), A. Philip Randolph (*to the left of the president*), President John F. Kennedy, Vice President Lyndon Johnson, Walter Reuther of the United Auto Workers Union, and Roy Wilkins of the NAACP.

The March on Washington, August 28, 1963.

(*photos courtesy of Fred Ward/Black Star*)

SNCC members and friends singing freedom songs—Julian Bond (*lower left*), James Forman (*center, in suit and tie*), and Annelle Ponder (*third from lower left*). *(photo courtesy of Danny Lyon/ Magnum Photos)*

Martin Luther King delivering his speech on the steps of the Lincoln Memorial. Bayard Rustin (*in glasses*) stands behind him. *(photo courtesy of Bob Adelman/ Magnum Photos)*

The crowd officially estimated at 250,000 listening to the speeches—the VIP seating is in the foreground. *(photo courtesy of Fred Ward/Black Star)*

By King's side at one of his many speaking engagements.

March 1964, St. Augustine, Florida. Police hold a group of demonstrators waiting for jail transportation after their arrest. *(photo courtesy of AP/Wide World Photos)*

Mrs. Fannie Lou Hamer leading voter education for the 1964 presidential election. *(photo courtesy of Black Star)*

Fall of 1964, arriving in Houston, Texas, for the voter registration drive following the Democratic National Convention with Dora McDonald, Martin's secretary *(far left)*, Rev. William Lawson *(third from left)* and Bernard Lee *(far right)*.

December 10, 1964, Oslo. Martin Luther King, Jr., receiving his Nobel Prize for Peace from Gunnar Jahn, chairman of the Nobel committee. *(photo courtesy of AP/Wide World Photos)*

By the light of hundreds of torches, King arrives at the University of Oslo Festival Hall to deliver his Nobel Peace Prize address, December 11. *(photo courtesy of AP/Wide World Photos)*

In Baltimore, Maryland, being greeted upon his return from receiving the Nobel Prize. *(photo courtesy of Leonard Freed/ Magnum Photos)* movement songs, and sung communally they provided a unifying force that captured the spirit of the movement.

The Albany movement displayed particularly striking voices, and a music possessed of a particular minor tonality that sounded African and distinctly different from the singing heard in other Southern cities. The key SNCC organizers, Cordell Reagon and Charles Sherrod, were great singers, and they in turn inspired recruits like Bernice Johnson (who later married Cordell, got her Ph.D., and received a MacArthur Fellowship for her work preserving the music traditions of African-Americans), Rutha Mae Harris, and Bertha Gober. All of them were great singers who themselves arranged freedom songs that were subsequently used in every city of the Southern movement. In fact, during the struggle in Albany they formed an SNCC Freedom Singers Quartet: Charles Neblett, Cordell Reagon, Rutha Mae Harris, and Bernice Johnson.

Somehow through the music a great secret was discovered: that black people, otherwise cowed, discouraged, and faced with innumerable and insuperable obstacles, could transcend all those difficulties and forge a new determination, a new faith and strength, when fortified with song. The music was not a political or economic gift to the people from the authorities, nor could it be taken away by them—music was the gift of the people to themselves, a bottomless reservoir of spiritual power.

Charles Sherrod likes to tell a story about holding a freedom meeting in a rural church near Albany. The sheriff and his deputies suddenly crashed into the church, and the people were struck with fear. The sheriff strutted around the church and made his point clear: "We don't wanta hear no talk 'bout registerin' to vote in this county . . . " But while he was speaking, the congregation began to hum "We'll Never Turn Back" softly. As the sheriff moved to the rear of the church and shouted, "There won't be no Freedom Riders round here . . ." the congregation commenced to sing, still softly. Then the singing became stronger and louder and some sister began to moan till you could hardly hear the sheriff over the singing and moaning. The sheriff didn't know what to do. He seemed to be afraid to tell the people to shut up. Finally, he and his men just turned their backs and stomped out. Those beautiful people sang that sheriff right out of their church! That was some powerful music.

A great many lessons were learned in Albany. It confirmed Martin's belief that whatever his role in a movement, he would bear responsibility for its failure. From that point on, Martin would not hesitate to assert his right to make final decisions regarding strategy.

We also learned that passion and enthusiasm were no substitute for sound, strategic planning. Everywhere we had problems it was because we had not planned and prepared. People only saw the movement when Martin Luther King showed up, so they thought that was all there was to it. Get Reverend King and put him in jail and things will start to happen. It was never that way. There were lots of boycotts, but none succeeded like Montgomery. There were many student sit-ins, but none were as successful as Atlanta and Nashville. When people operated purely on emotion, without organization and planning, it simply didn't work. We learned that you couldn't start the negotiation process after things got heated, because by then folks were so angry that they wouldn't meet with you. Perhaps most important, Albany was an out-of-town opening for the SCLC staff that was just coming together. The citizenship school component and I began to become a factor in SCLC's ability to organize a community, and in Albany I began to see areas of need in SCLC in which I could play a supportive role without creating further internal conflicts.

The gaps in the SCLC staff were gradually being filled and everyone, including Martin, who as our leader was only thirty-three, had gained much-needed experience. We would be needing every bit of that wisdom, skill, and knowledge in the years to come.

9

The Lord Is with
This Movement

Joshua fit the battle of Jericho.

—AFRICAN-AMERICAN SPIRITUAL

SCLC was for the most part a collection of thirty-something preachers who had followed various paths to arrive at a common commitment to end racial segregation. After Albany, many said we were beaten; but we were beaten the way a blacksmith hammers a blade. We emerged from Albany with the kind of unity and purpose that George Washington's troops found in the miserable snows of Valley Forge. We were more ready than we had ever been to wage our nonviolent campaign, and fittingly, we set our sights on the toughest town in the South—Birmingham, Alabama.

This was a turning point for the national movement for civil rights. In Birmingham, we truly broke the back of segregation. In so doing, we developed a model for nonviolent social change that can be applied in virtually any contemporary context. The Birmingham campaign was also a turning point for our leader. Martin had always been cautious, even reluctant about his leadership role. It had been thrust upon him in Montgomery, and there had been no time since his twenty-seventh birthday that he had not been subject to public scrutiny and criticism. Occasionally this still-young man would try to retreat from it all, but that fall in Birmingham marked a turning point in Martin. It was then that I believe he came to accept, finally, that he could never walk away from the awesome responsibility of the civil rights leadership that had fallen upon his shoulders.

Today it might seem that everything about the movement was intentional, that Martin Luther King was always a man with an enormously ambitious mission. But the Montgomery bus boycott, the student sit-ins, and the Freedom Rides were all events that Martin had become involved in reluctantly. He had embraced the movement in Albany only after his unplanned arrest. Birmingham, however, was a movement that Martin Luther King anticipated, planned, and coordinated from beginning to end.

Martin's mentor, the legendary Dr. Benjamin Mays, instructed his students that there was no shame in failure, the shame was in aiming too low. In Albany, we set our sights high and accomplished less than we intended, but rather than suffer discouragement, we became even more determined.

"All things work together for good, for them that love the Lord, and are called according to his purposes," is a verse Coretta Scott King often quotes. It had taken three generations of Baptist preachers to produce a Martin Luther King, Jr. The studies at Morehouse College, Crozier Theological Seminary, and Boston University, where he received his Ph.D. in theology, were only a small part of his preparation. Martin's leadership abilities were wrought and refined in the crucible of collective black experience. His grandfather on his mother's side, the Rev. A. D. Williams, had been treasurer of the National Baptist Convention, the largest organized group of black Christians in the world, with some seven million members. His father, the son of Georgia sharecroppers, had walked into Atlanta with his shoes slung over his shoulders and taken himself to Morehouse College because he knew the value of education. And Martin's wife, Coretta, the daughter of strong rural stock in Alabama, had worked her way through Antioch University in Ohio and the New England Conservatory of Music. A less dedicated or less determined lineage could not have produced this "Moses" of the twentieth century.

Daddy King, as Martin's father was called by almost everybody in the movement, would often end his message on Sunday mornings at Ebenezer Baptist Church with the cry, "I love the Lord, he heard my cry and pitieth every groan. Long as I live while troubles last, I'll hasten to his throne!" Martin had heard his father shout this affirmation of faith literally thousands of times as a boy and young man. It was a joyous, emotional proclamation that Daddy King continued even after the tragic deaths of first Martin, then his other son, and later, his wife. It was this statement of the King family faith and the sincere commitment to following it through, even in the face of great personal sacrifice, that produced such a leader.

But even such a leader as Martin Luther King could not produce a movement out of thin air. Rev. Fred Shuttlesworth had been laboring for racial justice in Birmingham, Alabama, since 1954, when he began his efforts to enroll his daughter in a white school in response to the Supreme Court's desegregation ruling. Tall and lean with a booming voice and an expansive style, Fred Shuttlesworth had the heart of a lion and was as fearless as if the entire power of the Birmingham establishment were with him, rather than arrayed firmly against his every petition.

As a first step toward making a decision about whether or not to make Birmingham our next movement city, the SCLC board decided to hold its annual convention there in September 1962, in order to appraise the situation. An omen of what was to come occurred during the convention itself when a white youth sitting in the front of the auditorium leapt up on the stage while Martin was speaking and punched him repeatedly before he could be subdued. Birmingham was destined to be both violent and stubborn.

For some time, Shuttlesworth and his brave group of local preachers who made up the Alabama Christian Movement for Human Rights (ACMHR) had an economic boycott of downtown merchants in force, and the SCLC convention was intended to be a show of support for Shuttlesworth's efforts, which we hoped would strengthen his hand in bargaining with the merchants over the desegregation of lunch counters. Upon learning of the forthcoming convention some of the merchants did agree to voluntarily desegregate their lunch counters, whereupon Shuttlesworth ended the boycott as a show of good faith. His good faith was misplaced, however, and the leverage supplied by the SCLC convention lasted no longer than the convention itself. As soon as Martin Luther King and the SCLC staff left town, the merchants reactivated their segregationist practices.

That same month, four black churches near Albany that were friendly to the movement were blown up. The nation was also transfixed by the violence in Oxford, Mississippi, over the admission of a black student, James Meredith, to the University of Mississippi, during which two people were killed. Seven years after the Supreme Court had declared segregated schools unconstitutional, more than ninety percent of all Southern school districts were still segregated, and black voter registration percentages in the South were still abysmally low. The national media were declaring the Albany campaign a failure (though we who were involved thought that was far too simplistic a judgment) and pronouncing that the direct-action phase of the civil rights movement was over. Given the tenor of the times, Martin and the SCLC board determined that they must go ahead in the near future with a major campaign, and that there was no better place to stage it than in Birmingham, Alabama.

Everyone involved, especially Martin, was determined that the campaign in Birmingham not get bogged down as the one in Albany had. Toward this end Martin called a planning meeting of the entire SCLC staff, along with key supporters and board members, for December 1962 to convene at the Dorchester Citizenship Program site. This was the first time the whole SCLC staff had been to Dorchester; I was pleased to have them there and proud of the center where we had trained so many dedicated community leaders. With its stately oaks, Dorchester was a beautiful and peaceful place to debate the lessons of Albany and formulate a strategy for Birmingham free of the relentless distractions of SCLC's Atlanta office. Martin, Ralph, Wyatt, Jim Bevel, Jack O'Dell, B. J. Johnson, Fred Bennett, Dorothy Cotton, and I participated in the strategy sessions, along with members of the ACMHR—Fred Shuttlesworth, Reverend Edward A. Gardner, and Abraham Woods.

Wyatt had developed a plan of action, which he presented to the group. It was somewhat abstract and intellectual, but basically good, and laid out very specifically the preparations that were needed for a successful movement in Birmingham. The specificity of Wyatt's plan was both its strength and its weakness. On the one hand, it laid out an organizational structure for enlisting the support of the entire community. However, it was a battle plan that assumed lines of authority and a rigid command structure that could never exist in a nonviolent social movement. Through demonstrations, workshops, mass meetings, negotiations, and personal relationships, we would have to persuade black and white citizens in Birmingham to take risks and make changes—many of which would involve real pain and suffering, emotional and physical. This dimension was absent from Wyatt's plan, which lacked adequate consideration for the psychology of the human beings involved in the struggle.

It was our tradition in Dorchester to include recreation as part of the daily program and this meeting was no different. We met in the mornings, had recreation time in the afternoons, and resumed meet-

ings in the evenings. We played softball and went over to a gym at
Fort Stewart to play basketball—most of us were in our early thirties
and still had a respectable half-court game. We arranged the three-
day meeting schedule to allow for periods of private, quiet reflection,
walks in the woods, a chance for personal prayer. We made it a point
to serve nourishing, tasty meals at Dorchester, and our cook, Mrs.
Smith, really burned some pots for us that weekend. Everybody knew
that Martin had a weakness for good food: our corn bread had never
been as rich, the chicken as crispy, or the greens as tangy.

The retreat at Dorchester marked a change in the role I played
with SCLC. In Albany, although I was more familiar with the community than anyone else in SCLC from my years as a pastor in
nearby Thomasville, I was not part of the initial decision making. I
had been an observer, offering assistance from the sidelines. This was
largely due to my newness to the staff and my position as director of
the Citizenship School Program. During the Albany movement I
began to see the gaps in the staff structure, places where I could contribute without treading on anyone's turf, and it was in Birmingham
that I had the opportunity to fill these gaps.

As executive director of SCLC, Wyatt's responsibility was relating to Martin and the press, while maintaining some oversight of the
business operations of SCLC. That was a full-time job, so that while
he initiated relationships with the community and the staff, he really
wasn't available to maintain a day-to-day relationship during the
course of the Albany movement. Citizenship training would be critical to training and mobilizing the demonstrators for the Birmingham
movement. Once I was on the scene in Birmingham, I would move
into regular communication with community leaders, most of whom
I would get to know during our workshops.

The negotiations process presented another area that was under-
staffed and needed attention. In the Gandhian theory, negotiations
are as important a part of the process of social change as demonstrations. Paradoxically, for a movement grounded in Gandhi's nonviolent methods, we didn't discuss theories of nonviolent change in our
strategy sessions. Most members of the staff developed strategies
based on their own experience, which basically involved being
thrown into some kind of confrontation and having survived it with
relative success. But that had been the pattern in Albany and it had
clearly been a flawed approach. This time we needed to be more
deliberate, to set our goals before we went into Birmingham. In the
citizenship schools we meticulously taught Gandhi's method, which
involved four steps: investigation, communication/negotiation, con-

frontation, and reconciliation. As applied to Birmingham, our discussions with Fred Shuttlesworth and holding the SCLC convention there served to help us ascertain the facts; I viewed the next step as communicating our concerns to the white leaders of Birmingham. People usually didn't want to hear the facts from us, didn't want to talk with us at all, but I felt it was partly because demonstrations too often started before the communication process began. I offered to initiate contact with white business leaders in Birmingham using some of my contacts through the National Council of Churches. My idea was that we needed to begin talking early, before the polarization started, and to keep talking to speed up the process of reconciliation.

Martin was very encouraging, and my offer to start negotiations was cheerfully accepted by all. Other members of the staff were able negotiators, but it was a job no one coveted. They thought it was a waste of time and perceived it as "sucking up to the white folks." In the National Council of Churches and even in my New Orleans upbringing, I had had a lot of experience relating to whites in fairly wholesome relationships. My father taught me that putting white people at ease was a survival skill that signaled my superior intellect rather than inferior social status. In my four years at the National Council of Churches I worked almost entirely with whites, and I had always believed that people were people. I had enough relationships with different kinds of people to know the individual differences in human beings were more important than the color of their skin. I understood that from a white Southerner's perspective we were trying to upset a world in which they had it made. The changes we were proposing were enormously threatening and we had to help white people embrace them.

I enjoyed the camaraderie of the retreat. The SCLC staff was competitive and a one-upmanship style prevailed on any point, no mater how minor. While egotistical, my colleagues were also good-natured and teasing, and playfulness came readily. It was a work hard, play hard group and in that respect not dissimilar to my Alpha Phi Alpha fraternity brothers at Howard. In fact, Martin was an Alpha. Only Wyatt felt a need to maintain a serious posture throughout. To him fell the unenviable job of keeping the meetings focused on the task at hand.

During the meetings I felt surges of adrenaline as I envisioned the coming campaign. I understood that people, black and white, were the key to the movement. Dorothy Cotton, Jim Bevel, and I would be training the black people for Birmingham and I would engage the white business community in sustained negotiations. I would not be a bystander in Birmingham. We emerged from the Dorchester retreat with the strategy for Birmingham set and our responsibilities divided. First, we would focus our energies on the economic power base of the city, particularly the downtown stores. As I had learned in Thomasville, a city's business leaders would feel the pinch of an effective boycott and in turn would persuade political leaders to act. We all agreed that the city's pocket was the best place to start applying the pressure.

Our plan was to begin in March 1963, when we would target several downtown stores where blacks shopped heavily with sit-ins. We would simultaneously impose a tight citywide boycott on the purchasing of Easter clothing or any goods other than those that were absolutely necessary. Such a boycott would reap the additional benefit of heightening community consciousness of the campaign, and provide for a large number of people the feeling they were "doing something" to assist the campaign and were not merely uninvolved bystanders. This consciousness would be particularly intense during the Easter season because this was the second most important buying period of the year, and in black communities across the South a time when families traditionally purchased new clothing. When we began the boycott, there were no black sales clerks in Birmingham, so our objective was not only the desegregation of all facilities in all stores but also the hiring of black sales clerks, especially in those businesses that thrived on black patronage.

Our secondary aim was to establish far greater control over our campaign tactics than we had had in Albany, where Martin was often caught reacting to events rather than creating them. We knew that no such effort, which depends on unpredictable social dynamics, can be completely controlled. But we hoped to make it clear that the leadership in Birmingham emanated from the SCLC structure. To establish a good working relationship with the community, we would rely on the advice and counsel of Fred Shuttlesworth and the Alabama movement (ACMHR), but we also planned to broaden our base of support by organizing an advisory committee of prominent local citizens who were active in the black business and professional community. In Albany, the black elite had cut a deal with the white establishment in exchange for vague promises of change. We wanted to avoid that kind of ad hoc action in Birmingham by opening channels to Birmingham's much larger black elite from the very beginning. Martin would take responsibility for making the contacts necessary to establish this broadened base through his talks to groups and in his personal visits. In the meantime, I would initiate discussions with the Birmingham business community through a contact from my days with the United Christian Youth Movement, Peggy Horne, who was working with the Episcopal Diocese in Birmingham.

Third, the kind of citizenship and nonviolent demonstration training we were providing at Dorchester on a monthly basis would be incorporated into our Birmingham campaign from the beginning. Martin was concerned that I come to Birmingham on terms that did not threaten the grant with the Field Foundation. I assured him that Wes Hotchkiss and Bob Spike wanted the movement to succeed and that there would be no problem with them. We could do recruitment and citizenship training of folks from Birmingham at Dorchester before the demonstrations began and we could move into Birmingham and continue training. Wyatt expressed concern that I stay out of jail, and all felt it was best that I not be assigned to demonstrations as part of my official responsibilities. Training demonstrators in nonviolence was not specifically in my mandate, but it was something I could stretch my mandate to include. So we all agreed that I would be assigned to Birmingham for the duration of the campaign to work on recruitment and training, along with Jim and Diane Bevel, formerly of SNCC, who joined our staff in the fall of 1962, and Rev. James Lawson, who was the organizer and philosophical force behind the Nashville sit-ins of 1960.

Jim Bevel came to SCLC from the student movement, where he was one of the key figures in the Nashville sit-ins. He had gone to seminary after a dishonorable discharge from the navy for insubordination. It's a story worth telling not just for what it says about Bevel, but for what it reveals about the navy during that period. The navy had the worst record in the armed services for segregation, and they had assigned Bevel to the kitchen, where a disproportionate number of blacks were sent to work. He told his superior officers that he would not work in the kitchen and proceeded to sit on the deck reading instead. My uncle Walter Fuller, who was truly a saint, also received a dishonorable discharge from the army, and he too was assigned to the kitchen. When he was ordered by some white officers to bury a dead mule, he protested that the mule was full of maggots, and he couldn't deal with that mule and then go back and cook food. When the officer insisted, Uncle Walt told him to go to hell. So I interpreted Bevel's dishonorable discharge from the racist armed forces as a sign that he was a man of great honor and principle—and he was. Bevel was eccentric in the extreme and as gifted as he was eccentric. He was passionate about the struggle against injustice, but he never lost his cool under pressure. In that sense, we were kindred spirits. The more chaotic the situation, the calmer both he and I became.

Our goal in Birmingham was larger than ending segregation in one Southern city. It was our hope that our efforts in Birmingham would so dramatize the plight and determination of African-American citizens in the Southern states that we would force the Kennedy administration to draft and push through Congress a comprehensive Civil Rights Act, outlawing segregation and racial discrimination in public accommodations, employment, and education. Clarence Mitchell, the NAACP's chief lobbyist in Washington, had been pressing for a comprehensive civil rights bill for years. We believed that ultimately the political pressure to enact a civil rights bill had to come from outside of Washington. Our demonstrations dramatized in graphic images the injustices endured by black Americans, calling attention to issues that were otherwise easy for white Americans to ignore. But Roy Wilkins and influential members of the NAACP were not pleased by SCLC's use of demonstrations and arrests. The NAACP's civil rights strategy was grounded on obedience to the law. If the laws could be changed, they believed, behavior would also change. Therefore black people must be scrupulous in their obedience to the law, otherwise they risked undermining the moral force of their own pleas for obedience to orders such as the Supreme Court decision on school desegregation.

At SCLC, we felt that changing laws was extremely slow and too dependent on just one sector of society—the legal sector. Nonviolent demonstrations attempted to change people's attitudes toward the situation by reminding whites of their economic interdependence with blacks. Our methods, resting on the foundation of court cases brought by the NAACP Legal Defense Fund, were quicker. We typically accomplished what we were attempting to do in ninety days, whereas a court battle could take nine years. It wasn't an either/or situation; we felt both approaches were useful in the right context. We never questioned the NAACP's role, but our strategy challenged the very core of NAACP belief. The NAACP built an entire strategy on the assumption that people will obey the law once the law is changed. We believed in law, but we also believed we had a moral obligation to challenge unjust laws. The laws we challenged were written by white people to repress black people. There was no doubt in anyone's mind that they were discriminatory, but the NAACP just wasn't comfortable breaking even unjust laws.

The differences between the NAACP and SCLC strategies were

in some ways generational, and my own family is a classic case study. Both of my parents were active in the Urban League and my father was in the NAACP. My brother was active in CORE, and I was in SCLC. If we had had a younger brother, he probably would have joined SNCC. SCLC and the NAACP shared the same objectives, we just had different approaches to achieving them.

When my father, a "race man" in the NAACP mold, was asked whether he thought whites would obey federal laws against segregation, he gave the standard NAACP answer: "They stop for red lights, don't they?" However, one thing that encourages people to stop for red lights is the possibility of being caught and fined if they don't. Since the end of Reconstruction, African-Americans had been in possession of paper rights—the right to vote and the right to equal schools, water fountains, and waiting rooms—rights with no enforcement mechanism. The Supreme Court had ruled segregation was unconstitutional, but individual lawsuits were impractical, cumbersome, and too expensive to serve as an enforcement mechanism. We needed a national law that created an affirmative obligation not to discriminate and established penalties for disobedience. The pressure for that kind of change would not be generated in meetings on Capitol Hill or at the Supreme Court. We needed a civil rights bill and we had to go through Birmingham to get it.

These were our aims, forged in the three-day December 1962 conference. They were ambitious goals: we knew Birmingham would be difficult but we left Dorchester with a sense of grim determination. After the planning meeting Martin set off on a whirlwind fundraising tour, and met in New York with longtime supporters like entertainer Harry Belafonte, his counsel, Stan Levison, and the attorneys from the NAACP Legal Defense Fund to apprise them of our plans for Birmingham. We all, and Martin especially, were convinced that the campaign in Birmingham would make or break our movement—and we were prepared to stay there for as long as it took to force change.

As we gathered at the close of the retreat, Martin used his favorite technique for dispersing the tension we all felt—he began to tease us by telling us how he was going to preach at our funerals. "Some of us are going to lose our lives in Birmingham," he said, actually joking about the danger ahead. He would then go around the room, taking some embarrassing aspect of each of our lives that he threatened to use in our eulogies.

These mock eulogies were first inspired by a story told about Vernon Johns, the eccentric pastor who had once presided at Martin's first church, Dexter Avenue Baptist in Montgomery. Dexter Avenue Baptist was where the black Ph.D.'s in Alabama went to church. People would drive all the way from Tuskegee to go to Dexter Avenue Church to show how sophisticated and intelligent they were. Its pastor, Vernon Johns, was at once brilliant and infuriating. He could quote Scripture in different versions and make the appropriate adjustments without cracking a Bible, and in his sermons he would recite long passages of Shakespeare and other classics. This was the side of him that Dexter folks loved. No one ever questioned his intelligence or moral authority. It was for very different reasons that he got fired and rehired in every place he ever pastored.

Vernon Johns was pastoring Dexter Avenue when a somewhat disreputable member of a very prominent family in the church was killed. Vernon Johns was willing to conduct the funeral, but he wanted to do it at the funeral home because, as he said, "He didn't come to church when he was alive, why you want to drag him in here now?" But the family insisted and persuaded the deacons to call a church meeting. At this meeting, the congregation voted that the family could have the funeral in the church sanctuary. Even in the Congregational Church, this was an extraordinary usurpation of a pastor's authority over the worship life of his congregation.

Vernon Johns appeared to concede to this decision, however, and presided over the funeral. When it was time for him to deliver the eulogy, Johns stood up and walked over to the pulpit. Martin loved to repeat Johns's legendary eulogy: "Amos Jefferson lived a trifling, meaningless, worthless life. He went around trying to be a bully and daring someone to cut his throat. The other night at the bar in the Bed Moore Hotel somebody obliged him. He lived like a dog. He died like a dog." And with a wave of the hand he added, "Undertaker, take the body." Martin loved to preach our eulogies in that manner, saying openly and frankly the most humiliating things about us, preaching our eulogies like Vernon Johns would preach if we had made him mad.

I had met Vernon Johns when Jean and I were living in New York. He was preaching a New Year's Eve service at St. Albans Congregational UCC, where we were members. We had wanted to go to the New Year's Eve service, but there was also a fraternity dance that night to which friends had invited us to go. We went to the church planning to go to the dance afterward. Usually a watch night service in a Congregational church ended shortly after midnight and at that hour the party would just be warming up. I had on my tuxedo and Jean wore a formal gown. When we arrived at the church, it was full.

The only remaining seats were in the front row and the usher took us right down front. When Johns got up to preach, he looked down at us from the pulpit and using his most stentorian tones said, "Now, don't bring these young people in here that are trying to get a little religion at the last minute and gon' run back out to party. I'll preach to them 'til the sun comes up." So when Martin started to sound like Vernon Johns, I knew we were in for a rough time.

When I returned to Atlanta after the intensity of the retreat, it was as if I had entered another world. Jean had begun teaching at Whiteford Elementary School in Atlanta, where she was surprised to find that the parents of her poor white students from public housing respected her as a teacher. With her activities at First Congregational Church, her new colleagues at school, especially Sammy Bacote and his wife, Joyce, and the girls' calendar of ballet and swimming lessons, Jean had developed a separate life. Her life was strictly Atlanta and mine was strictly movement, and only when I came home did they overlap.

For me, Atlanta was a haven, an oasis away from the intensity of citizenship schools and trips to New York to meet with the Board for Homeland Ministries of the United Church of Christ or the Field Foundation. But, while Atlanta called itself "A City too Busy to Hate" it was not without its own racial problems. The Atlanta NAACP had been trying to desegregate Atlanta schools for several years and was meeting with resistance. Housing was strictly segregated, much more so than in New Orleans. Middle-class blacks in Atlanta had comfortable homes compared to blacks in New York, but they paled in comparison to the generous, dogwood-studded lawns that surrounded the homes of middle-class whites. Jean refused to shop downtown, because black shoppers were relegated to the basement and first-floor levels of the major department stores like Rich's and Davidson's. So she shopped at Kmart, Sears, and the handful of other stores in the black neighborhoods. When efforts began to desegregate Rich's Department Store, Jean joined the picket line.

Thanks to the presence of the black colleges in the Atlanta University Center, black Atlantans were relatively well educated. In fact, when the schools finally were desegregated it was discovered that the average educational level of black teachers in the Atlanta public school system was higher than the average for white teachers. Another result of the strong influence of local higher education was the prevalence of black professionals. Our girls grew up knowing black pediatricians, dentists, and pharmacists, and we kept our accounts at the black bank, Citizens Trust. Jean endeavored to keep the girls enclosed in a secure world of church, school, and neighborhood on Atlanta's west side.

When I was in town and free to attend church at First Congregational, we enjoyed going out for dinner afterward at one of Atlanta's black restaurants. I had heard that the Holiday Inn chain had voluntarily desegregated across the country, and one Sunday Jean and I decided to take the girls to dinner there. It was a very nice restaurant, round and airy, with floor-to-ceiling windows. From the maître'd's station we could see cloud-white tablecloths and cloth napkins folded like little pyramids. The maître'd was clearly uncomfortable and looked startled to see us. He informed us that there were no tables available, although we could plainly see that most of the tables were vacant. Paula, who was still a toddler, began to cry loudly, "I'm hungry!" She scrambled out of Jean's arms and began running around the restaurant crying. I don't approve of children throwing tantrums, but in this case I made an exception. I later discovered that our oldest daughter, Andrea, who understood why we were being turned away, was afraid that we were going to jail and upset that she might have to go in her best dress. But I had not intended a confrontation, so we went home. It was a reminder to me that race relations in Atlanta still had a long way to go.

Eliza Paschal, a member of the Georgia Human Rights Commission, whom I had met in Albany, suggested that SCLC press for integration of Atlanta's church-affiliated private schools. So we began the process of applications and tests for enrolling Andrea and Lisa in Trinity Presbyterian School. Ralph and Juanita Abernathy also applied for their two girls, Juandalyn and Donzaleigh, to enter Westminster School, and Martin and Coretta applied to Lovett School for Yolanda and Marty. We did not expect that they would be accepted and were planning this as a test case. The Trinity Presbyterian congregation and their pastor were fairly liberal, however, and the congregation was associated with faith-inspired social action around Atlanta. Much to our surprise, Andrea and Lisa were accepted to Trinity for the following school year, and we had to scramble to scrape together the money to send them.

We were finally settled into the Atlanta house and really able to enjoy Christmas that year. Jean decorated the house with holly branches from a bush in the side yard and the girls loved the ritual of decorating the Christmas tree. Artificial trees were the latest fashion and Jean put a silver tree with blue ornaments on a coffee table in front of the picture window. I made eggnog, using my mother's recipe. When friends dropped by during the holidays, we'd serve eggnog spiked with rum and dance to records in the sparsely furnished living room. The girls loved the limbo pole, because they could go lower than any of the adults. Jean's dinner table was always welcoming staff and volunteers from SCLC and SNCC, many of whom were far from their families. Holiday meals and Sunday dinners would find Wyatt Walker's secretary, Edwina Smith, and her son Kevin, Dorothy Cotton, a couple of SNCC kids, and others around the table. Jean's signature dish was macaroni and cheese and there always seemed to be enough no matter how many folks turned up at dinnertime. It was a relaxed and enjoyable holiday, the calm before the storm.

The church Rev. Fred Shuttlesworth pastored was not the largest Baptist Church in Birmingham, nor was it the most prestigious. He ministered to the emerging working class of Birmingham, the veterans who earned middle-class wages in the steel mills and purchased modern homes in newly created subdivisions. Fred was tall, lean, dark-skinned, clean-cut, and very good-looking, and he took care with his appearance. When Fred preached, his collars were crisp and white, his trousers creased, and his shoes were spit-and-polish glossy. Fred became a leader, although I don't believe he was looking to lead a movement. Rather, he was trying to provide a good education for his daughter, an education to which she was entitled under the law. His parishioners supported Fred, because unlike the congregations of more prestigious churches, his members had no vested interest in the segregated system. Many upper-middle-class blacks in Birmingham were teachers in the segregated schools or professionals who thrived on an all-black clientele. For them, respect and status within the black community helped to soften the harshness of segregation, and they could adjust to segregation as had my parents. But the emerging working class didn't fit into prior patterns of segregation. They were not farmworkers or domestics and their income often equaled or surpassed that of many black professionals.

Shuttlesworth organized, along with a tiny group of other brave ministers, the Alabama Christian Movement for Human Rights in the late 1950s to in effect replace the NAACP, which was outlawed in 1956 by an Alabama court injunction because it refused to reveal its membership list to the state's attorney general. The ACMHR was isolated, lacked funding, and was met with angry opposition by the police and state legal authorities. Attempts by the ACMHR to encourage black voter registration were met with a continuous wave of retaliatory violence unequaled anywhere in the South, with the possible exception of Mississippi. Incredible violence was unleashed against them. When Fred tried to desegregate an all-white public school by enrolling his daughter, he was beaten and his wife was stabbed in the hip outside the school by white vigilantes, then they, not the vigilantes, were arrested. Rev. Charles Billups, one of the key ACMHR members, was kidnapped by the Klan, tied to a tree, and beaten; he barely escaped with his life and was only spared because he insisted on praying aloud for his kidnappers.

To grasp the extent of the violence that occurred in Birmingham, it is necessary to understand its rather unique history. Birmingham is the largest iron and steel center in the South. It is also Alabama's largest city, with a population of three hundred thousand, a significant percentage of which is black. It developed in the late nineteenth century due to its rich iron, coal, and steel mills and expanded rapidly along with the growth of the railway system, which made wide distribution of its manufactured goods possible. Because it was the first major industrial center in the Deep South, Birmingham was the target of heavy union recruiting and bitter attempts to win recognition for unions. Resistance to unionization by the plant owners was extremely harsh, however, and considerable violence characterized the Birmingham "union wars" of the 1950s.

Birmingham was virtually within walking distance of Alabama's black belt, and as farming jobs declined for the rural black population there was a massive movement into the city fueled by the availability of jobs in the steel and coal industries. Blacks were not paid as well as whites, but they were paid a great deal more in the mills than they had been on the farms. By 1960 the city had a large black community that maintained several stable businesses and a small professional class with a middle-income standard of living. It developed within a rigidly segregated system kept intact by tight police control. On the rare occasions when blacks attempted to protest segregation and racial oppression their efforts were met not only with heavy police crackdowns but also with the kind of vigilante violence by racist whites that had been common in the union wars.

Vigilante groups such as the Klan attacked blacks with the tacit, if not active, cooperation of the police. In the early 1960s, bombings in a middle-class area of black Birmingham were so common the neighborhood became known as "Dynamite Hill," even though the residents of that area were not actively protesting anything. This atmosphere of violent suppression of any sort of black assertiveness, along with a defiance of federal court orders to desegregate, was articulated in official state policy by Governor George Wallace, who rode into office in 1962 on the wings of his promises to vigorously oppose racial integration.

The Birmingham police department was overseen by Police Commissioner Eugene "Bull" Connor, a man who made no secret of his contempt for black citizens. Connor had become a sort of folk hero to racists everywhere. He and his police repeatedly arrested Shuttlesworth and other members of the Alabama movement. Fred's home was bombed, and he was the recipient of nightly threatening phone calls. It became dangerous to even be seen with Fred Shuttlesworth in Birmingham: he was greatly admired, but steadfastly avoided. The atmosphere in Birmingham toward "uppity blacks" was so hostile that popular singer Nat King Cole was attacked on stage by white supremacists when he performed there in 1956. It is a testament to his unselfishness that despite this history of harsh repression, Fred and the members of the Alabama Christian Movement were ready to commit themselves to a civil rights effort in Birmingham more extensive and possibly more exhausting than any campaign against segregation since the Montgomery bus boycott of 1955.

The Birmingham movement was designed to impact not just a city but a nation, and perhaps we should have anticipated the anxiety that we were generating outside the South. But we were totally unaware of the extent of FBI surveillance of SCLC. It has since been revealed in FBI documents of the time that FBI Director J. Edgar Hoover received authorization from Attorney General Robert Kennedy to wiretap the offices of Martin's close friend and counselor, Stan Levison, after Hoover led Kennedy to believe that he had evidence that Stan was some sort of communist. Stan was a gentle, soft-spoken man whom I considered conservative because he always encouraged Martin to look carefully at all sides before making important decisions. He made his money from Ford dealerships that he owned in New York and New Jersey and later had such significant real estate holdings that he didn't need to earn a salary or hold a regular job, so he really made the movement his life's work.

Stan Levison and Harry Wachtel, another progressive independent investor, along with Harry Belafonte, attorney Clarence Jones, and union leader Cleve Robinson formed Martin's New York kitchen cabinet. He depended on similar informal groups in Los Angeles and Chicago to advise him and keep him apprised of the perceptions of the movement in those cities. Stan in particular was essential in keeping us abreast of the intellectual and political climate in the progressive community in New York. If a book came out that he thought we ought to read, he read it first and gave Martin a review, noting key chapters. Stan also had personal contacts with Walter Reuther and members of the United Auto Workers board, and helped Martin build important relationships with leaders of the Northern industrial unions. Stan and his circle were admirers of social reformers like Eleanor Roosevelt and A. Philip Randolph who believed in an activist government supportive of poor and working people.

Stan and Jack O'Dell maintained the SCLC's New York office and were adept at soliciting badly needed funds from Northern liberals. One of the reasons Jack O'Dell had attended our strategy sessions in Dorchester was that he had been an organizer with one of the mine workers' unions in Birmingham and knew the organizing climate in Birmingham intimately. The Birmingham campaign was going to require more money than SCLC had ever raised. With Stan Levison's help, O'Dell used mailing lists from liberal organizations and publications like *The Nation* and the then liberal *New Republic* and put together a modern direct-mail operation for SCLC that I believe was the first of its kind. O'Dell also used newspaper ads to generate funds as well as political support.

Neither the FBI wiretap on Stan's home and office phones nor the microphone placed in his office ever provided any evidence that Stan was in communication with the Communist Party, which was the supposed reason for the bugs. Instead, this became a listening post for the FBI to learn about Martin's plans and strategies, and the first step toward full-scale monitoring of SCLC by the FBI. FBI memos attacked Martin for using "deceit, lies and treachery as propaganda" and this view was shared with publishers of black newspapers such as the *Chicago Defender*. Having labeled Stan Levison a communist, the Bureau proceeded to inform the attorney general and officials at the White House of the extent of his influence on Martin. Citing a "reliable informant," Hoover sent a steady stream of memos that seemed designed to give the impression that the FBI had a source within the Communist Party that was feeding information about Levison's work with King. In fact, the "reliable source" was the FBI's own wiretap. There is little indication that anyone in the Kennedy administration challenged the FBI's circular reasoning. The FBI alleged that Stan Levison was a communist and used their own unfounded assertion to generate concern over Stan's influence with Martin. While at the time we attributed any absence of support from the Kennedy administration to politics—Dixiecrats held power in the Congress and influenced the electoral votes that President Kennedy would need to

win a second term—it is now clear what deep fears Hoover's accusation of communism unleashed in the administration.

We had planned to issue our manifesto and initiate our campaign in
March 1963, but Birmingham was in the midst of a rather complicated election over the issue of whether the city would convert to a
mayor–city council system or retain its city commissioner system. In
the midst of this potential administrative change, a mayoral election
was to be held in April and Bull Connor, the police commissioner,
was a candidate. Fred and our Birmingham advisory committee
asked us to postpone the beginning of the demonstrations since while
they felt Connor would lose the election soundly, they were concerned that demonstrations might unleash a strong backlash vote for
him. Martin saw the reason for this delay, and agreed. The city went
on to adopt the mayor–city council system, and a few months later
Bull Connor lost the mayoral election to Albert Boutwell, a man we
didn't know much about but who seemed moderate in comparison
with the ranting and raving Connor. The election was inconclusive,
however, because Connor and the other commissioners filed a suit
contesting the validity of the change to a mayor–city council system.
    The newly elected Mayor Boutwell gave no indication he was
willing to even begin making changes toward desegregation. On the
contrary, we got the impression the white power structure felt
Boutwell's election should be sufficient cause for us to forgo our campaign in Birmingham altogether. Meanwhile, the issue of the city's
legitimate form of government remained in limbo, awaiting a court
decision, and Bull Connor stayed on as police commissioner.
    During early 1963, Jim Bevel, Dorothy Cotton, and I held work-
shops at Dorchester for community leaders of Birmingham chosen by
Fred Shuttlesworth. We planned to go into Birmingham with trained
leaders in every key neighborhood. The demonstrators in Birmingham
would be under tremendous pressure and we knew that a large number
of well-trained folk would be necessary to maintain discipline in the
face of the violence that was sure to come from Bull Connor and his
men. We did not want a repeat of the rock throwing that had derailed
the Albany movement. We had discovered there that thorough preparation and strict discipline were necessary in order to help people remain
calm and in control of the situation when they were arrested. In Birmingham, we were going to prepare them for jail. There would be no
kids clad in T-shirts freezing in their cells and nobody getting stir-crazy.
Demonstrators would come prepared for the harsh conditions of jail
with their toothbrushes, layered clothing, and other necessary items.

They were also trained to follow a daily routine of prayer, Bible study, and citizen education. This time we were going to be ready.

We set the day following the mayoral election for the beginning of our demonstrations. On April 3 we issued our Birmingham manifesto, calling for the desegregation of lunch counters, rest rooms, and water fountains in downtown stores, the hiring of blacks in local businesses and industry, and the forming of a biracial committee to work out a timetable for the desegregation of other areas of city life.

I had contacted Peggy Horne to ask for her help in setting up meetings with members of the white establishment in Birmingham. Peggy was working in Christian education in the Episcopal Diocese in Birmingham, and was one of the first women to hold such a responsible position with the Episcopal Church. She was charming and had the vitality one must have to work with young people, and her long skirts and modest blouses reflected an awareness that she was a churchwoman in the conservative South. Peggy was able to persuade Bishop George Murray to meet with me at the diocese's headquarters. I dressed in a suit for the meeting with Murray, who was as distinguished as one would expect an Episcopal bishop to be—tall, slender, with his hair tastefully graying at his temples. Bishop Murray agreed to use his good offices to set up a second meeting with Martin, Fred, and me that would include Sydney Smyer from the Board of Trade and a couple of other businesspeople.

Our first meeting was designed to show the local religious and business representatives that we did not sprout horns. I always made it a point to change out of my blue jean overalls into a business suit for these meetings—these were mature men of wealth and standing in their community and I was a thirty-one year-old preacher. In many ways these meetings were similar to my interaction as a young boy in New Orleans with the white men who sold the supplies and instruments essential to my father's dental practice. It was my responsibility to bring home the supplies my father had actually ordered. For a child, even checking the order without giving offense was an exercise in charm and tact, at a time when a white salesclerk might take offense at a black adult counting his change. I had had opportunities that segregation denied most people in Birmingham—black and white—and due to my upbringing in an interracial neighborhood and my years with the National Council of Churches I did not view white people as racial stereotypes. At Hartford Seminary, Camp Mack, and in church meetings around the country I had had overwhelmingly positive experiences with white Americans.

I did not view the white business leaders in Birmingham as bad people; they were people in a bad situation. My attitude was influenced by my understanding of Christianity and Gandhi, but there was also some of my father's quiet arrogance, that only a person of superior intellect and moral sensibility could negotiate under such circumstances. I was determined to be respectful and keep them always focused on the issues rather than give them any reason to form negative perceptions of me. We also did not want to draw the press's attention since the businessmen were anxious to avoid any public association with us.

The meeting went extremely well. We kept things very low-key, simply explained the dynamics of the movement, and suggested how issues pertaining to our demands in the manifesto might be resolved. There was no hostile lecturing or denunciation of us as troublemakers; Smyere and Murray seemed to be honestly trying to understand what our intentions were, and what they could expect from us in the near future. We wanted these community leaders to know that we did not consider them "the enemy." Our position was that the people in the room might not have created an unjust economic system, but that we were all—black and white alike—cooperating to maintain it. Our goal was to end the implicit collusion with injustice of which we were all guilty.

First, we discussed the theory behind the economic boycott: black citizens must be urged to stop spending their hard-earned money in stores where they could not get jobs or where they were required to submit to the humiliation of drinking at segregated water fountains or using "colored" toilets. We also informed them that our demonstrations would not only continue but escalate until, if need be, all of Birmingham became a jail. We made it clear that the fear of jail or even death could no longer keep us locked into a system that required us to accept a false inferiority, and in which white citizens enjoyed a superiority based solely on race. Once again, we spelled out our goals:

1. The desegregation of lunch counters, rest rooms, drinking fountains, and fitting rooms in all stores;
2. The hiring of blacks on a nondiscriminatory basis as clerks and cashiers, not just as maids and janitors, throughout the business community;
3. The dropping of all charges against every citizen arrested in nonviolent demonstrations;
4. The formation of a biracial committee to develop a strategy for school desegregation and for a continuing dialogue on racial conflicts and tensions.

A great deal of understanding grew out of these early meetings, and we established an important basis of trust. There was, however, no sense of urgency on the part of the white leaders to put an end to the demonstrations by agreeing to our goals, reasonable as they were. The white establishment was comfortable with the way things were in Birmingham and they were not going to change until we made them uncomfortable. It was not a test of reason or justice that we were being required to meet: it was a test of power.

We had not begun our discussions under any illusion that they would embrace our demands, but it was important to give them that opportunity and begin the demonstrations knowing that we had conveyed our purpose and our goals. But while we had not expected enthusiasm from the white community in Birmingham, we had hoped for more support from the black community in Birmingham as we began our sit-ins and other demonstrations. Fred Shuttlesworth had assured us that Birmingham was totally ready for a movement, but that was not the case. Birmingham was a dangerous town, and people rightly feared violent retaliation if they participated with us. Many adults working in the factories or for other white employers could lose their jobs if they were seen in a demonstration. We were able to recruit a few people to sit-in at the downtown stores, but participation in marches was thin and not many more than a dozen preachers gave Martin their full support. Many people seemed to take a wait-and-see attitude, standing on the sidelines to check out what would happen, expecting Martin Luther King to produce some kind of instant miracle.

After the first week, our economic boycott seemed to be going well enough, but the downtown merchants were acting as if they could afford to wait us out. In the white Birmingham community, in the national press, and even in many black Birmingham churches and other established black circles, our campaign was being described as forced, ill-timed, and unnecessary. Martin was portrayed by the city as an uninvited aggressor and an intruder into a "peaceful" Southern city attempting to undergo change according to its own pace and time-honored traditions—even though not one thing was being done, other than our campaign, to induce change. President John Kennedy and Attorney General Robert Kennedy well knew that our demonstrations were designed to bring about changes that had already been decreed by the federal courts, but we received no encouragement from them. The Kennedys had told Martin that the country was not ready for a civil rights bill. They didn't seem to understand that our actions in Birmingham would dramatize the need for such a bill.

While I now believe that Hoover's disinformation campaign was responsible for much of the Kennedys' initial coolness to the Birmingham movement, it was also certainly true that Kennedy was thinking like a politician. Kennedy needed Southern Democrats to enact his legislative agenda and he wasn't anxious to alienate them with a civil rights bill. Senator James Eastland's strategy was to oppose the civil rights bill on the grounds that it was communist-inspired. In a sense, President Kennedy and Attorney General Kennedy were caught between the movement on one hand and Hoover and Eastland on the other.

The Kennedys knew we were right, but as politicians with a white Southern constituency to protect, they wanted as narrow a bill as possible. SCLC's goal was to get as strong and broad a bill as possible. Our demonstrations were designed to dramatize the need for different provisions in the bill and we shifted demonstration sites around to show how broad employment discrimination was in the most ordinary positions. We took a group to a bank to ask for jobs, and no one in authority would even talk with us, so we knelt down inside the bank and prayed. The picture we were creating was of young black Americans praying for jobs in the financial sector.

Perhaps no one exemplified the absurdity of the practice of segregation in Birmingham more than Mr. A. J. Gaston, the owner of the motel that served as our base of operations. In addition to his hotel and restaurant, Mr. Gaston owned a funeral home, bank, insurance company, and a business school, which his wife ran. He was probably the richest black person in the state of Alabama. Gaston was in his seventies, small and bald; he always wore three-piece suits with a little watch chain. He was the very image of dignity and wealth, except for his brown skin. One morning we were holding our regular citizen education workshop at the Sixteenth Street Baptist Church. I asked the group, "What does segregation mean to you just in your everyday life?" Someone answered, "It's like having one arm tied behind your back. Everything is harder, you have to work harder to do anything, get anything, and you still don't get as much as the white guy." Someone else got excited. "Yeah, like I saw Mr. A. J. Gaston drive his big Chrysler car over to a Chinese restaurant, and he went to the back door, the stinking kitchen door! And he's the richest black man I ever heard of." Nothing could have better illustrated the injustice of segregation than the sight of a black millionaire forced to go to the back door of a Chinese restaurant in his own hometown.

Our demonstrations continued with a small, dedicated band of activists. The earliest volunteers for demonstrations in Birmingham were the elderly; a seventy-eight-year-old man led the very first demonstration. There was a wonderful older, church-oriented group that testified in our meetings each night: "We didn't have no opportunities when we was coming up, so we don't mind risking our lives for the grandchildren. What else we got to live for?" These wise elders had learned that belief in a cause worth dying for gave meaning and purpose to life. While the older people had perhaps come to accept the possibility of death, the children were simply without fear. In many ways the youth and the elderly were the two age groups in the black community that had the least to lose; they were the ones who were the most free, and, it turned out, they were the most willing to go to jail to become freer.

Each day began with a gathering at the Sixteenth Street Church. It was an old colonial-style church, but well maintained, with new carpeting down the aisles of the seven-hundred-seat sanctuary. Meetings were called for 9:00 A.M., but usually didn't get going until 10:00. Before the morning meeting, Wyatt Walker held background briefings with the press to explain what we were going to do and why.

It was important to us that the demonstrations be understood by the media, for the television networks allowed only two to three minutes on the evening news to tell the story, and we depended upon an accurate portrayal to get our message across. This was where my experience with CBS and *Look Up and Live* really came into play. At the Dorchester meeting, I had impressed upon Martin the importance of crafting a message that could be conveyed in just sixty seconds for the television cameras. Martin picked it up right away, reciting to me a favorite saying of Dr. Benjamin Mays, president of Morehouse College:

> *One tiny little minute*
> *just sixty seconds in it*
> *I can't refuse it*
> *I dare not abuse it*
> *It's up to me to use it.*

Chapel at Morehouse was compulsory, and Dr. Mays had recited that little poem at chapel almost every day. In fact, every time I heard Dr. Mays speak, he used that poem. So when I emphasized the need to have a message that we could convey in a matter of seconds, Martin would smile and say, "One tiny little minute, just sixty seconds in it."

That sixty seconds was what we were demonstrating for—that

sixty-second message to the world. We wanted people to know what was going on in the South, the reality of segregation. One important purpose of any nonviolent demonstration was to raise a particular injustice before the court of world opinion. But we didn't have a sixty-minute lecture or a fifteen- to twenty-minute sermon in which to do it. We had to craft a concise and dramatic message that could be explained in just sixty seconds. That was our media strategy.

Once the preliminaries were over and the demonstrators were checked to see if they had toothbrush, washcloth, and a small Bible for study, we would form a circle of prayer, sing "We Shall Overcome," and march out of the church by twos, down Fourth Avenue toward city hall, and on to jail. Each day a group was arrested within a few blocks of the church and Kelly Ingram Park.

I could not go to jail with them—my role was in organizational support and I had to adhere to it—but I found myself deeply moved each time I witnessed these individuals psychologically preparing themselves for the decision to go to jail. These were people who almost without exception had never believed they would face the possibility of imprisonment. They had to make the adjustment from thinking of jail as a place of shame to the idea of going to jail as a badge of pride and self-respect. For each individual there was a cost involved: a job that might be lost or seriously endangered, arguments with parents or loved ones. And yet these courageous people made the decision; we could not make it for them. Our movement was made up of thousands of individual personal decisions to overcome an inner doubt or crisis, each decision a story in itself as vital as the larger story. *Freedom* meant freedom from restraint—material or psychological—choosing to make a positive sacrifice for the betterment of self and of one's fellow man. In that sense, those who marched to jail, particularly the elderly, the seventy-year-old men and women, marched with the greatest dignity they had ever known.

With some important exceptions, most middle-aged or professional blacks were unwilling to risk their jobs by demonstrating, and we understood why—they were usually the sole breadwinners in their families. Schoolteachers were typical of this: though they had decent jobs, they depended on the white power structure to keep them. Workers from the Birmingham industries or mines would of course lose their jobs immediately if they became publicly identified with us. Black men in particular had reason to fear not just for their jobs but for their lives if they were identified as troublemakers. What we strove for, and what Martin continually preached to achieve, was the tacit support of those who felt they could not march. If they couldn't be with us on the lines, we felt that at least they had the responsibility not to actively oppose us.

Perhaps most hurtful to us was the resistance of the older, more traditional Birmingham ministers. After the SCLC convention in Birmingham, there was a vote among the black Baptist churches in Birmingham on whether or not Martin Luther King should start a movement there. The Baptist preachers as a group voted to oppose Martin's coming to Birmingham. Of the more than four hundred black churches in Birmingham, there were only fourteen that agreed to host the mass meetings that were our primary means of communicating with blacks in Birmingham. Part of the problem was that their established role as community elders was being challenged by a few younger, more militant, activist clergymen, and they saw us as part of that challenge. We were fortunate that by 1963 several younger ministers had recently accepted appointments in Birmingham churches, including Rev. A. D. King, Martin's younger brother; Bishop Linsey of the C.M.E. Church, whom I had met as a student at Lake Brownwood; Rev. John Porter at Sixth Avenue Baptist; Rev. Nelson Smith at New Pilgrim Baptist; and Rev. John Cross at Sixteenth Street Baptist. Martin sought immediately to construct a bridge between the movement and this new breed of clergy—and their courage and support made the Birmingham movement a beacon of hope for the world.

The clergy were crucial community leaders for several reasons. Most important, they were the only leaders whose livelihood was entirely dependent on other blacks. Ministers had an organized constituency—their congregations—and a place to meet—their churches. The congregations, especially the Baptist ones, were self-sustaining, and entirely independent of any external authority. No educated black person was less vulnerable to pressure from the white establishment than a black Baptist minister. The pastor had to answer only to his congregation and his God.

The movement's ties to the church were more than just practical, though. The movement used the Exodus story of the children of Israel and their escape from bondage to root our struggle for civil rights firmly in the African-American Christian experience. As Christians discovered in apartheid-era South Africa, a pastor could read directly from the Bible to make a point about freedom and justice. The books of Exodus and the prophets Isaiah and Amos are rich with such passages. The Bible provided ministers with the inspiration and strength to participate in the movement, as well as the language to communicate the movement to their people.

Our first sit-ins, at selected downtown stores, were easy to manage. The downtown commercial district was no more than a fifteen-minute walk from Sixteenth Street Baptist Church and Gaston's Motel. Both were located virtually at the center of the downtown black district in the same way Rampart Street was the center of downtown black New Orleans and Auburn Avenue the center of downtown black Atlanta.

The sit-ins were designed to work hand-in-hand with our boycotts of this downtown area. From the very beginning we spent considerable time organizing—even orchestrating—the image of our demonstrations. We intended them to tell a story, what Jim Bevel called "socio-dramas"; they were conscious efforts to dramatize the conditions and realities of segregation. The slogans we used were "Only food and medicine for Easter" and "Old clothes for Easter." We wore blue jeans to dramatize our solidarity with working people and our determination not to indulge in new clothing. Levi Strauss owes a lot to the movement, for it was this Birmingham campaign that introduced denims into college fashion. The blue jeans were a bold statement at a time when black college students wore pumps and nylons and shirts and ties to class and many ladies wore white gloves while shopping downtown. Everyday dress then was much more formal than it is today, so much so that Martin and Ralph tended to wear denim jackets to cover their shirtsleeves. One unintended side effect of this was that the denim was offensive to many middle-class blacks, who had worked hard to get out of the overalls of their sharecropping youth. It takes three or four generations of being middle class to feel secure enough to challenge the social order you have worked so hard to fit into. Martin and I were both third generation—we had had grandparents who were comfortable economically and well educated for their time. We had no anxiety about being returned to the fields, although Martin had spent a summer break from Morehouse picking tobacco in New England. We could readily dispense with the symbols of our middle-class status, because we took them for granted. For those whose suits, hats, and gloves were hard-won, adherence to the boycott constituted genuine sacrifice.

We ran a tight boycott. We leafleted the downtown area and monitored stores to gauge our effectiveness. If we saw blacks shopping in defiance of the boycott we did not harass them but asked them where they lived, in order to identify neighborhoods that had not been effectively leafleted. Blacks who were shopping always said, whether truthfully or not, "We don't know anything about any boycott."

When I came South with the Citizenship Program, it was my original intention to remain on the fringes of the movement. Now, I was part of the daily challenges of a major civil rights campaign. I saw my role as a behind-the-scenes catalyst. I ran from mass meetings, to press briefings with Wyatt, to negotiations, to strategy sessions with Martin and the lawyers, to workshops with Dorothy and Bevel, to demonstrations—only the wee hours of the morning were free for sleep and reflection. I realized that I was the only person with a holistic picture of what was actually happening, and I tried to keep Martin abreast of it all. I was operating on nervous energy and willpower. The intensity of the Birmingham campaign demanded the same concentration and focus as preaching without notes, except that a sermon lasts for thirty minutes and a movement was seldom resolved in even thirty days.

In the midst of all this Jean came to Birmingham to spend some time with me during her spring break. She left the girls with her cousin, Betty Lipscomb, a student nurse at Atlanta's Grady Hospital, and caught a ride with someone from SCLC. She wanted to feel more a part of what we were doing. Jean's family had always lived a philosophy of noncooperation with injustice. Unless there was no alternative, they spent money with black businesses only, even if it meant paying more. And within the confines of segregation, they had still insisted on their right to be treated with a certain level of courtesy. The first time Jean showed me around her hometown, she pointed out all the stores where her family refused to shop because her mother or father had been insulted there. So a boycott was second nature to her. The philosophy of the movement was something Jean had lived by all her life, and she wanted to be a part of the action for a change.

Jean was also lonely in Atlanta. She was lovely and vulnerable; this combination drew attention from men in the church, in SCLC, and others who knew that I was traveling a great deal. Mostly, the attention was in the form of help fixing things around the house or diagnosing problems with the car. I resolved in my own heart that I would not be jealous. My mother had always had male friends, so I had a model to follow. I knew that Jean was carrying a heavy burden with a job, a house, and three active children to care for all alone, and it would be unfair for me to resent the people who were part of the support system she was building for herself.

Jean stayed a few days and participated in some of the workshops, but I felt very uncomfortable with her there. I was still finding my own way with the staff at SCLC; my work demanded my full attention, and more. My days started early and ended late. The after-hours gatherings in Martin's room were where important decisions were made, conflicts aired, and bonds formed. If I missed those meetings, which went on until the early hours of the mornings, I was out of the loop. It was frustrating: if I went to the meetings I was neglecting Jean, but if I had dinner with Jean, I would miss the planning for the next day's demonstrations. I believed, rightly or wrongly, that as long as Jean was in Birmingham I had to be concerned primarily with her needs. She argued that I was being overly protective, that it wasn't necessary for me to be so continually concerned with her well-being. I felt pulled in two opposing directions, each requiring a different facet of my personality. With SCLC, I was hyperactive and dispassionate, emotionless; the work was so all-consuming; there were no predictable patterns and promises were difficult to keep. Jean came to Birmingham to be with me, and in part to reassure herself that my absences were genuinely the result of the demands of the movement and did not represent any lessening of my commitment to her and our daughters.

I was also concerned for her safety—events had proved Birmingham to be a very dangerous place. Jean argued that there were other women there—Dorothy Cotton, Diane Bevel, and Wyatt's secretary, Edwina Smith. But none of them went to jail in Birmingham, or even marched in the demonstrations. Edwina stayed in the office that we had set up in an insurance building across from the Gaston Motel. Diane, who had a new baby, and Dorothy were more involved in mass meetings and workshops than demonstrations. I had been brought up to respect women, and part of that respect was taking care for their safety. On the occasions that Dorothy or Diane did march, I stayed as far away from them as possible. I didn't trust myself not to fight to defend them if they were attacked. It was a struggle to retain my composure when my wife was being exposed to danger. I simply could not concentrate fully on what I had to do, day and night, while she was there. I could neither give Jean proper attention nor ignore her and allow her to participate in the movement as she liked. I was tense and distracted and I couldn't relax when we were together. After a few days of a mutually frustrating visit, Jean returned to Atlanta.

Shortly after our campaign began, the city of Birmingham sought and was successful in securing a state court injunction against demonstrations. The injunction was served on us at one o'clock in the morning at Gaston's on April 11, the day before Good Friday. Martin and our staff were determined that this injunction would not destroy the Birmingham campaign in the same way the federal injunction in Albany had stymied our efforts there.

Since we had been informed that the injunction was coming, Wyatt Walker alerted the press, and after it was served, we held a press conference in Gaston's restaurant. In his prepared statement upon receiving the injunction, Martin stated that we would not abide by it, for, "Alabama has made clear its determination to defy the law of the land. Most of its public officials, its legislative body and many of its law enforcement agents have openly defied the desegregation decision of the Supreme Court. We would feel morally and legally responsible to obey the injunction if the courts of Alabama applied equal justice to all its citizens."

We knew that further marches would result in certain imprisonment and probably even more public condemnation from those who hadn't wanted to see us there in the first place. The negative public attitude in Birmingham and the nation, the critical need for bail money, and the state court injunction set the stage for one of the great crises of the civil rights movement, and a critical juncture in Martin's leadership of it. Though he had denounced the injunction in his press statement, what we would actually do about it was the subject of an emergency meeting the next morning consisting of the SCLC staff and the local advisory committee in Martin's room, number 30, at the Gaston Motel.

Gaston's was just a small motel, even for the early sixties. The decor was tweed contemporary. The best suite in the motel was on par with an average room in a Holiday Inn. That morning about a dozen of us were squeezed into the living room area of Martin's suite. Some of us sat on the floor, others on the angular, brownish tweed sofa, others leaned against the wall. It was too warm and stuffy and some of the members of the local committee were smoking nervously. We were facing a difficult decision and our unity of purpose began to fray as various individuals argued from their own point of view.

Hundreds of our demonstrators had already been arrested in the first week of the boycott, and bail bonds had been set at higher and higher rates. One member of the local support committee said, "Martin, you've done all you can do here. Forget Birmingham for a while and go raise some money, so we can get these folk we've already sent to jail out." Another one agreed and said, "You can't put more of these people in jail now. We can't bail out the ones that are already in there and sending more people to jail is just out of the question." The local committee included prominent members of the black business community who were not only under tremendous pressure from whites already because of the demonstrations, but were entirely vulnerable to retaliation. The city of Birmingham could easily harass black businesses with taxes, permits, and inspections. The black businesspeople were dependent on suppliers, banks, landlords, and other businesses owned by whites. Their support for the movement required them to balance the possible future benefits against immediate negative consequences. And at this stage, they saw the chances of our eventual success dimming.

Fred Shuttlesworth spoke up, blaming the Kennedy administration. "I risked my life to get folk out to vote for that Jack Kennedy, and they act like they don't know nothing about us now. Where is the Justice Department? Where is Bobby Kennedy when we need him? They have just left us to the mercy of Bull Connor and George Wallace, to fend for ourselves!"

As for me, I was impatient with sitting around in a meeting arguing when I knew there was work to be done. I knew people were gathering at the church, waiting for instructions. We were committed to the movement and had devoted months to planning and preparing for it. I felt we could not leave Birmingham after only a few weeks. But I didn't feel I had yet earned the right to argue with movement leaders like Shuttlesworth, so I kept my own counsel in the meeting.

In this atmosphere of utter depression, Martin said very little. He lit a cigarette, and just listened, as I was coming to learn was his habit in high-pressure situations. I watched Martin's face, knowing that whatever the staff and the local committee advised, he would make his own decision as to whether he should abandon or drive forward with the effort in Birmingham. The arguments circled around the room, ricocheting like a marble in a pinball machine. Martin's countenance was sometimes placid, sometimes reflecting annoyance, and at some moments he looked as if he were far away from the stuffy room.

Abruptly, in the early afternoon, Martin rose and retired into the rear bedroom. As we continued discussing our options, I noticed Martin had been gone for quite a while. Ralph Abernathy must have noticed it too, because he also got up and went back to the rear bedroom. As other individuals became conscious of Martin's absence, the argument began to lose velocity, and the discussion in the front room finally slowed to a halt. Almost on cue, Martin and Ralph came out. I was surprised to see Martin had changed from his dark suit to denim jacket and jeans, our "work" uniform in Birmingham.

"There's no point in going on a speaking tour," he said. "We've already raised all the money we can right now. The only thing to do is for me to go to jail, and join those people already there. And stay there until people see what we're dealing with. Those who're going with me, get ready."

Martin knew that we could not afford to have our campaign interrupted at this crucial moment. Despite the crises—financial problems, morale problems, legal problems—his being jailed to dramatize the evils of Southern segregation was what must be done. The time had come for him to bear personal witness. I've never forgotten that day. Martin's decision to go to jail on Good Friday, 1963, made it possible for us to sustain both the Birmingham campaign and the movement throughout the South. But of course we didn't know that yet.

One of the key components of the Birmingham movement was our ability to use the Bill of Rights and the American tradition of an independent judiciary as part of the strategy to bring attention to the evils of segregation. The NAACP Legal Defense Fund (LDF), which under the leadership of Thurgood Marshall had won the *Brown* school desegregation case reversing the doctrine of separate but equal, contributed its innovative legal expertise. Norman Amaker and Leroy Clark, attorneys with LDF, had moved into Birmingham with us from the beginning. Martin had gone to meet with Thurgood Marshall and Jack Greenberg after the Dorchester meeting, and they had pledged LDF's support. It was the first time the LDF lawyers were on the scene of a movement full-time. Their style was such that they never discouraged us from anything. Their position was that they could not dictate the strategy of the movement but would be there to manage the legal ramifications of our decisions. Jack Greenberg, who succeeded Thurgood Marshall as LDF executive director, would say, "We'd like to discuss your plans with you, because there may be some things we can do to help you make your case," but he never tried to tell us what to do. Once Martin had decided to break the injunction, Norman and Leroy went to work drafting telegrams to the local law enforcement agencies and the FBI stating our intentions, telling them when and how we were going to march.

The telegrams explained that we were going to march on the sidewalk by twos, that we would stop for red lights, that we would not disrupt any traffic. It was our contention this was not a parade, and that therefore we did not need a permit. While we knew we would be arrested and convicted in Alabama courts, we were laying the foundation for a federal appeal. Martin determined the political strategy, and the LDF crafted a complementary legal strategy to minimize our exposure to legal sanctions. We were breaking the law because it was unjust, and we were willing to accept punishment, but we were not masochists. We wanted to minimize the punishment, wherever possible.

The march on that Good Friday did not last long. Martin, Ralph, and some fifty others, including several ministers, strode past Kelly Ingram Park, which was across the street from the Sixteenth Street Baptist Church, the headquarters for our nightly mass meetings. An unlikely setting for a confrontation, Kelly Ingram Park was the size of a city block, with huge hundred-year-old oak trees shading the crisscrossing walkways. It was a perfect setting for young couples promenading around the central fountain in their Easter finery, too picturesque for what was about to take place. As they drew near the park, Martin and the marchers were halted by a massive aggregation of police, who, expecting the march, had set up barricades just beyond the park. A huge crowd of black citizens gathered around the march, as news spread quickly through the black community that Dr. King himself would be leading a group that afternoon. I was among the people walking alongside, because I was not going to jail. With Martin in jail, a strong staff member would be needed to keep the movement going, and I was the logical choice. Soon, so many bystanders had gathered that it became difficult to tell who was in the march and who wasn't.

We were stunned by the aggressiveness of the police, who began to push and shove the marchers, including Martin, onto the paddy wagon. Wyatt, who wasn't supposed to be among those going to jail, protested the rough handling of Martin, and he too was thrown in the wagon. The crowd of bystanders became incensed, shouting, "Don't rough up Dr. King like that," screaming at the police, and cursing them. All of our confrontations with the Birmingham police had been tense little dramas: at a certain point no one knew what would happen. I tried to intervene, asking the police to pull back and allow the SCLC marshals to move the crowd back into the church. Ignoring my pleas, Connor ordered his police to go after the bystanders, and attempt to clear the park. Using nightsticks to jab people in the ribs, and with snarling and snapping dogs straining on their leashes, the police line advanced relentlessly on the demonstrators. The batons were impossible to avoid, and some marchers found themselves forced to walk backward with police and dogs steadily bearing down on them. Amid the confusion and terror, SCLC staff members tried to guide people into the Sixteenth Street Baptist Church. The potential for violence was heavy in the air; we had never seen the police so abusive and spoiling for a fight. People were streaming into the church, particularly women and children. Some of the boys and young men were still in the park, throwing rocks and cursing the police. Their resentment of the police invasion of what they considered "their" park was understandable, but at that stage of the confrontation we did not know what the police might do to quell their rage.

Before very long, the church was absolutely jammed full. Dorothy Cotton and I tried to calm the crowd. This proved to be extremely difficult, as people were seething about the roughness of the arrests, and the random violence of the police in the park. They wanted to retaliate, but didn't know how, and they were demanding that we *do* something. I was shaken by what had transpired, but I knew we had to reason with the people. If that crowd exploded out of the church there was a very good chance the police, in their ugly mood, might open fire. We couldn't let that happen, nor did we need people going home and returning to the park with the weapons we knew they owned; that would provide an excuse for Bull Connor to convert black Birmingham into a free-fire zone.

Dorothy, with her wonderful voice and knowledge of the freedom songs, began to lead the crowd in singing. "Oh Freedom, Oh Freedom, Oh Freedom over me. And before I'd be a slave, I'd be buried in my grave, and go home to my Lord and be free!" After several verses some of the intense energy had been redirected to what was happening inside the church, but to keep their attention now someone had to say something. The crowd in the church wanted to know what we were going to do, what they were supposed to do. As I looked around for someone to speak, I realized that everyone who usually spoke in such situations was either in jail or outside. Only Dorothy and I, among our staff, were in the church. So Dorothy turned to me and said, "You've got to say something to these folks, Andy."

I did not know what to say, but I could hear my father's voice again, telling me: "Keep control of yourself in a crisis and you can get through it." I entered the pulpit and spoke the first words that came to mind. "How many of you have ever been bitten by a dog?" I asked the people. About a third of the audience raised their hands. I raised my hand. Then I asked, "Raise your hands if you've ever been hit in the head with a baseball bat." A few men laughed and raised their hands. I raised mine again. "When you're bitten by a dog you can get a shot for rabies, and maybe a few stitches from the doctor. In a few days your scars will heal. Now, when I was hit by a baseball bat as a boy, I was dazed for a few minutes, but someone placed ice on the knot on my head, the swelling soon went down, and it wasn't long before I was itching to get back in the game. When I was first hit I thought I was dead. But, you see, we are hardheaded. We're hardheaded for the times when we get hit with a bat, times like now."

The crowd listened.

"But what happens if we let our fears get the best of us? How long does it take to remove the emotional, spiritual, and psychological fears brought about by racial prejudice and feelings of inferiority?" As I groped toward the ideas I wanted to express, I could feel a quiet coming over the church. "All we know is that for more than four centuries of slavery and segregation we have been the victims of social oppression, we've been treated as inferiors. We've watched our grandparents called 'Auntie' and 'Uncle.' Even at sixty they were still 'boy' and 'girl' to any teenager who might speak to them." Now I could hear a slight "A-men" coming from the people. "And we can't get a rabies shot from the doctor to cure the sickness and hurt of being treated as inferior. There's no way we can put ice on those scars and make them heal.

"We have to learn," I continued, "that the damage to us is so great, if we're going to heal centuries of racial sickness in America we have to be willing to risk whatever physical injury our oppressors subject us to. Police brutality is just part of an old story we know too well, and that's the obvious part of it. We've been hurt even more seriously in unspoken and subtle ways. Dr. King says, 'We've got to force the racial sickness of America out into the open so that the healing light of truth can shine on the cancer of racism.'" I felt the crowd was with me. "We want to make our case before the entire world. We want the Court of World Opinion to ask America if she can allow the abuse and humiliation of her people to continue while she presents herself to the world as the land of the free." I could hear many "A-men"s now.

"We have no choice as to whether we will die. We all will die. But we can decide that dying in the cause of freedom for our families, our friends, in the cause of justice, is preferable to dying in an automobile accident, or from cancer or alcoholism, or getting stabbed to death by a friend or girlfriend because of the violence, hostility, and aggression built up in us because we've been treated as inferiors. Dr. King says, 'A man who has not found something he is willing to die for has not found something he is willing to live for.' We want you to believe in that, and to support our movement, not for us, nor for Dr. King, but for your own interests, your own families.

"It is important for us to win this fight, but we must win it by elevating our white brothers and sisters to a new moral level. We cannot win if we sink to their level. They are relying on dogs and batons as instruments of violence. If we throw rocks and curse them, they will have succeeded in dragging us down to their level, and once we are on their level of violence, any violent act will be acceptable and approved. But if we refuse to be dragged down to their level of violence, then the moral victory will be accorded us on our own terms. They can always find more weapons of violence, but what happens if we force them to match our moral courage? They will either find new moral strength and begin to respond to us as brothers, or they will be defeated by our superior moral power.

"I know this is different than anything you've ever been taught, but we must admit that we cannot win a violent struggle; for their resources, from police to state troopers to national guard and even the U.S. Army, are violent powers that we can never defeat. But when it comes to love, to understanding, yes, even to suffering in a just cause, we cannot lose.

"We suffer in silence usually, but we suffer! The violence is internalized and we hate ourselves and our loved ones. But now we know that we are not to blame. This system of segregation imposes its violence upon us. We are not fighting white people, we are fighting the system of segregation. We could kill white people in Birmingham, but the system of segregation would prevail and maybe even be strengthened. But if we dare to love all people, even white people who fear us, what happens? Perhaps we can put an end to the system which is hurting us both—black and white.

"Frederick Douglass said almost a hundred years ago that the struggle for freedom is a struggle to save black men's bodies and white men's souls. Let's give it a try. You're not going to kill anyone today. You didn't hurt anyone yesterday and you probably won't hurt anyone tomorrow, but we are organizing nonviolently to change Birmingham. Give us a chance. Help us if you can, but please don't hurt us. The way you can hurt us is by trying to match violence with violence. By throwing rocks, cursing police officers and other retaliatory behavior. You can help us by 'being cool.' Don't let them make you fear, and don't let them make you hate. If you love, 'Perfect love casts out fear,' the Bible says, and if you are not afraid you will have no need to hate—white people, black people; nobody."

I asked them to leave the church peacefully, with dedication to the long struggle ahead. Our battle was not with the police, I reminded them, but with the leaders of Birmingham who continued

to oppress our people. I asked them to return that night to the Sixteenth Street Baptist Church for our meeting, and join our movement. Then Dorothy lifted her voice and led us into singing and clapping. "Ain't gonna let nobody turn me around, turn me 'round, turn
me 'round, ain't gonna let nobody turn me 'round, gonna keep on a-
talkin', keep on a-walkin', walking up to freedom's land."

It had been a long day, but there was much more to do. I was
running on pure adrenaline, with no time to eat or sleep. I wanted to
make sure Martin, Ralph, and those arrested with them were well. I
needed to make preparations for the mass meeting at the church that
evening, plan the strategy for demonstrations the next day, explain to
the news media our rationale for defying the court order, check on
the news reports to see what the national reaction was, and call Jean
in Atlanta to tell her I was okay and something about what had
taken place, as I knew she was concerned. Fortunately, by that time,
Wyatt had gotten out of jail by paying his ridiculously high bond.
One of the tactics used by the city of Birmingham was to set the bond
at one thousand dollars or more for each marcher. This was an
incredibly high bond for what was essentially jaywalking. Martin led
the marchers along the sidewalk and stopped for red lights, still they
were arrested for parading without a permit and their bonds set as if
it were first-degree murder. Wyatt and I conferred with the LDF
lawyers about the upcoming bail hearings. Eventually, we would need
to get these people out of jail, and as intended, the bonds were draining our coffers.

When Martin, Ralph, and the other ministers were brought to
the jail, Martin and Ralph were separated, and Martin was placed in
an isolation cell. No one was allowed to see him for a day or so, not
even our attorney, Norman Amaker. Martin was not allowed to make
a telephone call to Coretta, who had just given birth to their fourth
child, Bernice Albertine. Wyatt Walker attempted to get help from the
Justice Department but none was forthcoming. A *New York Times*
story that weekend quoted a Justice Department aide as saying, "Dr.
King's refusal to abide by the injunction against demonstrations has
further complicated the federal government's position. We believe in
the necessity of obeying court orders." When Wyatt Walker was
finally able to see Martin, he was in a very irritable mood as a result
of his isolation. He despised the fear that arose in him when he was
alone in any jail, and this was Bull Connor's jail. Martin snapped,
"You must resume demonstrations immediately. Don't let the local
support committee stop you. We have got to keep the pressure on
Birmingham." Wyatt tried to explain about the packed mass meeting,

the activities for the next day, the briefings with the press, the out-pouring of support. Martin replied churlishly, "But we don't see any-thing." Martin did not like being in jail, it was a cross he had agreed to bear, but it made him very moody and difficult to handle. He put tremendous pressure on Wyatt to maximize the impact and signifi-cance of his time in jail. Wyatt, in turn, came from these meetings with Martin pumped up and giving orders.

Wyatt was really in a no-win situation. He was under pressure from Martin, but when he came from the jail barking out instruc-tions, people resented it, especially Jim Bevel. Bevel told Wyatt, "You cannot order me to give my life. This is a movement, not a military operation." Wyatt considered this insubordination and later insisted that Martin fire Bevel. Bevel pleaded with Martin, "I can take orders from you, but Wyatt is just an unprincipled motherfucker." Martin refused to fire Bevel, and that left Wyatt feeling that Martin had given him responsibility without the authority necessary to carry it out.

The trouble was, Wyatt and Bevel proceeded from diametrically opposite organizational philosophies. Wyatt's view was hierarchical and authoritarian, in the tradition of Baptist preachers, and he felt himself totally responsible for the performance of SCLC staff mem-bers. Bevel was deeply steeped in Gandhian philosophy and he believed that in a movement where any act could cost a person his or her life, no one was entitled to give orders. I had few problems with Wyatt, because the grant I administered was outside of the line of authority which he scrupulously observed, so I tried to mediate the relationship with Wyatt and Bevel and ease their differences. There was little enough to attract talented, committed people to the move-ment and I believed we needed everybody we could get.

Despite Martin's impatience, the situation was already changing for the better. The news and images of the Good Friday arrests were sinking in. Photographs of Martin and Ralph being hustled off to jail were shown on television and published all over the world. The reac-tion was tremendous. For the first time we were receiving indications that the Birmingham campaign was being taken seriously. It was not long before we began receiving pledges of support from all over.

That same weekend singer Harry Belafonte, a committed sup-porter of our cause and a close friend, was hard at work in New York securing new funds to replenish the critically short bail money. By Monday, Harry reported he had raised fifty thousand dollars and that more would be forthcoming. To us this sounded like a miracle. Belafonte's effort was of psychological and strategic value also: it disproved the argument made by the local support committee that money could not be raised without Martin.

Easter Sunday dawned with Martin in jail and the moral power of his act of personal sacrifice dramatizing our struggle and its importance to all of black Birmingham. To take advantage of this enthusiasm, to sustain our momentum, and to show strong, visible and audible support to the people jailed, we planned a march from New Pilgrim Baptist Church to the city jail for the afternoon of Easter Sunday.

Throughout the morning service at New Pilgrim, whose pastor, Rev. Nelson Smith, was in jail, a tremendous crowd was building outside. By the time church ended some five thousand people had gathered, waiting for the march to begin. The people were all local Birmingham folk, many of them solid church people who probably never thought they would participate in a civil rights demonstration. They were dressed in their best Sunday clothes, which, due to the boycott, were last year's Easter outfits. Many of them had come over from other churches after their own Easter services were over.

We marched from New Pilgrim until we arrived at a point about two blocks from the jail, where the police had set up barricades to block us. They were out in full force, Bull Connor barking orders with his foghorn voice. Fire trucks blocked the street, and the firemen were ready with hoses. Water hoses might have seemed to the kids like playing in a powerful sprinkler, but being blasted by high pressure hoses was extremely painful and not at all funny to the adult church folk.

As we approached the barricades, marching slowly right up to them, Bull Connor shouted at us: "Y'all have to disperse this crowd. Turn this group around." But there were five thousand people behind us, and up ahead, two blocks away, were our people in jail who were surely watching what was happening from their tiny cell windows.

Wyatt Walker and I were leading the march. I can't say we knew what to do. I know I didn't want to turn the march around, whatever the consequences. So, to get myself together and as a holding action, I asked the people to get down on their knees and offer a prayer. The entire group dropped to their knees and began to pray. They were praying an old-fashioned kind of long-meter moan, mixed with singing. A couple of sisters began praying very loudly. While this was going on, Wyatt and I walked ahead to the barricades and tried to reason with Bull Connor. He stood there, looking like he was standing on the sidelines at a football game and revealing less emotion than Tom Landry with a secure play-off berth. We told him we simply wanted to march to the jail, sing a few songs and have a word of prayer, then march back to New Pilgrim. We were almost pleading our case with him.

Suddenly, Rev. Charles Billups, one of the most faithful and fearless leaders of the old ACMHR, jumped up and hollered: "The Lord is with this movement! Off your knees. We're going on to the jail!" And everybody in the front rows—they had been praying now for about five minutes—got up and started walking right toward the barricades and the amassed police. Stunned at first, Bull Connor yelled, "Stop 'em, stop 'em!" But none of the police moved a muscle. I've never seen anything like it before or since: they all just stood there watching us as if they were transfixed. Even the police dogs that had been growling and straining at their leashes when we first marched up were now perfectly calm. The firemen just stood there, holding their hoses. We were walking right past them and Bull Connor was yelling, "Turn on the hoses, turn on the hoses!" But the firemen didn't move either. I saw one fireman, tears in his eyes, just let the hose drop at his feet. Our people marched right between the red fire trucks, singing, "I want Jesus to walk with me." They were not rushing; it was a very slow, serious march. They just marched on to the park across from the jail, where we convened to sing to the people in jail.

Bull Connor stood there cussing and fussing. All of his resources had failed him. His policemen had refused to arrest us, his firemen had refused to hose us, and his dogs had refused to bite us. It was quite a moment to witness: I'll never forget one old woman who became ecstatic when she marched through the barricades. As she passed through, she shouted, "Great God Almighty done parted the Red Sea one mo' time!"

On Good Friday, when Martin went to jail, the white clergy of Birmingham issued a statement in the *Birmingham News* strongly condemning Martin and SCLC for the "ill-timing" of our campaign, and for not allowing the new city administration enough time to act; then they called for an end to the demonstrations. The same eight prominent white Birmingham clergymen (Protestant, Jewish, and Catholic) had taken out an advertisement in the *Birmingham News* in January calling for moderation in dealing with Birmingham's racial situation.

Martin was especially hurt by this attack because it came from clergymen. From his cell, the week after Easter, he began writing the reply, which would become his famous "Letter from a Birmingham Jail." He wrote in the margins of newspapers, and on the back of legal papers and slipped us the text bit by bit. Willie Pearl Mackey, one of the secretaries who typed it, had a terrible time reading Martin's handwriting. Most of the letter was brought in installments delivered from the jail by our attorneys, Clarence Jones, Ozell Billingsley, and Arthur Shores, during their trips to jail to visit Martin. I saw it arriving piece by piece, and read each installment eagerly, because I understood that in this document Martin was providing a comprehensive, far-ranging answer to all the objections to our campaign. He was also articulating the religious basis for the nonviolent protest movement in Christian theology. We had trained our demonstrators to maintain a certain discipline during their time in jail, but now Martin set the example. It always moved me to think about what Martin was able to create out of what most people would consider a painful period of deprivation.

Martin's letter answered the charge of "ill-timing" by reminding our critics that blacks had waited more than three hundred years for justice in America; we could afford to wait no longer. We must become protagonists, he said, and the new Birmingham administration "must be prodded." He answered charges that he was an "outsider" by citing biblical precedent for the mission of concerned outsiders. He then addressed the state court injunction against us: "There are two types of laws," he wrote, "just and unjust. One has a moral responsibility to disobey unjust laws." He went on to define an unjust law as "a human law that is not rooted in eternal law and natural law. All segregation statutes are unjust because segregation distorts the soul and damages the personality."

He pointed out the value of the societal tension created by our demonstrations. "Actually, we who engage in nonviolent direct action are not the creators of tension," he wrote. "We merely bring to the surface the hidden tension that is already alive. We bring it out in the open, where it can be seen and dealt with."

Finally, he concluded with a statement of our aims that in my opinion was the most poetic and profound of his career: "For more than two centuries our foreparents labored in this country without wages; they made cotton king; they built the houses of their masters while suffering gross injustices and shameful humiliation and out of a bottomless vitality they continued to thrive and develop. If the inexpressible cruelties of slavery could not stop us, the opposition we now face will surely fail. We will win our freedom because the sacred heritage of our nation and eternal will of God are embodied in our echoing demands."

When we typed and distributed Martin's reply as an open letter, it did not make an instantaneous impact, but its long-range reverberations were enormous. Within a few weeks, thousands of copies had been printed by the American Friends Service Committee and distributed around the country. The letter was published in national journals and in Europe, and was widely quoted from as a testament of the philosophical rationale behind the civil rights movement. More than any other written document or statement, Martin's letter helped to lay a strong moral and intellectual basis not only for our struggle in Birmingham, but for all subsequent movement campaigns in the South. It has become a classic in American literature.

Martin's arrest put the Birmingham movement in the headlines of the national news, and that in turn aided our efforts to organize locally. It was not easy to communicate effectively with the entire black community in Birmingham. We had found that the black radio stations would not give us any play; they were all white-owned. They would run announcements of mass meetings, but none of us were ever invited on the air for interviews to explain our positions, not even Martin. The Birmingham newspapers tried their best to ignore us, to act as if nothing of any importance was happening. Mass meetings and leaflets were our primary tools to spread the word about the boycott and invite people to join the movement. In addition, *Jet*, the national black weekly magazine, and its publisher John Johnson were a great boon to us. *Jet* was read in homes and barber and beauty shops that we might not otherwise reach. Fortunately, after the Good Friday arrests, there was a tremendous surge in national press and television coverage of the Birmingham campaign. Three minutes of television time each night on the three networks was worth an awful lot. In 1963, a minute of advertisement on the six o'clock news was selling for one hundred thousand dollars, so we were well aware that each night we were receiving close to a million dollars' worth of prime TV exposure. Accordingly, we attempted to plan our demonstrations so that a distinct message was conveyed each day, first to the people of Birmingham, then to the nation.

As the television networks continued to come to Birmingham, reporters began to ask for me by name. It turned out that my friend Al Cox, who was with CBS, had told colleagues from CBS and other news departments to look me up when they went down to Alabama. That gave me some credibility with the news crews, who didn't have a lot of experience covering blacks. By the same token, if someone mentioned Al Cox's name, I gave them some extra attention, figuring that they were likely to be sympathetic to what we were doing.

We maintained an attitude of openness with the press, as we did with the FBI and local authorities. Wyatt, who had a very good relationship with the press, carried primary responsibility for relating to them. He continued to hold press briefings at nine every morning, where he would give background on the planned marches or sit-ins for the day, answer questions, and explain the reasoning behind our actions. Wyatt was aware of the various deadlines for print, radio, and television journalists, and he made every effort to accommodate those deadlines and help reporters do their job. In those days, there were no mobile satellite hookups, and network camera crews had to take film to the airport by two o'clock at the latest to be sent to New York for processing for the nightly news. As a result, we timed our demonstrations to end by noon. Anticipating the needs of the press helped us to get our message out to the nation.

We provided the same advance information to the police and the Justice Department. On advice of NAACP Legal Defense Fund attorneys, we wired our intentions with respect to demonstrations to the Justice Department and we informed the local police, as well. This served to document that we were engaging in a deliberate violation of a law that violated our rights as citizens under the U.S. Constitution. In addition, our mass meetings and workshops were public events and we made no effort to screen for suspected police informants. We assumed they were present and we had nothing to hide.

Meanwhile, our work with the high school students had been so productive we were ready to move full speed ahead. The tremendous national attention the Good Friday arrests received had caused a flock of supporters, many of them celebrities, to flood into Gaston Motel during the week following Easter. There wasn't anything in particular for them to do once they got there, but they wanted to witness the history that was occurring—Gaston's Motel in Birmingham had become the place to be in the South for both black and white supporters of the civil rights movement.

Birmingham teenagers were in turn drawn to the magnetism and excitement generated by the celebrities who came, including Dick Gregory, Joe Louis, Al Hibbler, and Harry Belafonte. Al Hibbler, the great blind singer, was a native of Alabama and the first well-known artist to volunteer to participate in a downtown demonstration. When his group was being arrested, the police ignored him, but Bull Connor saw Hibbler standing there and yelled, "Hey, wait a minute! Don't forget that blind nigger over there."

While the direct-action demonstrations and sit-ins were effective primarily in dramatizing our cause outside of Birmingham, the economic boycott was what finally brought the campaign home to the local seats of power. Ultimately, any meaningful change was in their hands. The downtown boycott was almost totally effective. For nearly two months, black citizens had purchased very little but food and medicine. The lack of retail sales during the Easter season was visibly hurting our targeted stores, just as we had hoped.

The lesson of the power of the pocketbook had been indelibly impressed upon me when I was very young through a story told in my family, which I learned to understand more fully as I grew older. My grandfather Frank Young was a successful businessman in Franklin, Louisiana. At one point he came under harassment from the local sheriff because he wanted to keep his business open on Sunday. His white competitors were open on Sunday, but the sheriff told my grandfather he would not be allowed that privilege. No matter what my grandfather said to the sheriff, he could do nothing to change the situation. My grandfather became so discouraged he decided to close his business and move to New Orleans, where he thought he would have a better chance of succeeding.

However, as it happened, Frank Young was also the state treasurer for several influential black Masonic and fraternal organizations, and their funds were deposited in Franklin banks. When he went down to these banks and informed the officers that he wanted to withdraw all his accounts because he had decided to move to New Orleans, the bank officers were stunned—these statewide accounts were quite substantial. When one officer asked my grandfather why he was moving, my grandfather told him about the sheriff's harassment, and said he wasn't going to take it anymore. "Just give us a few days, Mr. Young, maybe we can do something about that," the bank officer quickly replied. They did, and from then on my grandfather never had any trouble from the sheriff. The banks controlled the town, and when it was in their economic interest to control the police, they did so. The strength of this point had only been reinforced for me when we were threatened by the Klan in Thomasville.

In Birmingham, blacks spent a lot of money downtown, but once again, the businessmen didn't seem to appreciate just how much until their black patronage was withdrawn from them. Until the impact of their Easter season losses was felt, they seemed to have little or no understanding of what was going on, and the local political leaders and the Birmingham press only reinforced their ignorance.

It was now three weeks into the campaign, and my days were a blur. Each day I began with workshops in the morning at the different churches. I would then monitor the demonstrations and their aftermath, and run by the jail. In the early evenings I'd come back to the Gaston Motel to shower and change into a suit for talks with our liaisons to the white business community, the Birmingham Board of Trade. I received a lot of teasing for this. When I came out in my suit, James Orange, a new recruit, and Fred Shuttlesworth would tease, "Andy's going to 'Tom.'" And everybody would laugh. I'd respond, "Any of you all are welcome to go with me, come on." But going to negotiate with white folks was not their idea of a good time. Negotiating was one job at SCLC for which there was no competition. Ultimately, our challenge to desegregate Birmingham would have to be resolved face-to-face in discussion with someone in a position of power to make a decision, but Bevel and others dismissed that. Bevel was single-minded about our campaign and not really interested in publicity or public recognition, but he felt that the power for change lay with the masses of people in the black community. He invested himself in his direct relationships with the people. I agreed with that, but my notion of "people" included not just the black masses but the people who controlled the Birmingham economy. The boycott was designed to pressure the business community to reach a settlement, but someone had to talk with them to elicit that settlement. It was actually easier to impact the business community than the elected officials in the government, who were secure unless we persuaded more than fifty percent of the registered voters to turn them out. The business community, on the other hand, had a ninety-day judgment period. They had to turn over goods every ninety days—and we were probably cutting into fifteen to twenty percent of their profits with our boycott. Because I felt the business community had the most power to respond to us to bring about change, I thought it was worth spending time with them.

The first day I went to Birmingham, I was trying to figure out how to get out. I saw the negotiations with the business community as the quickest way for us to achieve our goals and get out of Birmingham. I didn't like demonstrations. I didn't like to see people hurt, and I didn't want to be hurt either. I never let myself forget the danger that was all around us. I thought it was smart to be cautious, and I was not seeking martyrdom. Negotiations were not necessarily safer than demonstrations, though. When everybody else went to march, they were in groups and the press was always there, watching. When I went downtown for negotiations, I was mostly by myself, walking down the same streets where folks had been beaten up just a few hours before and where the same policemen who knew me as an SCLC staff person were patrolling the streets. I used to pray I wouldn't be set up by the Klan for a hit and run. I would vary my route as I walked the five blocks to evening meetings and avoided establishing any kind of pattern. I was trying to do a job and I wanted to avoid unnecessary risks. My primary responsibility with SCLC had been to train people to read and write so that they could register to vote: the negotiations, press work, and demonstrations were really extra. Of course, they turned out to be the most important things I did. But while I knew the demonstrations were essential, I didn't have to like them.

After the meetings with the business community, the SCLC staff would get together at Gaston's Motel to go over the day's activities. Wyatt convened these sessions as enough of us straggled in from the mass meetings and other gatherings. He would have some food brought up—it was usually my only meal of the day and too heavy for so late at night. I'd chew on a few ribs and mostly eat the greens. The food we ate in Birmingham really made me long for some New Orleans red beans or a sandwich of fried oysters on a loaf of French bread.

The intense media attention combined with the effective economic boycott began to put a lot of pressure on the power structure in Birmingham. While Martin was in jail, I had continued my meetings with Sydney Smyer and Bishop Murray, but they offered no counterproposals for the desegregation of Birmingham. We were caught by surprise when someone posted bail for Martin and Ralph on Saturday, April 20, after they had been in jail for eight days. We didn't want Martin out of jail because jail in the South was always perceived as dangerous and his imprisonment was focusing the world's attention on Birmingham. "Letter from a Birmingham Jail" had begun to catch on and was being read around the world. That Martin was willing to accept punishment for defying an unjust arrest placed us in a morally powerful position, and to bond him out would be to admit there was a legitimate purpose for the arrest. If the international attention had compelled the Alabama courts to release Martin voluntarily, it would have been an admission that Martin's arrest was wrong.

But, rather than seek a real settlement, leaders in the white business community had begun a full court press on members of the black middle class with whom whites had direct contact. Black businesspeople were in a precarious position; most wanted us to succeed, but at the same time they were vulnerable to pressure from white-owned suppliers and banks. I have always believed that it was A. J. Gaston himself who put up Martin's bond to persuade him to stop the demonstrations and leave Birmingham. A. J. Gaston was an

Uncle Tom in the best sense; he milked the system of segregation for millions of dollars. He owned a business school that trained most of the black typists and secretaries in Birmingham, had the largest undertaking establishment in the black community, and owned a bank and a motel. But Gaston couldn't sustain these enterprises without cooperation from the white establishment: suppliers could delay his deliveries; government inspectors could find violations of state codes in his service businesses; local banks could refuse to honor his credit. Gaston took the system as he found it and made it work for him and, it must be said, for us as well. It would have been much harder to run a movement in Birmingham without Gaston's motel and his restaurant. Gaston was a master at survival; he made money on segregation, and he made money during the movement—not one of us ever stayed a night free in Gaston's Motel. Notwithstanding his possible role in Martin's untimely release from jail, A. J Gaston played an important part in supporting the Birmingham movement.

Of course, no one could have persuaded Martin to leave Birmingham at that point. We planned to step up demonstrations and intensify the pressure, but despite the growing excitement and support for the movement we had to delay further protests to respond to a court injunction. Beginning on Monday, April 22, we were required to attend a daily court session at the Jefferson County Courthouse on the contempt proceedings brought by the city under the injunction of April 11. The trial, held before Judge William A. Jenkins of the Tenth Judicial Circuit, provided a lull in the storm of escalating events. Each morning during the week of April 22 we walked the three short blocks from Gaston's to the courthouse with our attorneys, Jack Greenberg, Constance Baker Motley, Norman Amaker, and Leroy Clark of LDF, and Arthur Shores and Ozell Billingsley of Birmingham. (I was named in the contempt proceedings, along with Ralph, Wyatt, Fred Shuttlesworth, A. D. King, and Bevel.) As part of our legal strategy, our attorneys instituted a counteraction in the federal courts to restrain the city from depriving us of our rights to peacefully march and demonstrate.

Our key concern during the trial was whether Martin and our other leaders would be found guilty of civil and criminal contempt. If Martin were found guilty of civil contempt, there was a good chance he might be jailed immediately upon sentencing, and held in jail until he "purged" himself of contempt. It was an interesting legal question with potentially heavy ramifications. However, either the city attorneys or Judge Jenkins—someone in a position of some power—realized they hardly wanted to create the spectacle before the world of holding Martin Luther King in jail indefinitely until he "purged" himself of his beliefs; certainly not after the circulation of "Letter from a Birmingham Jail." So on Friday, April 26, Judge Jenkins dropped the civil contempt charges, found each of us guilty of criminal contempt, and sentenced us to a jail term of five days and a fine of fifty dollars each, the maximum. Martin, Ralph, Wyatt, and A. D. actually had to return to Birmingham in October 1967, more than four years later, to serve four days in jail on this case, which we eventually lost in the U.S. Supreme Court. The charges against me were dropped by the Alabama Supreme Court in their appeal decision, which affirmed the other convictions.

Each day, while we were in court, the gatherings in the courtyard and restaurant of the L-shaped, two-storied motel increased. Gaston's was beginning to resemble Grand Central Station at rush hour. The motel bubbled with activity and discussions on a twenty-four-hour basis. It had become the site of a national meeting and greeting convention, an ongoing debating society on the pertinent questions of the movement, a place where supporters might meet or see or talk with Martin if he was available, a continuing educational seminar on the movement conducted by Wyatt for visiting reporters and supporters, and a magnet for the curious and for celebrity hounds.

The activity reached its peak each night when we held our mass meetings, usually at the Sixteenth Street Church. The church was packed to the rafters and filled with an electric excitement. The "old folks" arrived early to begin an old-fashioned prayer meeting. Their long, slow dirges conjured up powers derived from the slave religions. It was a calling forth of the spirit—the Holy Spirit—and while the words were English, the moan and meter was African.

The dirges gained power as they were interspersed with prayers from kneeling elders, who gave poetic utterance to their sins and sufferings and pleaded for God's forgiveness and deliverance: "You delivered Daniel from the lion's den, Jonah from the belly of the whale, the Hebrew children from the fiery furnace, so why not everyman?" The imagery of triumph over suffering was pure Old Testament. The God of Abraham, Isaac, and Jacob had found new children who placed their trust in his power of deliverance.

After an hour or more of the "old folks" prayers, the young people would begin streaming in, the men often still in their work clothes. The blue denim overalls were now all that the men wore, a proud symbol of the new freedom that was sweeping Birmingham.

The young adults then took over the service and began with the syncopated rhythms of a jazz-gospel organ. Some of the same songs of faith were now given a modern melodic treatment. Carlton Reese, a prominent church organist, organized the Alabama Christian Movement Choir, which performed at almost all of our mass meetings. The choir specialized in freedom songs, adaptations of old church songs like "I'm on My Way," "Lord, I'm Runnin', Trying to Make a Hundred, 99½ Won't Do," "Woke Up This Morning with My Mind on Freedom," and Reese's own "Marching on to Freedom Land." The up-tempo music brought a new vitality and power to the service of worship, praise, and mobilization for redemption:

> *Woke up this morning with my mind*
> *staaaaaaaaayed on freedom*
> *Hallelu, Hallelu, Halleluia*
> *Walkin' and talkin' with my mind*
> *stayed on freedom . . .*
> *It ain't no harm to keep your mind*
> *staaaaaaaaayed on freedom.*

Ours was an evangelical freedom movement that identified salvation with not just one's personal relationship with God, but a new relationship between people black and white. The fruit of this salvation was seen as personal as well as political liberation from the particular snare of the devil of racism. These songs, so powerful in their ability to inspire the marchers with the courage to face Bull Connor and his men, were very important in helping us keep the movement strong, dignified, and centered on our goal of nonviolent resistance, of maintaining the high road. It was a beautiful example of the power of music to fill people with God's strength.

By eight o'clock the tone had been properly set in prayer and song, and the speaking began. First the formalities of reports and evaluation of the progress of the movement. Then announcement of future meetings and training sessions for demonstrations, and finally, a report from the leadership in jail. This was the business of the movement. Costs and plans were all openly discussed, in spite of the fact that we knew our meetings were being taped.

Powerful folk oratory was necessary to preach people out of their fears, and it continued with speeches by one local leader after another as they rose to commit themselves to the struggle and urge others to observe the boycott, march in demonstrations, register to vote, and go to jail in the interest of their own freedom and that of their children.

Fred Shuttlesworth gave his thanks in fiery, determined, dynamic style; no fancy theology for him. He was a people's minister, tough and straightforward. Bevel presented a singular presence with his shaved head, high, ringing voice, tight dark skin, and an air of the possessed. He spoke about the mission of the days ahead, teaching in almost mystical Gandhian terms and in black folk language. Abernathy followed with his language full of images and rhythms that were very familiar in Birmingham—at his best he was a traditional Baptist preacher at one with this audience. Then Ralph would introduce Martin, always our last, or "altar call" speaker. Martin was invariably able to pull together everything that had been said, and to put our movement, and our trials in Birmingham, into its proper context as a world movement. He did this in strong biblical metaphors, drawing upon his scholarship and sophisticated knowledge. Martin had the ability to make us feel as if we were more than our daily selves, more than we had been—a part of a beautiful and glorious vision that was enabling us to transcend ourselves. It was a marvelous quality he had, not ever fully captured on the printed page or in recordings, to lift the people to another place so that they could almost feel themselves moving.

After Martin concluded to tumultuous applause, he would call for those who were there to join workshops and demonstrations the next day. Then we would all rise, join hands, and sing "We Shall Overcome." Sometimes while we were singing "We Shall Overcome" I would sneak a glance at the rear of the church to see if the Alabama police investigators and the observer from the White Citizens Council were singing with us. They never were. In Alabama the police were welcome to sit in on all of our mass meetings, and every night they dutifully came, sitting or standing at the rear of the church, talking to no one. They displayed no emotion, and I always wondered what their private thoughts were—about us, about what we were doing and what they were doing. When it came time to sing "We Shall Overcome" they usually slipped out into the night.

After the mass meetings, our staff would return to Martin's room at Gaston's for a time of fellowship. It was in these late-night meetings that the real decisions and directions of the campaign were determined. And, of course, there was food—Martin loved to eat— fried chicken or barbecued ribs, or both. I learned to love the ribs: there was something about the elemental act of chewing on bones that brought one back to basics and seemed to encourage honest searching among the staff, discouraging the usual ego battles or jockeying for favor with Martin. It's hard to put on airs when you're in the middle of eating a messy slab of ribs!

During the daytime meetings Martin always listened quietly and reflectively, but at night he came alive and dominated the gatherings with a mixture of playful preaching and joke telling, a side of his personality he rarely displayed in public. His manner set the tone for a relaxed analysis of the day's activities and a leisurely charting of strategy for the next few days. Often it was 2:00 A.M. or later before we began to drift off to bed, leaving Martin, Ralph, and A. D. the last ones to turn in. It is these fellowship gatherings that I remember most about that time. They were sheer joy, and Martin's energy and charisma were as dominant in this kind of small gathering as on any major speaking platform. Here he experimented with new ideas, borrowed phrases and turned them into oratorical masterpieces to be used later, though without the raucous laughter and raunchy humor present in our meetings.

Those days and nights demanded the stamina of a long-distance runner. I had to pace myself through the day, never knowing when a situation would require an extra burst of energy. Active days flowed into nights of planning meetings, problems to solve, and expectations for the days ahead. I've always been able to go long periods without much sleep when I had to; in Birmingham I took short naps after the demonstrations, was up until two or three in the morning and back at the church at nine. Those days after April 22, despite the trial, were so different from the gloom of just two or three weeks before and made us feel as if a massive sun was rising over us. We really *couldn't* sleep—none of us—even if we wanted to. There would be plenty of time to rest and sleep later. Right now our train was on the track and moving. We were moving slowly, but we knew we were picking up speed and passengers. For one of the few times we would ever experience in our lives, we felt that our people and ourselves were confined only by the limits of our own faith and our determination.

In sharpening my own sense of purpose, I also tried to assist Martin in areas where he needed help. The rush of unstructured events in Birmingham, particularly after Good Friday, was so rapid that he simply had no time to address all of them. On any given day he might have to deal with day-to-day strategy, staff deployment, the financial needs of the campaign, visitors and callers from around the country—all of whom wished to speak to him personally—the Justice Department in Washington, the Birmingham Advisory Committee, which jealously guarded their access, attorneys who needed to discuss legal strategies, press conferences and media interviews, and last, but not least, his responsibilities as the climactic speaker at our nightly mass meetings. All this was simply too much for one man to do—and though Wyatt Walker did more than his share as executive director, I found that I could also help with many of these tasks, acting as a surrogate for Martin. It was, above all, necessary that Martin be available to perform his role as spokesman for our cause, a role only he could play.

As I took on these new responsibilities and moved away from my sole responsibility to the Dorchester Citizenship Program, I made no particular effort to become a close personal friend of Martin's, nor did I go out of my way to compete for his favor. His real need at the time was for independent analysis that could only come from someone outside his close inner circle. I moved around speaking with members of the press, the street people, the white businessmen; their opinions were all needed for sound decision making. It became my role to be available to the doubters and malcontents among the students on the one hand and the establishment on the other. My personal friendship with Martin developed later, and over time. Ralph Abernathy and Martin's younger brother, A. D., were in Birmingham throughout the campaign, and they were Martin's intimates. But as the campaign progressed, I became more confident that Martin respected and relied upon my ability to craft sound judgments based on my interaction with diverse groups in Birmingham.

The energy of young African-Americans was essential to tumbling the walls of segregation in Birmingham. To direct that energy and build social consciousness, I collaborated closely with James and Diane Bevel, Dorothy Cotton, James Lawson, and Bernard Lee, a leader of the 1960 Atlanta student sit-ins. Bernard, who physically resembled Martin, had become friendly with him while they were in jail together in Atlanta. He adopted Martin as his role model and came to work for SCLC, remaining until the end as a personal assistant and close friend of Martin's. The more time Bernard spent with Martin, the more his voice, dress, and mannerisms reflected that association. On the phone, their voices were almost indistinguishable. As we increasingly realized that it was not safe for Martin to travel alone, the devoted Bernard provided him with a constant and utterly loyal companion. Ralph continued to accompany Martin to jail and major marches, but Ralph also had to serve West Hunter Baptist Church and he couldn't follow Martin as he spoke around the country. Bernard traveled with Martin on his many speaking engagements and was supposed to confirm flight and hotel arrangements, check luggage, and ease the hardships of travel. As it turned out, Bernard was not too dependable as an assistant. One morning in Atlantic

City, Bernard overslept and must have had too much to drink the night before because Martin couldn't wake him. Finally, in disgust, Martin picked up a bucket with melting ice from the dresser and dumped it on Bernard's head. Bernard slept on and Martin went on to Washington without him. Nevertheless, Bernard was a useful companion—he didn't have any aspirations, except to be around Martin, and he was very perceptive when it came to reading an audience. Bernard was one of the few people who would let Martin know whether he had misjudged an audience or made an effective presentation, though that was not often.

Prior to the Good Friday march, most of my time was spent working along with Bevel, recruiting and training teenagers for our demonstrations, providing them with a quick, basic introduction to the philosophy and techniques of nonviolent protest and the philosophy behind it. Our recruits were shown the American Friends Service Committee film on Gandhi's Indian movement, a Quaker film on the Montgomery bus boycott, and the NBC television documentary "The Nashville Sit-in Story." With this background, Bevel offered his dramatic lecture, "The Water Tower of Segregation." This tower, he said, is supported by four legs: (1) political disenfranchisement, (2) lack of economic opportunity, (3) alienation from God, and (4) lack of educational opportunity. In his presentations, Bevel reminded us that segregation could not last without psychological assistance from blacks themselves and a lack of faith in our own heritage and potential. In his talks there was a strong emphasis on positive affirmation, an early form of the slogan Jesse Jackson made popular a few years later: "I am somebody."

The young people we were concentrating on were, for the most part, drawn from Ulman and Parker, the largest black high schools in Birmingham, each with more than a thousand students. But getting to them was not easy, not the least because the principal at Parker would not allow us on the school grounds. We didn't try to fight him, but we knew we had to find ways to work around him. We invited interested students to meet with us at the First Congregational Church after school and sometimes we met at another friendly church located nearer Parker. Our drive to recruit students was boosted by the early recruitment of James Orange, a former Parker student leader and star football player who knew everyone there. Orange was a large and imposing young man with dark brown skin and a deep laugh that resonated around a room. He was a gentle giant, but he filled up the key on a basketball court and there was no driving inside on James Orange. His passion for sports was transformed into a passion for justice. He joined our staff permanently after Birmingham and became one of our most effective field organizers.

James was able to quickly begin recruiting in the high schools. His strategy was to first pull in the football captains at both Parker and Ulman High Schools. They were to go to jail first, then bail out and recruit their homecoming queens and student body presidents, who would follow them to jail. Since these were the idols of the schools, and Orange himself was a former star, within a few days we actually had to try to stem the flow of students who were ready to go to jail.

As for the ethics of taking teenage demonstrators out of school, we of course recognized the value of formal education, but we also knew that the most valuable education those students could possibly receive at that time, in April 1963, was to be part of the Birmingham movement. They were not immune to the pain of segregation. It had poisoned their lives, inhibited their growth, restricted the possibilities for their futures. It didn't matter if they found a way to become as rich as Mr. Gaston, they could and would still be sent to the back door of a third-class restaurant. At the time of the Birmingham movement, the top students in these high schools would not have been admitted to the University of Alabama. The problems they were confronting as teenagers, and the problems they would face as adults, could not be solved by a high school education. Something else was needed that would address conditions that had existed for centuries and that would work to their deprivation even if they achieved Ph.D.'s. In the movement, they could work to counteract historic wrongs. They could develop a sense of confidence, knowing that they had made an effort to create change in their own time for the betterment of their people. I wished I had had that opportunity when I was a teenager in New Orleans.

However, despite our strong belief in the importance of youth involvement, we were well aware of the tremendous risks we were asking these teenagers to undertake, and in the first two weeks of our campaign, we excluded youth under the age of fourteen. Later, when the demonstrations became even more popular, it was impossible to keep young children away. We always asked teenagers to obtain parental permission to demonstrate, knowing they would be going to jail. We tried to place youths in groups that included adults, so that when they were arrested there would always be an older person along with them in jail. And all demonstrators were required to sign written pledges that they would adhere to principles of nonviolence before they were allowed to go out on demonstrations. It read:

I hereby pledge myself, my person, and my body to the non-violent movement. Therefore I will keep the following ten commandments:

1. Meditate daily on the life and teachings of Jesus.
2. Remember always that the nonviolent movement seeks justice and reconciliation—not victory.
3. Walk and talk in the manner of love; for God is Love.
4. Pray daily to be used by God in order that all men might be free.
5. Sacrifice personal wishes that all men might be free.
6. Observe with both friend and foe the ordinary rules of courtesy.
7. Seek to perform regular service for others and for the world.
8. Refrain from violence of fist, tongue and heart.
9. Strive to be in good spiritual and bodily health.
10. Follow the directions of the Movement leaders and of the captains on demonstrations.

As it turned out, the discipline of prayer and Bible study that we maintained in jail was good for the teenagers. They went to jail with their pastors and saw faith in action. They saw religion providing support to challenge injustice in this lifetime, not just making promises for the next. The Birmingham movement was probably the largest and most effective youth evangelization effort this country has ever seen.

By Monday, April 29, we were ready to launch large-scale demonstrations by the high school students, and escalate them to a peak. All the work we had done in preparing the young people now manifested itself in tremendous enthusiasm; they were ready to go. We sent the athletic stars and homecoming queens out first on Monday, knowing the other students would follow. We were aiming for a massive march on Thursday, May 2, which we labeled "D-Day" for Desegregation Day. By then we expected the entire student bodies of Parker and Ulman and other schools to be involved in the demonstrations.

It was during this onrush of teenage volunteers that we discovered there were many students younger than sixteen who were determined to go to jail along with their older brothers and sisters. It was difficult to impose a cutoff age, and despite the criticism that came from some quarters about our "using children," we had no other option. The young kids were determined to join their older siblings, and in many cases they joined their parents in demonstrations. Our concern, and it was a heavy responsibility in the excitement of the moment, was to make sure that the children always had someone older with them so they would not get stranded in jail by themselves.

On "D-Day," Thursday, May 2, about a thousand students marched downtown in various groups, some as decoy groups, to stage sit-ins. About nine hundred were arrested, more than the city really knew what to do with. Two thousand five hundred more volunteers were ready to go, and as soon as the news of the arrests got around, more teenagers were eager to join their friends in jail. We knew this upsurge of activity would anger Bull Connor, as he may have been under the delusion that time had dimmed our determination. Until now, he and his police had been moderately well behaved, conducting themselves without resorting to too much violence. But when he was confronted with more than two thousand kids demonstrating all over the city on Friday, May 3, he made the fateful decision to order fire trucks into Kelly Ingram Park. Apparently, "D-Day" and "D-Day Plus One" were more than he could bear.

On that Friday, as groups of kids marched past the park headed for downtown, Connor issued the order to the firemen to uncoil their hoses. Police dogs had been seen before, and once again they were brought to the front of the barricades, straining at their leashes. But until now, the fire trucks had remained on the sidelines. Suddenly, fire hoses didn't seem like fun anymore, and the kids watched with trepidation as the fire hoses were unwound. They kept marching and their voices grew stronger with the comforting tunes of the freedom songs. It never ceased to amaze me, the strength that people drew from the singing of those old songs.

Suddenly, Connor ordered the firemen to open the fire hoses on both the marchers and the large crowd of onlookers who had gathered in the park. The water was so powerful it knocked people down and the line began to break as marchers ran screaming through the park to escape the water. Connor then ordered the police to pursue the terrified kids with angry dogs, and to our horror actually unleashed some of them. The police ran through the park, swinging their billy clubs at marchers, onlookers, and newsmen—anyone in the way. Kelly Ingram Park was exploding with insanity and terror.

We didn't fully comprehend at first what was happening. We were witnessing police violence and brutality Birmingham-style: unfortunately for Bull Connor, so was the rest of the world. Photographs and television images of people being attacked by dogs and sprayed with water hoses sped across America and around the world, causing an outcry of indignation and denunciation. Before this, so much of what Martin had said about Birmingham had been ignored, so much of what Fred Shuttlesworth had said and experienced had been dismissed. But this time the images of the violence in Kelly Ingram Park were too strong and too immediate to ignore or forget. Years later I attended a human rights conference in Algeria. Someone was showing a film on apartheid in South Africa that included a clip of young blacks running from a police assault. I said, "Stop the tape, and rewind that scene." They showed the scene again, and I told them, "That's not South Africa, that's Sixteenth Street Baptist Church and Kelly Ingram Park in Birmingham, Alabama, U.S.A."

But the display of violence by the Birmingham police did not discourage or deter us or any of the now thoroughly committed thousands of black citizens in Birmingham. In those days of miracles, it actually gave us renewed strength, and even more people prepared themselves to risk dogs, water, and jail. Some have commented that the drenching of blacks in Birmingham by the fire hoses was an act of baptism in the new movement for human freedom.

However, new problems developed as the students began to pack the jails. Once again members of the Birmingham advisory committee wished to slow things down. Their concern was that with thousands going to jail they wouldn't be able to come up with sufficient bail money. They felt the youth were out of control or, more precisely, out of their control. We were concerned also, but we knew we couldn't raise the support money to get people out unless enough people demonstrated their determination by going in. "We can't do that," I explained, "we can't tell these kids they can't go to jail." But the steering committee was still sitting up in room 30 of the Gaston Motel worrying themselves and us to death as the situation began to take on its own direction: "You've got to restrict the numbers," they protested, "you can't let all these kids go to jail." I listened, but I knew that the steering committee was not in charge of the movement. We had unleashed the spirit of people who longed to be free, and no committee vote was going to stop them now.

I went over to the Sixteenth Street Church to talk with Bevel, who was coordinating the marches there, and shared with him my frustration with the committee's wanting to limit the number going to jail to fifty people. Bevel looked at me and said, "They must be crazy. It's too late. There are already over five hundred kids from Ulman High School on the way. Ensley High heard that Ulman was going and they're about to go. It won't be long before Parker goes. Look," he went on, "we got four busloads of kids outside the church and they're all determined to go now. There's another group marching all the way in from Brighton High School. I know we don't have the money to rent buses to take them back to Brighton. And we don't have the food to feed them. But if we stop what's happening now it's going to be much more trouble than if we let whatever happens happen."

I agreed with him. So I went back and told the steering committee they had to accept that things were just too far gone for them—or for us—to turn around. They were upset with me, and I tried unsuccessfully to explain our position. But I knew that Martin understood what was going on. This was a movement led by the spirit. We had spent the better part of six months nurturing and drawing out that spirit which we now saw alive in the thousands of young people who were determined to go to jail to gain their freedom. Caution now would destroy the movement. The Birmingham movement had developed a momentum of its own.

10

Redeeming the Soul
of America

And the walls come a tumbling down.
—AFRICAN-AMERICAN SPIRITUAL

In fairness to the white business community of Birmingham, it
should be said that while it is true they were satisfied with the status quo of a segregated Birmingham, they were also justifiably
afraid of a backlash against them if they yielded to our demands to
desegregate. We were a nuisance, but unlike the extreme racist factions in white Birmingham, we were nonviolent and therefore less
threatening and more easily ignored. But while we weren't harmful to
them physically, they were slowly learning that our nonviolent tactics
could inflict a much deeper pain. By the week of May 6, 1963, not
only had black customers stopped shopping, but the daily demonstrations, the omnipresent police cars and sirens, and the anxiety and
tension surrounding the situation were also keeping white customers
away from downtown Birmingham. I like to think some of those
whites in Birmingham who stopped shopping did so because they
agreed with us that the time had come to put an end to segregation.

When Bull Connor unleashed his police dogs and fire hoses on
the crowd of kids in Kelly Ingram Park, the sentiments of the Justice

Department, which had ignored the movement for more than a month, became more sympathetic. At the same time, Robert Kennedy was getting his own initiation into the realities of racial politics in Alabama by having to deal with Governor George Wallace on the issue of desegregation of the University of Alabama. The federal courts had decreed that Vivian Malone and James Hood should be allowed to enter the university as its first black students. But Governor Wallace had vowed he would stand in the schoolhouse door and personally deny them entry before he would see the university desegregated. The Kennedys were getting fed up with Wallace and the intransigence of Alabama officials, and it gave them their own taste of what we were up against in Birmingham.

The courage of the young demonstrators and the viciousness of Bull Connor finally persuaded Attorney General Robert Kennedy that our movement in Birmingham was not only just but worthy of national attention and resources. He sent Burke Marshall, his assistant attorney general for civil rights, to Birmingham to make it clear to Mayor Boutwell that the Justice Department wanted to see some kind of settlement of the situation, and soon. Burke Marshall suggested the formation of a committee of one hundred business leaders to develop a plan for responding to our manifesto and the demonstrations. Meanwhile, President Kennedy gathered national business leaders like Roger Blau, the head of U.S. Steel, a major Birmingham employer, and urged them to make calls to key businesspeople. Harry Wachtel, a lawyer and a Democrat, was asked to intercede with the national chains like McCrory's and Woolworth's and direct their Birmingham stores to accept the desegregation plan.

After the D-Day demonstrations, downtown Birmingham was at a virtual standstill, and on the night of Tuesday, May 7, we received a message at Gaston's from local Birmingham attorneys Charles Morgan and David Vann that they had the power from the Committee of One Hundred to negotiate a settlement with us—and they would like to do so as soon as possible. Morgan and Vann, young liberal white lawyers who were comfortable with black people, were instructed to fine-tune the terms.

The business leaders may have wanted negotiations, but they certainly did not want to be seen negotiating. We agreed to meet at the home of John and Deanie Drew. John was a black insurance executive who served on our local support committee, and Deanie was a Links member, a society club woman who volunteered behind the scenes in the movement, working in the office, and ferrying people around town. Deanie, Ruth Barefield Pendleton, and other well-to-do black women had helped us to keep the demonstrations going. When the police placed barricades to keep students from marching downtown, Deanie, Ruth, and their friends would drive their Cadillacs and Buicks behind the Sixteenth Street Baptist Church and take demonstrators around the barricades to sit in locations downtown. Martin, Wyatt Walker, and I met Morgan and Vann at the Drews' modern ranch-style home. Fred Shuttlesworth, who had been privy to other attempts at talks, was absent since he had been injured by the water hoses on D-Day and was still in the hospital. Using cloak-and-dagger secrecy, we drove into the Drews' garage and closed the garage door before entering the house. We gathered in their spacious and tastefully decorated living room, two white lawyers representing the collective wealth and power of white Birmingham and three thirtyish African-American preachers.

I had set the framework for the negotiations from the beginning of the Birmingham demonstrations, but with Martin and Wyatt present I deferred to them. Martin began the initial discussion and then left Wyatt and me to hammer out the details. It was very natural for me and Wyatt and to play off each other as good guy–bad guy. Wyatt took the tough stance; he had put together the initial set of demands and established ground rules for the demonstrations with the black community in Birmingham. He was the hard-liner who was pressing them to the wall. Some observed that during the negotiations the preachers were cussing and the lawyers were weeping. At one point, Wyatt blew up. We were almost there, but Vann and Morgan started talking about what they couldn't do and Wyatt jumped up and started swearing and saying we'd go back to demonstrating. David Vann broke down and cried. The whole city was hanging on these negotiations. In contrast to Wyatt, I positioned myself as an unemotional facilitator, but obviously I wasn't neutral.

We reached a real stumbling block when Vann and Morgan proposed a ninety-day cooling-off period, after which time the downtown businesses would desegregate. This was totally unacceptable. Wyatt objected, saying, "What you want is for us to collapse the movement, fold up our tents and withdraw. If we do that, we'll have no credibility in this community. Those people will never follow us again."

I said, gently, "Look, this is not about you giving us something. What we want is good for Birmingham. We have thousands of people in jail and thousands who want to go to jail. We can't just shut that off. We are the only people who can guide this movement. The black citizens of Birmingham want an end to segregation now, and they are right. The Supreme Court says they're right."

In Nashville, a stair-step approach had been very successful, and since it was in everyone's interest to avoid unpleasant or violent incidents, I proposed a similar process, pointing out that this way changes could be implemented gradually, allowing people time to get used to new practices. But, as a show of good faith, on the day the settlement was announced they must take down the WHITES ONLY and COLORED signs from rest rooms, water fountains, and waiting areas. Also, the downtown merchants must start interviewing from within their own staffs to identify black employees they would promote to clerks and cashiers. Those things could be done quietly, without fanfare.

We also agreed to a ten-day cooling-off period between the end of the demonstrations and the actual testing of the changes. On the tenth day we would bring small, well-trained groups of black citizens to downtown lunch counters to be served. They would be regular customers who would sit at the counter for a simple meal like doughnuts and coffee. We would do this at one store per day for ten days, and if there were no incidents, we would expand the lunch-counter visits to several stores per day. From the tenth day on, small teams of trained activists would also make use of public facilities in downtown stores. We agreed to call the stores in advance and tell them when we were coming, hoping to avoid incidents and allowing time for the store's internal security to prepare for us.

These transitional provisions would be in effect for thirty days. After thirty days, there would be no conditions placed on access to public facilities: everything downtown must be completely desegregated at all times. And after forty-five days, each downtown business would begin to hire black clerks. At least one clerk was to be hired by each store. By the end of 1963 these stores were to agree to a comprehensive fair-employment plan.

The accord went on to state that the harassment of blacks attempting to register to vote must cease, and that businessmen were to take a lead in assuring this. Finally, the Committee of One Hundred was to work together with us on developing a plan for school desegregation during 1964.

We also fought long and hard that evening for the dropping of charges against arrested demonstrators, the release of those still in jail, and the canceling of bail. We later learned, however, that the city would not relent on the matter of the bail bonds, which had become an enormous expense of more than $160,000. With so much of their political currency at stake, the Kennedy administration was unwilling to let an agreement falter on the issue of bail money. Burke Marshall asked two unions—the United Auto Workers and the Maritime Workers Union—to post monies from their pension funds sufficient to guarantee the bonds of the demonstrators still in jail. The unions responded to what was essentially an appeal to their moral sense and their patriotism. They weren't really being asked to risk their members' pensions—it was only a paper transaction, since everybody knew the cases would be thrown out in federal court and no one would actually serve time on these offenses. The guarantees were essentially a face-saving device for the Alabama courts, but one that held the agreement together.

Our largest battle won, an internal battle within our own camp was just beginning to brew. Fred Shuttlesworth felt he couldn't accept the agreement. With the city finally on the run, and having been betrayed once already by the white business leaders, he saw no benefit for us in calling a moratorium on demonstrations. Fred was very emotional in his arguments, and a great deal of his anger was aimed at me, I suppose because I was the one who had made the initial negotiating contacts, and because I believed wholeheartedly that we should accept the agreement. He was also enormously suspicious of Burke Marshall, the Kennedys' representative, since Burke and the Justice Department had pushed extremely hard for immediate settlement.

This conflict was particularly intense and bitter because Fred, who had been injured by the police, had missed our meetings with the Committee of One Hundred. By the time he came out of the hospital, the business community had come to accept that they must reach an agreement, and Martin also felt it was time for a settlement, provided something concrete could be won. But events had moved so quickly that Fred felt he had been cut out of deciding the fate of the movement he had started.

On May 10, President Kennedy scheduled a press conference to announce the Birmingham settlement. Martin, Wyatt, and I were in room 30 of Gaston's with Fred and Joseph Dolan, John Doar's assistant in the Civil Rights Division of the Justice Department. We argued and argued over the settlement until in exasperation Martin finally said, "Well, what is it you want that's not in here, Fred?" But Fred just kept repeating: "We can't end this movement until Birmingham is freed." Martin finally threw up his hands in disgust and left Wyatt and me to go around and around in circles with Fred.

Fred had been able to muster a great deal of support for his position among the youth, many of whom wanted to keep the demonstrations going. He was now threatening to tell the demonstrators there was *no* agreement, and that they should just continue what they were doing. He made a move for the door and I had to physically restrain him. Meanwhile, Dolan was trying to get Robert Kennedy on the phone to reassure Fred of the validity of the agreement. I was prepared to do whatever I had to do to keep him from going out that door and embarrassing Martin Luther King in front of the whole world. Just as he was trying to push past me and I was steeling myself to tackle him to the floor, Dolan said, "The attorney general would like to speak with you, Reverend Shuttlesworth." Fred took the call, and thankfully it satisfied his principles, soothed his wounded ego, and saved me from punching him out. I think that Fred loved and respected Martin, but the resentment he felt toward Martin for having arrived at an agreement without him was something he could hardly express, so his anger was displaced toward me, King's operative. For my part, I felt we had accomplished what we came to Birmingham to do and I was tired. I hadn't had a full night's sleep since Christmas. I had exhausted all my tact and diplomacy obtaining that agreement, and I had none left for Fred. I wasn't about to let his emotions destroy what we had all been working toward since September.

Fred had been stricken with what I call "freedom high." The Birmingham movement was a heady experience. It was like being in an NBA championship series, each day more challenging and exhilarating than the next. But, unlike a basketball game, here the outcome really meant something. The Birmingham movement changed people's lives, gave them pride and dignity. After so many years of suffering and humiliation, for Fred and many of the students, the taste of victory felt too good to quit.

A similar phenomenon occurred during the student demonstration in 1989 in Beijing's Tiananmen Square. The student who was photographed facing down the tanks had "freedom high." It was a glorious moment, but the brutal confrontation with the Chinese military that followed virtually destroyed the student movement in China. Many of the more experienced student leaders had urged a strategic retreat from the square, arguing that it was better to preserve the movement for another battle. Instead, some of them got "freedom high": they pushed too hard, and when the government fought back with their greater resources the movement was crushed.

I admire Fred to this day, and I think even he would now agree that we were right to go to the negotiating table when we did. For one thing, we couldn't have sustained the campaign at that intense pace for much longer, despite our threats. There's a time in every

campaign when people have to see some sign of progress or they
become discouraged. Our supporters were paying a tremendous price
in time and emotional energy to keep up the daily pressure. The lives
of every one of us, day in and day out, were totally subject to the
demands of the campaign. If we had not produced an agreement then
that we believed was a victory, even though it didn't immediately
"free" Birmingham, we feared our level of popular support couldn't
help but weaken—and that eventually could only strengthen the
other side.

In assessing the Birmingham agreement it is also important to
remember our concern for the people who were still in jail. The
imprisoned demonstrators, old and young, had faith that we would
not leave them in jail; they expected us to work out the legal logistics,
to explore every possible means to bail them out and limit their personal liability. With thousands having been jailed since the inception
of the campaign and an agreement in hand, we now had to turn our
undivided energies toward solving this problem. The way we handled
this situation would also determine to a large degree the willingness
of demonstrators and supporters in other cities and towns to submit
themselves to arrest in future campaigns.

Perhaps more intense even than our fear of burning out our
base of support, was the administration's fear of alienating its base
of support among Alabama Democrats. The Birmingham movement
so dramatized the injustices of segregation and its incompatibility
with American principles that President Kennedy was persuaded that
a comprehensive civil rights bill should be introduced in Congress.
This decision could not be made public during the final negotiations,
but Martin received private assurances from the attorney general
that the adminstration would pursue it aggressively. As a result, the
administration was particularly concerned that the settlement in
Birmingham not offend Southern politicians unduly. The Alabama
senators, John Sparkman and Lister Hill, were Kennedy allies, loyal
to the national Democratic Party and relatively liberal for Southerners. It was critical to the success of the civil rights bill and the rest of
President Kennedy's legislative agenda that implementation of the
Birmingham agreement run smoothly. Any negative incidents
attributable to civil rights activists would have been used by the proponents of segregation as evidence that the races ought to remain
separated.

By and large, the Birmingham business community upheld their
end of the agreement, though not surprisingly there were problems.
They did employ a few black clerks in the stores, and they did begin

desegregating their services. This went forward despite the strong segregationist policy of Governor Wallace, and despite the fact that segregation was still a common practice in other Alabama cities, and very strongly entrenched in the small towns and rural areas. In fact, by desegregating downtown shops and lunch counters and public facilities, the business leaders of Birmingham were actually breaking the laws of the state of Alabama. Decades later I addressed the chamber of commerce in South Africa and, thinking of our experience in Birmingham, I urged them to agree with each other to ignore the apartheid laws. "Anything is legal if one hundred corporate citizens decide to make it legal. If one hundred influential businessmen decide to end apartheid, apartheid is ended." And, as it had been in Birmingham, in South Africa, ultimately, it was the effect of economic sanctions that persuaded the business establishment that the price of apartheid was too steep.

Tragically, an extreme white supremacist element in Birmingham was determined to demonstrate their vehement disapproval of the agreement. On Saturday night, May 11, while most of us were back in Atlanta for a brief rest, Gaston's Motel and A. D. King's home were bombed. It was a miracle no one was killed or seriously injured—but the intent was obvious: room 30, which had been Martin's room and our headquarters, was completely destroyed. That night the weary African-American community of Birmingham succumbed to the long withheld temptation to retaliate against the senseless violence it had endured. The police quickly labeled the situation a "riot" and moved through the community with sirens blaring, weapons out, and billy clubs swinging. Dorothy Cotton and Wyatt Walker were still in Birmingham. Bravely they went out into the streets and tried to help calm tempers. Back at Gaston's Motel, Wyatt's wife, Ann, was beaten by police and had to be taken to the hospital. Wyatt rushed to the hospital to see to his wife, and upon his return to the motel, he too was beaten by police.

At the time of the bombing most of the SCLC staff had left Birmingham for the ten-day cooling-off period that was part of the agreement. Martin had gone back to preach at Ebenezer and to see his family. I had gone back Saturday during the day; Jean picked me up at the airport and we had a real family dinner around our dining room table. The next morning, I was dressing to go to church with Jean and the girls when Martin called with news of the bombing. He told me to get back to Birmingham, lest we lose the agreement over violent retaliation by the African-American community. Jean grimly loaded the girls, hair combed and ribbons awry, into our blue Ford

Fairlane and drove down Stewart Avenue to the Atlanta airport. She and the girls went on to Sunday school and I went back to Birmingham.

On Sunday, May 12, it was quiet in Birmingham, although the wreckage of the bomb was still smoldering. The blast had blown off the end of the motel, destroying the room where Martin had been staying. Fortunately, at the time of the blast, the rooms were all empty. The churches and church folk helped to keep everyone calm that Sunday; the older people were almost matter-of-fact about the bombing, concluding, "That's just crazy white folk, still crazy."

The mayor assured us that our agreement would be honored. All day Monday we moved through the streets of the black community reminding people that we had won an important victory, that the agreement was in their best long-term interests, and that we must not allow the blatant strategies of the Klan and other Birmingham racists to destroy it. That we were able to calm the people down and prevent further retaliatory violence in the face of extreme provocation was one of the finest accomplishments of our campaign. We were able to achieve this not merely because of the power of Martin's appeal, but because of the relationships we had built with the young people in the community, who fully understood what was at stake because they had been directly involved in the achievement. To me this was an important lesson. Young people could be the strongest asset in a non-violent campaign, but without conscientious citizenship training, they could also easily be turned to violence.

When the community had settled down and the cooling-off period was over, we began the actual implementation of the Birmingham agreement. It was in our interest to see that desegregation proceeded without further incidents and setbacks, so we used our best-trained demonstrators and members of the Alabama Human Rights Commission, people like Abraham Woods and Edward Gardner, who had gone to jail for the right to patronize lunch counters and other public facilities in their own communities. We did not use Fred Shuttlesworth and Charles Billups, who were controversial and immediately recognizable. We started with one lunch counter a day; we would call in advance and avoid the busiest times. We wanted the community to gradually get used to seeing African-Americans sitting down, eating lunch. After several days, we sent people to four or five lunch counters a day, always offering to work with the business owners to address any problems and concerns that arose. Interestingly, when black folks not in the movement saw our activists eating lunch, they sat down too. And after a very short while, it was a natural part of life in Birmingham to see blacks and whites together in public eating establishments.

Our campaign in Birmingham proved that a sustained and comprehensive nonviolent, direct-action effort could bring about change under the most difficult circumstances. We had explained our purpose and our goals at the outset, offering the city's leaders a chance to avoid the protests. When they declined our offer, we moved onto the boycott, which served two purposes: it was a safe way for every black person in Birmingham to show support for the movement—no one would get fired because they didn't buy new Easter clothes—and it placed the kind of pressure on business leaders in Birmingham that they understood. At the same time, the demonstrations created additional pressure and attracted the national media to Birmingham. In the beginning the demonstrations were not large—only fifty people went to jail with Martin—but they were sustained and consistent: we marched every day. And we remained in dialogue with city leaders throughout the campaign, always placing as much emphasis on our goal of reconciliation as on the demonstrations themselves. Reconciliation was an essential part of our definition of a successful movement. We were trying to transform America, not triumph over white folk.

Martin used to say that America was a ten-day nation. The first ten days, no matter what we did it was wrong, and we were told we shouldn't be doing it at all. The second ten days, the opposition would admit there was a problem, but say that we were going about a solution in the wrong way. The third ten days, they would try to take the problem away from us, saying, "We were going to do something about this anyway, and if you hadn't interfered we could have solved it sooner." Getting to the third phase is the goal of a transformational movement. You *want* people to internalize and claim the changes as their own.

After the democracy movement succeeded in Poland, and Lech Walesa, leader of Poland's Solidarity Movement, came to the United States to address a joint session of Congress, a couple of his associates came to see me in Atlanta. They thanked me for the example of our movement, which they said had inspired them and taught them many things. One of the things they learned from us was to always give their opponent a face-saving way out of the confrontation. They understood from Birmingham that you couldn't win a protracted confrontation through nonviolent means. So, the Polish workers would end their strikes when the tanks and the military were brought in since they knew they couldn't win against them. But six months later they'd be back, organizing another strike. And in the interim, the government would have a chance to assimilate the demands of the strikers and discuss options among themselves, never seeming as if they had completely given in to the strikers.

The nonviolent approach is not emotional, although it is deeply spiritual. It is a rational process that seeks to transform, rather than defeat, the oppressor and the oppressive situation. Any kind of emotional outburst—violence, arrogance, intentional martyrdom—endangers the process of transformation. Emotionalism confirms the prejudices of those that nonviolence aims to transform.

The oppressed must be transformed too. They must learn to value and respect themselves, to understand the ways they support an oppressive system, and they must learn to forgive those who have hurt them. In the process of citizenship schooling, the boycott, mass meetings, and demonstrations, people grew in understanding and gained a sense of their own worth, power, and dignity. In the end, Birmingham and its citizens, black and white, were transformed to the greater good of all concerned.

One month after the Birmingham agreement was signed, President Kennedy fulfilled his commitment to introduce civil rights legislation. On June 11, 1963, he delivered a televised speech on civil rights and announced that he would be sending to Congress a comprehensive civil rights bill. The legislation, sent to Congress a week later, forbade segregation and discrimination in public accommodations and transportation, education, and employment. Our faith in Kennedy's integrity was revived. No American president had ever made such an unequivocal speech in support of the rights of African-Americans.

Our elation over President Kennedy's civil rights speech was short-lived, however; just after midnight on June 12, Medgar Evers, our friend and brother in the struggle, was killed by a sniper—shot in the back in the driveway of his home in Jackson, Mississippi. I had met Medgar two years earlier when I was touring Mississippi with Dorothy Cotton and Septima Clark on our first recruiting trip for the Dorchester Citizenship Program. He was wonderfully cooperative and friendly. Though he was state secretary of the Mississippi NAACP, Medgar knew the struggle for civil rights should not be limited by organizational boundaries, so he worked with everyone who came to Mississippi to organize. We all admired him for his fearlessness and dedication—I remember we thought no one would dare to shoot him because he consistently courted danger with so much élan and confidence.

His murder brought home to us our own vulnerability. Our tendency had been to ignore danger, even in the midst of potentially violent confrontations. Medgar's murder was one of many in the South that made us aware of how deeply the progress we had made had disturbed the racist psyche. We were now in uncharted psychological territory: never before had whites seen blacks as determined, as defiant as they were in 1963; never had blacks themselves been so willing to throw off the accumulated mental shackles of the days of slavery and postslavery. Blacks were staging smaller-scale campaigns across the South, and it appeared as if the white supremacists were launching a coordinated counterassault. An increase in the violence against blacks in the South during that spring and summer of 1963 seemed like desperate, blind attempts to murder our new spirit and resurrect the Old South by the same means it had been so long sustained—through acts of terrorism.

I was in Birmingham the night Medgar was killed, along with Dorothy Cotton and James Bevel, checking on the progress of the desegregation agreement and disposing of bail bond cases for people who had been jailed. Dorothy and I had just returned from a citizenship workshop, and we had learned a day or so before that Mrs. Fannie Lou Hamer and a group of women who were returning home with her from our session at Dorchester had been jailed in Winona, Mississippi. Not all of the people traveling with her were identified as civil rights activists, however, and a few of the women from the workshop had made it back to Greenwood to inform the other workers what had taken place. The sheriff at Winona would not confirm that he had arrested the women, nor would he let them make phone calls. But Mississippi movement people in Greenwood were able to ascertain that the indomitable Mrs. Hamer was being held, along with the petite, velvet-eyed Annelle Ponder, who had recently joined our staff to work on voter registration. Annelle beautifully embodied the spirit of nonviolent resistance: she gently, almost apologetically, withheld her cooperation from segregation. Rosemary Freeman, Elvester Morris, and perky young June Johnson, who was only fifteen, were also arrested.

Lawrence Guyot, a key SNCC worker in Mississippi and later chairman of the Freedom Democratic Party, had set out for Winona from Jackson with the intent of bailing the women out, but then he, too, had disappeared. No one had heard a word from him. He was traveling alone and we thought he certainly would have called in if he were not in danger.

Within an hour after we heard the terrible news of Medgar's

death, Martin called us at Gaston's. "I want you and Bevel to drive to Winona right now," he told me, "and see if you can get Annelle and Mrs. Hamer and the rest of those people out of jail. After the way Medgar was shot, there's no telling what might happen to them." Martin's call came at about one o'clock in the morning, but we were all still wide awake, having just heard the news about Medgar.

Winona is a tiny town located on Highway 82 between Starkville and Greenwood, Mississippi, about a five- or six-hour drive from Birmingham. Within minutes, Bevel and I were ready to depart, but then we realized we didn't have a car. Dorothy had just purchased a brand-new car, which she had driven over to Birmingham from Atlanta. We told her we needed her car and asked her for the keys. We were all exhausted, and our nerves were frayed from the shock of Medgar's death and the terrifying violence that seemed to be rising all around us like monsters from the soil. "If you're gonna take my car," Dorothy replied, "I'm going with you." We told her it was too dangerous for a woman to go, you never know what might happen in Mississippi and all that. "Those are women in jail in Winona," she answered. "If Mrs. Hamer's brave enough to challenge Mississippi, I'm brave enough to help get her out. You're being ridiculous!" she added. So we got into a really heated argument about the rights of women to be arrested, which lasted at least two hours. Now it was three or four in the morning and we hadn't even left for Winona yet. The truth was, Bevel and I didn't want to be bothered with Dorothy because we feared she might become emotional with the sheriff, who was apparently crazy, and blow up in his face. Then Martin would have to send somebody else to come to Mississippi to try to get *us* out of jail—if we were even still alive. Dorothy was accusing us of being male chauvinists, waking up whoever was asleep in Gaston's, screaming about how women had as much right to participate in the dangerous aspects of the movement as men. Finally, Dorothy said, "I don't need you people, I'll drive to Mississippi and get them out of jail myself!" Then she ran out to her car, got in, and started up the motor.

We dashed out after her and jumped into the car as she was pulling away. And so the three of us roared off toward Mississippi on a rescue mission. As Dorothy drove she was fussing and calling us names I won't repeat. The closer we got to Mississippi, the more Dorothy fussed and the faster she drove. She must have been doing about ninety. By the time we reached the Mississippi state line, she had calmed down some, but was still driving much too fast. Then, on a two-lane highway, she tried to pass a car on a curve. Just as she pulled out we saw a huge semi-trailer coming right at us. "It's all over," I said to myself. But somehow she swerved off the road into a ditch and then back up onto the road, miraculously avoiding the truck. The whole thing happened so fast I couldn't believe we were still alive. Then I lost my cool and screamed at Dorothy, "Damn you, woman, it's okay to be killed by white folks in Mississippi while trying to do something worthwhile, but I don't want you killing us on this highway for nothing!" Dorothy was so shaken up she just pulled over to the side of the road and stopped. We sat in silence for a while trying to collect ourselves. Then I told her I was taking the wheel, and I did.

When we finally approached Winona it was late morning. One of our cardinal rules was never to enter a small Southern town with the gas tank empty because you never knew when you might have to leave in a hurry. So about twenty miles before we reached Winona we decided to stop at a small service station to buy gas. By this time Dorothy was in the backseat, asleep, or so we thought. Bevel and I got out to jive with the old man as he filled up the tank, as was our habitual tactic. We made it a point to always make small talk with people in such situations, something I had learned from my experience with Sergeant Hamilton in Albany. We understood that whites were more afraid of us than we were of them and found that often if we took the initiative we could overcome the mutual anxiety.

While we were inside the store paying for the gas, we looked out the window and were startled to see Dorothy, her hips and red dress flouncing and bouncing above provocative high heels, striding purposefully down Highway 82. Bevel and I looked at each other, trying to conceal our alarm from the store owner, hoping he wouldn't spot Dorothy, become concerned, and call the sheriff. As soon as we finished paying for our gas we jumped into the car and raced off to catch up to Dorothy. We screeched to a stop beside her, yelled at her to get back in the car, and she said, as if it were any cheery June morning, "I'm going to get some orange juice from the store down the road." I lost all control of myself again and yelled at her, "Damn, woman, we're in Mississippi! We'll be lucky if we get out of this mess alive, and you're looking for *orange juice*!" Bevel was maintaining a stoic silence. I was sure that the man at the service station was right now calling the sheriff and telling him, "There's some crazy niggers on your highway you need to do something about." We finally coaxed Dorothy back into the car and drove on, but not until she went to the store to get her orange juice.

I think Dorothy's emotional reaction came from an overwhelming sense of guilt. She had invited Mrs. Hamer to Dorchester and felt responsible for her plight. It was as if she wanted to be in jail right along with the other women. We had sent more than ten thousand people to jail, but Dorothy and I hadn't been to jail ourselves. I did not make my decisions out of guilt, though, and I wasn't about to go to jail just because she felt guilty. My goal was to get everyone out of Winona in one piece.

A few minutes later we arrived in town and managed to find the sheriff's office and his jail. Once again I insisted that Dorothy remain in the car while Bevel and I went in to see the sheriff. I was scared to death because in Mississippi sheriffs had almost complete power; they were a law unto themselves. We went inside: the sheriff wasn't in. When Bevel and I returned to the car Dorothy was sitting in a swing under a huge tree—what looked like a hanging oak—reading Kahlil Gibran's *The Prophet*, which she'd brought with her to read in jail in case we were arrested. "Please, Dorothy," we pleaded, "don't sit in a swing reading in front of the jail. This is not the time or the place for that."

Just about that time the sheriff drove up. Fortunately, he ignored us and entered his office. We rushed in behind him. But when we got inside his office we clammed up, afraid to tell him why we were there, and he acted as if it was the most normal thing in the world for us to be hanging around that morning, so we began talking with him about the weather and other idle chitchat, without ever telling him we had come to get Mrs. Hamer and the other women out of his jail. This insane scene went on for quite a few minutes until the telephone rang. The sheriff answered the phone. We could overhear that it was attorney Wiley Branton calling from Atlanta about the women in jail. Wiley, the attorney for the Little Rock Five, was one of the most important and effective black civil rights attorneys during the Southern movement. He was also extremely light-skinned and he had an Arkansas twang that sounded like an authentic white Southern drawl. Wiley loved to tell stories about calling up Southern sheriffs and using his accent to his advantage: "You got 'er Negra boy there by the name 'er Jones? Well, that boy's mama works for me and ah need to get him out of jail."

Apparently Wiley was in great form with the sheriff. He must have asked the sheriff if I was there, because the sheriff looked over at me and said, "Boy, is your name Young?" Then he handed me the phone. Wiley explained that he was trying to get the sheriff to let the women go. He asked me what I thought. I answered very loudly, so that the sheriff could hear: "Well I *think* the sheriff is going to honor our bonds, I think he's going to let us bail them out in a few minutes." Of course, Bevel and I hadn't said anything to the sheriff about bailing people out yet.

Just about that time, an FBI agent strolled into the office. I asked Wiley to stay on the phone. We thought maybe the Justice Department had sent the agent, and maybe they had, but we soon discovered to our dismay that the agent was also the brother-in-law of the sheriff. The agent informed us in the most matter-of-fact manner that a federal brutality complaint had been filed in the case, and he had come over to investigate whether the sheriff and his deputies had been brutal. Wiley was still holding on the phone. It seemed as if an hour had passed since he first called. Finally, after a private conversation with the FBI agent, the sheriff asked us if we had the money to bail the people out. The bonds were three hundred dollars for each of the five women, and three hundred dollars more for Lawrence Guyot, who we discovered was in the same jail. When all the bonds were paid, hoping we could get out of there safely, I went back to the phone and shouted to Wiley. "Wiley, you want to thank the sheriff? He's been very cooperative."

The women and Guyot were brought out, staggering and injured; the sheriff and the FBI agent watched impassively, as if nothing unusual was happening. We cooperated in the charade and concealed our shock at their condition so we could get them away from Winona without further trouble.

Later, as we drove the group over to Greenwood they told us what had happened. They had been arrested because they tried to get coffee at "white only" counters first in the Columbus and then in the Winona bus stations. They had also tried to sit in the front of the bus. The driver was extremely abusive; he called them "niggers" and forced them to move to the rear. In jail they were all beaten; Annelle Ponder, Mrs. Hamer, and Guyot very badly. Annelle was beaten because she refused to say "YES, SIR" to the deputies and trustees. Mrs. Hamer was beaten even though she was in her fifties and obviously already in poor health. June Johnson, an innocent young girl of fifteen, had been made to strip naked before the leering deputies. After the women were beaten they were forced to wash the blood from their own clothing and from their bruises as the deputies cruelly attempted to remove the visible evidence of their brutality. As they had nothing else to wear, they returned to their cells in the same damp, clammy clothes. Guyot, who was massive and physically intimidating, had been arrested by state highway patrolmen on his way to Winona, beaten viciously on the highway and challenged to fight back, which he wisely declined to do. He knew that to do so would have given the patrolmen a perfect excuse to kill him.

We used to joke that Dorothy had initiated the women's rights movement on that mission to Winona. But all the women in the movement—those as experienced as Fannie Lou Hamer or as young and determined as June Johnson—made courageous sacrifices and took tremendous risks in the struggle for freedom. We probably too often tried to "protect" them, but there was really no way we could; there was no "safe haven" from the evils and abuses of the racist Southern system. June Johnson's ordeal reminded me of a haunting incident that had taken place when I was a pastor in Thomasville. There was some construction taking place at the elementary school near the church, and the kids confided in me that the white construction foreman was engaging in sexual relations with a sixth-grade black girl. I immediately went to report this to the principal, who responded, "That girl is a hussy." Soon after, the foreman was removed from that job, but no criminal action was taken against him. This was not an uncommon situation: black girls of tender age were often tragically vulnerable to sexual predators. And when the offenders were white, there was little black adults could do to protect their children. This vulnerability of African-American women under segregation was one of the bitter realities we had to face. Dorothy Cotton, June Johnson, Annelle Ponder, Mrs. Hamer, Diane Bevel, and countless women like them made us face that ugly truth.

Upon our return from Mississippi there was no time to really rest. Birmingham had spawned about a dozen smaller, simultaneous campaigns around the South, all with issues similar to those in Alabama. Leaders of these campaigns were constantly requesting that Martin come to speak for them, or that we devote financial and staff assistance to their campaigns, which we simply could not afford to do. However, when a request for assistance came in from Hosea Williams, a citizenship school leader down in Savannah, Georgia, Martin asked me to go and spend a few days there. Hosea was president of the Savannah Voters Crusade, an affiliate of SCLC, and had brought many of the Savannah youth into our Dorchester Citizenship Program; we felt an obligation to help him.

Hosea Williams is a fascinating, complex, and perplexing individual; the story he tells of the origin of his interest in the movement is at once typical and remarkable. He was born and raised in Attapulgus, Georgia, a small town in tough Decatur County near the Florida state line. He left Attapulgus as a youth to join the army during the Second World War, ended up in the European theater, and

there it was his misfortune to land in a foxhole almost totally obliter-
ated by German mortar fire. Of twelve soldiers in the foxhole, he was
the only one to survive, though he was seriously injured and knocked
unconscious by the shelling. When he regained consciousness, his
chest and stomach were blown open, and he was sure he was going
to die. He was then taken from the foxhole and placed in an ambulance, which was hit by mortar fire that killed the driver. Finally he
was rescued, taken to a medical station, sewn up, and somehow he
recovered. Hosea said this experience convinced him that God had
saved him for some purpose, though he didn't know then what it
was.

After recuperating for thirteen months in an army hospital,
Hosea was discharged into civilian life. A disabled veteran on
crutches, he made his way back by bus to Attapulgus. When the bus
stopped in Americus, Georgia, not far from Attapulgus, Hosea
entered the bus station to discover there were no waiting-room facilities for blacks. He limped over to the water fountain for whites and
drank. A policeman at the bus station saw Hosea drinking from the
fountain, jumped on him, and beat him up for violating Georgia segregation laws. It was then, Hosea declares, that he realized what the
Lord had saved him for: to fight racism and segregation.

He entered college at Morris Brown in Atlanta on the GI Bill,
completed his degree in chemistry, married, and settled down in
Savannah working as a chemist with the Department of Agriculture.
Not long after he moved to Savannah he became active in the local
NAACP and was a leader in the expanding protest activities against
segregation. The Savannah Department of Agriculture office viewed
his militancy and activism with extreme disfavor and tried their best
to fire him. It was in 1962, during the period Hosea was trying to
hold on to his job, that I first met him. Hosea had gravitated toward
our citizenship training activities in Dorchester, which was just a few
miles from Savannah. We became involved in his efforts to save his
job, which we knew was endangered only because of his civil rights
activities. Hosea in turn helped recruit youth from Savannah for our
Citizenship Program.

Savannah is a classic city of the Old South. The streets are laid
out in boulevards and squares. Live oaks hung with Spanish moss
line the wide streets. Savannah State, a black public college that was
part of the segregated system of colleges maintained in Georgia, provided the community with a small, conservative black middle class.
Like New Orleans, Savannah was a romantic coastal city, but its
local economy was just as cruel to black workers, with the exception

of the coveted jobs in the segregated longshoremen's union, most blacks in Savannah worked in lower-level service jobs in the tourist industry or as domestics in private homes.

The Savannah movement was loosely modeled on Birmingham's, and included a boycott and regular demonstrations. The local authorities were determined to crush the movement there. The police were issued blank arrest warrants by Judge Victor H. Mulling, a staunch segregationist, and they would approach anyone they thought had been involved in demonstrations or might become involved, ask their names, enter the names on the warrants, and then arrest them on the spot for "disturbing the peace." The entire active adult leadership of the movement had been arrested in this manner. To get out of jail they had to sign a pledge that they would not participate in or organize further demonstrations. When I arrived in Savannah, Hosea was in jail under a peace bond set at fifty-five thousand dollars. The unintended result of Hosea's arrest and absurdly high bond was to stir up people who had not previously been supportive of the movement.

When I arrived in Savannah, I went straight to the church where people were in line, ready to march. Willie Bolden and Ben Clark, who later became staff members of SCLC, were working with Hosea, and their plan was to march to the Holiday Inn, pass around a circular drive in front of the motel, pray, and return to the church to be dismissed. I walked along with them, taking care to stay to the side of the march.

As we marched along, I was distressed by the lack of discipline shown by the marchers. The mood was disorderly, there were no marshals, and no one led freedom songs—a clear sign of poor training. I tried to encourage Bolden and Clark to make them shape up but with no success. As we arrived at the planned turnaround at the Holiday Inn the police blocked the demonstrators from leaving the circle and started arresting them. I said to Bolden, "We can't let those kids go to jail by themselves. They don't know what they're doing!" I got no response from Bolden, so I went to one of the police officers and said, "Look, if you are going to take them to jail, you had better take me with them." He didn't say a word, just pushed me into the paddy wagon.

We were driven out to the jail, which was a work camp with old surplus army barracks. We weren't properly booked—they didn't even ask us to sign in—we were just herded into one of the large barracks. No sooner had they pushed us into the barracks than we were instructed to line up to go into a cafeteria for something to eat. For dinner, we were given a plate of grits with grease dribbled over them.

A couple of the kids said, "I don't want that." And next thing I knew the air was filled with metal plates flying around the cafeteria like Frisbees. I stopped them and calmed them down by telling them, "If you don't want to eat, you don't have to eat. You aren't in this jail to eat. You have better food at home. You are in this jail so that everybody can eat better." If the situation had gotten out of control, I feared the guards would have teargassed or maced everyone in a panic, out of their own terror and inability to maintain order.

After "dinner" I led the young demonstrators back to the sleeping area, which was filled with rows of military bunk beds. The bunks had mattresses, but no sheets or blankets. The kids had not been prepared or trained for jail. They had no toothbrushes or wash-cloths with them, no jail kits of any kind. I told them, "Everybody find a bed and let's just try to relax."

After everyone was quiet, I knew I needed to let Jean know where I was. I asked the officer on duty if I could use the phone. The policeman said, "We don't have a phone you can use, but there's a pay phone down the street at the end of the block." I asked, "Will that be all right?" He just shrugged. So I walked down the block to the telephone, called Jean, told her I was in jail (she wanted to know if I was in jail, why was I calling her from the street!), asked her to let the SCLC office know where I was, returned to the jail, and went to sleep.

The next morning we were loaded onto paddy wagons and taken down to the courthouse for hearings. The police officers packed twenty of us on trucks meant for eight. It was already hot and humid and the tiny windows were partially obstructed with metal bars across them. The crowd magnified the heat; it was like being in an oven. The kids in my paddy wagon panicked and started yelling, "It's hot, let us out of here!" The response of the police was to close the windows: now no air was circulating.

I said very calmly and quietly, "Look, they are trying to get you to crack up. They want you to scream and holler and plead. That would demonstrate that you are niggers who got out of your place. They will have punished you and put you back in your place and you'll be a good nigger for a long, long time. You can't let this get you down. You've got to use mind over matter." Then I said, "Every-body close your eyes, we're going to the beach. It's hot, we're sweat-ing. All the sweat is dripping off of us, but we're almost to the water. We've got about ten more steps to the water. When you put your self in the water, it's going to be cold, it's going to send shivers down your spine, and you're going to wonder whether you want to get in the

water, but we're going on. We're going to wade in the water." I
"walked" them out into the water until it was about waist deep.
Then I said, "Let's sing about it." We started singing soft as a whisper, "Wade in the water, wade in the water, children." When the
police officers heard us singing, they realized we weren't going to
crack up, and they let us out. From the looks on their faces, the officers were entirely disgusted with us.

By this time, Burke Marshall had called down to Savannah and
told someone in authority that I was there. He informed the Savannah officials that I had been instrumental in settling the demonstrations in Birmingham and recommended that they talk with me about
resolving the situation in Savannah. At the courthouse, I was pulled
from the group and taken to see the Savannah city manager, Arthur
A. Mendosa. He and I fashioned a way to get Hosea and the others
out of jail and established a structure for future negotiations. By then
Hosea had been in jail for sixty-six days, a longer consecutive period
of imprisonment than for any other movement leader.

With negotiations started, I returned to Atlanta to continue my
work on the Birmingham settlement and the citizenship schools. But
the poor preparation and insufficient training and organization of the
Savannah movement was a ticking time bomb, and soon violence
erupted. Three or four blocks of Savannah were burned down, and
the settlement process went down with them. The boycott of Savannah's downtown stores continued for fifteen months, but the white
establishment in Savannah was totally intransigent. As a result,
Savannah never reached a satisfactory conclusion.

Hosea wanted SCLC to launch a major campaign in Savannah,
and he wanted Martin to come down from Atlanta to lead it. But
after the Birmingham campaign we were simply exhausted. I also felt
it was important that we concentrate our energies on implementing
the Birmingham agreement, which meant we had to return there peri-
odically throughout the summer. For us to build up such a peak of
activity in Birmingham, then suddenly depart with no apparent interest in following through on the agreements so hard-won would simply not do. And SCLC just did not have the resources to mount the
kind of effort in Savannah that had just occurred in Birmingham.

In many ways, Savannah was a replay of Albany. The demonstrators had more enthusiasm than discipline. The community had
not been properly organized, and negotiations started much too late
in the process. The most delicate part of a movement, and the part
that determines whether it will ultimately be a success is whether reconciliation occurs: the same parties that are engaged in the con-

frontation must eventually be reconciled. And reconciliation requires all parties to grow, raising the situation to a new moral level. It requires a spiritual transformation to change the nature of the relationship. Part of the failure in Savannah was due to the fact that Hosea didn't fully understand the principles of nonviolence. He had a genuine passion for justice, but that passion cloaked a depth of bitterness from his own experience with segregation. In the Savannah movement, Hosea's goal was to win rather than to transform the relationships between the races in Savannah so that everyone could maintain their dignity and self-respect.

While every community needed its own movement to transform local racial arrangements, SCLC was not in a position to mount all of those movements at once. We had to focus on campaigns that would advance the national debate and change laws on the federal level. Birmingham made the case for the Civil Rights Act, and a strategy was now needed to get the votes necessary for passage.

The civil rights bill sent to Congress by President Kennedy was the most comprehensive package of civil rights proposals since Reconstruction. The Birmingham movement had given civil rights the moral high ground, but now the crafting of legislation was in the hands of the Justice Department and the NAACP's able lobbyist, Clarence Mitchell. Mitchell's work on the civil rights bill would earn him the title "101st Senator." The legislation faced political and constitutional hurdles, as comparable legislation passed in the 1870s had been invalidated by a hostile Supreme Court. One of the constitutional problems that had been raised by the legislation and had to be addressed was the separation of powers under the federal system. Desegregation of transportation and other public facilities could be mandated under the federal power to regulate interstate commerce. Similarly, employment discrimination in the states was deemed to be covered by the Fourteenth Amendment, which guarantees equal protection under the law. However, the problem of mandating desegregation in areas that were considered within the province of the states, especially schools and other matters subject to local governance, was more difficult. The technique developed by the Kennedy administration was to set standards for desegregation tied to eligibility for the receipt of federal funds. This breakthrough concept was surprisingly acceptable to members of Congress and neatly resolved the potentially fatal constitutional issues.

Once the constitutional problems were solved in a manner acceptable to congressional supporters, President Kennedy convened a meeting of several civil rights leaders, including Martin, at the

White House to discuss the political strategy for passing the bill. I accompanied Martin to the strategy session. After this meeting, John Kennedy invited Martin to take a walk with him in the Rose Garden. On that walk, Kennedy revealed to Martin the ongoing FBI surveillance of Martin's confidant Stanley Levison. The president told Martin that the FBI had uncovered information that two members of the SCLC staff, Stanley Levison and Jack O'Dell, had communist affiliations, an allegation we had received via Burke Marshall a few months earlier. Kennedy urged Martin to sever SCLC's affiliation with Stan and Jack: he was afraid Hoover would leak these allegations to segregationist Southern senators like Strom Thurmond, who would in turn use the information to defeat the upcoming civil rights legislation. Martin told the president he would give the matter serious consideration, but he did not promise Kennedy he would sever relations with Stan and Jack. He knew that the charge of communism was commonly and wildly bandied about by Southern politicians and right-wingers everywhere to attack anyone who advocated social change, particularly change that threatened the power of white supremacists. Martin himself was frequently and ludicrously accused of being a communist, despite the obvious incongruity of his status as a minister in the Baptist Church and his widely publicized philosophy of creative nonviolent protest based on Christian ideology. It wasn't as if Martin's ideas were any big secret. Yet, on highways all over the South, White Citizens Councils had placed billboard advertisements of a blown-up photograph of Martin at Highlander Folk School with the caption "Martin Luther King at Communist training school," and an arrow pointing to him.

As a lawyer, Stan had been involved in negotiating separations from the Communist Party for prominent persons who had been party members and who, when they awakened to the harsh realities of Stalinism, found themselves being threatened with blackmail when they attempted to walk away from the party. And Jack had been a union organizer for the Mine, Mill, and Smelter Workers' Uion, an organization often accused of having been infiltrated by communists.

Ironically, both Jack and Stan played extremely moderating roles in SCLC. They were experienced in some of the difficulties of social change in America and sought to keep the movement from falling victim to the kind of militancy that could become violent and self-destructive. Theirs were wise voices whose backgrounds unfortunately made them particularly vulnerable to red-baiting tactics. They were also among the few nonpreachers in our midst.

With all this in mind, Martin had pressed President Kennedy a little, asking him if he had proof Levison and O'Dell had communist connections, or if these might not be the same old political smear tactics. Kennedy answered that *he* didn't have proof, but that the FBI did. Martin felt this was hardly a satisfactory response. Besides, he knew there were sharp philosophical differences between Hoover and the Kennedy brothers themselves. What was "communist" to Hoover and the FBI might not be "communist" at all to the Kennedys if they were familiar with the facts. To assure Martin, Kennedy added that Burke Marshall would brief us on the details later. And that was the end of the discussion. Martin remarked as we were leaving the White House that "if Kennedy took me into the Rose Garden to talk about this, he must be afraid that Hoover is bugging him too."

If President Kennedy had taken the unusual step of speaking to Martin about this matter himself, he obviously was more than a little concerned, and we felt he must not trust Hoover and the FBI or what they might do with whatever allegations they were working up. So despite his reservations, when we returned to Atlanta, Martin tried to figure out how to deal with this problem.

Stan Levison was one of the first whites to offer help during the Montgomery bus boycott and was particularly key in national fund-raising. He was introduced to Martin by Bayard Rustin, the first labor union supporter of the boycott, with whom we maintained a working relationship throughout the civil rights movement. By the time Stan became interested in the Southern civil rights movement, he had severed some of his ties to the old left, and was, I suppose, looking for a new cause to devote himself to. In helping Martin, there was much that he could do, for Martin knew nothing about fund-raising. Stan established a New York office for the boycott and created the first Montgomery Improvement Association mail-solicitation efforts.

After Montgomery, Stan continued to assist Martin by offering his private counsel, and they became close personal friends. When Martin moved to Atlanta in November 1959, and the SCLC office there was organized, Stan served as an important New York supporter and fund-raiser—though unsalaried and without official staff status. Martin felt at ease around Stan because he was *not* aggressive with his advice, offered his analysis in rational and measured terms, and didn't jealously guard his influence among Martin's inner circle, as so many others did. Martin typically backed away from people who were too eager to volunteer unsolicited advice. I held many meetings with Stan as part of our New York organizational and fund-raising efforts, and I learned to trust and value his judiciousness.

When Stan and Martin first became friends, Stan had told him that he had many acquaintances from the old left who were former members of the Communist Party, and mentioned that he had been involved in legal cases defending several of these people in their attempts to sever themselves from the party. He also made it clear that he was not then, nor had he ever been, a member of the Communist Party, though he was then and had been for most of his life philosophically a socialist. He believed the American Communist Party had become outdated and authoritarian, particularly in its dealings with blacks, and was an obsolete and ineffective organization. It could not, in his view, play an important role in the movement for racial justice and civil rights. His sole activity in the area of social action was, therefore, now devoted to support of Martin and the civil rights movement. Martin believed Stan, and he believed that nothing Stan had done or said during the time he knew him was inconsistent with his revelations about his past or his work on behalf of the Montgomery Improvement Association or SCLC.

A native of Detroit, Jack O'Dell had studied pharmacy at Xavier University in New Orleans. After his junior year, he left college and shipped out to sea. While working as a merchant marine he became very active in the National Maritime Union. At that time, in the late forties and early fifties, the union was undergoing an internal fight for control between conservative and progressive factions. O'Dell was active in union politics with the progressive faction, which included several blacks. The conservative faction won control and, according to Jack, charged that the progressive faction was "communist influenced" in an attempt to tighten their control over the union. O'Dell and other blacks in the progressive wing were forced out. As a consequence of his union activity and the charges thrown around in the midst of the union fight, Jack's name had come to the attention of the FBI.

After being expelled from the union in the mid-fifties, Jack settled in Montgomery, Alabama, working for the Protective Insurance Company just at the time the Montgomery bus boycott was beginning. In Montgomery, Jack was supportive of the boycott and became very familiar with Martin and Ralph's early civil rights efforts.

In the late fifties, while still working for the insurance company, Jack became an organizer of the Prayer Pilgrimage March on Washington of 1957 and the Youth March for Integrated Schools in 1958, during which he met Stan Levison, who was also active in behind-the-scenes organizing for those marches. Levison was impressed with O'Dell's work, and soon asked him to leave the insurance company and come to work full-time for the new SCLC fund-raising office being established in New York.

When I joined the SCLC staff, Jack was already codirector of fund-raising, commuting between New York and Atlanta, where he served as the fledgling SCLC's first voter registration director. When I became coordinator of the Citizenship School Program at Dorchester, Jack proved to be an invaluable resource as a lecturer on black history. He was committed to the principles of nonviolence, and in all my experience with him he was an effective, highly intelligent, and efficient member of our staff.

There was no question in Martin's mind, or among any of our senior staff, that Stan and Jack were valuable and loyal members of the movement. While Martin always tried to cooperate with the White House, he did not yield to their pressures when his own heart and mind told him to stand firm: in both Birmingham and Albany, he had proceeded when the administration would have preferred he desist. Because of the president's concern, however, Martin felt we should contact Burke Marshall to give the administration the courtesy of hearing their evidence. When I called Burke Marshall, though, he said he could not discuss the matter on the telephone. Instead, he asked me to meet him in New Orleans at the old courthouse in Lafayette Square.

So I flew over to New Orleans for our rendezvous, feeling like an actor in a spy drama. He insisted we walk the halls of the huge, stately courthouse while we talked. When I pressed him for specifics, he said he had none; nor could he show me any documents to support the allegations. He just repeated that the FBI had evidence that Stan was a high-level Soviet agent. I asked Marshall if *he* had seen documents supporting this. He said, no, he had not. But he reiterated that the president was very desirous that SCLC sever ties with Stan and Jack immediately. In subsequent conversations with Burke Marshall, I continued to press him for supporting evidence, but never got any. At this date, more than three decades later, after the information released under the Freedom of Information Act and everything else we've learned, I can only conclude we never received any evidence supporting these allegations from the administration because there wasn't any.

After considerable discussion with the executive staff, Martin decided that he should meet with Stan and Jack in New York and talk with them as honestly as possible about these charges. Martin, attorney Clarence Jones of our New York support team, and I met first with Jack in New York to lay the problem out as plainly as we could. Jack went over with us his early union conflicts, which had occurred during the McCarthy period, and the subsequent FBI surveillance of him, of which he had been well aware. In this meeting, Martin told Jack he did not think there was any substance to the matter, but added that he was quite concerned that the charges would be used to attack the movement by its enemies. It would therefore be better that Jack resign, to prevent this from happening, and in the hope that FBI surveillance would let up; it was quite obvious to Jack that the New York office telephones were tapped, and he knew that agents were questioning his friends and acquaintances about him. (We had every reason to believe similar surveillance was being conducted in Atlanta, and when Martin was on the road.) Jack agreed to resign, and did so, though all of us felt uncomfortable about it. Martin wrote him a very cordial letter praising him for his service and dedication, a copy of which was sent to the Justice Department.

Martin had many second thoughts about Jack's resignation. He knew that this was McCarthyism, and he believed that you had to stand up to that kind of red-baiting. He complied only because of the effect the allegations could have on the civil rights bill, which he felt must not be jeopardized. I reminded Martin that he was not acting to protect his personal reputation but the reputation of the civil rights movement. Stan and Jack were very mature, politically astute individuals who were utterly committed to the movement. There was never any sense that they felt betrayed by Martin, and Jack offered his resignation like a good soldier making his sacrifice for the greater good. It was the best course of action in an unfair and unjust situation.

Ultimately Jack continued to do SCLC work, but without pay from SCLC accounts. I suspect that Stan paid Jack from his personal funds. But Martin always felt bad about asking Jack to resign, and so did I. When we began to reorganize the SCLC staff after Martin was killed, we asked Jack to return and he did. Later, in the 1970s, he worked for Operation Breadbasket in Chicago, and after that with Jesse Jackson's Rainbow Coalition.

Stan Levison was out of the country when we met with Jack. Martin talked with Stan later; Stan felt, after hearing the story of the administration's entreaties, that it would be better that he and Martin not see each other for a while and not speak over the telephone. From that point on, Stan ceased to participate in SCLC meetings, even as an observer. He didn't resign from anything because he was neither on staff nor an SCLC board member; his relationship with us had always been volunteer and unofficial. He received no salary or payment from SCLC, and he would not accept payment from Martin for his personal, legal, or editorial work.

But despite the decision that Stan would sever even his informal relations with SCLC, it was impossible for Martin to sever his personal connection with him, since he had come to rely so heavily on Stan's advice and friendship. As events later developed and the FBI surveillance of us did not stop, Martin increasingly felt there was no point in trying to hide relationships that he believed to be honest, beneficial to his work, and based on mutual respect.

During the period all this was going on we strongly suspected, though had no way of proving, that our office telephones were bugged. Little things like trouble with the phones, echoes, and weird sounds tipped us off. We did not become overly concerned with this invasion of privacy because we were conducting a consciously open movement, and we knew there was nothing we discussed that would prove damaging if the government knew what we were doing, or what we planned to do. Of course, if we had complained to the Justice Department that our telephones were bugged, they would have simply denied it. So we made jokes among ourselves about the "sound studio" we lived in. To us, basic civil liberties seemed secondary to our fundamental objective of destroying racial segregation and obtaining the power of the ballot. During this time plans were shaping up for a march on Washington. Jim Bevel had started talking about marching to Washington from Birmingham, to show the country what Birmingham was all about. He had gotten the kids excited about going on a dramatic march. Bevel's goal was to put eight thousand kids on Highway 11, a grand march from Birmingham to Washington in imitation of Gandhi's spectacular Salt March to the Sea in India. Birmingham is twelve hundred miles from Washington and the logistical problems of moving, feeding, and taking care of the physical needs of eight thousand people walking from Alabama to Washington was too daunting even to contemplate. Bevel assured us that people along the way would feed the kids, or that they could "live off the land." He said, "The worst thing they can do to us is put us in jail, and we've all been to jail." The cross-country march never came off, but out of the germ of Bevel's idea came SCLC's commitment to the famous celebration of August 28, 1963.

I called Bayard Rustin, a protégé of the great African-American labor leader A. Philip Randolph, and arranged for Bayard to talk to us about a march on Washington. A. Philip Randolph himself had at one time planned a march on Washington to dramatize the need for civil rights. But just the threat of such a march had persuaded President Franklin Roosevelt to sign an Executive Order forbidding racial discrimination in the war industries. I was interested in the idea, having been to the 1957 Prayer Pilgrimage that helped to convince President Eisenhower to pass a civil rights act that established a Civil Rights Commission and the Civil Rights Division at the Department of Justice.

Whitney Young, executive director of the Urban League, and Roy Wilkins, executive director of the NAACP, were initially against the idea of a march, saying it would not be advisable and that too many things could go wrong. But A. Philip Randolph's advocacy for the march began to make it sound respectable. Although the Kennedys were against the march and tried to discourage it at the White House meeting in June, when they realized the momentum was beyond their control, they began to try to manage the march. Concerned that an all-black march would hurt the chances for passage of the civil rights bill, they encouraged white union officials to get behind the March on Washington as well. The NAACP and the Urban League became even more enthusiastic once the Kennedys gave their support, calling it a March on Washington for Jobs and Freedom. The march became a joint effort, a coalition of conscience, black and white Americans of goodwill looking together for change that was long overdue.

The march that eventually evolved from the "Big Six" civil rights organizations (the Southern Christian Leadership Conference, Student Nonviolent Coordinating Committee, National Association for the Advancement of Colored People, National Council of Negro Women, Urban League, and Congress of Racial Equality), the unions, and some religious leaders was not the revolutionary statement Jim Bevel had originally envisioned. His vision was a grassroots march, a march made up of the people who went to jail and sacrificed for the movement. The March on Washington had become establishment, made up of middle-class blacks and liberal whites who had been reluctant to voice support for Birmingham in the early days. This was not a march in Birmingham denim, but one that required one's new Sunday go-to-meetin' suit. Bevel was angered by this turn of events, complaining, "You all turned my march into a picnic."

I had decided not to attend the march, either, not because I was angry like Bevel, but because I just didn't see the need to go. We had done our preparation work in the South, spreading the word, organizing buses, setting up transportation stations, and making arrangements for food and water to be on the buses that would drive all night. Most of the marchers could not afford to spend a night in a hotel, as I had for the 1957 Prayer Pilgrimage; they would ride all night to Washington, and all night back. I was exhausted from months of running back and forth to Birmingham, monitoring the settlement, getting people out of jail, putting out staff fires. Now my wife and kids were on summer vacation from school and I hadn't yet had time to see them. I reasoned that if the NAACP and the labor unions were prepared to organize for the march, I was happy to stay home and take my family for a much-needed vacation to Lake Alatoona.

The March on Washington for Jobs and Freedom took place on August 28, 1963, and Martin arrived in Washington a couple of days before the march to prepare his speech. There was an SCLC suite at the Willard Hotel and Martin had a private room on another floor. When Martin arrived and realized that Bevel and I were not among the SCLC staff present, Martin called to tell us to come. Jean got a baby-sitter for the girls and the two of us flew to Washington, but Bevel refused to budge and remained in the South. We took a room at the Willard, a very old and historic but rundown hotel, with a shabby grandeur, like European hotels after the war. Even so, it was far superior to Gaston's Motel in Birmingham.

There was tremendous behind-the-scenes haggling over the speeches and the order of speakers. Everyone knew that the early speakers would be the ones to make the television news programs, so Roy Wilkins and Whitney Young scrambled for the early slots. At first they had done everything in their power to stop the march, but once it was going to happen, they were determined to be the stars. After Martin had already finished laboring over his speech, he was told that all speakers were to be limited to three minutes each. In the order of the program, they left Martin until the end, after the cameras would be expected to leave to process their film.

The Willard overlooks Pennsylvania Avenue on the stretch that runs between Union Station and the Lincoln Memorial. The morning of the march I woke up early; it was difficult to sleep because I was worried whether enough people would actually come. I went out onto Pennsylvania Avenue, and there they were, walking, streaming from the train station and the bus station from the East. Then the buses began to pull in from the South, and I could hear the voices singing freedom songs, "Ain't gonna let nobody turn me 'round, turn me round, turn me 'round, ain't gonna let nobody turn me 'round we're gonna keep on a-walkin', keep on a-talkin', marching up to freedom land." I felt a huge surge of emotion and I realized I was glad I had come.

Jean and I were in the crowd at the foot of the steps of the Lin-

coln Memorial, where we had managed to squeeze into a reserved section. It was a hot and humid August day, the kind of day that reminds
you why anyone who can afford to leaves Washington in August. The
leaders on the platform were dressed in Sunday formality, but Jean
and I were spared that. Jean wore a simple lightweight cotton dress
and I wore khakis and a sports shirt. Our church in Thomasville was
often as hot as the Lincoln Memorial was on that day, so we knew
what to expect. I teased Jean for her longing looks at the marchers
behind us dangling their feet in the Reflecting Pool. There was a lot of
celebrity watching, which added some excitement to the mostly flat
speeches. We saw Lena Horne, Charlton Heston, Harry Belafonte
(Jean almost swooned), and James Baldwin in the crowd.

The speeches droned on. It got hotter and hotter, nearly as hot as
that paddy wagon in Savannah had been. Finally the time came for
Martin to speak. Surprisingly—and fortunately for posterity—the
cameras were still there. The press knew what the story was; they
knew that it was our work in Birmingham that had placed civil rights
at the top of the nation's agenda, and they weren't about to miss the
one who was responsible.

When Martin stood up, the restless crowd became still. He
began with familiar phrases from his "Bad Check" speech:

> We've come here today to dramatize a shameful condition. In a
> sense we've come to our nation's capital to cash a check. When
> the architects of our republic wrote the magnificent words of
> the Constitution and the Declaration of Independence, they
> were signing a promissory note to which every American was
> to fall heir. This note was the promise that all men, yes black
> men as well as white men, would be guaranteed the unalien-
> able rights of life, liberty and the pursuit of happiness. It is
> obvious today that America has defaulted on this promissory
> note insofar as her citizens of color are concerned. Instead of
> honoring this sacred obligation, America has given the Negro
> people a bad check; a check which has come back marked
> "insufficient funds." We refuse to believe that there are insuffi-
> cient funds in the great vaults of opportunity of this nation.
> And so we've come to cash this check, a check that will give us
> upon demand the riches of freedom and the security of justice.

Martin went on to paint a picture of the struggle for justice in
the South before moving into the now familiar cadences of his "I
Have a Dream" litany. Unfortunately, more than thirty years later,

that "bad check" continues to plague this nation. The despairing and often violent underclass in our cities is made up of those who went to redeem their promissory note at the bank of opportunity, only to have it returned marked "insufficient funds." America has accepted Martin's happy vision of equality without applying its full resources to enabling the dream to become a reality for all citizens. We are content to be swept away by the beautiful dream and are unwilling to recognize the painful realities that keep the dream from coming true.

There are two things the world will long remember about the March on Washington that day—Martin's speaking and Mahalia Jackson's singing. After Martin's inspiring words, the great gospel singer took the spirit of the crowd as high as the heavens with her rendition of "Soon I Will Be Done with the Troubles of the World," and brought the march to a thrilling close.

Martin's speech at the March on Washington revealed a dramatic shift in the civil rights leadership of the nation. The NAACP was the oldest civil rights organization and was widely acknowledged to be the preeminent organization as well. It was the NAACP that had had the audacity to advocate integration and develop the legal strategy that ended the legitimacy of "separate but equal." The Urban League began as a social work organization improving the conditions of rural African-Americans who migrated to the cities, especially in the North. Under Whitney Young, the Urban League had enlisted the support of corporate America in its urban strategy. This was important work, and Martin consciously avoided competition with either organization. But neither the NAACP nor the Urban League had a strategy to involve the great masses of African-Americans in taking control of their own destiny. The NAACP had based its strategy on petitioning for justice through the courts, the Congress, and the president. Its approach sought to shape interpretations of the law and to enforce obedience to it. Sit-ins and demonstrations operated on a theory of noncooperation with injustice that was contrary to the NAACP emphasis on legal means. There were many, including Thurgood Marshall, the author of the NAACP's legal strategy, who greatly resented Martin and SCLC's willingness to break the law, even unjust laws. They had crafted a decades-long strategy of promoting civil rights through obedience to the law and SCLC seemed poised to undermine that carefully nurtured strategy. As far as the established civil rights leaders were concerned, we were upstarts: young, brash, and irresponsible.

It is somewhat amusing to me when young people today accuse older civil rights leaders of being unwilling to surrender the torch. No one surrendered the torch to a thirty-four-year-old Martin King and SCLC. We took it by the strength of our actions. The nonviolent protest in Birmingham mobilized poor and working-class African-Americans to end their passive assent to their own oppression. When that power was unleashed, segregation ended in Birmingham, and a new force for civil rights had arrived.

SCLC filled a gap in the civil rights arsenal: we found a way to make civil rights live for the masses of African-Americans. It was always Martin's intent to work with the NAACP, the Urban League, SNCC, CORE, and other organizations toward our common goal of ending segregation in America. But whatever Martin's intent, it was difficult to avoid tension after his "I Have a Dream" speech at the March on Washington, where he emerged as the most recognizable and esteemed civil rights leader in the country. Most people were now looking to Atlanta for leadership, whereas for decades the mantle of racial leadership had rested with the NAACP. Other organizations resented Martin's ability to get headlines and attract attention and in turn Martin was hurt by their criticism that he was the "Lone Ranger" coming into any situation and taking all the glory. I maintain that everyone benefited by our success in Birmingham. When people saw civil rights moving forward in Birmingham, they were just as likely to send a check to the NAACP as they were to SCLC. It made people more attentive to the organization with which they had the best relationship. But perhaps naively, we really didn't understand how deep the resentment ran at times; we thought it was simply personal jealousy. Martin's historic speech at the March on Washington stole the show, and while it contributed greatly to the cause of civil rights, it did little to endear him to other civil rights leaders.

Immediately following the March on Washington, I left the United States for Switzerland. My friends and colleagues at the United Church of Christ were aware of the nonstop pace I had kept up throughout 1963. As a reward, Wes Hotchkiss appointed me as a delegate to a World Council of Churches Consultation on "The Church in the Development Decade," which took place at the Chateau de Bossey in Switzerland. In an attempt to make it a working vacation, Hotchkiss and Bob Spike booked first-class reservations for Bob and me on the Queen Elizabeth for the trip to Europe. Jean encouraged me to go although another school year was beginning for her, and the two older girls were starting their first classes at Trinity Presbyterian School. She had begun to assume that I would be unavailable for events like the first day of school, school plays, and PTA meetings.

We were still living our parallel lives, and the day-to-day responsibility for the children was within her sphere.

It was a miserable five-day trip. The ship seemed to be populated entirely by doctors' widows. There were no young people at all and Bob and I ended up serving as unofficial pastoral counselors to all these well-to-do widows. The one interesting person I met was an heir to the Dayton-Hudson department store fortune. We met in the finals of the Ping-Pong tournament. I was relieved when the ship finally docked in Europe, and I had to admit to myself that regardless of the luxurious surroundings, I just couldn't enjoy a vacation without Jean. Nonetheless, it was a welcome break for me from the intensity of my SCLC work and I returned from the conference refreshed and ready to face new challenges. But nothing could have prepared me for the terrible events of September 15.

On that Sunday morning the Sixteenth Street Baptist Church, the church that had hosted so many mass meetings during the Birmingham movement, was struck by a bomb. Four precious little girls, Denise McNair, Carole Robertson, Cynthia Wesley, and Addie Mae Collins, so like my own daughters in their best dresses and patent leather Mary Jane shoes, were killed while they listened to their Sunday school lessons.

This hit too close to home. I was rather cavalier about the possibility of my own death, but the murder of little girls in church defied every conceivable standard of civilized conduct. Their deaths, the bombings, the murder of Medgar Evers, the brutality in Winona, coming as they did after settlements, and after introduction of the Civil Rights Act, were senseless acts of violent retaliation from whites who could not or would not accept the changes that were coming, that had already begun. There was no better indication of my father's belief that racism was a sickness. Nonviolent change attempted to address that sickness, to help whites remove the racial blinders that prevented their seeing their own best interests. But while we spent hours negotiating with the representatives of the well-off business class and Martin spent several days a week speaking to middle- and upper-class whites in the North about our cause, we had no real access to poor and working-class whites in the South. Segregation gave status to poor whites, who were neither well educated nor well-to-do, simply on the basis of their skin color. The bombing of a church on Sunday morning was an ominous sign of the depth of the resistance that existed on the margins of the white community.

The Christian mystics talk about a "dark night of the soul," and for me the bombing of the Sixteenth Street Church triggered that experience. I could not bring myself to attend the funeral. But I heard from Bernard Lee how Martin transformed this tragedy with a sermon on the redemptive power of unearned suffering. Surely no suffering was more pure, more unearned, than the suffering of those little girls and their parents. If the redemptive power of that suffering was as great as their innocence, then the movement was about to experience a greater transformation of America than we could imagine. If our mission was to redeem the soul of America, I felt, the Cross would show the way.

11

Walking Through
the Valley

Oh Lord, keep me from sinking down.
　　　　　　　　　　　—African-American Traditional

A ny sense of our accomplishments in Birmingham was tempered
by the tremendous cost. There was no feeling of triumph; it
would have been inimical to the spirit of nonviolence. One of
the principles of nonviolence is that you leave your opponents whole
and better off than you found them. We didn't view success as defeating opponents, rather we wanted to make Birmingham a better place
to live and work and we were able to achieve that because of the
tremendous spiritual power of Birmingham's black citizens and their
willingness to forgive in the face of unspeakable provocation.

As we sought to consolidate and enforce the Birmingham agreement, the SCLC staff was exhausted and our cupboards were bare.
Stan Levison had been the volunteer organizer of our fund-raising
apparatus, and J. Edgar Hoover's false allegations had forced him to
the sidelines just as our coffers were exhausted. The rest of us were
too immersed in the field to mount effective fund-raising efforts.
Ironically, and once again proving that our successes benefited others,

the NAACP, SNCC, and CORE all had tremendous fund-raising success during SCLC's Birmingham campaign.

We needed time to relax with our families, regroup, and reorganize the staff. The time with our families was precious, made more so by the ever-present threat of violence that had hung over us since the brutal events of the previous summer. Martin liked to swim, and while the swimming pools in Atlanta were still segregated, the Ollie Street Branch of the YMCA, near Booker T. Washington High School in the heart of Atlanta's black community, had an indoor pool and occasionally we would all gather there, or at the home of Herman and Otelia Russell, for a family swim: Martin and his children, Ralph and his children, and me and my girls. I could swim underwater for the entire length of the pool and a favorite game was to surprise the children by sneaking up on them underwater. The children's giggles would echo off the walls and for a few moments we could shed the pressures of the movement and just enjoy being young fathers. The children were nine and younger, with all the exuberance that a happy and protected childhood had given them. That upbringing was mostly their mothers' doing, but being with Daddy was special and they were always on their best behavior on these outings.

Even as I was heavily involved with our efforts in Birmingham, Savannah, and the March on Washington, I continued to work with the Citizenship School Program, where we trained Birmingham activists and sent potential teachers to be trained at the monthly weeklong sessions. It was our intention that each movement leave in place a network of trained people to conduct voter education and registration efforts. During the intense phase of the Birmingham campaign, we suspended the regular monthly training sessions, but otherwise I usually made it there for a day or two. With Dorothy and me so immersed in Birmingham, though, it fell to Septima Clark to keep the citizenship training going for every other county in the South that we had identified in our original plan.

Because of some problems with the Dorchester facility, we ultimately moved our training sessions to Penn Center in South Carolina. Penn Center was closer for the students, most of whom were from the Carolinas and Virginia, although it was farther from home for me. It was while Septima and I were leading a workshop at the Penn Community Center that we heard the news, whispered in Septima's ear, that President Kennedy had been shot. We gathered everyone in the chapel and there we shared the sorrowful news. The chapel was comforting in its Quaker simplicity; the bare wooden floors and angular lines suited the somber mood that fell over the group. Somebody began to pray. This was not prayer as performance, standing regally in front of the gathered community grasping the security of a podium. This was heart-baring prayer. When it was your time to pray you got down on your knees, put your elbows on the seat of one of the cold, metal folding chairs and your head on your hands and begged for the comfort that only God can provide. The folk gathered there knew something had happened that could potentially change the course of the country and particularly their own lives. We had come to love John Kennedy, even though much of the time we were frustrated with him. We so often couldn't understand why he hadn't just enforced the law. It was hard to grasp why he had to wait for a political consensus to act on a matter of justice and morality. Still, he had gone further than any other president in advancing our cause, and because he had finally stood up and clearly articulated his support of the civil rights movement, everything that followed was made possible.

I cried, everybody cried. I don't know whether we cried for the Kennedys or for the country or for ourselves. Then someone began to sing the old dirges, and the sounds of mourning went around the room:

Oh Lord, Oh Lord, Oh Lord, Oh my good Lord
Keep me from sinking down
I know what I'm gonna do, keep me from sinking down
I'm gonna get me freedom, too
Keep me from sinking down.

At this point, among the SCLC executive staff, only Dorothy Cotton, James Bevel, and Ralph Abernathy remained, and Hosea Williams, Randolph Blackwell, and C. T. Vivian, a veteran of the Nashville movement, came on staff. Our immediate mission was to enforce the Birmingham agreement while tightening our organization so that it could continue to function on several levels and operate different projects simultaneously.

Randolph Blackwell, a college professor who had left academia to work for the first Voter Education Project in 1962, joined our staff as an administrator during the Birmingham campaign. Blackwell's real interest, however, was in forming rural economic cooperatives and small-scale economic development projects that would make it possible for a core leadership group to become independent of the "sharecropper economy" of the South. Black small farmers, sharecroppers, and farmworkers were entirely dependent on the large landowners in their county for consumer goods, supplies, and a market for their crops. Blackwell's thinking was that black farmers could develop their own cooperatives and pool resources to develop their own mills, purchasing arrangements, and market locations so as to be independent of exploitive plantation owners.

Blackwell was a tall, dark-skinned Renaissance man who prided himself on being able to recognize any piece of classical music. He would challenge his wife, Libby, to place the needle anyplace on a record and he could give the name of the piece. He had worked his way through college and graduate school and earned an MBA and law degree at the same time from Northwestern, and had believed that his achievements would prove that he was as good as any white person. He joined the Voter Education Project after he became disabused of the belief that personal merit would shield him from white racism. He hid his essential optimism behind a cynical and ironic sense of humor.

Libby Blackwell was a schoolteacher, like Jean, and she and Jean became great friends. Blackwell and Libby were a bridge between our separate lives. Libby was a totally unpretentious, fun-loving woman with a wicked sense of humor. The Blackwells' only daughter, Blanche, was the same age as our middle daughter, Lisa, and they were similarly thin. I teasingly called them skinny-minnies. Before long, Blackwell and his family had regular seats at our dinner table.

The SCLC staff continued to evolve as each local campaign revealed talented people committed to the movement. James Orange, a former short-order cook who quit his job to dedicate himself to ending segregation in Birmingham, became a permanent member of the SCLC staff. As director of education for SCLC, Dorothy Cotton took on more of the responsibility for running the Citizenship School Program as I was drawn into more facets of the movement. C. T. Vivian continued as director of affiliates; in the SCLC structure, preachers in cities and towns across the South formed local affiliates to conduct their own campaigns for social change and voter registration. The preachers who formed local affiliates had their own justice agenda, as had Fred Shuttlesworth in Birmingham. C. T., a tall, nut-brown angular man full of nervous energy and perpetually optimistic, was well suited to the task of nurturing these groups and keeping them encouraged, especially when actions like Birmingham were getting all the press and national attention. Local affiliates were key to the long-term effectiveness of SCLC. And while the national staff of SCLC was too small and had too little money to mount major campaigns in every town and county in the South, we could support them with assistance on strategy and training.

Meanwhile, Ralph Abernathy and Wyatt Walker began to drift away. Ralph had the major demands of a large Baptist church, which he pastored without a full-time professional assistant. Unlike Martin, he had no father who could fill in when he was away, preaching funerals and handling daily church administration. But Ralph was also becoming resentful of Martin's growing public prominence. He felt that he deserved more of the kind of attention that Martin was receiving and was upset that he hadn't been asked to speak at the March on Washington. When Ralph made a speech or went to support a local affiliate, he didn't receive the kind of press or public attention that Martin did. Ralph loved Martin, but as often happens with brothers, he was also jealous of him.

Wyatt had never resolved his frustrations over the conflicts that arose with Jim Bevel and other staff members during the Birmingham campaign. He felt that Martin should have supported him when staff members refused to recognize his authority, and he never quite got over Martin's refusal to fire Bevel when Wyatt insisted. Martin simply shrugged off Wyatt's complaint about Bevel, but issues of accountability, chain of command, and authority were important to Wyatt. If Martin was going to undercut his authority, then Wyatt couldn't fulfill what he saw as his responsibility. As a result of his disenchantment, Wyatt began looking at other opportunities, talking with Congressman Adam Clayton Powell about a position at his Abyssinian Baptist Church in New York City. In turn I began to fill in the gaps occasioned by Wyatt's absences.

After the Savannah demonstrations in the summer of 1963, Hosea Williams expressed an interest in joining our staff, and in the fall of that year Martin asked him to come on board to undertake the organizing and coordinating of voter registration campaigns on an expanded Southwide scale. "We need people who are confrontational," he said. "Some of us have a tendency to become too comfortable with injustice. Not Hosea. He's going to go out there and start something, and though we don't know what it might lead to, we need people like that."

Hosea was a chemist with the Department of Agriculture and was used to making a very good salary, more than any of us, so I had persuaded Gayraud Wilmore of the Presbyterian Church national staff to pay Hosea, as the UCC had done with me. The Presbyterians paid Hosea twelve thousand dollars a year, which made him the highest-paid person at SCLC. Martin received no salary from SCLC:

Ebenezer Baptist paid him six thousand dollars per year, and that was primarily what he and his family lived on. Martin believed in maintaining a simple lifestyle, but he also knew that it was dangerous for him to draw a salary from SCLC. Although he had been acquitted of the tax fraud charges leveled against him after the Montgomery bus boycott, he was very sensitive to the potential for tax harassment. Martin's income was supplemented by public speaking, although he gave most of his honoraria to SCLC, and the huge speaking fees of today were unknown. The precarious financial condition of Martin's family was of constant concern to Coretta.

Other SCLC staff used various means to supplement their income from SCLC. Ralph maintained his own church; Jean and Libby Blackwell taught school. Physicians like Bernard Bridges would treat members of our staff at little or no charge. Fortunately, housing in Atlanta was not expensive and some staff members cut expenses further by forming group houses. Our organizers in the field never had enough money though, and would not have survived without the in-kind contributions of local folk who fed them and gave them shelter. Of all the professionals who contributed their services and donors who contributed funds to SCLC, none gave more than the poor black citizens of the South's cities, towns, and rural areas who shared their tables and their homes with civil rights workers.

Although it would be months before I received the official title of executive director, I had begun to function in that role. I didn't think much of titles, really, but structure gives people a sense of security. Our core staff were strong and diverse personalities, so I had no illusions about being overly authoritative. I had learned from observing Wyatt's attempts to be dictatorial that such a style just wouldn't work in SCLC. Our staff people were innovative, headstrong, and competitive and that is the kind of staff Martin wanted. Our "work" was a commitment to social change in America and that required a unique quality of spirit and dedication. We were not a typical business or even a typical social service organization, nor did we want to be.

I thought of myself as a playmaker on the team; it was my job to keep the ball moving, it was not my job to score media points or call undue attention to myself. My job was to see that each one of my team of stars got the ball enough, had opportunities to score, and played some defense. Or, we might be compared to a jazz combo, where everyone is playing a different instrument, a different line, but the same song. Each person would get a chance to solo. I used those illustrations with the staff. The team approach is more in vogue now, and management workshops are full of talk of quality circles and skunk works, but then, the operative model was authoritarian. On one hand, Martin liked my style, but still he seemed less tolerant when my team approach didn't work than he was when Wyatt's more authoritarian style was ineffective. Martin was a Baptist preacher, the son and grandson of Baptist preachers, and the leadership style of Baptist preachers was authoritarian.

However, ultimately I knew that it was most important to Martin to see SCLC grow as an autonomous entity, to become less dependent on him and his constant presence. The easy way to conduct voter registration or organize a community was to have a big rally featuring Martin Luther King as the keynote speaker, but in the long term it wasn't effective. Since Martin simply couldn't be everywhere, I had to build a staff who were capable of taking their own leadership roles. People around the South thought that if Martin Luther King came to their town, white people would be so frightened they would do whatever local civil rights activists were demanding. It just didn't work that way, of course. Martin's presence without groundwork was what we had in Albany and it simply wasn't enough. For the future strength of the movement, we needed to develop the capability to organize a community and sustain movements without his presence.

Given the countless demands on Martin's time and energy, my role also involved controlling access to Martin. So when Martin didn't go along with the suggestions advocated by the executive staff, I was the one who caught hell. I was the "bad guy" because Martin didn't like to tell people no, a disinclination that I understood and accepted. He depended on me and a couple of other people to advise him concerning the many proposals, directives, requests for organizational endorsements, and so forth that came across his desk. In providing counsel, I never told him what I thought he should or shouldn't do. He expected me to review, summarize, and analyze the options. My practice was to say, "If you do 'A' it means this, and if you do 'B' it will probably mean that," and then give my reasons. For example, Hosea always had a dramatic scheme to change the world in one day and, like all of us, Hosea got his credibility from being able to deliver Martin. If I thought it was a good concept, I would recommend it to Martin, but if I thought it was a poor use of his time, if Hosea wanted Martin's attention to satisfy his own ego rather than provide a timely boost to the momentum of a movement, I would say no. I would then be blamed not simply for blocking access to Martin, but for blocking the progress of black people.

Martin eventually made all the decisions himself, and as often as not they were not what I privately would have preferred that he do. On those occasions when the entire executive staff wanted Martin to do something but he didn't want to, he occasionally would simply get "sick" until it was too late to do it. That was his way of saying no— at least to those of us who understood what it meant when he said he was "feeling tired." When Martin really wanted to do something he was never "feeling tired," no matter how little sleep he might have had.

On those occasions when the staff got carried away with its own enthusiasm and forgot the importance of timing for the movement, Martin would exercise his personal veto power over the group. I likened our staff to a team of wild horses, pulling in different directions, and all disliking anyone's hand on the reins. Martin understood, however, that the mantle of leadership had been thrust upon him and not us or the organization, and that it was his obligation not to squander his leadership on poorly planned, ill-timed, or nonproductive causes. Similarly, most of us understood that Martin had been given a special leadership role. It would never be written that Andrew Young had been wrong, or that SCLC had failed; it was always "the nonviolent leadership of Martin Luther King, Jr." that was on trial. But while he could be quite eloquent in defense of his position, it was always a most difficult job for him to say no to people who had suffered for centuries and saw in him a panacea for all their ills—social, political, and economic.

Martin was not interested in making "Amos 'n' Andy" plans. In that controversial television program, the characters had a new get-rich scheme every week that invariably ended in utter failure. One of Martin's favorite terms for what happened when you weren't organized or prepared was a "flunk." To explain this concept, Martin would begin one of his mock sermons about the preacher who left his sermon preparation until early Sunday morning and prayed for the Holy Spirit to speak through him: "He reared back and began to preach, but it wasn't the Holy Spirit, it was Flunk who came in and took over." Martin wanted planning that took into account what could be done and when it could be done, and he wanted to know whether we had the resources to do it. We always overstretched those resources, but at least we began with a realistic assessment.

I often played devil's advocate to new proposals or suggestions with questions such as "Well, how do you expect we can get that done?" or "What happens then?" If in a staff meeting discussion went off into outer space, it was my tendency to try to bring everyone back to Earth. Because I tried to present the most conservative options in our staff meetings, the staff began calling me "the Uncle Tom of SCLC." But within a volatile and imaginative staff someone needed to ask the hard questions, someone needed to think about the consequences of our planned strategies, someone needed to try to imagine the worst-case scenario, and it fell to me to be that person. And as with most humor in a competitive situation, the "Tom" label had an edge to it. It didn't bother me for the most part, because I was secure in who I was, but it was tiresome. It's easy to be self-righteous and accomplish nothing, but I was a pragmatist and I wasn't interested in wasting SCLC's efforts when there was so much that could be accomplished through rational means.

Sometimes I tired of being the person who always had to bring up the unpleasant realities. On one occasion I decided to willfully lend my enthusiastic consent to every suggestion, no matter how wild, that came from Bevel and Hosea. I even added a few grandiose touches of my own. First Martin began to look at me in a very concerned way. Then Hosea also began shooting suspicious glances. Dorothy looked startled. After the meeting Martin asked me if I was all right. I replied: "Listen, Martin, I'm sick of being the bad guy; if they're such 'geniuses' I'm tired of arguing with them all the time." This really made Martin angry. "I *depend* on you to bring a certain kind of common sense to staff meetings, and you know it," he said. "Now, if you decide you are going to start playing games, I don't see why I need you. I need you to take as conservative a position as possible, then I can have plenty of room to come down in the middle wherever I want to." After that discussion I decided I would maintain my role as the voice of common sense, and that no matter what any of the others might think, Martin needed me to do just that.

Despite that determination, staff meetings were never particularly satisfying for me. I really believed in the democratic process, that the way you discerned the will of God was to let everyone express their ideas and then choose what seemed the wisest and best course. But everyone on the staff was so high-strung, aggressive, and egotistical that it was hard to convey to them the concept of consensus building and discernment that I had in mind. I think Martin thought my way was very un-Baptist, which it was. He would have liked for me to come in with a program and sell it to the group. But Wyatt had done it that way and been totally frustrated. In any case, I didn't feel qualified to come into meetings with a prepackaged plan. I didn't presume to know where the movement was supposed to go; rather, I was constantly trying to read the signs of the times.

In my days with the National Council of Churches I had done a lot of work with group dynamics. I believed that the group could determine its own destiny. I had run experiments for adult leaders of youth groups in which we would get together as a group of adults and decide the agenda of the meeting and write it down. Then, without telling the young people our agenda, we would let the young people run the meeting their own way. Inevitably, they would cover exactly what the adults wanted covered and add things more crucial to their own needs and priorities.

Similarly, at SCLC meetings I saw no point in trying to stifle these strong egos and ambitions. I thought that it was counterproductive to even attempt it, and I doubt it would have been possible. But nobody else was used to working that way. They would get frustrated; they wanted me to come in with an action plan that they could all take positions against and then tear apart.

Martin understood the limitations of the staff in Atlanta and used the board and regional advisory groups to supplement what we lacked. Board members would often sit in on our staff meetings, people like Daddy King and Roland Smith, an authoritarian Baptist from Arkansas. If I asked Smith a question, before he'd answer he'd turn to me and say in his most arrogant voice, "Little nigger, don't you know nothing?" And I'd say, "I know I don't know, that's why I am asking for your input." But Daddy King would take up for me. "Don't play Andy cheap," he would say. "Andy knows what he's talking about." "Dad," as we called him, was a stabilizing presence. He attended only the important meetings, but was always available to share his wisdom and experience. I had the greatest respect for Daddy King, who had traveled a long journey from a sharecropper's shack to one of the most influential pulpits in Atlanta. Martin had developed interesting coping skills from his childhood under this strong-willed, even domineering man. Rather than rebel against older men, he courted authority figures, like his intellectual mentor, Dr. Benjamin Mays. "Dad" was Martin's spiritual mentor.

When he needed to make important decisions, Martin sought feedback from an informal network of "research committees" that included Harry Belafonte, Stan Levison, Clarence Jones, Bayard Rustin, and Harry Wachtel in New York; attorney Chauncy Eskridge, Jet's editor Bob Johnson, and historian Lerone Bennett in Chicago; A. M. E. Bishop Brookings of Los Angeles, Rev. John Hurst Adams, Rev. Tom Kilgore, and Rev. Amos Brown of San Francisco, and Reverend McKinney of Seattle on the West Coast. Through these groups he solicited feedback from important and influential regions of the country. Martin's network, which included many men he met at Morehouse, was an extremely useful tool that emerged from his ability to charm and win over powerful figures, thus avoiding the dangers of failed rebellion.

Rev. Fred Bennett became my confidant during that time of trying to fill SCLC's most impossible role. Bennett was a childhood friend of Martin's from the neighborhood around Auburn Avenue and saw himself as Martin's protector, even when they were kids. When Martin returned to Atlanta, Bennett began to serve as his driver, although by that time Fred had actually been called to the ministry and even had his own church. Bennett was a humble man who never forgot his childhood on the streets. He could never pass anyone begging and would give his last penny to someone in need. He loved Martin absolutely, and for some reason he found me worthy of his love as well.

Bennett never said anything in our meetings. He was utterly inarticulate, but his fumbling speech masked an incisive intelligence. In late-night get-togethers with Martin and me he could dominate the discussion as he poured out the insights he'd withheld during our meeting with the staff. Ralph resented Bennett's intelligence and his closeness to Martin, and he made a special effort to put down Bennett as a "chicken-eating" preacher. Bennett played the part of an old-fashioned Negro and acted the fool with most people. But while Ralph was a brilliant preacher, he was not able to offer the kinds of insights into politics and human dynamics that Bennett could. Bennett couldn't preach worth anything, but he was a genius when it came to human dynamics. Years later it would be Bennett who would persuade Daddy King and me to support Jimmy Carter in a long-shot bid for the presidency. It took a kind of genius to perceive the potential in a moderate, little-known, former governor of Georgia.

Bennett knew everybody in Martin's network and he understood people and preachers. After our meetings, I'd often be frustrated and I'd go talk to Bennett to vent. He was the one person, besides Martin, who was totally trustworthy, the only person with whom I shared my fears and anxieties. With the other staff members, you had to pretend to be something, to act important. Bennett never pretended to be anything—he always expressed his own sense of inadequacy and that encouraged me to express mine. And his insights were invaluable. Bennett could figure out the hidden agenda in any meeting, and never missed anything. He would advise me, "In the meeting tomorrow, pick up on Hosea's idea, and get him and Bevel to agree on it. That's what Dr. King wants to do anyway." We had a recurring joke about the staff; he would say, "The snakes are crawling," and I'd say, "Well, Bennett, I appreciate that, but I'm a sly mongoose." When Bennett went down to Jamaica with Martin while he was writing his book on the Birmingham movement, he brought me back a carving of a wooden mongoose to remind me that the snakes were always out to get me. The snake, of course, was the tempter, symbolic of all the egos stirring up trouble in the garden. It was the kind of biblically inspired joke one expects among preachers.

In the spring of 1964, Wyatt officially left the staff. He had been offered the presidency of the newly formed Educational Heritage Book Service, which planned to publish a series of encyclopedias on black American life. Martin gave me the title of executive director, a role I had already been filling for some months. My new title made little difference in my work or my colleagues' cooperation or lack thereof. I thought titles were an illusion anyway—I preferred to stand on energy and ideas. By this time, most of the staff members were people I had helped to bring in and hundreds of grassroots activists had been trained by our Citizenship School Program. They had looked to me for guidance even when Wyatt was more present with the staff. Wes Hotchkiss at the United Church of Christ, which continued to pay my salary, was totally supportive of my expanding work with SCLC. He wanted the church involved with the movement, and the more I did, the better he liked it.

The civil rights bill that had started with Kennedy's administration was gaining momentum and increasingly I maintained close communications with the Justice Department, particularly Assistant Attorney General for Civil Rights Burke Marshall and his assistant, John Doar. We, and all the civil rights groups, were concerned that the Justice Department move ahead with a comprehensive civil rights bill in 1964. In the wake of Birmingham, the March on Washington, and the Kennedy assassination, public opinion seemed to accept the need for such a bill, and President Lyndon Johnson had given assurances that his administration would move forward. Walter Fauntroy represented SCLC at the meetings of the Leadership Conference on Civil Rights. The Leadership Conference, a coalition of religious, labor, and civil rights organizations, was founded in 1950 by A. Philip Randolph, Arnold Aronson, and Roy Wilkins to implement the historic report of President Truman's Committee on Civil Rights. Roy Wilkins and Clarence Mitchell, the NAACP's Washington representative, had tremendous influence within the coalition. Gathered around the table of the Leadership Conference, civil rights organizations were given the opportunity for input as the bill made its way through congressional committees. Congress was inclined to narrow the scope of the legislation and we pressed back for the broadest possible law. Walter Fauntroy was a Baptist who went to Virginia Union, which has a reputation for producing great whooping preachers, and then to Yale Divinity School—a bastion of proper New England reserved Congregationalism. He effectively blended those two traditions and with his beautiful tenor voice could bring a congregation to a high emotional pitch, while his biblical scholarship remained sound. Given the egos I was used to working with, it was refreshing to work with someone so reasonable and even-tempered, and I always looked forward to his calls from Washington.

As the civil rights bill was moving through Congress, we became embroiled in our first major campaign since Birmingham down in St. Augustine, Florida. St. Augustine is the oldest city in the United States and it was also one of the most intractably racist. The black community there had been struggling in vain for five or six years to win desegregation of public accommodations under the leadership of Dr. Robert B. Hayling, an intrepid black dentist. By September 1963, conditions in St. Augustine were so horrible that Dr. Hayling and three other local black activists were kidnapped by the Klan and just barely escaped with their lives when the sheriff rescued them—though the sheriff was no friend of blacks. In February 1964, the homes of the two black families who had attempted to enroll their children in all-white public schools were bombed and Dr. Hayling's home was shot into, injuring his wife and children. The police conducted themselves outrageously in the black community, and Sheriff L. O. Davis and his deputies did little short of preventing actual lynchings to control the widespread Klan-like activity in the area.

Dr. Hayling had written to President Johnson and the Justice Department several times requesting that federal marshals be sent to St. Augustine to protect the civil rights of blacks, to no avail. The Johnson administration, meanwhile, had pledged $350,000 to St. Augustine to fund the celebration of its four-hundredth anniversary, an event meant for whites only, of course. That the federal government would provide funds to assist the tourist industry of such a bastion of racial segregation and violence while at the same time ignoring the pleas of its black citizens for equal protection under the law infuriated Dr. Hayling and his colleagues and in effect was the final straw.

Around this time, Hayling took his case to Martin and asked for his help, in the hope that national attention could be focused on con-

ditions in St. Augustine, thereby shaming the administration into
action. Martin was interested and assigned Dorothy Cotton to investigate the situation and to work with Dr. Hayling and his local organization. Dorothy returned after just a month to tend to the needs of
the Citizenship Program, and Hosea Williams, who was familiar with
the area, took her place there on a more long-range basis. Golden
Frinks of our staff was assigned to assist Hosea.

With Hosea's help and guidance, the St. Augustine civil rights
group expanded the scope of their demonstrations to include sit-ins
at lunch counters and challenges to businesses where blacks traded
but were not hired as employees. Hosea soon recommended that we
take on St. Augustine as a major SCLC effort, but I was not inclined
to agree; I thought all our efforts should be concentrated on pressuring the president and Congress to pass the proposed civil rights bill.
A major campaign in St. Augustine would, I strongly believed, only
be a diversion. Martin had not yet made up his mind.

While we were debating whether we would commit our staff and
resources to St. Augustine, Hosea was successful in persuading our
new Boston SCLC affiliate to recruit a few white supporters to come
down and join in the St. Augustine marches. One of those who volunteered was Mrs. Malcolm Peabody, the elderly mother of the governor of Massachusetts. No sooner had she arrived than Hosea took
her downtown to a drugstore sit-in, where the police promptly
arrested her and the incident made national news.

This arrest and the publicity it attracted only encouraged Hosea
in his argument that we should launch a major campaign in St.
Augustine. He felt we should use St. Augustine to dramatize the day-
to-day realities of injustice and racial oppression in the South, thus
facilitating rather than detracting from the campaign for the civil
rights bill. Hosea also believed St. Augustine was particularly vulnerable to change at that time, because consistent negative publicity
would damage their tourist trade and ruin their anniversary celebration. If we exploited the irony of America's oldest city being a capital
of racism, eventually either local officials, local businesses, or the
national government would be forced to make improvements. Hosea
had not been with the staff during Birmingham, and the movement in
Savannah had been basically unsuccessful, and I suspected that he
wanted to get embroiled in St. Augustine to compensate for his lack
of battle scars. I, on the other hand, was still trying to recover from
Birmingham.

I continued to argue against heavy staff involvement. We had
already committed James Bevel to work as our representative in the

Mississippi Freedom Summer of 1964 and we were also attempting to upgrade our voter registration efforts in Alabama, which we felt were very important. In addition, Martin thought it was time to tighten our organizational efficiency. He complained about things like the failure to answer mail promptly; and mail was arriving by the tons. Martin announced he wanted all financial contributions to be acknowledged within three days, and sometimes he would return to the office late at night to make sure for himself that this was being done.

Finally, I just had a gut feeling that we shouldn't go to St. Augustine. I sensed it was too volatile and I was not happy about the prospect of Martin leading demonstrations there. Most of the marches were taking place at night, a policy Hosea had adopted in Savannah, because almost all the black adults had to work during the day and it was impossible to recruit them to march in the afternoons. The destination of the marches in St. Augustine was the old slave market, which unfortunately was drawing large crowds of unruly whites who gathered each night to harass, threaten, and sometimes strike out at the marchers. And the demonstrators were receiving no protection from the sheriff.

There was one particular group of Klan-type vigilantes led by a fool named Holstead "Hoss" Manucy, who along with his "Ancient City Gun Club" rode on horseback to harass marchers whenever there were demonstrations. Their activities were coordinated by citizen-band radio, so whenever there was a demonstration, Manucy and his vigilantes would come into St. Augustine from all over the county. Sheriff Davis made no effort whatsoever to control them. Our fear, of course, was that they might one night open fire on a march, particularly if Martin was leading it.

To help resolve the question of whether we should make St. Augustine a major SCLC campaign site, in April I decided to go there myself to spend a few days observing the situation. As I drove into town, I realized that a mob had gathered around the town square and old slave market. They were whooping it up, drinking, and obviously there to make trouble. When I arrived at Shiloh Baptist Church, a mass meeting was in progress, and Hosea was speaking. When Hosea saw me, he announced grandly, "Now, I want one of you beautiful young ladies to lead the march tonight, walking beside the Rev. Andrew Young, our executive director, who has just arrived from Atlanta." Everyone turned around to stare at me. I hadn't even had time to drop my things off where I was staying. Although I had only intended to organize the march, Hosea had set me up so beautifully there was no way I could back out of leading it. So I did, while Hosea remained safely at the church, I might add.

When we reached a point almost a block away from the slave market, Hoss Manucy and his gang were there waiting for us. There were only a few of us marching, mostly women and children and a handful of men, including Willie Bolden of our staff who was a veteran of Savannah. Sheriff Davis was nowhere to be found; nor was there a city policeman in sight. The white onlookers were screaming for blood, and I was trying hard not to show my fear. We made a circle and I talked with the marchers. I had reminded our marchers at Shiloh Baptist Church that we would have no real protection from the police, and that we weren't in any position to take responsibility for anyone's life. "Now is the time to turn around," I said, "for any of you that don't want to go. We won't think ill of you, we won't talk about you, but some of us must go on." We prayed. A woman started singing "Be Not Dismayed, What E'er Be the Tide, God Will Take Care of You," a song that we sang so often during those days. Without waiting for the song to conclude, I started out the door of the church and headed toward the slave market downtown. Now, I love that song, but it's quite different believing in it in church on Sunday morning than it is when facing an angry mob outside on a Friday night.

I decided to do what I always do in confrontations; I walked over to Manucy and his people and was intending to talk to them, to at least try to defuse the situation. They stared at me like I was crazy, and as I was talking to one man, looking to my left, another guy slipped up behind me from the right and slugged me in the jaw. Then someone hit me in the head from the rear with a blackjack, and I don't remember anything after that. Network television cameras were filming, and when I watched what happened on film years later, I saw that when I fell to the ground, I instinctively tried to curl up as we had been taught to do, and then someone kicked and stomped me while I was on the ground. The fact that I grabbed my head probably saved me from serious injury. Willie Bolden rushed over and dragged me away from my attackers, back into the middle of our group.

I soon came back to my senses, and a short discussion followed as to whether we should resume the march. I remember saying, "We can't turn around, we have to go on. But let's stay together and not panic." So we regrouped and began moving slowly forward again. As we approached the slave market I spotted some of the same guys who had attacked me. I was probably only semiconscious. I didn't yet realize that I'd been severely beaten, and up to that point the pain had not really set in. A combination of my instinct for negotiation and a burst of adrenaline made me actually go right up to my attackers again. There was no sense of courage or heroism in this act, but neither was there any fear. I was too numb to really think, but all my training from the movement and from childhood made me get back to the front of the line, determined that violence would not be allowed to stop our movement. Suddenly a young thug, no bigger than I was, burst through the crowd, rushed up to me, and tried a running kick at my groin. I saw him just in time and turned to the side slightly so that the kick hit me on the inside of my thigh. As I bent over to escape the blow, someone else hit me once again, right across the head with a blackjack, but this time I didn't go down. I don't even recall being groggy, but in truth I was probably too dazed to feel anything.

My concern now was simply to get the marchers back safely to the church. As we approached the slave market we had to walk the gauntlet of hundreds of whites lining both sides of the street. It was as if we were reenacting an ancient pagan ritual; I felt like we were the martyrs on our way to the lion's den. That night the mob turned its wrath upon several reporters as well. We grabbed Nelson Benton, a CBS reporter who had become separated from his crew in the melee, and dragged him in with us to try and protect him. I believe a Danish cameraman was clubbed into unconsciousness. Then, as if sensing enough harm had been done in front of the cameras, the long-absent Sheriff Davis appeared and pushed the white onlookers back on to the sidewalk. We marched the last few feet to the slave market unmolested, knelt in prayer, then returned to the church without further incident.

After it was all over, I went behind the church and cried. The more I thought about it all, the madder I became, and the more the blows hurt. It was the first time I had ever been beaten up in a march. I bore those bruises for more than a year. After that night I became Hosea's strongest advocate for a major campaign in St. Augustine. I still didn't want to see Martin come down there, but I was determined to stay there myself until we had won something. It wasn't that I was personally vindictive, but I saw firsthand the courage of St. Augustine's black citizens in the face of the viciousness of the Klan. I felt it wouldn't be right to abandon those people to the Klan and the sheriff. It also dawned on me as it had on Hosea that the country should be reminded why we needed the rapid passage of the civil rights bill. Birmingham was a year in the past and Americans have short memories.

I would have preferred to rely on the lobbying skills of the NAACP, but those skills hadn't gotten the bill introduced, the action in the streets of Birmingham had. The demonstrations in St. Augustine might be necessary to overcome the filibuster that had been promised in the Senate. In addition, once in St. Augustine I realized we might as well see it through. It took remarkable courage for the people to decide to stand up for themselves after years of racial oppression. I couldn't say to them, "Thanks, but no thanks, your sacrifice isn't politically necessary at this time."

As I had suspected all along, quick progress was not forthcoming. When we asked Sheriff Davis for protection, he replied that he had only thirty-two policemen, and against a mob of five or six hundred his poor officers were powerless. "You shouldn't march" was his position.

But of course we continued to march. Sometimes the mob actually attacked us, sometimes they shot off firecrackers in an attempt to frighten us into thinking guns were being fired. We were determined not to be intimidated.

In contrast to the massive resistance we confronted, our demands in St. Augustine were quite modest. We asked for desegregation of public accommodations, the hiring of black policemen and firemen, and the establishment of a biracial commission to work out a plan for further desegregation of the city. But meeting with the mayor and city officials to negotiate our demands was simply impossible; they thought we wanted the moon and refused to even discuss our demands with us.

One weekend, Jean showed up at Shiloh Baptist. She had come down from Atlanta to march, but hadn't warned me in advance, since she knew I preferred that she not be there. She said later that reading about the violence in St. Augustine and watching the news briefs on television was just too frustrating for her; she had to take part herself for the sake of her own sanity, whether I liked it or not.

Once she was there, she acted as if we didn't know each other. She didn't even talk to me; she joined a group for a day march and went out. I stayed at the church and prayed for her safety. It was her first real movement march, and she was determined to be treated like everyone else, not as my wife. She told me later that the elderly woman she was marching with nudged her as they approached the slave market and the waiting mob and said, "Look at them, honey, ain't they sick?" All of a sudden she felt better, held her head high, and marched with more strength. She had been afraid to actually *look* at the jeering people. Seeing them for the first time, really seeing them, she felt it was *they* who deserved the pity, who needed help, not those marching.

We tried to keep Martin from coming to St. Augustine during the early phases of the campaign. He did come down later, though, insisted on marching, was arrested, and served a brief term in jail. My fear was that the vigilante Klan types in the area were setting a trap to kill Martin. There were just too many fanatics in that town. The archracist J. B. Stoner, who ran for president on a white supremacist platform, was there, stirring up things. In his speeches he would say things like "When you go to kill a nest of snakes, you don't let the little ones go, you kill the little ones too." This was his argument in defense of the bombing of the Sixteenth Street Baptist Church in Birmingham that killed four children.

I was determined to at least keep Martin from demonstrating at night. He would say, "Andy, I have to do everything everybody else does." I would answer, "No, Martin, that's not true. If you're out there and they're shooting at you, they're liable to miss you and hit some of us. If you stay here at the church they won't do any shooting." Whenever Martin was part of a demonstration the crowd went wild with hatred and vilification, so controlling when he would march was a way of protecting all of us. On this point, Martin reluctantly accepted my logic.

Throughout the movement, the men were usually the last to become involved, always using the reason that they didn't believe in a nonviolent response to violent provocations. This was more an excuse than anything else. I began challenging the men as they went into the pool halls and bars, attempting to shame them for letting the women and children carry the movement. I told them, "You won't have to turn the other cheek. Anytime there are fifty men in one of our demonstrations the Klan won't touch us!" Finally the men realized that their presence was essential. Usually we felt it important not to pressure anyone, but in St. Augustine the situation was so brutal we had to. Women and the elderly had borne the brunt of our demonstrations for far too long. We finally convinced one group in a neighborhood pool hall to leave their knives and guns at home and join with us one evening. The result, fortunately, was as we had expected. That night the mob shouted and threw a few rocks and firecrackers, but in general they refrained from violence. This mob had been beating up on unarmed groups of women, children, and old people, but they were far less willing to attack when the presence of young black men was added.

Considering the intransigence of the city administration, the incendiary atmosphere, and our fears of escalating violence, the St. Augustine campaign wound down to a surprisingly quick conclusion. A temporary local court ban had been instituted prohibiting any further marches on May 29. Soon after, we decided to go to the federal district court, asking protection for our marches in a case bearing my name, *Young v. Davis* (the sheriff). On June 9, federal district court Judge Brian Simpson ruled that we could resume our marches. In his decision he observed that the Ancient City Gun Club was nothing but another name for the Ku Klux Klan, and also found that many members of the gun club had been deputized by Sheriff Davis.

After the federal court injunction in our favor, Sheriff Davis, who had previously been willing to let us march through a sea of harassment and potential violence without any protection, changed tactics and began arresting and jailing our people before we could even get a block away from the church. Nor was there any decrease in the attacks on us. While staging "swim-ins" at the beaches, our people were attacked and some almost drowned. When an integrated group attempted to use a motel swimming pool, the manager came out to throw acid in the pool.

Finally we were able to get the Florida attorney general interested in resolving the situation. There was, of course, a danger that something might happen that would destroy St. Augustine's tourist trade and spoil the planned four-hundred-year anniversary celebration. The attorney general was also smart enough to realize that with the imminent passage of the 1964 Civil Rights Act, St. Augustine, along with other still rigidly segregated cities and towns in the South, was fighting a losing battle. The attorney general's representatives said, however, that they wanted to wait until the actual signing of the Civil Rights Act, which took place on July 2, before forcing St. Augustine to comply, so it wouldn't look as if they were capitulating to our demands. We didn't have a problem with this; I felt it was time for us to get the hell out of St. Augustine anyway, as long as we believed compliance would be forthcoming. The new legislation would achieve results not only in St. Augustine, but in many other towns as well, without us having to carry out torturous, dangerous, time-consuming campaigns in every locality. Even Hosea agreed with me that it was time for us to go, so we put St. Augustine behind us without the usual internal staff arguments.

In retrospect, St. Augustine turned out to be SCLC's most violent and bloody campaign. It took two months of continuous marching at night, demonstrations at lunch counters, motels, and beaches, plus a comprehensive boycott by the black community for several months to achieve what the Civil Rights Act was about to grant us all anyway. Still, it may be that we would not have had a Civil Rights Act without St. Augustine. We will never know whether the Senate filibuster would have been defeated if St. Augustine hadn't provided a vivid reminder of the injustices the bill was designed to address.

Even with the Civil Rights Act, a local civil rights movement changed the social order in a community in a way that legislation alone could not. Today, in cities like Nashville, Atlanta, and Birmingham, where there were strong movements, blacks have more social and political influence than in Jacksonville, Houston, and New Orleans, even though they're under the same national laws. A movement coalesces the consciousness of people as blacks serve notice that they will no longer be humiliated and white people learn that they will no longer rule the roost, that there will be consequences if whites make arbitrary decisions that affect the whole community. In a purely political change, blacks may win the battle for control of a city, but lose the war as whites abandon the city and take their financial resources with them. In a nonviolent civil rights revolution, the disruption is so great that all sides must participate in reconciliation. That healing allows the community to move to a new level of understanding. In that sense, the movement was certainly a good thing for St. Augustine.

Meanwhile, the Civil Rights Act of 1964 was steadily making its way through Congress and there was a massive lobbying effort by the churches under way. Under the leadership of Dr. Robert Spike of the National Council of Churches Commission on Religion and Race, and with the help and guidance of J. Irwin Miller, a member of the Business Round Table and CEO of Cummins Engine Corporation, as president of the National Council of Churches, we had a strong business voice. These resources complemented the work already being done by the leadership of the civil rights movement under Clarence Mitchell's guidance and the AFL-CIO. Spike and Miller, along with Fannie Lou Hamer and SCLC's Annelle Ponder, walked the halls of Congress, meeting with congressmen and explaining the importance of the civil rights bill. They swayed many votes, particularly among Midwestern members of Congress who really needed the issues explained to them. Mrs. Hamer and Annelle often told the story of how they had been arrested and beaten, simply because they tried to use a white waiting room on an interstate bus line. Mrs. Hamer's own story was one of the most powerful to come out of the movement.

More than a year after it was formally introduced by President

Kennedy, the civil rights bill passed through Congress. President Lyndon Johnson signed the Civil Rights Act of 1964 on July 2 in an extraordinary televised ceremony in the Capitol Rotunda. Through a deep Texas twang he made the strongest civil rights speech ever given by an American president. He had personally seen to the passage of the legislation in the Senate, where he had previously served as majority leader, twisting arms and calling in favors to defeat the Southern filibuster. It was a powerful symbol of America's awesome possibilities and her fascinating contradictions, that a president born and raised in a Confederate state was the one to sign the Civil Rights Act into law.

On July 5, 1964, we were finally successful in integrating the public accommodations of St. Augustine. We had decided that since the Fourth of July holiday usually involved a lot of heavy drinking, and the last thing the white racists in St. Augustine needed was to be fired up by alcohol, we would wait until everyone had returned to normal work schedules before we attempted to integrate.

To our surprise, we were really very courteously received by almost everyone. It was as though a great burden had been lifted from the store managers, waiters, and waitresses. Now that the law had been changed and the strife was over, they no longer had to categorically reject other human beings. In one of the restaurants we went to, a waitress very nervously poured my coffee to overflowing and then apologized profusely as she went to get a new cup. It seemed such a mundane incident. But I also remembered that many a night we had "walked through the valley of the shadow of death" in order to get these restaurants opened to all citizens, and I also remembered the rest of the words of the Twenty-third Psalm, which seemed especially apt at this time:

> Thou preparest a table before me in the presence of mine enemies: thou anointest my head with oil; my cup runneth over.
> Surely goodness and mercy shall follow me all the days of my life: and I will dwell in the house of the Lord for ever.

Hosea had always insisted that despite the steady progress toward the Civil Rights Act, it was necessary for the movement to stay on the front pages in order to keep America conscious of the reality and horror of racism, which quietly perpetuated itself through violence and bloodshed. Certainly our efforts in St. Augustine didn't hurt the movement, but I was always looking for the easiest way to freedom. Though I am almost grateful for my own encounter with violence there, I am still haunted by the sight of young women with blood streaming down their faces from head wounds, and the sheer terror of those racist mobs. It all seemed so unnecessary.

In addition, I was always suspicious of the competition for attention within the movement: the tugging at Martin's coattails, and the tension that existed between Hosea and James Bevel, each of whom felt the other was a menace to the movement, each of whom was prone to let his own personal competition and his own "movement images" interfere with the true needs of people to be free. Hosea could be abrasive and confrontational, but he could also be quite ingratiating when he felt like it. Bevel was ideologically pure to the point of irrationality, but it could not be denied that he operated out of a deep commitment to nonviolence; he genuinely saw himself as a prophet. Bevel could also transform himself into a wily diplomat when necessary. Each of them was an infuriating blend of ego-driven agendas and remarkably unselfish commitment to the cause of civil rights.

Martin was always philosophical about these internal tensions and about the violence that accompanied our efforts. "Andy, you are too rational," he would say. "You would reason your way out of segregation, but it takes more than just reason to get this country straight. You need some folks like Hosea and Bevel who are crazy enough to take on anything and anybody and not count the cost. The church bombing humbled us all. It reminded me of the religious aspect of our quest for justice, that it was a struggle to make our society whole. If you had your way, we'd never have a confrontation. But you need confrontation to bring the horror and violence of racism to the surface where it can be exposed to the light of truth and be healed."

And so I usually went along with them reluctantly, but I was never thoroughly convinced that there could not be an easier way. Yet despite my regrets, there is no question that a great deal of good came from our St. Augustine demonstrations. Among other things, the Ancient City Gun Club had been exposed by Judge Brian Simpson as a Klavern of the Ku Klux Klan. Judge Simpson symbolized the true strength of justice in our nation as he declared what was right and lawful at the cost of personal ostracism and public criticism from his former friends and colleagues. Because he upheld the law, old friends refused to socialize with him, and the poker game at which he had played every week secretly changed its location and he was never again invited to attend. *Young v. Davis* turned out to be a landmark decision that later protected our right to demonstrate in Selma,

Alabama, for the Voting Rights Act, and again in Charleston, South Carolina, in 1969 in an attempt to organize hospital workers.

The Southern judges—most of whom had been appointed by President Eisenhower—were the unsung heroes of democracy in these times. Our movement was able to progress nonviolently only because there was a court system that upheld justice. The importance of our courts can perhaps be best understood when we compare the United States with many places in the world, like China, where an independent judicial branch does not exist and where the success we had with our nonviolent movement would have taken much longer. Not that the judges and justices of the fifties and sixties were necessarily inclined to be liberal—the legal strategy that began with Thurgood Marshall and the NAACP Legal Defense Fund really involved a process of education in the judicial branch. But judges of that era possessed more life experience than I see on the federal bench today, whose judicial appointees seem to have lived fairly sheltered, suburban lives teaching the privileged and representing wealthy clients. The court system of the nineties seems familiar with the law, but not the land or the people. A movement today would begin to educate the members of our Supreme Court and dramatize the issues before them, and I believe they would become less conservative.

St. Augustine was in many ways a very personal experience for me. It helped me to grow, to complete a process of maturing in the movement. Martin never moved in to take over the movement in St. Augustine and Hosea was in jail most of the time, so I really ran the show once I arrived. And for better or worse, the beatings I took in St. Augustine helped to establish my movement credentials. Now I had been to jail, I had been beaten, and I had guided the movement to a reasonably successful conclusion. The snakes could crawl, but I was a sly mongoose.

12

International Acclaim, Domestic Harassment

Nobody knows the trouble I've seen.
—African-American Spiritual

The Civil Rights Act laid the foundation for a sea change in the position of black Americans relative to the rest of American society. It was our intention to create an affirmative obligation in white businesses and institutions, to remove the barriers that had served to exclude blacks. Across America, the visible signs of exclusion began to come down: signs were removed from waiting rooms and water fountains and seats became available at lunch counters. The invisible barriers became the subject of judicial review as well. Few people now remember when want ads were segregated by race and gender; when black police officers were forbidden to arrest whites; when an interracial meeting could not be held in an Atlanta hotel. These facts of life in the 1960s were changed by the Civil Rights Act.

We did not intend for black Americans to assimilate into white society and become culturally indistinguishable from whites. Nor did we expect that integration would eliminate the need for black institutions. Rather, it was clear that white America controlled resources to

which black Americans had little access. For decades, black Geor-
gians paid taxes to support universities like the Georgia Institute of
Technology, yet black students were never admitted. Today, Georgia
Tech has a thriving black alumni association and graduates more
black engineers than any other institution in the world. Integration is
not about rubbing shoulders with whites; it's about becoming engineers.

Martin talked about transforming America and we believed that
given the opportunity there were aspects of black culture that would
enrich the larger society. In the arts and humanities, sports and government, that has already happened, and increasingly, it is happening
in business and science as well.

I credit the religious culture of the South for the extent of cooperation that occurred with the Civil Rights Act. While white churches
were certainly not out in front challenging civil rights laws, I believe
that once the laws were passed white clergy urged forbearance.
Southern whites were religious, church-going folks and they had a
basic moral framework, though they excluded their black neighbors
from consideration under that framework. SCLC's nonviolent, Christian themes resonated with the strong moral foundation that was
characteristic of Southern culture. The movement helped people to
understand that segregation was morally wrong, and I believe that
most whites were actually relieved when the laws were changed. It
lifted from them a tremendous moral burden.

Another factor was certainly the courageous leadership demonstrated by President Johnson, all the more impressive because he
signed the Civil Rights Act in an election year. Rather than duck one
of the nation's most controversial issues, Johnson used his own prestige to overcome the filibuster by Southern senators and signed the
bill into law with a dramatic ceremony in the Capitol Rotunda just
before Independence Day celebrations were to begin. Johnson's
embrace of civil rights meant that the upcoming presidential election
would become a referendum on civil rights. If he lost, politicians
everywhere would attribute it to his position on civil rights and it
would be an incalculable setback for the movement. Black voters
were obviously beneficiaries of the new law and could be easily motivated to vote for Johnson. But two of the shortcomings of the new
law—the lack of a voting rights provision and the absence of protections for civil rights workers—meant that mobilizing Southern blacks
to vote for Johnson would be as difficult and dangerous as ever.

In the spring of 1964, while I was involved in St. Augustine,
SNCC had begun organizing college students from around the coun-

try to come to Mississippi for what was called "Freedom Summer." Liberal activist Al Lowenstein had approached SNCC chairman John Lewis with this concept, which resulted in scores of mostly white, Northern students coming to Mississippi to work as political organizers. At that time, the state Democratic Party apparatus was all white and they held whites-only conventions to choose delegates to the Democratic National Convention. Although white primaries had been ruled unconstitutional by the Supreme Court in 1944, the persistence of whites-only conventions in Mississippi was further evidence of the need for voting rights legislation. Black leaders like Aaron Henry and Fannie Lou Hamer had been persistent in their efforts to register voters and had met with vicious treatment at the hands of local authorities.

Lewis, Lowenstein, and local leaders in Mississippi developed a strategy to circumvent the exclusion of blacks from the state delegate selection process: they would create a Mississippi Freedom Democratic Party (MFDP), register people for the new party, and elect a slate of delegates to the Democratic National Convention in Atlantic City in August. The MFDP would be open to all people, regardless of race. At the convention they would challenge the seating of the state party delegates on the grounds that they were selected in a discriminatory process.

I had several misgivings about the Freedom Summer strategy. First, I thought that it was unnecessarily dangerous. There were no protections for civil rights workers and none could be expected for the idealistic students who were fanning out across Mississippi. John Lewis was well aware of this, since the omission of such protection was one of SNCC's key objections to the civil rights bill, and Lewis had expounded on this during his impassioned speech at the March on Washington. The presence of the national media was virtually the only inhibitor of official violence, and you simply could not get that kind of attention for people in dozens of little towns in Mississippi. One Bull Connor was dangerous enough, but the students would be confronting dozens of Bull Connors in dozens of towns with hostile judges, in hostile communities in a state with a hostile governor. If mature, experienced organizers like Hosea and Wyatt and savvy local leaders like Fannie Lou Hamer could be beaten and thrown in jail, how, I wondered, could a group of inexperienced college students avoid a similar fate.

Second, my understanding of rural black people was that they were extremely practical, and I felt there was nothing practical about a mock election for delegates to the Democratic National Convention. It was hard enough to organize voter registration, and now people would be registering for the MFDP and still not be eligible to vote in the November election. There was also a creeping influence in SNCC of self-styled black militants who were acting out of their own sense of frustration and inferiority. For my part, I felt that the students were manipulating community leaders and that Northern liberals, who wanted to radicalize the Democratic Party, were in turn manipulating the students into believing that this process would transform politics in Mississippi. Amazingly, the MFDP did transform politics in Mississippi by planting seeds that would be harvested later, as Aaron Henry, Unita Blackwell, Virginia Gray, and other local MFDP leaders ran for office in Mississippi. But at the time it seemed to me that the strategy was initiated to expose students and local leaders to unwarranted risk for an uncertain reward.

In contrast, SCLC's strategy was to register as many black voters as possible for the General Election in November. In Birmingham, St. Augustine, and wherever we built affiliates, organizers had turned to voter registration and mobilization. We wanted to change the politics in the South and establish a new relationship between blacks and whites, not to set up a separate party.

Despite my reservations about the Mississippi strategy, SCLC had always tried to be supportive of SNCC and this was no exception. We had not recruited or trained the students, but we had trained many of the adults who were the community leaders in Mississippi. These local leaders began to ask Martin to come to Mississippi to support their efforts to register people for the Mississippi Freedom Democratic Party. So, in July, we put together a tour of towns in Mississippi.

It was easy to be romantic about Mississippi. The rural black people in the Mississippi movement were the salt of the earth—good, strong, God-fearing people, survivors. Their courage and perseverance in the face of repression was awe-inspiring. Everywhere we went there was good singing, and every community had a local preacher who could really whoop. Something about folk in Mississippi really fed the spirit. We went to several towns in the Delta, including Greenwood, where violence had plagued the movement, and over to Philadelphia, where civil rights workers Andrew Goodman, Mickey Schwerner, and James Chaney were, at the time, still missing. Our assumption that they had been killed, probably with the cooperation of local law enforcement, was later confirmed. But in late July, their bodies had not yet been found and Mississippi officials were spreading rumors that their disappearance was nothing more than a SNCC hoax.

In Philadelphia, we met with an elderly black man who lived across the street from the remains of the burnt-out church the SNCC workers had visited on the Sunday they were abducted and murdered. This man had apparently witnessed the burning of the church, which the workers had come over from Meridian to investigate. He told us the killers had returned to his place later that Sunday night to kill him too, to remove him as a potential witness. They dragged him out of his house into his yard. His wife, the only other person in the house, ran out after them pleading, "Don't kill my husband, please don't kill my husband." The old man told us his wife had fallen down on her knees, and he just knew he was dead. He said he heard his wife's voice praying aloud: "Father, I stretch my hand to thee, no other help I know. If thou withdraw thyself from me, whither shall I go?" Then he said he didn't remember whether they beat him into unconsciousness, or whether he passed out, but when he came to, the men were gone, and he and his wife were in the front yard alone. He believed he had been saved miraculously.

Martin had insisted on going to Philadelphia. Between the presence of the FBI and knowledge that the killers could be anywhere, the visit kept me on edge until we had left that town far behind us. There was no violence on our tour, which simply confirmed my feelings that there was safety in numbers and in the presence of the press. Also, by this time the federal government had come into Mississippi to investigate the disappearance of Chaney, Goodman, and Schwerner. Once again, federal law enforcement was deployed only after a tragedy had occurred, and in this case, of course, one that included a white victim.

As the tour continued, we met with SNCC workers in the field and students who had come down from the North for the summer. We had a caravan of about five cars and we would drive to several towns in a day. One day we stopped for gas in the early afternoon at one of the little country stores with one gas pump that sold everything from fishing licenses to bubble gum. We hadn't eaten the entire day. On the counter was a two-gallon jar of pickled pigs' feet. Martin and Ralph and others in the caravan started buying pigs' feet, one by one. Then Martin just shrugged and bought the whole jar. They stood around this little country store in the middle of Mississippi eating pigs' feet like they were going out of style. Martin tried unsuccessfully to get me to eat one. "Come on, Andy," he teased, "you know they eat pigs' feet in New Orleans!" And he and Ralph had a good laugh at my expense.

When we were driving into Jackson, where Martin was to speak one evening, we stopped at a black-operated country kitchen near a

catfish farm. There is nothing like Mississippi grain-fed, deep-fried
catfish. We ordered the catfish platter and they brought out turkey-
sized platters each piled with about a dozen golden, crispy fried catfish, and set one in front of each of us. Now, I really had not grown
up eating much pork, since in New Orleans seafood was cheap and
plentiful, so fried fish was just what I needed. Martin and I each ate
an entire platter; Ralph ate two or three. When we were done, there
was nothing left to those catfish but the heads, tails and backbones.
They looked like fish from a Felix the Cat cartoon.

    Although the situation was deadly serious in Mississippi, the
tour was fun. It was a return to my roots; the people I met in the
small churches reminded me of the members of my congregation in
Beachton. I saw many old friends from the citizenship schools, the
natural leaders whom we had trained, prayed, and sung with at
Dorchester. Their courage, commitment, and persistence in the face
of the intransigence of officials renewed my strength and courage. I
felt humbled by the power of faith in these tiny rural communities in
Mississippi. I felt we had to respond to the call of these foot soldiers
of the movement, despite my deep misgivings about the overall strategy behind the MFDP. My problem was with the strategies that
SNCC proposed, never with the people of Mississippi, who had the
courage to rise to any challenge. But I thought it was the duty of
SNCC and any civil rights organization to be mindful of the risks we
were asking people to take and to ensure to the best of our ability
that the chance of achieving a meaningful goal was commensurate
with the risk. The students placed their faith in the grassroots black
people of Mississippi, and that faith was not misplaced; rather, it
asked too much.

The Democratic National Convention was held in late August in
Atlantic City, New Jersey, and Martin and I attended as honored
guests of Senator Hubert Humphrey. This was Atlantic City before
the financial influx brought about by gambling, and compared to the
huge convention Atlanta hosted in 1988 while I was mayor, it was a
modest event. The delegates and state party organizations had
booked rooms in the large, first-class hotels while Martin and I
stayed in an old hotel with fraying carpeting and no indication that it
had ever been grand in its day. Martin was often criticized for the
hotel suites supplied by his hosts when he was a guest speaker for a
national organization like the American Psychiatric Association, but
our Atlantic City accommodations were more typical of when SCLC
was footing the bill. At the convention itself, the media pool consisted

of a cadre of print journalists from the wire services and big-city papers, television network reporters, and radio network reporters. Since the gathering was so overwhelmingly filled with white, middle-aged males, Martin and I were noticeable everywhere we went.

We had two goals that were somewhat in conflict with each other. President Lyndon Johnson had just signed the Civil Rights Act and I believed that it was essential that he receive a resounding vote of confidence at this convention. The Republicans had just nominated Senator Barry Goldwater as their candidate, and his conservative platform was a threat to all we had accomplished and would certainly prevent further gains in the area of civil rights should he win. Moreover, the Democratic Party included a good number of conservative Southern Democrats. In 1948, many of them had walked out of the Democratic convention rather than support Truman. If that were to happen to Johnson, it would seriously jeopardize his ability to win the election in November.

Our second goal was to achieve recognition for the MFDP. The MFDP had held its election and sent an interracial slate of delegates to the convention, challenging the seating of Mississippi's state Democratic Party delegates. In its challenge, the MFDP accused the official party of holding whites-only meetings to select their all-white slate of delegates. Democratic officials in Mississippi were unrelenting in their hostility to voting rights for black citizens. The MFDP had come a long way and they were completely justified in challenging the official delegates, but Martin and I did not agree that the MFDP slate should entirely replace the official party delegates. We thought it would be a fair compromise to divide the number of voting delegates that Mississippi had at the convention between the two delegations—half to the MFDP and half to the traditional party slate. I thought it would be the wrong symbol for the MFDP to entirely supplant the white Democrats, and a blended delegation might promote some degree of mutual understanding.

We wanted as large a vote as possible for the MFDP, so we met with the various state delegations, trying to increase the support for seating the MFDP. And we went to platform sessions, where Martin spoke in support of a strong civil rights plank in the party platform and other reforms to make the party more inclusive. He was well received by the union folk in the Northern and Midwestern delegations. The Southern delegations were politely reserved; most were vulnerable to the same charges that the MFDP had brought against Mississippi.

I also met with the SNCC representatives at the convention and

tried to get them to tone down their rhetoric and to be more flexible
in their demands: SNCC wanted the entire MFDP delegation seated
and the entire official Mississippi delegation kicked out of the convention, a goal that we felt was both unrealistic and unnecessarily
divisive. Bob Spike of the National Council of Churches had
arranged for us to hold our meetings in the basement of a black
church near the convention hall. Jim Forman, executive secretary of
SNCC, and Cleve Sellers, SNCC field secretary, were passionate and
emphatic as they argued that it was all or nothing: either the MFDP
was seated or they were walking out.

"You just selling us out!" they cried. "How can you niggers
come here and sell us out! You ain't been getting your heads whipped
in Mississippi. While you niggers been staying in fancy hotels eating
chicken, we been sleeping on floors in Mississippi, glad to find some
grits. Y'all come through with nice cars, make a speech, and run back
to your fancy churches in Atlanta. It's bullshit! Don't come here with
this bullshit about what we ought to be glad to get!" Jim would say
angrily.

I would try to reason with them. "Look, Lyndon Johnson has
given us something we have been working for, been to jail for, got
chased by dogs and water hoses for."

"Andy, ain't no hose got you, no dogs, has your ass even been to
jail?"

"Look," I would insist, "this is a real election coming up, about
electing a real president. If you win and seat every nigger in Mississippi at this convention and Goldwater gets elected in November, you
have gained nothing."

John Lewis spoke more slowly, the sounds of rural Alabama in
his voice. "Andy, we have shed too much blood in Mississippi to
accept a compromise. You know we have shed blood. You were in
Philadelphia. That is the problem with the civil rights bill, it doesn't
protect us; it was open season on us in Mississippi this summer. People were murdered in Philadelphia, and there is no punishment.
When we try to register to vote, we get sent to jail, we are beaten, we
are threatened. We can't back down, we've come too far."

John was caught between our practical, Southern view and what
I considered to be the purely ideological Northern position of Jim
Forman and Stokely Carmichael. It was as if SNCC folk thought it
was more important to prove that nothing about the political system
was good than to work to redeem it. Subconsciously, I think, their
strategy was designed to bring down the system by showcasing its
very real faults rather than to try to change it.

However, Lyndon Johnson had pushed through a civil rights bill and Martin and I wanted to see him reelected. We wanted to change the Democratic Party, win genuine reforms for the next convention, and bring white Southerners in the party over to our way of thinking about the immorality of excluding black people from the democratic process. We certainly didn't think that getting a few seats in the Democratic National Convention was going to bring in the kingdom. To us this was not "protest politics"; it was real politics and a lot was at stake. We felt it would be counterproductive to win this battle in the convention and then lose the election. We took the Goldwater challenge very seriously and thought that Johnson needed the kind of boost that only a unified convention could produce. If the entire official Mississippi delegation was forced out, no one could predict who might walk out with them. A walk-out of white Southern Democrats could destroy the convention and all hopes of keeping Johnson in the White House.

I got the impression that many of the SNCC folk believed there was no important difference between Johnson and Goldwater. SNCC had continued to criticize the Civil Rights Act for its failure to provide a mechanism to protect civil rights workers, brushing over the many important provisions of the act. SCLC, on the other hand, was not interested in symbolic protest. Our goal was to get black folks into the political system and in so doing transform it from the inside. We strongly believed America was changing and could continue to change.

Meanwhile, Johnson's operatives were holding their own sessions. And, as he proved time and again, Johnson was ruthless in pursuit of his goals. He demanded utter loyalty from those he had helped, and he was angry and frustrated over the recalcitrance of the black delegates from the MFDP. Hadn't he just given them a civil rights bill? The president controlled enough delegates at the convention to win any vote on the convention floor. His real problem was to address the moral contradiction raised by the MFDP: having all-white delegations at the Democratic National Convention. Johnson pretended to negotiate with the MFDP, while making up his own mind about the most politically expedient solution to the conflict. Johnson misled his own negotiator, Joe Rauh, into presenting a solution to the MFDP that two delegates could be seated: Rev. Ed King, the white chaplain from Tougaloo College, and the state NAACP president, Aaron Henry. But, while the MFDP was still meeting with Joe Rauh, this proposal was being simultaneously presented to the convention with the inference that the MFDP had agreed to accept it. It was accepted by the convention.

This was an outrage. Perhaps Martin could have persuaded the MFDP to accept just two delegates, but the trickery of being presented with a fait accompli and not being able to select the two representatives themselves was too much for the MFDP to swallow. It was also difficult for Aaron Henry and Ed King to take a conciliatory stand and urge their colleagues to accept the two delegates because they were given seats. It was a brilliant Machiavellian move by Johnson; he placed the onus back on the MFDP to accept a tainted offer.

Martin spoke with the MFDP and agreed that Johnson had not dealt fairly with them. He was deeply disappointed in Lyndon Johnson, but he had also been dismayed by the unrealistic expectations of SNCC. I felt that Henry and King should have taken their seats. It was less than they deserved, but more than Mississippi black folks had won since the end of Reconstruction. On behalf of all those courageous people in Mississippi, they could have cast their votes for the Democratic Party candidate for president of the United States. They could have called Johnson's bluff. Martin agreed that the seating of two delegates elected from outside the traditional party structure was a remarkable achievement. The MFDP also inspired party reforms that transformed the rules that would apply at the next party convention. But like bad gamblers who never know when to quit, zealous activists often have a hard time knowing when they've won.

Despite the bad feeling, the legacy of the Mississippi Freedom Democratic Party is apparent at every Democratic National Convention, as democratically elected delegates of every hue, male and female, young and old gather to nominate the party's standard-bearer. Thirty years later, the state of Mississippi has more black elected officials than any state in the Union, many with roots in the gallant MFDP.

While we were in Atlantic City, Walter Reuther, the head of the United Auto Workers, had encouraged Martin to undertake a "get out the vote" tour for the fall. Before the convention ended, Martin and I flew to Washington to plan with Walter Fauntroy a twelve-city tour for October. After the SCLC convention in the fall, Martin set out on a tour of cities in the North, Midwest, and West where blacks were registered in significant numbers and where we had good connections with local preachers. I believe SCLC mobilized more voters for Johnson than any single group. We felt passionately that any further progress on civil rights would be almost impossible if Johnson were defeated, and Martin conveyed the importance of this election as a referendum on civil rights everywhere he went.

In many ways this trip was different from the tour in rural Mississippi. The churches we visited were large and made of stone or brick. The pastors had their own little offices tucked behind the chancel. In Mississippi the churches were small and made of wood. The pastor's "office" was the churchyard, which was also where church suppers were held, with food laid out on picnic tables. In the cities, churches had a fellowship hall in the basement, and generally their own kitchen too. During the mass meetings in the evening the aroma of fried chicken would float up into the sanctuary.

This tour was very hard on Martin. Everyone wanted his attention from the moment he stepped off the airplane—local preachers, local press, local politicians and union leaders. People came to the mass meetings to hear Martin preach and their expectations were very high. He felt compelled to try to give the equivalent of his "I Have a Dream" speech every night in every city. It was physically and emotionally draining for him to speak with such eloquence, passion, and power night after night. After the speeches and the dinners at the church, greeting everyone who came out for the mass meeting, walking through the kitchen and thanking the good sisters for the wonderful meal, Martin would be too wound up to sleep. He would pace the floor at the hotel, tell preacher jokes, and generally try to shed the mantle of being Dr. Martin Luther King, Jr. He would tell funny stories, contrasting his most stentorian tones with a deep dialect: "I was in Willacoochee, Georgia, looking for the Greater Mount Carmel Rising Free For All Baptist Church and I stopped by the road to ask directions. I saw a brother and I asked the way to the Greater Mount Carmel Rising Free For All Baptist Church and the gentleman replied, 'Weelll, Reverend King, it's like dis, you go down there past the cotton field an' you'll see a dirt road, but don't turn there and then you'll come to a creek . . . you know, now dat I think on it, you can't git there from here!' So, I thanked him for his time and drove on, but in my rearview mirror, I see the gentleman running and hollering after me, so I stop again. He's panting and out of breath. 'Dr. King, Dr. King, I ax my brother for the church an' he say . . . he say you can't get there from here, neither!'"

Or he would begin to tease, "Andy, when the Klan finally gets you, here's what I'll preach: 'Lord, white folks made a big mistake, today. They have sent home to glory your faithful servant, Andrew Young. Lord, have mercy on the white folks who did this terrible deed. They killed the wrong Negro. In Andrew Young, white folk had a friend so faithful, so enduring they should never have harmed a hair on his head. Of all my associates, no one loved white folks as much as Andy.'"

The next morning, it was time to board a plane and begin all over again in another city.

In his speeches, Martin did not endorse Johnson directly, but talked about the issues and what was at stake in the country. He spoke out against "Goldwaterism." Martin saw Goldwater as attempting to turn the clock backward and erase all the gains of the civil rights movement. Goldwater had opposed the Civil Rights Act, calling it "phony." He refused to denounce organizations like the John Birch Society, thought the United States should leave the United Nations, and was opposed to the progressive income tax: even within the Republican Party he was seen as an extreme conservative. However, Southern Democrats—the "Dixiecrats" known to be segregationists—were flocking to his bandwagon and changing parties.

One indication that a real shift was taking place occurred during the state Republican Party meeting in Macon, Georgia. Prominent black Atlanta businessmen and Republicans Q. V. Williamson, John Calhoun, and C. A. Scott, the publisher of the *Atlanta Daily World* newspaper, attended the Macon meeting. They had been accustomed to exercising some influence in the state Republican Party; during the Eisenhower years, they had even recommended candidates for the federal judiciary in Georgia. In 1964 in Macon, they found the party had been overrun with Dixiecrats like Bo Calloway. Williamson and Calhoun walked out of the meeting, but C. A. Scott remained, saying, "My daddy was a Republican, my granddaddy was a Republican and I'm going to be a Republican till I die. You all are not going to run me out of my party."

So it was that Southern Democrats began to make their home in the Republican Party: in the Republican primaries of 1964 Nelson Rockefeller would be the last moderate to make a plausible bid for the party's presidential nomination.

The changes taking place in the Republican Party as it moved to the right were reminiscent of the famous Hayes-Tilden Compromise of 1876, which had brought an end to Reconstruction. That year the Republican Party, the party that had freed the slaves, suddenly made a deal to elect Rutherford B. Hayes and agreed to withdraw all federal troops from the South. Without the presence of federal troops, each formerly Confederate state could now treat its "niggers" as it pleased. The South, which had seen the election of blacks to Congress, state legislatures, and even a black lieutenant governor of Louisiana, resegregated. Former slaves, freed without any financial compensation for a lifetime of forced servitude, became sharecroppers perennially in debt to landowners; "Black Codes" controlled the activities of blacks; and the Ku Klux Klan terrorized black people who had the temerity to act as if they were free Americans.

Similarly, in 1964 we had enjoyed nearly a decade of progress in civil rights, from the Supreme Court decision in *Brown v. the Board of Education* to the passage of the Civil Rights Act. And once again, history showed me that progress could always be turned back. A Goldwater victory would be another Hayes-Tilden disaster for the cause of justice for African-Americans.

Today no true moderate can mount a credible candidacy for the Republican nomination for president, and moderate Republicans in Congress are becoming an endangered species. The 104th Congress, led by Rep. Newt Gingrich of Georgia, has adopted all of the worst policies of Goldwater's 1964 platform: it is anti–civil rights, anti-labor, anti–United Nations, against humanitarian and development aid to poor nations, and against progressive taxation. What we fought so hard against in 1964, the country accepted as Gingrichism in the midterm elections in 1994.

In October, 1964, after the hectic summer was over, Martin entered St. Joseph's Hospital in Atlanta for a complete physical. There was nothing seriously wrong with him: he was simply exhausted and his doctors wanted to look him over. I was in his room at St. Joseph's on October 14, when Coretta phoned to say she had received a call early that morning from a newspaper reporter who said a report had come across the wire services that Martin had won the Nobel Peace Prize.

We knew Martin had been nominated for the Nobel Prize, but no one in our office thought he had a chance of winning it. And Martin never even mentioned it. Of course, we were all ecstatic. The Nobel Prize would endow Martin and our cause with worldwide prestige, and signify a new level of recognition for the American civil rights movement. We hoped this recognition would not only bring us renewed sympathy from white Americans, but also generate support from blacks that up to now had been reluctant to make a commitment to the movement. Martin and other movement activists were considered by many middle-class blacks in particular to be too controversial and remained aloof from them. We figured if they weren't impressed by "Letter from a Birmingham Jail," they might be impressed by the Nobel Peace Prize.

When Coretta called Martin to tell him about the prize, he had been asleep. She told him what the reporter had said and he muttered, "Uh huh, okay," and hung right up. Then he called her back about five minutes later and said, "Did you just call me? Or was I dreaming?"

That afternoon a small group from our staff took the day off to be with Martin. Friends came by and many called that joyous day, but I remember most vividly the visit from Archbishop Paul Hallanan of Atlanta. We were talking for a while around Martin's hospital bed; then I moved to the other side of the room to talk with some other folks. I overheard the archbishop ask Martin, "May I extend my blessings?" and Martin replied, "Yes, of course." The archbishop offered a prayer and extended the formal blessings of the Catholic Church. Then he got down on his knees beside Martin's bed and asked, "May I receive your blessing?"

The significance of this moment stunned me. A Roman Catholic archbishop on his knees, asking for and receiving the blessing of a black Baptist preacher named Martin Luther! Martin was so shocked he almost didn't know what to say, but he quickly collected himself and prayed very quietly, so that only God and the archbishop heard him. To me, the Catholic archbishop of Georgia kneeling for a blessing from Martin Luther King, Jr., was a symbol of the profound change that could and would come in the South. It said not only that we were right morally, but that we were beginning to win the kind of deeply felt support that would make real change possible.

But all the attention was not so positive. It was very soon after the Nobel Peace Prize announcement in October 1964 that we could not help but become conscious of an unmistakable and intensified harassment emanating from the FBI and Director J. Edgar Hoover. Martin had several times criticized the FBI for confining themselves to unresponsive "observer" roles when the rights of black citizens were being violated in the South. This was particularly true in Albany, and in cases like the Winona, Mississippi, jailing of Mrs. Hamer and the women traveling with her. We felt the FBI agents assigned to the South were far too friendly with the local police to be objective or effective in racial cases; sometimes they were outright segregationists themselves.

But we had never felt, until then, that we had a particular problem with Hoover. We were accustomed to Southern segregationists accusing their opponents of being communist and we assumed that that was behind President Kennedy's concern that some of our associates were communist. I remembered my experience with Highlander Folk School when Southern officials leveled charges of communism against it; even the House Un-American Activities Committee found no evidence of it, but the rumors persisted. We couldn't imagine that anyone seriously thought the movement was controlled by communists—to us the whole notion was simply ridiculous. We knew that the FBI was monitoring us, and we knew Hoover was right-wing. We were pretty sure our office phones were tapped and thought maybe our home phones were as well. And we were fairly certain we were being trailed by agents; but none of this really bothered us, naive as that may sound now. We took the position that since we weren't doing anything illegal, we had nothing to hide, and FBI surveillance would only bear out the truth of what we were about. We never protested the surveillance; we felt it would be useless to do so, anyway.

We knew that Hoover did not take kindly to our criticism, or any criticism, but it was not until his absurd remark in a November 18 press conference of women reporters, when he called Martin "the most notorious liar in the country," that we realized just how serious our problem with Hoover and the FBI was. At the time, I was with Martin and some of our senior staff on a brief working vacation on the isolated, undeveloped Caribbean island of Bimini, helping him prepare his Nobel Prize address. There was nothing there but a fishing lodge—no televisions, no phones in the rooms. We were trying to give Martin a peaceful place to think and write his acceptance speech, a speech that would explain our movement to the world, a speech worthy of the Nobel Prize. Suddenly, the tranquillity of the island was broken by an assault of helicopters; it was like an invasion. We had no idea what was going on until the moment Dan Rather jumped from his helicopter and began asking questions. As if they were a single, multibrained organism, the networks and wire reporters had descended on tiny Bimini to get Martin's response to Hoover's outrageous statement. We had to arrange a press conference at the Big Game Fisherman's Lodge, which only had one telephone. Suddenly we were immersed in the very kind of frantic responding to the urgent needs of others that we had come to Bimini to escape.

We worked out a very careful comment in which Martin said Hoover's remarks were "inconceivable" and that he was not going to try to answer them. Among ourselves, we conjectured that either Hoover was becoming senile or the unfettered power he had enjoyed for decades as the nation's most prestigious policeman had completely gone to his head. In private, Martin said slowly in his understated way, "Well, I guess the director's getting a little older." Hoover's remarks, however, made us look much more seriously at a series of worrisome occurrences and happenings that, up until then, we had not viewed as part of a pattern.

Our problems with the FBI, as far as we knew, dated back to the summer of 1963. It was in June of that year, after a White House meeting with civil rights leaders, that President Kennedy had asked Martin to step out into the Rose Garden with him for a private conversation and warned Martin that the FBI believed Stan Levison and Jack O'Dell were communists. As the time, President Kennedy also warned that our phones were tapped, although it was difficult for us to conceive of the extent of surveillance that existed.

After the president's conversation with Martin, we began receiving off-the-record calls from journalists, such as the *Atlanta Constitution*'s Ralph McGill, who said FBI agents were telling them incredible stories. They said the agents told them they had information that Martin was influenced by communists, was stealing money from the SCLC treasury and holding it in a secret Swiss bank account, and was guilty of sexual indiscretions.

When these stories began showing up from more than one source, we became concerned, and decided to try to get to the bottom of them. Walter Fauntroy and I decided we would see John Herbers of the *New York Times*'s Washington bureau, who had been friendly toward us, to ask him if he knew about the rumors, and if he had any information about their source. We met with Herbers and a few other *Times* reporters in Washington. We told them everything we had heard, and they told us the stories were definitely coming from the FBI. Walter and I asked for the name of the agent who was spreading stories, so we could actually confront FBI officials. Herbers said that as reporters they were not at liberty to provide us with the name since they were obliged to protect their sources.

Then we tried to get them to be more specific about what they had heard. We asked them if they had seen any evidence themselves. There were rumors that the FBI had photographs of Martin in "compromising" positions. They answered, "No, we didn't *see* them, but the agent we talked to says he has them." Once again it seemed stories were being spread by the FBI without any evidence or proof to back them up. In fact, I never talked to any newsperson who had actually seen or heard any evidence concerning the allegations against Martin.

There were several other strange incidents before Bimini to which I now wish we had paid more attention. First, there was a visit to Daddy King from Atlanta Police Chief Herbert Jenkins, with whom Dad was very friendly. Jenkins came right out and told Dad that the FBI was waging a campaign to discredit Martin. He said that J. Edgar Hoover had even tried to get him to cooperate in attacking

Martin. He also told Dad with disgust that he had once had a lot of respect for Hoover, but after his unscrupulous attempts to destroy Martin he had lost all respect for him. Such an admission, despite their relationship of informal friendliness, was most unusual. Jenkins asked Dad to warn Martin that Hoover was out to get him.

Around the time of that incident, Martin was trying desperately to complete a manuscript. He called me at the office from the Atlanta airport upon arrival from a trip out of town, and said he was going to check into a hotel for the day, because he simply had to get his writing done. Edwina Smith, my secretary, had had to enter the hospital a few days earlier, and Jean and I were taking care of her son. I had the keys to Edwina's apartment. I suggested to Martin that he go there to work.

I called Edwina and asked if it would be okay for Martin to use her apartment for a couple of days to write, and she gave her permission. I sent Martin the keys, and he went to Edwina's apartment. Later Martin told me that after he had finished his work, Bernard Lee had gone over to pick up the manuscript, and brought it back to the office for typing. Then Martin, who was exhausted, fell across the bed and went right to sleep. He did not know how long he had been sleeping when he was suddenly awakened by loud sirens and someone banging at the door. He staggered to the door, and discovered firemen and police who claimed they had a report there was a fire at the apartment. Martin told them there was no fire. He invited the police and firemen in to look. They all piled in while Martin stood there in a kind of daze. They looked around very thoroughly, searched every room, then finally left. It was clear to him that they thought Edwina or someone was there with him. The FBI had him under surveillance, had our office phones tapped, and had created the report of a fire in a silly attempt to catch Martin in an embarrassing situation.

Shortly after the meeting with the *New York Times* reporters, Walter Fauntroy received a call from someone who would not identify himself, informing us of the presence in one of the government agencies of a typed transcript of a long-distance conference call Martin had initiated concerning the language of his Nobel Peace Prize acceptance speech. The person who called Walter described how the transcript was set up, and said it included biographical sketches of each of the six people participating in the call. The informant said he didn't think the government's actions were proper and he wanted us to know we were under this kind of surveillance.

After the surprising media event in Bimini, these other incidents appeared more ominous and we felt we should try to meet directly with Hoover as soon as possible. Trying to find someone who could arrange such a meeting was difficult, but after some inquiries, we learned that Archibald Carey, a prominent black Chicago attorney and politician, knew Hoover and could handle it.

A meeting was set for December 1, 1964, in Hoover's office in the main Justice Department building on Constitution Avenue, and Martin, Ralph Abernathy, Walter Fauntroy, and I attended. What happened next has been wildly blown out of proportion. In fact, nothing happened, except that Hoover rambled on and on about the virtues of the FBI. He greeted us very cordially; his assistant, Cartha DeLoach, and one or two other officials from the Bureau were also present. Martin attempted to initiate a discussion that would touch on our differences, but Hoover quickly changed the subject, offering polite congratulations to Martin for winning the Nobel Prize, and saying he was glad to meet him after all these years. He took fifty minutes of the hour, talking, almost lecturing us. He said he had difficulty finding black agents, there were many problems the Bureau faced working in the South, and so forth. He was attempting to sell us on the virtues of the FBI, even the FBI in relation to civil rights. Hoover assured Martin that the FBI was making progress in the investigation of the deaths of Chaney, Goodman, and Schwerner, and referred to the difficulties the FBI had in getting cooperation in the investigation. We had no opportunity to express that we had reason to believe that the FBI agent initially assigned to Philadelphia was related to local law enforcement officials and had planted the idea that the disappearances were an SNCC publicity stunt. (An ABC News reporter, Paul Goode, was fired because he refused to report the FBI line.) It was as if Hoover wanted Martin to praise the FBI for finally finding the bodies; he also promised that after several months there would be arrests in the case.

But we never got around to discussing the "most notorious liar" business. Nor did we even get to mention the FBI surveillance, or the stories we were hearing from newspapermen. Hoover never raised the subject of communism, he never mentioned sex, and he expressed no opposition to the civil rights movement. On the surface, it may have seemed a very good meeting, except that we had given the director advance notice of our concerns, none of which he addressed.

After about an hour, Ralph thanked Hoover, then said there were some other matters we needed to go over with him, and since they involved Dr. King personally it might be better if Ralph and I returned at a later date to see Hoover without Martin. We hoped that without Martin present, we could have a less formal and more candid discussion. Hoover seemed agreeable to this. I was assigned to stay in touch with DeLoach to make the arrangements. We also agreed we would keep the FBI, through the Justice Department, informed about our forthcoming campaigns. They, in turn, agreed to inform us of any potential danger or threats against Martin's life. (We did receive subsequent information about threats against Martin from John Doar of the Justice Department while we were in Selma, but we never received any such warnings directly from the FBI.)

The smoothness of the meeting left us feeling vaguely dissatisfied because so much was left unsaid, but we assumed the meeting had shown him that we had nothing to hide. As we emerged from his office, we were confronted by a huge press contingent in his outer office awaiting a statement. Martin summarized the meeting for them, but in our presence, Hoover refused to talk to the press. FBI files made public years later, however, reveal that Hoover spoke with some members of the press after we left and declined to withdraw the "most notorious liar" statement. Somehow the rumor was later widely circulated that Hoover had threatened to "expose" Martin in the meeting, had shown him compromising pictures, and had told him, in effect, that he was going to do him in. This carried the implication that now Martin was in Hoover's pocket. Nothing like this ever came close to happening, but it worried me that such a false version of what had transpired gained such wide circulation. We wondered whether this rumor too was being deliberately circulated by the FBI. Meanwhile, the wiretaps on Martin, Stan Levison's home, and the office of Clarence Jones, our attorney in New York, continued. And the FBI regularly sent memos to the White House summarizing their interpretation of the content of these calls.

If it hadn't been for the persistent rumors, we would have thought there was no problem. It was as if there were two Hoovers: the one we met with was a perfectly respectable gentleman who acted like the head of the FBI; but we kept hearing about another Hoover who ranted and raved and called Martin names. Yet, there was nothing in our encounter with J. Edgar Hoover that suggested anything irregular in the relationship between Martin Luther King and the FBI.

In retrospect it was no coincidence that Hoover flipped out and called Martin a liar just after he had won the Nobel Prize. As absurd as it may seem, Hoover wanted the Nobel Prize himself. He had had his friends in Congress nominate him for the prize year after year. And despite the steady stream of nominations, he never surfaced as a leading candidate. When Martin was awarded the Nobel Prize, he won something Hoover had coveted for most of his career as director of the FBI. It was the Nobel Prize that elevated Hoover's strong dislike of Martin and mistrust of the goals of the civil rights movement to an obsession.

At the time, however, I could not conceive of the extent of our problem with Hoover and the FBI. I could not have imagined that significant resources of the nation's primary law enforcement agency would be devoted to examining details of the business of SCLC and those associated with it. We now know for a fact that our phones were tapped, and our conversations were recorded, transcribed, and summarized for transmission to higher officials in the Justice Department and the White House. There was also personal surveillance of Martin and other members and friends of SCLC at our meetings, in airports, at hotels. There were memos and reports on these activities. All that energy wasted on us, and this was the same federal law enforcement agency that insisted it did not have the resources to offer any protection to civil rights activists.

Hoover was not the only person angry and envious of Martin's Nobel Prize. Ralph, too, was upset that he had not received the prize along with Martin and thought Martin should rectify the oversight by giving Ralph half of the money. Ralph thought of himself and Martin as a modern-day version of the biblical David and Jonathan. And Ralph's estrangement was much more worrisome to Martin than anything he thought J. Edgar Hoover might do. Martin and Ralph had had an uneasy relationship since the end of the Birmingham movement. As SCLC grew in stature and as an institution, Ralph had difficulty adjusting to it. All along he didn't so much relate to the movement as to Martin, personally. Other, newer members of the staff, such as Bevel and Hosea, had taken on major organizing responsibilities. They had strong ideas and creative approaches to the challenges facing the movement. They were willing to do advance work for the movement, to engage in the unglamorous task of preparing the soil. But Ralph wanted press coverage. When he made a speech by himself, no press showed up to cover it. If he traveled with Martin, there was at least the possibility of getting his picture taken. Ralph would rather get his picture in the paper tagging along with Martin than go out by himself. He was a powerful orator who always made a contribution on his own, but he was unable to believe he was having an impact if he didn't generate press coverage.

The trip to Oslo to attend the Nobel Prize ceremony began with a fair amount of tension among the celebrants. We were able to pay the fare for only a few of our staff members, but when we could, we made loans against salary for staff persons who wanted to go. There were some thirty or forty people in our immediate party, which included Martin's family and personal friends, SCLC staff, and friends in the clergy. Unfortunately, there would be room for only ten or twelve persons from our party at the actual ceremony, which was held in a very small auditorium.

Jean did not go with us to Oslo. Unlike Juanita Abernathy and Coretta, she worked outside the home as a teacher, and would have had to take a leave of absence from her job and find someone who could stay with the girls while we were away. In her strong and silent way, she never asked to go and I was so immersed in the task of organizing the trip that I didn't really think about whether she ought to come.

It was quite a trip. On the first leg of the journey Martin spoke at St. Paul's Cathedral in London, before a massive crowd of three or four thousand—a historic event, as Martin was the first non-Anglican to preach there. Then we all flew to Oslo on December 8 for the ceremony.

I remember little things about that time, like the spontaneous singing of church and freedom songs one day in the lobby of the Grand Hotel in Oslo. Many black ministers are fine singers as well as orators, so we had no problem striking up an instant impromptu choir, led by Rev. O. M. Hoover of Cleveland, one of Martin's best friends. Martin, no lead singer himself, joined in with the "choir." Hotel guests wandered in and out of the lobby or, amused, stopped to listen. No one from the management complained, though I guess it could be said such an event was highly unusual, if not unprecedented. Odie Hoover was in wonderful form that day. When he sang "Precious Lord, Take My Hand," the most popular of all gospel songs, the Grand Hotel was transformed, as if by magic, into a black Baptist church at the height of spiritual emotion and fervor. I thought it beautiful that even here, in this cosmopolitan European setting, we could retain a sense of ourselves through our own music and culture. And it was fitting, for the Nobel Prize was more than a personal award for Martin. It was an acknowledgment of the struggles of all black Americans for survival and achievement during the long, arduous, and difficult century since emancipation.

The ceremony itself was formal and rather brief, held in the auditorium of Oslo University. Those few of us from Martin's inner circle who were able to attend had to smile when the Norwegian Broadcasting Symphony broke into selections from Gershwin's *Porgy and Bess* in an attempt to play music honoring black Americans.

Maybe they thought "Summertime, and the livin' is easy" was the perfect music to go with the police lines, barking dogs, and fire hoses of Birmingham, Alabama, but we could only feel amused. We knew they were probably ignorant of black symphonic composers such as William Dawson, Nathaniel Dett, and William Grant Still.

There was a brief speech, then the gold medallion was placed around Martin's neck, after which he gave his formal acceptance address. In his eloquent speech, Martin did not limit his vision to the struggle for equal justice in America, but emphasized the need for world peace and reaffirmed his strong commitment to the struggle against racism, poverty, and war throughout the world.

After the ceremony, outside the auditorium, we were thrilled by an enthusiastic greeting from hundreds of Norwegian students singing "We Shall Overcome" and chanting freedom slogans. It was an awe-inspiring moment when we realized, in a flash, that what we were doing—what had until now been an almost exclusively Southern American regional struggle—had transcended the limits of time and place and had become an international symbol of hope and freedom.

That night all of the SCLC "family" gathered in Martin's hotel suite, and I ordered a case of champagne. In the giddiness of the moment, in a pervasive atmosphere of jubilation, we fell into a series of elaborate toasts, everyone toasting everyone else. Finally, Daddy King rose to offer his toast.

"When I was a boy outside of Stockbridge, Georgia," he began, "I had to tend the animals in the morning before I went to school. My classmates used to kid me because I smelled so bad when I finally got to school. I vowed then that even if I smelled like a mule, I wasn't going to think like a mule. And I was determined that my children would not have to walk behind plow mules. But I never believed my children would ever come this far. We couldn't have come this far by ourselves, no, not *ever*!" he added, getting carried away. "I want us to toast the one who made it possible for us to be here tonight. I want to make a toast to *God*!"

So we raised our glasses, and a few of us nervously sipped champagne in honor of the Lord.

As I watched Coretta and Martin lift their glasses to each other in silent tribute, I missed Jean, deeply. I realized that I should have insisted that she come with us, not for my sake, but in recognition of all the sacrifices she had made to bring us to this wonderful day. Decades later, when I was serving as U.S. Ambassador to the United Nations, Jean accompanied me on virtually every international tour.

While I sat through official briefings, she visited the schools and hospitals and met with the women's nongovernmental organizations. And at the end of each trip, it was she who had the more accurate picture of the quality of life that existed for ordinary people in the country.

Harry Belafonte had graciously arranged a series of fund-raising concerts for us in Sweden and in Paris in December following the Nobel Prize ceremony. It impressed us how enthusiastically we were received by the French people and the press, but there wasn't even so much as a greeting from the American ambassador in Paris. In fact, our presence was generally ignored by American diplomats in Europe. It was as if the State Department did not approve of Martin's having been chosen for this award, and would have been much happier had someone else won it.

While we were in Paris, Belafonte played a practical joke on me. A small group of us, including Martin, were sitting around Harry's suite and he was kidding me pretty hard. "I got you now, Preacher. You're in Paris. You're on my territory. You've been running around here all sweet and innocent, but now you're where the Devil can really get to you." I said I didn't know what he was talking about. He went right on kidding me. "We'll see how you do when you really come face-to-face with the Devil's delights," he added.

"What are you talking about?" I said.

"We're going to find someone to tempt you," he said. "How about Brigitte Bardot for a start?"

"I never was attracted to her," I answered.

Harry feigned shock. "What's the matter with you?" he asked.

"Well, really, I've always been much more attracted to serious, more mature women," I said.

"Like who, for instance?"

"Oh, like Melina Mercouri, or maybe Simone Signoret." I thought I was being very blasé and sophisticated. So he said, "That's interesting," and he left the room. We sat there talking with his wife, Julie. Pretty soon he returned and said, "Come on, I want you to take a walk with me, Preacher." So Martin and Julie came with us and we all got on the elevator and went to another floor. Harry went to a room, rang the bell, and who should open the door but Melina Mercouri! She shook hands with Martin, but she threw her arms around me and hugged me. And when we went into the room she sat down on the couch with me and snuggled up to me, while Martin, Harry, and Jules Dassin, her husband, enjoyed my embarrassment—because I couldn't get a word out of my mouth. Martin and Harry really made the most of the moment: "You had your chance, boy, but your tongue got tied, huh? Sad." Martin liked to tell this story at parties whenever he got to talking about me.

On our return trip through Paris, Mrs. Freddie Henderson, who had handled Martin's travel arrangements for the trip, suggested that we couldn't come to Paris without going to one of the famous Parisian nightclubs. Freddie is a member of the United Church of Christ, not a Baptist; Mrs. Henderson didn't realize what a tempest an invitation like this could stir up among a group of Baptists!

Coretta, Christine King Farris, Martin's sister, his mother, and Dora McDonald, his secretary, all thought a night on the town in Paris would be a perfect ending to a wonderful trip. But Martin suddenly reminded everyone that he was a Baptist minister and he didn't go to places like that. Everyone tried to assure him that it was harmless. Nobody was really interested in drinking—you could drink Coca-Cola or ginger ale—but Martin wouldn't budge. "You all go on," he said. "I need to relax and get caught up on my reading. I still have to preach a sermon when we get back."

But then as everyone got dressed and began to gather in his suite to go out, Coretta came out in a beautiful burgundy velvet dress. It was one of the concert dresses that she wore in her musical performances for the movement, featuring an off-the-shoulder neckline. With her eyes sparkling with anticipation and the flattering dress, she looked more glamorous than the mother of three young children and pastor's wife we usually saw.

This was just too much for Martin. Coretta was too beautiful to be going out in Paris without him! Perhaps he was reminded that until she married him, Coretta had planned to study music in Europe, that evenings in Paris might have been a regular part of her life. Even if she was chaperoned by his mother and his sister she was too at home in Paris. He insisted that she change clothes and put on something more "dignified," but what he really meant was "dowdy." Even a Nobel Prize winner can panic at the sight of his wife going out on the town in Paris in her most alluring gown. Coretta, who had been managing Martin Luther King, Jr., for more than ten years, offered to stay home with him. That offer both reassured him and let him know that he was being selfish. He wrestled with his demons and finally relented, so Coretta, wearing the controversial dress, and the rest of us went to see the cancan without him.

This European tour was unlike any Martin had experienced. He was received by heads of state and royalty in the most elegant surroundings. As Daddy King had said, it was an incredible achievement for a young black preacher from Atlanta, Georgia. But, if some of us were awestruck, Coretta moved through Europe with the poise and dignity of a queen. She was gracious and seemed unfazed by the demands of protocol and social ritual. Martin was accustomed to seeing Coretta in the comfortable context of home and church. The ease with which she charmed Europe's elite was a reminder to him that the woman he married was a pearl beyond price.

When we returned to New York in late December 1964, Cleve Robinson of District 65 of the Retail, Wholesale Department Store Workers Union, one of our strongest supporters, sponsored a huge rally honoring Martin at the 169th Armory in Harlem. The rally was attended by many important black community leaders and government figures, including Governor Nelson Rockefeller. Malcolm X was also there. By then Malcolm had become a prominent figure in the media: his strong black nationalism and anti-integration views had been posed as an antithesis to Martin's agenda within the black freedom movement. Martin believed that Malcom's cynicism toward America stemmed from extreme frustration at rampant injustices in American society, but however psychologically appealing it was to blacks, Malcolm's approach offered no program for redress of those injustices.

I had met Malcolm before he became nationally known while I was living in Queens. Sometimes, when he was in Atlanta, Malcolm stopped by the SCLC offices, but he never had a chance to meet personally with Martin. Martin was always traveling so much, and their paths just never seemed to cross long enough for them to have a real conversation. Whenever we were in New York, Martin's schedule was full of speeches, meetings, and fund-raising events with little opportunity for courtesy calls. Moreover, the Black Muslims were somewhat problematic for Martin's core constituency of preachers, less because they were militant than because they weren't Christian. I appreciated the few opportunities I had to talk with Malcolm. I always found him a serious and sincere advocate for his belief in the need for blacks to develop a new sense of pride, and he made a powerful witness against black self-hatred. This was quite necessary, especially for Northern blacks. But it did not have to be seen as anti-white. It was an affirmation of blackness.

On his way to the stage at the armory, Martin encountered Malcolm in the passageway and the well-known photograph of the two of them was taken, though they only exchanged a few words. At the rally, I left the platform at the armory to go out and greet Malcolm and sit with him for a while.

While in New York we met with Governor Rockefeller, who had lost the Republican nomination to Barry Goldwater the summer before. Martin had decided to contribute all of his Nobel Prize money, fifty-four thousand dollars, to the civil rights movement. Rockefeller told him, "You can't afford to do that." Martin said, "I can't afford not to do it. I received the Nobel Prize, but it wasn't just my work, it was the work of the whole movement that was honored. I must share the money to sustain the mutual cooperation with the NAACP, SNCC, and the leading organizations." Rockefeller responded, "Well, if you can afford to give that money away, I can afford to match it." And on the spot he pledged fifty-four thousand dollars to civil rights organizations.

Rockefeller also offered his private plane to fly Martin from New York to Washington, where we went to the Justice Department to meet with Attorney General Nicholas Katzenbach and Vice President Hubert Humphrey. The meeting was cordial enough, but we had already decided we were going to push the Johnson administration to pass a Voting Rights Act in 1965; the Civil Rights Act of the previous summer, though historic and important, wasn't sufficient without guarantees of the ballot. "I'm sure we can't get a voting rights bill, not in 1965," Humphrey pleaded with us. "We passed the civil rights bill only a few months ago. It's too soon."

After we had talked with Humphrey for about an hour, he received a call and left the meeting. When he returned, Humphrey said Lyndon Johnson had invited us to meet with him at the White House. We couldn't help feeling that there had been quite a discussion over whether the president wanted to meet with Martin, and if so, how he should be received. Martin Luther King had been received as royalty across Europe, but even with a Nobel Prize, the president of the United States did not receive him with any pomp and circumstance. Just as the U.S. ambassadors had ignored our presence in Europe, the president held no reception or press conference to congratulate Martin Luther King for receiving the Nobel Peace Prize.

The resultant meeting with President Johnson was uneventful. Martin once again told the president that we desperately needed a voting rights act, and as soon as possible. However, there was no further discussion of this issue. Instead President Johnson spent almost the entire session talking about his federal programs. As we left the White House, Martin remarked, "Kennedy asked questions for an hour; Johnson talks for an hour. That's the difference between them."

The ambivalence toward Martin in America continued even in Atlanta. Rabbi Jacob Rothchild and Dr. Benjamin Mays, Martin's mentor at Morehouse, had planned a dinner to honor Martin for his winning the Nobel Prize, and the tickets were not selling. (Subsequent examinations of FBI records indicate that many Atlanta businessmen were discouraged from participating by officials of the FBI.) Finally, J. Paul Austin, the chairman and CEO of Coca-Cola, and Mayor Ivan Allen summoned key Atlanta business leaders to the Commerce Club's eighteenth-floor dining room, where Austin told them flatly, "It is embarrassing for Coca-Cola to be located in a city that refuses to honor its Nobel Prize winner. We are an international business. The Coca-Cola Company does not need Atlanta. You all need to decide whether Atlanta needs the Coca-Cola Company." Within two hours of the end of that meeting, every ticket to the dinner was sold.

Looking back at the year following the March on Washington, I now recognize that a major shift in attitudes toward Martin and the movement was taking place. We didn't perceive it at the time, but the criticism and the critics had begun to change. It was no longer only the profoundly ignorant people in the white community who were expressing reservations about Martin and what we were doing; even liberal whites in Atlanta were uneasy about his Nobel Prize. We were now beyond simple desegregation, pressing for changes that would require every American to alter his or her thinking and behavior about race. The Civil Rights Act didn't just change life for white Southern racists; it changed the rules for every American.

We soon discovered that our problems with J. Edgar Hoover were only beginning. On January 5, 1965, Coretta was opening mail and other packages forwarded to her by Martin's secretary. A couple of days a week, Dora would drive over to the house with mail and packages that Coretta would handle. When Martin spoke, people often sent him audiotapes of the speech, plaques, and other memorabilia. Coretta cataloged and generally kept track of those things. The volume of mail, people sending their good wishes as well as Christmas mail, had piled up during the trip to Oslo, and after Christmas she began to tend to all the boxes. One of the packages contained a bizarre anonymous letter that had been mailed to Martin at the SCLC offices. Along with the letter was a reel of audiotape. Dora had just included it in Coretta's regular mail without even unwrapping it. The package was postmarked from Miami.

Coretta opened the package and discovered a poorly typed letter that concluded with a threat something like: "King, we've found you out. This is just a sample of the goods we have against you. King, your end will come soon. You are done for, there is only one way out for you. You have thirty-four days before you will be exposed and publicly defamed." There was no question that there was a strong suggestion that Martin commit suicide in this sick letter, with its threats of "exposure" timed around the awarding of the Nobel Prize. Coretta immediately called Martin at the SCLC office.

Daddy King, Coretta, Martin, and I went to Martin's house on Sunset Avenue, where they had moved the year before when the Georgia Transportation Department decided to build a highway over their home on Johnson Avenue. Martin had insisted on remaining in the heart of the black community, but Coretta prevailed upon him to at least improve the modest home they purchased. Daddy King had to intervene with the state Department of Transportation to get full value for their old home. With the proceeds from the sale and another fourteen thousand dollars from Daddy King, Martin had purchased an old house on the edge of the Vine City slum. Coretta renovated the house, so that their three children had a playroom, and there was a powder room and a kitchen large enough to serve the constant stream of visitors. She also established an office in the base-ment to keep the mail and the archives that she maintained.

I set up the reel-to-reel tape recorder on the dining room table and we sat down together to listen to the contents of the tape. We had no idea what we would hear. Daddy King said, "Go ahead, Andy," and I turned on the machine.

It was a very poor quality recording. As far as we could deter-mine it was made at a party at the Willard Hotel in Washington the night after the March on Washington in August 1963. Coretta was with Martin at the march, but evidently she was not in the room when the bugging was done. SCLC had kept a suite for Martin at the Willard and a private room, where he wrote his speech. What some-one had recorded was a group of SCLC staff members, including Martin and Ralph, in a fun-filled and relaxed conversation after the triumph of the March on Washington. Bernard Lee and Walter Faun-troy were present, and Joe Lowery, SCLC's chairman, and Wyatt Walker seemed to come in and out of the suite.

The only section of the tape that was in the least damaging to Martin was when he started teasing Ralph. Ralph had started com-plaining that he hadn't been allowed to speak at the march. Martin responded with, "Ralph, you had to be the head of an organization to speak. What we have to do is find you an organization that you can be the head of, so that on the next march, you can have the right to speak." And everybody present agreed that the one organization

that Ralph was unquestionably the president of the "National Association for the Advancement of Eating Chicken." Martin waxed eloquent, saying, "No one could challenge your preeminence, you
would have no competition." And they all cracked on Ralph for
about an hour. Everyone would think of something different to say
about Ralph's organization. They laughed, big, deep, belly laughs,
releasing all the tension of the day.

After this locker-room talk came a section of the tape, replete
with distortions and pauses, that sounded like a couple having intercourse. Martin had a distinctive voice and it certainly wasn't his.
That's why Coretta wasn't upset. It was just the sounds of a couple
moaning and groaning.

There was no question in our minds that this scurrilous material
was coming from the FBI—for instance, the letter was purportedly
from someone black, but it attempted at one point to associate Martin's name with Henry VIII of England, an unlikely reference for a
black person in that context. And, of course, few people had the
capability of bugging hotel rooms except the FBI. It has subsequently
been suggested that the Washington police may have bugged the
rooms, but in those days the District of Columbia government was
wholly a creature of the federal government.

We had thought maybe the situation with Hoover had calmed
down some after our meeting with him in early December. Now I
was truly worried, and even Martin was concerned; we simply
couldn't understand the motive behind this type of activity. It seemed
that Hoover's personal vendetta against Martin was not the only
thing operating here: someone had made a conscious decision to try
to destroy Martin's reputation, thereby seriously damaging the movement.

As we discussed possible responses to the package, we determined it was time to meet again with Hoover's assistant, Cartha
DeLoach. We had agreed at our December meeting with Hoover that
we would discuss at a later date Hoover's charges and the rumors we
were hearing from newsmen, but we had heard nothing from the
Bureau about a follow-up. So I called DeLoach, and he set up an
appointment for Ralph, Walter Fauntroy, and me, to be held at FBI
headquarters in Washington on Monday, January 11, 1965.

At this meeting I was determined that we get to the root of the
problems, though that was difficult due to DeLoach's strange and
noncommittal attitude. I asked him specifically about Hoover's
charge that Martin was a "notorious liar," but he denied he knew
what that was about. I told him we had been hearing that the Bureau

was spreading rumors that SCLC was infiltrated by communists, that Martin had secret bank accounts in Switzerland, that he was some kind of sex maniac, and that FBI agents had offered newsmen incriminating photographs and recordings. DeLoach replied categorically that no FBI agent would do anything like that. We knew, of course, that this was not the case. I then took another tack: "If there is any evidence of communist attempts to infiltrate and take over our movement," I said to DeLoach, "we'd like to know about it. We don't have a communist movement, nor do we intend to. We are as anti-communist as you are."

DeLoach replied that he couldn't give us any information from Bureau files, but there were agencies that did keep and provide that kind of information. He mentioned the American Legion and the House Un-American Activities Committee. Ralph and I couldn't believe our ears.

"Look, Mr. DeLoach," I answered, struggling to remain calm, "the House Un-American Activities Committee is one of the most racist committees in Congress. They don't want us to have any rights at all. The fact that we want to vote in elections is a communist plot as far as they're concerned. So how can anyone take anything they have to say about communist influences with respect to us seriously?"

After a little more discussion about the issue of communist infiltration, I pressed DeLoach on the other two matters. "It's just impossible that Martin Luther King is confiscating any money," I began. "Virtually all the money we have in the organization is raised from his speeches and books anyway. This is how our salaries are paid. He doesn't even *take* a salary from SCLC, his only salary is from Ebenezer. Martin gave away the Nobel Prize money to SCLC and other civil rights organizations. He never has any money, he has to borrow money from his Daddy to pay his taxes every year. SCLC covers his expenses, and I can tell you just what they are, if you're interested. If he stays in a suite when he travels, it's usually the group he spoke for that paid for the suite. The idea of a secret bank account in Switzerland is totally ridiculous." I reminded DeLoach that an all-white jury in Alabama had found Martin innocent of tax evasion. That was the end of that discussion and DeLoach attempted no response.

Then DeLoach pointedly said to me, "Reverend, as a minister, you don't approve of abnormal sexual behavior, I'm sure."

"No I don't," I said, "but as a minister, I also don't think I should make judgments about anyone's sex life. That is something each person has to work out between themselves, their families, and their God. As far as I'm concerned," I added, "there isn't anything about Martin Luther King's personal life that interferes with his work, with our movement, or with his family." Then I spotted a photograph on his desk of DeLoach and his large family. "Now, by my own personal standards," I added, "it's rather abnormal to have a child each year. Because in our church we practice and teach family planning." He looked a bit shocked, and I continued, "It's very hard for officials, whether religious or secular, to define normal sexual behavior in a free society." That pretty much ended the discussion of sexuality, and on that note the meeting came to a close.

It was all so unfair. Here I was defending Martin against rumors that he had money in Swiss bank accounts, and his wife was struggling every day just to pay their bills while he gave away money that his family needed. Harry Belafonte was so concerned about the dangers Martin was facing that after the Birmingham campaign he personally took out one-hundred-thousand-dollar life insurance policies on Martin for each of Martin's children. Stan Levison set up the policies and Harry paid the premiums. Harry knew that Martin had no money to leave the children if he were to be killed.

I guess we should have expected the FBI to oppose us and to be fearful of our movement. But all of us had grown up believing that the FBI was fighting crime and evil in our nation, and all we were doing was fighting the evils of racism. It was not black citizens who were burning houses at night, dynamiting churches and synagogues, or shooting unarmed men in the back. We were the victims of this unlawful and violent activity, and we didn't expect to have to defend ourselves against the federal government too.

But we were advocating major and fundamental changes in the social order, and the FBI was desperate to protect the status quo. They did not see democracy as an evolving system, constantly perfecting itself by enacting changes to include and improve the lives of all of its citizens.

The FBI's constant allegations of sexual impropriety, what DeLoach chose to call "abnormal sexuality," were impossible to rebut. It was a classic "When did you stop beating your wife?" dilemma. There is just no way to disprove allegations concerning behavior that by its very nature takes place in private, without witnesses. This was simply an attempt at character assassination. Martin's private sexual behavior was not relevant to the movement, and I never saw any behavior that in any way undermined it. It was the FBI that did its damnedest to undermine the movement with these fabricated stories.

Martin did have a side to him that was comfortable with the streets. He had to develop that to thrive on Auburn Avenue during the depression. He liked to get down and talk like a street brother when he was relaxing, blowing off steam. He teased, he could crack on you, insult you until the whole room was laughing 'til they cried. But it was never in anger, never in bitterness, it was always in fun. Martin would never tease anyone he didn't love. He could only relax that way with people he trusted, his closest colleagues and personal friends.

None of us were saints. Saints could not have survived the rigors of the movement, could not have accomplished what we accomplished in so short a time. We were flesh-and-blood human beings, men and women. We got involved with the most pressing issue of our day; we got our hands dirty with the labors of social change. We associated with racists and white supremacists. We negotiated and compromised with people who opposed everything we were trying to achieve. We were flawed and imperfect and we fell far short of the glory of God. But we changed America. And we did it without harming anyone, except ourselves.

13

Give Us the Ballot

Ain't gonna let nobody turn me 'round . . .
—African-American Traditional

SCLC was always doing more than one thing at a time, and while Martin's Nobel Prize and our efforts toward Lyndon Johnson's victory in the presidential election were public events, behind the scenes we were planning a major campaign on voting rights. The SCLC convention had taken place in Savannah in the fall of 1964, after the Democratic National Convention and the painful conflict over the Mississippi Freedom Democratic Party, and before the reassuring Johnson landslide in November. As executive director, I was scheduled to make a major speech before the delegates, mostly Baptist preachers from the local affiliates across the South. As usual, people were late gathering and the mass meeting crowd that night was small. We needed Martin's speech to set the tone for the convention and it was typically the only news coverage we received. Martin's address had to be rescheduled from the night before, and, concerned that I would have to speak after him, he suggested that I give my speech another time. He wanted the delegates to hear what I had to say, to be impressed with me. And given the typical response to one of his speeches Martin didn't think that could happen if I spoke directly after him. I insisted that it didn't matter to me, I'd just as soon go ahead and get it over with.

Martin spoke with his usual eloquence and then it was my turn to address the convention. I gave an analysis of the political crisis in the nation caused by the stranglehold of several congressional committee chairmen elected from the South. Mississippi's John Stennis controlled the Senate Judiciary Committee and passed on judges for the entire nation, and Richard Russell ran the Armed Services Committee and used the military as a jobs program for the white South, while opposing domestic job creation programs such as housing and urban infrastructure. Russell, Stennis, Allen Ellender of Louisiana, and their counterparts in the House, rose to power through the seniority system that rewarded longevity above all else. In the conservative, one-party South, there was far less turnover in congressional delegations compared to the rest of the country, giving the South an advantage in claiming powerful leadership positions. These men were elected from states and congressional districts where black citizens were excluded from the electoral process through intimidation, literacy tests, bureaucratic red tape, and other legal and illegal means. My experience in Thomasville and the experiences of Amzie Moore and Fannie Lou Hamer were repeated in virtually every county across the South when blacks attempted to register.

After the speech, Martin expressed his admiration for the soundness of my presentation. "I didn't think I had left anything for you to say. I really learned something." That was high praise, coming from Martin. I wasn't afraid to speak after him, because I wasn't trying to compete with him. As far as I was concerned, there was only one Martin Luther King, who could challenge and inspire a mass meeting packed with great preachers.

Baptist ministers had a certain style of preaching and it was generally accepted that Congregationalists couldn't compare. But I was not trying to emulate a Baptist style, that was not who I was. My speech was short on emotion, but I tried to share my understanding of how the South used the denial of our voting rights to dominate the nation. Rather than confront head-on my position on the voting rights problem, I provided a well-researched assessment of the barrier that the denial of voting rights created for the full agenda of the movement and the nation as a whole. I wrote out the speech, which I rarely did, to ensure that my arguments were thoroughly explained. It was my contention that while it was possible to change a society through direct action, the restructuring of that society would require political action. We would need to continue with the direct-action strategy, but for the long-term transformation we were seeking, full participation from black Americans in the electoral process was essential. A campaign on voting rights was just the logical next step for SCLC.

Focusing on public accommodations in Birmingham had helped bring about a very comprehensive civil rights bill. Unfortunately, though the bill gave black citizens the right of access to public accommodations, it did not protect their voting rights, a forum in which they might actually help change the laws that kept them down. While the level of violent and unchecked intimidation, even murder, in Mississippi during Freedom Summer was extreme, threats, intimidation, retaliation, and virtually insurmountable bureaucratic hurdles were routinely used in the South to keep black voter participation low. Not coincidentally, the severest limitations on black voting were typically utilized in areas where the black voting age population was greatest. Strategies to prevent blacks from registering could be as simple as closing the registrar's window whenever blacks came to the courthouse to register or as drastic as putting a gun to Mr. Steptoe's head when he brought farmers in a wagon to register to vote in Amite County. Fannie Lou Hamer lost her job and her home because she led blacks citizens in Sunflower County to the courthouse to register.

Our citizenship schools trained local leaders to return to their communities armed with knowledge of their rights as citizens of the United States. Yet, in county after county across the South, their disciplined efforts to motivate their neighbors to register were met with subtle resistance and open hostility from the local authorities, sheriffs, judges, and clerks, who had reason to suspect that blacks would be unlikely to vote for them. While citizenship training was important, it did not offer any protection or redress for citizens in jurisdictions where the local authorities were determined to disregard the United States Constitution and the Bill of Rights. Having the law on your side wasn't enough, and, as a rule, voter registration occurred smoothly only in areas like Birmingham and St. Augustine, where there had been successful movements to desegregate.

Somehow, we had to dramatize the voting issue the way we took segregation in public accommodations to the national stage. In response, Jim and Diane Bevel developed a battle plan they called "G.R.O.W.: Get Rid of Wallace." Governor George Wallace of Alabama was a symbol of racist defiance of any attempt to provide equality for African-Americans. He proclaimed "segregation now, segregation forever," promising to keep black students out of the University of Alabama, though it was supported with their parents' taxes and labor. His intransigence was so severe it had opened Bobby

Kennedy's eyes to the realities of Southern resistance to desegregation. Yet, Wallace was governor of a state where nearly thirty percent
of the eligible voters were black.

To really change the South, it was necessary for COLORED signs
to come down, but it was also necessary to elect men and women of
goodwill to public office. Justice had to be institutionalized into the
body politic and not experienced just as a response to the massive
pressure of demonstrations and boycotts. As we had learned from
our study of the first Reconstruction, without real political power,
the changes achieved with demonstrations could well erode over
time. Blacks could not protect their newly won rights unless they
shared in the decision-making process of the political system. Federal
authorities had intervened in a few specific instances to enforce segregation, such as President Eisenhower's decision to send federal troops
to Arkansas to enforce a federal school desegregation order, but such
instances were rare. Typically, the federal role was initiated only after
the damage was done, as in the FBI's investigation into the murders
of the civil rights workers in Philadelphia, Mississippi. Neither President Johnson nor President Kennedy before him had any commitment to placing the South under the control of a federal occupying
army to ensure that desegregation continued to be carried out.

G.R.O.W. called for a statewide campaign. Unlike our other city-
based efforts, it was time to expand beyond Birmingham, in large
part because the black population there had done enough suffering.
There was only so much you could ask people to sacrifice. Diane and
Jim Bevel's plan involved all the big towns in Alabama: Montgomery,
Tuscaloosa, Anniston, Tuskegee, Huntsville, and eventually Birmingham. We looked at organizing the rural counties of Alabama's black
belt, which had large black populations and low black voting participation, though we were leery of organizing in small towns far from
media and airports. We had discovered in Albany that it was difficult
to generate national attention in a remote town, and the Mississippi
Freedom Summer was a recent and horrifying reminder of the dangers involved in rural organizing—so many long, dark, isolated
roads, so many opportunities for an ambush.

But as we reviewed various plans for a voting rights campaign,
in a series of formal and informal staff consultations occurring in the
midst of the Nobel Prize ceremonies and problems with the FBI,
events began to draw us to Selma, a small town on Highway 80 west
of Montgomery, in the center of the cotton-planting farmland of Dallas County. The Dallas County Voters League was created in 1960 in
an effort to spur black voter registration, but with very little success.

In 1964, no blacks were registered in Wilcox County, less than four percent in Hale County, slightly less than seven percent in Perry and Choctaw Counties, and less than three percent in Dallas County, where Selma was located. Registration of eligible white voters was more than ninety percent in each of these counties except Dallas, and in Wilcox white registration exceeded one hundred percent, a figure achieved by registering the deceased.

In 1962, Reggie Robinson, a SNCC worker, had gone to Selma to assess the feasibility of setting up a project there. In 1963, Bernard Lafayette and his wife settled in Selma and attempted to begin a full-fledged SNCC project. They hoped to win some converts to SNCC among young people at Selma University, but the administration of the school was extremely fearful, and they were banned from the campus. However, a few students did become active, and joined with adults like Mrs. Amelia Boynton, president of the banned NAACP, and the pastor of the Catholic Mission to form the beginnings of a movement. It did not take long for Bernard to establish himself in Selma, but he was viciously beaten by a group of whites in front of his home one night, and might have been killed had a neighbor not appeared on his porch with a rifle and chased the attackers away. Very soon afterward Bernard left Selma and was replaced by Worth Long, now one of the South's leading folklorists and a historian of the movement.

Selma was very much a SNCC movement and SNCC workers had tried a number of strategies to increase the number of registered voters with little tangible success. During the Birmingham movement, Jim Bevel, who was then a member of SNCC, responded to an invitation from the Dallas County Voters League to speak at one of their meetings. There were subsequent demonstrations and marches to the Dallas County courthouse to register, but whenever black citizens presented themselves at the courthouse during normal business hours, the registrar's office was closed or Sheriff Jim Clark and his deputies met the marchers with cattle prods. Nothing much substantive was gained as a consequence of these marches, though there were signs that the black community was beginning to wake up and take notice. In September 1963, SNCC's executive secretary, Jim Forman, and its national chairman, John Lewis, moved to Selma to try to step up activities. They were harassed, arrested, and abused. Refusing to give in, SNCC organized a boycott of city buses in early 1964 in response to the death of a pregnant black woman who was killed when a white bus driver drove away while she was trying to disembark, dragging her body along with the bus. The boycott did not achieve remarkable results; in July 1964, John Lewis mounted a strong voting registration march to the Dallas County courthouse, which resulted in widespread arrests of the demonstrators.

The July march was answered by an outrageous injunction imposed by James Hare, an avowedly white supremacist state circuit court judge, which prohibited the congregation of more than three blacks in public at any one time. It was absurd, and clearly unconstitutional, but Sheriff Jim Clark went about enforcing it diligently. Even children walking home from school in groups were harassed. By using this injunction, the city was able to prohibit further marches in 1964, but they were not able to alter the determination of the people.

With this recent history, Mrs. Amelia Boynton of the Voters League and a committee of fifteen citizens, mostly women, came to Atlanta to ask for our help. A stately, bronze-skinned former schoolteacher, Mrs. Boynton was determined and persistent. Like Rosa Parks, she was deceptively ladylike, a steel magnolia. The Dallas County Voters League provided minimal camouflage for what was essentially the program of the banned NAACP. I knew Mrs. Boynton from the citizenship schools and from Jim Bevel's visits to Selma, and she was a good friend of Jean's mother. So I took the group to see Martin, to make their case for his involvement in Selma. The NAACP in Selma had traditionally held an Emancipation Proclamation Day program, an effort that was carried on by the Dallas County Voters League. It would be a violation of the injunction to hold the Emancipation Day Program, but Mrs. Boynton was determined to hold it anyway, and the Selma citizens hoped Martin's presence would bring national attention and discourage retaliation by Sheriff Clark. One could not help being impressed with Mrs. Boynton and the brave history of her band of loyal activists. Martin agreed to speak on January 2, 1965, at Brown AME Chapel to commemorate the 102nd anniversary of the Emancipation Proclamation.

Meanwhile, Jim and Diane Bevel's G.R.O.W. plan was taking shape, and it was decided that the voting rights campaign would be launched from Selma. Selma did not meet many of our strategic requirements—it was both isolated and small. But the persistence, courage, and determination of the people in Selma were part of the equation. In little Selma, more people were committed to the movement before Martin's arrival than after months of organizing and two weeks of daily demonstrations in Birmingham. The people's commitment made it the right place for us.

I remembered visiting Selma when I was serving the Congregational Church in Marion during the summer of 1952. Jean and I had had our first real date in Selma, and occasionally drove down there to go to the movie theater. Selma was an insulated, isolated, hermetic Southern town in the middle of Alabama, seemingly untouched by Birmingham and Montgomery, even though it was not far from either city. From Montgomery you drive fifty miles through fields of cotton; suddenly you come upon Craig Air Force Base, the Alabama River, and Selma, and almost wonder how it got there, so desolate is the countryside surrounding it.

The site where Selma now stands on the Alabama River was the occasion of a meeting between Sieur de Bienville, founder of New Orleans, and the Alabama Indians in the early eighteenth century. When central Alabama was taken over by white men a hundred years later, Selma became the processing and merchandising center for the area's cotton plantations, mostly because of its strategic location on the Alabama River. It was also the largest slave purchasing and deployment center in the area, if not the entire new state of Alabama. As in New Orleans, there was in Selma a large black population, with many extremely dark-skinned direct descendants of West Africa. To this day Selma's black population is distinctive—it's almost as if one has been magically transported to Africa.

During the Civil War, Selma became a stronghold of the Confederacy and was virtually destroyed by the Union Army in 1865, an event remembered in Selma with extreme bitterness (it was frequently mentioned when we were there, as if we were the second coming of the Union Army). After the Civil War, Selma distinguished itself in the history of Southern white supremacy as the sometime home of Confederate General Nathan B. Forrest, the founder of the Ku Klux Klan; the birthplace of Birmingham's police chief, Bull Connor; and the home of the first White Citizens Council in Alabama, an organization created to promote defiance of the Supreme Court's ruling in *Brown v. Board of Education,* which made "separate but equal" unconstitutional.

Despite its legacy of racism and dearly held Confederate mythology, Selma had developed a strong, stable, and intact black community. It was a proud community as well. When I first saw it in the 1950s and when we campaigned there in 1965, it did not suffer the kind of destitution and hopelessness we all too often note today in the black communities of large urban areas. Nevertheless, blacks occupied the lowest rung of the economic scale and there was little employment for them except as maintenance help for white businesses, as domestics and gardeners for white families, and as laborers in the cotton gins and other cotton-processing industries. More fortunate blacks worked at Craig Air Force Base, probably the largest single employer in the area in 1965, located on the outskirts of town across the Alabama River. And despite the relative poverty of the Selma black community, it maintained two tiny church-affiliated black colleges, Selma University and Lutheran College, which served Selma and all the adjoining rural counties southward and westward toward the Mississippi state line.

One of the consequences of Selma's isolation, as the Alabama River became much less economically important in the twentieth century, was the unremitting victimization of the black community. Blacks were banned from participation in all aspects of economic or political life. This stemmed from the "bring back slavery" mentality of the white ruling class, but also from a strong resentment that Selma had been one of the few Alabama towns to elect a black congressman during Reconstruction. The idea in Selma was to "keep 'em down by force," and with few outsiders around to pass critical judgment, authorities like Sheriff Jim Clark had their way with the black community. Clark, in fact, was almost a reincarnation of the overseer of the old slave plantations. He didn't run this plantation, but he liked to act as if he did.

In 1965, Selma looked like it still belonged in the nineteenth century. It was nothing but a bridge and a main street. Large warehouses lined the river, empty reminders of the days of King Cotton. The central business strip occupied a few blocks along Broad Street, the main avenue that ran through town, lined by low buildings and large leafy trees and with ample room for angle parking on either side of the street. White folk tended to live in the southside of the city and black folks on the northside and it was possible to drive through town and miss signs of the black neighborhoods altogether. As in many old Southern towns, the blacks were tucked away out of sight, but near enough to be called upon when they were needed.

With its numerous churches, schools, tiny businesses, and Masonic organizations, the black community of Selma was old and strong. Yet they had no voice in the running of the city and somehow the appearance of the town reflected that political reality. It could be perceived from the looks on the faces of both races: blacks looked healthy and strong, but introverted; whites looked, talked, and behaved as if the only reality in the world was Selma, and Selma the only reality they cared to know about. In Selma, matters seemed set, predetermined, isolated from the rest of America and the world. With their neat white frame houses and their slightly worn, older, and larger houses and expansive gardens, with the town's blacks happily (they assumed) working in their kitchens, cleaning their homes, laboring in their gardens, and performing the hard physical work in the cotton fields and along the railroads for subsistence pay at best, the whites in Selma felt they were in the best of all possible worlds—there was no need for anything to ever change.

In their view, we had come to destroy their world, to urge the town's blacks to protest against inequities that had existed for as long as they could remember and that they felt were justified by the natural inferiority of the black race. After all, "their" blacks would never have known anything about the inequities without our "outside" agitation. In those early days of 1965, the white townspeople of Selma looked at us not only through eyes of hatred, but with minds and spirits that failed to comprehend in the least why we were there. Selma was symbolic of race relations in any small Southern town trapped in a time warp; we could have chosen any of a hundred similar towns, but we could not have found a more exemplary case of social polarity, or a more abused and oppressed black community. Ironically, the very isolation of Selma's black citizens made them determined to strike out against the source of their oppression, and Selma's isolation contained within it the potential to create an unusual rebirth of black racial solidarity.

Black people have always been courageous, but seldom have they been foolhardy. What so many observers have described as apathy is often just the protective attitude that is necessary for survival, like that of the dog who gets kicked all the time and who just moves out of the way whenever someone comes along. Martin used to tell of an old blues singer on Auburn Avenue in Atlanta who would sing "Been down so long, gettin' up don't cross my mind." In the tradition of the old slave songs with their double meanings, this song is about cultural adjustment to oppression. Slaves sang of a sweet chariot "coming to carry me home" while convincing the slave master that they were content to work now and wait until they got to heaven for shoes and dignity. In the sixties, many of these songs, both blues and gospel, gave rise to a new political beat—"Keep on Pushing" and "People Get Ready (There's a Train a Comin')" by Curtis Mayfield and the Impressions.

Selma had reason to feel like Martin's old blues singer. The court injunction had not only refused blacks the right to register, but further denied them even the right to walk down the street in groups of more than three persons. The approach in Alabama was like that in South Africa: intimidate and oppress and they'll stay in their places.

By 1965, the dog been kicked too many times. Selma was a city that had been bruised and abused long enough. Mrs. Boynton's plea was for Dr. King to give them the push they needed to get organized and finally win the right to vote without harassment.

Martin's "Give Us the Ballot" speech (a reincarnation of his 1957 Prayer Pilgrimage March on Washington speech) on the night of January 2 before a jammed audience at Brown Chapel challenged the injunction and served notice that we were willing to wage a determined campaign in Selma to achieve progress in the registration of black voters. The willingness of hundreds of people to violate the injunction was a powerful indication of the resolve of Selma's black citizens. In his speech to the enthusiastic crowd, Martin noted that Selma was "a symbol of bitter-end resistance to the Civil Rights Movement in the Deep South."

After the mass meeting, Jim Bevel and Albert Turner, an organizer from Marion, Jean's hometown, were assigned to organize marches to the courthouse, with Bevel in charge of the overall campaign. No one was more gifted at on-the-scene strategy than Bevel. Jim and Diane had a passion for the project that no one could match, and no small measure of what we saw as Jim's brilliance was due to Diane's rational thinking and influence. The preachers of SCLC were not advocates for women's equality at this stage of our moral and political development, and Diane was not on the SCLC payroll. As in the traditional church structure, a preacher's wife might direct the choir, run the Sunday school, and chair the women's fellowship without any compensation but her husband's salary. It is not to our credit that we followed that model with Diane.

Jim and Diane's connections with SNCC were another asset they brought to the Selma movement; both had come into the movement through the Nashville student sit-ins and were among SNCC's founders. SNCC had been working in Selma for years, and there was a potential for conflict and resentment of SCLC for coming in to take over "their movement," despite the fact that we had been invited by local leaders. Whenever Martin was present, he would dominate the media coverage. The flip side was that Martin's presence brought media attention that SNCC alone couldn't generate. Nevertheless, it created resentment among SNCC organizers. Bevel was effective in managing the conflicts with SNCC—he had come into the movement with many of the SNCC leaders and they trusted him.

We knew the only way we could sustain a movement in Selma was for some of us to move into the community, live there for a while, and work hand-in-hand with the local community as we had done in Birmingham and St. Augustine. Our fund-raising had made it possible for us to expand our staff greatly by early 1965, and we now had more than forty people working for us. Along with James Bevel and Albert Turner, Hosea Williams was assigned to run the field projects in Alabama.

I found it advantageous to virtually move into Selma myself, residing in the home of Mrs. Boynton. It was a gracious, white frame home full of antique furniture and lace curtains. Mrs. Boynton had two spare bedrooms, so Dorothy Cotton and Septima Clark stayed there as well when they came over to Selma. There was a small but clean black-owned Torch Motel, but it did not offer the meeting space and other advantages of Gaston's in Birmingham, and most of us stayed in private homes instead. We bought groceries and tried to help out some with chores, but Mrs. Boynton never charged us a penny in rent for the months we stayed in her home. When Martin came to Selma, he stayed across the street with Dr. Sullivan Jackson, an old friend and movement supporter and veteran. It was understood by everyone that Martin could not spend the majority of his time there, as he was keeping a growing schedule of national speaking engagements in order to spread the word about Selma. Martin was our chief spokesman and fund-raiser, and he could no longer be tied down with the specifics of a local campaign. As in Birmingham, he continued his speaking engagements and preaching at Ebenezer and rarely spent a full week in Selma. I would work with the press and our NAACP Legal Defense Fund attorneys and take care of all the intermediary details of coordination so he didn't have to be in Selma day in and day out.

Brown AME Chapel, a dark, reddish-brown old-fashioned brick building with twin towers, and First Baptist, with its beet-red brick, both on Sylvan Street, were the primary and secondary headquarters of the Selma movement. Surrounding the churches, which were about three blocks apart, was the George Washington Carver federal housing project, from which we drew many of the volunteers for our marches. Reverend Lewis of Brown Chapel virtually turned over his church to our needs; its role in Selma was comparable to that of Sixteenth Street Baptist in Birmingham. It took great courage for Reverend Lewis to be so supportive and cooperative since he well knew that the Sixteenth Street Church had been bombed, and four children killed, in retaliation for the support it had given to the Birmingham campaign. Acts of violence toward churches sympathetic to the movement were quite common, particularly in the Bible Belt of the South.

In undertaking our Alabama campaign, we had the advantage that many of our staff possessed important personal connections in the state. Martin had served his first pastorate at Dexter Avenue Baptist Church in Montgomery, had established himself as a national figure in the civil rights movement through his work with the Montgomery bus boycott, and had cemented his preeminent national leadership position during the Birmingham campaign. He was as well known and highly respected in Alabama as he was in Atlanta. And many of us involved in the campaign had roots in the area. The First Congregational Church in Marion, where I pastored the summer I met Jean, was just thirty miles from Selma. Coretta Scott King was a native of Perry County, just a few miles from Selma. Ralph Abernathy was a native of Marengo County, Alabama, and had served his residency in Montgomery; his wife, Juanita, was also a native of Perry County, Alabama. James and Diane Bevel had lived and worked in Birmingham, Montgomery, and Selma before we made Selma an SCLC project. Albert Turner lived in Marion, Jim Orange was a native of Birmingham, and so on. Therein lay a crucial secret of our success in Selma; though we were labeled "outsiders" by white Selma and the hostile Alabama press, we were all but locals and were never considered outsiders by the black community of Selma. The trials of Coretta Scott King's family were examples of the severe impact that political powerlessness had on black folk in that region of Alabama. When Coretta was growing up, her father farmed his own land and from that farm saved enough money to build a sawmill, but whites burned it down. He had no insurance and no bank would provide a loan, but he managed to build a store and went into logging only to have the store burned and the trucks sabotaged. Still, he persevered and rebuilt the store. Coretta had far more direct experience with the most painful realities of segregation than Martin.

Once, I was talking with Mr. Scott about his farming days and confided that I was able to pick cotton. He said, "Aw, you ain't never picked cotton." I said, "Yeah, I picked cotton for a whole day. I must've made about thirty pounds." He told me, "You ain't picked no cotton. Now, Cory could pick some cotton. She was the best cotton picker in our family. There was rarely a day when she didn't pull in two hundred pounds of cotton, and I've known Cory to pull in three hundred pounds when she had to." It is difficult for most people to imagine the regal Coretta Scott King on her family farm picking two to three hundred pounds of cotton every day until the crop was in, but that was the childhood that gave her such strength and character.

The Scotts were determined to give their children a better life, and Coretta attended the Lincoln Normal School in Marion. It was there that the music teacher, Olive Williams, a collector of spirituals, helped Coretta develop her musical talent as a vocalist. Another teacher, Fran Thomas, urged her to attend Antioch College, and within a few years Coretta had gone from cotton fields to the New England Conservatory of Music in Boston, where she met a young doctoral student, Martin King.

Quite the ladies' man, Martin had been dating the daughters of Boston's black aristocracy. Coretta was very different from those rather sheltered, prissy young ladies. Through her musical training she had developed the grace and poise of someone bred in sophisticated society, but she had strong convictions on social issues. Martin admired Coretta from the start, and Martin's roommate, Phillip Lenyard, saw Coretta as the kind of woman that Martin should be with. Together, he and Coretta gave a surprise party for Martin and invited all the young ladies that Martin was seeing. As their hostess, Coretta was all graciousness, thereby making it clear that she was in charge. It was a nonviolent way of dealing with one's opposition that Martin couldn't help but respect.

The tribulations of the Scotts were well known among black leaders in Selma and Perry County. Martin's marriage to "Cory" and our other local roots made this in many respects a homegrown movement. We needed that foundation, since to get things moving in Selma as well as in the neighboring towns and counties, our first task was to get more people involved than the Dallas County Voters League or SNCC had been able to do so far. To bring about change we had to attempt to sustain a movement for some time, and we needed the full participation of the local black population to do that. We had to get them to believe in the cause passionately since we knew from our experiences in Albany, Birmingham, and St. Augustine that involvement in demonstrations and the subsequent jailings caused a serious disruption of the lives of black citizens and involved tremendous economic sacrifices.

To achieve mass involvement we first attacked the apathy that was the product of almost a century of black disenfranchisement. Indifference born of long suffering and fear of economic reprisals were real factors; many blacks in Selma worked in jobs that were directly or indirectly controlled by the white community. Those who worked as laborers in the cotton industries and in Selma's businesses, or as domestics and gardeners, certainly had their pursuits controlled directly by their white employers, but, in a more indirect way, so did those blacks who worked at Craig Air Force Base. Public school teachers and principals were under the jurisdiction of white public

school administrators. In such an atmosphere of potential intimidation it was always the jobless, the elderly, and the youth who became
the first field soldiers of the movement. In Selma, we knew we had to
do better than that; we had to find a way to involve the middle-aged
and employed men and women with families, for they were the core
of the community. If they didn't find it worthwhile to be involved in
the struggle to vote we would not be successful.

The demonstrations in Albany had begun over the issue of segregated public interstate and intrastate transportation, despite the
edicts of the Interstate Commerce Commission and widening rulings
on desegregation by the federal courts. The Birmingham campaign
began over the issue of the inferior treatment of blacks in the downtown commercial area, and the policy of white businesses that made
a good part of their livelihood from black consumers refusing to hire
black clerks. St. Augustine began over the issue of widespread segregation at every level of city life, and the city authorities' toleration of
extreme violence in the name of maintaining it.

By early 1965, after the passage of the 1964 Civil Rights Act,
some measure of desegregation of public facilities in the South was
beginning to occur. But we all realized, particularly after the horrible
violence that followed the Birmingham movement, including the
killing of children, that our problems had far deeper roots than simply the personal prejudices and insecurity of white people and the
internalized apathy of the local black population. Martin had pointed
out the interrelationship between racism, poverty, and war in his
Nobel Prize lecture, and in Selma we began to see more clearly how
the South had used race to maintain a one-party political system in
which veteran senators and congressmen were able to use their
seniority to push for the spending of federal dollars—mostly through
military contractors—in their districts. Craig Air Force Base, Selma's
largest employer, for example, was kept open only by the efforts of
senior senators Lister Hill and John Sparkman. Once they retired, the
military "necessity" for maintaining an air force installation in Selma
would disappear.

So the movement in Selma was a much more serious threat to
the old South than anything we had done to date. Lunch counter
desegregation and token hiring of blacks had not changed the traditional lines of authority and power, nor had they seriously threatened
anybody economically. In fact, integration had contributed to the
economic development of the South in small ways. Racial tension discouraged outside investment in the South, but as people began to
work together the natural advantages of the South became more

attractive to investors. The South grew economically in inverse proportion to the amount of racial tension. An elderly white Georgia legislator from Perry used to say, "the best things that ever happened to the South were air-conditioning and integration." But almost every state in the Deep South had a powerful minority of potential black voters—twenty to forty percent—and to admit those voters into the democratic process could produce revolutionary changes. Of course, it was taken for granted that all blacks would vote together, and that they would vote against the Southern oligarchy.

The well-established relationship between political powers-that-be and the economic well-being of the region that the movement threatened to disrupt represented a real challenge to the status quo. Martin understood this well and joked about it as we made our plans for Selma. "Now when you start messin' with Mr. Charley's Senator, you're messin' with his jobs and that won't be easy. We'll have some funerals to deal with in the black belt of Alabama and we won't just be burying segregation, we'll be burying some of us," he would say.

Martin was always acutely aware of the imminence of his death. In 1958, while promoting *Stride Toward Freedom*, his book about the Montgomery bus boycott, Martin had been stabbed with a letter opener by a demented woman in Harlem and came very close to death. He might joke about it, but he was painfully conscious of his vulnerability. Late at night, when he couldn't sleep for worrying about the movement and the expectations he was compelled to fulfill, he would talk seriously about his experience of hovering near death. "I was lying in the hospital bed, and preachers were standing around me. I was unconscious but I seemed to be looking down on them and they were praying for me. Some of them were really anxious for me to die, hoping to take my place. I wanted to tell them 'I'm not gone yet!' but I couldn't speak. I could only look down at them and listen to their prayers. Now, I have to face my mortality, every morning when I stand in the mirror to brush my teeth." A huge cross-shaped scar remained on his chest from the operation that had removed the letter opener pressing against the aorta of his heart. And though he joked about preaching at our funerals and spoke of death very lightly, he knew that most of the risk and danger was focused on him personally. An awful burden for a man of thirty-six with a wife and children.

And there was tangible danger in what we were about to do. Sheriff Jim Clark was the Bull Connor of Selma: he was younger and just as aggressive, a prototype of a Southern white sheriff. Like Connor and Sheriff L. O. Davis of St. Augustine, he believed that Selma's black population could be suppressed and controlled through the use of force. Clark was assisted in patrolling demonstrations by a volunteer mounted "posse" of white citizens, half of whom came from the upper economic classes. The behavior of Clark and his posse was akin to that of the Southern sheriffs of antebellum times and the slave patrols that had hunted and captured runaway slaves, exercising the right to check slave "passes" whenever blacks were seen away from their plantations. These volunteer "police" were the forerunners of the Ku Klux Klan and the white leagues of post-Reconstruction. In Selma, they were accorded a cloak of respectability as deputies of Sheriff Clark. The sole purpose of the posse was, of course, to help suppress civil rights demonstrations.

Fortunately, Jim Clark was not the only authority in Selma. Wilson Baker was director of public safety, which was equivalent to chief of police in another city. A knowledgeable and moderate man, Baker taught criminology courses at the University of Alabama, and we always felt we could be reasonable with him. As was our practice, we tried to establish open communications with police officials and I had no trouble whatsoever talking with Baker; we maintained a good working relationship until the day we departed.

Baker always knew what we planned to do, both from his talks with me and through clumsy police surveillance of our public meetings in the churches. This knowledge was of no consequence in attempting to stop, or even frustrate, our demonstrations. On the other hand, Jim Clark was fired up by the "never, never" rhetoric of Governor George Wallace and his state chief of police, Al Lingo. We were never able to communicate or achieve any measure of understanding with Clark. Not surprisingly, Clark and Baker disliked each other intensely and often argued openly in front of us. Unfortunately, Baker could not restrain Clark, who was determined to have his share of the limelight during the demonstrations.

Bevel began by organizing citizens to go to the courthouse for scheduled registration days. Clark and Baker permitted group assembly in these instances and then would keep us waiting at the registration office for hours, finally informing us that the office was closed for the day. So once again we decided to institute an economic boycott of the type that had been so effective in Birmingham.

A kind of shadowboxing then went on for a couple of weeks with little of consequence occurring. Then one day in late January, in a demonstration led by local activist Rev. F. D. Reese, Clark lost control of himself and hit C. T. Vivian while the TV cameras were running. He pushed, shoved, and arrested Mrs. Amelia Boynton while she was monitoring one of the registration lines, because she "didn't move fast enough." Mrs. Boynton was so well known and the attack so unjustified, that her arrest and rough handling by Clark sparked an immediate increased interest in the demonstrations. In the next few days, over two hundred demonstrators were arrested. Once again, the opposition had become their own worst enemies in the attempt to sway public opinion.

For the next registration day, we organized a march of black public school teachers. In order to demonstrate, the teachers had to have the courage to defy the all-white Selma school administration, at the possible cost of their jobs. In Albany, Birmingham, and St. Augustine, we hadn't been able to get black teachers to openly demonstrate. In fact, in Birmingham, the black principal of Parker High had attempted to lock the students in to keep them from demonstrating. But in Selma, the teachers themselves marched to the courthouse to register to vote. At the courthouse, they were turned back by Sheriff Clark. Denied entry to the University of Alabama, many of these teachers had done graduate study out of state at some of the nation's best universities, and the march demonstrated pointedly that even the most educated segment of the population was being prevented from registering to vote. The teachers' march proved that the talk of blacks being "unqualified" to vote was a smoke screen. Shortly after, we organized a march of workers, scheduled to begin at six o'clock, to demonstrate that working black men were prohibited from the opportunity to register because, in addition to all the overtly racial barriers, the office was always closed during the hours when they were able to register. A march of veterans was designed to show the inequities in a society where men who had served their country in the military were being prevented from exercising the most basic of American civil rights because of their race.

In early February, Martin and Ralph returned to Selma and, as planned, led a march to the courthouse, whereupon they were arrested and taken to jail. Baker personally arrested Martin before he reached the courthouse: he was concerned that there might be violence if Jim Clark and his posse made the arrest. This also made Martin Baker's prisoner rather than Jim Clark's, and we were somewhat grateful for that. It was a day of massive arrests: almost five hundred people went to jail, including many high school students.

Once again, the arrest of Martin and Ralph brought tremendous national attention to the Selma campaign. To take advantage of this heightening national attention, we encouraged a group of concerned congressmen to come to Selma and observe conditions there. The group was organized by Rep. Charles Diggs and Rep. John Conyers, both black Democrats from Detroit, and Rep. Brad Morse, a white Republican from Massachusetts. Altogether fifteen congressmen, including Ed Koch of New York and Sid Yates and Abner Mikva of Chicago, descended upon Selma on a very cold day in February to see for themselves what was happening, and to talk with Martin and Ralph, who bailed themselves out of jail in order to brief the congressional delegation. We were encouraged that Assistant Attorney General Ramsey Clark flew down with the congressional delegation. I spent quite a bit of time with him, escorting him around and briefing him on conditions in Selma. Tall and lanky, like a modern-day Lincoln, Ramsey Clark was sincerely interested in the movement in Selma. As always, in speaking with officials from the Justice Department, I emphasized the importance of the administration's moving with dispatch toward a voting rights act. Clark conveyed the administration's belief that it would be impossible to convince Congress to approve such legislation in 1965, but his pragmatic responses clearly did not reflect his personal convictions.

While Martin was in jail in Selma, Malcolm X came for a brief visit. He was escorted over from Tuskegee by SNCC workers, where he had spoken briefly in support of SNCC's activities there. This was, as far as I know, Malcolm's first visit to the scene of a Southern movement campaign, though he had visited our offices several times in Atlanta when he was passing through. Coretta, James Bevel, Fred Shuttlesworth (who had come down from Birmingham), and I met with Malcolm at the home of Reverend Lewis. Malcolm made clear his intent to play a supportive role, and said that he wanted to pay his respects to Martin, who was still in jail. Malcolm and I went over to the jail together, but for some reason we were prevented from seeing Martin.

Later that afternoon, Malcolm was invited by SNCC workers to speak at Brown Chapel. Such an invitation was quite common, as our meetings were always open to visiting speakers. Though Malcolm was an excellent orator, his strident style was unfamiliar to most of the people in Selma, and despite the strong approval he received from the SNCC contingent, the Selma natives gave Malcolm a polite but lukewarm reception. They were more accustomed to the slow cadences and Southern accent of the Baptist preachers. In an insulated Southern community like Selma, Malcolm's rapid-fire delivery and Northern accent were almost incomprehensible.

Malcolm had said in our private meeting that day that he believed his militant public statements made it possible for other, more

moderate leaders like Martin to become more accepted by the mainstream. To some extent, I think this was true. Martin also understood
that Malcolm had to maintain a critical posture toward him in order
to establish his own individual image. Malcolm's visit to the South
and his interest in the great Southern movement, less than a month
before his death, may have been his way of showing a belated recognition of Martin's value, and the value of all those who struggled against
discrimination through nonviolent protest activities in the South. Just
three weeks later I would leave our campaign in Selma to return to
New York to attend his funeral, after his tragic assassination in February 1965. At the funeral I stood outside and participated as best I
could; the church was so crowded I could not even get inside.

Selma was an "open" movement, as were all our efforts. We
were there to educate, inform, and dramatize the injustices we were
working to change, and conflict was a necessary stage through which
we had to pass to reach our goal of social change and mutual understanding. We were never secretive about our strategies or tactics: we
let it be known that we planned to march, march, and march some
more until we obtained results. But Sheriff Jim Clark and the Selma
officials didn't know what an open movement was; they were constantly trying to spy on us, and eventually were able to place a small
secret microphone under the pulpit at Brown Chapel. In fact, before
his arrest, Ralph discovered the microphone one night in the midst of
one of his sermons. He first looked at it in puzzlement, then realized
what it was and became angry for a second; then he had an inspiration. He held it up so the congregation could see it; then he taped the
mike to the top of the pulpit and began to preach to it.

"Little doohickey," he said, "I don't know who you belong to or
who may be listening in on the other end. But I want you to tell them
for me, without static or interference, you tell them for me, that the
black people in Selma are on their way to freedom and nobody is
going to stop them!"

The crowd just went wild as Ralph continued to mock whoever
had hidden the microphone.

"Tell Mayor Smitherson, tell Jim Clark, and if you can reach
Montgomery I want you to tell Governor Wallace; then go on and
play the same tune for J. Edgar Hoover at the FBI and even President
Johnson in the White House.

"Tell them that we will keep on marchin' till hell freezes over if
that's what it takes, to bring down the walls of segregation. Tell them
that we intend to fill the jails in Alabama if necessary, because if
you're black in America you are already in jail.

"Tell them for me, Ralph David Abernathy, that 'we ain't gonna let nobody turn us around,' so they'd better wake up and start doing right. Right now!"

And everyone just howled. Ralph had cleverly turned the snooping around by showing we weren't afraid of this kind of surveillance of our public meetings. It made everyone there feel better, more in command of the situation, and pointed up the absurdity of the strategies the authorities were employing in the hopes they could stop us.

At the same time Martin and Ralph were arrested, we expanded the movement to the black belt counties surrounding Selma. It wasn't that we were disappointed with our progress in Selma, but we felt Selma needed a break: it was impossible to sustain demonstrations and massive jailings in a town so small for very long. People who had been in jail for a week or ten days could not afford to get arrested again and return to jail immediately after bailing out; they needed time to pull their affairs together. The original plan that James and Diane Bevel had developed called for demonstrations in several cities simultaneously, and though the press focused on Selma, we had been organizing quietly throughout the black belt for some time.

So we stepped up our demonstrations in Lowndes, Perry, Wilcox, and Marengo Counties. We were achieving good results in Jean's hometown, Marion, in Perry County, because of Albert Turner's excellent work. It certainly wasn't the same Marion I had known as a young seminary student. It was now activated. Our growing involvement in Marion also provided me with the opportunity of seeing Jean's parents often and of visiting with old friends.

The movement had become a family affair. Jean's mother, Idella Childs, began to run a sort of bed-and-breakfast for the movement in Marion. Jean's parents' old homeplace had been torn down for road construction, but their new ranch house had two spare bedrooms and a sleeping porch. Miss Idella, as her former students called her, was an old-fashioned homemaker who ironed sheets, made her biscuits from scratch, and would send you to her vegetable garden to pick dinner. The Childses' home became a primary meeting place for the Marion movement and, in the 1980s, Miss Idella served on Marion's city council and managed her grandson's wife's successful campaign for Perry County clerk.

It was during this period that the risks to Martin's life seemed to intensify. In mid-February, while we were visiting Marion almost daily, we received word from the Justice Department of a threat against Martin. Once, when we were in Marion, we were informed there was a car full of Klan members lying in wait for us on the highway to Selma. It was fortunate that I was with Martin on that trip, because I knew the back roads between Marion and Selma. I improvised an alternate route and we made the return journey without incident.

On February 17, following a tension-charged night march in Marion, a group of marchers and members of the press were brutally attacked by the Marion police and Alabama state troopers. During the attack, Jimmy Lee Jackson, a black Vietnam veteran, was shot when he went to the aid of his mother, who was also in the march. She was being roughed up by a trooper as she was hurrying into a black café, seeking safety. Within two days Jimmy Lee Jackson died.

Despite the tense atmosphere and the threat of violence that hung over all our campaigns, the death of Jimmy Lee Jackson stunned us. We were, of course, determined to go on, but with each explosion of violence around our campaigns, each death, something inside us died. We who were responsible for organizing and leading the demonstrations knew we had to plunge ahead. Looking back, listening to the doubts that naturally arose, allowing ourselves the luxury of feeling too much pain, might lead to a collapse. And we knew we could not afford to collapse.

In ways we could hardly have anticipated, the decision to intensify our campaign in the counties surrounding Selma, and the tragic death of Jimmy Lee Jackson, set the stage for the climax of our Selma campaign. The catalyst was our decision to conduct Jimmy Lee Jackson's funeral ourselves and have Martin deliver the eulogy. After the service, we planned a public march to the cemetery to accompany the funeral procession because there were so many people without cars.

The cemetery was located about three miles from the church in Marion. The day of the funeral turned out to be very bleak and cold, befitting the occasion, but we were cheered by the fact that the entire black population of Marion fell in behind the hearse to join us in the mournful procession. As we began the march it started to rain, a driving, cold rain, which soaked us to the bone. It was during this march that Bevel remarked it would be fitting to take Jimmy Lee's body and march it all the way to the state capitol in Montgomery, since a heavy responsibility for the racist policies in Alabama lay with the governor and the state legislature.

The funeral march, of course, was impossible; but we thought, why not a march to the state capitol building from Selma? In addition to bringing our grievances to Governor Wallace and the state legislature, this move would allow us to maneuver our rapidly accumulating docket of court cases away from the jurisdiction of Judge

Daniel H. Thomas, the conservative segregationist who sat in the federal court in Mobile and whose district covered Selma. Judge Thomas had consistently refused to use the power of his court to counteract violations of the civil rights of Selma's black citizens. We thought we would have a far better chance for justice in the court of federal Judge Frank M. Johnson, Jr., who sat in Montgomery.

Within a few days we had agreed to attempt the fifty-four-mile march from Selma to Montgomery and set Sunday, March 7, as the target date for our departure. We asked all of the groups participating in the Selma effort to join with us. However, for the week prior to Sunday, March 7, Martin was away on speaking engagements. He was also under a lot of pressure to be at Ebenezer, his home church in Atlanta, for a special program on that same date. So as the date approached, plans for the march were still tentative and it wasn't clear whether Martin would be present. I too had to return to Atlanta on Saturday, March 6, and by the time of my departure, no decision had been made by Martin, though our staff in Selma was planning to go forward with the march as planned.

Early Sunday morning, I received a call form Martin instructing me to rush over to Selma and postpone the march until Monday, when he could be there to lead it. I took an eight o'clock plane to Montgomery on Sunday morning with every intention of following his instructions and calling off the march. However, as we neared Selma that morning, driving over from the Montgomery airport, I was startled to see almost two hundred police officers lining up and monitoring traffic at the Edmund Pettus Bridge across the Alabama River, at the entrance to Selma. The officers included Clark's Selma police and Al Lingo's Alabama state troopers, along with some of Clark's deputies.

When we arrived at Brown Chapel, only a short ride from the bridge, there were four or five hundred people in the field beside the church preparing for the march. The group included a large contingent of people Albert Turner had bused down from Marion. I could see right away that we had a problem. To cancel the march, as Martin had instructed, after so many people had responded to our call, would seriously damage our credibility, and cost us precious momentum at a time when we were desperately trying to build it. There had been mixed feelings about the wisdom of the Selma-to-Montgomery march when it was first proposed, and many came despite such discouragement. For one thing, there were immense logistical problems involved in marching hundreds of people the fifty-four miles to Montgomery—such an effort would take four or five days. We were certain, though, that the march would be stopped by the police before it really got started, and we felt we had plenty of time to work out the logistics of an actual multistage march to Montgomery as we went along. However, the SNCC executive council, with the sole exception of Chairman John Lewis, had voted in Atlanta to oppose the march, which they saw as needlessly dangerous. SNCC Executive Secretary Jim Forman was among those who had rejected the idea. They preferred to intensify the demonstrations in and around Selma. We believed that the value of demonstrations in the small towns had been exhausted. Something more dramatic and compelling was needed to focus national attention on the denial of voting rights in Selma and throughout Alabama. This all had begun with a plan to get rid of Wallace, so it made good sense to put the spotlight on Wallace and the state's role in sustaining the disenfranchisement of its citizens.

Now we had about four hundred people ready to go—even if we did not know how far they would get. James Bevel and Hosea Williams, who were our chief organizers for the march, were both present and felt strongly we must go ahead, despite the police force massing on the other side of the bridge. Also present was John Lewis of SNCC, who decided to march as an individual despite SNCC's rejection of this idea. Bevel, Hosea, and I therefore decided to call Martin to see if he would change his mind and give us the go-ahead. Martin was at Ebenezer, and the church service had already begun. He left the pulpit to take our call.

"Look, all these people are here ready to go now," we told him, "the press is gathering expecting us to go, and we think we've just got to march, even if you aren't here. There'll probably be arrests when we hit the bridge." Martin reluctantly gave his assent. However, he added, "Listen, don't all three of you go. If John Lewis is going, let Bevel or Hosea go with him as coleader, and the other two stay behind as backup in case of emergencies." We ended the call with that understanding. A few minutes later Hosea, Bevel, and I decided we would flip coins among us and the odd man would march. Hosea lost—or won—depending on how you look at it. That's how he and John Lewis ended up leading the most dramatic march of the civil rights movement.

Once the march left the church and the first rows disappeared across the Pettus Bridge, I turned my attention to making sure the drivers for the Medical Committee for Human Rights, a group of Northern volunteer doctors and nurses who had come to Selma to support us, were in place. Within five minutes I could hear shouts

and screams coming from the other side of the bridge. Then I smelled
tear gas, all this before I saw the first of our people, those in the rear
of the march, come running back down the bridge onto Broad Street.
They were shouting that the troopers had stopped the march on the
other side of the bridge, then waded into the first rows of the march,
some on horseback with billy clubs swinging. I yelled at them to go
back to Brown Chapel, and tried to reserve our makeshift ambulances for those in the front of the march who might be injured. The
first of the wounded began staggering back down the bridge, confused, panicked, blinded by tear gas, and badly beaten.

To make matters worse, some of Clark's posse had secluded
themselves on the Selma side of the bridge, and when they saw our
people coming back across the bridge, they attacked and beat them
again. The people leading the march were also attacked: John Lewis
suffered a concussion, and Mrs. Boynton was knocked down right
behind him. They were trapped at the foot of the bridge and could
not run back up the bridge fast enough to escape the blows of the
troopers. Fortunately, the troopers did not open fire on the crowd,
but in the confusion, anything seemed possible. Frightened people
were running, choked and hysterical. At the same time we were trying to direct everyone, particularly the injured, back to the Sylvan
Street area and into Brown Chapel. The troopers and posse were
beating people all the way back into the black neighborhood, and
some actually rode their horses onto the steps of Brown Chapel, as if
they would ride right on into the church.

Meanwhile, an ugly scene was about to develop between the residents in the nearby public housing project, some of whom had relatives in the march, and the marauding police. Some rocks were
thrown from the project windows, though I doubt very many, and in
retaliation some of Clark's posse became enraged and began beating
anyone they could find, whether they were in the march or not. I
shouted to people to get back inside, because I knew a pitched battle
with the police could lead to a terrible disaster. Some of the state
troopers and posse may have been looking for an excuse to open fire,
and many people might have been killed. It was the same situation
we had seen in 1963 in Birmingham at Kelly Ingram Park where I
could almost hear the ticking of a bomb ready to explode. Our staff
and volunteer workers got the word around the projects that residents, many of whom we knew had weapons, should under no circumstances fire on officers, as one shot from an angry black person
that hit a policeman would have drawn a fusillade in retaliation. Fortunately, nothing like that happened. We were able to negotiate safe

passage for the dozens injured, who were taken to the infirmary, and Wilson Baker worked on coaxing the police out of the area.

It seemed inconceivable that the march had ended in this kind of violence. We knew when we began our campaign in Selma that Jim Clark and his posse were out of control, and that the troopers under State Public Safety Director Lingo were extremely violent, but up until March 7, the violence was directed only at several individuals. However, Clark, Lingo, Bull Connor, and folk of that ilk clearly believed that if they just unleashed the violence they were capable of, "the nigras" would retreat and plead for mercy. The attack on the Edmund Pettus Bridge was not only an attack on us; it was an expression of their fear that "racial relations" were changing—maybe forever—and that "their" South would never be the same again. Beating us back into our own community was like forcing us back into the concentration camp, back into the physical and psychological boundaries erected by the white power structure.

As soon as things calmed down somewhat, Bevel, Hosea, and I called Martin in Atlanta to tell him what had happened. He was still at Ebenezer and had not heard about the fate of the march. He was horrified. We quickly turned to the question of what to do next. Asking the Johnson administration for federal protection was out of the question; they hadn't wanted us in Selma in the first place. We decided instead that as soon as possible we would once again try to hold the Selma-to-Montgomery march—we chose Tuesday, March 9—and that we would put out a massive call to supporters all over the nation to join us in Selma immediately. In a statement to the press that night Martin addressed his "call" to "the Community of Good Will." Everyone on our staff went to work that night to get the word out to our friends in the movement, in the religious community, and in organized labor. Our staff in Atlanta burned the midnight oil, sending off telegrams to every person and every institution that had ever supported us.

We also asked Jack Greenberg and the NAACP Legal Defense Fund to file suit in the federal district court of Judge Frank M. Johnson of Montgomery, asking that Selma officials be enjoined from prohibiting us from carrying out the Tuesday Selma-to-Montgomery march. Our hope was that if Judge Johnson issued such an order the Johnson administration would be obliged to enforce it. We also hoped to bring our efforts to register Selma voters, the cornerstone of our campaign, before Judge Johnson. At that time, Frank M. Johnson was not considered a liberal on the Southern federal bench, but he did have a record of protecting the rights of black citizens when they were clearly violated, as in the case of the violence surrounding the Freedom Rides in Montgomery in 1961.

The national response to Martin's emergency call to the "Community of Good Will" surpassed our wildest expectations. Until that Sunday few people in America had ever heard of Selma, Alabama. After the beatings on the bridge everyone knew about Selma, and for a very good reason: the brutality was fully captured by television news cameras on the other side of the bridge. The newsmen were situated behind the mass of troopers, and while the troopers had moved them back to where they thought they could not get good pictures, the scenes they captured were vivid.

By an extraordinary coincidence, an extremely well-publicized documentary on the World War II war crimes trials, *Judgment at Nuremberg*, had been scheduled for broadcast on national television on March 7. The film was interrupted several times to interject updates and replays of the violence in Selma, and many viewers apparently mistook these clips for portions of the Nuremberg film. The violence in Selma was so similar to the violence in Nazi Germany that viewers could hardly miss the connection. The news film of the beatings on the Pettus Bridge produced such strong national and worldwide revulsion that prominent people from all over the country, both white and black, dropped whatever they were doing and rushed to Selma to join our demonstrations. Church groups also responded immediately; so did our friends in the labor unions. But most touchingly, many ordinary individuals, whose names we will never know, came down simply out of a personal sense of commitment.

Immediately after the march and his beating by Al Lingo's troopers, Hosea was angry with Bevel and me, accusing us of somehow cheating in the coin toss. But when the papers came out, and he realized how much national press he received, he was all right. Bevel and I shared a private joke. He said, "Why did Hosea and John let themselves get beat like that? Andy, if it had been us on that bridge, we could have talked Al Lingo into letting our folk go back to the church." "Yeah," I said, "I been beat before, it ain't worth getting your picture in the paper. Anytime you have the head of the Alabama state troopers in front of a bunch of television cameras, you ought to be able to cut a deal." Bevel and I thought we could talk our way out of anything. Hosea was proud of being beat up on that bridge and of all the times he'd been beaten in the cause of racial justice.

We immediately set to work preparing for a second Selma-to-Montgomery march. Hosea assumed responsibility for logistics. Plans were extremely complicated, and became only more so as armies of

volunteers flowed into Selma from all over by every means of transportation available. The Selma-to-Montgomery march had become a
media event overnight. But making it actually happen was a
formidable task. Martin had announced on Sunday night that we
would make a second attempt to begin the march to Montgomery on
Tuesday, March 9. By Monday night, though, we knew we weren't
ready.

At the hearings on Monday, Judge Johnson had made it quite
clear he did not intend to issue a judgment by Tuesday. We felt certain we would eventually get the injunction we sought from Judge
Johnson, but we had to convince him that we were prepared to feed
and lodge several hundred people for four or five days—the anticipated length of the march—and that we were capable of conducting
the march in an orderly manner. He further indicated to our attorney
that: (1) he would not issue a restraining order against the state
immediately, (2) he wished to hold hearings, beginning later in the
week, and (3) he wanted us to cancel the march scheduled for Tuesday, March 9.

On Monday night, March 8, we held a series of marathon meetings involving Martin, the members of our senior staff, Jim Forman,
John Lewis, Willie Ricks, and Fay Bellamy of SNCC, and James
Farmer, director of CORE, who had come to Selma in response to
our call for support. Martin's inclination was to follow Judge Johnson's informal but strong recommendation that we not begin a march
to Montgomery on Tuesday. He did not like to defy a federal judge,
especially one who we expected would eventually rule favorably in
our cases before him. He certainly didn't want to provoke a contempt
citation by sending back a message that he would ignore the judge's
suggestion. Moreover, Jack Greenberg made it clear that if Judge
Johnson thought we were going to actually attempt the first leg of the
Montgomery march on Tuesday he would serve us with a restraining
order. This would be disastrous: we wanted the federal courts behind
us, not against us.

But holding back the march wasn't quite that simple. We had
publicly announced we would begin another march to Montgomery
on Tuesday. Hundreds had responded to our call by coming to Selma
prepared to join us in such an effort. So we had to do something. It
was necessary to have some kind of march on Tuesday; we couldn't
let Judge Johnson, despite our respect for him and the federal courts,
take over the direction of the Selma campaign.

Caught in the throes of this dilemma, an argument broke out in
the Monday night meeting between us and SNCC leaders over the

course we should follow. The SNCC leaders were convinced we
should ignore the judge and start for Montgomery the next day. This
was a complete about-face on their part: the previous week they had
been arguing that a Selma-to-Montgomery march would expose people needlessly to danger and that, besides, nothing much could be
accomplished by marches anymore. Now they were arguing that the
march should proceed in spite of whatever dangers might be
involved, and the arguments were intense and bitter. SNCC activists
had a tendency to fall victim to "freedom high" and want to push
forward mindless of strategy and tactics. We were trying to make the
system work and wanted to cooperate with Judge Johnson insofar as
was possible and still attain our objectives. Martin felt he should hear
out the SNCC organizers, particularly since he knew that some of the
antagonism and bitterness had to do with SCLC once again coming
into a campaign SNCC had started and subsequently receiving all the
media credit for the effort.

But Martin rejected the SNCC argument and finally decided to
march on Tuesday across the Edmund Pettus bridge to approximately
where the Sunday marchers were beaten, hold a commemorative
prayer, then turn the march around and return to Brown Chapel.
Only the leadership of the march was informed of this plan. I think
most of the people sensed, however, that this was only going to be a
short march. They knew we were hardly prepared to begin the first
leg of a five-day trip to Montgomery.

Jim Forman accused us of selling out, as did some of the other
members of SNCC. But with so much at stake, I felt we had arrived
at an acceptable compromise. We could only go to Montgomery
when we were ready to go, and we wanted to go there with the blessing and support of the federal court and, hopefully, even the White
House.

Despite all this confusion, the Tuesday march was most memorable because of the broad cross-section of religious, civil rights, and
labor leaders who came and participated with us. Methodist Bishop
John W. Lord; Msgr. George L. Gingros of the Archdiocese of Washington, D.C.; Rabbi David K. Hunter of the National Council of
Churches; Fred Shuttlesworth of the Alabama Christian Movement
for Human Rights; James Farmer, the national director of CORE;
James Forman, executive director of SNCC; Mrs. Harold Ickes and
Mrs. Paul Douglas, wives of prominent members of the Kennedy
administration; and hundreds of concerned individuals felt it important to stop whatever they were doing and come to Selma to be a
part of this beautiful march.

We left Brown Chapel for the Pettus Bridge around three that afternoon with a contingent of about two thousand—ten times the number who were present at the fateful Sunday march. Everything went as planned. We did not inform Judge Johnson as to what we were doing, and he did issue a restraining order against us. We were prepared, however, to argue when hearings began in Montgomery on Thursday that we had not violated his order; his order had barred a march to Montgomery, not a commemorative march in the Selma area.

Tuesday night, after we had concluded our peaceful march, violence visited us once again. Some five hundred white students and ministers had come from across the nation to Selma in response to Martin's call. One of them was James Reeb, a young Unitarian minister from Boston. Early on Tuesday evening, after the march, he and two companions, both white, went to a local black café in the small downtown section of Selma to get something to eat. They were totally unfamiliar with Selma, of course, and after leaving the café they made a wrong turn. If he had turned right, he would have gone into the black community and been safe, but he turned toward downtown. Reeb walked near the Silver Moon Café, a hangout for white racists and thugs. Some people were gathered outside the Silver Moon, and they jumped and beat Reverend Reeb and his companions. Reeb sustained a heavy blow to the back of the head with a baseball bat or club, which caused a cerebral hemorrhage. At first, his companions rushed him to the Selma hospital, not realizing how severely he was injured, but the tiny hospital recommended he be taken all the way to Birmingham for treatment, a two-hour drive. The Selma hospital refused to take him in one of their ambulances, and precious time was lost trying to identify someone with a car who could find the Birmingham hospital. Reeb lost consciousness and never recovered; he was dead on arrival in Birmingham. We were in the church when we got word that he had died.

Reverend Reeb's death intensified the growing national sense of outrage. For the first time, the Johnson administration seemed inclined to offer us protection, and to get serious about the need for a voting rights act in 1965. They had stopped saying they couldn't get a bill through; in fact, they were working on drafting one. Clarence Mitchell and the NAACP already had several drafts of a voting rights bill that they had been urging the administration to adopt, but the demonstrations and the public clamor for action made the administration and members of Congress more receptive to their proposals. A few nights after the death of Reverend Reeb, we heard President

Johnson give a national address before an unusual evening joint session of Congress in which he spoke strongly for the need to protect the right of the ballot, even going so far as to adopt in his Texas accent the rallying cry of the movement: "We Shall Overcome." It was hard to believe and slightly unreal to us, but finally the national tide seemed to be turning in our favor. A recognition of the need for real, substantial changes in the South, and the realization that the federal government must play a stronger role in bringing about these changes, was growing. After all the work we had done, all the trials we had been through, and all the setbacks, it was almost impossible to believe that one day our dream could actually come true, and the tide of racism in the South could be turned back.

At the same time, we were painfully aware of the tragic irony that the killing of a white citizen—Reverend Reeb—created more media attention and national resentment of Southern racist violence than the prior deaths of a long list of blacks in the struggle for civil rights. The killing of Jimmy Lee Jackson certainly didn't receive the headlines that followed Reverend Reeb's murder. It was almost as if Jackson's death was to be expected, nothing unusual. To note this is in no way to demean the sacrifice of Reverend Reeb, but we couldn't help but feel bitter about the fact that it took the murder of a white minister to cause the federal government to become concerned about the safety of demonstrators and serious about ensuring our right to vote.

The following Tuesday, March 16, Judge Frank Johnson began hearings in Montgomery, during which we made it clear we were expending every effort to prepare an orderly and peaceful march to Montgomery. When he ruled, two days later, he found that we had not violated his restraining order with our Tuesday march, and issued a new injunction prohibiting the state from blocking our proposed march from Selma to Montgomery. This was the ruling we were hoping for.

Specifically, Judge Johnson's order approved the inclusion of as many marchers as we wished on four-lane sections of Highway 80, but restricted us to three hundred marchers on the two-lane sections. Our Legal Defense Fund attorneys and Hosea Williams worked out an elaborate support plan for the march to make that possible. We set March 21 as the departure date. The entire fifty-four-mile march would span five days. Night campsites were set up to accommodate the marchers after each day's leg. Food and medical support teams were engaged by the Medical Committee for Human Rights and the National Council of Churches Committee on Religion and Race.

Most important, President Johnson federalized the Alabama National Guard. This, we hoped, would provide us with protection against anyone who had it in mind to attack the procession. Assistant Attorney General Ramsey Clark was assigned by the president to supervise the entire federal end of the operation.

In the meantime, my thirty-third birthday came and went. My wife and children were far away, and I was too busy to think much about it. I called Jean to share the good news of Judge Johnson's ruling. "I'm coming to the march," she announced. "But Jean, what about the girls?" I asked her. "They're coming, too." She said it in a tone that did not invite discussion. Jean's family was nearby and she knew the area better than I did. Her parents were in the thick of the movement in Marion, where Jimmy Lee Jackson was killed, and there was no point in arguing. Instead, we began to talk about when she would come. Jean drove over to Marion that weekend, and if I harbored hopes that her mother would bake one of her famous pound cakes for me or that Jean and the girls were bringing birthday presents, they were soon dashed. There was no cake and no presents.

After that experience, I made a promise to be at home for my wife's birthday and other special family days. Recalling the hollow feeling of a forgotten birthday, I was not ashamed to decline speaking engagements or reschedule meetings saying, "I can't be away from my wife on Mother's Day." Jean's birthday, Christmas, Easter, and graduations were family time that could not be violated. But, in the intensity of being involved in national events, it's hard to have a perfect record on events that are important to individuals. Nearly twenty years after Selma, I was mayor of Atlanta when the city hosted the Democratic National Convention. My family was gathered in the mayor's hospitality suite on the first day of the convention, when we were stunned to see my middle daughter, Lisa, sobbing as if her heart would break. It was her birthday. No one had remembered.

On March 21, 1965, under the glare of intense national publicity, we departed Brown Chapel once again, this time with a nonviolent army of thirty-five hundred people. Leaders from all of the major civil rights organizations were there, as were famous African-Americans such as Ralph Bunche and Harry Belafonte, representatives from the religious groups and labor unions that had been supportive to the movement, and just plain ordinary people black and white who came to Selma out of an act of conscience, to walk along beside us. There was a contingent of Catholic sisters whom I asked to please wear their habits, saying, "Nobody's likely to shoot at us if we have nuns in habits along with us." All marched together behind Martin, Ralph,

Coretta, Archbishop Iakovos of the Greek Orthodox Church, Rabbi
Abraham Heschel, and Walter Reuther of the United Auto Workers,
as the cameras flashed and television cameras rolled. It was as though
all my heroes had come to our rescue.

There was a huge television camera truck preceding the first row
of marchers, which made our procession look extremely unnatural.
Their primary interest was in keeping Martin within the range of
their lenses, so whenever Martin was marching in the front row they
were there, and there wasn't anything we could do about it. One of
the cameramen confided to me, "If King is shot and I don't have it on
tape, that's the end of my job."

Despite my initial alarm, in the end I was very happy that Jean
came over from Atlanta and marched with us, bringing our daughters
Andrea and Lisa with her. Andrea was only nine years old, but she
was determined to walk the entire distance. Lisa, who was seven, but
petite, was happy for me to carry her on my shoulders occasionally.
Both got a chance to find out for themselves what their daddy was
doing when he was away from home.

I couldn't spend much time with my family, however. I was too
busy running from the beginning of the march to the rear, a span of
almost a mile of bodies, taking care of this and that detail. It was
exhilarating. If people toward the back were lagging, or hadn't
caught the song started in the front, I would walk and sing with
them, "Ain't gonna let nobody turn me 'round, turn me 'round, turn
me 'round, ain't gonna let nobody turn me 'round, I'm gonna keep
on a-talking, keep on a-walking, marching up to freedom land."

Our arrangement with Judge Johnson was that we would march
on the eastbound side of the highway while traffic flowed in both
directions on the westbound side. Meanwhile, we could use the westbound side to transport supplies like food, water, blankets, and medical necessities to our first stopping point. We could also rush anyone
back to Selma who became sick or otherwise needed medical attention. With all the media hullabaloo, the march may have seemed like
a massive picnic, but hiking seven miles, particularly in the dress
clothes that some of the marchers chose to wear, was no picnic. It did
warm up during the day, but by nightfall on March 21, the first day
of spring, it was quite chilly and everyone who planned to sleep in
the tents needed blankets.

Most of those thirty-five hundred people did not stay overnight
at the first seven-mile junction. For many, the march was an opening
ceremony, and by the day's end they returned home. Martin was
scheduled for speaking engagements that he simply had to make, so

he left also, planning to return for the final legs. Alabama National Guardsmen, federalized by the president, were stationed at intervals along the highway, though this did not deter hostile whites from heckling us as they drove along the other side of the highway, or prevent whites whose property we passed along our way from yelling epithets at us. I wasn't worried about the epithets—it was the possibility of physical violence that concerned me.

We chose the length of each day's journey according to the availability of campsites. The campsites were on land owned by blacks in the counties we passed through. The National Council of Churches provided food for the marchers, a heavy responsibility, which they satisfied admirably. The Medical Committee for Human Rights provided physicians and medical supplies. Charlie Loudermilk, a white Southerner who had started an innovative company called Aaron Rents, was willing to rent us the tents that we used for eating and sleeping. It was courageous for a Southern businessman to support the march and risk the disapproval of his white customers.

The first evening under the tents was like an enormous Southern church homecoming celebration, except that there were blacks and whites together, a rarity in our churches even today. There was tremendous energy and excitement after the long day's walk. The food wasn't bad and there was even after-dinner entertainment. Despite the discomforts of camping out, the people had an aura of contentment and satisfaction.

Jean and the girls got a ride back to Marion sometime after dinner. As the remaining marchers began to prepare to go to sleep, I rode back to Selma. I needed to make and return phone calls, check in with Martin, consult with the LDF lawyers, and prepare for the next day's march. After a couple hours' sleep, I was on my way back to the campsite by dawn.

The crowd for our second, third, and fourth legs of the March dwindled until we were down to our limit of three hundred people, as set by Judge Johnson's order. Lowndes County west of Montgomery is very sparsely populated, with hardly a town over five thousand people, and no towns west of Montgomery. In the section where Highway 80 becomes two lanes, rising and dipping with the hills and valleys, there is an eeriness, a gloomy strangeness.

The next-to-last leg of the march ended on the outskirts of Montgomery, at the City of St. Jude, a black Catholic school. It rained and rained and rained that night, until we were all slopping through a City of Mud. It was a real mess because by then our ranks had swelled again in anticipation of the final afternoon's climactic march to the state capitol. Martin and Ralph were back with us, along with many others who had marched the first leg from Selma.

Harry Belafonte pulled together a terrific outdoor program of nationally known performers, which went on, despite the downpour. There was the usual tumultuous confusion and bustling activity preceding a momentous event; as in Birmingham, we had built toward a peak. We always forged ahead despite confusion, lack of schedule, rain, tragedy, absence of sufficient resources, whatever the obstacles—they served only to remind all of us that it is possible to do unbelievable things if people are determined enough. It was this ability to make the impossible possible that was the most thrilling aspect of being in the movement. For a while, anyway, we saw that we could produce miracles, if we just believed. That night at St. Jude's, the magical musical celebration that went on in spite of all the problems and frustrations was a celebration of our determination to accomplish the dreams of our entire Selma campaign: to change Selma and towns like it forever. We were drenched with joy; in that sense, the relentless rain was in harmony with our spirits.

The next day, Saturday, as we prepared to regroup for our march to the state capitol, John Doar of the Justice Department ran up to me and whispered, "Andy, we have reports there's a sniper on the outskirts of Montgomery waiting to shoot Dr. King." There was a white neighborhood with several old houses along the march route that the FBI had not checked out thoroughly, and it was this stretch of the march that most concerned us. Doar wanted us to remove Martin from the march and drive him into Montgomery to rejoin the march at the capitol.

Trying to get Martin to step out of the march for his own protection was impossible. The only time I had been able to do it at all was in St. Augustine, during our night marches. I told Martin what Doar had said, and added that maybe he shouldn't march; it was too dangerous. "Yes, I should," he answered. "And I don't care what happens. I have to march and I have to be in the front line." I could see there was no point in arguing with him, so I hurried back to Doar and told him that Martin would not relent. Doar threw up his hands and said, "In that case, there's nothing we can do."

But I felt there was something I could do. Most crazy white folks think all black folks look alike anyway, so I asked every preacher who had on a blue suit like Martin's to "walk with Dr. King in the front row as we triumphantly enter the capital of Southern racism and bigotry." About fifteen ministers rushed to situate themselves in the front row, all flanking Martin, all dressed alike. They never did find out why they were there. But they loved it. I'll never know for certain whether my plan foiled a would-be assassin that day. But in any case, Martin led the march as planned, and we walked into Montgomery without incident.

By the time we entered Montgomery, most whites had left the city, though we had reports that Governor Wallace was secreted inside his capitol office, watching from behind drawn blinds. Rev. Joseph Lowery, president of the SCLC board, marched, as planned, to the entrance of the state capitol to present Wallace with our petition, but the governor didn't show his face; an assistant was there to accept the petition in his place. Reverend Lowery refused to hand the petition over to the assistant, however; he kept it until a few weeks later, when he and a delegation of ministers finally had an audience with Wallace.

Martin's speech in front of the state capitol was, fittingly, the high point of our five-day march. He reviewed our long struggle to arrive where we were now physically and spiritually. He spoke of the unrealized promise of American society. "How long," he rhetorically asked, "will it take us to realize the promise of justice in our society?" Repeating over and over the agonizing phrase "How long," he rededicated himself and our movement to the struggle for justice until we would achieve it in America. His voice, fraught with emotion, seemed to echo over all the hills and valleys of Alabama: "I come to say to you this afternoon: however difficult the moment, however frustrating the *hour*, it will not be long, because truth pressed to the earth will rise again." We all roared in unison, as he answered our shout, with the blood- and history-soaked refrain of the *Battle Hymn of the Republic*: "Mine eyes have seen the glory of the coming of the Lord. . . . His truth is marching on. . . . "

As the march dispersed and we retired to the Dexter Avenue Baptist Church, I could feel the tension slowly leaving me, and I thanked God that we had been able to get through these last five unbelievable days without violence, without tragedy, without disaster. We were talking excitedly among ourselves, reviewing the events of the past five days, repeating phrases from Martin's address and joyously imitating his memorable and mellifluous style. I had held so much emotion, so many fears within me—I always did during these marches. Now that it was over, I slipped away to the men's room of the church and locked the door. Then I just let the tears flow, tears of relief that we had completed the march without any more bloodshed, that we had actually pulled it off, this virtual strolling city of five days' duration across the lonely Alabama terrain, a feat we could not have possibly foreseen when we were beginning our campaign in Selma. Finally, when there were no more tears, I washed my face, composed myself, and went back out to rejoin my friends and coworkers. As far as they knew, I was then, as always, the "Andy" who never broke down or disintegrated into displays of emotion.

But the relief was short-lived. That night, as participants in the march were returning to their various homes, violence came winging swiftly toward us, as if to warn us we had not been forgotten. Mrs. Viola Liuzzo, a white homemaker from Detroit, one of those courageous volunteers who rushed to Selma after seeing television coverage of the beating on the Pettus Bridge, was helping to drive marchers back to Selma on Highway 80. That night she and young Leroy Moton of Selma, who had worked in the march, were ambushed and their car was fired upon by a car full of white thugs as they were returning to Selma. Mrs. Liuzzo was shot in the head and killed instantly as the car swerved off the road out of control and into a ditch. Young Moton would also have been killed but when the car came to a stop he wisely played dead. The murderers actually swung their car around on the highway and returned to examine what they had done, then left, satisfied that both their victims were dead. This kind of brutal and senseless killing occurring after the march, after the peak of our activities, served to remind us, as if we needed a reminder, that we would never be able to enjoy the luxury of relaxation from the presence of danger. During those days we never knew the meaning of psychic rest. When would the violence end? That was a question for which we had no answer; we could only trudge forward, knowing there would be more sacrifices, but never knowing when or where they would come.

Today, three decades later, Selma remains indelibly impressed upon our memories because of its unforgettable images—the violence at Pettus Bridge, the long march to Montgomery—and also because it was the strongest single dramatization of the need for new legislation protecting the right to the ballot for all citizens. Thirty years later, the importance of Selma clearly stands out. There were those who had thought a campaign in Alabama in 1965 to demonstrate the need for protection of the right to vote was premature. There were also many of our brothers and sisters who were upset because they thought we ended the Selma campaign too soon, the same criticism leveled against us in Birmingham. There were always movement workers who wanted to continue demonstrating and keep campaigns going. But knowing the proper time to make settlements and bring demonstrations to a conclusion hinges on having a strong and precise concept of the objectives of the campaign. If the objectives were too broad, then there could be no end to demonstrating, for the search for full justice is an ever-continuing struggle.

Our conflicts with SNCC in Selma once again had to do with the breadth of some of their objectives. Our objectives were simple: we wanted to clearly demonstrate to the nation that black citizens were being effectively deprived of their right to register and vote in Selma, Alabama, and that Selma was not an anomaly: it was representative of many other Southern towns in the black belt. Finally, we wanted everyone to know that we would continue to protest these conditions until the federal government passed legislation guaranteeing and protecting our right to the ballot. In my mind, we achieved those goals in Selma. The settlement was always the most contentious point in a movement. As in Birmingham, there were activists who wanted to keep marching, for whom incremental progress was unacceptable. But I always stressed that nonviolent social change requires reconciliation and forgiveness. The people in Selma had a lot to forgive, but without forgiveness, no real change could take place.

The monumental Voting Rights Act, which Congress passed and President Lyndon Johnson signed on August 6, 1965, just a few months after the Selma-to-Montgomery march, remains a lasting achievement of the civil rights movement. The Voting Rights Act helped to change the face of Southern politics in ways we could hardly imagine while we were still bogged down in Selma. In Alabama, in the space of just one year, black voter registration practically doubled—from 116,000 in August 1965 to 228,000 in August 1966. By 1990, there were more than 7,300 black elected officials nationwide, including the governor of Virginia. An amended voting rights act produced black members of Congress from Alabama, Florida, and North Carolina for the first time since Reconstruction. Rural black voters in Georgia and Louisiana sent black representatives to Congress as well.

The very real achievements under the Voting Rights Act must be attributed to the courage, vigilance, and persistence of local black leaders and a small number of attorneys in the states covered by the act. The provisions of the Voting Rights Act called for the placement of federal referees and monitors in counties with a clear practice of disenfranchisement. In my experience, that was virtually all of the more than seven thousand political jurisdictions covered by the Voting Rights Act. However, the Civil Rights Division began with a sadly limited view of its mandate and adopted an enforcement strategy that relied on the "smallest possible federal intrusion into the conduct of state affairs." The weak enforcement practices of the Civil Rights

Division reinforced my belief that President Johnson had stopped the
Southern filibuster against the Voting Rights Act by promising federal
restraint in its enforcement.

The Voting Rights Section of the Civil Rights Division was put in
the position of encouraging cooperation from the same officials who
had been beating people for attempting to register. Not surprisingly,
white officials in the South resisted the Voting Rights Act, continuing
to change polling places without notice, closing registration offices at
times it might be convenient for blacks to register, disqualifying black
candidates running for office on spurious grounds, annexing or dean-
nexing communities to prevent a black majority, and purging voter
lists between the presidential elections, when voter participation is
highest. The civil rights leadership in each county bore the burden of
alerting the Justice Department to irregularities, begging for election
monitors, and finally finding lawyers to bring lawsuits against local
officials. Largely effective when brought, lawsuits by private groups
to force implementation of the Voting Rights Act cost hundreds of
thousands of dollars in legal fees and research and often took years.
To this day, this burden is borne by private citizens who contribute to
organizations like the NAACP Legal Defense Fund and the American
Civil Liberties Union. Lawsuits must be brought in each individual
jurisdiction, and a successful lawsuit in one county does not ensure
compliance in the neighboring county.

One area where the Justice Department has been assertive is in
the enforcement of the preclearance provisions of the Voting Rights
Act. This has served as a critical enforcement tool to prevent Southern
officials from using race-neutral actions designed to reduce black voting strength. Changes in districts, voting procedures, or voting eligibility have to be submitted to the Justice Department for preclearance
and opponents of such measures are given an opportunity to explain
their objections. Still, local jurisdictions often ignore the preclearance
provisions and local black leaders have to take the initiative to inform
the Justice Department when these provisions are being violated.

The preclearance provisions are also used to monitor the redis-
tricting of congressional and state legislative districts that occurs after
every national census. In the redistricting that took place under the
1990 census, the Justice Department during the administration of
President George Bush took a very aggressive line on Voting Rights
Act enforcement, which resulted in a dozen new black members of
Congress from the Southern states. States like North Carolina, South
Carolina, and Alabama sent blacks to Congress for the first time since
Reconstruction. As of this writing, the conservative justices of the

Supreme Court have declared many of those districts unconstitutional.

We still await full enforcement of the Voting Rights Act. There were and are so many subtle tools to discourage blacks, other minorities, and poor people from voting. Local political establishments use many tactics: annexation; deannexation of black neighborhoods; petty crimes provisions in eligibility; consolidation of polling places to an area inconvenient for black voters; enactment of at-large election statutes; raising bonds for qualification to stand for office; purging voter lists; raising residency requirements. All these and more undermine the impact of black voters.

In Selma, our goal was to overcome the selective enfranchisement that had been characteristic of the United States throughout its history. It is my belief that a limited franchise and limited voter participation hurts our nation: in order to function as a true democracy, we must have full participation. Voting is not just a right, it's an obligation, like paying taxes. In this country, despite the passage of simplified voter registration provisions in 1992, there is a reluctance to see all Americans registered and voting. A nation committed to full voter participation would experiment with weekend voting, mail-in voting, proportional representation, and full enforcement of the Voting Rights Act until our participation levels were closer to ninety percent rather than below sixty percent.

Despite the flaws in its implementation, the Voting Rights Act did prohibit the use of the dreaded literacy tests, which were so abused by Southern registrars. In her book *Bridge Across Jordan,* Mrs. Amelia Boynton tells the story of taking an elderly gentleman to register to vote only to have him challenged by the white registrar because his writing was poor and the hostile attitude of the registrar made him nervous. But upon being challenged, he lifted his head and said, "Mr. Adkins, I am 65 years old, I own 100 acres of land that is paid for, I am a taxpayer and I have six children. All of them teachin', workin' for the government, got they own business, and preaching. If what I done ain't enough to be a registered voter with all the tax I got to pay, the Lord have mercy on America."

The franchise is a privilege, but it must not be restricted to the privileged. The spirit of the Voting Rights Act and the cause for which we marched from Selma to Montgomery was to extend the practical exercise of the franchise to all Americans. If America is a democracy, every adult must be encouraged to vote. Voting should take place on holidays and certainly our presidential election day should be a national holiday, a celebration of democracy and government "of the people, by the people, for the people."

14

Going to Chicago

They say this is a big, rich, town, but I live in the poorest
part. I was born on a dead end street, in a city without a
heart.

— Lou Rawls, "Dead End Street"

The march from Selma to Montgomery created an atmosphere
of general support for voting rights that permitted Lyndon
Johnson to make good on his pledge to pass a Voting Rights
Act. But we would not wait for the new legislation to pass before
planning our next move. The goal of the Alabama movement was to
register black voters in Alabama. The new law with its federal
observers, an end to literacy tests, and other protections would eliminate many of the barriers to registration. The new federal observers
were not responsible, however, for urging people to go down to the
courthouse and register—people who had gotten used to having no
votes and often couldn't believe their vote would mean anything. We
had to do that ourselves, along with the other civil rights organizations and the Negro Voters Leagues, those post–World War II prede-
cessors of the civil rights movement.

In pursuit of dramatic increases in black Southern registration,
SCLC assigned full- and part-time staff to 104 counties in the South
with large black populations to work on voter registration in anticipation of the passage of the Voting Rights Act. This program was

called SCOPE, the Summer Community Organization and Political Education Program, and was directed by Hosea Williams.

The difference between SCOPE and the Mississippi Freedom Summer was that while the Freedom Democratic Party was a largely symbolic protest demonstration, SCOPE was registering voters for one of the two political parties, who would be eligible to vote in national and local elections. Much of our focus was on Alabama, where we had dependable contacts across the state and had a record of successful movements in three important communities: Montgomery, Birmingham, and Selma. Our goal was to build participation in the two-party system. Before the election of John Kennedy to the presidency, many black voters were registered Republicans. In the South, Democrats were largely the Dixiecrats and Boll Weevils who defended segregation and white supremacy. We were in no way committed to registering only Democrats; rather, we were encouraging blacks to make their vote count for the candidate who would act most on our behalf, whatever party that candidate belonged to. In fact, during the lobbying for Senate passage of the Voting Rights Act, I paid a visit to Senator Howard Baker in his Washington office. Baker, a Republican from Tennessee, was perceived as a moderate on race in contrast to Southern Democrats like Strom Thurmond and Richard Russell.

Baker was not available, so I met with his key staff person, Lamar Alexander. I told Alexander, "Don't oppose the voting rights bill because you think it will register black Democrats. Many of us voted for Eisenhower in 1956 and we can be persuaded to vote Republican again. My daddy and Dr. King's daddy were Republicans. Don't write off the black vote." I don't think Alexander ever shared our conversation with Howard Baker. He was polite but unresponsive, and I had no further contact with Baker's office. In our hopes for a two-party South, we had assumed that the Rockefeller Republicans would challenge the Dixiecrats in the South. Instead, as the Democrats moved away from racially divisive politics, men like Rueben Askew, Dale Bumpers, and Jimmy Carter came to stand for the new South. In turn the Republican Party embraced race baiting as a way to win elections. The Dixiecrats fleeing a Democratic Party that stood for racial justice and equality, at least in principle, were welcomed by the Republicans.

One of the people who made SCOPE work was a young man named Stoney Cooks, who left college to come to Selma. Stoney was of medium height, with warm brown skin and a trim, wiry build. He had worked under my direction in Selma and I was tremendously impressed with his abilities. After the Selma march, Stoney was assigned to work with Hosea, recruiting students from colleges across the country to come South to work with SCOPE for the summer. An energetic organizer, Stoney threw himself into SCOPE with contagious enthusiasm. Stoney was a little too enthusiastic for Hosea, and Hosea didn't hesitate to put him in his place. After assembling the college students in the auditorium at David T. Howard High School in Atlanta to receive their training and assignments, Stoney stood up on the stage in the brightly lit concrete block gymnasium, with anxious students seated all around him on metal folding chairs. Stoney had recruited most of the students and had a sense of their strengths. Many of them had requested assignments to counties where they had some friends or family relationships, and Stoney had worked out an assignment plan based on this information.

Stoney began confidently calling out names and handing out assignments, when Hosea snapped. He called Stoney out in front of the entire group: "Little nigger, who put you in charge? You just got here. You ain't done nothing. You don't know any more than these other kids." Hosea figured he would get rid of Stoney and teach him a lesson. So he sent Stoney to organize Barbour and Bullock Counties in Alabama, George Wallace's home base. This was rural Alabama, tough to organize, and Stoney was sent there on his own with twenty-five dollars in his pocket. Fortunately, it was the kind of sink-or-swim challenge that Stoney, although a city boy from Gary, Indiana, could handle. He found allies among local leaders and conducted a systematic campaign with canvassing, small meetings, and voter education workshops—the hallmarks of effective organizing. A representative from these counties was among the first blacks sent to the Alabama state legislature, and black civil rights attorney Fred Gray was elected to the state senate. Many attributed that success to the political groundwork laid by Stoney.

Despite personality problems, the SCLC staff was in many ways like a big family. That summer Jean and one of my associates who had children the same age as ours discovered waterskiing, with the help of Arthur Robinson, a family friend and one of Joe Lowery's deacons. Deacon Robinson had a red Thunderbird, a black motorboat, and a generous spirit. While the white children at Lisa and Andrea's school spent the summers in cabins on Lake Lanier, those facilities were still closed to blacks when our children were young, and summer recreation for the kids was limited to poorly staffed segregated pools and sprinklers in the street. Thanks to Robinson, our families discovered Lake Alatoona, a man-made lake north of

The first march across the Pettus Bridge in Selma, March 7, 1965; Hosea Williams is at the head of the line (wearing a dark suit and tie). Alabama state police are in the foreground.

Police descending upon fallen and fleeing demonstrators during the first attack on the marchers.

A planning meeting following the beatings. Hosea Williams is in the foreground. Ralph David Abernathy is seated at right. *(photo courtesy of Flip Schulke/Black Star)*

The second march across the Pettus Bridge when marchers were given permission to occupy a single lane. *(photo courtesy of Flip Schulke/Black Star)*

During a lunch break on the Selma-to-Montgomery march. A group from Hawaii gave King the lei that he wears. *(photo courtesy of Dan Budnik)*

Drenched marchers walking to Montgomery. *(photo courtesy of Matt Herron/Black Star)*

Leading the marchers—also at the head of the group are Bernard Lafayette
at the left and James Orange to the right of Andrew Young.

On one of the long and lonely stretches between Selma and Montgomery.

(photos courtesy of Vernon Merritt/Black Star)

TOP: On the outskirts of Montgomery, King is camouflaged by ministers wearing dark suits—to the left of King are Ralph Abernathy and James Forman.
(photo courtesy of Bob Adelman/Magnum Photos)

CENTER: Leading the march, singing Freedom Songs as they enter Montgomery on March 25, 1965, are: *(from left)* Rosa Parks, Ralph and Juanita Abernathy, Ralph Bunche, Martin and Coretta King. Jean Young is marching just behind Martin and Coretta. *(photo courtesy of Bruce Davidson/Magnum Photos)*

BOTTOM: Farther back in the line of marchers entering Montgomery.

President Johnson reaches to shake hands with King
after presenting him with the pen he used to sign the
Voting Rights Act, August 6, 1965.
(photo courtesy of AP/Wide World Photos)

King and Jesse Jackson at one of the Frogmore,
South Carolina, staff meetings during the 1966 Chicago
campaign, just before Jackson was made the designated
staff person for Operation Breadbasket.
(photo courtesy of Bob Fitch/Black Star)

The side of King most never had a chance to see—teasing someone during the Meredith march through Mississippi in the fall of 1966. *(photo courtesy of Bill Strode/Black Star)*

A typical late night session during the Meredith march. (*From left*) Ralph Abernathy, Bernard Lee (obscured), Andrew Young, Bob Green, and Martin Luther King. Lying on the floor in the foreground is Stokely Carmichael. *(photo courtesy of Bob Fitch/A Lãos Photo)*

Martin and Coretta with James Meredith leading the marchers. *(photo courtesy of Bruce Davison/ Magnum Photos)*

During the Meredith march, King accompanying schoolchildren in Grenada, Mississippi. Two days earlier, black children had been beaten by townspeople while trying to attend school. Also in the second row is Hosea Williams and in the third row Joan Baez. *(photo courtesy of Bob Fitch/Black Star)*

Striking Memphis garbagemen marching past police with guns at the ready, 1968. *(photo courtesy of Fred Ward/Black Star)*

Ralph and Martin. *(photo courtesy of Ivan Massar/Black Star)*

Dora McDonald holds Coretta's arm as she stands by her husband's open casket. From left are Yolanda (age twelve), Bernice (age five), Marty (age ten), Dexter (age six), and Ralph Abernathy, Jr. In the right foreground is Christine King Farris, Martin's sister. *(photo courtesy of Costa Manos/Black Star)*

The funeral procession, with Yolanda, Marty, and Dexter walking next to their mother and Ralph Abernathy. *(photo courtesy of Dennis Brack/Black Star)*

Bobby and Ethel Kennedy visiting
with Coretta after the funeral.
(photo courtesy of Bob Fitch/Black Star)

Daddy King in Ebenezer Church,
soon after his son's assassination.
(photo courtesy of Flip Schulke/Black Star)

Giving mule rides to children in Atlanta during the Poor People's March.

Singing in Marks, Mississippi, May 1968, at the start of the Poor People's March. On the platform are Christine King, Coretta Scott King, and Ralph Abernathy. *(photo courtesy of Dennis Brack/Black Star)*

Leading the Poor People's March, *(from right)* Andrew Young, Juanita and Ralph Abernathy, Cesar Chavez, and Martin's brother, A. D. King. *(photo courtesy of Dennis Brack/Black Star)*

March through Atlanta in support of the Poor People's Campaign. Also in the wagon are Bill Rutherford (*far left*, obscured), Ralph Abernathy at the reins, Bernard Lafayette (behind Andrew Young, obscured), and in the rear of the wagon, Bernard Lee.

Resurrection City, Washington, D.C. (photo courtesy of Costa Manos/ Magnum Photos)

Ralph Abernathy speaking in Resurrection City with Juanita at his side. (*photo courtesy of Costa Manos/Magnum Photos*)

With Lisa, Paula, Andrea, and Jean on Solidarity Day.

The Solidarity Day Demonstration, June 19, 1968. *(photo courtesy of Robert Houston/Black Star)*

A Resurrection City resident being evicted from his nation's capital. *(photo courtesy of Dennis Brack/Black Star)*

Charleston, South Carolina, June 1969. A policeman watches as a group of striking hospital workers do some hand clapping and singing.
(photo courtesy of AP/Wide World Photos)

Celebrating the announcement of a settlement at Zion Olivet United Presbyterian Church, June 28. *(photo courtesy of AP/Wide World Photos)*

After winning the Democratic primary during the
first congressional campaign in 1970. From left are
Eldrin Bell, Maynard Jackson, and Julian Bond.

Campaigning for Congress
the first time around.

Election night in 1972 with Jean, Lisa, and Paula.

At the Washington, D.C., swearing-in celebration,
in the first row (*from left*),
Lisa, Andrea, Paula, Jean, Daisy Young, and Andrew Young, Sr.
In the second row are Jean's parents, Norman Childs
(partially obscured), and Idella Childs.
(photo courtesy of Bob Fitch/Black Star)

Atlanta where blacks could swim and ski. Created with federal funds to supply water and recreation as part of the Tennessee Valley Authority, the facilities at the lake were still segregated, and there was a single boat ramp for blacks to use, a roped-in swimming area, and an old wooden lodge that served as the snack bar. Except for the sand tucked in to make a beach not much bigger than the quilts we used for picnicking, the area was covered with pine straw from the tall limbless trees surrounding the lake.

Jean and the girls had been out skiing several times without me by the time I was able to join them. I discovered that Jean could ski, Andrea could ski, even eight-year-old Lisa could ski. This was a crisis. I thought of myself as a great athlete. I was the daddy. How could my wife and children ski, when I could not? Anticipating this first outing, I had read books about waterskiing. I was determined to come up on my first time on the water and resolved that I would not fall.

Robinson was behind the wheel of the boat and I tumbled overboard in my life jacket and skis and tried to get into position in the water. The boat took off, the rope tightened, but I didn't come up. I held on to the handle attached to the rope and my arms were being pulled until it felt like they were going to pop out, but I wouldn't let go. When I was at the breaking point, I came up to a full stand, remembering to keep my knees bent. I could see the girls cheering in the back of the boat. My male ego had been salvaged, but I wasn't taking any chances. Jean and the girls used two skis. To establish my superiority, I quickly learned to use just one.

Those were rare interludes when I was able to enjoy my family on a hot summer day. SCOPE required constant monitoring and I was continually receiving complaints from Hosea's SCOPE field staff about how they were being treated. Hosea was by nature a bully, and most people could not withstand the kind of browbeating that Hosea could dish out. They came to me for what was essentially counseling. I had to patch their cracked egos and send them back to work. But the complaints about money were more troubling. Field staff would call in need of funds that I knew had been disbursed to Hosea to distribute to them. When Hosea was confronted, it was always a "the check is in the mail" sort of thing. While there was not very much money involved, those kinds of problems created mistrust among the SCOPE field-workers. Martin trusted everybody. Our financial controls were designed to satisfy the IRS, and the Citizenship School Program kept records that satisfied Field Foundation audits, but other SCLC programs did not keep detailed accounts of spending. Expense account reports were very general and most payments were in cash. People were working under difficult circumstances with fairly small amounts of money, but the informality of some procedures left opportunities for petty leakage.

In general, staff issues were becoming more taxing on my time and energies. When the 1965 SCLC convention took place in August in Birmingham, we really didn't know what our direction should be after Selma. Our staff had grown from twenty-five to thirty to more than one hundred, and we were constantly trying to sort out who was responsible for what. As Wyatt had been, I was caught between the staff and Martin. Martin would not fire people, wouldn't discipline them, didn't even like to tell them when they had done something wrong. On one occasion Hosea printed up flyers on the SCOPE program to be distributed all over Alabama with Hosea Williams's name on them. SCLC and Martin Luther King were nowhere to be found on the flyers, although this was a major SCLC project. These things hurt Martin more than they angered him, but he would not confront those involved.

After the convention, I flew to New Orleans, where Jean and the girls were staying with my parents. This was supposed to be our family's summer vacation. With few exceptions, our typical vacations consisted of visiting relatives, since we couldn't afford anything else. Jean was amazing. All on her own, she would put the three girls and our dog, Snuffy, into our blue Ford Fairlane and drive, first to her brother's in Tuskegee, then to her parents' in Marion, where she would stay a day or two and visit her sister, Cora, over in Uniontown, and finally to New Orleans.

When I met her in New Orleans, all the tension of the previous months expressed itself in a searing migraine. Mother looked at me with deep concern when I arrived and began furiously stuffing crabs and frying oysters for me as I dived into bed in the guest room upstairs. Mother believed food was the answer to any ill. Jean administered periodic back rubs. The girls ran up and down the steps to a room over the garage that contained the pool table. The clinking of the porcelain balls made it feel as if they were rolling back and forth between my ears. The pain was excruciating. I seldom got sick during a movement, but when things slowed down and I became conscious of my exhaustion, I often got a migraine. The previous year had been nonstop activity: the Nobel Prize, the work in Selma, the march from Selma to Montgomery, the Voting Rights Act, the annual SCLC convention in Birmingham in August.

I had been getting migraine headaches since my early childhood.

I remember that when my mother forced me to take piano lessons, the headache and nausea resulted in my throwing up on the piano keys. I would get headaches when I didn't want to go to school, probably in response to the pressure of trying to keep up with kids older than me. In college I would get headaches on Sunday morning, usually when I didn't go to chapel. Somehow, if I got up and went to chapel, I didn't get a headache.

I just never knew how to say no. During a movement, along with all my other responsibilities, people came to me with their problems. We were always dealing with people's personal lives; some might lose their jobs because of the time they spent in jail, and I would feel compelled to help them. Others might need rent money. There were personal crises among the folks joining our demonstrations and coming to mass meetings. We attracted people who were already struggling and, for many, their participation in the movement prompted another crisis, such as Fannie Lou Hamer's eviction from her home. As executive director, I had access to some discretionary money and I was by nature a sucker for a sob story.

I was in bed with the same headache early Sunday morning when Martin called to tell me to meet him in Los Angeles. The day before, August 11, a black neighborhood had exploded in violence, a place called Watts.

The worst of the violence was about over when I got there. The immediate cause of the trouble was classic and all too typical: an insensitive action by white policemen in the black community. A man in Watts was speeding in his car to the hospital, taking someone to the emergency ward. He was waving a white handkerchief out the window as he drove, a common practice in the South in cases of medical emergency. A police car saw him, began chasing, and signaled him to pull over. A white policeman got out of his patrol car, and either did not see, or chose to disregard, the handkerchief. He approached the driver's window with his pistol drawn. As he spoke to the driver, the car lurched; either the driver was nervous or, in his fright, he actually intended to drive away. In any case, the policeman panicked and fired. The bullet hit the driver in the head, killing him instantly.

Unfortunately, this sort of tragic incident was, and still is, so common. Only the details change. This time the black community of Watts exploded into an expression of outrage and violence surpassing anything Los Angeles had ever seen, and with a greater sustained intensity than America had experienced for many, many years. The intensity was caused, of course, by the depth of a whole range of resentments long held over a myriad of problems, from police brutality to persistent and chronic unemployment. Soon Watts resembled an occupied war zone, with its burned-out shells of buildings, debris scattered over the streets, the military presence of the police and the National Guard, the constant sound of helicopters droning above the buildings, and the lingering smell of tear gas and smoke. Thirty-four people had been killed by police and the National Guard. A nightly curfew was in force. I was shocked by the deplorable condition of the area.

Martin was deeply disturbed by the violence in Watts. He understood its basic causes; he had said many times that "violence is the language of the unheard." But violence as retribution was against his principles, and he felt that the riot in Watts was evidence of his failure to get his message of nonviolence across to all black Americans. It was ridiculous for him to take this situation so personally, and I told him so. I thought Martin was mistaken to think we could prevent long-festering eruptions in the nation's cities by running around from city to city like volunteer firemen trying to put out the blazes. I also believed that violence was too ingrained a feature of American life and the American psyche to be easily eradicated. However preferable nonviolence was as a means of protesting injustice, it was hardly reasonable to expect that blacks in America would remain nonviolent in the face of white violence.

One of the main problems that emerged in Los Angeles was that the black leadership felt they were totally ignored by the power structure when they tried to voice community problems. This was not unlike the classic situations we had cut our teeth on in the South, from Albany to Selma. In Martin's meetings with the black leaders of Los Angeles, particularly the ministers, they asked him to help them achieve a more effective exposure of their community's problems. They wished to bring an appeal to the attention of the federal government: the rampant unemployment due to the effects of automation, decaying housing, police brutality, and so forth. "You all down South are making progress, and you've won national and international attention for your cause," they told us, "but in the ghettos of the big cities we're really suffering. Our situation has become worse, not better."

In many respects, blacks in the cities of the North and West were objectively better off than their Southern cousins. They did not face the most rigid barriers of segregation, there was a greater potential for finding a job, and there was generally less overt hostility to blacks seeking to uplift themselves. But while blacks in Los Angeles were perhaps better off, their lives were no longer improving, as they had during the war years: in the South, there was progress, real change for African-Americans, while in Los Angeles there was stagnation. We felt a real responsibility to help with their cause since white leaders in Los Angeles had proved supportive of SCLC in its efforts in the South. During the movement in Birmingham, one of the largest rallies held in our support was at the Los Angeles Coliseum with the support of Mayor Sam Yorty.

One of the things we did right away was to set up a public forum for the people of the community so that they could talk about their problems and vent their frustrations. We met in churches, even in California the only gathering places that blacks felt were truly under their control. We invited the press to come and hear their testimony. I was still in pain and feeling fairly irritable during the hearings and almost got involved in a physical altercation with one of the young men. He was outside, loudly denouncing our forum, screaming about "these goddamn preachers coming around here with all this bullshit." I really was in no mood for that, so I found myself saying out loud, "Listen, mutha fukkah, shut up and come in and listen to what the brother is saying." He was stunned. When he realized that we were not going to be intimidated by a few vulgar words, he suddenly calmed down. "We just came from Alabama where we were working to organize the South, but obviously you all aren't organized in L.A.," I continued. By this time there was no need to shout or cuss. I had established my street-corner credentials and we were able to move on to a more reasonable discussion.

I could scarcely believe this was the Watts I had known as a college student less than twenty years before. After World War II, Los Angeles was a land of opportunity for blacks fleeing segregation in Louisiana. The summer before my first year at Howard I had driven out to Los Angeles to stay with my Aunt May. I thought I could get a job, but the wartime production was over. My mother insisted that I work or go to school, so I enrolled in a botany course at the University of Southern California (USC). I was the only black student in the class, but I had no difficulty registering, and no problem with the course.

I thought California was heaven. Black people lived in single-family homes with green lawns and palm trees. Unlike black neighborhoods in New Orleans, Watts had public parks and swimming pools. The weather was more pleasant than a New Orleans summer, and I ran back and forth to USC, just for the joy of running. On the streets, which were now littered with the debris of the riot, I had walked without fear, day or night.

Watts surfaced issues of class and poverty that went beyond the largely middle-class focus of the Southern movement. The sit-ins in Greensboro had been started by college students. Birmingham was about access to public facilities, shops, and parks that middle-class people had the means to enjoy. Selma was about even the most educated black college graduates being denied the right to vote by virtue of their color. Even the Montgomery bus boycott was mostly beneficial to employed members of the black community who used the buses to go to work. Watts was a cry for help from the unemployed, the displaced, the disinherited. Many of them had come from the South in search of an elusive opportunity. When dreams failed, they were far from the stable family and religious structures of their rural roots that had helped their parents and grandparents persevere in the hardest of times. The movement had addressed many issues for blacks who were economically stable and prepared for the job market, but were held back solely because of their race. But for African-Americans whose lives were not successful, who were victims of poverty and inadequate education, the movement had yet to provide answers.

The immediate emergency ended, we returned to Atlanta. Very soon after we left Watts, SCLC began seriously considering the possibility of undertaking a major campaign in Chicago. Several of the staff had been lobbying for a move North. I think the idea finally took shape in Martin's mind because of an offhand remark Robert Kennedy had made about the Watts riot. Kennedy said the civil rights movement, in focusing on the South, had neglected the problems of the North and the cities. Kennedy may not have had Martin specifically in mind when he said that, but Martin took the remark personally and was wounded by it. "He's right, Andy, we have neglected the cities of the North." The whole thing made me angry. I said, "Look, Martin, here we are with about a half-million-dollar budget and maybe a hundred staff members and this rich boy who has the resources of the entire federal government at his disposal is telling us we haven't done enough? I think we've done a helluva a lot. I am very pleased with what we have done, and I'm not going to let anybody make me feel guilty that I should've, could've done more." But Martin took it very seriously. He never thought he had done enough and Bobby Kennedy's words ate at him.

Martin had visited Chicago several times in response to requests from community organizations there. In fact it was the stress of running back and forth between our Southern efforts and Martin's grueling tour of several Northern cities that had led to my migraine attack after the convention. I did not believe it was practical for SCLC to move North and felt we could help the Northern cities more by continuing our work to register black voters to change the political climate in the South and, thereby, in the nation. We had neither the resources nor the staff to sustain two major campaigns in far-off geographical areas. And in terms of population, there were as many black folk in a city like Chicago as in all of Alabama. We had been successful in Alabama because we knew everybody, we understood the culture and the people, white and black.

Helping to fuel the interest that Chicago activists had in Martin was the presence of several veterans of Southern civil rights campaigns. Diane Bevel had returned to Chicago, her hometown, after Selma, and Jim was traveling to Chicago at every opportunity. Bernard Lafayette, one of the first SNCC workers in Selma, was working with the American Friends Service Committee in Chicago and collaborating with the newly created Coordinating Council of Community Organization (CCCO), an alliance of about seventy-five civil rights groups. The first objective of CCCO had been to force the dismissal of School Superintendent Benjamin Willis, who, in the opinion of the black groups, was dragging his feet on school desegregation. De facto segregation in Chicago was as real as in any city in the South. Along with this separation along color lines, the school system spent about three times more to educate a white child on the North Side than to educate a black child on the South Side.

Rev. Al Raby, chairman of CCCO, and Bill Berry, director of the Chicago Urban League, had asked SNCC and Martin to join with them in protest marches to city hall against Willis in July 1965, and Martin and I did so for three days. But I felt the Chicago marches were extremely nonproductive. Really, *all* they were doing was marching. Marches are minidramas designed to focus attention on particular problems, but for them to be successful some substantive effort at economic leveraging has to be going on beneath that surface display. People all across the nation saw the Birmingham demonstrations on television, but it was the economic boycotts that brought the power structure of Birmingham to the negotiating table. There was no such strategy in Chicago. They weren't even thinking that way.

Nevertheless, CCCO asked SCLC to come to Chicago to launch a massive campaign in the mold of Birmingham and Selma. We would focus on the deplorable housing conditions in the black ghetto of the South Side, on the pernicious problem of unemployment, and on the lack of economic opportunity for blacks. At a marathon two-day executive and "kitchen cabinet" SCLC staff meeting in the

Atlanta Airport Hilton Inn in September 1965, we argued the pros
and cons of accepting this invitation.

For this meeting all our senior staff were present: Ralph Aber-
nathy, Hosea Williams, Dorothy Cotton, Jim Orange, Bernard Lee,
C. T. Vivian, and Diane and Jim Bevel, who had come down from
Chicago. The more senior members in attendance were Bayard
Rustin, who had counseled Martin since the Montgomery bus boycott; Stanley Levison, who Martin still called on occasionally despite
his agreement to have Stan sever all ties under pressure from the FBI;
Harry Wachtel, a New York attorney and more recent addition to the
New York fund-raising and legal teams; Cleveland Robinson, treasurer of New York Local District 65 of the Service Employees Union,
an increasingly active and important supporter and an invaluable aid
during our moments of need in Selma; and Clarence Jones, who handled most of our legal work in New York and who was a close
adviser on fund-raising. Chauncey Eskridge, a bright young attorney
from Chicago who handled SCLC's tax affairs, also attended the session. It was Chauncey who won an acquittal for Martin when the
state of Alabama tried him for tax evasion. Dora McDonald kept the
record of the meeting.

In such meetings it was Martin's habit to open discussion by
putting the issues on the table and then letting everyone have a say.
He liked, even encouraged, people to take extreme positions, which
indeed we did. Our crucial staff meetings were usually extremely
argumentative and have become legendary among the SCLC inner
circle. They could go on forever as we debated the issues, strategies,
and tactics from each position. Martin believed that to hear an issue
discussed properly someone had to be strongly for it, and someone
had to argue the opposite position just as passionately. Of course,
arguing the opposition point of view typically fell to me. Since Bevel
and Hosea (and later Jesse Jackson) were always trying to get Martin
to *do* something, they were the ones pushing; it was left to me to
point up the problems and the drawbacks along with the proposed
action, as Martin expected me to do. After Selma, the executive staff
knew that if Martin consulted with anyone before he made a final
decision, I was that person. Thus I was often accused of undercutting
staff meeting arguments in later, private conversations with Martin.
But Martin didn't like advice; he liked to hear from me what I
thought his options were, period. Martin always made his own decisions in the final analysis, and nothing I said or did could have dis-
suaded him from what he felt he must do.

Jim Bevel was the main champion for undertaking a major campaign in Chicago. Bevel always marched to the beat of his own drummer; he was knowledgeable, persuasive, and instinctive. It had been his idea that we make Selma the site for a major campaign to dramatize the need for a voting rights bill. Now he argued that we should take on Chicago as an important test case for nonviolent protest techniques in the North. "We ought to reply to those people who say nonviolence won't work in New York or Chicago by going there and showing them it will. We shouldn't just let 'em take shots at us and Dr. King like that, and act like we accept the validity of their arguments. Some people are saying folks in Chicago are too unruly to listen to Dr. King. He ought to challenge that!" When someone commented, "Well, Bevel, Chicago *is* different from Mississippi and Alabama," he answered in his characteristic style: "Chicago is not that different from the South. Black Chicago *is* Mississippi moved north a few hundred miles. If you can organize people in Mississippi and Alabama, you can organize them in Chicago. It's the same people."

Bayard Rustin, who had coordinated the massive August 1963 March on Washington, assumed the opposing position. He was a veteran of labor and pacifist activism, and the protégé of patriarch A. Philip Randolph, the first prominent black in the American labor movement and organizer of the all-black Brotherhood of Sleeping Car Porters. Rustin immediately recognized the potential of Martin's theories of nonviolence during the Montgomery bus boycott and had moved to Alabama to help in the boycott by offering his organizational skills and contacts.

"I think SCLC has to continue to focus on the South," Rustin said slowly and deliberately, "and leave the Northern urban areas to other groups. SCLC's special mission is to transform the eleven Southern states. There won't be any real change in American politics and in the American social situation until that is done. Now, SCLC simply isn't strong enough, with its limited staff, to take on the old-line Southern politicians like Eastland, Byrd, and Ellender, who control Congress, and start a fight with Mayor Daley in Chicago at the same time."

A long discussion on the complexity of Chicago politics followed. We considered how our problems there would be different from what we were accustomed to in the South. What remained unstated in this discussion was the possibility that if Martin undertook a campaign in Chicago, he would eventually get bogged down in reforming Chicago politics.

In the beginning, Hosea argued against a move to Chicago, but he played a tricky game and after a while changed direction. By late 1965, Hosea and Bevel had become so competitive that he wanted to keep Bevel as far away from him as possible. Hosea had a full-time operation in SCOPE, our Southern voter registration program concentrating on implementation of the Voting Rights Act, and he figured if Bevel and everyone else were preoccupied with Chicago, he would have the South all to himself.

Dorothy said, "I'll do whatever Dr. King decides. Of course, as long as I have responsibility for keeping Dorchester going, I can't afford to devote too much time to Chicago. And we must realize we won't be able to transport people all the way from Chicago to Dorchester to train them. That's too expensive."

I added my voice to those who saw plenty of problems with a Chicago campaign. I thought Rustin's reasoning, whatever his motives, was sound. I first met Bayard when I was a student at Hartford Seminary and he came to give an address on nonviolence. It was only a few years after Gandhi's success in India and few people knew very much about it. In his speech, Rustin argued that "repentance need not be multilateral," that nonviolent solutions can provide justice without demanding surrender by either side. The speech was very intellectual, except that he closed by singing spirituals with a lovely tenor voice in a way that was very moving. I trusted Bayard's passion for justice and his commitment to nonviolence and I respected his tremendous depth of experience.

However, I also knew that Bayard was an employee of the AFL-CIO and that Richard Daley was a favorite of the Northern Labor Democrats. Behind Bayard's arguments was a concern that a move into Chicago would drive a wedge between big labor and the civil rights movement and between the movement and Daley. Nevertheless, Bayard's reasoning was sound and no one at that table could claim purity of motive.

"Let's not abandon the South now," I pleaded, "not when we've just finished working so hard to get the voting rights bill passed. We just can't walk away from it, we *know* it won't be implemented unless somebody stays in the South to force implementation. Hosea can't do it all by himself and the Justice Department isn't going to do anything unless we make them do it, no matter what Nicholas Katzenbach [Bobby Kennedy's replacement as Johnson's attorney general] promises." I went on to argue that in leaving the South, we would be walking away from our strength as organizers. Our field staff, built up during the Birmingham and Selma campaigns, possessed a mastery of the black communities of the South, particularly in Alabama. In Chicago they would be working unfamiliar territory. I reminded everyone that even if we began with the intent of maintaining a large staff in the South, eventually they would get diverted to Chicago; to conduct successful marches we had to have our veteran organizers. "We're just kidding ourselves if we say we can do Chicago and maintain the same presence in the South," I insisted.

Even after the dramatic victories in Birmingham and Selma, SCLC had a staff of just over a hundred persons and our budget was less than a million dollars annually. We received no federal funds and had only a small grant of fifty-five thousand dollars from the Field Foundation for our citizenship education program. The practical, administrative details of maintaining a national organization on such a limited budget were already almost unmanageable. No matter how much it drained us and our limited resources, if a job needed to be done and we committed ourselves to do it, the funds always came. As a group of preachers we were often quoting, "I was young and now I'm old, but I've never seen the righteous forsaken, nor his seed begging bread."

Given our already taxed bottom line, I further argued that the problems in Chicago, or anywhere in the North for that matter, required a level of funding we just didn't have. We would have to bear the cost of transporting people to Chicago, renting offices, hiring new people, and instituting a strong legal campaign to attack the rigidly segregated neighborhood housing patterns in Chicago—all of which necessitated an increased level of income I didn't believe we had the capacity to raise. While SCLC seldom allowed practical considerations to override moral ones, it was my role on the staff to point out the very real problems associated with a particular course of action. I appreciated the sound counsel of Bayard and Stan Levison, because like me they were rational pragmatists. I found virtue in taking a conservative position on the implementation of progressive ideals. I wanted Martin to understand fully the risks of a Chicago campaign.

Martin, as was his habit, hardly said anything, though he listened intently to everyone as they spoke. When we had finished our meeting his only remark was, "Well, it seems to me we've got to begin dealing with the North sometime. We can't just concern ourselves with the South if we call ourselves a national movement."

He didn't say much more than that, but from this statement I knew Martin was "going to Chicago." Bevel's argument that Martin should expand his leadership outside of the South and Robert Kennedy's remark that the civil rights movement had neglected the cities were, I believe, the key factors in his decision. And he felt we might as well begin a Northern campaign in Chicago, with its broad coalition of black community and civil rights groups already in place. Finally, as he remarked one day shortly after our meeting: "We've been responsible through the nonviolent movement for giving the downtrodden hope. Not just in the South, but all over the country. People are rioting because their rising expectations, engendered by us, are not fulfilled in the North. So we can't act like we have nothing to do with them, like they aren't our people too just because they live in Chicago."

It was decided that we would accept CCCO's invitation to lead the movement in Chicago, and Jesse Jackson was brought onto the SCLC staff to serve as our liaison with CCCO. Dr. Alan Pitcher, a professor at Chicago Theological Seminary, was also a key member of CCCO coalition. As a student at Chicago Theological Seminary, Jesse had brought students down to Selma in response to our call for solidarity for the march from Selma to Montgomery. In Selma, I was impressed with his willingness to assume responsibility, which set him apart from other students from the North. One night after the terrible attack at the Edmund Pettus Bridge, members of the SCLC staff were monitoring barricades outside the Brown Chapel AME Church. By that time, most of us had gone several days without rest. Jesse volunteered to monitor the situation, saying, "You all go relax. I'll keep watch here for you." I didn't know at the time that he was a veteran of the student movement in Greensboro, while he was studying at North Carolina A&T. Tall and handsome, Jesse had an air of confidence and was willing to take the initiative. He had proved himself to be responsible and levelheaded in Selma and, unlike the SNCC students, Jesse did not have a romance with the proletariat: while SNCC was striving for a nonleadership model and saw themselves as antiauthoritarian facilitators, Jesse's model for leadership was the traditional Baptist preacher. He was eager for the leadership mantle. We didn't know exactly what was driving Jesse, but Martin appreciated Jesse's desperate desire to lead and encouraged it.

I always suspected that Jesse's childhood as the son of a single mother created in him a constant psychological need for a father figure. And his leadership drive was a product of that need for attention and approval. As a student, he seemed drawn to the glory of leadership and looked to Martin as a paternal authority. While neither Martin nor I had any trouble being a brother to Jesse, we were struggling ourselves with our own identity development and in no position to play a fatherly role. Yet Martin was always tolerant of the different neuroses that drove his individual staff members and in fact found a creative tension in it. Martin used to say that I was actually too well adjusted to be in the movement. He would say, "Andy, you would be helping people to adjust to segregation. You're too normal." He put Walter Fauntroy, SCLC's Washington staff member in that category, as well. Of course, I felt like I was left to pick up the pieces when Hosea lost his temper and chewed out a kid or he and Bevel viciously attacked each other in staff meeting.

It was Martin who came up with the idea of dramatizing the Chicago campaign, which would focus on inadequate housing, by renting a fourth-floor walk-up apartment in a dull, brick-front building at 16th Street and Hamlin Avenue. The idea was that Martin and his family would live there in the ghetto while he was in Chicago, thus demonstrating his solidarity with the people. Actually that idea didn't quite come off. Bernard Lee went up to Chicago and rented the apartment all right, but when the real estate company discovered in early January that the apartment was intended for Martin, they panicked and tried to spruce it up at the last minute. Martin hardly even used the apartment, but I ended up staying there a lot; 16th Street and Hamlin Avenue became our unofficial Chicago headquarters. The place was cold, in poor repair, and depressing. It would have taken an archaeologist to discern the intended color of the walls and the flooring was worn and coming up in places. We leased all the furniture and paid rent of about $150 a month.

When we began our campaign on January 6, 1966, the idea of Martin, the national leader and Nobel Peace Prize laureate, living in a Chicago tenement did draw considerable press, for those who were familiar with the area knew that Hamlin and 16th was a center of drugs, prostitution, and racketeering. But at least initially our neighbors in the building and those adjoining were not in the least impressed. They took a cynical view of our presence there and hardly paid any attention to us. I suppose they felt whatever we were doing didn't relate to their daily struggles, so why get excited? I have to say that I felt a little bit of an adrenaline rush, because it was the first time I had ever lived in a tenement. In Chicago, after long days of meetings and conferences, I often returned home to the tenement apartment late at night. Frankly, I was afraid for my life, in a way that I had never been in the South. I was truly frightened that some junkie was going to knife me for twenty dollars. My feeling was that it would be one thing to be killed by the Klan in the South—that was an acceptable martyrdom—but to be murdered by a junkie in

Chicago seemed to me the ultimate absurdity. When walking up those four dark, creaky flights of stairs late at night, my heart would pound and wouldn't slow for some time after I was within our apartment with the door securely bolted.

After we had been there for a few weeks, and it became known that there were SCLC people at the apartment, a few people in the neighborhood began to trickle by to complain about conditions in their buildings. They really had no one else to complain to. We decided to try to organize them into neighborhood groups on the basis of who their landlords were. People who rented from the same absentee landlord learned to know one another, compare notes, and formulate some means of protest against the deficiencies of their tenements. We called this first small effort the Movement to End Slums.

One unforgettable day in February 1966, the temperature hit a frigid sixteen degrees below zero. I was wearing my overcoat inside our apartment. We thought it was freezing in our flat, but at least we could hear that there was some heat attempting to escape from the old banging radiators. Then some shivering neighbors knocked on our door and told us they had no heat at all and had had none in weeks. They wanted to know if we could do something to help. So we all—Martin, Bevel, Bernard Lafayette, and Al Raby—went over together in a group to their apartment. The family had no blankets. A newborn baby was covered with newspapers and wrapped in a cotton sheet. I don't know how that baby survived. It seemed even colder inside their rooms than it was outside. We went down to the basement to check the furnace. It seemed in good shape; all it lacked was coal. So we called a coal company and asked them to come right over and said we would pay them.

News of what happened that day spread like wildfire in the neighborhood. Now people in the immediate area began to flock over in droves with every conceivable problem all hours of the day and night. We set up a system whereby people who suffered from long-standing violations could, if they chose, pay their rent to us, which we placed in an escrow account. From that account we were able to make some repairs. But our primary purpose was to force the owners of such tenements to go to court against us to get their rent money, and in so doing to expose their extreme negligence. We hoped that the court would then force them to make substantive repairs. The landlords and the city raised a big stink, charging that we were "grabbing tenements," but the people were very enthusiastic and involved; in effect, they took over management of their own houses.

With our help, they began to paint, clean up, make repairs, and purchase coal with their rent money. Surprisingly, we were also able to receive considerable support from Chicago labor unions—the unions really pitched in and helped finance the Movement to End Slums. I suppose the local unions viewed repairing slums preferable to integrating the working-class neighborhoods of their white members. The idea was novel: renters would form a union and bargain collectively with landlords to ensure basic services and the correction of grievances. The landlords and the city sued us, but their attorneys realized it would take them forever to get the rent strikes declared illegal, so they eventually abandoned a court fight.

Then we decided to take things a step or two further. In conjunction with the City Mission Society, now known as the Community Renewal Society, we hired architects to evaluate the buildings involved in our rent strikes. They discovered that most of the structures were physically sound and renovatable if sufficient funds were made available. And so the Community Union Movement, a nonprofit housing corporation, was created. We applied for a Department of Housing and Urban Development (HUD) grant to renovate the structures. The next step was to offer to buy the buildings involved in rent strikes from their owners, none of whom lived in those properties. These were absentee owners in the truest sense: sometimes they had never even seen the properties, which were managed by real estate companies. The owners were glad to sell after all the negative publicity about the condition of their properties. Slum property provided regular income with virtually no costs for maintenance and upkeep. There was profit in slums, but only when the tenants were passive. Our efforts took the obscene profit margin out of the tenements we organized.

The Community Union Movement was awarded a HUD grant, and architects redesigned and renovated about twenty buildings, which were converted into low-income cooperatives, a process that took about two years to complete. Then the cooperatives, outfitted with new washing machines, refrigerators, stoves, plumbing, wiring, and so forth, were resold to the people who lived there. This conversion process was undertaken under the name of the Urban Renewal Society, an organization we set up with the help of the City Mission Society, to administer the HUD grant and complete the project. Whereas people had previously been paying $140 to $180 per month in rent, they now were buying their apartments and paying notes of $85 to $120 per month.

This was one of the most successful but least publicized achievements of our Chicago campaign. Bevel and Bernard Lafayette were passionate about the program and put all their organizing skill and experience into it. The rent strike work was Bevel's way of proving that Martin had not made a mistake in choosing to go to Chicago. As a result of that experience in Chicago, I too became convinced that the way to improve housing for poor people is to help them own their homes.

While quite limited in scope, considering the plethora of bad housing in Chicago, the Urban Renewal Society served as a model for what could be done when people took control of their own lives and refused to be victims. In a sense that was about all we could do anyway—provide a few models that, hopefully, people could pick up on and carry forth themselves, imparting a new sense of control, of "somebodiness," to use Martin's term, to their children and their children's children.

Operation Breadbasket was another important aspect of our Chicago campaign. An idea originally developed by Rev. Leon Sullivan in Philadelphia, its fundamental objective in Chicago was to get corporations and businesses located in the black community to provide jobs for blacks—jobs on several levels, not just menial labor—and to encourage these same companies to deposit at least some of their assets in black-owned banks. We also asked supermarkets that often realized high profits in the black community to stock products manufactured by blacks when possible. Though these supermarkets were located in totally black neighborhoods, products manufactured by black companies, such as Johnson Beauty Products and Joe Louis milk, were not available. We systematically undertook negotiating agreements with such businesses and were, of course, prepared to use consumer boycotts against those that had problems seeing the light. In fact, the name "Breadbasket" had derived from our boycott of the hiring and investment practices of bread companies in Atlanta, such as Colonial and Sunshine, who had been our first targets in the spring of 1962. Rev. Fred Bennett, Martin's old classmate and close friend, had administered our original Breadbasket program in Atlanta. The program was so successful at economically empowering and improving the black community that when Ford Motor Company built a new assembly plant in Atlanta a small group of black ministers visited the plant manager at his office to encourage him to hire black workers. When the manager was not only unwilling to consider their request, but was also rude, the ministers came to Bennett, and with Martin's help they contacted Henry Ford and told him he was going to have a hard time selling Fords to black consumers in

Atlanta. Ford came to Atlanta and settled the issue personally. Ultimately, about a third of the labor force hired at the plant was black, producing middle-class incomes for hundreds of black families. The same kind of economic enfranchisement was needed in Chicago, and remembering that supportive ministers had been the means of spreading the word during the Atlanta bread company boycott, we went to the ministers of Chicago to request their support for Breadbasket community boycotts and negotiating efforts there.

In Chicago, Jesse was assigned to staff Breadbasket and assist the chairman. One of the more effective features of Breadbasket in other regions was that the chairmanship rotated monthly among the board members, encouraging involvement by a broad base of community leaders. Each board member knew that every ten or twelve months, he would be the chairman of Breadbasket and the spokesman for its programs, and it kept them active. Jesse changed that design and became the spokesman himself, although his role continued to involve keeping the rotations working, supporting the chairman, and maintaining consistency among the programs. Breadbasket expanded under Jesse's leadership and provided him with an organizational vehicle long after the Chicago campaign ended. But it was another example of how Jesse's ambition undercut his genuine potential. It would have been a slower process, but had Jesse maintained the original structure of Breadbasket, he would have developed a much stronger organizational base for his endeavors, strong enough to challenge the Daley machine. Nevertheless, Breadbasket was a success by any measure.

So, despite my deep apprehensions over the move into Chicago, and the whole new set of problems we were facing, we were beginning to find meaningful ways of helping people there. SCLC was stretched very thin, but Chicago was fascinating, if intensely challenging. Despite Bevel's passionate assertion that people in Chicago were the same as those in Mississippi, it wasn't true. In Alabama, we worked mostly with children and older people. I felt like I was always learning something—from the unvarnished honesty of the children to the cultural depth of the elders. In Alabama, when you got weary, there was always some good sister to remind you, "I don't feel noways tired . . . I don't believe God brought me this far to leave me." There was more spiritual strength in the South, a reserve that I had learned to draw from. Chicago lacked the unity of purpose of the South. In Birmingham, whether you were a welfare mother or a millionaire, segregation was a problem, you still had to go to the kitchen door of a Chinese restaurant. In Chicago, a mother in the slums was

concerned about her baby being wrapped in newspaper on the cold-
est night of the year, while a black millionaire might be more concerned about selling his products in the local supermarket. These
were very different issues. There were upwardly mobile black parents
of all economic strata who were concerned about their children's education and there were the liberal whites and the young, black urban
professionals who were anti-Daley. They wanted to undermine the
Daley machine so that in the name of political reform, they could
gain political power. But as fast as they would organize a neighborhood, the Daley forces would come in and offer a preacher a city
contract for subsidized day care in his church. The rub was that
while such maneuvering was hard on CCCO it was ultimately good
for the community, which despite the dishonest means was getting a
fairer share of the city's resources. In the same movement we had
people who wanted major reform of the entire political system in
Chicago and others who just wanted the chance to improve their
material lives in a very fundamental way—a job, a better school, a
home with heat.

This was different from movements in the South, which focused
themselves around issues of dignity and citizenship, through which
all blacks were affected equally. In Chicago, poor people had tremendous, immediate material needs. It was not the place of comfortable,
middle-class people to condemn a local preacher for abandoning
CCCO for day care, commodities for a feeding program, or city
grants for a seniors program. I grew up in church-sponsored day care
and sent my own children to them. I was not prepared to argue that
the Chicago movement was defending a higher principle than day
care or food for the hungry. By organizing, churches serving
Chicago's poor gained the attention of city hall and more of their tax
dollars were returned to the community. In many respects the competing interests had more to do with process than result.

To find the Southern spirit in Chicago, you had to go to the
churches. Chicago was a good church town and had a gospel tradition that rode the rails straight up from Mississippi. Ministers like
Clay Evans, Patterson Jackson, and John Thurston invited us into
their churches and gave support to the movement. During the course
of the Chicago movement, I must have preached in fifty Baptist
churches. It was an indication that our Chicago effort was as controversial as any in the South that no black Congregational Church
invited me to preach. The middle-class Congregationalists were comfortable with the status quo. Educated in the American Missionary
Association schools of the South, they came to Chicago in migrations

after each world war possessing skills and a top-flight education. They owned businesses, taught school, worked in the post office, and accommodated the Daley machine. Like me, they were too well adjusted.

Just as we were settling deep into our Chicago campaign, James Meredith was shot on Highway 51 just inside the Mississippi state line. He was shotgunned in the leg, though fortunately not seriously injured, by a crazed white Mississippian almost immediately after beginning his "March Against Fear," a planned two-week walk from Memphis to Jackson.

In 1962, James Meredith had become the first black student to be enrolled at the University of Mississippi. This was accomplished only after a long legal campaign waged by the NAACP Legal Defense Fund and a virtual military campaign waged by the federal government against the state of Mississippi. The governor of Mississippi, Ross Barnett, had refused to follow United States Supreme Court orders to desegregate the university and allow Meredith to enroll, and his defiance of the Court order received a great deal of popular support from the heavily segregationist white populace of Mississippi. The vicious race hatred of the local population created an explosive atmosphere on the night in September 1962 when Meredith was installed in a University of Mississippi dormitory under the protection of more than a hundred federal marshals. A riot ensued on the campus during which two people (one a foreign newsman) were killed.

After graduation from the University of Mississippi and law school at Columbia University, Meredith, for reasons I never understood, decided he would undertake a march, virtually alone, from Memphis through the heart of Mississippi to the state capitol in Jackson. He called it a March Against Fear. I always believed that marches should be designed to promote or dramatize long-term, concrete, community goals, not to express one individual's personal psychological needs. And I certainly didn't see the point in waving red flags at crackpots who were crazy enough to shoot at you. That wasn't the idea of the civil rights movement as far as I was concerned, and I didn't see how it would lead to anything beneficial for the people as a whole. His plan struck me from the start as stemming from an excessive desire for media attention and as an invitation to every racist nut in Mississippi.

When the news flashed on the radio that Meredith had been shot, we were in the midst of a staff meeting in Atlanta. The first report we heard was that Meredith had been killed. Hosea said, "If they killed James Meredith we gotta do something." He wanted us all to jump on a plane and go right over to Memphis. But we were already in the middle of running back and forth to Chicago, trying to keep that effort going, so I said, "Wait a second. Let's take a minute and decide what to do." "No!" Hosea yelled, "we can decide what to do on the way to Memphis." He was furious with me because he thought I wasn't angry enough over the shooting of Meredith. We almost came to blows right then and there.

Everyone did finally go to Memphis, including Martin, leaving me and Bevel, who also refused to go, in Atlanta. Bevel and Hosea were still not getting along, and Bevel stayed away from wherever Hosea thought it important to be. Bevel was operating the nuts and bolts of the Chicago campaign and receiving a lot of publicity; Hosea was stuck down South with voter registration, laboring out of the limelight once again. I felt Hosea saw the Meredith march as a perfect opportunity to get something dramatic going in the South accompanied by an army of reporters; and with Martin now devoting most of his time to the new project in Chicago, Hosea would have much of the limelight to himself. While the debate over our Northern thrust was ostensibly over, the resultant infighting among staff was still going on. With the freedom Martin allowed his staff, executive staff members were always trying to pull the organization, and Martin, in whatever direction they advocated. My job was to ensure some balance and keep the infighting from becoming self-destructive, but I never felt I could control the tension between Bevel and Hosea.

In Memphis, Martin and leaders from other civil rights groups active in Mississippi, SNCC, and CORE gathered around Meredith's hospital bed and vowed to him that they would continue his march from the exact point at which he was shot and march on until they reached Jackson. When Meredith became well enough, he would rejoin them. The leaders sent out a national call for support, as we had done in Selma, and all the veterans of the movement were urged to rush to Mississippi to join the march. Despite my personal reservations there was some logic to the decision to go. There was an unwritten pact among the civil rights leadership that where there were violent attacks to block our civil rights efforts, other organizations would come in to intensify the movement. Violent opposition could never be allowed to stop a movement; that would simply encourage Klan members and racist bullies to believe that violence could be effective in halting social change.

However, to my mind Meredith was a lone individual who made

a unilateral decision to risk his life. His march was not the work of SNCC, NAACP, CORE, or any national or local civil rights organization. It was an ego trip by one man. I thought it was wrong to allow SCLC's priorities to be set aside by Meredith's actions. We were beginning to win trust and support in Chicago and this kind of blowing with the wind was exactly the sort of foolishness that had led me to oppose going to Chicago in the first place. There were times to go with the spirit. This was not one of them.

When Martin called to tell me we were assuming major responsibility for the march and that he wanted me to come over to Mississippi immediately, I had to repeat to myself my daddy's teaching like a mantra: "Don't get mad, get smart." I had had my say. So, like a good soldier, I went. It was my responsibility to make the best of a bad situation.

To that end, we managed to provide some continuity with our work in Chicago by recruiting a group of gang members, the Blackstone Rangers, to join us on the march in Memphis. These young men, who were so tough and swaggering on the streets of Chicago, became very meek away from their home turf. Once in Mississippi, they caused no trouble and seemed awed by the fact that the SCLC staff members were not afraid to be in Mississippi. When the Rangers returned to Chicago, they viewed the SCLC staff with new respect. They realized that we had not adopted the philosophy of nonviolence because we were afraid to fight—nonviolence required genuine courage. After we had earned their respect, these gang members became excellent marshals for our demonstrations in Chicago. From them we learned an important lesson about working with gangs and respecting their potential as a form of community organization: gangs include many of the natural leaders in a community and in any effort to organize a community where gangs are present, they must be mobilized as a constructive force or they will eventually undermine your efforts.

As we began our march from Memphis, an open conflict between SNCC and SCLC quickly broke out, and the press picked up on it instantly. SNCC had just undergone an internal power struggle in which a small group of Northern workers took control, symbolized by the election of Stokely Carmichael, who replaced John Lewis as chairman. Stokely was a sharp, fast-talking rhetorician, with a strong record of SNCC organizing in Mississippi and Alabama. But he was generally unknown to the public and the media. The Meredith march was his first exposure to the press, and he went right to work attempting to establish a more militant image for himself and

SNCC. We felt a lot of the focus on his distinct image had to do with his resentment of Martin's preeminence and of the overwhelming media focus on Martin. So the same problems that first appeared in Albany, and had worsened in Selma, were now flaring up again during the Meredith march.

Early in the march Stokely became enraged at a Mississippi state trooper and charged at him. Martin, Bob Greene, and others in the front line had to grab him and hold him back. To me, this was just the height of stupidity. What was he going to do, I wondered, beat up an armed state trooper single-handedly? Apparently the trooper had pushed him or something, and Stokely got mad and started screaming, "To hell with nonviolence. If someone shoves me, I'm going to shove him back." The problem was, Stokely wasn't responsible for only himself. We were in the midst of a march involving a group of people, including women and children, and if someone broke discipline and caused the march to be attacked, then everyone was endangered. If you're by yourself and you say, "If someone pushes me I'm gonna push them back," then that's your business. If you're in a group demonstration, you willingly exchange some of your personal freedom for the shared discipline of the march. Stokely's stunt was a bad omen, but it wasn't the only one.

Bob Greene, one of my closest friends, took a leave of absence from his professorship at Michigan State University to join us to work with the Dorchester Citizenship Schools Program after I left, and has since achieved a fine career in the academic world. But on the Meredith march Bob acted like a frustrated classroom intellectual trying to prove his "movement credentials." In the town square of Grenada, one of those horrible, bigoted little Mississippi towns, Bob climbed up onto the statue of Jefferson Davis and draped the American flag over his head, yelling, ". . . we want brother Jeff Davis to know the South he represented will never rise again!" He performed this act while state troopers stood by, trying to control their anger, and all the hostile white townspeople hung around the courthouse square, seething. Then, a few miles farther down the road, as a train approached a crossing, threatening to split our march, Bob ran down the tracks toward the slowly approaching engine, climbed up on it, and yelled at the engineer, "You better stop this train! Stop this train now!" I felt that this sort of grandstanding had more to do with being in Mississippi defying the image of Mississippi all-white omnipotence than anything else. He was caught up in "freedom high" as if in overcoming his fear he had lost all sense of reason. Maybe this is what Meredith had meant by "a march against fear."

With the defeat of the Southern and spiritually strong John Lewis as chairman, SNCC began to turn away from the spirit of nonviolence that had characterized it up to that point. A nonviolent movement did not seek to defeat its opponent but to be reconciled in a fairer and more just relationship. But under Stokely, the rhetoric of SNCC became more hostile, although its actions remained nonviolent. The slogan "Black Power" came to be associated with Stokely Carmichael and the Meredith march. But in fact the slogan was coined by Willie Ricks, another SNCC organizer, not Stokely. Chants and group singing were characteristic of our marches, as a way of reinforcing group spirit, picking up the step, and keeping the energy level high. When we reached Greenwood, Mississippi, a SNCC stronghold of the early sixties, Ricks improvised on the old call-and-response chant while we were setting up tents: "What do we want? Freedom now!" became "What do we want? Black Power!" Stokely picked up on this, as did some other members of SNCC, and the few reporters on the march perked up their ears. Within hours the chant "Black Power" became the lead sound bite for the newspeople reporting on the march, along with "dissension in the movement" and "a new militancy in SNCC." The real point—racism in Mississippi and in the South—was ignored by the press. Reporters immediately ran to Martin to ask whether he approved of the slogan.

Black Power, as a militant expression, was born out of the bitterness and disillusionment that grew from the youth and impatience of SNCC students. Optimistic and naive, they had underestimated the cost and suffering that change required. They truly expected the police, the courts, and the FBI to practice democracy. As ministers who were a few years older, we in SCLC had a more realistic view of the power of sin in individuals and institutions and were more cautious in our struggle and moderate in our expectations. We didn't expect to change the world with one summer or one campaign, but rather looked to a lifetime of struggle and perhaps losing our lives in the struggle.

It was about this time that Frantz Fanon's justifications of Algerian terrorism in *The Wretched of the Earth* became available in an English translation and copies of Mao's *Little Red Book* were beginning to be seen around the movement. The provocative rhetoric of SNCC reflected the influence of those books and a Northern leftist approach to social change. To me it really symbolized a crisis in faith, for it was faith that had sustained the movement through beatings, jailings, setbacks, and betrayals since the early days of Montgomery.

The Southern-born SNCC students like John Lewis were steeped in religion, but many of the Northern students, black and white, were drawn to SNCC for political reasons and lacked the spiritual resources that the movement demanded. Without a mature, personal faith, one could not make sense of the suffering, forgive the persecutors, and be reconciled with oppressors. For me, the true embodiment of Black Power was Amzie Moore, the Mississippi postal worker who had had the courage to face down a group of armed hoodlums that had come to kill him. His was a powerful, personal spiritual presence who stood strong in the face of violence and threats through many decades.

Now, we had no quarrel with the concept of Black Power. On the contrary, all of our campaigns were designed to counter the economic and political impotence of the black community. Our selective buying boycotts, economic cooperatives, voter registration efforts, and political organization were all, we thought, very much about the empowerment of the black community. But Martin was uncomfortable with the rhetoric and tone of Black Power, rhetoric with no real pragmatic substance behind it. Black Power was just a chant with no program. At our nightly interorganizational meetings in the tents Martin would say, "Listen, when people talk about Catholic power, all Catholics deny it, because they *have* power. When people talk about Jewish power the Jews get angry and declare there is no such thing. When you really have power you don't go around shouting about it, you're too busy developing it and exercising it. By yelling 'Black Power' all we're doing is advertising the fact we don't have any. Power is like money in the bank, the less you use it the more you have."

But Martin knew what all this was really about: SNCC's attempt to stake out a separate, more militant image for itself. Though Martin was disappointed by the media's wallowing in the Black Power controversy, he was not really dismayed. He said, "Listen, Andy, if Stokely is saying the same thing I'm saying, he becomes like my assistant. Stokely and the students are struggling to develop their own identity. We just have to accept that."

Despite the well-publicized split between SNCC and SCLC during the march, in substance there was never that great a difference between the two organizations. But the press loved to exaggerate our clashes. On one occasion during the march, Martin concluded his speech by outlining an economic and political strategy, one that retained respect for person and property. Stokely concluded by chanting, "We need Black Power." The national press reported "a major departure" by SNCC from traditional civil rights movement ideology. In fact, Martin and Stokely were saying essentially the same thing. Their styles were different, and Stokely's style was new, startling, and attention-getting. There were those who found that style grating, of course. Some who worked closely with Stokely grew a bit weary of his tendency toward self-promotion and went so far as to dub him "Stokely Star-Michael."

None of this, however, destroyed the strong and binding personal relationships between SNCC workers and those of us in SCLC. Stokely and Martin were friendly, though not as close as John Lewis and Martin had been. I thought of our two organizations as an older and a younger brother, with the younger brother craving more respect than he was receiving. SNCC and SCLC needed each other, however, and worked together more closely than any of the other major civil rights groups, even when we were arguing. From the removed perspective of three decades, I now realize that if we were older, more settled, and more conventional in our thinking, we needed the energy and daring of the younger people, though we may not have liked to admit it. Conversely, SNCC needed our steadiness, and while they may have resented it at the time, they benefited from the exposure that Martin's charisma brought to any campaign. In practical terms, they also needed whatever financial assistance we could provide.

The wrangling that occurred was less an issue of ideology than it was a by-product of SNCC's internal evolution. During this period, SNCC was moving abruptly toward becoming an all-black organization. SCLC had always been a black-controlled organization, because its organizational basis was young ministers of the Southern black— essentially Baptist—church. After its first sit-in stage, however, SNCC had become an integrated organization, and very fluid in terms of who the controlling members were. By 1966, the black students from the South who had founded the organization were not in control anymore, and they and the liberal white and black students from the North found themselves at odds with one another. The religious, spiritual grounding that was typical of Southern students like John Lewis, Jim Bevel, and Bernard Lafayette came under pressure from both black and white Northern students, many of whom saw the violence of Mississippi Freedom Summer as a call for SNCC to become more militant. John Lewis and the other SNCC workers who came out of the Southern religious tradition had come to grips with their own fear of death. They were angered by the violence, but they knew the South too well to be surprised by it. Through faith, they would stand their ground and persevere, as blacks always had in the South. Lacking this spiritual grounding, the militants were responding out of their own fear and insecurity. With the election of Stokely as chairman, militant black students asserted dominance and eventually even the white students who were so enamored of Stokely and the militant posture of the new SNCC leadership found themselves pushed aside by the all-black policy.

Complicating the racial issues in SNCC were gender dynamics. During the Mississippi Freedom Summer, the male leadership of SNCC had a way of riding around in cars playing macho on two-way radios, while the actual door-to-door canvassing was done by women. Some of the young women confided to me that the brothers were playing the white and black women against each other to gain sexual favors. A man would approach a young, white college woman and if she turned him down he would accuse her of racism, until she relented. The same man would then approach a young, black college woman with the argument, "the white girls are doing it, why are you so stuck up?" Mary King, later an official in the Carter administration, and Casey Hayden wrote a position paper on the role of women in SNCC that was presented anonymously at a SNCC retreat at Waveland Conference Center in Mississippi. It created a lot of controversy in SNCC amid accusations of disloyalty, and it forced into the open what had already been the accepted practice—that in SNCC women and white men could play supportive roles, but the leadership roles were reserved for black men.

Once the unspoken genie was out of the bottle, the illusion that SNCC was a pure, egalitarian democracy could not be maintained, and its emerging leaders were not inclined to reform themselves. Mary circulated the document to women in progressive organizations around the country, a first attempt at articulating the dilemma faced by women in organizations that purported to seek justice, equality, and social change. The white students left SNCC and took that experience into other social movements. Eventually, Mary and Casey went to Chicago and started feminist consciousness-raising groups. Tom Hayden went from SNCC to Students for a Democratic Society, which initiated the radical student movement against Vietnam.

My dispute with the phrase Black Power was less about what those espousing it might do than it was about how the words might be misinterpreted. Some in the media automatically associated violence with the words *Black Power*. But Stokely never advocated violence, nor did anyone in SNCC either before or after the Black Power phase. And as far as I know, no one in SNCC ever committed any violence, despite their posturing during the Meredith march, and their subsequent rhetoric.

Those of us on the march decided, however, that *we* would brave violence by detouring from Highway 51 to visit the town of Philadelphia, Mississippi, where civil rights workers Goodman, Chaney, and Schwerner were murdered in 1964. Our idea was to march to the town square and hold a brief memorial service for the slain civil rights workers at the courthouse. By that time it was well known that key law enforcement officers in Neshoba County (where Philadelphia is located) had been involved in the murders.

We began the march at the little country church that was burned during Freedom Summer. This church had been the only one in Neshoba County that had opened its doors to civil rights workers and it was rewarded with shocking violence. By now it had been rebuilt by the community, and the Meredith march was to continue there, then travel a few miles into downtown Philadelphia to the courthouse, where we would hold our commemorative rally.

Trouble came early. While we were striding down the dirt road toward town, a pickup truck swung onto the road ahead of us and sped directly at us. We could see it roaring down the road kicking up dust, headed toward a group who were marching and singing in front, unaware of the truck's speeding approach. We screamed at them to jump out of the way and they just barely made it as the truck hurtled all the way through our ranks, as if the driver were bent on crushing every last one of us. The Mississippi State Highway Patrol, which was supposed to be protecting us, did nothing.

As we neared the courthouse we had to march past hostile mobs on either side, who were cursing and throwing things at us, while we fought to maintain discipline. It was like St. Augustine all over again. When we finally made it to the courthouse to have our rally, Martin—as he was fond of joking later—called on Ralph to pray, "Since I sure wasn't about to close *my* eyes." Martin, in telling this story, always added, "Ralph prayed, but he prayed with a wary eye open."

At one point in his prayer, Ralph asked forgiveness "for the murderers" of the three civil rights workers. Both Sheriff Rainey and Deputy Sheriff Price, who had been implicated in the murders and were eventually tried on federal conspiracy charges, were in the surrounding crowd. "Some of the murderers are wel-l-l-l within my voice," Ralph intoned. Someone in the crowd yelled back, "You goddamned right. And we ain't through yet!" It was a chilling moment.

Canton, Mississippi, was the last major stop before our final day's march and culminating ceremonies in Jackson. In 1962 and

1963, Canton had been through a bitter and hard-fought struggle to register voters, similar to the effort in Greenwood, and in the process had developed outstanding leaders who later headed the statewide movement. In many ways, Canton resembled Selma: it was similarly isolated, and the same forms of oppression and dominance were used to keep blacks "in their place." The white power structure there had much to fear given its existence in a seventy-percent black county, in the heart of the black belt. The potential shift in political power should enough blacks exercise the franchise was tremendous, and the efforts of the local black community were met with bitter hatred.

The leaders of the Canton movement had arranged to house, feed and entertain us on the grounds of McNeil Elementary School, where we set up a speaker system as soon as we arrived so that various people, including Martin, could speak. We were about to set up tents to house the march for the night, when it came to our attention that the issue of whether we would be allowed to use the school grounds was still being debated. Several speeches had been made when, late that afternoon, I observed state troopers moving into position across from the school. The commander of the troopers said nothing to us, nor did he tell us to stop speaking. Then I saw the troopers take out their gas masks and adjust them on their faces. Still, nothing at all had been said nor was there any attempt to communicate with us. I told the minister who was then speaking, standing on top of a trailer truck, "You better get down from that truck. Something's going to happen." Everyone on top of the truck platform climbed down, and I climbed up to say something to the people.

No sooner had I reached the top of the truck than the troopers opened fire with tear-gas modules. People started screaming and falling down and running every which way. I was shouting instructions through the bullhorn: "Be calm," "Get close to the ground," "Put a handkerchief over your face," "Don't panic." Then I got hit with a terrific whiff of gas while still there on top of the truck. I don't know how high I was off the ground, maybe about nine feet, but I leaped off that truck in one bound.

I had inhaled too much gas and I started choking and vomiting. It was the same combination of tear and nausea gas they had used on us in Selma. I panicked, the only time during the movement when I think I lost my cool completely. I had been through the mob and knocked woozy in St. Augustine, been in the middle of the attacks in Birmingham and Selma, and withstood the vicious crowds in Philadelphia, Mississippi, but this was the first time I was thoroughly teargassed. I thought I was going to die. Suddenly, I was just running.

Normally, I would be the last to run; I was always checking to make sure Martin was safe, to make sure the women and children were safe.

This time I left the children behind and probably ran over some women. I ran right into more gas. All I would have had to do was walk over to the right to evade the drift; instead I was flying along *with* the gas. I ran until I reached the fence of the school grounds, a wire fence about six feet high. The minister who had been speaking was running beside me. We both hit that fence and went over in one leap.

Once we got over the fence, we ducked behind a house to try to escape the heavy fumes. Slowly, I began to catch my breath and gathered my wits about me. As soon as I was all right, I went back out to the grounds. The people who were sensible had simply moved off to the right of the fumes and were not seriously affected. Martin was among those who had remained calm and moved upwind, away from the gas. The troopers moved in after the gassing and beat people who had fallen to the ground, as they did on Selma's Edmund Pettus Bridge. Fortunately, no one was seriously injured.

One of those who was not hit by the gas was Willie Ricks. Ricks was on top of an automobile shouting, "We ain' gon' take this shit, we gon' get these mothers," as if challenging the troopers to come back and beat us again. I jumped on top of the car, grabbed Ricks by the collar, and said, "Look, those motha fuckahs out there got machine guns. And they're crazy. And you got nothing but your mouth and some bricks and bottles. If you want to get yourself killed, go on. But you are not sending women and children over there to get killed. If you want to fight somebody, fight me." Willie shut up, thankfully, and got down.

Stokely was gassed badly, and he couldn't seem to get himself together. Long after everyone else had recovered he was still hysterical, screaming and crying like he was in shock. Several young women were trying to comfort him and calm him down. I suspected his reaction had to do with more than being teargassed. The year before, Stokely had been standing between Jonathan Daniels, an Episcopal seminary student, and Richard Morrisroe, a Roman Catholic priest from Chicago, during a demonstration in Lowndes County, Alabama, when a deputy sheriff shot and killed Daniels, wounded Morrisroe, and Stokely came away without a scratch. That sort of memory is horrible to live with; the survivor's guilt is overwhelming. Those who have been that close to death, but were not injured solely because of luck, suffer long, long after the event has passed. Stokely raved all night long, "They're gonna gas us again. Everybody get moving!" Finally, Martin just took him by the hand and said, "Stokely, let's go somewhere and sit down and talk."

The final rally at Jackson was uneventful. I was never in favor of this twenty-seven-day side trip into the psychological zone, so I was thankful when it was all over and we could get out of Mississippi and back to Chicago. Though I had returned to Chicago a couple of times during the month, I had spent most of my time on the march, the longest and most sustained of the movement, trying to deal with people and keep things from flying apart at the seams.

The Meredith march solidified and intensified my belief that the need to prove oneself by doing something, almost anything, to defy the myth of black submissiveness, was a *Northern* black phenomenon, and purely psychological. Native black Southerners were more interested in survival than defiance, and infinitely more skilled at the subtle methods of survival. My respect went to older black folks who had lived in Mississippi for years, struggling and scratching for every inch of progress they could obtain, learning how to absorb or dodge the blows and keep moving in order to struggle and scratch another day. Even if their small gains didn't look like much, in accumulation they were substantial. Such gains in the economic and political arena are the result of tough compromises that seldom provide dramatic or colorful flags to rally around. Yet this is the way social change usually occurs in America. I was becoming even more convinced than before that the changes we were seeking would also occur in slow, painful accretions, for the most part behind the scenes, long after the media glow of our demonstrations and marches had faded away.

The real work of the struggle is not sensational, it does not garner headlines. Black Power was a dead end. It provided emotional release and the illusion of manhood, without the content. The original Black Panther Party was formed in Lowndes County, Alabama, one of SNCC's projects, before Huey Newton founded his party of the same name in Oakland. I found it counterproductive to organize black citizens into a separate political party, particularly one that used a symbol that was certain to frighten and intimidate white people in Lowndes County, just adding insult to injury. Ultimately, blacks and whites in the same community had to be reconciled. It was critical that black citizens dialogue with white citizens on a level of honesty, and that black citizens withdraw their support from social and economic structures that were oppressive. But a successful movement requires white citizens to change in fundamental ways, and fear and race baiting are not conducive to constructive change. The advocates of Black Power had failed to master their own fears. With their posturing, they could trigger polarization but not genuine social change. But it was easy for the media to glamorize Black Power advocates. They were often handsome, charismatic, articulate; perhaps most important they posed no threat to business as usual in America. If anything, many of their tactics wound up contributing to the racial division rather than eliminating it.

After the Meredith march, Victoria Gray, one of the founders of the Mississippi Freedom Democratic Party called with the news that Charles Evers, the brother of Medgar Evers, was in jail in Natchez and would I please come. I flew into the little airport and there were state troopers on the roof with machine guns; I got the distinct impression they were ready to use them. When I arrived at the church, it was full of crazy kids talking about how it was time to do battle and they didn't have so much as a stick to throw. It was a highly volatile situation, people were feeling very passionate and emotional, but a march into those machine guns would have been suicidal. I had to find a way to express all that anger and frustration and get the crowd under my control, so I gave a speech that made Malcom's speeches sound like those of an Uncle Tom. By first validating their anger, I was able to convince the crowd not to march and persuaded people to go home and let the lawyers get Evers out of jail. I called Martin, extremely proud of myself. But, to my chagrin, the *New York Times* reported my speech as the birth of a "new militant voice" in the civil rights movement, just the opposite of what I was trying to do. That was just "preaching" not policy. Sometimes militant preaching was necessary to keep policy and strategy moderate and rational.

As soon as the Meredith march was over we returned full-time to Chicago to intensify our campaign there. Mayor Daley and his political machine, including his black lieutenants and field soldiers, were then taking the position that they were as interested in abolishing slums and improving conditions for the underprivileged as we were. In fact, they intimated they would take care of everything if we would just get lost. Daley controlled the city as it had never been controlled before or since, and he had a strong organization in the predominantly black South Side, which did help assure certain minimal services for the local population—if, of course, you played ball with his team. But despite all the promises, there were never any substantive changes. In the Chicago political gumbo, black electoral strength wasn't strong enough to demand meaningful change for those who most needed it; under the Chicago system of political patronage the people on the bottom rung were simply ignored.

Our problem was how to find a way to force the Daley machine and the Chicago establishment to get moving. But it was tricky: we had to create momentum without getting tied up in partisan politics. As Martin said, "We're not anti-Daley, we're anti–economic and political injustice." But walking such a tightrope was difficult, because many of the leaders and organizations in the Chicago movement coalition clearly were anti-Daley, even if they were also genuinely concerned about the issues affecting the poor and disenfranchised of the city. Al Raby, the head of CCCO, who invited us to Chicago, would eventually wrest city hall away from the remnants of the Daley machine with the election of Harold Washington, Chicago's first and only black mayor.

Bayard Rustin's warning about the complexity of Chicago politics was becoming ever more relevant. Many factions within CCCO, which was a coalition of organizations with differing agendas, were unalterably opposed to Daley. SCLC could not take on responsibility for running Richard Daley out of Chicago, and we weren't sure we wanted to, even if it were possible. Despite the hostility to Daley in CCCO, there was a lot to admire in Daley's political operation, especially compared to the political dispensation in other big cities. Blacks in Chicago had relatively more access to the political machinery compared to black communities in New York or Los Angeles during the sixties. People like black Congressmen Ralph Metcalfe and William Dawson had helped to build Daley's political machine and Daley's ability to place Illinois in the Democratic column on election day had given the country John Kennedy and helped to solidify the Johnson landslide. In fact, one of SCLC's most successful fund-raisers had been held in Chicago with the sponsorship of Mayor Daley and Mahalia Jackson: SCLC took home virtually all the money that was contributed. Daley and his operatives actually persuaded vendors not to charge us for expenses. This was not the kind of thing Martin forgot.

In short, Richard Daley was no Bull Connor, so it was frustrating to me when CCCO leaders tried to tar Daley with that brush. Martin would explain, "The truth is, if *I* were mayor of Chicago, it would take me at least ten years to make an impact on many of these problems." Daley had become the symbol of all that was wrong with big cities, when he had been relatively effective in managing the competing interests of an ethnically and economically diverse city. To really find the source of slums, urban decay, and joblessness one had

to look beyond Daley to the postwar federal policies that were draining the cities of resources and funneling them to the suburbs.

While we pursued housing equity in Chicago, my own house in
Atlanta was becoming overcrowded. Our three-bedroom, one-bath
home was often overflowing with visitors, and when my or Jean's
parents came to visit, we had to give them our bedroom and sleep on
the living room couch. Our three girls were becoming too large to
bathe together in the one tub, and they were becoming modest about
sharing the bathroom at all, which was beginning to make mornings
impossible.

As in Chicago, blacks in Atlanta were artificially hemmed in,
prevented by custom, real estate practices, and restrictive covenants
from moving into the more spacious neighborhoods that many
Atlanta blacks could afford. One such area was on Peyton Road in
southwest Atlanta. White homeowners on Peyton Road were so
determined to prevent blacks from buying homes in the neighborhood that they built a wall across the street near what is now Martin
Luther King, Jr. Drive. North of the three-foot-high wall, black construction companies had built lovely homes on large wooded lots for
members of Atlanta's black elite. As the white landowners intended,
the wall had the effect of preventing anyone from driving directly
from the nearest black neighborhood down Peyton Road; but it also
deprived white Peyton Road residents from a quick route downtown.

The wall was an embarrassment for the "City Too Busy to
Hate," and it became fashionable to hold vigils at the wall, singing
freedom songs and praying. The media called it Atlanta's Berlin Wall.
One afternoon, I rode with my family out to the wall and the girls sat
on top of the wall singing freedom songs and kicking their feet. We
felt no danger, or even apprehension. City leaders were so embarrassed by the negative publicity about the wall that it soon came
down. Meanwhile, real estate companies and developers discovered
that desegregation could be profitable as white flight created markets
for new homes in the suburbs.

The undeveloped acres on Peyton Road were soon available
through black real estate companies, and I approached a friend,
Atlanta businessman T. M. Alexander, about a lot. Once we identified one, we needed a house to go on it and T. M. introduced me to a
young white architect, Paul Muldawer. Paul and I met at T. M.'s Red
Carpet Car Wash, a car wash so clean and modern my daughters
considered it a treat to go there after church and watch the car go
through. I stretched out on the floor of T. M.'s carpeted office and

Paul and I sipped a glass of wine, while I fantasized about Jean's and my dream house.

Before long, Paul returned with floor plans of a house that was perfect for the particular needs of my family. Then the problem became how to pay for it. The house would cost forty-two thousand dollars to build, and we would have to finance the construction while still paying the mortgage on our present home. We just did not have enough money.

Jean and I began to drive through the once-forbidden neighborhoods south of Peyton Road looking at the roomy, brick ranch homes out there. Realtors had discovered "blockbusting" and it was opening new neighborhoods to black families. There was a tremendous pent-up demand for housing among Atlanta's well-educated middle-class black community, and many blacks were eager to move into all-white areas if it meant more space for their families. Realtors could exploit this by informing white neighbors that a black family had moved to their block. Sometimes, one phone call was all it would take and the realtor had two more houses to sell. The speed at which neighborhoods turned from all white to majority black was astonishing. White families fled southwest Atlanta neighborhoods in fear of the black lawyers, doctors, teachers, and other professionals who were moving in. More and more Sunday afternoons, our family drove leisurely through the winding, hilly streets looking at the houses behind "for sale" signs.

In Chicago, SCLC and CCCO were continuing to search for strategies to help bring attention to the issues of poverty and inadequate housing. We decided to declare Sunday, July 10, 1966, "Freedom Day." It would be marked by a massive rally at Soldier Field, then a march downtown to pin on the door of Chicago City Hall ninety-six demands for comprehensive improvements, which Martin called his ninety-six "theses," evoking Martin Luther's historic act nailing his Ninety-five Theses on the door of the Wittenberg castle church in 1517, which marked the beginning of the Protestant Reformation.

We were quite aware that pressuring the city to at least acknowledge there were major problems in Chicago would be a new test of the reach of the nonviolent protest movement, particularly now that Stokely Carmichael and other advocates of Black Power were receiving a great deal of attention and comment in the wake of the Meredith march. We were hearing the criticism in the national press, from SNCC and CORE, and in Chicago itself, that our methods of bringing issues to the fore were "outdated" and that a more militant approach was now required. Of course, it was never specified exactly which more militant tactics would be effective in the situation we were facing in Chicago, or what exactly militant tactics had accomplished thus far.

The rally at Soldier Field on July 10 was moderately successful. About thirty thousand people showed up; we had hoped for more. Mahalia Jackson sang, and Dick Gregory and many other nationally known performers participated. Martin spoke with his unique combination of passion and thoughtfulness. Then we set off on our march to city hall. But it was a scorching day—in the high nineties—and Martin could not withstand the heat. He rode part of the distance, then rejoined the march at city hall, thus drawing criticism from some folks. Martin pinned his "theses" on the door of city hall, and the next day he met with Daley, who acted as if he was being extremely put upon and promised nothing.

However, on Tuesday, July 12, Mayor Daley's calm and confidence was shattered when violence broke out in the black community. Once again a small incident started the trouble. A common practice by youth, black or white, in poor urban areas on hot summer days is to unplug the fire hydrants, thereby creating a refreshing sprinkler that can provide some relief from the oppressive heat. Chicago tenements were as hot and airless in summer as they were cold and drafty in winter. The streets offered little shade and, unlike suburban lawns, tenements do not routinely require a hose and sprinkler. The fire hydrant was the sprinkler. A group of black kids on the South Side opened a fire hydrant and the police turned it off. As soon as the police were out of sight, the kids opened the hydrant again. This time the police rushed over to turn the water off and roughed up the kids. The kids started throwing rocks and within a few hours the sounds of children playing in the street had become a full-scale riot of resentment and boiling rage.

We were meeting in the West Side Organization headquarters, just a few blocks away from the site of the original incident, so we arrived at the scene just a matter of minutes after the trouble began. The black youths involved had gathered in a nearby park and the police had moved two blocks away to wait for backup. During this lull in the fighting we were able to talk with some of the kids. Their complaint was not just that the police had harassed them for turning on the fire hydrant, but that right across Roosevelt Boulevard they could see white kids playing in a fire hydrant unmolested. When they pointed this out to the officer he merely said that was not his beat.

The injustice of the situation was what had moved the kids to start the rock throwing, and soon every hothead in the neighborhood was getting in on the action. One young man, clearly crazy, stood by, preaching from the Bible about this being the beginning of the Lord's wrath and the Day of Judgment. He urged the kids to "burn down this Babylon." We tried to get the police to come into the park and take him into custody: he obviously needed help. His rantings were oil on flames. But their strategy was not to prevent further violence, only to contain it. They were willing to let this four-square-block area be destroyed in the hopes of isolating the rioting to one area. However, while they may have had the kids isolated and in view, their older brothers were elsewhere and angry about the total disregard the police had shown for children trying to cope with the heat. The big brothers knew the alleys better than the police did, and once they got worked up, they escaped the cordoned-off area and began to spread the fires of destruction.

We had hoped the movement would channel frustrations away from violence that summer. We knew the prime victims of such explosions were always the helpless in the black community. We also knew we would be blamed for the riot by the city and the press, and we were. Burnings and looting continued for two days, during which 2 people lost their lives, 56 were injured, and 282 arrested; Governor Otto Kerner called out the Illinois National Guard. Fortunately, Mayor Daley, after publicly charging us with abetting the disturbances, held a meeting with Martin, during which he asked that we help calm the situation. Daley also announced a few cosmetic concessions, such as setting up temporary swimming pools in the troubled area.

After the rioting, gangs like the Blackstone Rangers were vowing revenge against the police, but after a protracted meeting with Martin, and with our core staff diligently working with them, especially Bevel and James Orange, even the Rangers saw that continued violence would be counterproductive. They, along with our staff, deserve far more credit than the National Guard for bringing the situation under control.

That summer was a study in extremes as I went from watching riots in Chicago to strolling the boulevards of Paris. The United Church of Christ Board for Homeland Ministries continued to support my work with SCLC and pass through the grant for the citizenship schools, which were now run by Dorothy Cotton. Through the UCC, I was selected to serve on the board of the Programme to Combat Racism of the World Council of Churches. The board was meeting that summer at Chateau de Bossey just outside of Geneva and I insisted that Jean go with me. We hadn't been to Europe together since our college work camp experience. My parents came to Atlanta to stay with the girls. At the WCC gathering, I met for the first time Sam Nujoma, the leader of the SWAPO liberation movement, who is today the president of Namibia, and Jose Chipenda of Angola, who is now the general secretary of the All-Africa Council of Churches.

Jean and I returned to the United States by way of Paris and I followed her around to the art museums that she adored. The museums were probably the only thing Jean missed about New York. We were café-hopping and window-shopping when Jean saw a blue and green silk scarf that she admired. I urged her to go inside and look at it, but when she picked up the scarf she saw that it cost the equivalent of sixteen dollars. "It's too expensive," she declared. "Jean, let me get it for you. When will you have a chance to buy a genuine Parisian scarf?" But she hated to spend money on herself and she refused to buy it. I bought the scarf anyway. In our modest pension Jean fussed and fumed about the scarf, "I could feed our family for a week on sixteen dollars!" I would not take the scarf back, though. "Jean, our family is going to eat, even if you have a scarf from Paris." She was still mad about that scarf, but she kept it long after she had designer silk scarves from all over the world.

Back in Chicago, despite the housing accomplishments and the now proven status of our organizational abilities, we still weren't getting anywhere. Our method had always been to use our marches to make a clear point to the nation, and we decided it was time to design marches that would point up the rigid neighborhood segregation, not only racially, but ethnically. Chicago had a functional policy of "ethnic purity" taken to an extreme. The initial stage of integration of all-white neighborhoods that I experienced in Jamaica, Queens, when we lived there in the late fifties wasn't even being thought about in Chicago. Blacks were simply not allowed to see or apply to purchase homes in all-white neighborhoods—a system with which the real estate agencies colluded. There were blacks who lived in Chicago who had never seen areas other than the South Side and downtown, and they feared entering areas where no blacks lived. Once, a black youth had wandered into the all-white Chicago suburb of Cicero in search of a job without realizing the danger. When darkness came and he was still there he was accosted by a gang and beaten to death. On another occasion, efforts by a black family to purchase a home in Cicero resulted in a full-scale riot.

We therefore decided to institute a series of marches into the all-white "forbidden" area bordering the South Side to bring this pattern of housing discrimination into the open. Mayor Daley himself lived in a rigidly all-white area, as did all the whites in Chicago city government. By holding the marches we were in effect violating a gentleman's agreement between white and black politicians: the control of ethnic areas and de facto recognition of their existence had never been challenged in Chicago political life. In fact, all-white areas were segregated even amongst themselves into rigid ethnic neighborhoods formed by the European immigrant groups who had come over during the late-nineteenth and early-twentieth centuries. Even crossing these borderlines might mean serious peril for the transgressor, and we knew that.

Our decision to undertake the open housing marches met with considerable criticism from some of the members of the Chicago coalition. They felt it was impractical to concentrate on opening up the possibility of purchasing homes in all-white areas because few blacks would be financially able to avail themselves of such opportunities in any case. They believed we should concentrate instead on improving conditions in the black ghetto and forget about open housing.

We knew we had to do both. Our rent strike and housing programs were designed to improve conditions in the ghetto, though such improvements were admittedly slow in coming and confined to only a few housing units. But such improvements were doomed to be even slower unless we found ways to get the message across about the existence of racial discrimination in all aspects of Chicago's housing. Until our efforts in effect touched the white power structure where they lived, we would never be able to force the city to acknowledge improvements were needed and to develop programs to rectify the situation.

We also realized that we had to assume full responsibility for forcing a crisis: we weren't going to receive any assistance from President Lyndon Johnson and his administration in Chicago otherwise. The president's relationship with the Chicago Daley machine and his stronghold in the Midwest were formidable obstacles indeed. Since we had come to Chicago we were definitely feeling the cold shoulder from the White House. When Martin asked for federal protection after the teargassing and beatings in Canton during the Meredith march, he hardly even received a reply from the Justice Department. And during the previous month, when the White House had held an expensive, well-publicized conference on civil rights called "To Secure These Rights," Martin had been invited to attend, but not to speak, although Roy Wilkins, Whitney Young, and Thurgood Marshall, then solicitor general, addressed the meeting. Amazingly, the conference on civil rights was held, and all the progress of the 1960s discussed, with no mention made of Martin or SCLC.

In this new climate of increased criticism from within the black coalition and outright coldness from the federal government, we made the mistake of holding our large housing discrimination marches on weekends. Our incursion into the "forbidden" areas on days when all the neighborhood residents were home gave them the perfect opportunity to amass hostile crowds to greet us, the likes of which we did not fully anticipate. It was just insane; folks charged the police in an attempt to get at us, even though the police were often from the same neighborhoods as the people who were hurling curses, bricks, and bottles at us.

If I had to choose the march I would most like to forget, it would be the one through Chicago's Gage Park on August 5, 1966. About ten thousand screaming people showed up to harass, curse, and throw debris on us that Sunday, aided and abetted by crazies from the American Nazi Party and similar folk. At one point I was walking just ahead of Martin when I was called to the rear of the line for something. I asked someone to march in front of Dr. King while I ran to the back for a second. No sooner had I taken a step or two than a bottle came flying through the air, hitting the man I had placed in front of Martin in the face. Bottles were flying and cherry bombs were going off. We felt like we were walking through a war zone. Thirty years later, seeing some of that film footage still frightens me. It seems bizarre and unreal. But this was America. In the "enlightened" North.

During another such march, when we finally returned to our starting point, we discovered our cars had been completely destroyed. The Ford I had rented had been set afire and rolled into a lake. All I could see was the tail end of my car sticking up out of the water. We didn't know how we were going to get out of there. Fortunately, the police sent for buses, and we were able to escape under heavy police guard. Even so, the buses were showered with bricks and other debris as we were leaving. It was a lynch mob howling for blood, one worse and more frightening than what we had encountered in St. Augustine or Mississippi. I expected such behavior in the South, but it was a surprise, and an ominous sign, to find such vicious animosity in the North.

We were realizing along with the rest of the country that the movement had passed the stage of easy solutions. Integrating lunch

counters and waiting rooms did not require whites to sacrifice anything, except maybe some of their prejudices. Genuine school integration, housing integration, and employment opportunity for poor
blacks was going to require real sacrifices. For instance, to equalize
the spending on white and black students, either spending on white
students would have to come down or taxes would have to be raised
to increase spending on black students. Jobs and unions in Chicago
were not just racially exclusive, but they were often dominated by
certain white ethnic groups who risked a loss of their corner on political power. Housing was perhaps the most threatening issue. For
most Americans, their home is the most important investment they
make; it is their major asset, it represents most of the wealth they
have to pass on to their children. In the well-kept streets of Chicago's
working-class white neighborhoods, blacks were synonymous with
slums. They believed that if blacks moved in, it would result in the
destruction of their neighborhoods, their way of life. Sadly, such fears
and prejudices by white homeowners and real estate agents often
became self-fulfilling prophecies.

Violent eruptions in the cities seemed to be everywhere during
the summer of 1966: riots broke out in the black sections of Cleveland, Dayton, Newark, and forty other cities across the nation. Discussions about civil rights in the media and within the black community seemed to be hung up on the inevitability of violence as an
expression of social and racial conflict. Talk about violence, and the
fear of it, was shifting emphasis away from the basic issues of social
and economic inequities that lay beneath the outbreaks, and eclipsing
the need to derive methods to combat these inequities. For those who
did not wish to see change come, the emphasis on violence was most
convenient, for it provided an easy excuse for championing the status
quo, and brought about tougher police responses to any form of
social protest. Even Martin was accused of violence. Behind his back
people said, "He says he believes in nonviolence, but violence follows
him everywhere he goes," as if Martin could be held responsible for
the actions of those who opposed and vilified him.

In mid-August we announced we would not be deterred or discouraged by the threat of violence and the assaults in Gage Park. We
would hold a march in the feared all-white Chicago suburb of
Cicero. It was ultimately this threat that drove Mayor Daley to establish a negotiating conference at Palmer House, consisting of seventy-
nine participants who represented key organizations in Chicago's
social, political, and racial life.

Once again Martin's decision to enter the negotiating process was roundly criticized by other black leaders. There was little glory in negotiations. The idea of the proposed march in Daley's backyard thrilled some of the younger militants; they wanted to cross those boundaries uninvited. Martin, on the other hand, wanted to use the threat of the march to force Mayor Daley and the real estate agencies to make a commitment toward open housing.

The "summit agreement" of August 26 was signed as a result of the Palmer House meetings and included commitments by the city's Real Estate Commission to carry out a fair and open housing policy and establish a process to investigate complaints. There were no guarantees on implementation, but we felt we had taken a significant step forward. For the first time, they had acknowledged a pattern of injustice in Chicago housing practices and had promised to do something about it. Viewed from the perspective of the mid-1990s, when the memory of strict housing discrimination has nearly faded away, it should be said that the Chicago agreement was far more advanced than it may now seem. We felt we had done well, considering the tremendous pressure we were under in Chicago. We had been attacked by the mayor, who resorted to the courts in an attempt to halt our marches and rent strikes, by local and state politicians who denounced us, by the national media, which treated us as if we were presumptuous to attempt a campaign in Chicago in the first place, and by Archbishop John Cody, who was the leader of the populous and wealthy Diocese of Chicago and was the most powerful Catholic clergyman in America. Within the Chicago coalition there were also attacks by CORE and, of course, by the Chicago chapter of SNCC. The Chicago coalition groups did reunify for a moment behind the idea of a Cicero march, but when we canceled the march upon signing the agreement, SNCC and CORE were vociferous in their opposition.

Settlements are never popular. SNCC didn't support the Civil Rights Act of 1964, since its failure to prohibit interference with civil rights workers fell short of their ideals. Negotiations demanded compromise on all sides, even ours. But when people marched and chanted for months on end, "Do you want your freedom? Oh Yeah! Do you want it now? Oh Yeah! Naaa, Naa, Naa Naa Naaa, Naa, Freedom NOW!" it was easy to lose sight of the modest goals that began the campaign.

The reconciliation and negotiation process was the aspect of SCLC and Dr. King's nonviolent approach that even our supporters least understood. The settlement was always less than people needed. It was less than they deserved. I understood that it was hard to see value in compromise with a power structure that had caused so much pain in the black community. But compromise and reconciliation were essential phases of a successful movement.

Almost inevitably, the coalition splintered over the settlement. Some members of CCCO declared they would go ahead and march in Cicero without us, thereby effectively destroying whatever negotiating value there was in the threat of a massive unified march. Martin understood that a march in Cicero was more effective as a threat than as a reality. He wanted to continue to hold out the march on Mayor Daley's neighbors as leverage over implementation of the agreement. In order to restrain the dissenters, Martin assured them that the march to Cicero was only postponed.

While we tried to settle housing problems in Chicago, my housing situation in Atlanta took a dramatic turn for the worse. The Federal Highway System was digging up the earth around my Atlanta neighborhood and all the construction disturbed rats living in the ground. Soon they began to invade our house—one night I looked out of the kitchen window and saw a big rat calmly eating peaches that had fallen from the tree in my backyard. That was it. We moved to a brick ranch house on a 1.5-acre lot. Jean wanted a living room facing the garden and no grass, as it had been years since she'd seen me with a lawn mower. We found a four-bedroom house that met those criteria and had three bathrooms—one per daughter.

Later that fall, the SCLC staff met on retreat at Frogmore outside of Savannah to assess the movement in Chicago and attempt to resolve some of the ongoing staff conflicts. The meeting did not go well. Hosea, who had favored the move to Chicago, complained that the South was being neglected. Jesse and Bevel teamed up against Hosea, defending the achievements in the Chicago movement. Martin was calm during the sessions, but privately chastised me for not staying on top of the multiplicity of staff issues. We were all exhausted. Martin had conceived of a pilgrimage of five thousand people to the Holy Land, the largest such trip in recent memory. In addition to monitoring the Chicago movement, managing the negotiations, and giving oversight to SCLC's other projects, I was responsible for the Holy Land tour. I was carrying a heavy load and criticism from Martin was the last thing I needed.

I left the Frogmore meeting early, and Fred Bennett drove me to the Savannah airport to catch an evening flight to Atlanta. Jean and I would meet there and fly to Israel the next day. I waved Bennett away, telling him he didn't have to wait for me, and went to the rest room. The next thing I knew I was stretched out on the cold, damp tile of the bathroom floor with Bennett standing over me. I had just passed out.

After assuring himself that I was fully conscious, Bennett contacted Jean to let her know what had happened so that she could be sure to meet me at the gate. I traveled so frequently that our usual arrangement was that she would meet me at the curb outside of baggage claim. Despite my protestations that I was really fine, Bennett saw me to my seat on the airplane and secured promises from the flight attendants that they would keep an eye on me during the flight. There was no thought of staying in Savannah. If I really needed medical attention, I was better off in Atlanta.

Jean met me at the airport with Dr. Jim Palmer, an internist who was one of Atlanta's "movement" doctors. The "movement" doctors typically treated movement activists for little or no charge. SCLC did not provide health insurance, although I had it through Jean's employer and the United Church of Christ. My brother Walter's dental practice in Louisiana was also a resource for the movement, providing dental care for the activists in the South.

Jean's brow wore a deep frown, more than her usual concerned expression. Jim Palmer's round, fair-skinned face was typically pleasant and belied no anxiety about my condition. In a matter-of-fact way I was hustled over to Holy Family Hospital for a full examination. I decided I might as well let Jim and Jean take charge, since I had had my fill of arguments at the SCLC meeting. Jim found nothing wrong with me and approved my trip to Israel. He said, "Andy, given the schedule you've been keeping, a trip to Israel counts as a vacation. R and R is the best prescription I can give."

The next day, Jean and I flew to Tel Aviv, where I was to negotiate arrangements for a five-thousand-person pilgrimage to the Holy Land conceived by Martin and Dr. Sandy Ray, a prominent Baptist minister in New York City. Israel alone lacked sufficient hotel space to accommodate a tour of this scale, and I had to drive to Jordan to make arrangements there as well. I negotiated with both sides for the opening of the Mandelbaum Gate in Jerusalem and to allow our party to pass between Israel and Jordan through Jerusalem. I found officials in the Israeli and Jordanian tourism offices to be highly receptive to our plans. Both Israel and Jordan agreed to cooperate to build an amphitheater on the Sea of Galilee, where Martin would preach from the water. This tour would bring a great deal of money to both countries so they had good reason to be agreeable.

Martin and Sandy Ray's notion of it was that the economics of the Middle East would require Jews and Arabs to work together. If we could demonstrate the tourist potential of this pilgrimage, that was the best way to heal some of the wounds. I believe that a pilgrimage of five thousand led by Martin Luther King could have changed the history of the region by demonstrating how much everyone had to gain by working together, but it was not to be. The first Egyptian jets were shot down over Gaza the day we left Tel Aviv, and the Six Day War in June 1967 ended all hopes of a five-thousand-person tour to the Holy Land.

That was my first experience in the Middle East. When I became U.S. Ambassador to the United Nations more than a decade later, people accused me of being naive about that region's ancient conflicts. However, I understood very well the depth of the hatred and bitterness between Jews and Palestinians. But I also understood that they would have to learn to live together as brothers or perish together as fools.

Before I left Frogmore, the SCLC staff resolved to continue Operation Breadbasket and the Movement to End Slums and to push for increased voter registration. As a rule, registration in Chicago required a trip downtown, and the local Democratic Party seldom held well-publicized voter registration drives among black Chicagoans. In addition, Bob Greene and Stoney Cooks came to Chicago and developed a literacy and job placement program. They trained around a thousand unemployed residents of Chicago and helped them find jobs, putting us in direct competition with Daley's machine. Daley wanted all patronage to come through his organization and he found ways to undermine SCLC's literacy and job placement efforts. We obtained federal grants for our job-training programs, and despite our success rate, the grants were not renewed.

Meanwhile, it was clear that the Chicago machine had enough registered voters for its purposes and was not inclined to encourage additional registration. In our canvassing of the neighborhoods and other organizational work, we discovered that few of the tenants in the rundown slums of Chicago were registered voters. Voter education workshops had been a regular part of the Chicago movement as we trained people to take more control over their own lives, but now it was time to actually get people registered. We sought permission from the Cook County Registrar for off-site voter registration using deputy registrars. We were assigned January 30, 1967.

We set up registration sites and volunteers canvassed neighborhoods around the sites informing residents of the date, time, and location of the nearest registration table. The organizers had taken care of every detail, save one. Snow began falling in the morning as we opened the voter registration sites at churches and other public places. Snow is no rarity in Chicago and we waited for folks to come out to register. But it soon became clear that this was no ordinary snowstorm. The snow was falling thick and steady and soon it reached my knees. At that point I remembered that Chauncey Eskridge's apartment was nearby and I had a key—Martin and other staff members often stayed there on trips to Chicago. The four volunteers with me were all women, two black and two white. "Let's get out of here," I told them. "I know where we can ride out the storm." The five of us walked the three or four blocks to Chauncey's apartment.

It was small, very spartan, with just two bedrooms and without even a television. There I was, snowed-in in this little apartment with four women who were very unhappy about the whole situation. They just didn't like each other and every attempt at civil conversation deteriorated into fretful complaints and general fussing. It was like Sartre's hell. Finally, I got a book and went into one of the bedrooms and closed the door for the rest of the night. In the morning, the snow had stopped and I was free. I could understand why people in Chicago were so afraid of Richard Daley. Even the weather seemed to be part of his organization.

Ultimately, the Daley machine and other big-city political organizations hurt themselves by keeping voting rolls low. It would have been far better for Chicago if blacks had been encouraged to register in large numbers and vote Democratic. Instead, the disenfranchisement of blacks was eating away at the cities as the suburbs were growing, and suburban voters were casting votes for antiurban candidates in state and national elections. The real enemy of the machine was not the black voter in Chicago, it was the downstate Republican voter, and in his shortsightedness, Daley contributed to the decline of Chicago's power and influence.

The right to vote in America began as a privilege of white, male property owners and many of the voting requirements that persist favor stable, middle-class property owners. Efforts have continued to make voting easier for all Americans, but especially for those who tend to be younger, more mobile, poorer, such as hourly workers who are easily discouraged by residency requirements and trips to the courthouse. The most recent success at easing voter registration was the enactment of so-called Motor Voter legislation in 1995. The legislation required states to provide voter registration at public agencies, such as driver's license bureaus, unemployment offices, and other locations. The law generated a great deal of controversy and complaints from the state about the potential for fraud and the extra paperwork that would be required, but virtually all complied. The two states that failed to conform to the law were Illinois and Mississippi, proving that old habits die hard.

Many commentators, both at the time and since, pronounced our Chicago campaign a failure. They concluded that we were effectively subverted by the Daley political machine, and hopeless in the face of the enormity of Chicago's problems, problems both explicit and subtle, and immensely difficult to address. In the South, segregation and overt racial discrimination were clear and visible targets; the problems in the North were more amorphous. How does one make real progress in addressing a range of social problems like poor housing, lack of economic opportunity, and inadequate political representation? The problems were so large, comprehensive, and intertwined.

Much of the disappointment expressed in our efforts, and in the summit agreement, had its roots in the unspoken expectation that out of this mire we could produce a miracle; that Chicago, after we left, would be changed forever. But by our interpretation, in Chicago we *were* successful in focusing national attention on urban problems that were plaguing all large American cities. In the mid-1960s there was no national policy devoted to addressing conditions of urban decay, though the Johnson administration's "War on Poverty" was a beginning in that direction. We knew instinctively that real change in a city like Chicago would take a long time. And we knew then as we know now that ultimately this work will have to be done by the people of Chicago themselves, by those who have a passionate commitment to the productive future of the city.

And, of course, many of the problems we brought to the surface in our Chicago campaign still persist thirty years later. Some of the specific programs the Chicago coalition initiated were both effective and innovative, and could have enormously positive results in today's Chicago. Operation Breadbasket, under the leadership of Jesse Jackson, achieved excellent results by bringing economic strength to the black ghetto over a period of several years following our Chicago campaign. Rent strikes, as a means through which otherwise impotent and impoverished tenants could deal with negligent landlords, were extremely effective when efficiently run. The same can be said for the Movement to End Slums, whereby tenants collectively purchased their own buildings. I continue to support the development of such programs. Rather than build public housing projects that encourage the dependence of tenants, we should enable poor people to buy their own homes. If people, however poor, have an investment in their own living space, they will seek to enhance its value.

Chicago marked a turning point for SCLC. Our work there forced Martin and me and other creative thinkers within our circle to concern ourselves more directly with the multifaceted implications of urban poverty and to direct our attention more pointedly to its underlying causes. We knew that poverty, abetted and supported by a history of oppression and discrimination, equaled powerlessness. From 1966 on, as an organization we would increasingly concentrate on ways to attack it at its roots. And more than ever before, Martin would lend his eloquence to the voice of the powerless, whether they were trapped in the cabins of the Mississippi Delta or the rundown tenements of Harlem, Watts, or Chicago.

By 1966, the walls of overt racial segregation in the South, encrusted with almost a century of regional law, had almost completely crumbled. These barriers, which marked and delineated the world I grew up in, were the first target of the civil rights movement. Now, as the outer crust of American racism and oppression was falling away, deeper, more recalcitrant patterns of discrimination lay exposed before us: the very nerve and bone structure of American racism. As Martin pushed forward, there was no way we could have anticipated the hostility he would encounter as he became an even more strident advocate for the economically and politically impoverished in America, and plunged into the bitter national debate over the war in Vietnam.

15

War and Poverty

Gonna lay down my burden, down by the riverside, ain't gonna study war no more.
— AFRICAN-AMERICAN SPIRITUAL

The war in Vietnam was a defining moment in American political history, leaving wounds as deep and lasting as the pain of thousands of parents who lost thousands of sons. Americans retain, even cherish, intensely emotional perspectives on the war, more than twenty years after the last American helicopter left Saigon. Our international policy is polarized between those who are ashamed that we lost the war and those who are ashamed that we fought it, and regardless of which side you are on, shame is the common denominator. America's posture in the world lurches between policies born of those two contradictory impulses.

Martin Luther King came to his position on Vietnam as he had come to his position on segregation, through an examination of his own heart, the teachings of Jesus Christ, and his commitment to nonviolence. The "just war" theology that Christian churches used to support World War II simply could not be stretched to cover the U.S. involvement in Vietnam. There was no Hitler, no clear aggressor in Vietnam, except for the colonial French, whose fallen banner the United States had taken up. Martin's opposition to the war was also grounded in the general principles of nonviolence. He had noted the destructiveness of war, without referring specifically to Vietnam, in his Nobel Peace Prize acceptance speech. War, poverty, and racism were increasingly linked as related evils in his speeches from 1965 on. Martin always believed the war in Vietnam was ill advised, and a classic illustration of America's misunderstanding of the worldwide drive for self-determination.

We watched along with the rest of America during 1965 and 1966, as hope after hope was dashed that the conflict in Southeast Asia would move toward peaceful negotiation. We hoped the administration would see that it was merely duplicating the mistakes of the French a decade earlier in Southeast Asia and not learning anything from their experiences. Instead of movement toward resolution, we witnessed escalation and a growing commitment of American personnel and equipment to the tar baby of Vietnam.

Despite his despair over American involvement in the war, Martin was conflicted about adding his voice to the growing criticism of our policy in Vietnam from both political and religious leaders. For one thing, it was only with the greatest reluctance that Martin would publicly criticize President Johnson. After all, it was Johnson who had steered home the civil rights legislation we had fought so hard for: the Civil Rights Act of 1965 and the Voting Rights Act of 1965. And by late 1966, with the backing of the federal government through the Justice Department, both were being enforced. Martin believed that Johnson was basically in our corner on the issue of equal justice for black Americans, despite the fact that most of the administration's actions were often unwilling responses to heavy pressure from direct-action campaigns.

There was also the belief held by most major black leaders, except perhaps those in SNCC and CORE, that the multifaceted objectives of the civil rights movement—correcting historic injustices in the South, addressing the problems in the cities that were exploding like time bombs throughout the nation, and counteracting a growing white backlash—all precluded them from criticizing the president on the war. In other words, they felt they could not at the same time be effective as both civil rights leaders and critics of American foreign policy. They had to choose between the two. Martin was repeatedly admonished by other black leaders who cautioned, "We need President Johnson. Now you're attacking him and making him our enemy." This also was no time, he was told, to test the cohesion of the already fragile coalition of civil rights organizations, particularly when the coalition was asking the federal government to allocate more money and attention to the needs of black communities.

In 1966, the civil rights movement and the growing peace movement were considered two different forces with two distinctly different constituencies. The peace movement, in the beginning, was primarily a movement of white radicals, a few black radicals, socialists
and leftists. The traditional civil rights movement was, in its leadership, basically middle-class, religious, black America, and its gains
were most meaningful to mainstream, upwardly mobile black Americans. In viewing these two movements as interrelated, Martin was
taking a departure from traditional civil rights thinking. But for more
than a year, Martin had been moving beyond the narrow field of the
traditional civil rights movement of the South. One of the first steps
in that direction had been our work in Chicago focusing on economic
issues, housing issues, and on broadening our vision to include the
cities of the North as well as the South. As a human being with a
keen social conscience, he could not ignore what was happening in
Vietnam, and he felt that speaking out against it was not only his
responsibility but a logical next step in unifying America's, and the
world's, downtrodden.

In Chicago, Martin began interjecting criticism of the war into
his speeches. At this point he did not accept invitations to participate
in peace demonstrations, but he often asked Coretta to appear in his
stead. She had joined Americans for a National Nuclear Policy in a
picket line in front of the White House in 1965, to express opposition to the war and urge negotiations to end the conflict. Coretta had
a long association with the peace movement, going back to her student days at Antioch College in Ohio, when she was active in
Women's Strike for Peace. Philosophically, Coretta was a pacifist. In
fact, her intellectual understanding of nonviolence and her deep personal commitment influenced Martin in the development of his own
views. Always a good speaker, she had maintained an active connection with the Women's Strike for Peace and possessed a thorough
knowledge of the issues and many of the personalities of the peace
movement. While it must be admitted that Martin was traditional in
his view of the role of women, it should also be recognized that in his
marriage to Coretta Scott, he chose an intellectual equal with her
own deeply held convictions.

Around the end of 1966, Martin began to make a definite turn
toward a public statement on the war. The SCLC board was uncomfortable with the issue of Vietnam, however. They requested that
Martin refrain from making further criticisms of the war, despite the
fact that for some time several members of the SCLC staff had participated in the peace movement, and that both SNCC and CORE had

endorsed strong antiwar positions. Jim Bevel in particular was becoming more and more obsessed with the need to speak out against the war in every way possible; in fact, as our work in Chicago became less important to him, the antiwar movement seemed to occupy his every thought. He was determined to persuade Martin not only to intensify his criticism of Johnson's Vietnam policy, but to assume an active leadership role in the American peace movement.

One winter's morning in Chicago, while we were planning our ill-fated voter registration day, Bevel burst in on me, trembling with excitement. "Andy," he said, "we have got to stop the war in Vietnam. We've got to. The Lord came to me and told me we've got to stop it."

"Calm down, Bevel," I told him. "Tell me what this is all about."

"Well," said Bevel, "last night I was in the laundry room in the basement of my building. You know, babies mess up a lot of clothes. When I looked up from loading diapers into the washing machine, there was the Lord, sitting on the dryer. I said, 'Lord, what have I done now.' And the Lord told me, 'James Bevel, my children are dying in Vietnam, my children are suffering. They are your brothers and sisters too. You must help them.' Then, he disappeared."

Bevel truly believed that he had seen a vision of Jesus Christ. Whether he actually received a holy visitation, Bevel felt that neither he nor Martin Luther King could take a stand for justice while ignoring the immoral nature of the war. Always one of SCLC's most innovative strategists, Bevel thought that we should gather a delegation of prominent Americans and go out in the Vietnam countryside, which was the target of the bombing raids. At that time the U.S. military was contemplating a bombing action that would destroy the dikes that enabled rice production in the Mekong Delta, erasing the efforts of centuries of civilization. To prevent this, he reasoned, perhaps optimistically, that the U.S. military wouldn't drop bombs on American citizens. But it is a testament to Bevel's brilliance that his suggestion anticipated a strategy that the peace activists would later use in Central America to protect the targets of death squads—accompaniment. During the war in El Salvador, courageous Americans would accompany leaders of the democracy movement who were targeted by right-wing death squads on the theory that the presence of an American would protect them.

I encouraged Bevel to talk directly to Martin, who was in Jamaica working on his book *Where Do We Go from Here?* Martin had already had conversations with Dr. Benjamin Spock, who had urged him to join the peace movement, and with a prominent Buddhist monk, Tric Na Han, who sent us excellent behind-the-scenes information about the war and general conditions in Indochina. Tric Na Han was an advocate of a third-force solution, explaining that it was not only the communists in South Vietnam who were against the Thieu-Ky regime, which he was convinced was not a popular one and was only able to remain in power because it was propped up by the American government. These conversations helped Martin to see the war as a very complicated political situation—certainly not the simplistic evil communist–good noncommunist framework presented by the State Department. While in Jamaica, Martin read books on the Vietnam conflict by Bernard Fall, the brilliant French-American critic of American Vietnam policy whose arguments were based on his research of the recent French catastrophe in Indochina. With the contingent of American combat troops in Vietnam increasing steadily and the intensified bombing of North Vietnam, which had begun in 1965, it was obvious that the American military effort was not de-escalating but snowballing, and that we were well along the road to repeating the mistakes of the French. For a man of faith, it was even more difficult to ignore the self-immolation of Buddhist monks, the most dramatic symbol of America's failure to comprehend Vietnam.

When Martin returned from Jamaica at the beginning of February 1967, his mind was made up. He would speak out against the war. "I'm not going to segregate my conscience," he said. When he was invited to be a keynote speaker at the huge mobilization against the war march scheduled for April 15 at United Nations Plaza in New York, he decided to accept.

I had no problem with Martin's, or anyone else's, opposition to the war. Had we been attacked by a foreign nation I would have felt differently: every nation, every people, every person has a right to self-defense. But the war in Vietnam was clearly not a war of self-defense. I believed then, and still believe, that if the issue at hand was the threat to American economic interests in Southeast Asia, these interests could have been much more successfully defended and preserved through aggressive diplomacy.

I also knew that within the black community, the war was creating a great deal of bitterness. Too many black families had seen their sons sign up for the military because they could not find jobs at home—either in rural areas of the South or in the cities of the North. They were being sent as foot soldiers to the front lines in Vietnam in disproportionate numbers, then returned in less than a year as corpses. To the black community, the war was doubly destructive; it drew attention away from chronic domestic needs, and it was a devastation upon black male youth. Those black youth who survived the war often returned maladjusted, ill-prepared psychologically to participate in society, and embittered, knowing they had sacrificed so much for a war that meant so little and returned to a country with no respect for them. Martin's decision to oppose the war was courageous, but it did not run counter to the prevailing sentiment in the black community. Negative attitudes toward the war were widely prevalent among blacks well before massive protests began. Few black leaders, however, were willing to come out and give public expression to such community sentiments for fear they would alienate the president and the federal government and be charged with a lack of patriotism.

My personal feelings about the war aside, though, at a meeting of our New York "kitchen cabinet" to discuss our participation in the spring antiwar mobilization campaign, I told Martin that I was uncomfortable with the mobilization committee as it was then constituted. In preparation for our participation, I had been to a meeting attended by all the component groups: Youth Against Fascism, several Socialist groups, and some Northern white radical groups. I came away greatly disturbed. There was simply too much confusion about the aims and tactics of the event and the only person there who seemed rational was the delegate from the Communist Party. I also told Martin I did not feel he should try to assume leadership of the antiwar movement. It was basically a Northern movement made up of Students for a Democratic Society (SDS) and various leftist groups whose tactics and overall orientation were different from ours. And I felt they were not all that appreciative of Martin's participation, even though they had invited him. Frankly, I felt they resented Martin, and I didn't trust them. I feared someone would deliberately do something to embarrass Martin, something much more destructive than our antagonists in SNCC would ever think of doing. Many of the young leftists were talking about bringing down the system. They saw Martin as a reformer—which he was—and they weren't interested in reforming the American system. They wanted to destroy it. Stan Levison agreed with my apprehensions. He always resented my calling him a conservative, but he was, in the true sense of the word—not ideologically but in his cautious manner of analyzing issues and tactics.

I said to Martin, "You're gonna get up there at the UN Plaza, trying to give a reasoned speech, and you'll find yourself speaking between Stokely Carmichael and somebody else. You're not gonna be able to get your points across. And there will be so many speakers you'll only have ten minutes. You can't say what you need to say the way you want to say it in ten minutes." I advised Martin that it would be better to deliver his initial statement against the war in a forum where we would have more influence. I was adamant that we not enter another rally over which we had no control. I said, "Listen, Martin, why don't you let me contact John Bennett [of Union Theological Seminary] and Rabbi Abraham Heschel [of Jewish Theological Seminary] and let them help us set up a forum for you." Dr. Bennett and Rabbi Heschel had formed a group called Clergy and Laity Concerned About Vietnam. Martin agreed.

I made the calls, Dr. Bennett and Rabbi Heschel responded with enthusiasm, and they set up a forum for April 4, 1967, at Riverside Church, the Protestant cathedral built by John D. Rockefeller and Harry Emerson Fosdick on the Upper West Side of Manhattan. Riverside was across the street from the Interchurch Center, the headquarters of the National Council of Churches. Once again, my connections with national religious organizations proved helpful. Martin would speak, followed by a panel discussion with Dr. Bennett, Rabbi Heschel, and historian Henry Steele Commager participating.

Martin's thoughtful Riverside Church speech was one of the finest and most important of his career. He began by saying he had made a decision to "break the betrayal of my own silences and to speak from the burnings of my own heart." He made it clear that he was addressing the concerned of his own nation, not Hanoi, the National Liberation Front of Vietnam, China, or Russia. He first addressed the detrimental effects of the war on the domestic struggle for social and economic reforms: "A few years ago there was a shining moment in the struggle. It seemed as if there was real promise of hope for the poor—both black and white—through the Poverty Program. . . . Then came the build-up in Vietnam and I watched the program broken and eviscerated as if it were some idle political plaything of a society gone mad on war, and I knew that America would never invest the necessary funds or energies in rehabilitation of its poor so long as adventures like Vietnam continued to draw men and skills and money like some demonic destructive suction tube." As for the black poor: "It was sending their sons and their brothers to die in extraordinarily high proportions relative to the rest of the population. We were taking the black young men who had been crippled by our society and sending them 8,000 miles away to guarantee liberties in Southeast Asia which they had not found in Southwest Georgia or East Harlem."

He discussed the negative effects of the war and reviewed the history of the Vietnam conflict in the light of the American refusal to work diligently for a negotiated settlement. He advised young men facing the draft to seek the "alternative of conscientious objection." And he reviewed the depressing process by which the American stance in Vietnam was producing widespread mistrust and hatred of our nation throughout the Third World, and among all peoples struggling for self-determination. "Such thoughts take us beyond Vietnam, but not beyond our calling as sons of the living God."

Martin concluded with a call for a cessation of the bombing of North Vietnam, the declaration of a cease-fire in an effort to induce negotiation, and the setting of a date for the removal of all foreign troops from Vietnam in accordance with the demands of the 1954 Geneva Agreement. "A nation," he warned, "that continues year after year to spend more money on military defense than on programs of social uplift is approaching spiritual death."

The media reaction to the Riverside Church speech was so hostile and acrimonious Martin was stunned. He was prepared for criticism and controversy within an atmosphere of debate, but not for the immediate and widespread condemnation from both the establishment and the black press that followed. The Riverside Church speech did dominate the news for a while, however, and contributed to the phenomenal success of the April 15 mobilization march and rally at the UN Plaza. I marched with Martin from Central Park down Fifth Avenue and across 42nd Street to UN Plaza. The crowd seemed to extend as far as the eye could see. I believe more than a million people demonstrated their opposition to the war in Vietnam that day. At that rally, Martin's speech was tremendously well received by the huge crowd. Basically, he used the same text he had delivered at Riverside, but at the UN Plaza Martin added some of his most memorable phrases: "The promises of the Great Society have been shot down on the battlefields of Vietnam. The bombs in Vietnam explode at home; they destroy the hopes and possibilities for a decent America." He added: "I am disappointed with our failure to deal positively and forthrightly with the triple evils of racism, extreme materialism, and militarism. We are presently moving down a dead-end road that can only lead to national disaster."

After these speeches, President Johnson and the White House wasted no time in pressuring black leaders to denounce Martin. Roy Wilkins of the NAACP and Whitney Young of the Urban League made particularly strong statements criticizing Martin's antiwar stance. They felt that Lyndon Johnson had done more for the black community than any modern president and should not be criticized for policies unrelated to civil rights. We believed that the Vietnam policy hurt the black community and Martin's criticism of the Vietnam policy was not intended to be a personal criticism of the president. Even leaders of the black clergy were called in an effort to get them to denounce Martin, though this effort was less successful. This campaign against Martin's Vietnam stance was managed by Louis Martin, a black former publisher on Johnson's White House staff. Louis Martin invited black publishers from all over the country to the White House, where they met with President Johnson. Johnson reportedly told them that King was misled and was following the lead of white leftists rather than his own black constituency. After the meeting the publishers came out against Martin and his position on Vietnam.

This greatly accelerated policy of White House–directed criticism of Martin followed a campaign by President Johnson just a few months earlier to persuade Martin and other civil rights leaders to support the administration's war policy. The president had asked Martin to meet with Arthur Goldberg, then U.S. Ambassador to the United Nations, ostensibly to discuss Vietnam from the perspective of the administration's inside knowledge. I went along with Martin to the meeting.

Goldberg strained to explain the administration's position that the policy was justified because there were North Vietnamese troops in South Vietnam; therefore, the North Vietnamese had violated the Geneva accords. But Martin believed that the Geneva Accord of 1960 had provided for a temporary separation of Vietnam that neither North nor South Vietnam had agreed to. The United States was supposed to reconvene the Geneva conference, but President Eisenhower had never done so. Goldberg went on to talk about how dangerous the Chinese were; Martin argued that Goldberg and the State Department should be communicating with the Chinese.

Not only did we remain unconvinced by this discussion, we came away with the impression that even Goldberg himself was not all that sure of the rightness of the war. After our meeting, Martin was asked a question by a reporter about the issue of our diplomatic nonrecognition of China. He responded that "eight hundred million people are not going to disappear because we refuse to admit their existence." This reply was about as understated as could be, but the press really went wild. These were the members of the press who covered national and diplomatic issues and knew Martin only superficially as a controversial black leader. International relations in the

1960s were largely the province of an elite club of upper-class white males. I think they were as surprised to find a Southern black preacher with strong and sophisticated opinions on international policy as by the opinions themselves.

Martin was extremely well versed on the facts and issues relating to the Vietnam conflict. In fact, my impression was that our information was better than Goldberg's. In addition to his own reading, Martin had received a thorough briefing from a Swedish journalist, Sven Oste, who had spent a month in South Vietnam and a month in North Vietnam. A Swedish superliberal, with the cynical edge common among experienced journalists, Sven had spent a month with us in Selma, so we felt confident that his research was thorough, and we trusted his political acumen. He gave Martin a briefing on what he termed the "ten commandments of Vietnam" and Martin took notes on the back of an envelope, which he kept with him for easy reference. Furio Colombo was an Italian journalist, now a member of the Italian parliament, who developed a prizewinning series on Vietnam for Italian television. We knew Furio from Birmingham and Albany, and he shared his insights on Vietnam with Martin.

At one point during this period Martin and Whitney Young attended a dinner at the home of a wealthy white philanthropist in Great Neck, Long Island, where they got into a terrible argument over the issue of Vietnam. Martin had been stung by Whitney's public criticisms of him, and told him so at the dinner. I was not present, but Martin told me later he said to Whitney, "I don't believe you have to say everything I say, or agree with everything I say. But I do expect you to defend my right to say it." Whitney got mad. He accused Martin of alienating the support of President Johnson, and so forth. They almost ended up in a shoving match after the dinner, and neither of them ever forgot it.

It was a difficult period for Whitney. I believe he had been tricked into supporting the administration, and he was in inner conflict over it. President Johnson had asked him to go to South Vietnam to certify an election, and he had gone. Meanwhile, his daughter, we heard, was on a hunger fast in opposition to the war, along with her fellow students at Bryn Mawr. Whitney's family, of course, was not alone in being enmeshed in internal conflict over this destructive and demoralizing war.

After Martin's Riverside Church and April mobilization speeches we noticed that the FBI surveillance and harassment, which had slacked off for a while, picked up again. Whenever we traveled we were aware of cars trailing us and the office phone was making suspicious noises, just as it had in 1964. In fact, very soon after our meeting with Goldberg, Walter Fauntroy received a call from someone who identified himself as a government worker. He said he had a file transcript of a conference call Martin had arranged with twelve staff members and supporters from New York to discuss the Vietnam War issue and our upcoming meeting with Goldberg. In the transcript was the name of everyone who participated in the call, with a biographical sketch of each person. So the informant was either someone in the FBI who was trying to intimidate us with his knowledge or someone who acted on his own conscience to warn us that our phones were being tapped, even on the road.

We tried a counterattack against the administration's pressure campaign. I organized a meeting of Southern black ministers in Atlanta to give Martin a platform at which to present his views on the war. We also requested that Martin be included among the speakers at the National Negro Publishers Association's annual meeting in Cleveland during the summer of 1967. This was especially important because Lyndon Johnson had invited the black press to the White House and encouraged them to denounce Martin. Martin King had always had an excellent relationship with John and Robert Johnson, the publisher and editor in chief, respectively, of Johnson Publishing Company. Bob Johnson and Lerone Bennett, the publishing company's house historian, were classmates of Martin's at Morehouse. Bob Johnson edited the weekly publication *Jet*, which was read by an estimated nine million black Americans. Between *Jet* and *Ebony*, the monthly picture magazine, Johnson publications were read in virtually every black community in the nation, and their coverage helped make it possible for the civil rights efforts to become a national movement. Because Bob Johnson knew Martin personally and trusted him, he was always open to Martin's view of an issue, and this was no exception.

With the assistance of Bob and John Johnson of *Jet* and *Ebony*, the black publishers were persuaded to allow Martin to address them at a luncheon during the convention. Martin explained the moral basis for his opposition to the Vietnam War and the impact the war had on the struggle to end poverty in the United States. His command of the facts and familiarity with all the issues turned the publishers completely around. In speaking before black groups, Martin always made it clear that his opposition to the war was not a result of his having been co-opted by the radical left. Rather, he explained that his decision to speak out was based on the damage the war and the sharply increased defense budget was doing to domestic programs intended to help all, and especially black Americans. He also stressed his strong moral and pacifist convictions. When Martin spoke about Vietnam before the black publishers' association without notes, revealing his detailed knowledge of the war, he made a strong impression. The black publishers had been told at the White House that Martin was misinformed, that his anti-Vietnam position was an indication that he was being influenced by communists and a lot of other foolishness. But in addition to Sven Oste and Furio Colombo there were several other European journalists supplying us with up-to-date information on Vietnam—and it was all contradictory to administration claims that we were "winning the war." Even the official body counts provided by the administration were in some dispute. We surmised President Johnson was being manipulated by his own military.

During the summer and fall of 1967, Martin was on fire with determination. He was argumentative and assertive, though sometimes even he would slip into depressions, almost reduced to tears by the stridency of the criticism directed against him. He was most hurt by the *Washington Post* and *New York Times* editorials. They didn't say he was wrong or that his criticisms were not well founded; they challenged his very *right* to take a position. They said he was a civil rights leader and didn't have any business talking about foreign affairs. He saw this as a racist attempt to confine him to a limited and acceptable role the establishment approved of. He sensed the risks he was taking in criticizing his own government, but he was determined to push his case. His hours were more ridiculous now than ever. He would stay up until two or three in the morning talking and arguing with us, and he carried forth his arguments on the war and on domestic conditions as strongly with us as with his critics. Among ourselves, we said, "Martin is not only waging a war on the war, he's waging a war on sleep." The situation became so bad I spoke to him about his deteriorating health and also spoke to Coretta and Stan Levison about it, encouraging them to plead with Martin to take better care of himself.

In early 1967, Martin had one of his last conversations with Lyndon Johnson. It was absolutely off-the-record and totally unplanned. We were in New York at the Americana Hotel. Martin was going on and on about the war to me, Bernard Lee, and one or two other people. Bernard got kind of tired of listening to him and said, "Listen, Martin, you don't need to tell us that. You need to tell that to President Johnson." Martin shot back testily, "You think I'm afraid to tell Johnson that? Well, I'm not." Then he started preaching to us about something else. "Well, then, I'll get him on the phone," Bernard muttered off-handedly, as he walked toward the bedroom. Martin wasn't paying any attention to Bernard and went right on talking. Bernard says he dialed the White House and told the operator, "Dr. King would like to speak to President Johnson." Usually, the White House would take a message and maybe someone would call back the next day. That night, after a short delay, Johnson himself came to the phone. Bernard came out and said, "All right, Martin, there he is." Martin said, "Who?" Bernard said, "President Johnson." Martin said, "What do you mean?" Bernard answered, "You wanted to tell the president about his war. Well, there he is waiting for you on the phone." So Martin had about a half-hour impromptu conversation with Johnson.

But Johnson seldom listened to anyone. When you met with him, *you* listened. Johnson's defense of his position was that he was a moderate in his own administration. "Some of these generals want to bomb Vietnam right up to China and end it all," he said. He said he needed Martin's support and the support of the civil rights establishment to help him keep the generals under control. But as Martin remarked later, "We have to keep pressure on *Johnson* to make sure he remains a restraining force on the generals. That's what I intend to do."

I later learned the extent of Lyndon Johnson's bitterness toward us as his presidency became mired in the morass of the war. Many years after, I heard from someone who was close to Johnson that the president, in a despairing mood, blamed Martin for his troubles, and was overheard fuming in the White House about "Martin Luther King, that goddamned nigger preacher."

Of course, we didn't know all that then. If Johnson had decided to run for reelection in 1968, Martin probably would have supported him, with the proviso that he begin looking immediately for a diplomatic solution in Vietnam. It wasn't Martin and those in the peace movement who brought down the president. Johnson fatally injured himself through his mistaken belief there could ever be a victory in Vietnam without our destroying ourselves and everything we were supposed to stand for.

Martin did, in my opinion, enhance the respectability of the peace movement. All the noise Whitney Young, Roy Wilkins, and others made in support of the administration could not negate either the logic or the effect of Martin's criticism. This was particularly the case within the black community. Every American war during the twentieth century had won the general support of the black community, which had rendered willingly and uncritically the sacrifice of its children's lives only to discover afterward that there was little improvement in the general condition for blacks at home, despite our support and sacrifices. The experience Hosea Williams had at the water fountain in southwest Georgia was only one of thousands of such incidents. I thought at the time that the war in Vietnam squandered capital that could have been directed to the War on Poverty. In fact, federal tax policies and economic growth in the Johnson era provided sufficient revenue for him to pay for the war in Vietnam and the War on Poverty. It was moral capital that we squandered in Vietnam, more precious and more difficult to accumulate than money.

The pivotal year for Lyndon Johnson's presidency was 1965. That year, he signed a Voting Rights Act, which committed this nation to protecting the franchise for all Americans, and he signed Medicare into law, which provided health care for the elderly. But the decision to bomb Vietnam and commit U.S. combat troops also took place in 1965. Just as World War II had put an end to Roosevelt's plans to extend the New Deal, the expansion of the war in Vietnam drained Johnson's political, fiscal, and moral resources for enacting his ambitious and badly needed Great Society programs for education, health care, protection of the environment, jobs, civil rights, and urban development. On domestic policy, Lyndon Johnson was a great president. He exhibited tremendous moral courage on the issues of race and poverty in America. His political skills were phenomenal. But neither he nor his closest advisers could comprehend the real meaning of the war in Vietnam and the aspirations of the Vietnamese people. Had he refused to escalate the Vietnam War, I believe Lyndon Johnson would have been elected president in 1968 and fulfilled his Great Society agenda. Instead, Senator Eugene McCarthy ran in the New Hampshire primary as the antiwar candidate and did well enough against Johnson that Robert Kennedy, by then a senator from New York, entered the race. Even so, I believe Johnson would most likely have won the Democratic nomination had he not withdrawn. And while I would have preferred Robert Kennedy as president, I would have supported Johnson as the Democratic nominee.

As President Johnson concentrated his energies on the war in Vietnam, Martin's concern over the continuing crisis in the cities increased. There were twenty-one major riots in 1966 and another seventy-five riots in 1967. Despite the progress in ending segregation laws, despair was growing among blacks in the urban centers, and our experience in Chicago left us with no illusions about the complexity of the problems. These problems had been exacerbated by federal policies, and it would require several policies in order to solve them. Two decades of federal policies had encouraged a drain of jobs and resources from the old central cities to the suburbs. Federal highway construction, water projects, and home loan programs subsidized the middle-class flight. In the rural areas, agricultural crop subsidies, soil banks, and tax breaks for mechanization sharply and steadily reduced the demand for farm labor and sent the unskilled, rural poor to the cities in search of jobs that were no longer there. In Birmingham and Selma we had been able to dramatize the issue of segregation and voting rights to move the nation to action, but we struggled to do same for the problem of urban poverty.

Martin was encouraged by his informal research committee to try organizing a Northern city less demanding and less politically pivotal than Chicago. Carl Stokes's campaign in Cleveland to become the first black mayor of a major American city provided an opportunity to test strategies for the Northern cities. During the summer of 1967, we took a major portion of our staff and considerable financial resources to Cleveland to organize the get-out-the-vote effort on election day, bringing together the organizational expertise developed in Chicago and Alabama.

We brought all our resources to bear on this campaign. Martin, especially, never let up. Once, we were driving to a meeting in Cleveland during the mayoral campaign when we stopped for a red light in the heart of the rundown black ghetto. Several prostitutes were working the area, and one lady approached our car while we were stopped. She peeked inside, recognized Martin in the front seat, beckoned to a friend, and yelled, "There's that Uncle Tom, Martin Luther King. What's *he* doing here?" After we had gone about a block Martin said, "Bernard, turn this car around. I want to talk with that woman." Bernard moaned, "Oh, Doc, don't pay any attention to those women. They're just ignorant." He just kept driving straight ahead. "TURN THE CAR AROUND, BERNARD!" Martin shouted. He hardly ever raised his voice like that.

Bernard turned the car around and we returned to that very corner. Martin got out, found the woman who had made the remark, and told her, "If you'll allow me the opportunity, I'll tell you why I'm here. I'm on my way to a meeting now, but we're staying at the Sheraton Cleveland Hotel, and if you and your friends meet us there this afternoon at three o'clock we'd like to have a chance to talk to you. Bring as many friends as you want." When we returned to the hotel there was a delegation of ladies waiting in the lobby! They had told the desk clerk they were waiting to meet with Martin Luther King! We arranged for a meeting room and ordered coffee, and Martin began a discussion on the necessity for them to register and vote if they ever hoped to get off the street. "We can get rid of this ghetto if we go to work politically," he said. Maybe he only convinced a few of them, but I'll always remember how he insisted on going back and confronting them, not willing to give up on anyone whose mind he might change.

It was extremely gratifying to us after the polls closed in Cleveland and it appeared that Carl Stokes would indeed become the next mayor. Martin returned to his hotel to rest after a long day of getting out the vote activity for Stokes. We were assured that the campaign would call when the mayor-elect was heading to headquarters to make his acceptance speech. But the campaign never called, and after several weeks of organizing on behalf of Carl Stokes, Martin watched his acceptance speech on television.

The next morning an embarrassed Carl Stokes came by to thank Martin for all of his hard work, but I was deeply offended that a black candidate would demonstrate that level of hypocrisy. Martin Luther King was still sufficiently controversial that candidates wanted his help behind the scenes, away from the television cameras. It had been that way when Martin worked to get out the vote for President Johnson and now for Carl Stokes.

In September 1967 Martin received a visit in the Atlanta office of SCLC from attorney Marian Wright (later Edelman), who was then director of the NAACP Legal Defense Fund office in Mississippi. A slim, articulate, no-nonsense, light brown–skinned woman, she was accompanied by four black men in their forties from the Mississippi Delta who were out of work. In fact, they had not worked since the government farm programs began paying farmers not to grow crops. These were responsible men who had been their families' breadwinners. They were desperate to do something, and after we listened to their stories, Marian proposed that Martin and other religious and labor leaders join them in a protest in Washington with a sit-in and fast at the office of Secretary of Labor Willard Wirtz. Either something would be done about the problem of chronic unemployment, or they would stay there until everyone was jailed.

Marian was very persuasive and determined. It was as if a whirlwind had entered Martin's small office. The energy of her presence filled the room and gave force to the sad but familiar story of the unemployed farmworkers. Marian made a point and presented a plan that exhibited the kind of sound strategic thinking that Martin respected. These were qualities that would lead Marian Wright Edelman to found the Children's Defense Fund and become a champion for America's children.

After Marian's group had left, Martin and I sat around his office discussing whether he should demonstrate along with the men from Mississippi. The idea was right, Martin believed, but he didn't see much point in holding a fast and sit-in in Washington with only a handful of people; he felt fasting didn't impress the American public. The more we discussed it, it seemed that a campaign designed to dramatize the extent of poverty in America might work if a couple of thousand people went to Washington instead of just a few, and if they were prepared to stay there until something happened.

A few weeks later Martin and I met with the editors of *Time*, *Life*, and *Fortune* magazines. The editors expressed great concern about the riots in the cities, which were becoming an annual summer event. They felt the situation had reached the point of no return and that something must be done to alleviate the underlying causes of these riots. America would not survive if urban violence continued on the level we were then witnessing, they felt. The fear was that if the situation continued unchanged, we were either headed toward a state of total anarchy and chaos, or a right-wing police state. Of course, neither outcome was desirable. Moreover, they believed that President Johnson's antipoverty program was insufficient to cope with the scope of the problem, and its jobs and programs were getting bogged down in bureaucracy and not filtering down quickly enough to benefit the masses. Too much of the money was going to consultants, studies, and evaluations. This is what we thought too, but we were surprised to find that these journalists, who represented the power of American media, were thinking along the same lines.

Shortly after this meeting, Martin and Bernard were in New York for a meeting that psychiatrist Kenneth Clark had set up, which included young militants. In the course of this discussion, Martin pressed these young people for their views on violence. They explained they were not exactly advocates of violence, but they expressed their opinions in strong language meant to reflect the seriousness of our racial condition. When Martin took the time to explain what we had been able to do in Birmingham and Selma through nonviolent direct-action techniques, they replied, "Well, why don't you try that in another Northern city? If you undertake a massive large-scale protest in Washington, we'll support it." The outline of Marian Wright's concept was beginning to gain substance. We all thought that such a campaign would have to be large enough and of such duration that it would disrupt the ongoing machinery of the city and the federal government. Either the government would deal with the substance of the protests or everyone would go to jail.

The underlying reason for this sense of desperation and determination was the explosion of America's black ghettos into fires of devastation. The flames of the riots destroyed more than property. The fragile moral consensus that had been building around the need to address the conditions of blacks was also disrupted. The violence of the riots became an excuse not to do more for the cities, and could be used as proof that poor, urban blacks were unworthy of assistance. Far from being mobilized to address the harsh conditions in the inner cities, Congress refused to pass a rent supplement bill, local governments were stymieing federal antipoverty and model-cities programs, and Congress went so far as to ignore a bill to kill rats in cities.

President Johnson, who had responded so nobly to the nonviolent campaign in Selma, was absorbed in issuing hopeful and visionary statements about ultimate victory in Vietnam. The War on Poverty became a casualty of the war in Vietnam. It was as Martin had prophesied: "The bombs you drop on Vietnam will explode at home in unemployment and inflation." It was as if violence had become fashionable; the philosophy of nonviolent protest seemed a distant memory, almost forgotten, as if Birmingham, Selma, and Albany, within just a few years, had become signposts of another time. But we all knew riots were essentially self-destructive and thoughtless outbursts of rage. They were producing a reaction, particularly from political and civic authorities, that had the effect of making the police response only more extreme, and the designation of protest activities as criminal and a threat to the national security. We even feared the establishment of secret government concentration camps for detainment of the "suspicious" if the riots continued and police powers continued to expand. Unfortunately, much that we have learned since regarding the Justice Department's counterintelligence program and the actions of J. Edgar Hoover has revealed there was substance to our fears.

While we were very much aware that black Americans were on the bottom of the economic ladder, we believed, initially, that black poverty was largely a function of the lack of political power. We thought fundamental economic change in America would come as a result of increased black voting and political activity in the South. We had hoped, for instance, that the Voting Rights Act would be a strong factor in retiring forever some of the old-line Southern conservative congressmen who supported policies that drained resources from the cities. However, by 1967 we knew this wasn't going to happen. For one thing, President Johnson chose to invoke the act in only one hundred counties out of a possible nine hundred. The Justice Department simply would not assign referees except under persistent and concerted pressure from us or other civil rights groups about specific abuses in specific counties. To make the Voting Rights Act really work at maximum effectiveness, we would have had to spend the next ten years in the South creating "little Selmas." And "little Selmas" were hard to create. After 1965, we faced a wave of harassment arrests any time we entered a community to conduct voter registration drives, arrests that required as much as forty thousand dollars in bond money. The financial burden finally was too much. Even though black voter registration in the South was steadily increasing, real social and economic reform would not come in the near future through electoral politics alone; something else was needed.

In the Chicago campaign, we learned that slums existed in part because they were profitable. Efforts to help poor blacks came into direct conflict with the financial interests of many politically connected whites. This was in contrast to our experience with demonstrations against segregation in the South, where the local economic power structure usually eventually came around to our side. They knew we had the power of the Constitution behind us, and that through Supreme Court decisions ultimately we would always win. The private sector also supported us because we made them realize through our boycotts that they couldn't afford to sacrifice the patronage of the black community and because they quickly realized, to their surprise, that integration brought them even more business. The integration of public facilities in the South didn't cost the economic power structure anything; in fact, integration was a boon to businesses throughout the South.

However, once we moved North and began to target the deeper, more entrenched problems of poor urban blacks, the private sector turned against us. Now their interest was in favor of maintaining the status quo. Cosmetic or token changes were fine, but not fundamental changes that in the long run would provide a more equitable and healthy society. The nature of the changes we were now seeking would have required a major redistribution of wealth. This, of course, was a very threatening situation. Now *we* were the problem.

Even the big labor unions, which supported the movement's efforts to end segregation, were less enthusiastic when it came to social justice for the poor. There was a big gap between the wages earned in heavily unionized industries and the wages of workers in industries that were not unionized—the working poor were not among the members of the big unions. In the late sixties, there was an unfortunate level of complacency in the union movement. Its leaders were slow to recognize that huge numbers of unemployed people were a drag on union wages.

Because the private sector—and labor unions—so strongly resisted substantive change, Martin and other civil rights leaders concluded that any change that would alleviate the causes of the riots and reverse the escalating economic inequities in American society must come through public policy. But there was tremendous criticism of our demands that the federal government become more active in improving conditions for the poor and disadvantaged; the criticisms from conservatives on this issue were as strong as the attacks against Martin over his stand on the war. Federal programs that would alleviate conditions for the most needy in our society—welfare, social security, legal aid, unemployment compensation, and various programs instituted through the War on Poverty—were labeled as "creeping socialism." The federal government should not "interfere" with the free enterprise system, it was said.

Yet we noted that leaders of the free enterprise system did not hesitate to turn to the federal government when they needed help. "Socialism" was just fine when it was socialism for the rich. Government intervention was perfectly acceptable when it benefited business interests. When steel prices drop slightly, the government buys steel whether it needs it or not. That is called "price supports" for the steel industry. If big oil needs a little money to play with, they have the "oil depletion allowance." The airlines receive governmental support: federal tax money pays for the construction of new airports and the salaries of air-traffic controllers and other employees involved in air travel safety and security.

Meanwhile, U.S. farm policy had been a disaster for black people in the South like the men Marian Wright Edelman had brought to meet with us. SCLC researchers found that in Mississippi alone in 1967, six wealthy farmers were each receiving more than a million dollars a year not to grow food. The government assistance they received was not called "welfare," but "parity." Meanwhile, the poor farmers or sharecroppers that made a menial, but to them absolutely essential, wage working the lands of the huge owners were now out of work and criticized if they received a tiny welfare payment.

These and other federal programs designed to help American businesses to prosper cost far more than all the social programs to benefit the poor put together. Yet, the only complaints we heard were about food stamps, welfare benefits, and other proposed federal programs "leading us to socialism." Meanwhile, wealthy farmers were not only receiving federal assistance for not planting food or cotton, but also converting their land to cattle grazing and making a good profit from the sale of cattle. So this policy made the rich richer, while the working poor became unemployed. And there was no plan to retrain agricultural workers displaced by these programs. The complaint of "creeping socialism" somehow only arises when the government is spending money on poor people.

The movement of people from rural communities into cities faster than the cities could absorb them had reached a crisis level by 1962. Displaced and dislocated workers came to cities seeking an opportunity that never materialized. The resulting alienation from American society was not only economic, but psychological, and continues to pay negative dividends in terms of crime and general social dysfunction. This psychological condition of alienation and despair almost defined what was being called in the sixties the "black ghetto." The original meaning of the term "ghetto" evoked a place where people were gathered so that they could be exterminated. The activists who began referring to black slums as "ghettos" intended to evoke the horror of genocide. A "ghetto" was inhabited by people the society had designated superfluous. The "ghetto" was marked by high unemployment, costly but rundown housing, a declining public education system due to the absence of a strong inner-city tax base, lack of strong black businesses that would invest in the community, inadequate health facilities and higher rates of disease, and the ugly manifestations of the confluence of all these factors: a high, spiraling crime rate and a bitter, violent turning of the community on itself by its most trapped, most hopeless, most desperate, and most ignorant inhabitants. This sort of ghetto crime is like a series of small, personal "miniriots": individuals striking out blindly at the symbols of their frustration without purpose or design. The residents of the ghettos of our big cities were as fenced in by their economic, political, and psychological barriers as the people of Selma had been by segregation. People in the ghetto, in fact, were even more trapped because they often lacked the hope and determination demonstrated by people in Southern towns like Selma to take charge of their lives and work for change. In an important sense, our marches in Chicago were not so much marches to integrate forbidden all-white housing areas, but marches to break the physical and psychological barriers of the mental and legal restrictions placed on the citizens of the ghetto.

The strategy for what we had begun to call the Poor People's Campaign was intended to challenge those same barriers on the national stage. Poor people in America were out of sight and out of mind. Policies that created slums and kept people in poverty were perpetuated almost unconsciously. For politicians, there was no real need to consider the impact of policy decisions on the poor, since they were powerless in the political system. Using the techniques of nonviolence, we intended to confront the nation with the reality of poverty in the world's wealthiest society. We intended to arouse the conscience of the nation around issues of poverty as we had challenged the nation to reject segregation. We hoped the process of training and mobilization would empower poor people in a new social movement that transcended race.

The Poor People's Campaign was to be a more massive, long-range campaign of civil disobedience than we had ever previously undertaken. We intended to bring fifteen hundred demonstrators to Washington from fifteen regions of the country, an effort that Bernard Lafayette would organize and oversee. The demonstrators would live in Washington in temporary housing we would construct and begin the petitioning of government agencies and Congress for what was, in effect, an economic Bill of Rights. During the Great Depression, Bonus Marchers, Veterans of World War I, had come to Washington and camped out, demanding a promised "bonus." In many ways, the Poor People's Campaign was part of a constitutionally protected tradition of Americans petitioning the government for the redress of grievances.

Undergirding the initial fifteen hundred demonstrators, who would be well trained in nonviolent protest techniques, we planned for a second wave of fifteen to twenty thousand volunteers from selected regions around the country who would coordinate local demonstrations with the actions of the core group in Washington. It was also our hope that the initial core group would organize college and high school students in the D.C. area. We believed that if everything went well, we could rally as many as fifty thousand youth in the nation's capital behind our cause. We expected that many of them would be white youth, a testimony that we believed would be very effective.

We were prepared to stay in Washington on this campaign as long as we needed to, and we were expecting a period of heavy repression by the government, which we anticipated might mean jail terms for all of us for possibly as long as a year, far longer than any of our staff had spent incarcerated. We were also prepared to ask the backup wave of twenty thousand demonstrators to come to Washington, if necessary. We set a target date of April 15 for the first demonstrations.

The Washington Poor People's Campaign was announced by Martin at an Ebenezer Church press conference on December 4. We did not completely formulate our plans until January 1968, however, and by February it was evident that there were serious problems in implementation. For one thing, not everyone on the senior SCLC staff was as committed to the Poor People's Campaign as Martin was. Bevel wanted to expand the peace campaign into a stop-the-draft movement. He had also become enamored with Wilhelm Reich's theories on war and sexual repression, which had him more than ever before marching to his own drummer. Jesse Jackson, who had undertaken Operation Breadbasket in Chicago, was hung up on what Martin called "the image of Breadbasket" and what others of us used to call his "little Empire." He didn't want to leave Breadbasket-building to devote major time to the PPC. Martin was becoming a bit agitated with Jesse because he felt Breadbasket by itself was not going to solve major economic problems. He wanted to continue the program, but he felt, as I did, that a major structural reform of the American economy was needed, and that Breadbasket was too limited an approach to achieve this. Breadbasket, like other programs, dealt with neighborhood businesses and national franchises that depended on black patronage, but by late 1967, Martin was convinced that a substantial increase in jobs would have to come from the public sector; private businesses simply weren't going to provide enough jobs to ease the huge problem of unemployment. Changes in priorities and policies must be affected.

Some of our board members had never been impressed with the wisdom of the Washington campaign, particularly Bayard Rustin and Marian Logan, the wife of a prominent New York physician, but recalcitrant board members and counselors weren't much of a problem as long as Martin was strong in his conviction. Reluctant staff members, however, were a problem—they had to make the campaign work.

And it was a difficult job. Bernard Lafayette had little difficulty finding three thousand poor people who would go to Washington, but by February, the actual training of individuals by our staff had not even begun. We had set up plenty of contacts with social-action organizers, but we had not yet worked directly with the people. "There's no masses in this mass movement," Martin complained in one of our meetings. And there were organizational and budgetary

problems. Bill Rutherford, who became SCLC's new executive director when I was named executive vice president toward the end of
1967, strongly recommended that to pull PPC off we would have to
close down all our other activities for a while and devote ourselves
entirely to the campaign in Washington.

Meanwhile, Martin was running around the country desperately
trying to rally support for the campaign. I was doing the same with
selected groups like churches, labor unions, congressmen, and other
potential supporters. Most of Martin's contacts were made through
speeches, mine through behind-the-scenes meetings. I spent a lot of
time with local committees, and so did Bernard Lafayette. I met with
several black militant groups to ask them, in effect, to give us one
season in Washington to try out our program, free from the strife and
internal criticism that was hurting our movement almost as much as
criticism from the racist and conservative opposition was. I wanted
to move to Washington for a while and work there on organizing
support and making arrangements. But Martin wanted me to stay
with him on his tours and help pin down the details of commitments
made by those who promised to support us. I enjoyed traveling with
Martin, but it meant that my duties as executive vice president of
SCLC were neglected. Most members of the staff were eager for a
chance to travel with Martin, but not too many wanted to tend to
correspondence and budgets in Atlanta, so I made it my policy to
travel with him only when he specifically requested that I go along.

In February, hoping we could move things along a little faster,
we sent out calls to representatives of other ethnic minorities to support or join the campaign. We were happily surprised at the positive
response from Cesar Chavez and the California Farm Workers,
groups in the Appalachians, and Native Americans. I remember
meeting with Cesar Chavez in his office in California. He was a small
man with a soothing, spiritual presence. In his long-running battle
with California lettuce growers over the rights of the farmworkers,
he had reached what he thought was a gentleman's agreement on a
strike and sent workers into the fields to bring in the lettuce crop. I
was with Chavez when one of his associates brought word that the
growers had reneged on the agreement. In fact, the growers maintained that no agreement had ever existed. This was a betrayal of
three years of work by the California Farm Workers Union. Chavez
allowed himself one controlled expression of emotion. He whispered,
"The dirty motherfuckers!" Then he looked at me with eyes that
expressed the kind of loving determination with which the apostle
Paul spread the Gospel, and said, "I should have been more careful.

It's going to take us a little longer." There was not a trace of despair. He never raised his voice. Chavez explained to me about the agreement, that these were distinguished leaders in the community, the largest farmers. You shouldn't have to hold people like that to a written agreement. His workers didn't have a contract; you agree to work and you expect to be paid. He considered himself naive for not insisting on a written agreement, but, of course, he said, if the growers were determined to be dishonorable, they would have found some technical reason to invalidate a written agreement. Chavez was disappointed, but not bitter. So often the people who have a real right to be bitter learn that it is not productive.

The media coverage of our plans for the Poor People's Campaign caused great consternation in official Washington. Now that the PPC had the potential of unifying protest across a wide spectrum of ethnic and underprivileged groups in America, it could also raise massive civil disobedience to a new level in American life. Far from attempting to cooperate with our demands, the White House moved quickly to stop us. In Congress Martin was widely condemned. Senator Robert Byrd of Virginia was most strident in his criticism. He called Martin a "self-seeking rabble-rouser" and declared that the Poor People's Campaign would be responsible for bringing "violence, destruction, looting, and bloodshed" to Washington. Even liberal congressmen denounced the campaign. Senator Howard Baker of Tennessee said "the march on Washington is like striking a match to look in your gas tank and see if you're out of gas." Senator John Stennis of Mississippi declared: "I want to give a word of advice and counsel to the colored people and to any others who may be inclined to come to Washington from Mississippi. It is to stay out of the march. Nothing good for them or for anyone else can come from it."

Years later, when I read my daughter Andrea's college thesis on the Poor People's Campaign, for which she had compiled press clippings from before, during, and after the campaign, I remembered again the extraordinary extent to which we were opposed by members of Congress, the administration, and the media. As they saw it, the conditions of poverty and oppression in America weren't the enemy—we had become the enemy. We did not realize the extent of the panic we were engendering in the capital. Had we understood the level of concern, we might have acted to either soothe the fear or at least take advantage of it. We wanted to challenge the president and the Congress enough to make them take seriously the problems of poverty and act to help poor people. We believed that as segregation was immoral in a democracy, poverty was immoral in a nation as wealthy as the United States of America.

What had begun as a movement for racial equality had evolved until Martin could no longer ignore the role that war and poverty played in the oppression of people of color in America and around the world. Racism, war, and poverty were intertwined. Only when we removed the first layer of segregation did we see clearly the cancer of poverty eating away at the hope and strength of black people in America. Segregation nourished that cancer, but the elimination of segregation could not eradicate it. But, by attacking poverty, Martin was calling into question fundamental patterns of American life. There was scarcely any power center that was unaffected by his challenge.

16

Let Us Slay the Dreamer

The trumpet sounds within my soul, I ain' got long to
stay here.
— AFRICAN-AMERICAN SPIRITUAL

During March 1968, Martin, Ralph, Fred Bennett, Bernard Lee,
and I were on a national tour to drum up support for the
Poor People's Campaign. We scheduled mass meetings where
Martin was the featured speaker, networked with local leadership,
and left someone from our staff in each town to help recruit on an
ongoing basis.

While we were in Newark, Martin received a call from Jim Lawson in Memphis requesting that he come down and speak in support
of a garbage workers' strike there that had been going on since
February 12. Jim Lawson was an old friend, an organizer of the
Nashville sit-in movement who was instrumental in organizing our
Birmingham nonviolent protest workshops. He had moved to Memphis to become pastor of Centenary Methodist Church, had become
active in support of the garbage workers, and had been named chairman of a community-wide support committee. All the workers
involved were black, and what had started out as a union grievance
had by February widened into a racial and civil rights struggle,
because the black community identified so strongly with the plight of
the workers. Lawson explained that they were trying to bring down

civil rights leaders to build community and national support for the embattled workers, and Martin was needed only to make a speech. Lawson knew we were busy trying to get the Washington campaign together.

I felt it would be a mistake for Martin to leave our tour even for a day. Trying to get the Poor People's Campaign off the ground was a difficult enough task. And I had been down that road enough times to know that to become involved in any way in the garbage workers' strike in Memphis would really mean taking on another campaign. We had been through this too many times to think Martin could just go to Memphis, make a speech, and leave. Albany had started with just one little speech. The Meredith march had taken nearly a month out of the middle of our Chicago campaign. I was constantly in the position of urging Martin to focus our limited staff resources and resist the temptation to respond to every worthy cause.

There was no question about the importance of the issue in Memphis. The strike began in the wake of the death of two workers who were accidentally crushed by their own garbage truck machinery when they took shelter inside the rear of their truck during a hard rain. They were forced to seek such perilous shelter because the workers, particularly the black workers, were not allowed to seek cover in the cabs of their own trucks, or in stores in the neighborhoods they were working in. They either had to sit inside the rear compartments of their trucks along with the garbage or be drenched. In those days especially, picking up garbage was backbreaking, nasty work. Workers walked into backyards, lifting and emptying rusty metal cans full of rotting food and trash. The deaths were symptomatic of the disrespect with which garbage workers were treated, and the workers had a long list of legitimate grievances. They were extremely poorly paid and, to make matters worse, the city of Memphis didn't provide workers' compensation or any other family benefits or insurance. In addition to dealing with the shocking deaths of their loved ones, the families then had to try to scrounge up the money to pay for their funerals.

The situation was worsened by the obstinate and inflexible attitude of the new mayor, Henry Loeb, who had been elected in January against the almost total opposition of the black community. Loeb's election and his hostility toward the black community followed directly in the wake of the depressing defeat of a very strong black candidate, A. W. Willis, and seemed to intensify the black community's feelings of alienation from the Memphis power structure and from the usual forms of political relief. Loeb vowed he would never recognize the garbage workers' union, and he refused to negotiate. The city hired nonunion workers to replace the striking workers and pulled out a large contingent of police to protect the nonunion workers while they worked their daily routes.

In response, Community on the Move for Equality (COME) brought together the relatively conservative constituencies of the NAACP and middle-class churches of Memphis and unified them behind the concerns of working-class black people. For a while it seemed as if their efforts were having an impact; in mid-February Lawson and the COME organizers had undertaken negotiations with the city council on behalf of the workers, and these negotiations almost resulted in a compromise settlement. But on February 23, the compromise fell through because of pressure by the intransigent and image-conscious Mayor Loeb. When COME organized a march on the night of the twenty-third to protest the collapse of negotiations, many of the marchers, including ministers, were attacked by police and beaten, which further angered and unified the black community. COME retaliated against the police brutality with a tight economic boycott of downtown Memphis as well as a boycott of the Memphis daily newspapers, which were extremely hostile to the striking workers and biased and inflammatory in their reports.

So in response to Jim Lawson's request on March 18, Martin went to Memphis. He spoke and received an ovation from a fired-up audience of more than ten thousand that filled the cavernous Masonic Temple. I went with him; the enthusiasm was just incredible. This was a larger crowd than we could ever have assembled in one hall in Birmingham or Selma, but it had that same energy. Buoyed by the euphoria of the moment and the spirit of the people, Martin promised that he would return on Friday, March 22, to lead a march downtown in support of the workers. Lawson and the local COME organizers were overjoyed, because the daily marches were not moving the city; they anticipated that a march led by Martin would bring out their largest crowd ever, substantially escalate their campaign, and create the desired national publicity.

After the speech we drove down to the Mississippi Delta to make contacts and arrangements for the Washington campaign. We spent time in particular in the impoverished black sharecropping community of Marks, Mississippi. Marks was in the poorest county in the United States, according to the 1960 census. Conditions were so bad Martin actually cried when he saw how people were living. We determined right then and there that the Poor People's Campaign would originate in Marks. A caravan from the Marks community would depart by mule train and be the first to arrive in Washington.

Martin was unable to return to Memphis for the march on Friday the twenty-second; it was canceled by a freak snowstorm and rescheduled for Thursday, March 28. Just prior to the rescheduled march, we were recruiting in Newark and New York for the Poor People's Campaign while holding meetings with Congressman John Conyers, Mayor Dick Hatcher, and Harry Belafonte to discuss the direction of the movement, raise the question of future political efforts, and get their reactions. We had reached no conclusions, but I remember that Hatcher was pushing for a Black Americans for Democratic Action organization that might be considered an arm of the Democratic Party, but would define political issues from a black perspective. As always, I was against an all-black party. The civil rights leadership had become the moral leadership of both parties, Democratic and Republican, and I saw our role as defining the issues and motivating people of goodwill, leading what Martin termed "a coalition of conscience." We all agreed that the next step for the movement was electoral politics, but we were grappling with how to accomplish that aim.

I proposed moving the Washington campaign back to June. April was almost upon us, and we still hadn't worked out all the details. Everyone was frantic; Martin was staying up nights calling all over the country trying to get things organized, and I was on the phone constantly as well. Besides, some of the board members were still not behind the campaign and this concerned Martin. As for the executive staff, we were not all on the same wavelength either, though there were no outspoken objections. In the midst of this rapidly closing deadline for the Poor People's Campaign, and all that we still needed to do to pull it off, I wished fervently that Martin had not agreed to go back to Memphis, despite my appreciation of the importance of the garbage workers' strike, and the obvious value of Martin to their struggle.

On Wednesday night, March 27, we were up very late in our New York hotel and the only plane Martin could catch to Memphis left very early Thursday morning from Newark. The march was scheduled for nine o'clock. Martin was so anxious that he would oversleep and miss the plane that I don't think he ever went to sleep. By the time he, Bernard, and Ralph arrived in Memphis, Martin must have been so fatigued he was almost in a daze. I was to go to Washington later that morning to begin PPC meetings there. Martin, Ralph, and Bernard were to meet Walter Fauntroy and me in Washington later in the afternoon, after returning from Memphis.

It was when I arrived in Washington early that afternoon and called Walter Fauntroy that I first heard the disturbing news that the march in Memphis had disintegrated into violence and that Martin had temporarily canceled his plans to return to Washington. He was tired and disgusted, had checked into a hotel, and was planning to meet with Lawson and the organizers of the march later to find out what went wrong.

Only much later were we able to piece together what I believe happened. About twenty thousand people showed up at the downtown Clayborn Temple site for the march, a far larger number than for any previous Memphis march. The march was scheduled to get under way at 9:00 A.M., but either the plane was late or they could not find a plane to get them there that early, so Martin, Ralph, and Bernard didn't arrive at the site until around 11:00, and it was 11:30 before they were in position to begin departing from the church.

While they were waiting for Martin to arrive, all kinds of problems were brewing up at the site. Many excitable young people were leaving their high schools to join the march, though the schools were trying to prohibit them from going. At one of the largest schools, Hamilton High School, a skirmish developed, police were called, and a black girl was injured. By the time the story reached the crowd outside Clayborn it had ballooned into a rumor that the girl had been shot or killed by police, so many of the young people were in an extremely agitated and angry mood, and as the crowd milled, waiting, their mood grew worse.

In addition, it was discovered that many "street people," unemployed folk who tended to hang out near bars and corners and who did not intend to join the march, were congregating on the sidewalks along the march route and were drinking. Later, after an investigation by his group into what happened, Lawson came to believe that several of these people were petty thieves who made a living stealing from the stores that lined the Beale Street area, the center of black downtown shopping. Since the economic boycott had kept blacks from the downtown area, they had been prohibited from "plying their trade." The committee felt these individuals were simply waiting for an opportunity to use the march as cover for break-ins during which they could replenish their stock and make up for lost time. The lack of a strong police presence along the march route left wide open such opportunities.

Finally, Lawson and the COME organizing committee simply hadn't properly anticipated trouble. But conditions were ripe for it: in a divided city with a history of injustices and inequities, and with tension building toward a peak no one could control, the committee had attempted this massive march. And those assigned to marshal the participants were not trained in leading such a demonstration. This last problem I had not anticipated. Jim Lawson was a veteran nonviolent organizer. The movement he led in Nashville was a textbook example of how to organize for social change. In fact, everyone who ever attended a citizen education workshop was briefed on the Nashville campaign. I assumed that Lawson was as well organized in Memphis as he had been in Nashville. That assumption proved to be inaccurate.

Our experience with marches everywhere had taught us that to have a successful nonviolent march, the participants *must* have some prior knowledge of what kind of behavior is expected of them, particularly if they're going to undergo abuse or attack from bystanders or police. They must give up the freedom to react the way they might normally, because they're in a demonstration with more than their individual emotions to be concerned with. You simply cannot draw a crowd of twenty thousand people, line them up six abreast, and march them down the street, and not expect to have problems, particularly if your march includes highly excitable and undisciplined high school kids.

Apparently, when Martin and Ralph finally arrived and it was time to begin the march, they and Lawson sensed the disorganization. Martin and Ralph were supposed to *lead* the march, but there were people lined up ahead of them ready to go. There was a brief discussion of whether to delay until the crowd was better organized, but since the start was already more than two hours late Lawson decided to go ahead. So they began.

The group strode down Hernando Street, turned left on Beale Street for two blocks, then right on Main Street en route to downtown and city hall. Even among the leadership, there was insufficient discipline. Most of the ministers, who as marshals should have spread themselves over the six-block length of the march on both flanks, instead crowded behind or beside Martin and Ralph. This left the rear of the march, which was made up of a heavy contingent of youth, completely unsupervised.

By the time the leadership of the march had gone a few blocks along Main Street, the sound of windows breaking in the rear was heard. These were the windows of shops back on Beale. Lawson and the other Memphis leaders, along with Martin and Ralph, became alarmed, and Lawson made a quick run to the rear to ascertain what was happening. When he returned, he made two decisions. First, he decided to abort the march, turn it around, and return to Clayborn Temple. Second, he told Martin and Ralph it would be better if they left immediately and went somewhere their safety would be assured. It was difficult to know what violence might take place upon the arrival of the massive group of police who were running toward the scene, having also heard the sound of breaking glass.

At first Martin protested that he did not want to leave—he had never done so previously when trouble developed—but Lawson insisted, and a group of the Memphis march leaders encircled Martin and Ralph and moved them off to a side street. Meanwhile, Bernard ran to the corner, stopped a passing vehicle, and asked the driver, who was black, if they could catch an emergency ride. A passing policeman in his patrol car saw what was happening, got out of his vehicle, and ran over and asked Martin where he wanted to go, saying he would escort them. Usually Martin stayed at the black-owned Lorraine Motel when he was in Memphis, but the officer said it would be impossible to get there because that would take them back through the area crowded with marchers. Union officials had reserved rooms for Martin, Ralph, and Bernard at the downtown Peabody Hotel, but that route was also blocked. The policeman therefore escorted them to the Holiday Inn Rivermont, which was located toward the Mississippi River. Martin, Ralph, and Bernard, exhausted and dazed from the rapid series of events, checked in.

Meanwhile, back at the march site, the situation was deteriorating from bad to worse. The marchers had a difficult time reversing themselves—there were many elderly folk as well as young children in the lines—and the breaking and looting of stores increased rather than lessened. Some of the youth in the march used the wooden sticks of their picket signs to break windows. This was just mindless violence, but those waiting for an opportunity to loot were running into clothing and liquor stores along the route and taking out everything they could carry. The police arrived and began to beat people and shoot Mace and tear gas indiscriminately as marchers sought to scramble inside the church, and Lawson and his aides were running around screaming at people to stop looting. Nevertheless, some of the youth got into pitched battles with the police by throwing rocks at them, as blacks from a nearby project entered the melee to also throw rocks at police in what was becoming a battle in the streets. The police did not help the situation when they fired tear gas *into* Clayborn Temple, where women, children, and the elderly had sought safety, and into the Memphis committee office adjacent to the church.

The disruptions at the march site quickly spread throughout the city, and within a few hours martial law had been declared. Later that afternoon, a black youth, Larry Payne, was shot and killed by police.

Martin was extremely depressed by the breakup of the march in Memphis, but he was not angry; rarely, if ever, did he display anger. However, what was supposed to have been a brief detour in support of comrades-in-arms had turned into an absolute disaster. He was tired, worried, and probably confused, and he crawled into bed, but could not sleep. Bernard and Ralph *were* angry, because they felt Lawson and the Memphis committee had brought Martin into a situation that they did not have under control. This was the first time a march Martin was in had been disrupted by violence on the part of blacks: previously, whenever there was violence, as in Selma or Chicago or Mississippi, the marchers were victims, not perpetrators.

As Martin, Ralph, and Bernard listened in their rooms to television reports of the breakup, they were further horrified to discover that the Memphis media was reporting that Martin had run from the march in fear once trouble began. The violence, or at least the beginning of it, was blamed on a group of young Memphis militants called the Invaders, of whom we had no knowledge whatsoever. And now not only was the news of the disastrous march flashing quickly around the country, but added to it was the false information that Martin had fled.

Within a few hours Lawson and other members of the Memphis committee came over to try to explain, or at least figure out, what had happened and assess the dire implications. It was obvious that none of the Memphis leaders had anticipated trouble, and they did take responsibility for not imposing sufficient discipline. But the problems for us were long-range; as Martin told Lawson, "I can see a lot of our critics now saying, 'You can't have any more nonviolent marches and you can't come to Washington.'" Opponents of the Poor People's Campaign would eagerly seize on the violence in Memphis and use it as an example of what could happen in the capital if we launched a campaign there. In fact, they did so almost immediately.

By late afternoon the press had discovered where Martin was staying, and they were milling around the hallway outside his room trying to get him to comment. So Martin and the Memphis group quickly drew up a statement and held a press conference in which Martin stated he would return to Memphis at the earliest opportunity to hold another march, on Friday, April 5, and insist that it be nonviolent. Lawson supported Martin's statement and added that it was *he* and members of the Memphis COME leadership who had forced Martin to leave the scene, even though Martin had not wanted to go. The press picked up the announcement of an additional march, but largely ignored Lawson's explanation of why Martin had left; they reported that Martin was staying at a "safe" luxury hotel instead of in the dangerously volatile black community, as if he had deliberately chosen to go to the Holiday Inn in Rivermont.

The next morning, Friday, March 29, three leaders of the Invaders came to Martin's room. They explained they wanted to tell Martin personally they were not responsible for the violence at the march, and that they were being falsely blamed by the media and others. Pretty soon Martin came out of his room and met with them, along with Ralph. One of the founders of the Invaders was Charles Cabbage, a graduate of Morehouse College, Martin's alma mater, who was at one time supposed to do some work for SCLC, so Martin was acquainted with him. On a note of comradeship, Cabbage honestly stated that the leaders of the Invaders had not participated in the march, and their nonparticipation was deliberate, because Lawson and the COME leadership had ignored them in their efforts to build community support for the strike. They did admit that some of their followers and youths wearing Invader jackets were in the march and probably participated in the breaking of windows and stone throwing. Martin reminded them of the futility of violence and of the possibility that many innocent people, particularly the elderly and children, might be injured in any situation where the police are provoked. Cabbage blamed the deterioration of the march on Lawson, saying, "Lawson kept us out. If he had been listening to us, we could have warned him there was likely to be trouble." Calvin Taylor, another Invader leader, added, "Memphis is much too tense and potentially explosive to conduct the kind of march Lawson attempted. He should never have invited you here in the first place to lead a march under these conditions. Memphis wasn't ready for this."

SCLC had always been careful to enlist all members of the community—young, old, employed, and disenfranchised—so Martin immediately perceived the need to correct the COME leadership's error in not including the Invaders in their plans. Martin asked the Invaders about their program, which focused on working with youth, especially in the colleges, to develop black consciousness. They felt they had been unfairly tagged with a militant and strongly antiwhite image, and as a result it was impossible for them to obtain financial support. Martin replied that he liked the idea of their program and wanted to help them, but said first there had to be a successful nonviolent march in Memphis. He turned to Cabbage and said, "Cabbage, what must be done to have a peaceful march? Because, you know, I have got to lead one. There's no other way out of this."

Each of the Invader leaders pledged that they would help ensure a peaceful march if *Martin* wanted their support. Martin, in turn, pledged that when he returned to Memphis the following week to prepare for the announced march on April 5, he and members of the SCLC staff would meet with them to discuss ways their program could be bolstered, as long as it remained constructive and nonviolent.

Early that afternoon, Martin, Ralph, and Bernard returned to Atlanta. Martin had the entire executive staff called in for a meeting on Saturday. Meanwhile, he secluded himself and was totally unreachable. I remained in Washington on Friday, but returned to Atlanta for the staff meeting on Saturday, March 30, which was to be held in the conference room at Ebenezer.

Ralph, Hosea Williams, Jim Bevel, Chauncey Eskridge, Jesse Jackson, and Dorothy Cotton had all been called to Atlanta for the meeting. It was obvious from the beginning that Martin was in an agitated mood. Never before had I seen him so aggressive in dealing with us. He wanted everyone to drop what they were doing and return with him to Memphis. But the staff was upset with him also. There was criticism of his going to Memphis in the first place, and going ahead with a march when he and Ralph sensed trouble and apparent disorganization. I didn't join in the criticism because even though I had been against the Memphis detour initially, now that the march had so dramatically disintegrated I knew Martin had to go back. I also knew, because I had been with him, how tired and rundown he had been by the time he arrived in Memphis and that he had probably been incapable of making a decision, once there, whether to go ahead or not. Martin didn't usually make those decisions anyway—he depended on us to organize demonstrations and make them work. But we weren't there. If he felt he had no option but to return and attempt another march the next week, then we *had* to be there, and that was all there was to it. In our original plan, the garbage strike was simply a detour. Now, however, Memphis had become a necessary stepping-stone to Washington and the successful launching of our Poor People's Campaign.

Several senior staff members complained about having to interrupt what they were doing to go to Memphis for we knew not how long. There was a general tone of lecturing Martin: "You shouldn't have done this, you shouldn't have done that." I felt it really was not the time to tell him about his mistakes. There in the wood-paneled room where Ebenezer trustees counted the Sunday offering, Martin became the pastor berating his wandering flock. He quite emotionally reminded us that he had gone to Memphis for the same reasons he went anywhere: he was asked by the people who were fighting for basic civil and human rights, and, in this case, the issue in Memphis was consistent with the broader aims of the Poor People's Campaign. "Memphis is the Washington campaign in miniature," he argued.

"Everyone here wants to drag me into your particular projects," he protested. "Now that there is a movement that originated basically from Mississippi-born folk, not from SCLC leadership, you don't want to get involved." He added that he felt the executive staff was not taking the Poor People's Campaign seriously enough. No one was fired up about it. Several people had other private agendas. "Now that I want you to come back to Memphis to help *me*, everyone is '*too busy*,'" he charged.

Succumbing to their own egomania, some members of the staff had begun to feel that they were more important to the movement than Martin. When they were really feeling their oats, Hosea, Bevel, and Jesse acted as if Martin was just a symbol under which they operated. Bevel was so arrogant as to think he was smarter than Martin. Hosea wanted to focus on voter registration and running black candidates for state offices; his rationale was, "If we get out the vote, we elect the president and tell him what to do." Even now, I can hear Bevel saying, "Aw, that's just a bunch of bullshit. We don't need to be hanging around Washington, we need to stop this war." He was still talking about getting together a delegation to go to the Mekong Delta and place themselves between Americans and the North Vietnamese and either force a cease-fire or offer themselves up as a sacrifice to the futility of war. Meanwhile, Jesse was busy building his own empire up in Chicago. Operation Breadbasket was in its prime, and Jesse's focus was on the economy and forcing white business to open its doors to blacks. He was very good at Breadbasket and he felt his approach was better than Martin's. "Look," Martin told Jesse pointedly, "whenever you needed me or wanted me to come to Chicago, I've always been there supporting your efforts. Now when we're trying to get a national movement going, I don't really have your support." He told Bevel he was a wonderful worker, "But you don't like to work on anything that isn't your idea. Bevel, I think you owe *me* one."

Martin said that the media might blame the disruption of the March 28 march on the youth group, but he was sympathetic toward them. *He* didn't blame them. He could understand how black kids could feel hostile and bitter. And there was no question that the Memphis incident was being used by the police and the press to undercut what we were trying to do nationally, so that had to be dealt with. Everyone had to decide whether they were going to be part of the SCLC team or whether they were merely using SCLC to promote themselves, he declared. Then he stormed out of the meeting.

We had never seen Martin explode that way, not with us. After he left, people were so stunned they finally began to listen. I talked about the Bonus Marchers during the depression, and how their coming to Washington as veterans helped to set the climate and agenda for the New Deal. While there would not be a legislative response to the Poor People's Campaign before the elections, by coming to Washington in the context of the elections, we could force the nation to deal with the issue of poverty. Poverty had to be addressed in a comprehensive way, just as we had approached segregation and voting rights. I told them that while what Jesse was doing was very important, and what Bevel wanted to do on the war was important, if we had a nation committed to ending poverty, it would in effect end the war in Vietnam and there would be more opportunity for black workers. As somberly and seriously as we had ever done anything, we decided we would support Martin in any way he needed us and we would all return to Memphis the next week to help prepare for the march planned for Friday, April 5. When Martin finally returned, we told him our decision, and for the first time in a long while our individualistic and freewheeling staff, the "team of wild horses," was as one.

On Tuesday and Wednesday mornings, April 2 and 3, our staff headed to Memphis on several flights to prepare for the upcoming march. But before we could get under way there was a bad omen. Our plane was held up in the Atlanta airport for an hour and searched because of a bomb threat called in against Martin. Martin laughed about the threat and the delay, but there was no question that the widely reported sharp criticisms of him were taking their toll on his psyche, as we found out that night when he spoke in Memphis.

When we arrived, we settled in at the familiar Lorraine Motel, taking several rooms. The Lorraine was a typical two-story motel with doors to all the rooms opening directly outside. The decor was sixties contemporary, which seemed so modern then and so frightful today. Martin called the Invaders leaders very soon after we arrived, and a meeting was set up for that afternoon between them and our staff. I wanted to be present, since I still considered working with youth one of my specialties.

One of the revelations of the meeting were rumors of the presence of paid provocateurs in the Memphis march. I later met with individuals who confessed that they themselves had been paid to disrupt the march. I have always believed that the FBI was behind it, as a way of preventing us from coming to Washington with our Poor People's Campaign. The presence of paid informants and infiltrators was a persistent one throughout the movement. We tended to assume that the most violent, hostile, and angry people were the plants, so much so that I became automatically suspicious of anyone who was supermilitant and wanted to fight and kill people. My tactic was to challenge them, "How many people did you kill last year? Last week? If you didn't kill anybody last week, what are you waiting for? Why are you in here talking about violence? Either work with us or get out of our way." You had to expose the supermilitants for the windbags they were; otherwise, they would get people stirred up to do stupid things, as happened in Memphis. People in the movement had very serious grievances and some of them were angry enough to kill if they were provoked. SCLC's way was to train people to channel that anger into constructive, nonviolent action. We always had to be on guard against those who would use individual rage to destroy the movement.

The Invaders agreed not only to participate in Friday's march, but to act as marshals. The absence of well-spaced marshals along the full length of the march had been a major contributor to the deterioration of the first march. Martin emphasized that the march must not only be nonviolent, but also be a much-needed public show of unity. He told them, "If at any time there is a meeting with me or our staff and we argue and disagree, once we leave the meeting we aren't to let anyone suspect we argued. Let's not air our differences in public." Martin asked the Invaders leaders if they respected his integrity. He said he respected theirs and their sincerity. In other words, no working arrangement could be set unless it was based on mutual trust. They gave their word that they would support us.

Martin promised that he himself would intercede on behalf of the Invaders and their Black Organizing Project (BOP) to help them raise funds. I offered to meet with Cabbage on Thursday morning to go over their organizational structure and to tighten it so that the

BOP would be eligible to receive funds. There was some discussion of the possibility that the BOP would be taken over by the SCLC budget, but we didn't have sufficient funds to take on any more than we were already doing.

In the midst of our meeting with the Invaders, we were served at the motel with an injunction prohibiting further marching, brought by the city of Memphis and issued by U.S. District Judge Bailey Brown. The injunction banned any march unless the judge approved it, which meant we would have to go through a period of hearings. It also meant that the march tentatively scheduled for Friday was off, as there was no way hearings could be concluded by then. Martin asked me to represent SCLC at the hearings; Lawson would represent the Memphis community leadership backing the striking garbage workers. Lucius Burch, a white Memphis ACLU attorney and noted liberal, came over to the Lorraine when he heard news of the injunction and offered to represent us in court free of charge. Chauncey Eskridge of Chicago, who represented us in various legal matters, flew down from Chicago Thursday morning to assist Burch.

A mass meeting was planned at the Masonic Temple for the night of April 3. Martin didn't feel well, and after a day of meetings, he was suffering from a sore throat. He said he preferred not to go to the mass meeting and said Ralph should take his place while he rested. The weather was horrible. It was cold, raining intermittently, and storm warnings had been issued. We were sure there would only be a handful of people at the church. But when we arrived, the hall was packed with thousands of enthusiastic supporters waiting for us, despite the bad weather. And it was obvious they were disappointed when they did not see Martin arrive with us. It was then that Ralph called Martin and told him, "You need to come on over here, even if you don't do anything but say hello, because these people came out to see you."

So Martin dressed and came to the church. That night Ralph ended up getting into a very long introduction of Martin, unlike anything I had ever heard him do before. Martin had told Ralph, "Just take your time, because I'm just going to say a word or two, you make the major speech." But rather than speak about the Poor People's Campaign or the Memphis movement, Ralph preached about Martin for at least an hour. He began with their association in Montgomery, how he had watched Martin grow and overcome all kinds of obstacles. It was Ralph's way that he was led by the Spirit, especially when he was in the pulpit. His instincts there were nearly always sound. He loved Martin like a brother, and although he sometimes let

his jealousy of Martin get the best of him, it didn't change the deep
affection they shared.

That night, Martin was tired and depressed and Ralph used the
pulpit to build Martin up; he made Martin feel good about himself
and created a situation in which Martin would simply have to
preach. And Martin responded. He used a speech that I had heard
him give at other times when he was struggling with his fears, and it
seemed as if he were buoyed by waves of inspiration, discovering,
while speaking, renewed confidence in our struggle, even while the
storm, lightning, and thunder raged outside. He began by observing
that he would have chosen, if such choice was possible, to live in
these times. He noted the current revolution in world power and
human rights, the struggles of oppressed people all over the world.
He placed in that world context the struggle of the Memphis garbage
workers to better their condition.

He then reviewed the history of our campaigns in Albany, Birmingham, and Selma, noting that the twists and turns of a long journey had brought us to Memphis. He assured us that we could garner
strength to overcome our present obstacles in the same way we had
overcome seemingly insurmountable obstacles in the past.

> These are years when the masses of people are rising up. And
> wherever they are assembled today, whether they are in Johan-
> nesburg, South Africa; Nairobi, Kenya; Accra, Ghana; New
> York City; Atlanta, Georgia; Jackson, Mississippi; or Memphis,
> Tennessee, the cry is always the same: "We want to be free."
> If something isn't done in a hurry to bring the colored
> peoples of the world out of their poverty, these long years of
> hurt and neglect, the whole world is doomed. . . . I'm just
> happy that God has allowed me to live in this period to see
> what is unfolding. And, I'm happy that He's allowed me to be
> in Memphis.
> We aren't engaged in any negative arguments with any-
> body. We are saying that we are determined to be men. We are
> determined to be people. We are saying that we are God's chil-
> dren, and that we don't have to live like we are forced to live.
> The issue is the refusal of Memphis to be fair and honest in its
> dealings with its public servants who happen to be sanitation
> workers.

He referred to the threats against his life, and the fact that his
flight from Atlanta had been delayed because of a bomb threat. But

he literally sang forth: "I've been to the Mountaintop." This was not the first time Martin invoked the image of the "Mountaintop." It had always symbolized for him both a vantage point from which he could view the past, and a vision of moral justice in the world. The "Mountaintop" also represented a peak of personal achievement and fulfillment and commitment in this world.

I think in a rare moment born of inner turmoil, inner questioning, and self-doubt during those days in which his leadership was sorely questioned and challenged, he may have seen, as we could not, that his time was passing, that he had done all he could on earth. Possibly he even sensed what was coming in the clarity of that rare moment of vision when he could see everything in his life in harmony: "He's allowed me to go up to the mountaintop and I've looked over. I've *seen* the promised land. I may not get there with you. But I want you to know tonight, that we as a people will get to the promised land. . . . I'm not fearing any man. Mine eyes have *seen* the glory of the coming of the Lord."

We were all awed and shaken by Martin's speech. But Martin seemed buoyed by inspiration. Later that night they went to the home of Ben Hooks, then a judge, banker, and the pastor of one of the largest black Baptist churches in Memphis, where they discussed the strike and the march until about two in the morning. When they returned to the Lorraine Motel at about three, they discovered that A. D. King, Martin's younger brother, had driven in from Florida; he just thought he should be there. Martin was overjoyed to see him, and they stayed up talking until daybreak. I went to bed.

I arose early Thursday morning, April 4, because I had to spend the entire day in court attending hearings on our attempt to get the temporary federal restraining order removed. I testified for more than an hour on how we conducted marches, our training process for demonstrators, and our philosophy of nonviolence. In my opinion, the hearings were going very well, and I felt there was an excellent chance the judge would approve a march for Monday, under certain guidelines.

The federal court hearing lasted until about four o'clock. It was almost five before I arrived back at the Lorraine Motel. Martin and some other SCLC folk were gathered in A. D.'s room on the first floor. Ralph was there. They were just sitting around clowning in an extremely playful happy-go-lucky way, in complete contrast to the tension of the last few days. When I came in, Martin yelled, in mock anger, "Lil' nigger, just where you been?" Of course, he knew where I had been, but he was enjoying the pretense of being angry with me, and Ralph joined in. "You ought to stay in touch with me," Martin said, keeping it up. "You're always running off doing something without me knowing about it."

Then he sprang up from the bed, grabbed a pillow, and swung at me. The next thing I knew, both Martin and Ralph were beating on me with pillows. After all the tension we had been through, this kind of childlike play was exhilarating. It was a big room with two double beds, so I dodged and ducked my way over to the other bed, grabbed a pillow, and fought them off. Pretty soon our nervous energy was expended and I explained what had transpired in court.

Then Martin and Ralph left to go upstairs to room 306, which they were sharing. Martin had told us we were all invited to a soul food dinner at the home of Rev. Billy Kyles, an old friend and a long-time supporter of the movement in Memphis. Within a few minutes, Kyles would be there to pick us up.

It was by then almost six o'clock. I decided to wait for Reverend Kyles downstairs in the motel parking lot, in front of the rooms. Martin and Ralph's room was on the second floor, toward the middle. Several of the staff—Jesse Jackson, Bevel, Jim Orange—were also milling about, waiting in the parking lot. Shortly before 6:00 P.M. Reverend Kyles arrived with a limousine to take our party to his house. Kyles went up to Martin's room. A few minutes later Kyles came out onto the balcony. Martin soon followed, now dressed. He stood at the railing of the balcony, leaning over and talking to some of us down in the parking lot, while waiting for Ralph to join us.

James Orange and I got into a shadowboxing match in the lot. It was something we did all the time, like pillow fighting. Orange weighed about 260 pounds and I weighed only 160. We must have looked ludicrous. I realized it had suddenly become cooler, the wind had picked up. Someone told Martin he should go back and get a coat. I wasn't really paying much attention to Martin, but from the sound of his voice, he seemed still to be in an exuberant mood.

Suddenly we heard what sounded like a car backfiring or a firecracker. I looked across from the motel to see what might have caused the noise, then I glanced quickly up to the balcony where Martin had been standing at the railing. He was no longer standing. I could see from where I was that he had fallen down, fallen back. I remember that for a moment I thought he was still clowning; he had been in such a playful mood. But he wasn't moving. I leaped up the balcony stairs. Billy Kyles, who had been waiting on the stairs, was just ahead of me. Kyles glanced quickly at Martin, then ducked into room 306 to try to get the telephone operator. Ralph rushed out of the room and over to the fallen Martin.

As soon as I reached Martin I could see he had been shot. A bullet had literally exploded into the right side of his chin. His chin bone had been ripped away as though severed by a knife. He was bleeding profusely; there was a huge pool of blood underneath his head. All this took place within the space of no more than half a minute.

Ralph was desperately trying to force Martin, whose eyes were open but not focusing, to say something. He had fallen back and was stretched out between the wall and the railing. "Martin, this is Ralph. . . . Can you hear me? Can you hear me . . . ?" Martin seemed to be looking at him, but there was no way for us to ever know if he saw anything. Within what must have been only two or three minutes our entire staff was surrounding Martin, plus others who spilled out of their rooms on the second floor. Someone brought a pillow to lay under Martin's head, someone else brought a towel to try to stem the flow of blood; then blankets were brought to cover him. Acting on some superstition, Ralph actually tried to collect Martin's blood in a jar. Almost immediately after the realization hit us that Martin was shot, a large group of plainclothes and uniformed police were running toward us; I rose from Martin's side and pointed them in the direction I instinctively thought the shot had come from—across the street from the motel. But they paid no attention to me, they all kept running up to the balcony to look at Martin. The photo of several of us on the balcony standing beside the fallen Martin with me gesturing to the police was taken by a black South African photographer who was staying in the motel a few doors down from Martin. When he heard the shot, he came out, saw what happened to Martin, and ran back to his room to get his camera.

I knew when I first reached Martin and saw the severity of the wound and the amount of bleeding and looked into his eyes that he would not survive. But none of us could verbalize that then. Ralph was still trying desperately to get Martin to say something, but I have always felt he never said anything. Martin probably didn't even know he had been shot: the bullet had severed his spinal cord before he could have heard the explosion. I felt for his pulse—it was barely discernible; his eyes were losing focus. Ralph was moaning; others were screaming in the courtyard.

I don't know who called the ambulance. It was there within five minutes, but it seemed like centuries. Martin was placed on a stretcher and rushed downstairs to the ambulance, and Ralph and Bernard jumped in with Martin. Chauncey Eskridge and I raced to the limousine Reverend Kyles had readied for the dinner party. I drove and followed the ambulance.

When we arrived at St. Joseph's Hospital, Ralph and Bernard went with Martin into the operating room. There was an emergency medical staff there when we arrived; apparently they had been alerted. I ran to a phone booth in the hallway outside the operating room to call Coretta. I was able to reach her at home and told her that Martin had been shot in the neck and that it was very serious, but he was not dead. Coretta sounded extremely calm, almost serene. She had already heard Martin had been shot and was hurriedly packing to rush to the airport to catch a plane for Memphis.

I then called Jean. We spoke only briefly.

As soon as I hung up, Ralph and Bernard were walking toward me from the emergency room. Bernard said softly, simply, "He's gone." I don't believe I even stopped, paused to reflect, or said anything. I walked into the operating room. The doctors had finished. Martin lay there, still, his wounds cleaned, and in the most profound sense I know, he rested.

Medical personnel were milling about the operating room, but there was no excitement, only a controlled calmness. No one spoke above a whisper.

A small army of press were gathering at the hospital. Ralph, Bernard, Chauncey Eskridge, and I held hands and said a brief prayer. Pretty soon one of the doctors left the emergency room to announce that Martin was dead. After that, Ralph made a brief statement. Then we left. I was numb, drained.

To be frank, my memories of the remainder of that night are jumbled. So much happened, but I don't believe I want to remember. My reaction to stress is to deny emotion, if possible, at the time of impact—the emotion comes later when I'm alone.

No matter how one tries to prepare for death, the reality is difficult to accept. Now that Martin's death, which had always lurked just below the surface of our consciousness, had actually occurred, we were, I suppose, all struggling to find a way to accept it. My first gut reaction was classic anger and denial: Martin couldn't leave us with all this mess. It seemed unfair that he was "free" from innumerable problems, while we, the living, were left to try to cope without him. We had been just getting by with him, how could we get along without him?

We left the hospital and went to the airport, where Coretta was expected. When we arrived, we were informed that Coretta had received confirmation of Martin's death at the Atlanta airport; she had decided against coming to Memphis and had gone back home to be with her children. As we prepared to leave the Memphis airport, we were informed that an autopsy would be performed on Martin's body, and one of us would have to go to the Memphis morgue to identify the body. I went with Ralph to the morgue, where Ralph performed the seemingly needless formality of official identification. From there we returned to the Lorraine.

There were police everywhere, the area around the motel had been cordoned off, and a curfew had been imposed on the city. Memphis was rife with rumors that the black community was exploding in rage; in fact, we heard en route to the Lorraine that someone else had already been killed. Lawson and other Memphis leaders were at the black radio stations pleading for calm. People in the streets seemed to be hurrying home; there was hardly any traffic in the black areas around the motel. We heard that as news of Martin's death spread, whites on their way home during the rush hour were trying to avoid traveling on thoroughfares that took them through black neighborhoods.

Back at the Lorraine there was a palpable sadness. I was still numb; all of us seemed to be sleepwalking through the night. We didn't watch television—there wasn't coverage of Martin's death anyway, it was too late for the news. Police were all over the motel, questioning us. I called Jean and talked to her for a long time, explaining as best I could what had happened; she had just returned from the King house. She said Coretta was holding up. I called my parents; they were, of course, overly concerned about me, but I assured them I was fine. I remember calling Harry Belafonte, such a close and loyal friend and supporter of Martin's—I knew he would want to know from someone other than the news media how it had happened. I also called Stanley Levison, with whom Martin had talked several times since he came to Memphis; Martin had confided to Stan his worries and doubts and hopes ever since Montgomery and had defied the FBI and the president of the United States for their friendship. I knew he too would want to hear from one of us personally.

Finally, I called Dorothy Cotton, the only one of the old faithful inner circle who was not in Memphis when Martin was killed. Dorothy had flown over with us on Wednesday but had returned earlier in the day to prepare to go to Dorchester for the monthly session.

Meanwhile, A. D. was having an awful time. He simply could not get himself under control. A. D. had always seemed on the emotional edge, and his attachment to Martin, and dependency on him, was extremely strong. Just a few hours before, hours that now seemed timeless, he and Martin had been tussling on the bed like boys, calling their mother and playing affectionate tricks on her by pretending to be each other, imitating each other's voice. Now Martin was gone, and though it was difficult for any of us to believe, A. D. didn't seem to be able to accept it at all. He was crying and drinking and screaming as he raged around the room that he was going to get a pistol and "kill all the motherfuckers who killed my brother." Then he would shift abruptly into another state, tearfully admonishing himself, "I've got to be nonviolent. That's what Martin would expect. Martin wouldn't want me to take revenge. Why am I saying I want to kill someone?"

There was no point to reminding him that we didn't have the slightest idea who had killed Martin; there was hardly anything anyone could do to alleviate his pain. In my opinion, the pain never did heal: A. D. died prematurely of a heart attack. Part of him, a part of him none of us was ever able to touch, could never overcome the awesomeness of his brother's death.

As the night wore on toward midnight, we learned from growing television news reports that rioting had already begun in Memphis and around the nation. We could hear the police sirens' awful scream all through the night. After watching for a little while, I snapped the television off again; it was enough to deal with trying to pick up the pieces without having to comprehend what was happening elsewhere. Around three o'clock in the morning we decided we *must* have a meeting then, and not in the morning. Sleep was impossible anyway. So we gathered in room 306 once again—Ralph, Hosea, Bevel, Jim Orange, Ben Hooks, Billy Kyles, Jim Lawson, Bernard, and me. Jesse had already flown back to Chicago and appeared on television with blood on his jacket.

Bernard was trying to pack Martin's things while we began the meeting, and he could hardly do it; he kept breaking down. Finally, Bevel broke a mournful silence and said, "Now we've got to pull ourselves together. Martin's dead and we just have to deal with that. We don't have Martin to lead us anymore, we don't have Martin to raise money for us anymore, so we have to stop messing around and work harder. Now we can't let Martin down by staying in the graveyard with him. He wouldn't want that. Everything he planned has to go forward. Ralph Abernathy is our leader now and we have to go to work behind him." Years before, the board had chosen Ralph as the guaranteed successor to Martin, and while many on the staff might not have made the same decision, we knew that nothing could destroy us as fast as we could destroy ourselves. We were determined to avoid an internecine struggle.

We, each of us, agreed; thus Ralph was chosen by staff acclamation as Martin's successor. The board had already made that decision for us, but that night we wanted Ralph to know he had our spiritual blessing. The staff ran SCLC anyway; no one paid much attention to the board. Ralph's only reply was, "I won't ask any more of you than I gave to Martin."

We reminded ourselves that Martin was surely not the only intended victim of the murder; the whole civil rights movement was the assassin's target. Martin had always said that in the event of his death—and he thought it certain he would not live out his days to old age—we should continue on, not pausing for one minute. "If you do this," he had told us, "you'll prove a movement can't be killed by killing the leaders." Furthermore, we agreed we could not let ourselves be consumed by revenge or anger directed at Martin's killer or others we thought were responsible for his death. If we did, we would fatally stifle our creativity, our productivity, and would be "remaining in the graveyard" as Bevel had said. So we pushed back the tears and steeled ourselves for the coming days, whatever they might bring.

That night we pledged to one another that the Poor People's Campaign in Washington must go forward. Any doubts we had had before, any reservations about the wisdom of the campaign, were pushed aside. We *had* to do it; there was no choice.

We moved on to a brief discussion of services for Martin, difficult as that was even to consider. We decided that we would like to have two services—one private for the family and SCLC staff, the other public and open to anyone. We realized, of course, that we must defer to the wishes of Coretta and Martin's parents, so we made no final decision that night.

By then it was about 4:00 A.M. on Friday. We called Mr. R. C. Lewis, the owner of a Memphis funeral home, who had graciously provided Martin with a limousine and driver each time Martin came to Memphis. It was his limousine that had been waiting to drive Martin to the Kyleses' on that fateful night. We asked Mr. Lewis to go to the morgue, pick up Martin's body, and take it to his funeral home to prepare it for the trip back to Atlanta. Coretta would be arriving later that day to return to Atlanta with Martin's body. Two carloads of us made the trip to the funeral home, arriving at about 4:30 A.M. We were to select a coffin. We all wanted to be there. Martin was there, and even though we all knew that we, the living, must move on with our lives, with our movement, we wanted to be near Martin for as long as we possibly could.

After we returned to Atlanta on Friday, I remember most vividly the experience of talking with the King children—Marty, Yoki, Dexter, and Bernice—about the death of their father. They seemed so utterly prepared. Yolanda was twelve, Marty was about ten, Dexter and Bernice were hardly more than babies. Dexter said to me, "This man didn't know our Daddy, did he? Because if he had known Daddy he wouldn't have shot him. He wouldn't have been able to." And: "Daddy wouldn't want us to hate the man who killed him. He was just an ignorant man who didn't know any better." It was obvious Martin had talked with them about the possibility of his death, and as best as one can prepare children for the eventuality of certain death, he had prepared them.

But that seems too easy to say. I wondered if my children would have been "prepared" if it were me who had been killed. And I wonder if it is possible to really prepare for a violent death like Martin's. Those of us who worked with him could "accept" his death, honor his life, and, through faith, go on and try to make our lives purposeful. Coretta and his children would have to do the same, with the additional emotional pain of having to face every day the loss of a husband, the loss of a father.

I wasn't concerned, then or now, with *who* killed Martin Luther King, but rather focused my concern on *what* killed Martin Luther King. Martin was murdered at a time of pervasive fears about race, a lack of confidence in America's ability to confront the issues of poverty, a paranoia about global and domestic communism. Martin survived challenging America's racial status quo and accomplished changes in segregation and voting rights that few could have imagined the decade before. But when Martin began to address poverty and war, he began to challenge in an even more fundamental way the basic structure of the American economy.

While I believe that there was an element of conspiracy and a degree of involvement by some segment of the U.S. government, I have always felt that my task was to continue Martin's work and not to solve the mystery of his murder. Nevertheless, I cannot dismiss the role of the FBI in nurturing hostility toward Martin among influential members of American society, including the president. The FBI campaign against Martin was outrageous, unconscionable, a violation of his constitutional rights and a breach of the FBI's duty to uphold the Constitution of the United States. It was a smear campaign rooted in racism and all the more tragic because the FBI's right to engage in the campaign was not even questioned by the media or high-level government officials.

The vicious campaign against Martin had three themes: communism, misappropriation of funds, and sexual impropriety. The electronic surveillance of the movement began with allegations of communist influence that the FBI was never required to substantiate. Later rumors of sexual misconduct were circulated—again, never substantiated—and the FBI was never required to justify its extraordinary incursion through pervasive wiretaps into the privacy of dozens of American citizens. Despite the intense surveillance of the movement, no charges were ever brought against any full-time employee of SCLC relating to sexual misconduct, fraud, or financial negligence.

But that's almost beside the point, since clearly the campaign against Martin and the movement was less about sex than about fear of sexuality. Deeply buried but intense sexual fear of black males, illustrated by the sexual nature of attacks on black men by whites who seek to control or destroy black aggressiveness, has been a persistent pattern in the South since the advent of slavery. From the systematic destruction of the black family during slavery to contemporary barriers for black males attempting to protect and provide for their families via the imposition of strong societal and economic proscriptions, there is a recurrent theme: controlling black men. The theme was ever-present at lynchings of black men for allegations of rape or for flirtation with white women, and is always evident somewhere in the heavy punishment awaiting black men who assert or advocate the interests of their people. The FBI campaign was very much consistent with this neurotic white Southern racist tradition.

FBI memos released under the Freedom of Information Act reek with racist language and a determination to "get" something dirty on us that would ruin our reputations. Agents were instructed to be on the alert in the search for indiscretions in Atlanta or wherever Martin traveled. It is shocking that memos containing personal information gleaned from telephone calls and other conversations were widely and indiscriminately circulated around the Justice Department and even sent to the White House, where they were apparently eagerly read by Lyndon Johnson. At one point late in Johnson's administration, Cartha DeLoach of the FBI actually moved into the White House West Wing, where he personally fed the president results of FBI wiretap surveillance. These items were of no possible use to Lyndon Johnson or anyone else except insofar as they satisfied their base curiosity. Some inkling of how bizarre this obsession became was revealed to Martin during one of his last conversations with Lyndon Johnson about his opposition to the war in Vietnam. The president complained that he was so hurt by Martin's criticisms that he felt as if he had discovered that Martin raped his daughter. That remark was so off-key it stunned and puzzled Martin, and suggested to him he was dealing with more than ideological and policy differences.

In his frustration over Martin's opposition to the war in Vietnam, Lyndon Johnson released his most ferocious attacks on Martin, reportedly referring to him as that "goddamn nigger preacher" in one of his trademark tirades. His anger seemed increasingly personal in a way that was difficult to understand, unless one considers that he was receiving reports on SCLC's conversations and staff meetings from the FBI. One of Jim Bevel's favorite pet theories was that white men went to war to hide their feelings of sexual inadequacy—if that kind of offhand comment in the midst of an SCLC staff meeting was reported to Lyndon Johnson, one can imagine his hostility becoming personal and even irrational. While I think Johnson did not wish Martin any harm, his anger, nurtured by FBI officials, could have given some elements within his government a sense that the death of Martin Luther King would not be unacceptable to the president. One gets the feeling, after reading the released FBI and Justice Department memos and the communications from the White House, especially during Lyndon Johnson's administration, that on the surface we were being smiled at and granted grudging support; below the surface we were distrusted, resented, and undercut.

Ultimately, I do not believe that James Earl Ray possessed sufficient intelligence to escape from Memphis, much less acquire a passport and develop a plan to leave the country for what was then Rhodesia. A number of theories have been proposed and I am glad that people are investigating these events, since the possibility that there was a conspiracy within the U.S. government represents a serious threat to our democracy and the principles and rights that all U.S. citizens should hold dear.

There are several troubling coincidences and unexplained deaths of people who were influential opponents of the war in Vietnam that prevent me from dismissing the possibility of a conspiracy. Martin was killed one year to the day after his speech at Riverside Church in which he outlined his opposition to the war in Vietnam. Other outspoken opponents of the war died prematurely, including Bob Spike, my good friend and colleague from the National Council of Churches. As chairman of the National Council of Churches's Commission on Race and Religion, Bob had been instrumental in organizing national church support for the civil rights movement, the March on Washington, the Civil Rights Act, and the Voting Rights Act. He was probably the single most active church movement leader, though he did not become widely known outside of church circles. He was also an early opponent of the war and was influential in the decision of the National Council of Churches to oppose the bombing of North Vietnam, the first major church pronouncement against the war. He was murdered in 1966 in Columbus, Ohio, at an Ohio State University guest house. No one was ever convicted of the crime.

Bernard Fall was killed when he stepped on a land mine in Vietnam, but I've always thought there was more to this story than has been told. Orphaned as a youth in France during the Second World War, Fall had grown up as a teenage member of the French underground. When France was liberated, he somehow joined up with the U.S. Army and began attending college through an extension course offered in the military by the University of Maryland. After working with the U.S. Army at the Nuremberg trials, he emigrated from France to the United States, where he earned a doctorate in International Relations at the Maxwell School of Citizenship of Syracuse University, writing his dissertation on the French Indochinese War. His masterful knowledge of what had occurred there in 1955 and 1956 was the basis for his early warnings that America was repeating the same mistakes in Vietnam that the French had made a decade earlier. I have always found it hard to believe that someone who virtually cut his teeth in battlefield situations and was so intimately familiar with war zones would accidentally kill himself by stepping on a mine. At the time he was killed, Bernard Fall was the most knowledgeable critic of American policy in Vietnam.

Then there is the case of Thomas Merton, an influential theologian and outspoken opponent of the U.S. policy in Vietnam, who died in Thailand in 1968. Merton was found electrocuted by a hand-held hair dryer that had fallen into his bathwater. This was especially suspicious since Merton was bald and would have had no reason to use a hair dryer. He was found dead in the bathtub. It seems there were just too many convenient deaths of key opponents of the war—those who sought a more humane and peaceful solution to the problems in Southeast Asia. Throughout the 1960s, beginning with the plane crash that killed United Nations Secretary General Dag Hammarskjöld, so many friends of justice and peace suffered premature deaths—famous, outspoken people like Martin, but also quiet, behind-the-scenes people like Bob Spike.

Today, almost three decades later, Martin's legacy looms even larger than we thought possible in the days immediately after April 4, 1968.

And as the details of his travails, his struggles, and the atmosphere of turmoil and contention have receded into broad strokes of black and white, Martin has become a larger-than-life symbol, almost a deity, rather than the flesh-and-blood man I knew. There is a danger in this. We should not lose our sense of how the civil rights movement happened, because if we do, younger generations, along with ourselves, will lose a sense of how new opportunities were fought for, and won. In blurring, or ignoring, the context of the struggle, the veneration of Martin Luther King becomes devoid of depth and context, and the ability to use his model to renew the struggle for a just and equitable society is lost. In these days of "everything for me," Martin's decision to devote his life to social change seems almost of another age. But if his life teaches us anything, it is that real leadership must be grounded in the interest and institutions of the people, and leadership must appeal to the most moral, disciplined, and determined qualities in our nature. This can only come from a process of continual questioning, the capacity to overcome mistakes, and the ability to follow a path courageously once it is chosen, all of which was Martin King's essential nature.

In the profoundest of terms, my work with Martin gave my life a purpose and sustenance I could have hardly dreamed of when Jean and I left New York to return to the South in 1961. He left his mark on me, both in indelible memories and in the spiritual and practical lessons of our trials and triumphs. It is by the quality of those days that I have come to measure my own continuing journey.

PART III

1968–1972

17

City of Hope

Done made my vow to the Lord and I never will turn back.
—African-American Spiritual

After Martin's death, we went forward on faith. There was the matter of his funeral, which had to be settled in consultation with Daddy King and Coretta. Since Ebenezer Baptist Church, where Martin, his daddy, and his granddaddy had been preachers, was not large enough to hold even a fraction of the mourners, it was not going to be possible to hold Martin's funeral there. Condolences and donations to SCLC and the family were pouring in from all over the world. Martin's would be the equivalent of a funeral for a head of state, although SCLC and the King family did not begin to have the resources for an event of such proportions. It was fitting that his body lay in state at Ebenezer, but a larger place would have to be found for the funeral.

Martin's mentor, Benjamin Mays, offered the historic quadrangle of Morehouse College as a venue for Martin's funeral. To comply with Martin's wishes for a simple funeral, we proposed to carry his coffin in the back of a mule-drawn wagon and process down Auburn Avenue and over to Fair Street and the Morehouse campus.

As it turned out though, the football stadium at Georgia Tech was the only facility in Atlanta that could have accommodated all the people who came to pay tribute to Martin. At the time of his death,

Martin was too controversial in Georgia for that venue to have been available to us. But, more than two decades later, a multiracial crowd filled that stadium to hear Nelson Mandela on his first tour of the United States following his release from a South African prison.

The crowds that followed the rough mule-drawn wagon on its journey through the narrow streets of Atlanta were frighteningly enormous. There was simply not enough room in the quadrangle for all the people in the march. Jean and the girls were almost left outside the gate and they were near the front of the march. What began as a cool day grew hot in the afternoon. Those of us inside the Morehouse compound were hemmed in on all sides. We had to trust that everything would be all right, that everyone in the crowd inside and outside the gate would behave with dignity and restraint.

The service was long, with one speech after another, each preacher trying to outdo the last in praising Martin. I had had no time to mourn the loss of my leader, my brother in Christ, my friend. The service was in many ways just another situation for me to manage, another grand idea to break into manageable pieces and administer. I was preoccupied with worrying about the crowds, about the rows of dignitaries that we were unable to protect in the event of a crisis. I also worried about my own family in the midst of that sea of mourners.

Then Ralph began to speak. He preached from the story of Joseph, "Let us slay the dreamer, and see what shall become of his dream." He called each of us to take up Martin's cause and to dedicate ourselves to the fulfillment of his dream. Of all the speeches by intellectual giants that day, Ralph's preaching is all that I remember. It has since been borrowed many times, but it was Ralph who evoked the Dreamer Joseph, the great patriarch of Israel, in reference to Martin: "What shall become of his dream."

I located Jean and the girls for the slow, stately procession to the historic Southside Cemetery where Martin was first entombed. When they sealed Martin's body in the tomb, I wept. Whenever I visit his tomb, I weep, even after nearly thirty years.

With Martin buried and checks coming in from all over the world, a new conflict arose. While Martin had often talked about his death, he made no provisions for Coretta and the children. Now, money was coming in as a result of Martin's death and Coretta needed it for her family. But there was no sensitivity to that among Ralph and many SCLC board members. They argued, with some merit, that the funds were to continue Martin's work. But, the fact remained that many of the checks were made out to Coretta and she could not be ignored. There were a lot of contestants for Martin's legacy and Coretta wanted to take up the mantle, too. She had always seen herself as a civil rights leader, not just as a wife in the background. She was pregnant most of the early days of the movement and we used to tease Martin that every time he went to jail and came out she got pregnant. But, Coretta had come into her own when she began representing Martin at rallies and demonstrations against the war in Vietnam. Martin could keep her "in her place" so to speak, but there was no way Ralph, Joe Lowery, Hosea Williams, or any of us were going to tell Coretta what to do. She was determined to do more than raise children. She was committed to seeing that her husband's work was carried on.

This caused incredible tension within the SCLC staff. Ralph and the board wanted to use Coretta to raise money for SCLC, but they didn't want her to play any kind of policy role in the organization. The men in SCLC were incapable of dealing with a strong woman like Coretta, who was insisting on being treated as an equal.

Coretta had her own sense of mission and she perceived her role differently from the role of SCLC. Martin used the parable of the Good Samaritan to illustrate the different roles that people must play in the movement for social change. He cautioned against condemning those who hurried on to their meetings, because it wasn't enough to help the injured person, someone had to address the conditions on the Jericho Road that led to his injuries. Martin would say, "I think we ought to have some police officers on that road. My role is not that of the Good Samaritan." Coretta did not see herself as the Good Samaritan either, nor did she see herself filling Martin's role. In her view, it was the role of SCLC to carry on the movement that was part of Martin's legacy. She wanted to train people in nonviolence and, to follow Martin's analogy, she wanted to train city planners to improve Jericho Roads all over America. Almost unavoidably, Coretta became a prominent spokesperson for Martin's legacy and many people resented her because of it. It was painful to see people that Martin had nurtured openly criticizing his widow. Nevertheless, Coretta tenaciously set about establishing the Martin Luther King Center for Nonviolent Social Change to preserve and share Martin's legacy into the twenty-first century.

We were compelled to go ahead with the Poor People's Campaign in the late spring of 1968, though what we really needed was a long break before attempting to rekindle our energies. This was not the time to rest, however. For one thing, we believed that the ulterior motive behind Martin's murder was cancellation of the campaign. I felt it was my responsibility to hold things together. I didn't really grieve, I just let work consume me. I didn't want to feel anything, because the feelings would be too painful, so I just went numb. For better or worse, there was so much to do that I didn't have the luxury of self-examination.

We didn't hold many illusions about the success of the Poor People's Campaign. Without Martin, it would be very difficult to convey our message. Truthfully, without Martin, keeping the staff focused on our message would be almost impossible. Not unexpectedly, in the confusion and tumult following Martin's death, the Poor People's Campaign got completely out of hand. Once again we were faced with an almost insane reversal of fortune. Before Martin's assassination we were desperately trying to drum up volunteers and support; now we were deluged with more volunteers than we could handle. Our original intention was to carefully select the first wave of demonstrators and train them rigorously in nonviolent philosophy and techniques. Demonstrators had been identified, and most had been trained in nonviolence. Now we were expecting many more demonstrators, many of whom were not a part of the basic organizational structure that had been set up for the campaign. People were pledging to come to Washington, people we hadn't trained, didn't really know, and couldn't necessarily control.

On April 19, Ralph announced we would go ahead with the Poor People's March to Washington. Before Martin Luther King's death we had planned on fifteen hundred well-trained demonstrators; by the time of the march we had received commitments from more than three thousand in addition to the core fifteen hundred people who had pledged to support the PPC by coming to Washington.

Walter Fauntroy, Marian Wright, and I coordinated the lobby efforts of the Poor People's Committee of 100. The committee was multiracial and multiethnic and included Chicanos, Puerto Ricans, Native Americans, and whites as well as African-Americans. Old and new allies from the peace movement, religious organizations, and the labor movement were also represented. We did not appreciate it at the time, but with Martin's death, the Poor People's Campaign became the venue through which his coalition of conscience came together. This broad-based committee met with congressional leaders and officials in the Johnson administration to convey our intentions and the demands of the PPC before caravans of poor people began camping out in the nation's capital.

As in every campaign since Birmingham, we wanted the authorities to understand fully our aims. The declaration we issued in 1968 is just as relevant today:

1. A meaningful job at a living wage for every employable citizen.
2. A secure and adequate income for all who cannot find jobs or for whom employment is inappropriate.
3. Access to land as a means to income and livelihood.
4. Access to capital as a means of full participation in the economic life of America.
5. Recognition by law of the right of people affected by government programs to play a truly significant role in determining how they are designed and carried out.

The Committee of 100 held three days of meetings sharing the general declaration and their specific demands of federal departments, such as Agriculture, Health, Education and Welfare, Labor, Housing and Urban Development, Justice, and the Office of Economic Opportunity. Meanwhile, Hosea coordinated the caravans of poor people that began leaving Mississippi, Chicago, and Boston bound for Washington, D.C. We kept Martin's pledge that a mule train would leave Marks, Mississippi. The mule train eventually met up with the buses for the long trip from the South to Washington. In an echo of Martin's funeral procession, we drove a mule train down Atlanta's Auburn Avenue to kick off the Poor People's Campaign there. I rode on the back of a mule and offered rides to children along the parade route. It was a rare moment of contentment, the calm before the storms that awaited us in Washington.

A site in West Potomac Park between the Lincoln and Washington Monuments was temporarily allotted to us by the District of Columbia. It was lush and green with fresh spring growth but surrounded by the cold white marble of official Washington. A local architect volunteered his services and designed plywood structures to be erected on the site to provide shelter. We named the village Resurrection City, to symbolize the idea of rebirth from the depths of despair and oppression. We wanted to name it "City of Hope" but a charity of the same name objected. Bernard Lafayette coordinated the extremely complex task of constructing Resurrection City, a raw city of tents and plywood structures for the poor in the capital of the world's richest nation.

The first poor people arrived in Washington on May 12, and by May 19, Resurrection City was a good-size town with a legion of logistical problems. First, there were simply too many people— almost seven thousand at our peak in June. And the larger the population, the greater the problems. In a few weeks Resurrection City had become almost a microcosm of an overcrowded big-city ghetto. Our staff became weighed down by the problems of housing, feeding, and governing. There was even a baby born in Resurrection City. Ralph formally baptized the child.

We simply weren't used to relating on a daily basis to several thousand people at once. For the Selma-to-Montgomery march we saw to the food, shelter, and medical care for three hundred marchers for about a week. Resurrection City demanded similar care for thousands for nearly two months. The SCLC staff became the "establishment" of the city—all frustrations were directed toward us. I began to feel a new sympathy for Mayor Daley. To make matters worse, there was dissension within SCLC. There was a power struggle between Jim Bevel and Ralph: they both wanted to be "mayor" of Resurrection City. The mayor held a press briefing every day, which made the title so attractive, I suppose. The entire business was so absurd. Had I known then as much as I now know about the structure of city government I would have accommodated Bevel with the title of city manager. But I had no patience with the kind of insecurity that led people to fight over titles when there was work to be done. So since Ralph was president of SCLC he declared himself mayor. But he wasn't there on a daily basis to deal with the problems. There were conflicts in the tent city that required regular mediation, but Ralph was primarily interested in the ceremonial functions of the mayor, such as baptizing a baby born in Resurrection City and holding press conferences.

Nature did not cooperate either. Washington was drenched by torrential rainstorms during June, and Resurrection City became a quagmire. The grounds of our city never had a chance to dry out because people continually trampled through them. The lovely green grass had become a sea of mud. In some of the holes, you could step in mud up to your knees. There was no place to dry off or clean up but an unheated plywood shelter. Miraculously, the roofs on the shelters didn't leak, but there were only canvas flaps to keep water from blowing in on the sides. And unfortunately, although Resurrection City was intended simply to house demonstrators, in the press coverage it became the focal point and symbol of the Poor People's Campaign.

Resurrection City was not the only residence for supporters of the PPC. Native Americans were housed in a school in southwest Washington. Many of the Hispanics also resided outside the tent city. Ralph and several staff members kept quarters at the Howard Johnson's across from the now-famous Watergate Complex. I found myself shuttling from Resurrection City to the Howard Johnson's to Capitol Hill in an attempt to keep everyone from running off on their own agendas.

Our plan had been for committees of demonstrators to visit the appropriate federal departments to pressure them to act on specific issues concerning the poor. Using Birmingham as a model, each demonstration was to be a little drama that told the story of a particular injustice. But it had been Martin's role to interpret our little dramas for the press. When Martin spoke, that became the story and it allowed us to control the message. Without Martin to focus the message, the press ignored many of the substantive issues around poverty that we came to highlight. The press had apparently made up its mind to condemn the Poor People's Campaign and Resurrection City long before we even arrived in the capital. The Washington press in particular didn't know anything about the civil rights movement, and even the black reporters were surprisingly unfamiliar with our philosophy and history. With few exceptions, reporters were interested only in dirt-digging—unearthing the internal conflicts, disputes, and backbiting from our sea of mud. There was no real interest shown in the issues we were attempting to elucidate. When physical examinations we provided revealed that a large number of people were suffering from medical problems, the press saw an "epidemic," not the deeper truth that poverty and health problems go hand in hand. It was as if the doctor who discovered a cancer was blamed for it.

Hosea held a series of demonstrations outside the Agriculture Department to highlight its little-known role in administering the food stamp and commodities programs. Its programs were also a flagrant example of "welfare for the rich," since big landowners received enormous subsidies and put poor people off the land. Hosea took his small band of poor people with their placards and picketed the ornate marble-trimmed building graced with seasonal flowers that housed the office of the secretary of agriculture. But when we called a press conference to ask the newsmen to focus on the food stamp program, not one of the twenty reporters present knew how the food stamp program worked. Martin could have held their attention long enough to begin to educate them about these programs and our concerns about their operation. Martin had always dominated and managed the press by the power of his personality. He knew how to do more than hold his own in press conferences—he could turn hostile questions to his advantage and get his message through. Without him, the Washington press corps saw no reason to understand food stamps or any other program that might help poor people. Consequently the negative tone set by the press prevailed.

Our difficulties were exacerbated by attacks from hostile congressmen. Most members of Congress made it quite clear that they had little interest in the needs of poor people. Senator Carl Curtis from Nebraska maintained that the "poor people who are colored, who live in the nation's capital, were against the march." Rep. Wayne Aspinall of Colorado said that since the Bonus Marchers, the veterans of World War I who came to Washington during the Depression to demand a promised cash bonus, had been evicted from Washington, poor people had even less right to come.

We were also certain that Resurrection City was infested with undercover agents and agents provocateurs. I believe the National Park Service and other government agencies sent in officers posing as poor people, and it was the infiltrators who kept people stirred up against us inside Resurrection City. For example, there were complaints about the food. Well, for poor people from Mississippi, beans and salami were nothing to complain about, and it was a fairly decent meal. Yet there were those inside Resurrection City who created distractions over food that hampered our efforts to raise the issue of hunger for poor people all over America. And I believe that was the intent.

My usual role was to negotiate with the appropriate officials and articulate the demands of a campaign. In the Poor People's Campaign I found myself mediating conflicts within our own ranks. There were power struggles everywhere. It was a great achievement to unite poor people of so many backgrounds and ethnic groups behind one movement, but the different groups had no experience working together. There was tension, not so much between black and white poor—their issues were largely the same whether rural or urban. But Hispanics and Native Americans brought issues that were entirely new to us— issues concerning language, treaties, and culture. One of the Hispanic leaders from New Mexico, Reis Tijerina, seemed more concerned about the Treaty of Guadalupe Hidalgo, which established the border between Mexico and the United States, than he was about poor people. Some leaders began agitating that their issues were being neglected.

Then there were the ongoing power struggles among the SCLC staff. James Bevel and Jesse Jackson wasted time and energy expressing their dissatisfaction with Ralph's leadership, while Bernard Lafayette was overburdened with directing the campaign. I kept them on the team as best I could. I told them all, "Whatever you may think about Ralph's leadership, this is neither the time nor the place to have a leadership struggle. This campaign is whipping our butts, we don't need to fight amongst ourselves." The *Washington Post* got wind of some of what was going on and began to speculate that Hosea or I would make a better president for SCLC than Ralph. Meanwhile, rather than arguing about and planning strategy with Congress and President Johnson, I was trying to keep SCLC staff members from turning on one another. All of this directed attention away from the basic issue of the Poor People's Campaign—what was America going to do about the poor?

I was in a daze, functioning on autopilot. I remember thinking that there was no way I was going to jail with this crew. The original planning for the PPC had anticipated civil disobedience that would likely result in longer jail sentences than we had ever served. We couldn't expect the federal courts to be on our side when we were disrupting Washington. I had been prepared to spend a year in jail with Martin. That would have been productive, meaningful, and perhaps even a spiritually enriching experience. But I had been to jail with a group of undisciplined people, and I had no desire to spend time in jail with people bickering and fighting with one another. I had never felt so despondent.

Our one remaining hope was the presidential election. All the presidential candidates had been asked to respond to the demands of the Poor People's Campaign and the responses of the Democrats were a source of hope. Eugene McCarthy had entered the campaign as the antiwar candidate, but he showed a genuine concern for issues of social justice. Hubert Humphrey was an old friend, although somewhat tainted by his tenure as Johnson's vice president. Then there was Robert Kennedy, who embodied all that was good and promising about his brother John and the best ideas of the Johnson era. Kennedy was openly supportive of the Poor People's Campaign and seemed to have a genuine passion for our agenda. There was comfort in knowing that the Poor People's Campaign, however flawed, was laying a foundation on which a President Robert Kennedy could build.

Then on June 5, just two months after Martin's death, Robert Kennedy was shot in Los Angeles; he died the next day. Deep in the recesses of our subconscious, we always expected that Martin would eventually be killed, but the death of Robert Kennedy shocked us into a state of disbelief and incomprehension bordering on total despair.

I was not a fan of Bobby Kennedy's when his brother was in the

White House. I knew he had immense political presence, but I felt he had taken advantage of his ability to appeal to the black community directly without bothering to work together with the black leadership. I viewed that as a kind of rich-boy arrogance. I was also angered by his charge after the Watts riot that the civil rights movement had neglected the cities. In my opinion, Bobby Kennedy had no right to suggest that Martin Luther King and other civil rights leaders weren't doing enough.

My impression of him changed, however, in the wake of Martin's assassination. In Atlanta, as we were preparing for Martin's funeral, Earl Graves, founder of *Black Enterprise Magazine,* arranged for Bobby Kennedy to speak privately with SCLC's senior staff: Daddy King, Dorothy Cotton, Jim Bevel, James Orange, Hosea Williams, Fred Bennett, T. Y. Rogers, Bernard Lafayette, C. T. Vivian, Bernard Lee, Jesse Jackson, and Randolph Blackwell. As I looked around the room, each face mirrored the pain and grief that pressed against my own heart. In sincere and personal terms, Kennedy spoke about his own grief at the death of his brother. He described the risk to all of us working for social change through politics and nonviolence as equivalent to the risks in times of war: "My brother survived a torpedo in a PT boat in the middle of the ocean, but when he came home to stand for the same ideals he fought for in that PT boat, he was killed in his own country. The struggle for freedom is as dangerous as the struggles against an external enemy, but we have to carry on. Those of us who are left must carry on." For the first time I could see some of the warmth and emotion and passion for meaningful social change that lay behind his seemingly cold, calculating political demeanor. He and his staff went on to support the Poor People's Campaign and Resurrection City when most national politicians were denouncing us and some black leaders avoided us as if we were a contagious disease.

The night Kennedy was shot, Coretta King and I sat in the genteel shabbiness of the Willard Hotel numbly watching the television screen, listening to the depressing medical reports as life faded from him. After he died I sank into a depression so deep it was impossible for me to go on. We had thought we might be able to rebuild a forceful national consensus around Kennedy, salvaging at least something in the wake of Martin's death. Now even that hope was gone. It had been a long while since my spirit suffered such an enduring low. Washington was at the end of a long road that just seemed to have deteriorated into a narrow track leading to a swamp. My colleagues and I had begun at a frantic pace back in January and by April everyone was physically spent. Then came the shock and emotional exhaustion of Martin's death. But we forced ourselves to go ahead. By the time we reached Washington we simply weren't functioning very well. The SCLC staff didn't have the energy or the willpower we had had in Birmingham and Selma—none of us were up to it either physically or emotionally. We were all trying to pretend that Martin's death had not devastated us, but it had. And with the compounding shock and grief of Robert Kennedy's murder, I couldn't even pretend anymore.

We had to salvage an end to the Poor People's Campaign and get out of Washington with some degree of dignity. Our initial plan had called for a Memorial Day rally, which we later rescheduled for June 19, a symbolic date. "Juneteenth" was celebrated in the black community as the day black slaves actually heard of the Emancipation Proclamation in the cotton-producing country of the Deep South. We pulled the staff together for a contentious strategy session and agreed to focus our demands on hunger, organize for a successful rally on June 19, close out Resurrection City, and go home. As an issue, hunger had the clearest moral dimension, there were programs that could be expanded or revised, and it was an issue on which all factions could agree—Native Americans on reservations, poor whites in Appalachia, Hispanics in barrios, and blacks in Harlem and Mississippi. Also, a blue-ribbon panel had recently issued a study on hunger, so the facts were available from a source the Washington press corps might respect. It had been Marian Wright's idea to focus our demands on hunger, and I was supportive, because I knew it was critical that we salvage some actual gain from this massive undertaking. Bayard Rustin, who had organized the March on Washington in 1963, disagreed, arguing that the campaign should address the causes of poverty rather than its symptoms. Hunger was a symptom of unemployment and low wages. Because Rustin believed in this so strongly, he left the coalition in protest.

Jean was beginning to worry about me. The Solidarity Day Rally was scheduled after the end of school in Atlanta, so she decided to come to Washington. She could check on me, attend the rally, and take the girls to some of the museums. I couldn't spare the time to meet Jean at the airport, so she took a cab to the Howard Johnson's where Ralph maintained his headquarters. The next day, I took Jean and the girls to muddy Resurrection City. We had to walk on plywood walkways to get to the A-frame shelter where we would spend the night. The sound of the rain against the shelter kept us all pretty restless. During the night, I would get up and walk around the sleeping community, making sure that everything was as right as it could be. Standing watch over Resurrection City was the tall obelisk we know as the Washington Monument, with a red light blinking steadily through the night. Depending on one's perspective, the Monument was either a guardian of liberty or a giant Klansman.

The next morning, I took Jean and our daughters to the school where the Native American delegation was staying so they could take a hot shower. At Resurrection City, personal comfort and hygiene had to be maintained without the benefit of indoor toilets and hot water. From the school, I dropped Jean and the girls at the Mall near the American History Museum and returned to my work.

Jean and our daughters were probably the only residents of Resurrection City to spend their days at the Smithsonian. Unlike Birmingham, where I felt Jean's presence was a distraction, I was happy to have my family in Washington. It was disorienting for the girls, however. Children like predictability, and my schedule was anything but. Jean was trying to keep an eye on my emotional state and entertain the three girls—ages six, ten, and twelve—at the same time. I'm not sure which one of us had the more demanding job.

The Poor People's Campaign culminated in the Solidarity Day Rally for Jobs, Peace and Freedom. More than fifty thousand people gathered in front of the Lincoln Memorial on the hot afternoon of June 19. This crowd was less tentative than the group that had gathered five years before for the March on Washington, dressed more casually, and was less inhibited about cooling themselves in the Reflecting Pool. Where toes had dangled in the pool in 1963, denim-clad bodies now waded. In many ways, it was the March on Washington without Martin's transcendent conclusion—just a long day filled with dull speeches.

At the time I felt it was something to be endured. Looking back, I can see that it marked the emergence of a broad-based progressive coalition: poor people who were black, white, brown, and red; religious leaders; union leaders; peace activists. Jobs, peace, and freedom would be linked, sustained through a loose, shifting, but persistent coalition of organizations. Among the people gathered were some who would go on to head organizations and become members of Congress and elected officials from small Southern communities. But in my despair in June 1968 it was difficult to see the possibilities emerging from the Poor People's Campaign. It seemed that despite our marches, press conferences, and civil disobedience, the only image that ever came through in the press was Resurrection City, beset with turmoil, symbolic of the very problems the nation preferred not to face. Despite my feelings, Solidarity Day was the high point of the Poor People's Campaign. Ralph delivered the keynote address: "We have brought to the attention of the country more vividly than ever before the plight of the poor in America. We have made America see the hunger and the deprivation, the terrible and shameful spectacle of children starving while a nation diets."

Our permit for Resurrection City was due to expire on Sunday night, June 23rd. The tension in Washington grew as the date neared. One night, the D.C. police surrounded the tent city and threw tear-gas canisters inside, while residents slept. I dashed out to the police line and asked for the commander in charge. The police were all wearing gas masks and they looked like aliens. I said, "Look, people are in there sleeping with their kids. How would you feel if someone was throwing tear gas in on your family while they slept? If you all have a problem with something going on here let's talk about it. But this is just going to create trouble where it doesn't need to exist." The commander took off his gas mask and stopped the attack. A lot of his officers were ashamed of the teargassing. We found many gas canisters that hadn't been triggered, and we had to restrain some hotheads from throwing them back at the police. Fortunately, most residents had already departed and no one became hysterical from the tear gas. The police claimed that someone inside Resurrection City was throwing rocks at motorists and for that they were willing to teargas the entire community.

The Department of the Interior had agreed to allow a brief period for an orderly departure from the tent city after the expiration date. On June 25th, police and National Guardsmen surrounded Resurrection City, but only a few dozen people remained. We were being systematically run out of town by our own government. Ralph and three hundred others staged a demonstration at the Capitol during which Ralph was arrested. This was just the last in a series of independent, uncoordinated actions by members of SCLC's executive staff that contributed to the disorganization of the Poor People's Campaign. By nightfall, the muddy ground was all that remained of the City of Hope.

There were many creative ideas for resuming the Poor People's Campaign in Washington in the fall of 1968, but Bevel and Jesse had resisted the emphasis on economic justice, even when Martin was alive. The team of wild horses was now really running wild; each person was trying to push his own pet projects and we sorely missed Martin's unifying leadership. Ralph was unable to get everyone mov-

ing in the same direction, and he was also going through some difficult days; Martin's shoes were hard to fill. Ralph had been handed
the position of Martin's successor because of his genuine loyalty to
Martin. I tried to support Ralph, to shore up his weaknesses, but he
was frustrated by his inability to be Martin Luther King. Ralph
would complain that I didn't write powerful speeches for him as I
had done for Martin. I would try to explain that I didn't write
speeches for Martin, I gave him points, notes on specific issues and
outlines. He didn't understand that Martin could preach and quote
Shakespeare or Aristotle from memory and Ralph accused me of giving Martin better speech material than I gave him. No matter how I
urged him to be Ralph Abernathy, the powerful preacher and committed activist, he kept trying to imitate Martin rather than developing his own style of leading SCLC.

Ralph was not a strategist and could not fill the role that Martin
had played in staff meetings in choosing a direction for SCLC to
take. In truth, that task had become increasingly difficult even for
Martin, as the staff became more and more impressed with their own
abilities. Now clashes among the senior staff over organizational
direction were even more frequent than before, and the fireworks
were unfortunately intensified by the fact that we actually had more
money than ever, as contributions to SCLC flowed in the wake of
Martin's death. Arguments over the substance of programs became
bitter disputes over who would get what percentage of the budget.

To me, this distressing period was symbolized by an actual physical fight between Hosea and me during one staff meeting, which I
now attribute to our worn nerves. Hosea was chiding me about being
"middle class" in a way I didn't like, and I decided I had had enough
of his bullying. Sometimes, the only way to deal with a bully is to
fight him, so I jumped over the table and grabbed him and we wrestled to the floor.

Clearly, we were all fraying around the edges, and around this
time I decided that maybe what we needed was a staff psychiatrist,
someone who would join the staff permanently and could be available to everyone for this very stressful period. We invited Dr. Price
Cobb and his associate, Mrs. Betty Brandon, to work with us. Most
of the people in SCLC thought this was ridiculous: "We're not sick,
it's the society that we live in," they protested, which was true
enough. But we weren't functioning like the old team, and there was
no point trying to blame our deterioration on the state of racial
progress, or lack of it; I felt we had to look within ourselves for a
solution. The psychological impact of losing Martin was difficult for

all of us. Dr. Cobb and Mrs. Brandon were able to help us bring some of our buried feelings into the open.

The presidential campaign that fall provided some focus. In the wake of Bobby Kennedy's death, Hubert Humphrey came out of the Democratic National Convention with the nomination. But the activists in the country were so bitter and disillusioned they could muster no enthusiasm for Humphrey after experiencing true love for Kennedy and getting "clean for Gene." Further diluting support for Humphrey, Black Power advocate Eldridge Cleaver and satirist Dick Gregory ran for president as independent candidates. We tried to rally voters behind Humphrey, to encourage voter registration and mobilization on election day, but Lyndon Johnson's party became a victim of his decision not to send monitors and federal registrars to counties across the South. The Voting Rights Act was still not fulfilling its potential, and doubts about Humphrey persisted. Was he the liberal Hubert Humphrey of his Senate tenure, or was he so compromised by his term as LBJ's vice president that he would merely continue Johnson's policy toward the war in Vietnam? Activists were becoming single-issue oriented, and among antiwar students and black militants, Humphrey was condemned as merely the lesser of two evils, only marginally better than his Republican rival, Richard Nixon.

I was a strong Humphrey man. One of the first things I remember about electoral politics was the Democratic convention of 1948. My daddy called me to the radio to listen to Senator Hubert Humphrey speak in support of a civil rights plank for the party platform. During the movement, he was a senator we could count on to introduce legislation for civil rights, educational opportunity, and the alleviation of poverty. For me, there was no comparison between Humphrey and Nixon. Humphrey had proven himself a friend of justice for the previous twenty years.

In a now-famous clash, student protesters at the Democratic National Convention were met with Mayor Daley's riot police. The harsh crackdown on their protests only deepened the peace activists' suspicion of Humphrey. Activists mourned for their lost icons and elevated them to an even higher status than they had held in life. It became unfashionable to hope. Hope was in the grave with John, Martin, and Bobby. Like teenaged girls longing for the unattainable rock and roll star, those left in the Democratic Party could summon little passion for Hubert Humphrey.

Then George Wallace came out of Alabama with a third-party candidacy that increased our sense of urgency about the election.

Here was a symbol more clear than Goldwater: Wallace was the per-
sonification of white resistance to civil rights. But SCLC could not
duplicate Martin's "Get Out the Vote Tour" that rallied black voters
to block Goldwater. We made every effort to motivate SCLC chapters
and our citizenship school teachers to mobilize voters in their communities, and there was a good response, although not as overwhelming as the turnout for LBJ in 1964. But we simply could not
attract the crowds and the press that a tour by Martin would have
generated. There was a cynicism that reverberated through the black
community after the assassinations of Martin and then Bobby
Kennedy that created a kind of nihilism. Black voters supported
Humphrey, but the support lacked the intensity that was needed.

In November 1968, Richard Nixon was elected president of the
United States. He beat Hubert Humphrey by less than one vote per
precinct. The left wing of the Democratic Party paid a high price for
its self-indulgence, as did the nation.

That election shaped many of my views about politics and the
dangers of symbolic candidacies. A vote is too precious to spend on a
symbol, a candidate that cannot win. I felt that everything Martin
Luther King stood for and gave his life for began to lose ground
because we could not keep our eyes on the prize.

18

===

What Shall Become of His Dream

I'm so glad, trouble don't last always.
—AFRICAN-AMERICAN SPIRITUAL

In 1968, it seemed that everything that could go wrong did go wrong. Even after the assassinations of Martin and Bobby Kennedy and the chaotic Poor People's Campaign, the year could have been salvaged by Hubert Humphrey's winning the White House. The original strategy of the Poor People's Campaign had been to put poverty at the top of the agenda for the next administration. Humphrey as president would have been exceptionally responsive to those concerns, and just as the March on Washington had paved the way for the Civil Rights Act of 1964, the Poor People's Campaign would have paved the way for effective, comprehensive initiatives to end poverty. But Humphrey's razor-thin loss to Richard Nixon meant that we would have to struggle just to hold on to the gains that had been achieved.

One of the high moments of a painful and difficult year came when the Atlanta sanitation workers, no doubt inspired by the workers in Memphis, decided to strike for higher wages. When the workers union, the Association of State, County and Municipal Employees

(ASCME), asked for SCLC's support, we had no choice but to respond. The senior SCLC staff members based in Atlanta, Joe Lowery, Hosea Williams, and I, organized local ministers to go out and join the union demonstrators who were going to position themselves to block the sanitation trucks as they left the storage yard. Altogether, about a dozen garbage workers and preachers sat down, arms linked, blocking the driveway through which garbage trucks would have to pass to go on their routes. As the drivers cranked up the trucks people began maneuvering for the middle of the line. I didn't realize what was going on and I remained on the end of the line. I suddenly realized that the garbage trucks were high—as the trucks continued to roll, the people in the middle could lie down and the wheels wouldn't roll over them, but those of us on the fringe might get caught by the big double tires.

The Atlanta police were called in to clear the driveway and arrest us, if necessary. I started talking to them as soon as they came on the lot: "Now, officers, you ought to come and get in the line right behind us because your pay is not much better than the garbage workers'. We have garbage workers in the city of Atlanta that are making less than the poverty line, that are working all week long, and they are entitled to better pay. Now, policemen are underpaid, too. You are being used to arrest these folks, and as soon as they get a raise, don't you think you are going to get a raise, too? Don't your children need shoes? How are you going to send your kids to college? Do you have enough health insurance if your wife or kids get sick? These are the things that the union is trying to provide sanitation workers and they are things you need as police officers, too." In fact, in that speech I planted the seeds in my own mind for helping to organize the police officers after I got to be mayor.

I didn't persuade them to join us, but the officers did arrest us a little more nicely. I appreciated that because I never liked getting thrown around and beat up. We were taken to the jail and released without being booked. Mayor Ivan Allen did not want to see this escalate into a major confrontation. He had been elected with black community support and he wasn't running for reelection, but having presided over the "City Too Busy to Hate," I think he wanted to leave office with his progressive reputation intact.

Mayor Allen sent over a proposal to offer the garbage workers a two-step increase. We went over to the union meeting at an old auditorium, but when Hosea spoke he got the union workers so inflamed that they rejected the pay increase. Joe Jacobs, an attorney who was Ivan Allen's representative in the auditorium when the offer was rejected, reported to Allen and informed the union leadership that Allen could not see how the city could make a better offer. I started talking to the union leadership and I said, "You know, this offer is a good thing." They said, "It is good, it's as much as we could hope for." I said, "Why didn't you say something? Why did you let them vote it down?" But they said, "Well, we prefer to let the workers decide." I asked the ASCME leadership to call another meeting where I would present the mayor's proposal to the membership of the union.

The next morning, I stood in front of the assembled workers with a blackboard and chalk. I put a line down the middle of the blackboard and began to write numbers and dollar signs. I spoke as I wrote: "This is what your salary is and this is what your raise is, this is how much it adds up to a paycheck each month. If you agree to accept the mayor's offer, this is what you get starting now, plus they will give you two weeks' back pay for the time you have been on strike." I added it in one column.

"If you stay on strike," I said, "this is what the strike is costing you." And I wrote down lost wages, less a small stipend the union provided. "You can strike for another two weeks or four weeks, and the most you could get is another step. But let's say you got two more steps. It would still take you this number of months to make up what you are losing by being on strike. I'm not talking about what the union wants or what the mayor wants. I'm talking about what you and your families want. This is not a civil rights vote, this is a pocket-book vote, and you ought to vote your own pocketbook and your own conscience."

When I finished speaking, the union leaders put the offer to another vote. This time, it passed easily. After that, I had friends in the local labor movement and I had made a new friend in Mayor Allen.

In 1969, the increasingly contentious staff at SCLC was saved from the jaws of total disintegration once again by the timely strike of black hospital workers in Charleston, South Carolina. Charleston was almost made-to-order as a focus for the energies of an SCLC staff embroiled in the intrigue of succession. In contrast to the Poor People's Campaign, the strike by Charleston hospital workers in the spring of 1969 had clearly defined and achievable goals. This was something we knew how to do and we leaped at the chance to show that SCLC could function without Martin Luther King at the helm.

I felt that this would be a good campaign for SCLC. Even in my worst days, my energy level had remained high and now my basic optimism was returning. Martin had given his life in an effort to organize garbage workers in Memphis and I felt that left us with an obligation to work with the unions. The South was antiunion and since black workers tended to have the lowest wages and worst working conditions, unions would be a great benefit to the black community—increasing both the personal dignity and economic security of black workers.

Charleston had remained one of the most inert Southern cities during the earlier major campaigns of the civil rights movement, despite considerable student protest activity in other South Carolina cities, particularly Orangeburg, where South Carolina State College was located. But the Charleston area did possess the legacy of the trail-blazing voter registration work of Johns Island's Esau Jenkins and my longtime coworker and mentor Septima Clark.

Charleston was established as a center of trade for the rice plantations that line the Ashley and Cooper Rivers. Rice cultivation was labor intensive and for much of Charleston's early history, the black population in the area exceeded the number of whites. The city's ruling class maintained the habit of strict oppression of the black community, a legacy of the need to control a black population on whom the white oligarchy was wholly and utterly dependent. The graciousness of life for the owners of the elegant homes on Charleston's Battery could not be sustained without cheap labor. To maintain that labor force, the first shot in the Civil War was fired at Charleston's Fort Sumter, a matter of some pride in Charleston. While losing the Civil War increased the cost of labor, Charleston, like New Orleans and other Southern communities, used Jim Crow laws, gentleman's agreements, and other means to prevent the wages of black workers from rising too high. Charleston is often compared to New Orleans in its uniqueness as a historic Southern city, and indeed it possesses many of the qualities I did not like about New Orleans. Like my hometown, it was tradition-bound, facing the past rather than the future, and second-class status for black people was among the most treasured traditions. Charleston and the off-shore Carolina Sea Islands were and still are the repository of strong African cultural remnants, but in 1969 only rarely, if ever, had this cultural strength been converted into meaningful political or economic action.

It must have come as quite a shock to the white community, therefore, when a few black hospital workers attempted to organize a union at the South Carolina Medical College Hospital. Not only were none of the hospital workers unionized, but unions of any sort were anathema in South Carolina at that time. Since there were no local unions to lend support, Local 1199 of the Retail, Wholesale and Department Store Workers (AFL-CIO), headquartered in New York, offered to support the Charleston workers.

As soon as the Medical College administration discovered what was in the wind, on March 20, 1969, they summarily fired the twelve black workers they thought were spearheading recruiting efforts for the union. Almost immediately, 450 other workers walked off the job in support of those fired. A week later, 60 black workers struck Charleston County Hospital in support of the Medical College workers.

We had known about the efforts to organize a hospital workers' union in Charleston from the beginning, through our national contacts with Local 1199, and we encouraged them to go forward. Martin had supported Local 1199 in their long, bitter strike to organize hospital workers in New York in 1959–60. In appreciation, Local 1199 had been extremely supportive of us in all of our campaigns throughout the 1960s, sending financial assistance and sometimes volunteers to the South. It followed quite naturally that when Local 1199 asked us to join them in Charleston and fight that battle together, we decided to accept, creating the first partnership between a union and a civil rights organization in a campaign to gain recognition of a labor union. In fact, we were as eager to participate in the Charleston strike as Local 1199 was to have us; the hospital workers' strike, like the garbage workers' strike in Memphis, fit perfectly into our desire to combat fundamental economic inequities and was consistent with the long-term aims of the Poor People's Campaign as we had originally conceived it in 1968. In addition, in Septima Clark we had a staff person who knew intimately the personalities and tendencies of black and white leadership in Charleston. This in-depth knowledge of the key players was always a crucial factor in the success of a campaign.

James Orange, the gentle giant we discovered in Birmingham, really came into his own in Charleston. He was a gifted organizer who possessed an innate empathy for the issues that confront workers. Ralph was available to preach at mass meetings, something he did very well, but otherwise he left it to me to oversee the movement in Charleston. The striking workers and their families provided a ready-made force for pickets and demonstrations, so we didn't have to recruit people to help us. The hospital workers were mostly black women—responsible, attentive to detail, well organized, and caring. It was like being surrounded by mothers and aunts, sisters, and an

old girlfriend or two. After the miseries of the previous year,
Charleston was like the Langston Hughes poem about Sugar Hill.
When I think about being in the midst of all those nurses, I have to
chuckle.

Charleston could have been the beginning of a new model for
labor organizing and the labor movement today would do well to
study our experience. While we had support then from national
labor—even Walter Reuther came down to Charleston with a delegation of East Coast labor leaders to support the strike—the big unions
have not met the challenge of organizing the South. Union membership has declined in recent years, in part because of a lack of commitment to organize black and Hispanic workers. Too often, union leaders have been content to preside over a shrinking union rather than
bring new workers into the mix. At their best, unions have helped to
bridge the barriers of race and unite workers behind the common
cause of economic justice. But unions have also defended a status quo
that apportioned jobs by race and gender. In Charleston, labor and
civil rights leaders came together for the benefit of all.

The Charleston strike lasted 113 days. The key demands in the
strike were: (1) union recognition, (2) an end to racial discrimination
in wages and hiring, and (3) rehiring of the twelve fired workers. In
our phase of it we helped to organize the entire community in support of the workers and held daily marches to dramatize the strike.
We also organized a tight economic boycott around King Street in
downtown Charleston, asking people to purchase nothing but food
and medicine. Blacks who maintained charge accounts with downtown stores were asked to cancel them.

As in Birmingham, we made statements to the national media
whenever we had the opportunity and held nightly public meetings at
the old Morris Brown United Methodist Church pastored by Rev.
John Goodwin. Those mass meetings were a balm for my spirit. The
church was filled to capacity almost every night. Someone from
SCLC or a local preacher would speak; local choirs would sing. People would sway side to side in the pews and tap their toes on the
wood floor. I recall Walter Fauntroy had come down to Charleston
from Washington and once he was the featured preacher for the
evening. As a preacher, Walter is an interesting mixture of an old-
style Baptist tempered by Yale Divinity School. He also possesses a
wonderful tenor voice, which has earned him a lot of ribbing from
colleagues. He really had the crowd going at the mass meeting. When
he broke into "Impossible Dream" from *Man of La Mancha*, what
should have been a corny moment was transformed into a transcen-

dent expression of all our hopes for the Charleston movement and our grief for Martin. When Walter sat down, the entire congregation was weeping. "Impossible Dream" became Walter's signature song, but his performance was never more powerful than it was on that warm summer night in Charleston, South Carolina.

As the strike wore on into June, we requested national boycotts of the products of the powerful South Carolina textile industry and mills, coordinating this effort from New York. This last move turned out to provide us with significant leverage because these industries were themselves desperately resisting unionization, and we knew it. Out of pure self-interest, textile industries were also supportive of the governor and the ruling structure of the state in their efforts to prevent the formation of a hospital workers' union, so by challenging them we were in effect challenging the governor.

By June 20 there was still no indication from the hospitals that they were prepared to begin negotiations. We then asked the black longshoremen of Charleston to plan a sympathy strike, which would have closed Charleston's extremely lucrative port. The longshoremen had closed the port on the day of Martin's funeral, so the city was well aware of the negative economic impact of a port idle for just one day.

I recall sitting in the office we had set up in Charleston, talking with my assistant, Stoney Cooks, about the strike. Stoney brought in an article on the head of the Medical University. I said, "Let's just take a chance and call McCord, and see what happens." Dr. William Mellon McCord was president of the Medical University and responsible for firing the initial workers. My hunch that we might be able to negotiate with McCord was based on an article about him. We had read that McCord had grown up in South Africa, where his parents were Presbyterian missionaries.

I made the call and was able to get right through to Dr. McCord's assistant, William Huff. Previously, we had been unable to even have a conversation with the hospital administrators. I was very surprised, therefore, to find myself having a friendly telephone conversation with Mr. Huff. We spoke for a few minutes—he must have been alone in the office because he remarked candidly that he was a native of New York City, was familiar with the first Local 1199 hospital workers' strike of 1959, and indicated that he himself had no problems with unions. Of course, he admitted that he had no control over the situation, but he did agree to set up a meeting with Dr. McCord, which he did, within a day or two.

Stoney went with me to the meeting. For forty-five minutes we listened to McCord blow off steam, as he blamed us for leading a virtual slave rebellion in South Carolina. Dr. McCord was a man in his late fifties who had probably never conceived of relating to blacks on an equal basis. But I was ready for all that; my experience with negotiation had taught me to expect abuse and accusations from the other side before the talk began to come around to a possible settlement. The older white generation in the South simply could not approach changing racial relations dispassionately; there was always in their initial meetings with us a need to express personal outrage that we were challenging what was, to them, a perfectly acceptable status quo, and a deeply felt resentment that we had brought long-standing but generally ignored inequities into the open. It seemed as if they resented the breach of traditional Southern racial etiquette even more than the challenge to their power represented by the issues on the table. Whenever this happened, I knew it was better to just let them blow off steam without trying to reply. I remember Martin used to say he always knew the other side was ready to settle when they began meetings by asking "Reverend King to open our meeting with a prayer." Up until then, *King* had been only a despicable four-letter word.

When McCord was through with his tirade, I sensed he was ready to talk business, and we arranged for a series of meetings with his assistant. McCord was under pressure—not from us, but from the business community of Charleston—to settle, because downtown Charleston businesses had lost an estimated fifteen million dollars in tourist income since the inception of the strike. Also, the governor's office and the textile industries now wanted to see the strike settled, in the hopes of containing the idea of unionization.

It took only a few days for the hospital to agree to recognize the union through a dues checkoff system. The other issues—a general raise in pay and the rehiring of the original twelve dismissed workers—took longer to settle. Jay Iselin, a New York attorney, was instrumental in successfully negotiating these issues through contacts he set up with the governor's office. On June 26, 1969, it was announced that the union was recognized and the strike was over.

Charleston was a campaign in which we put our tried-and-true strategies and techniques to work with excellent results. Perhaps most important, we were able to bring the black churches, the most stable institutions in the black community, into the battle; the union could not do it by itself. As in Memphis, the strength of the Charleston movement relied upon a coalition between workers and churches, with the clergy sharing leadership roles with the spokespersons for the workers. Jack O'Dell, who had recently rejoined our staff, pointed out in the quarterly *Freedomways*: "Charleston forged a unity between the community organizing techniques developed during the civil rights era of the Freedom Movement and the working-class organizational techniques of strike action developed by the labor movement."

But sadly, Charleston was the first and last partnership of this type, and the last major campaign waged by SCLC. We had hoped that Charleston would be the beginning of something new; but it turned out to be the end of the direct-action phase of the movement for us, and of the application of the direct-action techniques developed in the sixties.

When I think of the Charleston strike today, I remember the ebullient spirit of the people, not the negotiating sessions or what we gained from the settlement. Charleston was the singingest, preachingest, clappingest movement since our days in Albany and Selma. In the mobilization of the community, there was a spirituality infused into the marches and the meetings that will always remain with me as an enduring memory.

Charleston was the end of an era. The election of President Richard Nixon in 1968 and the subsequent policies he initiated signaled a markedly conservative trend and a new, rigid antagonism toward social change. It was almost as if the ideas and issues brought forth by the civil rights movement, the antiwar movement, and the general challenge to the status quo had subjected traditional American myths and values to such pressure that conservative and middle-of-the-road national forces rebelled in one last gasp, striking back in an attempt to protect what they perceived as their interests against any change. In the case of blacks, who had broken down the walls of segregation and made measurable incursions into the American economic and political system during the sixties, white America seemed to be saying, "Enough is enough." As for black discontent and frustration as expressed through urban violence and talk of rebellion, the reply from the government and middle-of-the-road whites was, "No more discussion of causes of problems; we'll deal with rebellious blacks through police actions and larger prisons." Much of this hardened attitude was expressed in the pronouncements of Vice President Spiro Agnew and Attorney General John Mitchell.

The attitude of the Kennedy and Johnson administrations, particularly in the early days of the movement, had been at least to try to use the power of the federal government to redress long-standing social and economic inequities. The new attitude in Washington was one of complete intransigence. This meant that the major civil rights organizations still functioning (SNCC and CORE had each come apart at the seams in the late sixties over internal ideological and racial splits) were thrown into a quandary over the question of how best to deal with the situation. Within SCLC, every direction except violence was given vehement expression: traditional direct action, union organization, political alliances, economic development, retreats into the black community with quasi-religious solutions, black militancy. But we could not agree to concentrate on any one direction.

I do not wish to sound condemnatory of us or other civil rights groups. The opposition to social change was far too hardened, and this opposition had now become national, not merely regional. In a sense, we had become the victims of our own success. We had achieved surface change: the abolition of segregation, a spectacular increase in voter registration, and so forth. But now none of the groups could do much more against an entrenched American economic system and the Byzantine subtleties of institutionalized racism. I thought we had to face the bitter reality that another level of progress would take possibly a generation or two longer, and that the various devices of direct action had taken us about as far as they could.

I was also becoming frustrated because our organization was drifting and lacked leadership. The executive staff had accepted Ralph as our leader to avoid a divisive fight over the issue of succession after Martin's assassination. We knew that Ralph had weaknesses, but there was a logic to his ascension on which we could all agree. I was next in line in terms of authority within the organization and I was handling most of the fund-raising and supervising the administration of the Atlanta office and our fieldwork. Most of the staff looked to me to solve problems when things went wrong. But I was a Congregational minister in a movement dominated by Baptist preachers. I thought that I could support Ralph, protect his flanks, and keep our movement going. But the major flaw in this strategy was that Ralph could neither lead nor inspire us. One aspect of Martin's genius was his ability to give his staff freedom, yet pull everyone more or less together when we had to work together. Ralph simply wasn't able to do that. There was no way Ralph could automatically inherit Martin's authority. And despite his close friendship with Martin, Ralph had not performed a decision-making role on a day-to-day basis while Martin was alive. We were facing difficult times now, which called for new ideas. And we weren't coming up with any.

It wasn't long before our internal disputes and conflicts came to a head. Looking back, I feel a turning point occurred in 1970 with the way we handled a dispute involving Jim Bevel. By 1970, Bevel was pretty much operating autonomously from the rest of the staff. During that summer he did something that was absolutely bizarre and unnecessary, which frightened some members of our staff. It was an emotional breakdown and battle fatigue from a decade of stress and pressure. A senior staff meeting was called to discuss this incident and to deal with Bevel's continued presence on the staff. People were saying they didn't understand what Bevel was doing and accused him of running his own civil rights movement, which had nothing to do with SCLC policy. The situation was exacerbated by the fact that Bevel, in an executive staff meeting a few months previously, had proposed that Ralph resign "because it was obvious he wasn't doing his job," and that he be replaced by Jesse Jackson, a proposal that Ralph categorically rejected. Bevel knew Jesse had a tremendous natural talent for inspiring people to follow him and Bevel figured that he could provide the substance behind Jesse's charisma. Though we all had our problems with Ralph's leadership, Bevel's lack of tact made the whole matter embarrassing.

Now this scandal involving Bevel gave Ralph a perfect excuse to go after him. Bevel had been the chapel speaker at Spelman, Atlanta's prestigious women's college. In those days, the college was very protective of the young black women who were its students. Chapel was mandatory, men weren't allowed in the dormitories, and the campus gates were locked at midnight. The chapel service was rigidly scheduled from 11 A.M. to noon on a Friday, but when the lunch bell rang, Bevel was still talking. He said, "Niggers don't need to eat, you been eating all your lives, anybody who wants to be free needs to just stay here and listen. I'm not through yet." The chaplain, Rev. Norman Rates, a very gentle man, went to Bevel and calmly told him that while they really appreciated everything he had to say, they had to close the chapel. Bevel responded, "We can continue this under a tree, we don't need any building." The group of women he took outside missed lunch and classes as they sat under a tree all afternoon listening to Bevel.

Toward evening Bevel was told he needed to leave the campus, so he invited the students back to his room at Paschals Motor Hotel, where he had a two-room suite. Once at the hotel, Bevel continued preaching and lecturing until Monday morning. He used the walls as blackboards and wrote on them with Magic Markers. On Monday,

Mr. Paschal, who was a member of my church, called me to ask who would be responsible for Reverend Bevel's expenses. Not realizing the extent of the situation, I assured him that SCLC would take care of it.

Then I heard from James Orange, who by that time had been to the hotel. He said, "Man, Bevel's got about fifteen or twenty gals over there, he's been there all weekend ordering food and holding workshops, writing all over the walls. Bevel is really out of control this time."

Joe Lowery and I immediately went to Paschals to look for Bevel and extend our apologies to Mr. Paschal. Together we were able to resolve the crisis. It was this fiasco that set off the staff meeting at which we considered whether Bevel should be fired. Bevel was not present at the meeting. Now I had no illusions about Bevel and his problems or his unpredictability, but I argued strongly against dismissing him, and not just because of our close relationship in earlier campaigns. Bevel had been singleminded in his commitment to the movement for the previous ten years. I felt that releasing Bevel would undermine our original staff concept as it had existed under Martin. Martin believed in a nonauthoritarian, nondirective style of leadership, and so do I. I inherited that from my father, and I had seen it work under Martin. Martin had understood, and now I was arguing, that the most important quality of our staff was its creativity and mobility, not its organizational discipline, and we could not have any creativity if senior staff members did not retain great independence. In effect, we had always depended on staff to inspire the original ideas in SCLC: the ideas and strategies came up to Martin from his staff, rather than from Martin down, as in most organizations.

I lost that vote. John Lewis was the only member of the SCLC board who voted against Bevel's dismissal. After the vote, John and I went to my office and closed the door to debrief. John showed me a copy of a letter that he had sent Julian Bond, urging him to run for the Fifth Congressional District seat. Julian was one of the first movement activists to enter electoral politics, and his opposition to the Vietnam War had prompted the Georgia legislature to bar him from taking his seat. He had received a tremendous amount of national publicity when he was nominated for vice president at the tumultuous 1968 Democratic National Convention, and his press interviews reflected his low-key, informed, and intelligent approach to controversy. Julian seemed a natural choice for the congressional race. There had not been a single black congressperson elected from the South during the entire twentieth century. Now, there were signs of growing opportunity for blacks in electoral politics. Maynard

Jackson had challenged Senator Herman Talmadge in the 1968 election and while he had not prevailed, the race positioned Maynard for a successful campaign for vice mayor of Atlanta in 1969. The municipal election that year also increased the number of black aldermen from one to five. Atlanta, with its concentration of well-educated African-Americans and a tradition of progressive politics, was a substantial part of the Fifth Congressional District. Even though blacks represented only just over thirty percent of the registered voters in the district, community leaders believed that a congressional campaign by an African-American candidate would likely be successful.

We called Julian from my office to see how he had responded to John's letter. I encouraged Julian to run, but he declined. Then he and John suggested that I should run for the seat. I told John that I had to catch a plane for New York; Harry Belafonte was planning a series of fund-raisers for SCLC and I had a meeting with him that evening. I promised John that I would give the matter serious thought and I rushed off to the Atlanta airport.

Until this point, I really hadn't thought about running. I wasn't nearly as well known as Julian was, and although I was interested in politics, I had never thought of myself as a potential candidate. I always saw my role as helping others to get elected. However, when I began to think about it, I became very excited about the possibility. Of course, there were serious obstacles. I wasn't a native Atlantan. I had lived in Atlanta for almost ten years, but much of that time had been spent on the road with SCLC. Still, if I were supported by key black leaders in Atlanta, like Daddy King and the old-guard religious, business, and education establishment, I might be able to overcome the fact that I was not a native.

Then there was the money problem. I had none of my own, and I did not know how much I would be able to raise in Atlanta. At my meeting with Harry later that evening, I gave him a copy of John's beautiful letter to Julian and told him that Julian had decided not to run for Congress. I shared with him my conversation with John and Julian. "They're suggesting that because what's needed is someone who isn't afraid to talk to white people, could raise money outside the city, could get young people to work as volunteers, that maybe I ought to think about running."

Harry just got up and called his wife, Julie, and said, "Get Sydney and Lena, we have to do a benefit. Andy's running for Congress." I said, "Hold on, Harry, I haven't decided, yet. I haven't even talked to Jean." He said firmly, "Oh yes, it's decided."

When I came home and told her all that had happened, Jean

said, "That's good, Andrew." She never flinched. She had always
been supportive of the things I felt called to do, from leaving
Thomasville for New York, to leaving New York for Atlanta. She
had even been willing to go to Highlander in the hills of Tennessee.
Jean could be volatile about small things, but she was amazingly matter-of-fact about the big things. The bigger the challenge, the more
calmly she went about it. She didn't get excited about my running for
Congress, but I could sense her pride. With Jean's blessing, I began to
seriously explore whether I had the resources to win the congressional race. I was not interested in a symbolic candidacy; I wanted to
assure myself that there was a realistic expectation of success.

In Atlanta I began to make the rounds of influential black leaders. Daddy King assured me that I could count on him to get support
for me from local preachers, that he would urge his white friends to
support me and help me raise money. There was no hesitation on
either his part or Coretta's to support my candidacy.

However, no one helped us more than Paul and Carol Muldawer. Paul is a prominent Atlanta architect, and he and his wife
Carol were our earliest nonblack supporters. They were also friends
of the Carters—I had recently met Jimmy Carter at their house when
Carter was preparing to announce his entry into the race for governor. At my request, Carol and Paul arranged a get-together for me
with some of their most conservative white friends and acquaintances. I wanted to meet people I was sure would vote against me to
see if I could at least talk with them. If I couldn't get my ideas across
to them at all, I thought it would be very difficult to win a campaign
in Atlanta. I saw this as a kind of test and I enjoyed the challenge.
Some of the people that showed up were Goldwaterites, and there
was one near John Bircher. I sat on the floor in the modern, wood-
beamed living room that Paul had designed, sharing my ideas and
fielding questions. The meeting turned out to be a very intense two-
hour discussion, during which I am sure I made no converts, but at
least I felt they left the Muldawers' with some respect for me. They
learned that I wasn't the mad bogeyman from the movement, after
all.

Thanks to Teamster lawyer Tony Zivlich I had good relations
with Atlanta's labor unions. Zivlich was a Croatian-American from
Chicago who came to Atlanta to work as a Teamster organizer and
went to Emory University Law School. While he was an attorney, he
maintained a working-man persona, never wore a tie, and talked like
a truck driver. In the mid-sixties, he asked Martin to speak with a
group of white workers who were on strike. When Martin wasn't

available, Tony asked me to come. I drove to the union hall in south Fulton County, an area I thought of as Klan territory. I had recently been involved in the movement in St. Augustine, where working-class whites who looked a lot like the guys sitting around this union hall drinking beer had thrown rocks and bottles at women and old people. I wasn't sure what to say, and I wasn't familiar with their issues, but I spoke anyway. My speech was repeatedly interrupted by applause and I received a standing ovation as I concluded. They were glad to hear from someone who cared about their situation. After such an enthusiastic reception, I had no choice but to offer my assistance to settle their strike.

When I spoke with Tony about running for Congress he was very encouraging. Based on my experience with the Teamsters, I thought I could persuade white union workers to support my candidacy.

Meanwhile, I knew I was ready to leave SCLC. I had had seven good years of training with Martin Luther King, and it was time to go in a new direction. Jean understood that it was time for me to go and she was ready to help me through a long, uphill campaign.

The more I thought about it, the happier I was with the idea of running for Congress. It seemed like a natural culmination of so much we had worked for in the sixties. No objective of our Southern campaigns was more well focused than our voter registration drives, which we knew would affect politics in the South forever. As the direct-action phase of the movement began to fade, and as civil rights organizations and alliances began to splinter, I became convinced that our participation in the political system was all the more imperative. An active black electorate could preserve the gains the people had won at such a dear price and could become a means for opening up other opportunities we were sorely in need of, especially economic opportunities. Perhaps, in a time of increasing national conservatism, black elected officials could serve as a brake on the tide and become a force for pulling the country back to face the hard realities of oppression, poverty, and racism.

Electoral politics also seemed right for me personally. The essence of the political life is working with people and representing people to help them better their condition, and working with people is what I had come to accept as my gift. I had chalked up quite a bit of experience in my years with SCLC and had developed many national contacts, which I believed would be of benefit to the people of the Fifth Congressional District and to Atlanta. I knew that some would see my style as unorthodox—I was never one for excessive formality, and I did not like the image of the well-dressed authoritarian "leader" who stands above the people he or she represents. I did not plan to alter the informal, conversational style of socially relevant activism, which I saw as an extension of my religious commitment to the people. I saw electoral politics as a natural extension of my concept of a relevant ministry, not a departure from anything I had done in the past.

The only real question remaining was whether it was wise for those of us who had actually worked in the civil rights movement to enter politics ourselves. When we worked to assist Carl Stokes in his mayoral campaign in Cleveland in 1967, Martin had observed that it was necessary for us to encourage and support greater black participation in the electoral process, but he felt we ourselves should not become candidates because we would get bogged down by the system and thereby lessen our freedom to be objective and critical of the system.

But that was in 1967. By 1970, the sixties movement was disintegrating, and it was necessary that those of us who had worked in the movement now move into the political arena ourselves, applying our skills, contacts, and experiences to this previously forbidden area of activity. I saw political office as a way of sustaining what we had done and needed to do again rather than as a deviation from our history of collective struggle.

So much of my life was tied up with SCLC. There was a spiritual bond among the contentious SCLC family that I did not want to disrupt by leaving on unpleasant terms. It was not easy to explain my decision to Ralph and the senior SCLC staff, but they were not surprised—they knew I had been investigating a congressional bid. My colleagues had a lukewarm reaction to my decision, though, and seemed to feel that I was running out on them. I explained that I was not leaving the movement, just taking it to a new arena.

Harry and Julie Belafonte sponsored an elegant fund-raising dinner for me in New York, at the Hotel Pierre on Fifth Avenue. This was a long way from the modest Atlanta neighborhoods where I would seek votes, but a campaign required money and New York was where the money was. I was not unknown to New York, through my work with Martin and the National Council of Churches, and my congressional race was something of a novelty—a black man running for Congress in Georgia.

Ivanhoe Donaldson, a former SNCC organizer, came to Atlanta to manage my campaign. Ivanhoe was meticulous in his attention to detail in managing the campaign and everything else. Campaign staff often gathered at my home for dinner and late-night strategy meetings. One evening, when everyone was ready for the meeting to begin, Ivanhoe was nowhere to be seen. I checked the kitchen and found Ivanhoe instructing one of my daughters on improving her dishwashing technique, pointing out spots she had missed on the bottom of a pot.

The campaign also attracted idealistic students from around the country, who volunteered to work long hours canvassing neighborhoods, calling potential supporters, and organizing events. Our main office was downtown at 41 Exchange Place. We had satellite offices on the west side of Atlanta in the old Amos Drugstore, an institution in black Atlanta that had closed its doors the year before, and another on the north side in Atlanta's upscale Buckhead area. The campaign offices were noisy as volunteers stuffed envelopes, made phone calls, and formed teams of canvassers. We went all over Atlanta and Fulton County leafletting neighborhoods, meeting people in supermarket parking lots and block parties. Thanks to my father's training, it was second nature for me to put out my hand to a stranger and say, "Hello, I'm Andrew Young, and I'd like to be your congressman." Our slogan was "Think Young," and I would take a team of college students and greet people returning to their cars with groceries and ask if I could put a bumper sticker on their car. The kids would scamper through the lot with tremendous energy.

One of the revelations of that campaign was the blossoming of the shy, country girl I had taken out of Marion, Alabama, fifteen years before. Her work with the Atlanta public schools and the First Congregational Church, as well as her civil rights involvement, had taken Jean into sections of Atlanta that I hadn't known existed. She knew people and, more important, there was scarcely anyone—students, teachers, administrators, community activists—who knew Jean who wasn't fond of her. Jean and the girls eagerly accompanied me to campaign cookouts and coffees and sat through countless speeches. After nearly a decade of Jean and me living on parallel tracks, our lives were more intertwined than at any time since those honeymoon years in Thomasville.

Jean had also developed into an effective public speaker. Watching her confidently address a group of strangers, it was difficult to remember how shy she had been about delivering the Women's Day message at Bethany Congregational Church. She had agonized over her speech, worried that she would run out of things to say, and put notes on three-by-five cards to take into the pulpit. Once she began, the congregation was so responsive, the amen corner kept her speaking for forty-five minutes.

I worked hard in the 1970 campaign, and managed to win the Democratic nomination. My opponent had been Lonnie King. Lonnie was a "Grady-baby," a native Atlantan who had been active in Atlanta's student movement. It was a tough contest, with LONNIE KING yard signs turning up on my own street, but I prevailed. It was the first time since Reconstruction that a black candidate had won a major party nomination for a congressional seat in the South.

I was running on a Democratic ticket that included Jimmy Carter as the gubernatorial candidate and Lester Maddox as the candidate for lieutenant governor. I was determined to campaign in every part of the district, even though a marine had become violent at one of Jimmy Carter's campaign meetings. One afternoon, I was shaking hands in a strip shopping center in south Fulton County, a white working-class area, when a big pickup truck with a gun rack across the back window drove toward me. I was tempted to walk the other way, but the truck stopped and the driver opened the door right in front of me. I had no choice but to stick out my hand and say, my voice a little higher than normal, "Excuse me, sir, I'm Andrew Young, and I'm running for Congress. I sure would like your support." The big, beefy, middle-aged white man grabbed my hand and said, "Goddamn boy, I sure am glad to meet you. I was telling my wife the other day, it's two people I want to vote for, you and Lester!"

That gentleman confirmed my instinctive belief that the campaign was not just about ideas. People take an emotional snapshot of you and if they like you, feel that you are trustworthy, they'll vote for you. Sometimes they will support you even if they disagree with your beliefs, if those beliefs are genuine. I never pretended to agree with people for the sake of getting their votes. I would try to explain carefully why I disagreed, while respecting their opinion.

My opposition in the general election was a conservative Republican first-term incumbent, Fletcher Thompson. Thompson had unseated moderate Democrat Charley Weltner in the last election, and he pulled out every stop in his campaign, including the distorted use of a statement I had made condemning the police killing of Chicago Black Panther leader Fred Hampton, to portray me as some kind of insane black militant. The Thompson campaign got a copy of the interview and played a portion of it in white neighborhoods throughout south Fulton County. Because this was before videotape recorders were in every home, a film projector and screen were required, so it was no small undertaking. The interview included one of those impossible hypotheticals, "If the only way for the Third World to emerge was through the destruction of Western Civilization, would you support that?" I said, "I probably would." On television, with its sixty-second sound bites, you don't have a chance to argue the faulty premise, that Western Civilization was the best hope for the emergence of the Third World. In any case, in 1970, the Fifth District was only thirty percent black, so unless I picked up a fairly good percentage of white votes I was doomed. But the white vote, particularly in conservative, blue-collar south Fulton County, flocked to the polls as never before, and they didn't vote for me.

Jean and I sat in a downtown hotel room watching television on election night, waiting, waiting for the three heavy-voting black precincts on Atlanta's west side to report in, confident that they would help me overcome the lead that Thompson had held all night, but they were actually already in. When we realized that our votes were in, I went downstairs to face my supporters and perform the ritual of a gracious concession speech to my opponent. I had been taught good sportsmanship, and my disappointment did not overcome my upbringing. The excitement of deciding to run and winning the Democratic primary had led me to believe that I was going to win with little or no trouble. I had won the competition for the black voters in Atlanta, overcoming the charges that I was an outsider. Traditionally, the general election was a formality for a Democratic nominee, but in my case, despite good black voter turnout, I was soundly defeated. I failed to win a large enough percentage of the white vote.

After the election I was exhausted. Jean and I took a few days' vacation in Jamaica, we talked things over, and right then and there we decided I was going to go for it again in 1972. Within a week after election day in 1970 I was aiming at the congressional campaign of 1972.

After the 1970 census, a reapportionment was required to reflect the new population figures. The district reapportionment drawn up by the Georgia legislature seemed designed to knock me out of the running forever—the Fifth District lines were drawn so that they actually excluded my house by one block. The new boundaries also left the home of Maynard Jackson, then Atlanta's vice mayor, outside the district. But thanks to the Voting Rights Act of 1965 we were protected from exactly this kind of attempt to undermine black voting strength. The Southeastern Region of the American Civil Liberties Union, attorney Laughlin McDonald, staff member Patsy Morris, and Chuck Morgan—one of the negotiators in Birmingham—and others wasted no time in going to court. The result of their suit was a legislative committee assigned to work on new boundaries, and when the revised district was created, I was back in the district, and the percentage of black votes had increased to thirty-eight percent. Several of the more conservative white precincts were placed in the Sixth District. Under the new boundaries, the Fifth also gained in youngish middle-class, urban-oriented whites who lived near Emory University. The result of this reapportionment was a much more favorable district for a black candidate than it had been in 1970.

In the meantime, Atlanta's new mayor, Sam Massell, appointed me to chair the Community Relations Commission. I have always believed that Joe Jacobs, Ivan Allen's attorney, suggested me because of my work on the Atlanta sanitation workers' strike. This was a position that had been held by the late Rev. Samuel Williams, a professor at Morehouse College, pastor of Friendship Baptist Church, and president of the Atlanta NAACP prior to his untimely death. The Community Relations Commission provided me with a staff and the opportunity to work with a broad-based group of respected citizens from all segments of the Atlanta population. This commission conducted regular meetings at city hall and was empowered to entertain citizen complaints about discrimination and other civic issues. It so happened that during 1971 there were a series of unusual wildcat strikes in Atlanta at the Mead Packing Company, Sears Roebuck, and Nabisco plants. In each of these strikes racial discrimination was a key factor. A group of young white socialists had obtained jobs at these factories and were instrumental in raising issues of long-standing racism that were as critical of the unions as the employers.

At Mead Packing Company, the trouble began when a woman who was diabetic came to work and told the supervisor she had forgotten her insulin. She asked permission to go home during the lunch break to get her medicine, but she lived too far away to make it back before the lunch period ended. The supervisor told her that if she wasn't back on time, she would lose her job. So, the employee stayed, and around three o'clock in the afternoon, she fell into a diabetic coma. When the ambulance took her to the hospital, the workers walked off the job. These were human dignity issues as much as pure union issues, but they were important and could mean the difference between life and death in many instances.

Nat Welch was the executive director of the Community Relations Commission, and he knew that I was planning to run for Congress again. He did things that the commission had never done before that were not only good for the commission, but also excellent exposure for me. We organized a series of neighborhood hearings, just to let people talk about problems in the city. That gave me a chance to get to know neighborhood leadership firsthand in a context where I didn't have to do anything but listen. It was very good preparation for a congressional race. When I ran again, I knew a lot more about the politics of the collection of neighborhoods that were the city.

In preparation for the 1972 congressional campaign, my old SCLC assistant and close friend Stoney Cooks, who had succeeded me as SCLC executive director, decided to leave SCLC to manage my campaign, a tremendous stroke of good fortune because Stoney was a brilliant organizer. (Ivanhoe Donaldson had moved on to become active in politics in Washington.) We also acquired the advantage of working with a computerized voting list that included every person who had voted for Maynard Jackson, who had voted consistently for the Democratic Party, and/or who was a black registered voter. So we were able to develop an excellent concept of our target constituency. With the help of volunteers, we contacted each of these people through our telephone banks, through the mail, and through a door-to-door canvass of key neighborhoods. Our goal was to contact each targeted voter three times. We also registered twenty thousand new black voters through a heavy registration drive.

Rev. Fred Bennett, a close friend from SCLC, sat me down and gave me his analysis of my loss in the first campaign. He lectured me on the realities of Atlanta politics. "Andy, you've got to have Jesse Hill. Most of the black folk in this town that vote are registered because of Jesse Hill. It's not enough for him to be with you. You need him really working on your campaign." After the Voting Rights Act had passed, Bennett had gone to Jesse Hill, an executive with the Atlanta Life Insurance Company, and persuaded him to fund a series of voter registration drives that had substantially increased black registration in Atlanta. Bennett and I met with Jesse Hill in his office on Auburn Avenue and convinced him to take an active role in my congressional campaign. Bennett also chastised me for not spending enough time talking with neighborhood leaders. He took me in hand to make the rounds of community leaders like Mrs. Ella Brayboy, a motherly woman whom we persuaded to operate our get-out-the vote effort.

In addition, we also learned to use the media better. We actually had *less* money than in 1970—roughly one hundred thousand dollars for the entire campaign. But in 1970 I had made the mistake of attempting a Kennedy-style media campaign, using most of our budget for television spots. In 1972, we cut almost all the television, and concentrated on radio advertising, especially on black radio stations.

Of course, radio time was also much cheaper. New York advertising executive Carolyn Jones wrote our campaign song:

> *One man goes to Washington*
> *the people all stay behind*
> *but the man who goes to Washington*
> *has to keep the people in mind*
> *he has to speak like a million people*
> *speak out loud, speak out strong*
> *Andrew Young is going to go to Congress*
> *And Atlanta's going to go along.*

We had a soul music version, a pop version, and a country version of the tune. We also found that buying time on black radio would encourage the disk jockeys to make other nonpartisan announcements about voter registration and election day.

The little television advertising we did was designed to introduce me to the young, educated white voter. And we took inexpensive commercial ads on late-night movies, such as "creature features," which we discovered some blacks watched. Since we didn't have big money we had to use what we had sparingly, and wisely.

We gained important and unprecedented help from key young whites in the district that we didn't have in 1970. Stu and Fran Eisenstadt really went to work on Atlanta's north side. Stu was a young Atlanta attorney who, after my campaign, joined the Jimmy Carter team and played a key role in the White House during the Carter presidency. I'll always be proud that Stu Eisenstadt's initial political involvement was with my congressional campaign. Jack Watson, later Carter's chief of staff, was also active and extremely effective in organizing young attorneys for the 1972 campaign.

In the first campaign, Jean was very supportive and filled the traditional role of a candidate's wife. We had not been accustomed to working together and she did not want to be seen as meddling in my campaign. This time I encouraged Jean to give us the full benefit of her knowledge of issues and Atlanta. Jean brought all of her resources to the table, participated as a strategist, and organized a network of women. Jean, my sister-in-law Sonjia, and our good friends Joyce Bacote and Carolyn Moore formed the nucleus of a group of black and white professional and businesswomen who canvassed, organized fund-raisers, issue forums, and other events to fully engage women in the campaign. They drew on networks of teachers, churchwomen, social clubs like the Links and Jack and Jill, and independent businesswomen. Rather than have her substitute for me at an event, we organized coffee klatches especially for Jean. Jean's effective organizing was all the more remarkable because she was pregnant with our son throughout the campaign, a blessed result of our spending so much more time together.

Atlanta people knew me as an SCLC official and an aide to Martin Luther King—even with my work on the Community Relations Commission very few people, even blacks, really *knew* me. Saying someone was "an aide to Martin King" does not tell much, though it might seem to. I also had to carry my old cross of being dubbed Martin's "middle-class assistant."

One of my primary opponents initially was a photographer and a black Fulton County commissioner, Henry Dodson. Dodson really unintentionally helped me out. He made a point of heckling me during a black radio station interview in which we were both participating. I was just barely able to retain my self-control during the interview. As soon as the program was over and we were leaving the station, I told him, "Listen, don't you ever do that to me again." Dodson became angry and shot back, "What if I do? What you gonna do about it!" I told him just as forcefully as I could, "I will kick your ass, right out here in this parking lot, that's what!" Well, Dodson had his tape recorder turned on—he had been taping the interview. So for the next few weeks he ran around trying to get the black radio stations to run the tape of me threatening him. "I'm a believer in nonviolence and a follower of Martin Luther King," he would say, "and Andy Young is threatening to commit violence on me!" No one ran the tape. But a few weeks later we met face-to-face for a debate before the student body of Morris Brown College. Dodson spoke first, and ran through his "violent Andy Young" routine. When it came my time to speak, I answered his accusation. "When I was with Martin," I said, "I was always nonviolent because the safety of the entire movement depended on it. But whenever there was a situation one-on-one and someone tried to pull the kind of chickenshit Dodson is pulling, I would tell Martin Luther King, 'I'm gonna kick his ass.'" And the kids roared. That was the end for Dodson. And, fortunately, it was also the end for a good while of my too-nice-to-be-tough image.

I won the Democratic nomination, after a runoff with a young white attorney, Wyche Fowler. Wyche was remarkably gracious, and conceded the race almost as soon as results began coming in.

This time I knew better than to rest on my laurels. The general election was going to be a real contest. My opponent was Rodney

Cook, a rather liberal Republican. Fletcher Thompson, the incumbent who had defeated me in 1970, decided not to run again, so neither Cook nor I had to face the extremely difficult task of unseating an incumbent congressman.

With a more scientific campaign and better data on voting patterns, I could concentrate my efforts on neighborhoods where voters had some liberal inclinations. In 1970, I had had only the returns from Maynard's race against Senator Talmadge to analyze. This time, we had the returns from my previous campaigning and Maynard's election as vice mayor of Atlanta.

I had to find a way to reach out to white voters in a way that didn't create a backlash. In my neighborhood meetings, I listened to voters' concerns and responded to the issues they raised. If I was meeting with mothers on Atlanta's affluent north side who raised concerns about their children, I talked about childbearing and shared my concerns as a parent, and I tried to be as open and honest as I could be.

This was frustrating to my campaign staff, because I never stayed on message. I read their briefing papers and then said what was in my heart. In the back of my mind I remembered Martin saying, "Leaders have to be thermostats more than thermometers. What's wrong with most leaders is they're always trying to take the public's temperature and conform to it. We need leaders who will set the moral temperature in Atlanta." So I spoke the truth, even when I wasn't sure my audience wanted to hear it.

I could never predict what issue might be a priority for a neighborhood. Many progressive whites in Atlanta were beginning to be concerned about the environment and they wanted a federal recreation area on the Chattahoochee River just outside of the city. Another group was concerned about the persistent flooding of their homes caused by Peachtree Creek. I wasn't sure why that was a federal issue, but I was willing to learn. I had considered myself pretty sophisticated about the extent of federal influence in generating prosperity in America, but I was constantly hearing from downtown business groups about federal rapid transit money, from developers about federal road money, from educators about federal education dollars, from neighborhoods about federal funds for parks and recreation, from art lovers about federal funding for the arts and humanities. There was no area of life in Atlanta that couldn't be improved by the right federal grant. In this case, it turned out that the Army Corps of Engineers had responsibility for a flood-mitigation project upstream that was delayed. The project had been approved, but the funding had not been appropriated. Since this required state cooperation, I asked Governor Jimmy Carter to come with me on a fact-finding mission to Peachtree Creek. I didn't know Carter very well at that point, so I felt a little awkward when he showed up in one of his trademark plaid shirts and a pair of jeans. I was wearing a suit. I later learned to appreciate that Carter's informal style was completely genuine.

I nearly always wore a suit to campaign, even to tramp through the mud. Early on in my political career, I was scheduled to attend a neighborhood block party and fish fry in a lower-middle-class black neighborhood. I asked my host what I should wear, if a sport shirt would be appropriate. I have never forgotten what he said, "You wear a coat and tie to go downtown and meet with white folks, you wear a coat and tie to come over here."

In the five years since Martin's first major speech against the Vietnam War, the antiwar movement had grown tremendously. In the 1972 campaign, I assumed a strong stance against unnecessary defense spending. Cook accused me of taking a "meat axe approach to defense spending." I said, "Yes, I do. Let's cut away all that fat." And I discovered, to my own slight surprise, there were many people out there who agreed with me. Georgia was very dependent on defense spending, but the Vietnam War was also bringing heartbreaking casualties home. I talked about the need to convert defense-industry giants such as Lockheed into companies that promoted life and development instead of investing in death and destruction. I suggested that Lockheed subsidies could be better spent building rapid transit cars for our cities. Today, due to decades of subsidy for the military and neglect of domestic infrastructure investment, there are no transit cars built in the United States: we have to import them from countries such as Italy and Japan.

All politics is local and my campaign was no exception. But I was campaigning in a national political atmosphere that was being poisoned by the politics of fear and division. Throughout the campaign I tried to appeal to people's hopes and aspirations rather than their fears. This had always been the challenge in SCLC's campaigns for social change—to help people grow toward their hopes rather than letting a fear of change overwhelm them. I saw President Nixon's and George Wallace's presidential campaigns as exploiting fear and insecurity about the enormous changes our nation was experiencing. There was no question that the surge of freedom and the new assertiveness of oppressed groups was unsettling. My daughter's Afro hairstyles were unsettling even to my own mother. But the new pride and self-confidence emerging from African-Americans, students, women, and the poor were also releasing productive energy that in the past was not available to fuel our nation's development. I saw in the upheaval a chance for a better, more prosperous America. A recurring refrain in my speeches called for an America where everyone shared the unprecedented material wealth of the nation: "Rich and poor, young and old, black and white, we must work together for a better America."

After more than two years of work, five elections, a federal court battle over the district, painstaking analysis of voting patterns, fundraising, phone banking, canvassing, hours of handshaking at bus stops and in parking lots, coffee klatching, candidate debates, and the development of an extensive get-out-the vote organization, it would all be decided on one election day in November 1972. When that day dawned, all I could do was to look up at the skies and cry, "Lord, why are you doing this to me?" It rained all day, one of those incessant, depressing rains that makes you want to stay home and do nothing. Or just sleep.

I had been projected to lose the election by four percentage points. So there was no choice; we had to get out the vote, particularly the black vote. Blacks own fewer private vehicles and typically have fewer resources enabling them to vote at their own convenience and have less control over their own time than white voters. They usually vote before or after working hours, when the lines are longest, so in poor weather conditions the black vote is typically low. People have other things they just have to do.

Fortunately, Stoney had done a brilliant job of organizing the seventy precincts we concentrated on and we had five hundred volunteers ready to drive people to the polls. We had phone banks operating to call identified supporters to remind them to vote and offer a ride to the polls. We had sound tracks and bands on flatbed trucks that went into critical neighborhoods as canvassers knocked on doors to urge people to vote; cars patrolling behind them were ready to transport voters to the appropriate polling place. We carried an estimated six thousand people to vote. The Quaker Oats Community Affairs Department made a documentary of my 1972 campaign. When I watched it after the election, the image that stuck in my mind was of me running, running, running; running from door to door as the polls neared closing. That wasn't a media-created image. We really were hustling to get people out, down to the very last minute.

What happened that day was beautiful and unpredictable. The very harshness of the downpour, it seemed, created a get-to-the-polls-to-make-up-for-them-that-won't flurry of activity in the black community. More people voted than if it had been a perfectly sunny day. Once we began to perceive the extent of the black vote, as reports began to filter in from our precinct workers, we began to feel hopeful, despite the expert forecast of a Cook victory.

After the polls closed, Jean and I went home to get a little rest. Jean was six months pregnant and was working as hard as anyone on the campaign, and I had been at the bus stops before dawn asking for votes. Later, we headed back to our headquarters on Piedmont Street. A huge crowd of supporters and friends were gathering in anticipation of an upset victory. Results were very slow coming in. We had our experts over at the courthouse looking at the first returns, however, and they were phoning in positive indications, despite the lack of anything conclusive on television. The mood in our headquarters was joyous; people were coming from everywhere, whether they were friends or not. Stu Eisenstadt, who was monitoring the vote counting, called from the Fulton County Courthouse to say he thought we had won. I decided to leave headquarters and go to the television stations to do interviews, but I was also hoping to get quicker reports of results. Finally, around midnight, one of the stations projected me as the apparent winner, barring the absentee vote count.

Jean and I returned to headquarters after midnight to greet the throngs of jubilant campaign volunteers. I walked through the crowd shaking hands and hugging everyone in my path as I made my way to the platform. As I reached the platform, the noisy crowd became even louder and I grabbed Jean's hand and held it high. Campaign signs were pumped up and down: ATLANTA'S GOT YOUNG IDEAS. Surrounded by my children, my brother Walter and his wife, Sonjia, Coretta Scott King, and Jesse Hill I searched the crowd for Stoney, Fred Bennett, and Paul and Carol Muldawer, waving them to the stage. "This was your victory," I said, hoarse from months of intense campaigning. I thanked Rodney Cook for a fair contest. I thanked the volunteers who made the phone calls and canvassed the blocks, especially those who drove people to the polls. Then Jean and I went home and tried to sleep.

I slept a little, but not much. In the turmoil of the day and in the rush of the long campaign there had been little time to think of history. Now, as I tried to rest, I realized that if the figures held up, I would be the first black person to be elected to Congress from Georgia since Reconstruction and, along with Barbara Jordan of Houston (who had already been declared an easy winner), one of the first blacks to go to Congress from a Southern state in the twentieth century. In doing what seemed so right and natural, "firsts" like that didn't really mean much to me, though I fully recognized they might mean a great deal to others. What meant more to me was the realization that my winning in Atlanta, and Barbara Jordan's victory in Houston, was the satisfying culmination of a decade's worth of hard work. Both a culmination and an important beginning. It made me feel good just to imagine the satisfaction Martin would have felt about this election. Though Martin had believed that those of us working in the movement should not be the ones to run for office, I knew he would understand and would have shared with me a wonder at the unpredictable course that had brought me to this point. I had always been the behind-the-scenes person, the organizational man, the nonimage staff person. Now I knew I would be called on to perform a new role, and I really didn't know whether I was ready for that. I knew I would not change. I would be the same Andrew Young I was the day before, or year before.

But these were heavy thoughts, and I was tired; tired physically, but *not* psychologically. I offered a prayer of gratitude for the victory. Then I woke Jean up and whispered, "Jean, I'm going to get up early. I'm going down to Peachtree at six tomorrow morning, just like we've been doing, and thank the people at the bus stops. *They* did it for us!"

Thanking the voters the morning after election day was one of the most memorable and joyous experiences of my life. These were the hotel workers, the hospital workers, the custodians and janitors of Atlanta who were off to work early, and who changed buses downtown as they came from the black neighborhoods going to the white areas where they were employed. These were people who braved the rain to vote after they got off from work, and my guess is a goodly number of them had never before voted in their lives. I had been campaigning hard at these bus stops during the last few weeks, shaking hands, begging for their support. They were genuinely surprised to see me out there again, the morning after the election. There was a warmth in their greetings that made me feel so good, it seemed far more than a mere political victory. In a sense I could never underestimate, it was the beginning of a new promise that had its origins in days of endless marching, in years of meetings and campaigns in Alabama and Chicago and Memphis, in the urgency of Martin's voice, in the communion of singing "We Shall Overcome"—all that and more was there in their faces that joyous morning.

===

We Still Have a Long Way to Go

M y election to Congress took place nearly a quarter century before the publication of this book. Walking the halls of Gilbert Academy and later the lonely Highway 80 from Selma to Montgomery, I could never have imagined myself in the halls of the United States Congress. In my lifetime, we have come so far, but we still have a long way to go. As a pastor in Thomasville, I saw daily the effects of racial segregation on members of my congregation. It placed limits on their freedom to use their talents and abilities; it distorted family relationships and unbalanced the allocation of resources. And so, when I began my sojourn with Martin King in 1961, the elimination of racial segregation and racism was the focus of our stated goal to redeem the soul of America.

However, as the movement progressed our understanding of the problems facing America deepened, and the focus of our efforts likewise evolved. We came to see that racism walked hand in hand with war and poverty, and all were stealing away the soul of a potentially great nation. We accepted the responsibility to save our nation from these ills. We did not view ourselves as radicals or revolutionaries. Rather, we sought transformation, believing that the principles on which America was founded were fundamentally sound. Martin called on the nation "to live out the true meaning of its creed, that all men [and women] were created equal."

The efforts to eliminate the pervasive exclusion of black Americans from the ordinary pleasures and privileges of American life—the hot dog enjoyed at the ballpark, the water fountain, the public park, the library, the comfort of a seat on the city bus, the expectation of a room at the inn—were by and large successful. As SCLC's direct-action campaigns addressed discrimination in public accommodations, employment, and voting rights, in each instance, policies on the national level changed to reflect the emerging consensus around fairness and equality in America's public life. The expansion of employment opportunities created a new kind of black leader that had scarcely existed before the civil rights movement—one who supervised white employees and led historically white institutions from the U.S. Commerce Department to the state of Virginia to Smith College.

Our relative success in removing the visible barriers of racial discrimination in the United States revealed more complex factors perpetuating second-class status for persons of color the world over. We became acutely aware of this as our confrontation with the legal structures of racism within the United States soon brought us face-to-face with the international military apparatus established to maintain "white privilege" abroad as well. The battle against any totalitarian system, whether fascism or communism, we overwhelmingly supported, but all too often we saw the United States use its military power to defend not freedom but colonialism. In Vietnam, in the southern African countries of Rhodesia, Namibia, Mozambique, Angola, and South Africa, our government involved the U.S. military and intelligence networks in alliances that we knew to be against the right of self-determination, respect for human rights, and the precepts of our own Declaration of Independence. The stand against the war in Vietnam and against white minority rule in southern Africa was a stand against American alliances with forces that were antidemocratic but justified on the grounds of fighting communism. We challenged the notion that such alliances were the only plausible alternative to conceding to the spread of communism. The redemption of America from a strictly military toward a human rights emphasis on self-determination and free economic choice is one of the significant, yet incomplete, influences of the Southern civil rights movement. Our movement for civil rights educated American policy makers, enabling them to examine international events through a human rights lens rather than the geopolitical framework that had been the exclusive viewpoint. While often unable to resist the temptation to support covert or military action, since 1968 the United States has increasingly responded to conflict by serving as an honest broker for negotiations among combatants. In Central America, Angola, Namibia, and the Middle East, negotiated peace settlements were achieved with U.S. assistance. In South Africa, the focused involvement of the United States over a period of years paved the way for the most inspiring democratic transition of our time—Nelson Mandela's government of national unity.

One of my most treasured memories is of a conversation I once had with a lieutenant of Lech Walesa, who rose from leading rebellious workers in Poland's Gdansk shipyard to leading the entire country to democracy. He shared with me the inspiration and strategic lessons he had taken from his knowledge of SCLC's Birmingham movement. Similarly, whenever Irish, Polish, East German, Hungarian, Chinese, and Russian human rights forces sing "We Shall Overcome," they are acknowledging their moral and spiritual connection to Rosa Parks, Martin Luther King, Jr., and the thousands of students who nonviolently and spiritually endured jail for freedom's sake.

If dealing with racism, war, and poverty were SCLC's stated goals, then it must be acknowledged that our progress against racism and war has been more successful than any of us could have imagined or predicted thirty years ago. In confronting the problems of poverty, though, problems that surely undermine this country's greatness, we didn't anticipate that the opposition we would face would be more violent and intransigent than Bull Connor—and certainly more powerful. Nor did we comprehend, initially, the daunting complexity of the problem.

Our movement began as a struggle for freedom, but we discovered that racism was a symptom of even deeper issues. Despite important gains in education and economic opportunity, for black Americans without education, political power, or wealth, their condition remains as Martin once described, "a lonely island of poverty in an ocean of material wealth and affluence." We launched the Poor People's Campaign, the last march that Martin planned, because we understood that the root problem of the vast majority of our social ills was poverty. Poverty breeds crime and interferes with economic growth, and in a society based on free enterprise, it is too expensive to tolerate. People who think education is expensive have never counted the cost of ignorance. Today, poverty remains this nation's most intractable problem.

Poverty persists, in part, because our society is willing to invest in punishing the criminal behavior that is one of the symptoms of poverty, but less willing to invest in preventing the poverty itself. The cost of prison in my home state, Georgia, is five times the cost of tuition at a state university. And while four years of college makes people productive, tax-paying citizens, comparable time in prison has little impact on the reform and rehabilitation of inmates, and most often has quite the reverse result. In effect, a ten-year mandatory sentence costs the state $250,000 to give a prisoner a Ph.D. in crime, when a four-year investment in college would be around $20,000. At the same time, I must praise Georgia for its HOPE scholarship program, financed by the state lottery, which awards state college scholarships to high school students with a B average or better. Not surprisingly, many of the advocates for the scholarship program were people in the corrections system. Georgia has the highest incarceration rate in America, which in turn has the highest incarceration rate in the world, and Georgia corrections officials are constant witnesses to the hardening effect that prison has on most inmates. The irony and the tragedy is that the prison guards are often products of the same poverty and lack of opportunity as the prisoners. In the absence of a plan for economic growth for both rural and urban areas, prisons have become a rural industry for the export of urban decay. Rural white poverty and urban black poverty feed on each other in a no-win situation for the poor of either race, thus continuing a cycle begun generations ago when poorly educated rural poor were driven to the cities by government subsidies to mechanized farming.

Clearly, we must go beyond addressing the symptoms of poverty to treating the causes of poverty. Toward that end, the challenge is to evolve an economy that includes everybody and accords a fair chance to every American. The persistence of poverty and racial discrimination in America has generated communities and individuals isolated from the economic life of the country. If this country's monumental problems are to be solved to everyone's betterment, the disenfranchised must be given a realistic opportunity to apply themselves to economic achievement. In order to achieve that goal of shared prosperity, fairness as well as logic requires that special consideration be given to people who have been locked out of the economic mainstream.

My own city, Atlanta, provides example after example of the kind of economic growth that can occur when opportunity is extended to all. Atlanta has become a great city because it developed a fairness formula for ensuring that the benefits of development were disseminated throughout the various communities that made up the city. This practice emerged not from any particular ideology, but from pragmatism. In 1969, the city proposed the development of a mass transit system, supported by the business community. A referendum was required to approve the sale of bonds and a local sales tax to finance the system. The first time the referendum was on the ballot, it lost by a wide margin, largely due to opposition within the black community. In response, Mayor Sam Massell met with black businessman Jesse Hill to develop a strategy for winning black voter support. Mayor Massell negotiated with Mr. Hill and community leaders to produce an agreement that assured the black community had a stake in the growth of the transit system. At the time of the MARTA (Metropolitan Atlanta Rapid Transit Authority) referendum, less than one percent of city contracts were offered to black-owned businesses in a city that was nearly fifty percent black; the agreement provided that twenty percent of the contracts on the project would go to minority companies as well as thirty percent of the management positions, a tremendous increase, and one which no one could argue was unfair. In addition, during construction, bus fare was reduced to fifteen cents, to compensate for the regressive impact of the local sales tax. These minority contract provisions achieved extraordinary results, and not just for black Atlantans. By giving black voters an economic stake in the transit system, Atlanta got a twenty-year jump on other Sunbelt cities in the area of mass transit and created greater opportunity for all.

That fairness model was extended during the administration of Atlanta's first black mayor, Maynard Jackson. When the city needed a new airport, Mayor Jackson and black members of the city council withheld their support until an agreement was reached to provide twenty-five percent of contracts to minority firms and establish joint ventures for the concessions. The new airport, which quickly became the second busiest airport in the world, opened on time and under budget.

Atlanta's commitment to the economic empowerment of the city's black community continued to expand during my service as mayor of Atlanta. Increasingly, business, academia, and even cultural organizations learned that a project that excluded women and people of color was going to have a tough time gaining acceptance in the city of Atlanta. In many respects, Atlanta's hosting of the centennial Olympic Games was a product of the successful racial diversification of Atlanta's economy during the seventies and eighties. Billy Payne, who came to me with the idea of bringing the Olympics to Atlanta, and I were men in midlife with a religious sense of service and fond memories of sports glory in our youth. The Olympic bid was an interracial effort from the first moment, and from that base it expanded to include the diversity that was Atlanta's business, social, and cultural reality. The strategy to promote Atlanta as the host for the centennial Olympic Games was developed largely by Ginger Watkins and Linda Stevenson, former Junior Leaguers who understood the universal appeal of the American South's reputation for hospitality and graciousness.

When International Olympic Committee members came to inspect Atlanta as a potential site for the games, we hosted them in private homes. Regardless of the nationalities of the delegates, we could introduce them to prominent Atlantans with whom they shared a religious, cultural, or ethnic heritage. African representatives of the International Olympic Committee who came to Atlanta saw African-Americans in key positions in business and government. Latin American representatives of the IOC came to Atlanta and were impressed when they were greeted in Spanish by Roberto Goizueta, the chairman of our largest corporation, Coca-Cola. Atlanta's small Asian population included R. K. Seghall, who transformed Law Engineering into a multinational company. Women delegates saw women in nontraditional positions in local government, such as the Department of Parks and Recreation. Beverly Harvard, who was deputy chief of police at that time was Atlanta's chief of police by the time the Olympic Games were held.

As Atlanta won its Olympic bid on the strength of its diversity and inclusiveness, there was scarcely any need to argue that forty percent of the construction contracts be awarded to minority- and women-owned firms. With two billion dollars in spending on the Olympics, Metro Atlanta led the region in economic growth during the 1990s, and no one had reason to complain that they weren't part of Atlanta's boom.

Perhaps just as important as the Olympics in Atlanta's growth during the 1990s was a Pulitzer prize–winning article by the *Atlanta Constitution* on the practice of redlining by Atlanta banks. This series of articles revealed a pattern and practice of denying capital to Atlanta's black neighborhoods, despite the education and affluence of the residents of those neighborhoods. While admitting no wrongdoing, Atlanta banks began to look at their loan portfolios and at the neighborhoods they had neglected.

In doing so, Atlanta banks and investors discovered an underdeveloped country in their own backyard, a country with the same laws, currency, language, and value system. The only difference was the color of the skin of the residents. Atlanta's steady economic growth and global prominence—surpassing other Southern cities like Birmingham and New Orleans—is due to the emergence of a free trade agreement with Atlanta's black community. The fairness formula developed twenty years ago gave Atlanta's black citizens a stake in the economic growth of the city. As economic opportunity expanded for black Atlantans, the economy grew for all Atlantans. Atlanta's experience—investing in its own black community—can serve as a model for stimulating economic growth in every American city. Investments in our least-developed communities, where unmet needs and pent-up demands are greatest, will produce returns without the uncertainty of currency fluctuations and unfamiliar legal systems.

A national free trade agreement with black America would provide the kind of growth in American industry that could solve the problem of persistent, intergenerational poverty that plagues this nation. Even underdeveloped, the spending power of black America represents a market larger than Mexico and Canada. When Martin King became involved in the Montgomery bus boycott, the earning power of black America was around eighteen billion dollars annually, larger than the economy of Canada. Today, in 1996, that figure is closer to four hundred billion dollars, larger than the economies of Canada and Mexico combined. While I support the North American Free Trade Agreement, there are more benefits with less risk to be had from a free trade agreement with black America.

One of the myths inhibiting the growth of investment in the black community is the false perception that the increase in black prosperity has come at the expense of white Americans. One has only to look at the South, where the increase in educational and economic opportunity for black Americans has contributed to the economic expansion of one of the most economically vital regions of the world—the Sunbelt. Universities where a governor once stood in the doorway barring any black students, where black students were physically threatened for attempting to enroll, now offer scholarships to enable and encourage black students to attend. Businesses that once refused to interview blacks for any job located above the basement floor now set goals to increase hiring of black managerial staff. Governments that once granted no contracts to black businesses now set guidelines that ensure that contracts spending taxpayer funds are distributed with a concern for the diversity of the taxpaying community. These efforts represent that fairness and good government have generated prosperity for the South. However, the myth of preferential treatment threatens to undermine much of that prosperity.

We can embrace our diversity, find strength in it, and prosper together, or we can focus on our differences and try to restrict access to resources by members of ethnic and racial groups different from ours and limit prosperity for all. So many of California's ongoing economic problems are only exacerbated by the divisiveness that has entered the state's political climate. From Proposition 13, which artificially restricted the resources available to provide government services to a growing and diverse population, to the recent battles over affirmative action in California's stellar public universities, the state's political leaders have promoted division and envy rather than fostering every community's interest in a prosperous California. One result is that companies and talented individuals are beginning to leave California, taking the prospects for economic growth with them. California, with its rich diversity and one of the largest economies in the world, should be a model of pragmatic inclusion. If part of the mission of a state university is to train leadership for the state, then some kind of proportional representation is necessary to fulfill that mission. In addition, black and Hispanic taxpaying citizens will not long tolerate a state university system that denies access to the brightest young people in those communities. The role of responsible political leadership is to search for solutions that persuade all communities that they will prosper, together.

My conservative friends seem to have a Marxist worldview that the economy is a fixed pie, that in order for the poor to get more, the rich must get less. But the experience of the South is that free enterprise produces an ever-expanding pie. The more people included in the economy, the more growth and the larger one's slice becomes. In an economy that is producing equitable growth, wealthier citizens find they may have a smaller percentage of a much larger pie, but the result is greater wealth all around. However, the inequitable growth that has left millions of Americans in poverty has given America's wealthy a larger percentage of a smaller pie. Rather than improve the economic status of all Americans, this country has grown in part by making middle-class children consumers of junk—junk food, junk entertainment, and trendy clothes. How much better it would be to expand the economy by including America's poor, women, and minorities as full participants and consumers of homes, business services, and manufactured goods.

In an equitable society, you give the people who need the most a little more assistance, encouragement, and support. This is a crucial role for government. When rural citizens, black or white, move into your cities from areas where they have been unable to receive good education or job training, the only intelligent thing to do is to give them encouragement, education, and job training so that they may become self-sufficient, contributing citizens. And when one group has been systematically denied access to resources it is only fair to establish a period of affirmative action to provide an opportunity for members of those groups to gain access to the resources, rights, and privileges that they were denied for so long.

Ultimately, the success of a community and a nation requires sound, positive values. A community cannot succeed economically without political power, education, and a basic religious awareness of who one is as a child of God. The religious values of the black community in America sustained us through generations of slavery and segregation. Hard work, education, and faith in God did not prevent the oppression of black people, but they allowed us to resist the dehumanization that could have resulted. Our movement emphasized the importance of those fundamental values. One of the great tragedies today is that absent a strong personal faith, young people anesthetize their pain with narcotics. In a society that grants them more freedom than ever before, they are prisoners of the poverty of their own spirits. The young people that marched in Birmingham had far fewer material comforts than almost any young American today. But they were far richer in spiritual resources. They believed that they were children of God and that gave them the strength, courage, and discipline to overturn segregation. Values prepare a person or community to take full advantage of the opportunities a society provides.

At the same time one must question the values of a society that tolerates the kind of poverty that exists in the United States. Policies that deprive workers of a living wage, undermine educational opportunity, and seek to balance budgets by cutting assistance to the poor, the sick, and the vulnerable do not reflect the values of the America I love. The model set by such policies is "everyone for himself" rather than a democratic community working for the common good.

Put differently, for effective governance, hollow ideology cannot compare to pragmatic democracy. After World War II, Allied leaders looked at the wreckage in the aftermath of global war and proposed a Marshall Plan featuring access to low-interest capital, management skills, and markets. Implemented over the objections of isolationists who would have tolerated a Europe and Africa dominated by Hitler, the Marshall Plan not only worked for Europe, but expanded the global economy and created new opportunities for growth of the U.S. economy. Some of these Europeans had been our enemies. Yet, wisely, we learned the lessons of our failures after World War I to continue our involvement politically and economically with Europe and invested U.S. tax dollars in a global future. Today, the same leaders who look wistfully at that period of postwar prosperity are incapable of applying the lessons of the Marshall Plan to our present domestic crisis. Investment generates prosperity for the investor. It would seem an easy burden for America to do things for her own sons and daughters that we did for our former enemies.

America is so important to the world at this moment in history as we seek a new vision for our world. As I travel around the globe, I am reminded that the heads of state and people of nearly every country look to America for leadership. Yet, the poverty in our midst undermines our will and ability to respond to the call to global leadership and to meet the challenge of global poverty and environmental degradation—a far greater threat to future generations than even the Cold War.

When I served as United States Ambassador to the United Nations, I became aware of the intense appreciation that the Japanese delegation had for the U.S. role in rebuilding Japan after World War II. That experience led many Japanese businessmen to advocate a global fund for strategic infrastructure projects that would improve the environment, facilitate sustainable development, and generate jobs. They identified fifty such strategic projects, including the English Channel Tunnel (which the British built themselves), a natural gas pipeline across Africa from the Nigerian oil fields to the Mediterranean, and a sea level canal through Nicaragua. Without enthusiastic backing from the United States, a new global infrastructure fund could not move past the visioning stage, yet no nation would benefit more from such projects than the United States. For example, the practical benefits of a canal across Nicaragua to accommodate modern supertankers are at least twofold: given the cost and dangers associated with the long voyage around South America from the Atlantic to the Pacific, the canal would pay for itself in short order. Moreover, a canal under international governance would provide the basis for long-term economic growth and resulting political stability for U.S. neighbors and trading partners in Central America. Investing in development in Central America would produce far better results in reversing the immigration flow than the punitive measures presently finding political favor.

This is the kind of forward thinking that is required from American leadership today: investing in the future to solve problems and prevent problems. How much better to build a canal than to build a wall. How much more effective to support the creation of jobs in their own regions for workers who presently risk life and limb in pursuit of a better life in the United States, rather than to put forward yet another plan for making illegal immigrants' lives only more miserable once they're here. Our nation's prosperity rests on the vision of leaders who invested in and built bridges, roads, canals, communication networks, and national parks. These are the things that make for peace.

In an expanding economy people are too busy making money and accumulating material goods to fight over ancient prejudices. Had there been growth rather than recession in Europe when Bosnia and Serbia became independent of the former Yugoslavia, I doubt we would have seen the kind of bitter carnage that we have witnessed in that region of the world. The frustration that erupted in riots in South Central Los Angeles were rooted as much in the steady withdrawal of jobs and resources from that community as in the tragic beating of Rodney King.

Our own budget deficit has become the new excuse for ignoring growing problems in our midst and shirking our global responsibilities. But America does not have the luxury of attempting to shrink its way out of deficits; we only enlarge our problems when we withdraw resources from cities, schools, rural communities, infrastructure, parks, health care, and environmental protection. We undermine the integrity and vitality of our communities and we trigger dangerous recessions that breed conflict and violence. Surely responsible and dedicated Americans of all races can, based on the dictates of our minds as well as our hearts, pull together to meet the present challenge of poverty in all its complex manifestations both at home and abroad.

I am considerably older than I was in 1961, and I hope I'm wiser and certainly much more experienced after having moved through the Congress, the United Nations, the city of Atlanta, and the private sector. I have yet to find a reason to question or doubt the faith that we had in America then. Everything I know now convinces me that the struggle to eliminate racism, war, and poverty is a burden, but in America, with all the freedom and opportunity afforded us under our Constitution, in the most productive society in human history, it is an easy burden if we undertake it together.

Acknowledgments

T here is always a ground crew behind the scenes making the flight, the movement, or the book look easy. In this book I have tried to mention the names of as many people as possible who contributed to the nonviolent revolution we know as the civil rights movement. It is impossible to include all the names. This book is dedicated to that ground crew, men and women like Dana Swan, Big Lester, Tom Offenberger, Fred Bennett, Samuel Wells, Sunshine, Abraham Woods, Reverend Lewis, Albert Turner, Victoria Gray, Vera Pigee, and the many others whose names I never knew. The unnamed but forever remembered include the six thousand students in our citizenship schools, the people who marched in demonstrations, who canvassed, who fried chicken and baked pies, who offered their homes to strangers, who offered their churches for mass meetings, who sat in, sat down, and stood up for their rights as Americans. Their courage and patriotism is an inspiration to all who love freedom.

For helping to make this book a reality, my thanks go to:

Tom Dent, my childhood friend, a talented writer and cultural historian who helped and encouraged me to tell this story,

Lawrence Jordan, who never lost faith in this project,

Peternelle Van Arsdale, my editor at HarperCollins, who was supportive and enthusiastic about this project and whose fine insights helped to strengthen the book.

My ground crew for *An Easy Burden* included Magdelene Womack, Lisa Young Alston, Bo Young, Diane Wisner, and Doug Gatlin, all of whom helped me to juggle the many demands on my attention and created space for this book. I would also like to thank the ground crew at the Lawrence Jordan Literary Agency: Aitza Ponce, Magalie McDonald, Sherry Bailey, Telma Benvenuti, Lisa Rodriguez, and Myra Warren who typed and proofread the manuscript. Thanks as well to the good people at HarperCollins, especially Kristen Auclair.

Janet Hulstrand and my son-in-law Rev. Knighton Stanley read several versions of this manuscript and offered constructive criticism. Carol Muldawer and Susan Ross were of great assistance in collecting photographs.

And finally, my greatest gratitude and appreciation are reserved for my daughter, Andrea Young, our family historian, who continues to keep alive many of the memories and emotions of this period, and for Jean Childs Young, my late wife of forty years whose spiritual strength and love guided us through these exciting times.

INDEX

TIMELINE
1957–1972

1957

FEBRUARY 13 Southern Christian Leadership Conference organized in New Orleans with Martin Luther King as president.

MAY 17 Washington Prayer Pilgrimage March in support of civil rights.

JULY 19 Daughter Lisa Young born in Thomasville.

AUGUST Andrew Young joins executive staff of Youth Division, National Council of the Churches of Christ USA in New York.

SEPTEMBER President Eisenhower sends federal troops to Little Rock, Arkansas, to back integration of Central High School.

1960

FEBRUARY 1 Four students from North Carolina A&T College sit-in at Woolworth's lunch counter in Greensboro.

APRIL Student Nonviolent Coordinating Committee (SNCC) organized at Shaw University in Raleigh, North Carolina.

NOVEMBER 8 John Kennedy elected President of the United States.

1961

MAY 4 Freedom Rides begin, initially organized by the Congress of Racial Equality (CORE).

JUNE 6 Daughter Paula Young born in New York City.

Andrew Young joins Citizenship School Program housed at SCLC in Atlanta.

SEPTEMBER 22 Interstate Commerce Commission issues ruling prohibiting segregation on interstate buses and facilities.

DECEMBER 15 Martin Luther King arrested in Albany, Georgia.

1962

SCLC leaves Albany without conclusive settlement.

SCLC Convention held in Birmingham, Alabama.

1963

APRIL 3 Martin Luther King press conference launches Birmingham Movement.

MAY 10 Settlement agreement announced in Birmingham.

JUNE 12 Medgar Evers, field secretary for the NAACP, assassinated in Mississippi.

AUGUST 28 March on Washington in support of Civil Rights Act. Martin Luther King delivers "I have a dream" speech.

SEPTEMBER 15 Bombing of the Sixteenth Street Baptist Church in Birmingham kills four little girls.

NOVEMBER 22 John Kennedy assassinated in Dallas.

1964

APRIL St. Augustine, Florida, becomes a major focus for SCLC.

JULY 2 Civil Rights Act of 1964 signed by President Lyndon Johnson.